The American Foreign Policy Library
Edwin O. Reischauer, Editor

The United States and Poland

Piotr S. Wandycz

Harvard University Press
Cambridge, Massachusetts
and London, England 1980

Library of Congress Cataloging in Publication Data

Wandycz, Piotr Stefan.
  The United States and Poland.

  (American foreign policy library)
  Bibliography: p.
  Includes index.
  1. United States—Foreign relations—Poland.
2. Poland—Foreign relations—United States.
I. Title.   II. Series.
E183.8.P7W36   327.73'0438   79-11998
ISBN 0-674-92685-4

For Teresa

Foreword

by Edwin O. Reischauer

Poland has never loomed large in the American mind or in American foreign policy. Some 4,600 miles away, landlocked through much of its history, and more often than not in modern times under the domination of one or more of its great neighbors, Poland has had relatively little direct contact with the United States. In fact, during the two centuries of American national existence, Poland has been a fully independent nation for only twenty years. When the "Polish question" has figured in American thinking, it has largely been as an element in our relation with other greater powers or as a symbol of some broad world order. This was certainly the case in the Wilsonian "fourteen points" and "self-determination," which contributed to the rebirth of Poland in the aftermath of World War I. It is again the situation today, when Poland in the American mind figures more as a borderland and satellite of the Soviet Union than as an entity in its own right.

The tendency in this country has been to ignore Poland in our concern for larger countries and those with which we have been more directly involved, either as friend or foe. The result has naturally been an ignorance of Poland on our part, making this book by Professor Wandycz all the more needed. The largely unhappy history of Poland has made it a subject of controversy and deeply held feelings. An understanding treatment required intimate perceptions from within and not merely objective analysis from without. Professor Wandycz fortunately brings both perspectives to his remarkably evenhanded analysis. A resident of the United States since 1951, a citizen since 1960, and at present a professor at Yale, he is himself of Polish birth and upbringing and served in the Polish army in exile before completing his higher education in England.

The underlying tragedy of Poland has been its location on the great plain of Eastern Europe, virtually bereft of natural boundaries and pressed between two larger ethnic groups—the Germans and the Russians. It has been the battleground for other peoples and the pathway for great invasions—Napoleon into Russia in the early nineteenth century, the Germans into Russia twice in the twentieth, and the Russians in a return of conquest most recently. As a result, Poland has had a disconcerting tendency to wander over the map, and it even disappeared completely for one long period of time. The three successive partitions of Poland between Russia, Prussia, and the Austro-Hungarian Empire in 1772, 1793, and 1795, left no politically visible Poland for more than a century.

The shift of the nation's borders roughly 150 miles to the west in the post-World War II settlements is the most recent case of this geographic instability. This latest move, however, was accompanied by a massive reshuffling of peoples that gives some promise of greater stability in the future. In place of the jumble of Polish minorities in other countries and a multitude of other peoples within Poland, the contemporary borders encompass almost all Poles and only two percent or less of minority groups.

Poland's history has inevitably been closely intertwined with that of Eastern Europe as a whole. It is a complex story that Professor Wandycz recounts, though he does so with clarity, balance, and in considerable detail, especially for the period since the outbreak of World War I, which accounts for three quarters of the total. It is a long history dating back to the tenth century and the conversion in 966 of the Polish Duke Mieszko and his people to Christianity. The adherence of Poland to Catholicism, underscored today by the startling fact that for the first time in history the Pope is a Pole, has been a dominant theme in Polish history. This has been particularly true in recent centuries, when this situation deepened the cleavages between the Poles and the Protestant Prussians to the west and the Orthodox Russians to the east. Today it leaves Poland in the dilemma of being "basically Western" in culture "yet operating within an Eastern, Soviet bloc," as Professor Wandycz puts it.

Like most of the volumes of the Foreign Policy Library, this book is essentially a history of the country it treats, but Professor Wandycz, unlike many of the other authors in the series, has taken to heart the opening words of the customary titles of these books, which are "The United States and . . . ." One of the most interesting features of this work for Americans is his treatment, not just of the political relations between the United States and Poland, but of their cultural contacts and the attitudes of Americans and Poles toward each other.

Naturally the United States has loomed larger in Polish thinking than Poland has in American. During the unhappy years in the late eighteenth century when the successive partitions of Poland obliterated the country and its revolutions were quelled, the success of the American Revolution and the country it spawned caught the imagination of Poles with special poignancy. Poland's rebirth after World War I was in no small degree influenced by the concepts of President Wilson, and its fate after World War II again depended in part on American attitudes. Throughout, the promise for mankind that the United States held forth and the vigor of its culture had a strong impact on Poles.

The return impact has been less strong and little noticed. People and cultural influences from Poland, however, have left their mark in America, from the Poles who turned up at Jamestown in 1608, through the Revolutionary War heroes, Kościuszko and Pułaski, to Zbigniew Brzezinski in Carter's White House. Paderewski, Artur Rubinstein, and a host of other Poles have served as cultural links. Americans have repeatedly become exercised over the "Polish question," as during the early days of our own national existence, when a conference was held at the Harvard Commencement of 1792 "Upon the comparative importance of the American, French and Polish revolutions to mankind," and again in the prolonged debates over the postwar settlements of the two world wars.

For the United States the most significant factor in our relations with Poland has been the large number of Polish immigrants and their descendants, whom Professor Wandycz refers to as "Polonia." According to recent calculations, the 30,000 people of Polish origin in the United States before the Civil War had grown to 800,000 by 1889, and another 3.6 million poured in between then and World War I, making the Poles the largest of all Eastern European ethnic groups in this country.

The checkered and complex history of Poland and the indirectness of most American involvements with that country have left "The United States and Poland" a little known subject to most Americans. Involving, as it does, a complex national history and a still more involved set of international relations, it is by no means a story that is easy to analyze or to recount. Professor Wandycz, however, has accomplished both tasks with admirable balance and skill.

Preface

> [The historian] needs something more than sympathy,
> for sympathy may be condescending, pitying,
> contemptuous . . . Sympathy there must be . . . but it must
> be sympathy of the man who stands in the midst
> and sees like one within, not like one without, like a native,
> not like an alien. He must not sit like a judge exercising
> exterritorial jurisdiction.
>
> Woodrow Wilson

This book is a survey and a tentative synthesis. Based largely on published studies and documents it necessarily reflects the paucity of works in this field. This is particularly true for the treatment of Polish Americans; new contributions using more sophisticated research techniques are only beginning to appear. The main thrust of this study is the relations between the United States and Poland, which explains why the Polish emigration to America is treated only insofar as it affected these relations. Given the importance of the First and Second World Wars, for which more abundant although not always more reliable literature exists, I have explored some relevant archival materials for 1914-1918 and 1939-1945. I have done the same for the interwar period, and my task there was facilitated by the research papers of three graduate students, Robert Biskupski, Peter Hayes, and Neal Pease; some of their findings are included in the fourth chapter. Unfortunately, K. Lundgreen-Nielsen's *The Polish Problem at the Paris Peace Conference* (Odense, 1979), which throws new light on Wilson's Polish policies, came out too late to be used here. In attempting to explain the nature of American-Polish relations to the American reader, I found it necessary to survey the broad currents of Polish history that are likely to be unfamiliar to him, and devote some space to an analysis of Poland in the twentieth century. Detailed narrative, which figures large in several writings of Polish American historians, notably in the pioneering works of Miecislaus Haiman, is reduced to a minimum, and the reader may miss some colorful episodes connected with

Kościuszko or Puɫaski. Since American-Polish contacts must not be
viewed in a vacuum, particulary in the last half century, I attempted
to place them in the broader framework of East-West relations. The
short last chapter, "Reflections," contains generalizations and
speculations that range wide over the entire field of study.

If my efforts will help the American reader to get a better
perspective and understanding of Poland and aid a Polish reader to
overcome a tendency to view America in terms of either wishful
thinking or bitterness engendered by deceived hopes, I shall
consider myself amply rewarded. My approach to the subject is
admirably expressed by President Wilson, whose remark made in
1904 at the Congress of Arts and Sciences I adopted as a motto for
this study. Whether I succeeded in following his wise counsel is for
the reader to say.

I am obliged to several people and institutions for the assistance I
received. Comments by my colleagues at Yale, Professors Edmund
Morgan and David B. Davis, helped me to a better grasp of some
issues that appear in chapter one, and I am indebted to Professor
Robert R. Palmer who read extensive parts of the manuscript.
Professor Jean Seznec of All Souls College, Oxford, kindly read the
second chapter and gave me the benefit of his wise advice. Dr.
Zbigniew Pelczynski of Pembroke College, Oxford, read and
extensively commented on the seventh chapter. Professor Zbigniew
Landau of the Central School of Planning and Statistics (SGPiS) in
Warsaw patiently answered my many questions and elucidated
problems concerning the economic side of American-Polish
relations. Several colleagues in this country and Poland were kind
enough to keep me informed about recent publications. I am
grateful to my children, Katherine, Joanna, and Antoni, for help in
preparing the index.

Thanks to the financial assistance of the Yale University
Concilium on International and Area Studies and of the Council on
Humanities, I was able to do research in several American archives,
particularly in Washington and Hyde Park, and to travel to the
Bellagio Study and Conference Center of the Rockefeller
Foundation. I am grateful to the foundation for granting me the
residency at Villa Serbelloni and to the director of the center, Dr.
William C. Olson, and his wife, for making my stay there
intellectually fruitful and most pleasant.

The book is dedicated to my wife.

P.S.W.

New Haven, Connecticut
1979

Contents

Contents

Maps

The United States
and Poland

A Guide to Polish Pronunciation

ą	as in French *bon*	ś	soft s as in *sure*
c	ts	u	oo as in *brood*
ć	soft tch, as in *champ*	w	v as in *van*
ę	as in French *main*	y	as in *whim*
h	as in *humble*	ź	soft zi
i	ee as in *beet*	ż	as in *measure*
j	y as in *yield*	dż	dj as in *journey*
ł	w as in *war*	ch	h as in *loch*
ń	soft n as in *canyon*	cz	ch as in *church*
ó	u as in *true*	rz	zh as in *measure*
s	as in *sister*	sz	sh as in *ship*

Throughout the text Polish names are spelled with diacritical marks even though Pulaski, for instance, is better known in this country than Pułaski. But in the case of Pulaski Day and other names habitually used without diacritical marks, such as Brzezinski, the marks are left out.

1

Partitions of Poland and the Rise of the United States

From the Origins of the Polish State to the Union of Lublin

THE birth of the United States almost coincided with the demise of the old Poland. The year of the Boston Tea Party was also that of the ratification of the first treaty dismembering the Polish-Lithuanian Commonwealth. The third and last partition, which wiped Poland off the political map of Europe in 1795, preceded Washington's Farewell Address by less than a year. It is hardly surprising that this coincidence affected American thinking about Poland. American success contrasted with Polish failure, and few people stopped to think that the Revolutionary War did not have to end the way it did or that Poland's collapse was not necessarily the unavoidable outcome of that country's past.

Writing in 1919, the American historian Robert Lord aptly remarked that for most outsiders the partitions "have overshadowed all the preceding period of Polish history." These foreign observers "have fastened their eyes too exclusively upon the deplorable conditions into which Poland had fallen just before her dismemberment and have concluded that her history is chiefly made up of a tissue of mistakes, sins and follies, interesting only as furnishing a terrible example of how a State ought not to be governed and of how badly a people can mismanage its national life."

Indeed the country that was partitioned by its neighbors had behind it several centuries of rich, varied, and productive life. Poland had shared with the rest of Europe most of the important historical

1

trends and traditions, and celebrated its millennium a decade before the United States observed its bicentennial in 1976. To overlook this past in a study of American-Polish relations during the last two centuries would be to deprive them of a perspective and a depth of understanding that are indispensable.

The following brief outline of Polish history prior to the partitions is highly selective; it attempts to dispose of clichés and indicate the complexities of Polish historical tradition. At the same time it seeks to highlight the events and individuals who have permanently affected the national image. All too often Poland has been pictured as a land of anarchy, oppressed peasants, persecuted Jews, bigoted Catholics, and ungovernable aristocrats. Admirers have countered with an equally one-sided image of a land constantly invaded by greedy neighbors and defended by heroes and patriots endowed with saintly virtues. It is obvious that such black and white contrasts cannot satisfy a historian.

A historical overview might begin with the tenth century, when the first references to a Polish state apeared in contemporary chronicles. More important, since some form of statehood already existed, it was the baptism of Duke Mieszko and his people in 966 that decisively affected the character of the state. The acceptance of Christianity meant entry into European medieval society and Western civilization with all it implied: an international language (Latin) and alphabet and Western scholarship, philosophy, politics, and socioeconomic relations. The medieval language of symbols expressed through church architecture spread throughout the country, as embodied in the Romanesque and Gothic buildings preserved to this day. At the same time, one must remember that the Polish state, located roughly in the same territory as it is today, lay in the "new Europe" that had never been part of the Roman Empire and its civilization. It could not build upon the rich foundations existing in the western and Mediterranean parts of the Continent. Nor was it a large state territorially or demographically. According to calculations by Polish historians the population amounted to 1.25 million, as compared with the 5 million inhabitants of Germany, 7 of Italy, 9 of France, or even 2.5 of England. The nucleus of early Poland was the Gniezno area inhabited by the Polanie tribe who gave their name to the nation; from there the state began to expand.

As throughout all of early medieval Europe, Poland's economy was based on agriculture, but the husbandry was more primitive and extensive. Development was relatively slow, although Mieszko's control of Cracow, Wrocław, and the Pomeranian towns brought

Poland into international commerce. Urban units were hardly more than rural agglomerations assuming the economic function of towns. The existence of so-called service villages specializing in the production of certain goods indicated a primitive stage of market economy. Crafts and mining industries developed gradually. Social structure, originally composed of freemen and slaves, showed signs of stratification; a warrior elite merging with the descendants of tribal chieftains anticipated a later knightly or magnate class. Slowly some of the poorer natives sank to the level of servitude on the land. Wars with neighbors were fought less for control of territory then for loot and captives, who were settled as slaves to cultivate the victor's land.

Internationally, the relationship to the two pillars of medieval Christendom, the pope and the emperor, constituted the crucial problem of the Polish state. The adroit policy of Mieszko of avoiding dependence on German ecclesiastical hierarchy and cultivating Rome reached a new stage under his son and successor Bolesław the Valiant (992-1025). Regarded as one of Poland's great rulers, Bolesław became associated with the short-lived plans of Emperor Otto III, who sought to promote a universalist concept of the Holy Roman Empire. Otto thought of Bolesław as the head of "Sclavinia" comprising Poland, Bohemia, and the Slav lands between the Odra (Oder) and Elbe rivers. Although the failure of Ottonian plans destroyed the chance of the emergence of a western Slav bloc, Bolesław achieved international recognition of an independent Polish ecclesiastical organization headed by the archbishop of Gniezno; to stress his own status he assumed the royal crown.

German-Polish struggles, which continued under Bolesław's successors, must be viewed largely in dynastic terms. To regard them as an early version of a German *Drang nach Osten* is to transfer modern concepts to a medieval past. Polish dukes and kings were at times obliged to recognize the feudal overlordship of the emperor. Still, this temporary relationship never developed into a regular association as in the Czech case. Poland was not included in the Holy Roman Empire nor did its rulers become electors of the emperors. By struggle or diplomacy it thwarted the imperial ambitions.

Early medieval Poland developed following general European patterns. The arrival of Benedictine and Cistercian monks from the West in the eleventh and twelfth centuries, followed by the mendicant orders of Dominicans and Franciscans in the thirteenth, stimulated cultural developments. The first chronicle, by Gallus, was written in Latin in the twelfth century. It was probably the work of a foreign priest, the cosmopolitan medieval church being the vehicle of cultural advancement, but at the beginning of the thirteenth century Gallus was followed by a native Polish chronicler, Bishop Wincenty Kadłubek. The great Investiture Controversy between the empire and the papacy affected Poland, which sided with the pope, but there were simultaneous internal struggles between the ruler and the church hierarchy. Bolesław the Bold (1058-1079) clashed with the bishop of Cracow, Stanisław, later canonized, in a conflict similar to that between Henry of England and Thomas à Becket. In both cases it ended with the martyrdom of the bishop.

The early rulers had not established a clearly stated principle of primogeniture, and the problem of succession to the throne caused frequent internal divisions and fighting. To safeguard the succession under conditions of gradual weakening of the central power, Bolesław III the Wrymouth (1102-1138) in his will provided for the oldest son to preside from Cracow over principalities assigned to younger sons. With the spreading feudalization of society Bolesław's testament contributed to growing subdivisions of Poland. For the next two hundred years or so, the all-Polish ecclesiastical organization and the titular senior prince in Cracow were all that remained of the unified kingdom. Feudalism, although different in many ways from the classical Western model, became established in the principalities. The upper clergy and the magnates began to emancipate themselves from princely control by acquiring immunities and privileges.

At the turn of the twelfth and through the thirteenth century—a real turning point in Polish medieval history—the country entered a period of significant economic development. Economic opportunities and need for manpower led to calls for settlers, foreign and native, to come and work under novel and attractive conditions. Special charters were granted to transform and develop old town settlements or to found new cities endowed with municipal autonomy. The model for this self-government was taken from Magdeburg, hence the expression Magdeburg law. In the countryside, new and renovated settlements came into being through fief-like contracts; the settlers became rent-paying tenant farmers. The system was first known as the German law and gave rise to far-reaching assertions by German and some Western historians about the civilizing German colonization in the backward Slav lands. Given the long-range political implications of these assertions it is not surprising that much heated discussion, often conducted in nationalist or almost racist terms, ensued. Recent Polish research seems to have arrived at a fairly balanced presentation. Without denying the importance of German migrations into the lands of Eastern Europe and their economic, social, and legal contributions, Polish historians argue for more complexity. The numbers of German immigrants were found to have been exaggerated and progress noticeable in areas they did not penetrate. Polish economic know-how was not so low as to preclude evolution without foreign aid. The thesis that German law per se brought freedom for the peasant masses appears highly debatable.

A gradual replacement of serfdom by rent-paying tenantry was less the result of legal provisions and more of the changing socio-economic realities. German law and its local variation, the Polish law based largely on payments in kind, served as incentives to attract colonists and make the local population work more efficiently. These arrangements were made in response to an existing need. Mobility of tenant farmers became in some respects more restricted under the German and Polish law, yet peasants continued to move into towns, either bypassing regulations or migrating illegally. If a man stayed in the city for a year and six weeks he became a burgher. As the contemporary saying put it "the city air makes one free."

Cities made important progress during that period and many towns of present-day Poland, such as Cracow, Wrocław, and Poznań received their charters in the thirteenth century. A majority of the burghers was German-speaking then but the population slowly became polonized. The status of the peasantry improved and so did its contribution to the economic growth of the country. Granting privileges to the peasants, the lords in turn insisted on their own immunities, particularly financial, from the ruling princes—a semi-feudal manorial economy was developing.

Politically, the divided Polish principalities could not play an important part in international relations. Southern Poland and part of Silesia were devastated around 1241 by Mongol (Tartar) invasions. The memory of the battle of Legnica, where Polish troops fought the Mongols, has become part of the national tradition. The Mongol attack on Cracow gave rise to folktales and legends; one version appears in the American novel by E. P. Kelly, *The Trumpeter of Cracow*. Much more serious than the Mongol raids was the arrival of the crusading order of the Teutonic Knights, called in by the Mazovian Prince Konrad in 1226 to protect his principality against the pagan Prussians. The knights conquered what later became known as East Prussia and colonized it so effectively that the word Prussian lost its original meaning. The Teutonic Order began to pose a threat to Polish lands in the north; this

German colony became a cradle of the future might of Prussia. Polish presence on the Baltic Sea became seriously jeopardized.

During the period of division into principalities the concept of a united kingdom, *corona regni,* was never entirely lost. After one brief attempt at unification, the crown of Poland passed in 1300 to the last members of the Czech Přemyslid dynasty, Václav II and Václav III. The contest between them and a Polish claimant, Władysław the Short, has been too often presented in purely national terms—Poles versus Czechs and Germans. Even though one can observe the growth of *national* consciousness at this period, the complex struggles that culminated in the reemergence of a Polish kingdom under its own native ruler seem to have been at least partly a contest between the model of a feudal monarchy and that of a monarchy based on estates. When Václav II was issuing privileges for the clergy, magnates, and towns, and building a new type of administration, he seems to have been promoting the latter model. When Władysław eventually defeated the towns, which had supported the Přemyslid king, he may have decisively damaged their political power as an estate. The rise of a new class of lower gentry emancipating itself from the magnates further undermined the possibility of evolution toward an estates-based kingdom. The way was open for the predominance of one estate: *szlachta,* or the gentry. Its identification with the Polish nation, *natio,* eventually led to the phenomenon of the "noble nation." These developments were crucial for the subsequent evolution of Polish constitutional and political life.

The weakening of towns as a political factor in the early fourteenth century was not tantamount to a loss of their social and economic importance. In fact, towns participated fully in the economic boom. True, the reunited kingdom did not comprise two of the western and most urbanized provinces: Silesia (Śląsk) and Pomerania (Pomorze). The local princes of the former had sided with the kings of Bohemia. Pomerania with Gdańsk (Danzig) was lost to the Teutonic Knights, who thus effectively cut off Poland from access to the Baltic. These losses were keenly felt by Władysław's successor, Casimir the Great (1333-1370), the only Polish king to bear this name, which was originally given to him because of his height. Casimir was undoubtedly a great statesman and diplomat. He was also a political realist who sought to strength his kingdom internally and externally, leaving the task of reconquest of lost provinces to his successors. His acquisition of Ruthenia, later known as Eastern Galicia, has been sometimes regarded as turning Polish attention from the west to the east. But one must not forget that the control of that province, which opened the Black Sea trade routes, provided Casimir with important means of economic pressure on the Teutonic Knights and Silesia. Thanks to the new trade routes, Cracow, Sandomierz, and the newly acquired Lwów (Lviv, Lvov) went through a phase of growth and development. Cities were still significant enough to be included as signatories in international treaties. The story of the Cracow merchant Wierzynek entertaining Casimir and several foreign monarchs at a sumptuous feast in his house, often retold in Polish school readings, attests to the high position of the urban patriciate.

Economic prosperity rested above all on agriculture, but trade, much of it transit trade, and mining industries were of considerable importance. Grain surpluses appeared, methods of cultivation improved, the landless peasants supplied the labor force on the estates of the nobles and the church as well as on the land of the wealthy peasant tenants. The lines dividing social classes were not yet rigidly drawn, and for the next century or so many a burgher or a peasant was richer than a noble landowner. Polish industrial production during the Middle Ages and the Renaissance has not yet been exhaustively studied, but we do know of growing trends as well as competition of cheaper foreign imports, such as cloth, which may have affected the local crafts adversely.

Did late medieval Poland narrow the gap that had separated it from the more advanced countries of western Europe? In socio-economic terms it seems to have done so, although the sparseness of population—6 to 7 per square kilometer as compared with 30 in France—and the relatively small size of towns—the capital, Cracow, had only 12,000 inhabitants, Poznań some 5,000 to 6,000— placed it behind the urbanized West. In that respect the loss of the more advanced Silesia and Pomerania was keenly felt.

Casimir the Great was the last member of the Piast dynasty, which had ruled Poland since the dawn of its history. After his death the crown passed to his nephew, Louis of Hungary, and subsequently to Louis's daughter Hedwig (Jadwiga), who in 1386 married the grand duke of Lithuania, Władysław Jagiełło (Jogaila in Lithuanian). A new chapter in Polish history began.

The extinction of the Piast dynasty necessitated the adoption of the elective principle, which naturally affected both the royal power and the growth of popular representation of the noble nation. The union with Lithuania (at Krewo in 1385) raised a host of issues that can be more easily understood if one realizes what was the Grand Duchy of Lithuania in the fourteenth century. A huge country stretching from the shores of the Baltic south to the Black

Sea, Lithuania comprised, in addition to ethnic Lithuania, virtually all of present-day Belorussia and the Ukraine. Lithuania proper had been pagan until Jagiełło introduced Christianity there after he ascended the Polish throne, but the Belorussians and the Ukrainians were Orthodox. Culturally more advanced, they had dominated Lithuania, and their language, rather than Lithuanian, was the language of the grand ducal chancellery, administration, and courts of law. At that time Lithuania and Muscovy were locked in a struggle over the control of these "Russian lands," which had once been part of the medieval state of Kiev. Poland, by uniting with Lithuania—although until the late sixteenth century the union was only personal and dynastic—became drawn into the labyrinth of Eastern problems: international, constitutional, cultural, and religious. Poland-Lithuania eventually engaged in a formidable duel with Muscovy over what was in essence the issue of domination over Eastern Europe.

Historians, both foreign and Polish, have been divided in their opinions concerning the Polish-Lithuanian Union. Francis Dvornik thought that had Lithuania embraced Orthodoxy instead of Catholicism and merged, together with all its "Russian lands," with Muscovy, the subsequent Polish-Lithuanian struggle against Russia would have been avoided. Poland, remaining aloof from the Eastern problems, might have acted as a "friendly transmitter of Western culture to the Orthodox Russians." Some Poles have contrasted the westward-oriented Piast tradition in Polish history with the Jagiellonian eastern orientation. The latter, it was said, overtaxed Polish resources, involved the country in insoluble problems, and accelerated its eventual downfall. The Jagiellonian defenders have countered by arguing that the union gave Poland the unique opportunity of rising to the level of a European power. The small Polish monarchy of the last Piasts was too weak to deal alone with the Teutonic Knights. Against a united Muscovy-Lithuania it would have been utterly powerless.

Contemporaries viewed the situation in different terms. The marriage of Jagiełło with Jadwiga and the Christianization of and union with Lithuania seemed to offer obvious advantages. Lithuania was a natural ally of Poland against the Teutonic Knights, and Jagiełło was determined not to let Ruthenia slip away from Poland. The future economic potential of a union was also attractive, as was the general strengthening of Poland's power.

The intricacies of the relationship between Poland and Lithuania, after the original act of union, need not concern us here. The anticipated merger of the two countries did not take place, and each retained its separate state identity. Lithuania, however, began to evolve in a direction that made its socioeconomic and administrative-political structure similar to that of Poland. Linguistically and culturally, the Lithuanian upper classes became polonized. In international affairs the combined effort of the two countries resulted in their great victory over the Teutonic Knights at the battle of Grunwald (the Germans call it the battle of Tannenberg) in 1410. Although the victory was not immediately exploited, its symbolic significance was great for Polish history and tradition. Undoubtedly the battle undermined the might of the Teutonic Knights, but it took another long war in mid-fifteenth century to wrest the province of Pomerania from the order. The Peace of Toruń (Thorn) in 1466 restored Polish access to the Baltic and control over the habor city of Gdańsk. What was dubbed the Polish Corridor after World War I came into existence in mid-fifteenth century, except that at that time it separated the essentially colonial state of the Teutonic Knights from the lands of the Holy Roman Empire.

Given the later importance of the German-Polish controversy over this territory, a few words need to be said about it. Pomerania with a small part of East Prussia (Warmia, Ermland) became part of Poland under the name of Royal Prussia. Its nobility and a strong town patriciate were then mostly German or germanized. They had, however, fought on the side of the king of Poland against the Teutonic Order, and had Polish military strength been greater it is likely that all of East Prussia would have been absorbed. As it was, the bulk of it remained with the knights, who reluctantly recognized a feudal tie to Poland. Royal Prussia enjoyed wide autonomy, linguistic and political-economic, and its loyalty to the Polish crown was unshaken in the centuries that followed. The same was true for Gdańsk, although its jealously guarded autonomy and virtual monopoly of Polish Baltic trade caused several conflicts with the kings of Poland. The latter did not always have the upper hand.

Polish recovery of Pomerania was not followed by a recovery of Silesia, which remained as part of the Czech crown. True, from the 1490s to 1526 the Jagiellonians sat on the thrones of Bohemia and Hungary, in addition to those of Poland and Lithuania. A short-lived Jagiellonian bloc of states came into existence, parallel to the Habsburg and Valois systems, making Poland a pivotal state of Eastern and Central Europe.

From the late fifteenth through most of the sixteenth century Poland enjoyed its golden age. The population was increasing more

rapidly than that in the West and economically the country was far-
ing well. In the cultural sphere humanism and Renaissance reigned
supreme. Already under Casimir the Jagiellonian (1447-1492), the
king who recovered Pomerania and whose death coincided with
Columbus's discovery of America, Italian humanism had penetrated Poland. The Jagiellonian University, originally founded in
1364, became a foremost European center of mathematics and
astronomy. Its greatest pupil was Nicholas Copernicus (Mikołaj
Kopernik). Polish historical writing marked new achievements with
Jan Długosz, a famous chronicler and teacher of royal princes.

Just as the Gothic style had been adapted to the Polish surround-
ings, so the Italian Renaissance, promoted by King Sigismund the
Old (1506-1548) and his Italian wife, Bona Sforza, acquired local
characteristics. These were particularly noticeable in the rebuilt
royal castle, Wawel, and the Clothiers' Hall in Cracow. The transition in sculpture can be appreciated if one turns from the magnifi-
cent late Gothic altar of Wit Stwosz (Stos) in Cracow's St. Mary's
church to the Sigismund chapel, comparable to the Medici chapel
in Florence. Polish Renaissance music was represented by remark-
able native artists. Erasmus of Rotterdam, who corresponded with
scholars at the Jagiellonian University, congratulated them on the
flourishing of jurisprudence, morals, and religion. Poland, he felt,
now rivaled the most glorious of European nations.

Between 1503 and 1536 the city of Cracow alone printed as many
books as all of England, and indeed Polish literature achieved
heights not to be equaled until the Enlightenment or maybe even
the Romantic period. Mikołaj Rej may be justly called the father
of Polish vernacular literature; Jan Kochanowski was one of the
greatest poets of the country, perhaps of contemporary Europe. Political writings reflecting the great ferment of ideas received a powerful impulse from the Reformation, which made important strides
during the reign of the last Jagiellonian, Sigismund Augustus (1548-
1572). Lutherans, Calvinists, and especially the socially radical Unitarians (Polish Brethren, Arians, anti-Trinitarians or Socinians) left
their stamp on the debates that encompassed religious, political,
and social themes. It is useful to recall, given the later identification
of Poles with Catholicism, that in the sixteenth century some of
the leading figures were Protestants or included toward Protes-
tantism. It is to Poland's credit that during the age of burning
stakes and St. Bartholomew's Night religious toleration prevailed in
the country, and the king stressed that he was not the ruler of his
subjects' conscience. Not only Protestants but also Moslem Tartars
were allowed freedom of worship and enjoyed citizenship rights.

Differing in this respect from much of contemporary Europe, Poland also began to diverge in the development of its socioeconomic and political-constitutional patterns. The resulting problems were crucial for subsequent Polish history and require some analysis.

The turn of the fifteenth and beginning of the sixteenth centuries witnessed the birth of the much-debated "second serfdom" as well as of closely related trends that made Poland a "republic of the szlachta." The rise of capitalism in the West has often been contrasted with the rise of second serfdom in the East, yet the causes and the character of the latter are still not fully explained. The Polish historian Jerzy Topolski sees a general European phenomenon of decreasing incomes of the noble class and the emergence of a new nobility which had to turn to economic pursuits that differed in various parts of the Continent. In Western Europe a market for agricultural products grew and so did the prices. This trend, combined with the more plentiful and more easily controlled labor in Eastern Europe, led to important changes in that region. In Poland it became profitable to concentrate on grain production and to export it to the West through the Vistula River and Gdańsk. Although only some 12 percent of the crop was so exported, it affected the total price structure in the country. At roughly the same time the peasants' mobility became restricted by legal edicts, leading eventually to peasants' attachment to the soil. The peasants became dependent, economically, personally, and legally, on the szlachta.

The connection between West and East European developments produced sweeping assertions that West European capitalism grew on the imports of East European raw materials—implying a semi-colonial relationship—or that the new type of economy ruined the Polish towns and made the peasant a destitute serf. These assertions cannot be fully substantiated. Westbound exports, which increased tenfold in the sixteenth century, seem at first to have brought prosperity not only to the noble landowners but also to the wealthy burghers and peasants. A large part of the exported grain actually came from peasant holdings, which did not yet differ substantially in size from noble estates. Peasant obligations to perform some labor on the land of the lord, an important aspect of serfdom, were not increased overnight and it is likely that the better-off peasants sent their hired hands to do the work. Finally, the laws attaching peasants to the soil often proved ineffective in practice; one may also recall that the peasant did not cease to be a legal person. These facts might perhaps explain why peasant uprisings common in other parts of Central Europe were almost nonexistent in Poland.

As for urban development, some 20 percent of the population—a sizable figure—lived in mid-sixteenth century towns which showed signs of a vigorous economic life. True, the biggest of them, Gdańsk, with 30,000 inhabitants, Cracow with 20,000, Lwów, Toruń, Elbląg with over 10,000, and Warsaw, Lublin, and Poznań with around 10,000 each, approached the size only of an average European town and could not compare with the great Western cities. Also, new laws prevented burghers from acquiring land and barred them from high ecclesiastical offices. Practice was often different and sons of peasants and burghers could still be found among the leading figures of the Polish Renaissance. As another Polish historian, Andrzej Wyczański, has concluded, until the late sixteenth century Polish economy—developing in all sectors with agriculture predominating—showed a pattern that was not yet dissimilar from that of the rest of Europe.

The decline of *political* importance of towns, however, was a fact and resulted from a combination of various factors. The presence of a large foreign element in the cities was an important but not the single cause; the German urban element had been stronger at an earlier time when the cities did play a role in the political life of the country. Granted, the successful integration of various ethnic groups on the level of the szlachta had no real counterpart on the town level; an integrated all-Polish burgher class or estate had failed to materialize. It may well be that the largely German-Lutheran character of the patriciate in the most urbanized province of Pomerania helps to explain its townsmen's lack of cooperation with Cracow, Lublin, or Poznań. At the same time, the Pomeranian cities were represented in the provincial diet which satisfied their local interests. The largest city, Gdańsk, was virtually a self-governing republic that treated directly with the king. Some eastern towns, for instance Kamieniec Podolski, had not one but three municipal councils—Polish, Ruthenian, and Armenian—which doubtless made external representation difficult.

A certain parochialism of the towns was encouraged by the rulers. Free to levy municipal taxes, the kings had little incentive to promote the rise of a burgher estate and played on the rivalries between cities. Casimir the Jagiellonian shielded the cities from more flagrant abuses by the nobles but failed to give them a role in government. When the gentry became a leading element in the country's economic life as mass producers and exporters of grain, the king was deprived of the possibility of successfully playing the cities against the szlachta. It is likely that the towns preferred to deal directly with the king or magnates than to engage from a position of relative weakness in the risks of all-Polish politics.

The relationship between the king and the noble nation was the crux of Polish politics. The noble nation comprised two distinct social classes: the gentry (szlachta), whose new role as a land-owning and market-producing group stemmed from the contemporary economic evolution of the country, and the magnates, whether of old or new vintage. The noble nation was not a thin crust on the top of the social pyramid. One ought rather to picture it as a layer going from top to bottom with a considerable amount of upward and downward social mobility largely determined by wealth. The magnates at first favored a political estates model of government in which the magnate-dominated royal council, strengthened by representatives of szlachta, higher clergy, and cities, would be the center of power. The szlachta strove after a gentry democracy under the crown, and succeeded in significantly improving its position.

The theory that the king was the lord of all the land and that noble landowners held their estates in exchange for military services, still holding under the last Piast king, made room for the interpretation that military obligations were of a legal-public nature and did not stem from a vassal-lord relationship. Under Louis and Jagiełło the szlachta achieved significant concessions. Their estates could not be confiscated, and a Polish version of habeas corpus (and preceding it) called *Neminem captivabimus* (1425) protected the nobleman against arbitrary arrest. In the course of the fifteenth and sixteenth centuries other privileges followed. Military obligations became circumscribed, the szlachta gained exemption from export duties, and taxes could not be levied without the approval of the diet *(sejm)*. As finally constituted, it consisted of three equal components; the king, the senate, and the chamber of deputies.

Making their voices heard at the local dietines *(sejmiki)* and when mass levy *(pospolite ruszenie)* was decreed, the gentry was able to score against the king. But it also sought emancipation from the magnate tutelage and succeeded in making the chamber of deputies fully elective and independent of the senate. It then faced the magnates, demanding among other things the restitution of royal domain leased out or granted by the ruler to the lords. In the magnate-gentry conflict, the Jagiellonian kings pursued an inconsistent policy, shifting their support from one group to the other. Still, the enhanced position of the gentry became evident and was envied by the Lithuanian boyars subject to a much greater control by their magnates. The Poles proudly contrasted their liberal parliamentary system with the despotism of an Ivan the Terrible in Muscovy.

In the international sphere, one of the most important single events of the early sixteenth century was the secularization of the Teutonic Knights and the creation of a Duchy of Prussia under the former grand master, Albrecht Hohenzollern. In 1525 he rendered homage to Sigismund the Old and recognized the king of Poland as his overlord. This picturesque ceremony at Cracow's Market Square has often been recalled with pride in Polish literature and been the subject of historical paintings. The arrangement later gave rise to a heated controversy—Poland, it was said, had missed the chance of annexing East Prussia. The contemporaries were more optimistic and looked to a future inclusion of the duchy into Poland by peaceful means.

In 1569 the eventful real union of Poland and Lithuania took place. Under the pressure of the last childless Jagiellonian, Sigismund Augustus, Polish and Lithuanian representatives agreed at a joint session held in Lublin to the creation of a confederate state, a *Respublica* (commonwealth) of the two nations.

The Polish-Lithuanian Commonwealth until the Partitions

The newly established commonwealth, with its population of some 7.5 million inhabitants and 815 thousand square kilometers, was one of the largest states in Europe. It was also highly heterogeneous. Its two main parts were Poland proper, usually referred to as "the Crown"—to which the Ukraine had been transferred on the eve of the Union of Lublin—and the Grand Duchy of Lithuania. The two had one jointly elected king and a bicameral sejm, and constituted one customs area. Administration, legal systems, treasuries, and armies remained separate, each institution in the Crown having its counterpart in Lithuania. The term Poland and Polish began to be increasingly used to denote the entire commonwealth, the name transcending and not replacing the term Lithuanian. Had another term been coined equivalent to British, which comprises English, Scottish, and Welsh, some of the confusion between Polish proper and Polish in the sense of state-nationality would have been avoided. In addition to the Poles and Lithuanians, the commonwealth comprised Ukrainians and Belorussians (whose lands were described collectively as Ruś), Germans, a sizable Jewish community, and several smaller ethnic groups. The Catholic religion and Protestant denominations prevailed in the western parts of the state; the eastern borderlands were predominantly Orthodox. Jews lived in several areas, and given the importance of the Jewish question in Polish history, a few words needs to be said about the group.

A recent study of Jews in Poland before the partitions by Bernard Weinryb clarifies many misconceptions especially current in the West. Jews began to come to Poland during the Middle Ages, forming larger communities by the thirteenth and fourteenth centuries. They settled at first in urban centers, and unlike in the West, were not only money lenders but also debtors. They engaged in trade, crafts, and later became occasionally tax farmers and real estate leaseholders. While the burghers opposed them as competitors, Polish princes and kings protected them. Privileges were issued, the earliest of which was the famous Kalisz Privilege of 1264, which served as a model for later charters. Polish Jews were generally exempt from jurisdiction of the cities, not heavily taxed, and regarded as free men with rights to their own autonomous life. Unlike other European states, Poland did not treat these privileges as subject to arbitrary cancellation. Nor were the Jews usually referred to as serfs of the royal chamber (*servi camerae*), to be given away, sold, or mortgaged. Again, unlike in Western Europe, there were no separate Jewish ghettos in Poland, and Jews were not constrained to wear distinguishing garb or badges. Regarded in a sense as an estate, Jews enjoyed a status which in many respects seemed halfway between that of the szlachta and the burghers. It was not unusual for Jews to bear arms and be called upon to perform military obligations in the cities.

Although the early history of Jews in Poland is not free from discrimination or riots, the Jews were not entirely defenseless or lacking influence in the state. As Weinryb put it, Polish-Jewish contact was less "of the theological Christian and the theological Jew" but more human, which may explain "the more favorable development of the Jewish group in Poland." The Jews themselves characterized their living conditions as reasonably secure, and emphasized that there was "no fierce hatred of us as in Germany." Successive Polish kings of the sixteenth and seventeenth century were praised as friends of Israel; a mid-seventeenth century writer spoke of "Poland the admirable." Another one writing in the eighteenth century commented that Jews enjoyed a perfectly free exercise of their religion and civil liberties. While noting the existing anti-Jewish trends and sporadic outbreaks. Weinryb still concludes that to speak of anti-Semitism in prepartition Poland is to misunderstand or even to falsify the past.

The Jews did not constitute a religious or a political problem for the state, but the Orthodox did. Although at the time of the Union of Lublin the Orthodox part of the noble nation was equal with the rest, the question of church hierarchy and its place in the state structure remained unresolved. Given the possible attraction of Moscow, particularly in view of Russian territorial expansion at the cost of Lithuania, both religious and political considerations called for an arrangement with the Orthodox that would strengthen the Polish-Lithuanian state. The result was the Union of Brest (Brześć) of 1596, which, had it embraced *all* of the commonwealth's Orthodox hierarchy and lay leaders, would have been a perfect solution. As it was, the Greek Catholic (or Uniate) church that emerged, with a special status under Rome, produced splits and caused new tensions and animosities, particularly in the Ukraine.

The Ukraine was in fact a distinct third component of the commonwealth but was not recognized as such. Rich but sparsely populated it became the object of a double colonization: by peasants from central Poland who merged with the local population, and by magnates, local and Polish proper, who received grants of huge tracts of land. Dominated by an oligarchy that was polonized and becoming Roman Catholic, the Ukraine had no native counterpart of the lesser Lithuanian boyars who had negotiated with the Polish szlachta in the past. The group that began to be gradually regarded in the Ukraine as the defenders of Orthodoxy and as spokesmen for that country were the Cossacks. But the Cossacks had a long way to go before they could become a political elite, a partner of the szlachta. Half-peasant, half-free, living largely from loot taken from the Tartars and Turks, partly placed on the regular army register by Polish kings who recognized their military value, partly a self-governing fraternity in Zaporozhie on the Dnieper River, the Cossacks did not fit easily into the existing socioeconomic structure of the commonwealth. This became fully evident by the mid-seventeenth century.

The death of the last Jagiellonian, Sigismund Augustus, in 1572 raised the difficult question of royal election. The Piasts had ruled by right of hereditary succession; the Jagiellonians had been elected, but as reigning dukes of Lithuania faced no real competitors because no one wished to see the two countries drift apart. In 1572, however, the election became genuinely free and open to all. Afterwards, all the successful candidates, starting with Henry of Valois (later Henry III of France), had to sign a veritable contract with the noble nation. Called Pacta Conventa and Henrician Articles, this contract significantly restricted royal power. The sejm, meeting biennially, now decided on war and peace, decreed the general levy, and imposed new taxes—monopolies were expressly forbidden. Already since the so-called *nihil novi* constitution of 1505, all new laws and taxes required the approval of the sejm. The king engaged himself not to promote absolutism through the election of a successor during his lifetime, a method then used effectively by the Habsburgs in Bohemia and Hungary to establish a hereditary monarchy. The burden of financing a small standing army was placed on the royal treasury. More specific provisions varied according to circumstances accompanying a given election.

Much has been written about Polish anarchy, the nobles who knew neither how to govern or be governed, and the powerless king. This description is largely inapplicable to the sixteenth and early seventeenth centuries. The sejm functioned reasonably well and the deputies, although officially bound by instructions from their local dietines, often disregarded them and acted as a body. The king still enjoyed considerable power of patronage and had great influence and prestige. While much of his sizable domain was alienated through grants and leases, he was by no means a pauper. True, the principle of free election undermined continuity of royal policies and led to new concessions to the szlachta. The choice of several kings was unfortunate. But the view that no monarch after Sigismund Augustus could successfully manage the sejm is debatable. It is also worth recalling that in spite of a strong opposition to hereditary kingship, the szlachta showed a tendency to elect rulers from the same dynasty, for instance the three Vasa kings who reigned between 1587 and 1668.

The issue of republicanism, understood as a conflict between liberties of the noble nation and royal power, did not yet degenerate into anarchic individualism. Nor did the magnates' promotion of oligarchy in itself imply a tendency toward anarchy. Oligarchic rule can also be a stable form of government. The political contest between the kings and the szlachta, with the magnates joining one side or the other, enhanced the lords' power, but the bad consequences were a result of numerous other factors, political, social, and economic.

The Polish constitution combined advanced notions of a parliamentary regime and democracy with antiquated feudal elements. It was not an easy system to operate and much depended on the ability of the rulers and the political maturity of the szlachta to make it work well. The noble nation, which a Polish historian recently described as medieval in its estatelike character and modern in its all-national activity, was by now a numerous group. It constituted about 8 to 10 percent of the population of the entire commonwealth and around 25 percent of the ethnic Polish-speaking people. By comparison the French nobility did not exceed 0.3 percent of the total population. The number of voters in Poland was the highest in Europe, and it is legitimate to speak of a kind of political democracy prevailing in the country. Sovereignty was really vested in the noble nation and to criticize it as confined to one class is misleading, since the szlachta ranged through various socioeconomic strata, from the poorest to the most wealthy, and should not be equated with the aristocracy.

By the early seventeenth century the political and socioeconomic picture began to change and to affect grievously the szlachta, hitherto the most active and productive force in the country. The 1606-1609 Zebrzydowski *rokosz* (the term denoted a noble uprising against the king accused of violating the constitution) marked a certain decline of gentry democracy while it also enhanced it in theory. Economic trends, notably the passing of the boom for agricultural products in the West, operated to the disadvantage of the gentry. Landowners had to produce more and to lower the cost of production, which they tried to achieve by increasing peasant labor obligations and selling grain directly at Gdańsk rather than through local markets. These suffered in consequence. The directly run manorial estate *(folwark)* increasingly relied on serf labor, thus impoverishing the peasantry.

The officially proclaimed equality of all nobles, symbolized by the rejection of titles, could not obscure the growing gap between the szlachta and the magnates. The former, especially as they were getting poorer, tried to make up for it by jealously guarding their privileges and distancing themselves from the commoners. To engage in crafts and trade was demeaning for members of the gentry and was now forbidden. Yet the szlachta never became a fully closed caste, and its ranks grew by ennoblements and even more frequently by fraudulent passing into it by plebeians.

The magnates were able to adapt more easily to the changing economic conditions. The latifundia in the Ukraine which more than made up for some of the lost royal grants enabled them to play the role of "little kings." The magnates provided patronage to the middle and small gentry, maintained their own armies, built towns that enjoyed no autonomy, and attracted craftsmen and merchants who operated outside of guild restrictions. The little kings often pursued policies that were economically disadvantageous for the state; cities already affected by the contracting domestic market were further hurt by foreign luxury imports that the magnates promoted. Politically the great nobles were contributing to what the Polish constitutional historian, Bogusław Leśnodorski, has called the "decentralization of sovereignty."

All these processes accelerated and took on a more ominous character as a result of the wars and devastations that took place in the mid-seventeenth century. Polish experiences of foreign invasion and occupations in more recent times tend to make us forget that since the early fifteenth century Poland had fought wars along the borders or in enemy territory. While the country lost occasional battles it won the wars, and the late sixteenth and early seventeenth centuries saw several spectacular victories. Although Lithuania had lost one third of its eastern lands to the state of Muscovy, the territorial integrity of Poland proper remained intact. What is more, a dynamic eastward-directed Polish expansion related to demographic growth persisted, and the Ukrainian "wild steppes" offered opportunities for colonizing activities.

The Union of Lublin had been realized largely because of the ever increasing Russian danger to Lithuania, which called for concentrated efforts in the east. The struggle with Muscovy for Livonia (present day Latvia) under Sigismund Augustus brought one part of that country under the commonwealth's rule and made the Duchy of Courland a fief of the Polish crown. A large scale offensive against Muscovy took place during the reign of Stephen Batory (1575-1586), one of the best known Polish monarchs. Ably assisted by the chancellor and grand *hetman* (commander-in-chief) of the Crown Jan Zamoyski, the king scored heavily against Moscow; the commonwealth held the upper hand in the eastern conflict.

The successful union with Lithuania made Polish politicians and the szlachta regard unions with neighboring states as an excellent instrument of foreign policy. The thought of a dynastic union with Muscovy was voiced on several occasions, but eventually after Batory's death the Poles elected to their throne Sigismund Vasa, the crown prince of Sweden, whose mother was a Jagiellonian. The election seemed to open the way for a powerful Swedish-Polish union, but Sigismund III (1587-1632) proved to be a liability rather than an asset. A fervent Catholic and believer in Counter-Reformation, he could not maintain himself as king of Sweden and involved Poland in the Swedish conflict, highlighted by the victorious battle at Kircholm (Salaspils in Latvian) in 1605. Then Poland was dragged into an intervention in Russia, originating with the adventure of the False Dimitri, who claimed to have been a miraculously saved son of the Russian tsar. The story was immortalized in Mussorgsky's opera *Boris Godunov*.

Russia was now in the midst of its Time of Troubles, and the

Polish army led by the grand hetman Stanisław Żółkiewski defeated the Russian troops at Klushino (1610) and occupied Moscow. As a result of Żółkiewski's negotiations with the boyars, they elected Sigismund III's son, Władysław, as tsar of Russia. The event was of tremendous significance. As the Russian historian Nikolai Karamzin wrote, although Władysław had been elected by the city of Moscow alone, he stood a good chance of becoming tsar. Had this happened the autocratic regime in Russia would have changed and with it the fate of Russia. And Karamzin added that perhaps "the fate of Europe would also have changed for many centuries." But Sigismund would not approve the arrangement and claimed the crown for himself. The result was a powerful Russian reaction, a protracted war with Poland, and the surrender of the Polish garrison in the Kremlin. Russian hatred of the West as represented by Catholic Poland received a powerful impetus. Sigismund's concealed intervention on the Habsburg side in the Thirty Years' War also operated to Poland's disadvantage. The Habsburgs were allowed to recruit Polish cavalrymen—Rembrandt's famous painting of such a rider is in the Frick Collection in New York—whom they used against Transylvania. Since that province was under Turkish overlordship, Turkey reacted with an attack against Poland. In 1620 on the field of Cecora (Ţutora in Rumanian) the small Polish army was annihilated, and Żółkiewski killed.

By the 1630s peace was restored on all the fronts, and under King Władysław IV (1632-1648) Poland experienced a decade of stability. Contemporary noble writers extolled the Polish political, social, and economic system. Poland was a model of a successful constitutional government as opposed to arbitrary and absolute regimes of other states. Not unlike the ante-bellum South that placed its faith in "king cotton" Poland thought of itself as the irreplaceable granary of the West. This complacency rested on serious misconceptions, domestic and international. Władysław IV's efforts to strengthen the monarchy by internal devices and by a grandiose plan of liberating the Balkans from Turkey misfired. In his plans Władysław had assigned an important role to the Ukrainian Cossacks, restless and rebelling against magnates' attempts of subjecting them to serfdom. The failure of his plans precipitated a crisis, and in 1648 the exasperated Cossacks rose in rebellion under the leadership of Bohdan Khmelnitsky. An experienced warrior and politician, whom some contemporaries and historians compared to Cromwell, Khmelnitsky concluded an alliance with the Crimean Tartars and defeated the Polish troops. Soon all the Ukraine was in flames. The szlachta, the priests, and the Jews fell victim to large-scale massacres.

The sudden death of Władysław IV deprived Poland of leadership, and two trends emerged: one favoring negotiations and compromises, the other, represented by one of the little kings of the Ukraine, Prince Jeremi Wiśniowiecki, advocating war until victory. The prince did not succeed in defeating the Cossacks but rendered a negotiated peace impossible. In the course of the struggles, in which the battle of Piławce became the symbol of a shameful Polish defeat and the defense of Zbaraż an example of great bravery, the character and the goals of the Cossack uprising changed. Originally an upheaval directed mainly against the oppression by the magnates and favoring a stronger monarchy, the uprising became a sociopolitical revolution with religious and national objectives. The Ukraine emerged as a political unit and the Cossack leadership sought to determine its fate.

Successive Polish-Cossack peace treaties, including one signed after the victorious battle of Beresteczko of 1651 in which the new king John Casimir (1648-1668) distinguished himself, brought no lasting solution. They provided for varying schemes of autonomy for the Ukrainian provinces, an enlargement of the Cossack registered host, and grants of nobility to its leadership, but failed to satisfy all parties. Khmelnitsky decided then to seek the protection of the tsar and recognized his authority in the Pact of Pereiaslav, in 1654. To Khmelnitsky this was a palliative and not a permanent merger of the Ukraine with Muscovy, as Russian historiography tends to represent it. Pereiaslav', however, meant a Polish-Russian war; the conflict was becoming internationalized. While Khmelnitsky advanced in the south and the Muscovite armies drove deep into Lithuania and occupied its capital Wilno (Vilnius in Lithuanian), the commonwealth faced another invasion. In the summer of 1665 Swedish armies entered Polish and Lithuanian territory. The nobility in western Poland accepted Charles X Gustavus as king, and the grand hetman of Lithuania, Prince Janusz Radziwiłł, signed an act of union with Sweden. Luckless John Casimir, abandoned and defeated in the field, sought refuge in Silesia. Virtually all of Poland proper found itself under Swedish control.

The Polish szlachta at first thought that it had merely exercised its sovereign power by accepting a new ruler. It was quickly deceived. Treated as conquered subjects and delivered to the brutalities of mercenary troops, the Poles quickly rose against the Swedes. The successful defense of the monastery of Jasna Góra in Częstochowa (a famous Marian shrine) became a symbol of patriotic resistance to foreigners and Protestants. This aspect acquired great significance and Polish Protestants were accused of collaboration with the Swedes. Similar charges, though seemingly less well founded, were made against Jews. The war against the Swedish invaders proved long and costly and occasioned the growth of an extensive system of alliances. In the course of the fighting the name of Stefan Czarniecki, the hero of partisan warfare, became famous and eventually was remembered in the Polish national anthem.

The Swedish war finally ended and the Treaty of Oliwa was signed in 1660. It involved no territorial sacrifices. The treaty confirmed, however, complete independence of Prussia, which had shifted sides during the war and had to be bought off by this important concession. Since Poland had also recognized the succession of the electors of Brandenburg to Prussia, the Hohenzollerns now encircled the Pomeranian "Corridor." In the east hostilities against Russia continued for seven more years, the Ukraine occupying the center of the conflict. In 1658 Poland succeeded in negotiating the Agreement of Hadziacz (Hadiach) with Khmelnitsky's successors. It stipulated the establishment of an autonomous duchy within the commonwealth composed of the Ukrainian provinces, with its own administration, its own Cossack and mercenary army, separate courts, and two academies of higher learning. Large numbers of Cossack leaders were to be ennobled. Unlike the Union of Lublin, the Agreement of Hadziacz could not be changed save in agreement with the Ukrainian side. This bold scheme came too late, yet one can argue that it could not have come earlier. It was only at this point that the Ukraine produced its own elite composed of the Cossack upper crust and the local gentry which could have been a political partner of the Polish noble nation.

The Agreement of Hadziacz never came into practice. Poles, Russians, and the Cossacks (divided into hostile factions) fought over the Ukraine until the Polish-Russian treaty of Andrusovo, which in 1667 split the country into two parts divided by the Dnieper River. The commonwealth lost sizable territories; the Ukrainian question received no solution; the real victor was Russia whose might compared to the commonwealth had increased in every respect.

The 1648-1672 period is of crucial significance for Polish history. Immortalized in the great historical novel, the *Trilogy,* by Henryk Sienkiewicz, recently made into a series of films, it is remembered as the "deluge," a flooding of the country by Cossacks, Tartars, Swedes, Russians, Transylvanians, Turks, and Prussians, countered by a valiant Polish defense against great odds and treachery. The historian sees it as a period of profound crisis that shook the very foundations of the commonwealth and started the country's decline.

The devastation of the country was terrible. Main cities such as the old capital Cracow, Warsaw (the country's capital since the early seventeenth century), Poznań, and others lay in ruins. Much of the inventory, agricultural implements, and cattle had been destroyed throughout the countryside. The population, which stood at roughly 10 million inhabitants in the early part of the century, declined by some 30 percent. Recovery was slow, and the manorial system adversely affected the economy of the country. Ruined towns could not be quickly rebuilt owing to bad market conditions; many peasants who had been particularly badly hit shifted to a barter economy; the richer gentry and particularly the magnates weathered the storm better, but largely by making their estates more self-sufficient and shifting the burden on the peasants. There is no doubt that the purchasing power of the population contracted significantly. Yet to assert, as some Marxist historians do, that the serf-based manorial economy made recovery impossible is not convincing. This interpretation fails to explain why some attempts made to convert peasant obligations to rents, in other words abandoning serfdom, produced no remedy. It is clear that additional factors operated that had to do with both internal and external markets.

The decline of a demand for grain in the West was very serious. By 1660 the export trade via Gdańsk fell to one third of the early seventeenth-century figure. The term of foreign trade became distinctly unfavorable for Poland. Native production fell off, and it is likely that the economic levels of the sixteenth century were regained only in the decade 1750-1760.

Political and cultural decline accompanied the economic slump, and they affected each other. As a result of wars fought against Lutheran Swedes and Germans, Orthodox Russians and Cossacks, and Moslem Turks and Tartars, Polish patriotism became closely associated with militant Catholicism. Poland came to be represented as a bulwark of Christian Europe against Islam, the *Antemurale*. The apogee of the idea came in the late seventeenth century. Traditional Polish religious toleration was breached by the expulsion of Unitarians accused of having collaborated with the Swedes, although the expulsion was prompted more by political than religious reasons. Other Protestant communities remained unmolested, in contrast to their persecution in contemporary France under Louis XIV and in the Habsburg lands.

The period also saw the growth of Sarmatism, so called after the mythical ancestors of the Poles, the Sarmatians. This was an ideology asserting a unique Polish way of life, and it came to reflect the gentry's pride in their own and Poland's superiority over others. While it may have served as a bond keeping the noble nation together and reinforcing republicanism, it also led to xenophobia and parochialism. The West was believed to have nothing to offer by way of example to the Polish state and society.

In 1652 the notorious *liberum veto* (free veto) made its triumphant entry. A single deputy vetoed the prolongation of the sejm session, and his objection was recognized as a valid reason to dissolve the diet. The principle of unanimity had been, of course, an old idea and practice; it has survived to the present day in the United States in jury trials. One tends to forget that the system of majority vote presupposes the fulfillment of certain difficult conditions and arrangements. The votes must be considered equal and a system of counting them must be acceptable to the voters. If a minority is to conform to majority decisions a strong executive capable of enforcing such decisions must be on hand. In Poland many of these conditions were hard to satisfy and the vagueness of sejm procedural rules left great latitude for different interpretations. General consensus was regarded in the past as sufficient, and on occasions majority decisions were imposed on a reluctant minority. Only a few sejms prior to the mid-seventeenth century had disbanded because of their inability to agree on legislation. Nor were confederations (leagues of nobles at times of national emergency) ever affected by liberum veto.

The liberum veto must not be regarded as the cause of Poland's decline but rather as its symptom. The loss of royal prestige and continued emancipation of magnates from the king's influence distorted the political balance. It is revealing that liberum veto was used much more frequently by deputies from the eastern lands, where the great latifundia prevailed, than from central and western parts of the commonwealth. Represented as the surest safeguard of individual liberty ("golden liberty") against royal corruption of the diet, it became an instrument wielded by the magnates, occasionally by the king, and finally by the neighboring powers. Paralyzing the functioning of the legislature, the veto reflected a demoralization of the country and the decline of public spirit. Narrow interests and privileges were seen as tantamount to patriotism; political sovereignty became ever more fragmented.

After the deluge the unpopular John Casimir attempted reforms to strengthen the monarchy and improve the lot of the peasantry, which had played an important role in the partisan warfare against the Swedes. The maladroit royal initiative provoked an armed rokosz and civil war. Nothing useful was achieved and the king abdicated, prophetically warning the nation of black days that lay ahead. His successor, Michael Korybut Wiśniowiecki (1669–1673), the son of the little king of the Cossack wars, ruled shortly and ineffectively. A Polish historian, Władysław Konopczyński, remarked that Michael spoke seven languages but had nothing interesting to say in any of them. Under his reign Poland became involved in a war with Turkey over the perennial Ukrainian question and forced to sign a humiliating peace that abandoned parts of Podolia to the Turks.

The hero of the Turkish wars was Jan Sobieski, elected king in 1674 and reigning until 1696 as John III. Some signs of internal stability and economic recovery appeared during his reign, and Poland's position seemed to improve. Whether Sobieski's foreign policy was best calculated to assist the country is debatable, and for better or worse Poland became involved as an ally of the Habsburgs in a new great war against Turkey. The relief of Vienna by the Polish and imperial armies under Sobieski's supreme command in 1683 was the last of those victories that have become part of the national tradition. The war, however, dragged on until 1699 and brought no great advantages to Poland save the recovery of Podolia. The seventeenth century enjoyed only thirty-two years of peace and saw 90 percent of the budget spent on military needs that had sapped Poland's strength.

The first half of the eighteenth century became truly Poland's dark age. While the country was continuing an economic recovery, the first of the two kings from the Saxon Wettin dynasty embroiled it in the Northern War against Sweden. The result was new occupation, devastations comparable to those of the deluge, and civil strife. The ruler, Augustus II (1697–1733), was primarily interested in the greatness of his house and sought to enhance it through attempts at absolutism in Poland. At one point he even tried to achieve his goals in cooperation with the neighboring powers, and schemed Poland's partitions. In the prevailing turmoil, Peter the Great of Russia rose to be an arbiter between the king and his subjects. The commonwealth was turning into an object of international politics and a Russian protectorate. The neighboring powers saw to it that no meaningful reforms were carried out. The Polish army, never large, fell alarmingly behind those of Russia, Prussia, and Austria, in both numbers and equipment. Towns continued to decline, serfdom became harsher, economically the country was in chaos. The cultural level sank low and the descendants of highly educated families were often barely literate.

Coteries and factions of magnates struggled with each other and against the indolent Augustus III (1733–1763) who succeeded his father. The War of the Polish Succession, fought on the Rhine between Russia and Austria against France, assured Russian predominance in Poland. The French-supported rival king, Stanisław Leszczyński, the father-in-law of Louis XV, had to leave the country. Compensated with the Duchy of Lorraine, he made his court an important center of Polish national revival. Certain processes had indeed begun to take place in mid-eighteenth century Poland that shaped its subsequent development. A period of peace encouraged agriculture and grain exports rose again. The magnates began to build factories some of which produced for the latifundia, operating as economic units, while others had a wider range and produced for the national market. Warsaw expanded as an urban center of banking and credit. An economic revival became noticeable although it was still largely one-sided insofar as it profited mainly one class, that of great landowners.

By the 1740s there were signs of intellectual revival. Political writings appeared, criticizing the existing conditions and calling for reforms, among others by former king Leszczyński and the Piarist educator, Stanisław Konarski. Konarski founded an elitist academy, Collegium Nobilium, and introduced curricular reforms in the network of Piarist schools. This heralded a new era in education. Jesuit schools followed suit by overhauling their educational systems. Numbers of institutions and pupils began to grow, and Western ideas of the Enlightenment penetrated the country, often through the Freemasonry.

In political life, which was still characterized by crude methods of corruption, intimidation, and anarchy, new trends began to form. If the Potocki-Radziwiłł "republican" faction orienting itself toward France and Turkey was highly conservative, the Czartoryski "Family" advocated a coherent program of reforms. They wished to eliminate the liberum veto, overcome the king-diet dualism exploited by the oligarchs, and make the reformed *sejm* a real center of power. Related to the Czartoryskis through his mother, the young Stanislas Augustus Poniatowski believed that the solution lay rather in strengthened royal power and hereditary monarchy, but otherwise he agreed with his uncles that a thorough reform of the state and society was essential. He also shared their belief that this could only be accomplished in cooperation and with the approval of Russia.

In 1764 Catherine II of Russia made clear that she favored the election of Stanislas Augustus as king, and the Family, albeit reluctantly, threw its power behind him. The new king began his reign (1764–1795) under the stigma of being a creature of Russia, in addition to having been one of Catherine's lovers. Yet he was no Russian puppet, and attempted to pursue policies of his own. Stanislas Augustus, a monarch much maligned by contemporaries and many historians, was a highly cultured and intelligent man. Generally acknowledged as patron of arts and letters, he also was a politician of considerable talent—a typical product of the Enlightenment, with all the virtues and vices characteristic of this age.

The electoral sejm had accomplished certain reforms, and the king concentrated on putting order in the country's finances, sorely inadequate for its needs, and on promoting education. In 1765 he founded the Knights' School, a secular military academy which trained the country's elite in modern scholarship and civic virtues. Due to his inspiration a periodical, the *Monitor,* was founded to campaign for a modernization of state and society. It bitterly attacked Sarmatism and religious intolerance, and advocated improving the lot of the peasantry and extending civic rights to the burghers. The king clearly sought to gain a basis of power in the country by organizing his own supporters in the sejm and the local dietines. He struggled against heavy odds: inertia of the gentry, vested interests of the magnates used to conducting their own policies and cooperating with foreign courts, and the designs of St. Petersburg.

Catherine II wished Poland to be a half-ally and a half-vassal of Russia. She was not opposed to limited reforms that would strengthen the country but not to the point of emancipating Poland from her tutelage. Stanislas Augustus' efforts to be his own master and his timid but independent moves in the field of foreign policy evoked deep suspicions in Russia. The developments have a familiar, twentieth-century ring. As for Prussia, Frederick II was adamant that Poland be "kept in lethargy" and he worked to that end both in Poland and in St. Petersburg.

The first attempt at reforms presented to the sejm in 1766 broke down in the teeth of Russo-Prussian opposition. The two powers threatened war if liberum veto were abolished, and insisted that religious dissenters—Protestants and Orthodox—whom they used as pawns to keep the country in check, be granted equality. The conservative szlachta was easily induced to oppose constitutional reform; however, it was quite determined not to give equality to the religious dissenters. Russia encouraged the forming of confederations directed against the king, and having thus checkmated him, proceeded to press him for concessions to dissenters. Magnates and

church leaders who had unwittingly played Russia's game by opposing Stanislas Augustus in the matter of reforms now took a strong
stand against the king and Russia when the religious issue came to
the fore.

The king found himself in a terrible situation. Russian-inspired
confederations had forced him to desist from constitutional reforms.
Now he had to fare the conservatives over the religious issue, and
appear to be a Russian tool. A new union of nobles known as the
Bar Confederation (1768) combined an almost fanatical Catholic
zeal with republican and anti-Russian slogans. The confederates
received support from France and Turkey; the latter even declared
war on Russia. Historians have not been unanimous in their appraisal of Bar Confederation. Some have stressed its patriotism,
others pointed to its conservatism. It attracted the attention of
contemporary French philosophers, notably Jean Jacques Rousseau,
who offered written advice on how to reform Poland. It stimulated
writings about politics, as by Claude de Ruhlière whose *Histoire
de l'anarchie en Pologne* popularized the Bar legend and affected
Western thinking about the incurable Polish political faults. Finally, the Bar Confederation when taken together with the Turkish-
Russian war accelerated the first partition of Poland.

Was there a way out for Stanislas Augustus and the Poles? Had
the king been utterly ruthless and unscrupulous he might have sided
fully with the Russians. St. Petersburg had invited him to join in
the Turkish war and to crack down unmercifully on the confederates. Had he chosen such a course he might have regained the full
confidence of Catherine even at the price of losing all his popularity
in Poland. But the king refused, partly perhaps on moral grounds
but also because he could not believe that Russia would go to the
extreme of partitioning the commonwealth. Yet this is precisely
what happened.

The first partition of 1772, strongly advocated by Prussia and
finally decided upon by St. Petersburg—Austria followed reluctantly
but still managed to seize a considerable part of Polish territory—
resulted from the need to reconcile the interests of the three powers.
Russia and Austria resolved their Balkan conflicts at Poland's expense, and Prussia gained from the deal. This was the application
of the balance of power principle in its extreme form of *système
copartageant,* as Albert Sorel had called it. It is useless to seek
religious, ethnic, or historic justifications for the decision of the
three courts. As Stanislas Augustus wrote at the time, "the only
motive of the enterprise" was "the force of these powers." The commonwealth lost roughly one third of its inhabitants and territory.

Prussia now barred Polish access to the Baltic, and Austria had seized the rich and densely inhabited southern Poland with the old capital of Cracow.

Edmund Burke called the partition "the first very great breach in the modern political system in Europe" and prophetically pointed to its long-range consequences for international relations. It is obvious that the country's weakness made the partition possible, and the two or three generations of Poles preceding it bore much responsibility for what had happened. This is not, however, the same as saying that Polish historical evolution had made the partitions inevitable, or that the entire Polish history has to be viewed from the partitions' vantage point.

It is not easy to perceive the main trends in the history of a country; even harder to define them as characteristic or unique, yet I shall try to do it by way of a summary. In the field of foreign policy the idea of expansion through union rather than through conquest was characteristic, at least from the late fourteenth century on. Poland was relatively free from the military-imperialist tradition of other states, the reason being largely the reluctance of the noble nation to be involved in wars that could strengthen the monarchy and open the way to absolutism. In the political-constitutional field the characteristic feature appears to have been a failure of the estates model, and the growth and decline of gentry democracy. The stress had been on the rights and liberties of the noble nation and on opposition to royalism. The so-called monarchic interpretation in Polish historiography ascribed the principal weakness of the state to the absence of a strong royal power; the republican emphasized the vitality of a mixed system of government through which the noble nation effectively restrained absolutism. The monarchists point to a causal relationship between anarchy and the first partition. The republicans draw attention to a resilience and inner strength of the mixed system which permitted survival even in conditions of anarchy.

By adhering to its unique form of government, Poland proved unable to develop an efficient bureaucracy, a large standing army, and a sound financial basis for the state. And these were precisely the elements which proved decisive in the transformation of the neighboring Prussia, Austria, and Russia into first-rate powers.

The growth of anarchy was at least partly due to the imbalance in development between the agricultural and urban sectors, between the szlachta and the middle class. Yet modern research shows that this imbalance started to become pronounced later than it was originally thought, and was greatly affected by the outside European

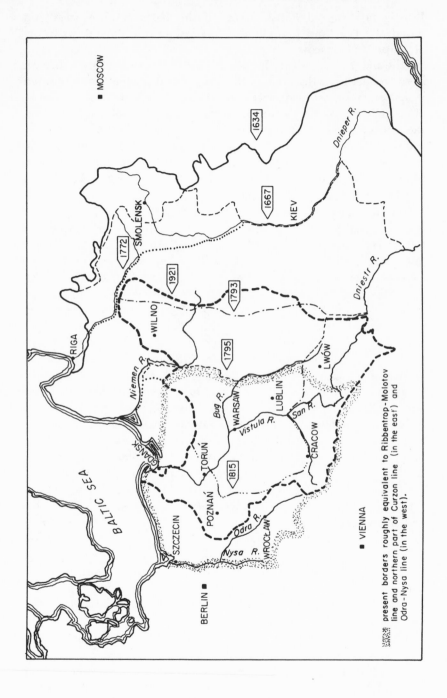

1. Poland's receding borders in the east

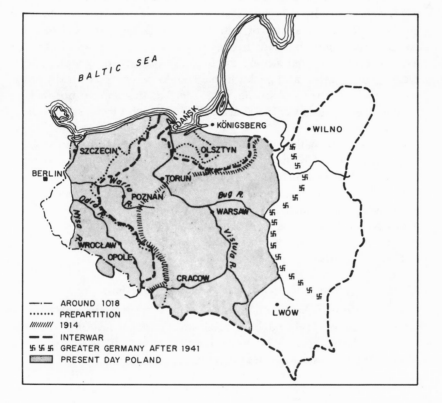

2. German-Polish borders in the course of history

market. Similarly, the question of peasant serfdom is more complex than formerly believed, and legal norms do not always provide a key to an understanding of realities. Finally, the socioeconomic structure characterized by serfdom was not unique for Poland but prevailed in all of Europe east of the Elbe River, roughly the area of the present-day Eastern Bloc. What was unique in Poland was the combination of serfdom with a republican regime.

In the vast field of culture and civilization, toleration for different races and religions, especially during the period of the highly heterogeneous commonwealth, was a marked Polish phenomenon. The noble nation itself emerged as an amalgamate of different ethnic groups, and the attraction of Polish culture rather than deliberate polonization made the state a cohesive whole. This integration was not, however, achieved among the broad masses of the people. But even if parochialism and backwardness could be observed in the late seventeenth century and in the Saxon period, this should not make us forget the splendid cultural achievements of the Renaissance and Reformation.

Neither Spain which was in full decline by the eighteenth century, nor England with its rotten boroughs, Gordon riots, and political instability—which made some contemporaries compare it to Poland—experienced the Polish fate, but then their geopolitical position guarded them against such a danger. The Polish-Lithuanian Commonwealth could not afford the luxury of weakness, were it even temporary, and its geographic position proved a basic factor of Poland's undoing.

The American and Polish Revolutions

A discussion of American-Polish relations in the late eighteenth century must be prefaced by a brief survey of earlier contacts. It is evident that people in both countries knew very little about each other. Columbus's discoveries attracted scant notice in Poland which was then only beginning to become interested in maritime trade that was in any case largely confined to the Baltic. Still, a letter from Columbus to Raphael de Santis dated April 1493 appeared in Poland in a German translation a few years later. German humanist writings provided additional information on Columbus, and in the seventeenth century there was some debate in Polish academic circles whether the new land should not have been called Columbina rather than America. One of the oldest known references to North America is made in a book entitled *Introductio in Ptholomei Cosmographiam* . . . by Jan of Stobnica published in Cracow in 1512. America appeared on a Polish-made globe, but cartographers did not get everything right. Florida, for instance, was represented as an island, and it was only at the turn of the sixteenth and seventeenth centuries that New France and New England were mentioned for the first time.

Other references to the new continent may be found in a section of Copernicus' work, in a passage of Marcin Bielski's chronicle, and in a poem by Sebastian Klonowicz. Sixteenth-century Poles were chiefly interested in the Catholic Spanish American empire; only two hundred years later did the Protestant colonies in the north attract real interest. Some analogies began to be drawn between American and Polish experiences. The westward movement brought to mind Polish activity in the Ukrainian steppes and the east; pioneering settlers could be compared to gentry colonists and Red Indians to Tartars.

The year 1608—during the reign of Sigismund III Vasa—is traditionally considered as the date of the arrival of the first Polish settlers to America. A group of artisans specializing in the manufacture of glass, pitch, and tar, which contemporary Poland exported to England, were brought to Jamestown. The work of these Polanders was praised by Captain John Smith, and it may have been Smith who, having once passed through Poland, was responsible for bringing them to Virginia. Some ten years later the Jamestown Poles protested their disfranchisement in local elections and went on strike. Virginia Company resolved the dispute in their favor. In the second half of the seventeenth century other Poles and Lithuanians came to the American colonies. Perhaps some of them were Unitarians expelled after the Swedish wars. One finds them mainly in New Amsterdam, although a few had moved south and west. A Protestant nobleman, Albrecht Zaborowski, settled in New Jersey founding the Zabriskie family; there were Poles in Pennsylvania who usually settled among Germans, probably for religious reasons. A fort built by Stuyvesant on the Delaware was called Fort Casimir, a popular Polish name borne at that time by King John Casimir.

In the early eighteenth century some Polish Brethren (Unitarians or Socinians) settled together with Czech Brethren in Virginia. Roughly at that time Antoni Sadowski, reputed founder of the Sandusky family, came to Philadelphia. His descendants were later active in Kentucky. Whether these people remained in touch with Poland is not known; no letters or communications have been discovered so far. Information about other American-Polish contacts is scarce. There exists an open letter addressed by William Penn to King John III Sobieski interceding on behalf of Quakers allegedly discriminated against in Gdańsk. It appears that Polish potash and starch sporadically reached America. The carriers may well

33

have been Gdańsk ships that occasionally sailed across the Atlantic in the seventeenth and mid-eighteenth centuries. Some poetry and prose (notably the political tract by W. Goślicki, *De Optimo Senatore*) was translated into English at the turn of the sixteenth and seventeenth centuries and published in England. It may well have been known in America as well. When in the late 1790s Julian Niemcewicz visited the Harvard College library, he noticed there the *Bibliotheca Fratrum Polonorum*. It is likely that other Polish books were there as well.

The last four decades of the eighteenth century saw the rise of Polish interest in America and vice versa and constituted the beginnings of an American-Polish relationship properly speaking. This relationship was obviously restricted and operated on divergent levels. American leaders, engaged in political debates of constitutional issues, made references to Polish experiences. Some Poles, notably Kościuszko and Pułaski, came to participate in the Revolutionary War. In Poland, the example of the United States was invoked within the context of the reform movement that swept the country in the late 1780s and early 1790s. Personal contacts between Americans and Poles multiplied. As dissimilar as American and Polish developments were at the time, an occasional comparison of the two nations was made. After the first revolutionary outbreaks took place in America, Edmund Burke thought that the Virginians were acting rather like the Poles. R. R. Palmer has observed that the American colonists and the Poles had belonged to those Europeans who had paid the lowest taxes in the eighteenth century.

The American press, for instance the *Virginia Gazette,* informed its readers about political developments in Poland, and the *Gazette de Leyde,* published in Holland in French, devoted considerable attention to Polish affairs. Jefferson was among the Americans who subscribed to this newspaper. The state of affairs of the Polish commonwealth looked gloomy, and Benjamin Franklin, commenting on the 1764 election of Stanislas Augustus, wrote ironically about the Poles "cutting each other's throat." He remarked that their neighbors had really no right "to disturb them in the enjoyment," and noted that the Russian army had entered Poland to secure "freedom of the election." Poland, which John Adams classified together with England as a "regal republic," seemed to offer the worst example of a misgoverned and disorganized country. Adams cited with approval Jean Jacques Rousseau's view of the state as hopelessly dominated by the nobility. In the *Defence of the Constitutions . . . of the United States*—two letters in which contained the first American-written outline of Poland's history—Adams opined that the country had been ruined by one-class rule, oppression of the peasantry by the gentry, and faulty forms of government. James Wilson would characterize Poland a little later as "composed only of slaves, headed and commanded by a few despots," in brief a country without a "people."

Arguing the case of the right form of government for the United States, Adams used Poland as an example "of the effects of 'collecting all authority into one centre,' of neglecting an equilibrium of powers, and of not having three branches in the legislature." Campaigning for a federalist regime in America, Hamilton and Madison called Poland a country equally "unfit for self-government and self-defense." Jefferson felt that the crisis in Poland was self-inflicted, and in a letter to Madison cited the frightening example of foreign interference in the elections of Polish kings. Should presidency for life be adopted in America, a similar danger could arise there. The pitfall of unanimity as exemplified by the Polish liberum veto was also to be avoided.

In criticizing Poland, the American observers did not seem to have noted the growing Polish movement for reforms. As for the first partition in 1772, they disapproved of it on moral grounds—Adams reporting to the Congress in 1779 called it "shameful"—but otherwise devoted little attention to it. A somewhat contemptuous note crept into Franklin's letter to his son of May 1772 about "miserable Poland" that was going to be "pacified" if the entry of "more foreign armies into it, can produce peace." Adams wrote that 12 million people would never allow their country to be dismembered if they lived under an English or American constitution. One can hardly find any American echoes of the astute appraisal of Edmund Burke about the significance of Polish partitions for international relations. Perhaps Gouverneur Morris' remark in 1790 that Prussia's control of Gdańsk and Toruń will make it a naval power and provide it with a key to the "great granary of Europe" comes closest to Burke's view. Events in Poland were of no genuine concern for the colonies struggling to be free.

In his report to the Congress, Adams had pointed out that the truncated Poland had "no occasion for the productions of America"; he saw "little probability of commerce, and less of any political connection between that nation and us." Hamilton opined in 1777 that the Prussian seizure of Pomerania might make Frederick II interested in maritime economic schemes and thus favor the cause of American independence. There was one interesting instance of a connection, albeit indirect, between the Declaration of Independence and the first partition of Poland. While analyzing the reasons that prompted the Congress to declare formal independence in 1776, the American historian James H. Hutson points to the fears of an impending partition of North America between England, France, and Spain. He cites the Philadelphia journals sounding alarm in the spring of 1776 and speaking of the "partition spirit" prevailing in Europe, as exemplified by the case of Poland. Richard Henry Lee, among others, made references to Poland and warned of the dangerous precedent of greater powers dismembering weaker states.

Although far away and preoccupied with her own problems, Poland followed with considerable interest the Revolutionary War in America, and some of its citizens crossed the Atlantic to participate in the fighting. In 1776 the young captain of engineers, Tadeusz Kościuszko, having left Poland for France as a result of an unhappy love affair, volunteered his services to the American cause. Dispatched with a group of French officers, he spent the next eight years in this country performing most creditably and making a genuine contribution to the war effort. He was present at Ticonderoga and helped to win the battle of Saratoga. Sent to fortify the defenses along the Hudson, he distinguished himself by constructing the formidable fortifications at West Point. Transferred later to the command of General Nathaniel Greene, Kościuszko earned his praise and friendship. In 1783 he received the rank of brigadier general from the Congress and was admitted to the prestigious Society of the Cincinnati. A year later he returned to Poland.

Although George Washington described Kościuszko to the Congress as a "gentleman of science and merit," there seems to have been no real intimacy between the two men. Kościuszko, who later became an object of admiration in America and a symbol of early Polish-American relations, was then but a junior, although exceptionally gifted officer of engineers, who could not easily leave a mark on America's leaders.

The other Pole who came via Paris to America in 1777 was Kazimierz (Casimir) Pułaski. Franklin recommended him as an officer "famous throughout Europe for his bravery and conduct in defense of the liberties of his country." A former leader of the Bar Confederation, with good contacts in French circles, Pułaski presented a contrast to Kościuszko. A flamboyant, fiery, and proud gentleman who felt that to be on par with Western aristocrats he must use the title of count to which he had no right, Pułaski was a dashing cavalryman. His experience had been largely with the irregular confederate troops, and he lacked the sound military training Kościuszko had received at the Knights' School and in Paris. Appointed by the Congress to the newly created post of Commander of Horse with the rank of brigadier general, Pułaski has sometimes been called the father of American cavalry, possibly an exaggeration if we think of other existing cavalry units. Not easily amenable to discipline, Pułaski organized, equipped, and assumed the command of a special legion composed mostly of cavalrymen and foreign volunteers. Displaying a banner offered by the Moravian Sisters of Bethlehem, the legion—later rendered famous by Longfellow's poem—fought with great bravery in the south relieving Charleston and charging at Savannah. It was at Savannah in 1779 that Pułaski was wounded and died on board the brig *Wasp*.

Pułaski seems to have caught the imagination of contemporaries to a greater extent than Kościuszko. Perhaps his death on the battlefield was partly responsible for it. He was, of course, better known, having begun his career as a brigadier general while Kościuszko became one only at the end of the war. Already in 1779 the Congress voted that a monument to Pułaski be built, but this was not done, though a column with a bas-relief commemorating Pułaski was erected in Savannah in the 1880s. A monument to Pułaski was built only in 1910 with Polish American contributions.

A complete list of Polish participants in the Revolutionary War is hard to draw up. Some of the fighters were settlers of Polish extraction; some arrived through France or England. Insofar as is known, none came directly from Poland. The fortunes of the unknown Kościuszko in America were of little interest to the Polish public; only his family found out about his departure to America through Franklin. Pułaski's name was familiar to many Poles, and a Polish newspaper mentioned his stay in America and printed the news of his death. The press also noticed the death of another Pole, Paweł Grabowski, whose family was close to Stanislas Augustus and who had gone from England to fight on the British side.

Kościuszko returned to Poland in 1784, but "our American hero," as a contemporary referred to him, was unable to find a position in the small Polish army. He joined it with the rank of brigadier general only in 1789 when the army underwent major reorganization and expansion.

The Kościuszko-Pułaski contribution to the Revolutionary War became a symbol of Polish attachment to American liberty, particularly dear to Americans of Polish descent—and is very important in that sense—but we shall not dwell on it here any longer. Instead let us turn to the impact of American developments on Poland which also deserves attention. In the second half of the eighteenth century Polish awareness of the New World grew. As a result of educational reforms the Jesuit schools introduced world geography into their curricula. Schools organized a little later under the Commission of National Education adopted new textbooks that contained references to American colonies and the Revolution. The very word American used thus far to describe Red Indians began to be applied to the colonists.

The great unheaval in America attracted close attention of Polish governmental circles and political groups. The king and his collaborators were critical of England's handling of the colonies; being pro-English they hoped for Whig ascendancy in Britain and a speedy end of the conflict. Stanislas Augustus felt that from the Polish point of view it was most important that London have free hands to deal with European matters. When the Revolutionary War developed into an international conflict, Polish diplomacy, although unable to exert any influence, watched the course of events with anxiety. The likely weakening of both England and France as a result of the war worried Warsaw. Contacts with American leaders, particularly Franklin in Paris, were established, and in 1786 the king enlisted the services of Lewis Littlepage of Virginia as his agent. Two years later the well-known Italo-Virginian Philip Mazzei became a collaborator of Stanislas Augustus and a link with the West and America.

The enlightened public in Poland was quite familiar with events across the ocean. Polish journalism had grown rapidly under Stanislas Augustus' reign; newsmen read about the colonies and followed reports in the Western press. One of the leading Polish reformers, Ignacy Potocki, had books in his library dealing with America. The writings of Jefferson, Adams, Thomas Paine, and Joel Barlow were known to the Poles. Franklin forwarded a copy of the Articles of Confederation to Stanislas Augustus. Among books on the American Revolution translated into Polish were T. G. Raynal's work and a German apologia edited by the Rev. Paweł Kollacz. The daily *Warsaw Gazette* (Gazeta Warszawska) appearing since 1774 and the monthly *Historical-Political Memoir* (Pamiętnik historyczno-polityczny) which began its publication eight year later, translated and reprinted the Declaration of Independence, the Articles of Confederation, and the Constitution. In 1783 the *Memoir* carried a lengthy article entitled "What effect will the freedom of America have on trade and the political state of Europe?" There were comments on the possible competition of American wood and potash with Polish exports of these articles. Somewhat later plans were entertained in Warsaw of cultivating Virginia tobacco and American cotton in Poland.

Except for some early writings in the *Warsaw Gazette,* the press adopted a pro-American position. Even Polish conservatives were impressed by such watchwords of the colonists as defense of property and liberty. Somewhat patronizing remarks about Washington, Franklin, and Adams because of their lowly occupations as farmers, printers, or tradesmen, soon gave way to a veritable cult of these leaders. This was especially true for Washington and Franklin, whom numerous Poles visited in Paris. Jefferson and Hamilton seem to have been less noticed. Pro-American sentiments occasionally took somewhat bizarre forms, as when the palatine of Mazovia, Piotr Mostowski, proposed to the Continental Congress the establishment of a New Poland in America and offered as his contribution to the American cause a healing balm. The Polish Masonic Order of Knights of Divine Providence wrote to Washington asking him to nominate American members to this organization.

The poet Kajetan Węgierski, who visited America in 1783 and left what is the oldest Polish eyewitness description of that country, was forcefully struck by the contrast between American success and Polish misfortunes. In a letter to John Dickinson (which was long believed to have been penned by Kościuszko) Węgierski wrote: "When I think, Sir, that with three million people, and without money you have shaken off the yoke of such a power as England, and have acquired such an extensive territory—and that Poland has suffered herself to be robbed of five million souls and a vast country— I acknowledge, I do not understand the cause of such a difference." Węgierski called on the Americans to preserve their newly won rights and added that if the gods showed no pity to Poland he would tell his countrymen: "Come, cross the seas, and insure to your children liberty and property!"

The news of troubles, economic, political and constitutional, growing in the United States in the mid-1780s worried pro-American Poles. The editor of the *Memoir* voiced his fear that given the instability and disunity of the thirteen states America might have become free too soon. Some years later he lamented that "all our hopes were mere dreams." In turn, the worried Kościuszko wrote to his former commander General Greene asking for information. But by 1789 the editor of the *Memoir* struck a more optimistic note. Washington was elected president, and even if conditions in America seemed chaotic, the Polish liberum veto was far worse. The mention of the veto at this point was not accidental, for Poland's diet was just then embarking on a major program of reforms.

The revival under Stanislas Augustus, intellectual, political, and economic, had gathered momentum since the first partition. True, serious obstacles to sweeping reforms continued to exist. The truncated Polish state, while still one of the largest in Europe, had an odd geographical shape and ethnic composition. The vast Ukrainian and Belorussian areas were still part of the commonwealth; the densely populated, ethnically Polish lands to the west had been lost. Gdańsk had successfully resisted absorption into Prussia but its geographic connection with Poland was severed. Polish trade had to reorient itself to the southeast: a Black Sea Trade Company came into existence. Feverish economic activity saw the growth of industrial enterprises producing for the national market; joint stock companies made their appearance. Overambitious attempts to build in record time a network of diverse factories in the royal lands of Lithuania ended in failure. It was not easy to carry out an economic revolution from above in a country that had no mercantilist traditions or absolute government. A great deal, however, was accomplished. Canals were built, banks established, factories came into existence. Between 1764 and 1792 the population of Warsaw grew from 30,000 to 120,000—an urban center capable of providing leadership to the burgher class throughout Poland.

The influence of physiocratic ideas in Poland was part of the general impact of the Enlightenment. Polish society was going through an intellectual upheaval patronized by the king and several progressive magnates. Painting, architecture, theater, journalism reached new heights. Among several outstanding literary figures the satirical poet, Bishop Ignacy Krasicki, deserves special mention. A critical history of Poland came from the pen of Ignacy Naruszewicz. A score of prominent scientists, philosophers, and educators lent luster to the culture of Stanislas Augustus' Poland.

The most characteristic feature of Poland's Enlightenment was, as the Polish historian Emanuel Rostworowski has aptly remarked, the alliance of politics and education. It was felt that without a thorough program of schooling and learning political reforms stood little chance of acceptance. The work of the Commission of National Education, the first European ministry of education, and its impact on higher and secondary schools was therefore of immense importance. There was also progress in other domains, notably finances, municipal affairs, and administration; the Permanent Council, a form of collegiate cabinet, assured a new degree of centralization. The council, introduced on Russian initiative and conceived as a channel through which Russia could more easily control Poland was, however, universally hated, and the Poles bitterly resented the virtually proconsular prerogatives exercised by the Russian ambassador in Warsaw. Although Poland was still an independent state, its relationship to Russia was almost that of a satellite. The king and the various political parties in Poland were never allowed to forget it.

Poland's fate hinged on a favorable international constellation that would give the country a breathing space and permit a sweeping reform of its political and socioeconomic system. Such a chance came in the years 1788–1791 when Russia became absorbed in the Turkish war, Austria and Prussia were estranged, and a Triple Alliance of England, Prussia, and Holland emerged. Poland faced the choice of either trying to gain greater confidence of Russia which would permit domestic reforms, or joining with Prussia and the Triple Alliance in a showdown with St. Petersburg. Stanislas Augustus tried the first alternative; rebuffed, he turned to the second. The majority of present-day Polish historians criticize his policies and regard the king and his advisers as bad diplomats, duped by Prussia. Robert Lord and recently Jerzy Łojek a Polish historian, take the opposite view. They argue that Russia, which sought to absorb Poland, represented a far greater danger than Prussia. True, the latter sought some territorial concessions (notably Gdańsk and Toruń) but seems to have been genuinely interested in assisting Poland against the empire of the tsars. The advocates of joining the Triple Alliance, Łojek argues, envisaged not only political but also economic gains—a commercial treaty with England, for example, where Poland would have taken the place of Russia as a possible partner.

Although Warsaw signed the controversial alliance with Prussia in 1790, it did not fully exploit the international situation. The Poles hoped to preserve their neutrality should it come to a war between Russia and the Triple Alliance, and by their policies weakened the hand of Pitt. When Britain's parliament rejected his warlike schemes against Russia, the fate of Poland was sealed. Isolated, Prussia had no longer any interest in cooperating with Warsaw against Russia and switched her position by coming to terms with St. Petersburg. The net result was the second partition of 1793.

But the short breathing spell of 1788–1791 gave Poland a chance to carry out the great work of internal reforms. The reconstruction was undertaken by the sejm that met in 1788, a year after the Federal Convention at which Poland was invoked in constitutional debates. Because of the long duration of the diet's session it is commonly known as the Four-Year or the Great sejm. The slow pace of its deliberation was unfortunate because time was pressing and the country had to make the best use of the existing international configuration. Yet the reforms that were attempted were so fundamental and revolutionary that they could hardly have been achieved overnight. Contemporary France took over two years to move from the Declaration of the Rights of Man and Citizen of 1789 to the constitution of 1791; the Poles moved only a little less rapidly.

Debates in the sejm were accompanied by rich polemical literature. Among the most avidly read authors one finds two burghers and a priest of lesser gentry background; Stanisław Staszic, Józef Pawlikowski, and Hugo Kołłątaj. With their backing the party known as the Patriots came into being. The Patriots originally favored a republic presided over by the king, but based on an enlarged electorate of taxpayers. Gradually they recognized the need for strengthening the monarchy and came to favor the hereditary principle. The remodelled sejm, as they saw it, would represent the propertied classes, landowners and burghers; the landless gentry which constituted the magnates' clientele was to be disenfranchised. To make the presence of burgher deputies in the diet more palatable to the szlachta, the Patriots considered the possibility of ennoblement for that class. Liberum veto, magnates' oligarchy, and peasant serfdom were, of course, evils to be gradually eliminated.

The reform as proposed by the king and his supporters put more emphasis on hereditary monarchy (preferably in the Poniatowski family), which they wished to make the true pillar of stability. The king would retain all his prerogatives, have exclusive initiative in legislation, and influence over the judicial branch. He would preside over a council of ministers responsible to a sejm elected in turn by property-owning voters. Liberum veto would be abolished and a small number of town deputies included in the sejm and the ministries. Burghers would have equal rights with nobles, and peasants would be no longer attached to the soil but placed under state protection. The status of the Jews, to which Kołłątaj also gave some thought, would be regularized.

The third trend in the sejm and the country was represented by the conservatives, who identified patriotism with noble privileges, oligarchic rule, and the old regime. They voiced demagogic republican statements and glorified Poland's past. Two influential magnates, Seweryn Rzewuski and Szczęsny Potocki, argued that monarchy was really superfluous. Potocki further claimed that only a weak Poland would not antagonize its powerful neighbors and advocated a federated republic, an obvious heaven for the oligarchs.

In 1789 the sejm elected a committee to prepare the text of a new constitution. A City Delegation representing the union of towns—a sign of changing times—worked on it along parallel lines. Bases of the Form of Government were made public, but the struggle between the factions continued. At first little progress was made.

The sejm was destroying the entire system based on the Permanent Council, and the building of a new model took time. Still, the landless gentry was excluded from the local diets, and a hundred-thousand strong army was accepted in principle. The conservatives succeeded, however, in making the exclusively noble units of National Cavalry an unnecessarily large part of the future force.

By 1791 an alliance took place between the king and the Patriots. The nation was to be reconciled with its king, and jointly they could pass the constitution. In feverish secret debates, the royal project underwent changes to meet the desires of the Patriots. For tactical reasons the peasant question was left open so as not to antagonize the szlachta; that reform was to come in a second stage after the constitution won acceptance by the sejm.

Before discussing the constitution itself let us turn to the American theme running through the debates of the sejm. Terms such as "revolution," "insurrection," and the use of "the People" in a new sense appear to have been introduced or popularized thanks to the American revolution. Debaters, however, invoked American ideas and experiences to argue opposite points of view. Thus the Patriots and die-hard conservatives clashed on their interpretation of American notions of liberty and equality. An anonymous defender of nobles' privileges attempted to strengthen his case by saying that those who governed America were landowners and great merchants. The Americans, he argued, had escaped the "fictitious liberty of the hereditary monarchy" and had achieved "real freedom and liberty." Angrily, Kołłątaj accused the conservative spokesmen of trying to pervert American revolutionary ideas. Franklin and Washington, he declared, were concerned with human freedom; Polish conservatives cared only for freedom of the nobility.

In the course of debates on the status of cities and the peasantry, the American constitution was invoked (although its silence on Negro slavery was condemned) as well as American views about social inequalities in Poland and France. Americans, asserted Kołłątaj, described the lower classes in these countries as "abject slaves." Another Patriot, the writer and deputy Julian Ursyn Niemcewicz, exclaimed that "No one knows to whom Washington owes his birth, and no one knows who Franklin's ancestors were. Yet it is to these two famous men that America owes its liberty and independence."

While advocating a federal republican regime for Poland, the arch-conservatives also invoked the example of America. If the United States could manage so well without a king, why agitate in Poland in favor of a hereditary monarchy? In reply some Patriots voiced doubts whether America would be able to preserve its freedom without becoming a hereditary monarchy—both they and the conservatives assumed that presidency in the United States was by definition a weak form of executive power—and regretfully admitted that Poland could not imitate the present American, Dutch, or Swiss republican form of government. The Patriot Ignacy Potocki argued that "neither Lycurgus nor Franklin can meet her [Poland's] needs. Poland can only be a monarchy." Kołłątaj further explained that the American republic, protected as it was by the ocean, marshes, and deserts, was in a very different position from Poland, which bordered on powerful despots. Besides, "what are we compared to the Americans," he asked, "but an old man full of bad habits compared to a well brought-up youth whose heart has not had time to be tainted by bad example?" Stanislas Augustus privately advanced just the contrary reason why American ideals were not applicable to Polish conditions. "We have not reached that level of maturity," he wrote Mazzei.

After the adoption of the constitution on May 3, 1791, the Patriots felt that they could be proud of their achievements. Stanisław Małachowski, introducing the document, referred to the two famous "republican governments"—English and American—"the latter improving on the faults of the first," and stated that the Polish constitution takes from both what is best and most suited to Poland. The propagandists of the constitution went further by claiming that the Poles no longer need to envy "the free American states of Franklin and Washington, having such legislators of our own as Małachowski" and others.

The constitution of May 3, 1791, was a revolutionary document adopted in semirevolutionary conditions. Contemporaries were fully aware that they were witnessing a historic event, as enthusiasm swept the chamber and the city. For the moment effective opposition was silenced, although individual conservatives voiced their indignation. The reaction of Prussia, however, was ominous, and Berlin warned that it would not consider itself bound to defend the new Poland. The Prussian minister Hertzberg privately said that by adopting a constitution that was superior to that of England the Poles had inflicted a mortal blow on Prussia. What he meant was that a revived and strengthened Poland would be capable of retaking the Prussian share in the first partition. How could Prussia defend her long frontier against "a numerous and well-governed nation"?

Celebrated as a national holiday until after the Second World War, the May 3 constitution introduced a regime that combined the best Polish traditions with late eighteenth-century political ideas. The monarchy remained elective in the sense that dynasties, not individuals, would be elected. After Stanislas Augustus the crown would pass to the Saxon house. The king, no longer regarded as one of the three estates of the sejm, was the chief executive but ministers responsible to the diet had to countersign his decrees. The chamber of deputies was to be elected on the basis of property qualifications by reorganized local diets which no longer had the right to issue binding instructions to the deputies. The senate lost the right of legislative initiative and its veto was circumscribed. Twenty-four town deputies were to come to the sejm even though their participation was restricted to municipal affairs.

Burghers received the right to own land and hold offices; *neminem captivabimus* (a version of habeas corpus) protected them against arbitrary measures. Town autonomies were restored, and even if this applied only to royal and not to private towns, it was a revolutionary change. The constitution left the peasant question open but referred to the peasantry as the bulk of the people, making clear that the concept of nation was to include all inhabitants. It promised peasants the protection of the law and of the government. Catholicism was declared the state religion but full toleration was extended to other creeds. Finally, the constitution ended the dualist structure of the commonwealth, and in a special document called the Reciprocal Warranty of Both Nations it set up a centralized state. Lithuanians, however, were assured equal representation in all offices.

Social and economic problems were to be tackled in a subsequent document, an unfinished draft of which exists. According to it the peasants were to hold land in full property, their obligations to the landlords being fixed through contracts under the control of the state. A national bank providing credits for factories and crafts was meant to encourage economic development. A Jewish reform bill was also in a project stage. Time did not allow the completion of these reforms.

Poland as transformed through the May 3 constitution was emerging as a modern, constitutional parliamentary monarchy. None of the neighboring powers possessed a similarly elected parliamentary body with such wide prerogatives. In none of them were the burghers free to acquire land and control city government. A German historian, Jörg Hoensch, has shown that Poland's governing class, by agreeing to transform the state into a modern nation, was not oblivious of the socioeconomic evolutionary trends, as older German and Russian historiography had asserted. To the contemporaries the change in Poland was truly part of the international "democratic revolution," to use R. R. Palmer's term.

American voices discussing and approving the Polish events were not lacking. From Paris Jefferson informed John Jay and Washington about Polish developments; he had even seen the first draft of the Polish constitution. George Washington wrote the American envoy in Lisbon that Poland "appears to have made large and unexpected strides toward liberty," which reflected great honor on the king. The envoy in turn sent a poem to Kościuszko lauding Stanislas Augustus, the "Paragon of Kings whom both Worlds admire and all the Muses sing." Joel Barlow in his poem spoke of the king who "points the progressive march, and shapes the way that leads a realm from darkness into day." The American press widely acclaimed the May 3 constitution and toasts to it were drunk in Philadelphia and Richmond. The *Gazette of the United States* referred to the event as a "most wonderful revolution," a great and important event "in favor of the rights of man." The paper lauded the revolution as "begun without violence or tumult." The London *Critical Review* in a survey of American, French and Polish developments opined that the Poles had caught the revolutionary spirit from the Americans. At the Harvard commencement on July 19, 1792, there was a conference "Upon the comparative importance of the American, French and Polish revolutions to mankind."

Some of this publicity, especially the comparisons to the French revolution, embarrassed Stanislas Augustus, so he turned to Philip Mazzei, who had earlier propagandized the American cause, to do the same for Poland. From the point of view of Polish relations with the neighboring powers it was most desirable to present the May 3 constitution as a moderate and not a revolutionary event. In a short time the Polish constitution became "a game of ideological football," to cite Palmer again. It was praised or criticized not so much on its own merits but for purposes of partisan polemics. Once again Poland played the role of an example to be invoked to score an ideological point.

The May 3 constitution must not be viewed as imposed on the country in the teeth of national opposition. During the twelve months of its existence, the king very adroitly won for it the support of the majority of local dietines. All of them voted thanks for the constitution and the majority officially endorsed it. True, the Club of the Friends of the Constitution, operating as a pressure group, almost a modern political party in the diet, smacked of Jacobinism to the frightened conservatives. It was also clear that the szlachta would have opposed any radical moves in the peasant question. Still, the first anniversary of the constitution was celebrated with some fanfare. At that moment, however, the Russian-sponsored Confederation of Targowica was already preparing an intervention in Poland.

The word Targowica has become in Polish a synonym for base treason, and its leaders have been called Judases. One can even speak of a Targowica complex from which many Polish aristocrats suffered throughout the nineteenth century. To be fair, one must say that the principal plotters, the conservatives Potocki and Rzewuski, were not paid agents of St. Petersburg. They belonged rather to the European "aristocratic resurgence" that had no qualms to call in foreign troops against the revolution. To use Rostworowski's apt phrase, they were "guardians of the magnate-republican *raison d'état* maddened by pride and doctrine." Catherine II, determined to prevent the reconstruction of Poland, was ready to use as her instruments any malcontents in the country. She was lucky to have found prominent magnates who seemed to lend some legitimacy to her action. The Act of the Targowica Confederation, a counter-revolutionary manifesto couched in theoretical political terms, was drawn up under Catherine's guidance in St. Petersburg in late April. It was officially announced in the little Polish-Ukrainian town of Targowica and post-dated May 14, 1792.

Russian military intervention on behalf of the Targowica Confederation invoked Catherine's guarantees of the old Polish constitutional regime violated by the May 3 constitution. Promised that the intervention would not lead to another partition, the Targowica leaders may have felt that they were saving the country from worse evils. As the Russian troops advanced driving back the smaller Polish armies, commanded among others by the king's nephew, Prince Józef Poniatowski, and Kościuszko, the number of Targowica adherents grew. But it was clear even to Potocki that most of them were mere opportunists. Stanislas Augustus tried to negotiate directly with St. Petersburg but Catherine forced him to contact the Targowica leaders. After a vote in the cabinet the king decided to join the confederation himself.

The ways of Polish politicians split. Targowicans were deceived as Russia proceeded, together with Prussia, to a second partition of Poland in 1793. Stanislas Augustus made frantic efforts to save what could still be saved in Poland. Some of the leading reformers and military commanders, including Kościuszko, left the country. A political emigration began, gravitating toward revolutionary France.

From Kościuszko's Insurrection to the Congress of Vienna

It is hard to imagine that the oddly shaped band of territory that constituted mutilated Poland after 1793 could have survived as an independent state. The May constitution was abolished, the Russian might had triumphed. Yet Polish emigrés believed that a supreme military effort that had not been made in 1792 was the only way of regaining independence. In 1794 Kościuszko, whose activity in the emigration won him an honorary French citizenship (but no promise of French assistance), returned to Poland, assumed the title of Chief (*Naczelnik*), and raised the banner of insurrection. Bypassing and isolating the king, the insurrection instituted a temporary form of government with radical overtones. Kościuszko issued the Połaniec Manifesto to the peasantry, promising them personal freedom and security of tenure. In Warsaw, Polish Jacobins resorted to acts of terror against the Targowica dignitaries. The Polish war effort was considerable and large numbers of peasants joined the insurrection. The attack of a peasant detachment armed with scythes on a Russian battery at the victorious battle of Racławice became a symbol of the united national struggle for independence.

The insurrection contributed to a popularization of the American image in Poland and of Poland in America. Already in 1792 an alleged letter of a Polish soldier appeared in the *Dunlap's American Daily* which said that it was the "example of the Americans who sustained many defeats before they achieved the glorious conquest of liberty" that inspired the Polish troops. In 1794 Kościuszko was being referred to as the pupil of Washington, and Polish historians have seen American influence in his organization of the militia and in some political acts issued during the insurrection. Whether the French revolutionary model of a nation in arms or the American example was more important is still debatable. Although obviously events centering on France claimed most of American attention, Polish actions were also noted and commented upon in this country. James Monroe wrote that a 'formidable head has been raised against Prussia and Russia" and noted that the insurrection was "under the direction of Kosciusko who acted with us in America." A clergyman, the Rev. William Gordon, wrote to Washington of his hope that God who had made Washington the instrument of American deliverance, commissioned Kościuszko "to deliver the Poles from under slavery." A poem written at the time addressed Kościuszko in the words: "May fated Poland yet be free and find a Washington in thee." Kościuszko's name apeared in many contemporary toasts drunk in America.

The insurrectionary troops were unable to defeat the Russian armies, later joined by Prussian troops. Kościuszko was wounded and taken prisoner; after nearly nine months of fighting the insurrection collapsed. The third and last partition (of 1795), in which Russia, Prussia, and Austria participated, wiped Poland off the political map of Europe. In the atmosphere of utter dejection and gloom, Polish patriots came to believe that this was the end of the nation. The fall of Poland was compared to that of Carthage and Troy. The former Targowica leader Potocki wrote that he was now Russian forever. The *Columbian Centinel* shared these views when it wrote on November 23, 1797: "Poland is no more. Its Stanislaus is dead—its nobles scattered abroad, and that it ever existed, will speedily only be remembered by the Historian, the Geographer, or the Newsmonger."

What was the American verdict on the partitions that had destroyed Polish statehood? Indignation over the immorality of the act mingled with a severe judgment of the Poles themselves. Jefferson writing to Colonel William Duane in 1811 invoked the Polish lesson, "the example of a country erased from the map of the world by the dissensions of its own citizens." In his correspondence with John Adams a few years later he referred to the partitions as a "crime" and a "wound" inflicted on the "character of honor in the eighteenth century." He felt, however, that only one great power (Austria) that had "character to lose" had descended to the "baseness of an accomplice"; Russia was a "barbarous government" and Prussia was "still scrambling to become great." True, France, England, and Spain also shared some responsibility insofar as they allowed the partitions to take place. Adams wrote that there was "no difference of opinion or feeling" between him and Jefferson concerning the Polish partitions. Noah Webster, the lexicographer, wrote that when Poland was dismembered an "outcry was raised by all lovers of freedom—and justly." Russia, at least partly because of its bad treatment of the first American envoy to St. Petersburg, became an object of particular scorn. Catherine II, once praised for her alleged refusal to send Cossacks to subdue the colonists, was now reviled. A toast was drunk in Baltimore in 1795: "Execration to the abominable tyrant—May the blood of Poland crying from the dust bring down Heaven's vengeance on her."

One cannot easily find American references to the partitions as affecting the international balance of power. The connection between Polish events and American developments was remote, although Hamilton, speaking of the second partition, remarked that the involvement of the three powers in Poland had constituted an obstacle to the launching of a counterrevolutionary crusade against

49

the United States. As already noted, the contrast between American success and Polish failure seems to have been taken for granted, although John Adams feared that if the tug-of-war between the pro-British and pro-French factions in the United States continued "all the corruption of Poland" would be introduced into the country. Charles Adams, John's grandson and editor of his works, was one of the few to speak later of the influence of outside forces that had no necessary connection with achievements or failures. "The Polish constitution of 1791," he wrote, "was immediately overthrown by the interference of neighboring powers interested to destroy it. The constitution of the United States has survived until now . . . But, if we could for a moment suppose the geographical position of the two countries to have been exactly changed, looking back at the nature of the political controversies which agitated America for many years, it is at least open to question, whether as marked disorders would not have been developed under the constitution of the United States, as were ever found in the worst of times in Poland."

In 1797 Kościuszko, freed from his imprisonment in Russia by Tsar Paul, came to the United States. Accompanied by Niemcewicz, he received a hero's welcome. Newspapers had previously written about Kościuszko's release; now the *Kentucky Gazette* published a poem beginning with "Welcome great Kosciusko, to our shores." The reception in Philadelphia was moving; people unhitched the horses and pulled Kościuszko's carriage to his lodgings. There were receptions in his honor and encounters with many former friends. Although formally invited, Kościuszko refused to visit Mount Vernon, which may indicate the coolness of his relations with Washington, but he renewed his former acquaintance with Jefferson, then serving as the Democratic-Republican vice-president in Adams' Federalist administration. The acquaintance grew into a friendship, and Jefferson wrote in a letter to General Gates that the Pole was "as pure a son of liberty as I have ever known." It appears that Kościuszko's contacts with Jefferson placed him in an awkward position with regard to the Federalists, who began to take an unfriendly attitude toward the Polish general. Jefferson later tried to explain to Niemcewicz that "however cold" to Kościuszko's merit "some in this country have been," he wished to assure him that "the mass of our countrymen have the highest veneration and attachment to his character."

In 1798 Kościuszko abruptly and secretly left the United States. The reasons are still not absolutely clear, and some historians conjecture that he may have been entrusted with a secret mission to France. Upon his departure Kościuszko instructed that his property in America be used after his death for the purpose of buying out Negro slaves and providing for their education as defenders of liberty and of their country. Jefferson was named as the executor of Kościuszko's will, but for various reasons its provisions were never implemented.

Kościuszko first settled in Paris and later moved to Switzerland, continuing his correspondence with Jefferson until his death in 1817. It concerned mainly personal matters; politics and the Polish question occupied very little place in it. In 1800 Kościuszko was commissioned to write a text on *Manoeuvers of the Horse Artillery* for the use of the American army. Translated from the French at the initiative of the superintendent of West Point, it was published in New York in 1808. Also in 1800, Kościuszko inspired the writing of a Polish pamphlet, anonymously published under the title *Can the Poles Fight their Way to Independence?* The pamphlet, which later exercised a considerable influence on Polish conceptions of partisan warfare, contained several important references to America. Drawing its illustrations from the American Revolutionary War, it proposed among others a Congress to act as a central Polish insurrectionary institution. The American model was indeed judged as most worthy of imitation.

Withdrawing into seclusion, Kościuszko saw his legend grow even during his lifetime. America commemorated his death in 1817 by a speech in the House of Representatives by William Harrison. Kościuszko's favorite rock garden at West Point received his name. Invited in 1821 by the Republic of Cracow to help collect funds for a Kościuszko memorial, Jefferson urged President Monroe to give his blessings to this initiative which, however, had no sequel. A Kościuszko monument was erected in Washington only in the first decade of the twentieth century.

Kościuszko's aide and companion, Niemcewicz, remained in the United States until 1807 and became an American citizen. Moving in leading American circles—among others he visited George Washington, John Adams, and Albert Gallatin—he became a member of the Philosophical Society in Philadelphia. He recorded his observations and also wrote a brief biography of Washington published in Warsaw in 1803. Niemcewicz was impressed by the egalitarian nature of American society and commented on the modest life of the country's legislators. He noted the "astonishing progress of human labor and industry" and the fact that there was "no poverty visible." Only the treatment of Negro slaves, which he deemed far worse than that of Polish serfs, shocked him.

Niemcewicz's reminiscences are also valuable for American attitudes and comments regarding Poland. It is obvious that the United States had no intention of becoming embroiled in European affairs because of Polish problems. True, in 1795 Gouverneur Morris had advocated a scheme by which England and Russia would rebuild a Polish kingdom composed of parts taken by Austria and Prussia and use such a Poland against Berlin and Vienna. Jefferson listened to Niemcewicz's ideas that Austria and Russia be compensated with Turkish territory so as to release their hold on Poland, and wrote to him in 1798 that if France and Austria resumed the war "'your country will again arise into the map of the earth."

These may have been pious wishes meant principally to comfort the Polish exile. Niemcewicz later described in a poem how Washington had wept over the fate of Poland, and a sentence of Washington's letter to Niemcewicz gave rise to assertions that the great American was one of the best friends Poland ever possessed. Actually, Washington wrote: "That your country is not as happy as her efforts were patriotic and noble, is a misfortune which all lovers of sensible liberty and rights of men deeply deplore, and were my prayers during this hard struggle of any good, you would be now 'under your own vine and fig tree', to quote the Bible, as happy in the enjoyments of these desirable blessings as the people of these United States enjoy theirs."

American foreign policy had been clearly set in Washington's Farewell Address of 1796. It described European interests as of "none or a very remote relation" to the United States and warned against entangling alliances save "in extraordinary emergencies." Relations with Britain and France could indeed fall into this category; Polish problems did not. Jefferson, as President of the United States, wrote Niemcewicz on the eve of his departure for Poland in 1807 that he considered Europe "as a world apart from us, about which it is improper for us even to form opinions, or to indulge in any wishes but the general one that whatever is to take place in it, may be for its happiness." Jefferson added that he would not offer any comments regarding Poland's present lot and its future, and "for the same principles of caution" he did not write "my friend Kosciuszko."

Niemcewicz's return to Poland was closely connected with a series of developments culminating in a partial liberation of Polish lands by Napoleon's army. To appreciate these events, one needs to retrace his steps and briefly survey Polish vicissitudes during the decade which Niemcewicz spent in America.

The Poles had challenged the partitions already in 1797, the year of Kościuszko's and Niemcewicz's arrival to America, by forming a legion attached to Bonaparte's army in Italy. Commanded by General Jan Henryk Dąbrowski, the Polish legion fought for its country's independence only to see its hopes shattered by French peace with Austria. Some of the legionnaires returned to Poland, others remained in French service and were sent to fight in Santo Domingo. A few made their way to America. Despite these failures, the Polish legions in Italy were of great significance for Polish history. They were an armed protest against the partitions and a school of civic virtues and democracy. They produced a cadre of trained officers and men who proved invaluable for the army of the future Duchy of Warsaw. The legions gave Poland its national anthem with its stirring opening words "Poland is not yet lost as long as we live."

The temporary failure of an armed attempt to regain freedom spurred another kind of effort in the homeland. Its promoter was Prince Adam Czartoryski, the cousin of the last king of Poland and a close friend of Tsar Alexander I. Involved in the work of modernizing Russia and becoming that country's foreign minister, Czartoryski sought to reconcile Russian and Polish interests. Named curator of the Wilno educational district which comprised nearly all the eastern lands of the former commonwealth, Czartoryski turned the city into a center of Polish culture and education radiating over the whole partitioned country. In 1805 Czartoryski urged Alexander to assume the Polish crown and to recover the Polish provinces of Prussia in the eventuality of a Russo-Prussian war. He was unsuccessful, and so the second trend which may be regarded as a forerunner of policies of evolution rather than revolution, limited cooperation rather than armed struggle, also failed to advance Poland's political cause, although it brought cultural gains.

The Polish problem, however, reemerged and came to the fore as a result of the 1806–1807 war between Napoleon and the Russian-Prussian coalition. French troops entered Prussian-held Poland as liberators, and at the famous encounter between Napoleon and Tsar Alexander I at Tilsit a small substitute Polish state, called the Duchy of Warsaw, was officially established.

To the Poles this was at best a partial solution. The duchy, composed only of Prussian acquisitions from the second and third partitions, seemed but a token. To France, the duchy was a valuable military outpost on the Vistula, but Napoleon was careful not to commit himself to a restoration of Poland which would mean burning his bridges to the three partitioning powers. The size of the duchy and its population significantly increased after the 1809 war against Austria; the state had now within its borders the three major cities:

Warsaw, Cracow, and Poznań. Although the word has been carefully avoided, it was clearly a Polish state. Napoleon granted it a
constitution which resembled other Napoleonic constitutions but
also took into account specific Polish conditions and political traditions. Administrative and political arrangements need not concern us here, but socioeconomic provisions and practice deserve
mention. The constitution provided for equality of all citizens before the law, and the Napoleonic Code was introduced. At the
same time two groups of people, the peasantry and the Jews, failed
to receive absolute equality, and the constitution blurred but did
not do away with the traditional division into estates. Serfdom was
abolished and the peasant became a free man, but his right to the
land was not established. The peasant who failed to perform labor
obligations was free to leave, but the land and agricultural implements reverted to the lord. As a contemporary saying put it, the
peasant lost his chains together with his boots, and became as free
as a bird.

Throughout its eight-year existence the Duchy of Warsaw, ruled
from Dresden by the king of Saxony, enjoyed only three years of
peace. Its economy was strained by the upkeep of a disproportionately large army and by devastations of the French military campaigns.
It had to adjust to the Napoleonic Continental System which meant
further economic hardships. Never a master of its own destiny, it
still exercised, as a Polish entity, a great psychological and political
impact on the nation. Its existence contradicted the verdict of partitions; the Poles were now fully aware of the fact that "a nation
always remains a nation," as expressed in a contemporary poem.
The duchy was affected by processes of modernization of a special
kind, and judicial and political reforms from above preceded spontaneous social and economic transformation. This produced certain
discrepancies, as in the case of partial emancipation of the peasantry.
At the same time institutional changes stimulated structural changes,
social mobility, and more advanced types of economic activity. A
laicization of society was reflected in education and culture. The
army was a place in which a peasant could be a first class citizen,
and it was a source of pride and glory for the duchy. The exploits
of Polish troops during the Napoleonic wars—the charge at Somo-
sierra or the battle of Raszyn—attested to a rebirth of the martial
spirit. The army which survived the Duchy of Warsaw and existed
as a separate Polish force until 1831, for more than a generation,
was the main vehicle of the Napoleonic legend and an important
link with France. The Napoleonic legend engendered illusions
about Western aid to Poland and strengthened the faith in the value

of military efforts, thus causing many bitter disappointments later. But it also contributed to an identification of the Polish cause with the general struggle for progress and national self-determination.

Other institutions survived the duchy. Basic reforms in the political field remained in force until 1831; in the administrative sphere until the late 1860s; in the judiciary until the 1870s. Notions of civil law derived from the Code Napoléon survived until the middle of the present century.

Historians have so far failed to reveal any significant American-Polish contacts during the period of the Duchy of Warsaw. The Kościuszko-Jefferson correspondence has already been mentioned. In 1810 Niemcewicz nominated Jefferson to be a member of the Society of the Friends of Learning in Warsaw which the latter acknowledged with a "sense of honor." There might have been other instances of scholarly cooperation. In his historical-political treatise begun at that time, Staszic contrasted the French revolution, the excesses of which he condemned, with the American more moderate revolutionary model. Other Poles indicated a similar preference. It would be interesting to compare the impact of the Duchy of Warsaw on the Polish nation with that of the War of 1812 on the American people. While the war was ill-starred and to some extent senseless, still, in the words of Commager and Nevins, it "did a great deal to make the republic more mature and more independent; to knit it together and to strengthen its character." As Gallatin observed, Americans "feel and act more as a nation." The same was true for the Poles.

The war against England placed the United States on the same side as the Duchy of Warsaw, involved in 1812 in the French invasion of Russia—the "Second Polish War" as Napoleon called it. The war offered to the Poles a chance of reviving prepartition Poland, or at least coming close to it should the vast lands taken by Russia be joined to the Duchy of Warsaw. Napoleon played on these hopes to spur the Poles to a maximum effort without committing himself to the cause of a reborn Polish kingdom. The eventual collapse of the Great Army in Russia and the invasion of the Duchy of Warsaw by Russian troops put an end to these expectations. Alexander, meanwhile had been making advances to Polish leaders and many of them felt that since Napoleon had used the Poles as an instrument of his policies, realism now demanded that they strike a bargain with the tsar. They urged the commander-in-chief, Prince Poniatowski, not to jeopardize national chances by resistance; even the Saxon ruler ordered him to sign an armistice. Poniatowski, however, refused to follow the example of numerous statesmen in Europe who were abandoning Napoleon. Rejoining the imperial army with his troops he was killed at the great battle of Leipzig in 1813, and his name, like those of Kościuszko and Dąbrowski, became part of the Polish legend.

What significance did the fact of Americans and Poles having enemies in common have for their mutual relations? One touches here on the question of Russia, which in the centuries to come increasingly cast its shadow on American policies toward Poland. During this period Americans were split in their views on Russia. The Federalists were for the tsar and England; the Democrats-Republicans opposed them and, largely out of Anglophobia, paraded their pro-French feelings. The first group could invoke several important reasons for its stand. Russia had recognized the United States in 1809 and in 1812–1813 Alexander offered to mediate between England and America. Russia's interest demanded that Britain, the ally against Napoleon, not be diverted from Europe. But the Russians did not wish to depend too much on England as a sea carrier and viewed America as a replacement. Hence, a weakening of the United States was contrary to Russian objectives. Indeed, in the long run an American navy might serve as a useful counterweight against the Royal Navy. All these considerations plus the fantastic growth of American exports to Russia reinforced Russophile feelings in several quarters in this country.

The anti-Federalist *Niles' Weekly Register* represented a different point of view, and in its articles on Russia brought in the Polish aspect. The paper had devoted unusually long and detailed accounts to an 1812 ceremony in Warsaw proclaiming the re-creation of a Napoleon-sponsored Kingdom of Poland. In April 1814, a lengthy article entitled "Russians and Cossacks" illustrated the barbarism and imperialism of the tsars by referring, among others, to Russian policies toward the Poles. It recalled the massacre of Warsaw's suburb of Praga by Suvorov's troops in 1794 and made several references to Russian treatment of the Poles during the three partitions. Clearly, the article was written to convince those Americans who were pro-English and anti-French. There were other examples in *Niles' Weekly Register* of biting criticism of Russia and its "parricide" tsar. Russia, the paper observed, consisted of *"conquered countries, usurped provinces and ravaged territories."* The Russian takeover of the Duchy of Warsaw after Napoleon's defeat disturbed the *Niles' Weekly Register*. The paper also noted that "Poland seems the 'bone of contention' among the folks at Vienna." This was certainly the case.

The Congress of Vienna (1814–1815) devoted a good deal of time to the Polish question. Tsar Alexander, supported by Czartoryski, sought to retain as much of the Duchy of Warsaw as possible and transform it into a Kingdom of Poland under his scepter. The other powers opposed what seemed an undue strengthening of Russia, and England's Castlereagh somewhat disingenously proposed the reconstruction of the pre-1772 commonwealth. In the final settlement a compromise solution was found. A small Kingdom of Poland linked with Russia came into existence. The *Niles' Weekly Register* commented that this kingdom would not have its own foreign relations and spoke scornfully of the "boasted independence which the magnanimous Alexander has been promising that unfortunate country." It concluded that Poland would be "nothing more than a province of Russia." Even if prophetic, this was perhaps unfair to Alexander's intentions and indicative of the way in which Americans tended to oversimplify Russian-Polish relations. In the course of the next century American public opinion would veer between wholeheartedly pro-Polish or pro-Russian outlook. In the arena of governmental policies the story would be somewhat different, for Russia was one of the great world powers and the Polish nation was no longer a real factor in international affairs.

2

The Polish Question in the Nineteenth Century

The November 1830 Insurrection:
Before and After

HE absence of a Polish state tended to distort the nature of American-Polish relations. The view that such absence precluded interstate friction and promoted a friendship between the two nations is highly dubious, for geography alone would have minimized the chance of a clash of interests. Instead of a country with which normal contacts would have existed there was the thorny and vexing Polish question. Americans could pity and even admire Poland for its fortitude in dealing with adversity but did not think of it as part of international society. American attitudes thus assumed a moralistic and moralizing character, and while European statesmen and politicians did on various occasions approach the Polish question in terms of the balance of power, the United States, which had never had diplomatic or economic relations with a Polish state, saw it largely as a humanitarian and somewhat academic issue.

The nineteenth century occupies a unique place in Polish history. At a time when most of the Western world was going through profound change and expansion, connected, to put it in the simplest terms, with the American, French, and Industrial revolutions, authoritarian Prussia, conservative Austria, and autocratic Russia were blocking or delaying the trends of political democracy and social and economic modernization that moved from west to east. Poland, under their triple rule, was thus "missing" much of the nineteenth century because its lands were increasingly integrated into the three empires. Only one part of the old commonwealth, the kingdom set up in Vienna in 1815 and hence popularly known as the Congress Kingdom, was genuinely affected by the Industrial Revolution. Polish peasantry was emancipated at different times in Prussia, Austria, and Russia, which interfered with a uniform social evolution. The partitions had destroyed the raison d'être of the szlachta as a political power, but accelerated the emergence of another elite, the intelligentsia, that took over some of the gentry's outlook. In contrast to the West where the chief components of modern society were the bourgeoisie and the proletariat, Polish society was largely a conglomerate of gentry, peasants, and plebeians.

The partitions affected the growth of Polish nationalism. The May 3 constitution had initialed the process of a gradual extension of the idea of the nation, and in view of the religious base of the commonwealth (85 percent of Roman and Greek Catholics), and the continuing polonization trends, it is likely that the bulk of the population would have eventually become Polish. The collapse of the state interrupted this process, and Polish nationalism became that of the underdog. During most of the nineteenth century it was shaped by the pursuit of political independence, liberalism and democracy, with emphasis on native culture. Only in the last decades of the century did a different type of nationalism emerge, based on ethnic Polish masses rather than on the historic concept of the nation. It inevitably clashed with a rising "integral" nationalism of the Ukrainians and Lithuanians. Yet the old attraction of Polish culture did not altogether disappear during the hundred odd years; many a German and some Jews and Ukrainians were assimilated and became Poles.

Deprived of statehood, with economic development distorted and processes of social modernization affected by the policies of the partitioning powers, Poland still remained a reality to its own politically conscious strata. In the existing conditions the role of intellectuals and of the intelligentsia acquired special importance. The age of Romanticism reinforced the spiritual leadership of the poets and writers, the greatest of whom became known as national bards *(wieszcz)*. They shaped to a large extent the nation's outlook and political philosophy, its way of thinking and behavioral patterns. As Lewis Namier rightly observed, it became easier for the Poles "to attain sainthood than to preserve a sense of proportions," and indeed many of the so-called Polish characteristics are traceable to this period; idealism, romanticism, lack of realism, heroism, ethnocentrism, and national exaltation. The Poles had to learn how to make sacrifices, struggle against odds, endure and resist. They had much less of a chance to learn how to live a normal, regulated, secure life. The word "compromise" acquired a pejorative meaning in the political dictionary, for it stood for sacrificing principles and accepting collaboration with the enemy. A German historian characterized Polish nineteenth-century efforts by entitling a book on the subject "All or Nothing." Poles acquired the reputation of heroic revolutionaries, rather than of realistic politicians or capable businessmen.

Like all sweeping generalizations the above assertions are only partly true. To prevent absorption by the partitioning powers the Poles often had to resort to actions that offered little prospect of success. In the words of a famous writer, Stefan Żeromski, they had to keep their national wounds bleeding. But they were also faced with agonizing questions of how to further the national cause. Would violent resistance—insurrection or revolution—or slow socioeconomic and cultural betterment ("organic work") be proper weapons in the struggle for survival? Realism or idealism, struggle versus conciliation, native efforts or attempts to rely on foreign aid; all were tried, sometimes even by the same men at various stages of their careers. Not all the Poles were utopian romantics all the time, but there were limits to policies of accommodation or loyalty toward the partitioning powers. In the final analysis no Pole could in the name of cold reason accept the partitions as final and irreversible. To do so would mean accepting national obliteration, and political realism is not tantamount to national suicide.

Life under three different political and socioeconomic systems conditioned the mentality of Prussian, Austrian, and Russian Poles, yet in spite of these differences the concept of a single Polish nation never disappeared. Common culture, language, historical consciousness, experiences of opposing the foreign rule, and the Catholic faith served as unbreakable ties that held the fragmented Polish nation together.

What to the Poles was the Polish cause, to the outside world was the Polish question. At various times it elicited sympathy, commiseration or even support on the part of individuals, whether liberals, radicals, socialists, or even conservatives. To their governments the Polish question had a nuisance value to be used to embarrass the partitioning powers. At other times it was ignored for the sake of the Concert of Europe. Generally it served to strengthen the solidarity of Prussia, Austria, and Russia, but there were moments when one exploited it against the others. West European politicians often found Polish efforts to reopen the question of their independence irritating and unrealistic. Even the polonophile Englishman, Lord Stratford de Redcliffe, spoke of Poland's revival as a "regular flying Dutchman. Never is—always to be."

When seeking Western aid the Poles exhibited at times optimism and wishful thinking. They mistook words of sympathy and encouragement for political commitments. Disappointed, they felt used, abandoned, or deceived by the powers and bitterly criticized their selfish interests. Polish relationships to the West often recalled a one-sided love affair.

There was never much likelihood that the Polish question would receive more than passing attention from the United States. Throughout the nineteenth century every administration in Washington resisted calls raised in America for aid to nations struggling to be free. Similarly the United States refused to use the instrument of withholding recognition from de facto governments in Europe, however abhorrent they might appear to the Americans. Secretary of State John Quincy Adams declared in 1821 that whenever the banner of freedom and independence was or would be unfurled, there would be America's "heart, her benedictions, and her prayers" but no active involvement. Monroe in his famous doctrine restated this position in 1823. A similar stand was taken toward the revolutions of 1848. The American contribution to European national liberation struggles took the form of providing a living example of a successful democracy. One could best help the freedom-seeking Europeans by keeping, in Clay's words, "our light burning on this western shore." A combination of moralistic attitudes with hands-off policies naturally applied also to the Polish question. But an additional aspect that affected this stance was the Russian angle. Polish struggles primarily concerned Russia, and American attitudes toward Poland became at times reflective of the United States relationship to the empire of the tsars.

The Congress of Vienna brought about a redistribution of Polish lands, which with minor changes survived until the First World War. West Prussia and the Duchy of Posen (Poznania) were under Prussia; Galicia under Austria; the city of Cracow with a small surrounding area became a free and neutral republic; finally Russia ruled over the eastern borderlands, held since the partitions, and extended its sway over the Kingdom of Poland which comprised the bulk of the former Duchy of Warsaw. Paying lip service to the idea of Poland, whose dismemberment hardly squared with the avowed principle of legitimacy, the Congress of Vienna had stipulated for freedom of commerce and navigation within the pre-partition borders, and called on the monarchs of the partitioning powers to grant their Polish subjects national rights compatible with their state interests. But there could not be economic unity that cut across the existing frontiers. As for respect of Polish nationality, it was assumed to be more applicable to Poznania than to West Prussia; the tsar took it far more seriously than the Austrian emperor.

In broad strokes, during the first fifteen years after 1815 Galicia stagnated politically and economically under the Metternich regime; in Prussia, the Poles made vain efforts to obtain some genuine autonomy, but the only important development there was a gradual emancipation of the peasantry. As conceived and carried out, it favored the larger farmers, and in the long run made the Prussian-Polish provinces a granary for Germany. Galician and Prussian Poles naturally looked to the Congress Kingdom, the only part of the old commonwealth that bore the name Poland and that, given Alexander's liberal ideas, could conceivably become the nucleus of a reunited Polish state.

The restricted use of the term Poland had an unfortunate impact on the outside world, and as time went on Poland began to mean to the West not the old prepartition commonwealth but the small Congress Kingdom. This way of thinking became so ingrained that when the question of Polish independence emerged in the course of the First World War, Polish aspirations to lands outside Congress Poland appeared wild and imperialistic.

The kingdom was linked with Russia through the tsar, who was also its king. He endowed it with a fairly liberal constitution, and the kingdom had a separate government, a bicameral parliament called by the old Polish name sejm, an army, and its own internal social, economic, and juridical organization. The separate nature of the kingdom was emphasized by its own borders, citizenship, and passports. The constitution contained an impressive section on personal and civic liberties but, as a wit put it, nobody noticed that. Apart from the loopholes in the constitution that were soon used to undermine its spirit, there was something anomalous in the very existence of a liberal kingdom tied to the autocratic empire of the tsars. The second anomaly in Polish eyes was the unjustifiable distinction between the former eastern provinces treated as an integral part of Russia, and the Congress Kingdom. Prominent Poles including the old Kościuszko had tried to persuade Alexander that only a union of the kingdom with the former provinces could provide for a healthy Russo-Polish relationship comparable to the Austro-Hungarian model. Alexander was not insensitive to such views, and in the first few years following the Congress of Vienna gave the Poles to understand that the two anomalies might be resolved. The kingdom, proving to be a successful experiment of constitutional government, could serve as an example for the liberalization of the empire. An eastward extension of the kingdom was also mentioned, and some steps taken in the Lithuanian provinces which even cautious politicians took as an earnest of more to come.

All these plans were anathema to the Russian ruling classes. The thought of giving up any territory to the Poles went against all the tradition of Russian expansion. It was roughly in the 1820s that the term "western provinces" began to replace the hitherto used name "Polish provinces" or "provinces detached from Poland and united with Russia." No one in St. Petersburg could envisage giving them up. The constitutional kingdom in turn appeared a hotbed of Jacobinism and a threat to the stability of tsardom. Many Russians believed it to be economically unviable and a burden to the empire. On all these grounds they favored its absorption.

Personalities weighed heavily on Russo-Polish relations. Alexander himself was a liberal by sentiment and education and an autocrat by temperament and in virtue of his position. He may have wanted his constitutional experiment in Congress Poland to succeed, and yet he considered himself above the constitution and would not hesitate to violate it if it meant opposition to his ideas of government. Acting in an extra-constitutional way, he made his neurotic brother, the Grand Duke Constantine, the commander of the Polish army, and the sinister intriguer, Senator Nikolai Novosiltsov, a special imperial representative. The position of viceroy went to a servile old Polish general rather than to the comaker of the kingdom, Prince Czartoryski, who had once been a trusted friend and collaborator of the tsar. Czartoryski may well have been the only statesman capable of working out a modus vivendi between Warsaw and St. Petersburg.

The complex story of Russo-Polish relations during the years 1815–1830 can only be briefly sketched here; some of its aspects have uncanny analogies with the present. On the Polish side, a wide political spectrum ranged from unqualified collaborators and opportunists through those who attempted genuine cooperation with Russia, down to a liberal opposition in the parliament and secret societies driven to espousal of revolutionary means against the tsarist government. With Alexander's retreat from liberalism and Russian conservatism triumphant, policies of repressions and violations of the constitution began to prevail. The analysis of the regime by one of Poland's most original political writers of the nineteenth century, Maurycy Mochnacki, has a strangely familiar ring to students of the Soviet Bloc.

The Poles gained martyrs, as for instance in the person of Major Walerian Łukasiński, the leader of the secret Patriotic Society, a man of great integrity and iron will who spent most of his life as a half-forgotten prisoner in the fortress of Schlüsselburg. In a series of reprisals in Lithuania, the Wilno University was closed, putting an end to the principal Polish cultural outpost in the former eastern lands. Their reunification with Congress Poland was now clearly out of the question. The chances of a satisfactory Russian-Polish political relationship grew ever more slender.

In the economic sphere, the outstanding Polish minister of finance, Prince Ksawery Drucki-Lubecki, showed that the kingdom could register impressive progress. A state-directed industrialization program was initiated: coal mining developed and the output of iron and zinc increased. A textile industry grew around the little town of Łódź, the future Polish Manchester. Steam-driven machinery made its entry into Polish industry. Drucki-Lubecki reoriented the kingdom's trade eastward and Russia became an important market for Polish exports. But the minister's strong belief that the kingdom needed above all schools, industry and trade, and armament factories, seems to indicate that he aimed at making Congress Poland more independent of Russia.

Was the armed insurrection which began in Warsaw in November 1830 unavoidable? Could cautious policies of strengthening the country economically and not antagonizing the tsardom politically have produced better results for the Poles? Even if one forgets for a moment the European revolutionary context of 1830 that influenced the insurrection, some historians argue that Russo-Polish relations had by then reached a deadlock which the new tsar, Nicholas I, was eager to break by force. The original hopes of Czartoryski had been dashed, the liberal opposition in the sejm was suppressed, the secret societies were in danger of liquidation, even the policies of Drucki-Lubecki, which depended on Russian cooperation, were running into difficulties.

The November 29, 1830, insurrection began as a revolutionary coup perpetrated by youthful conspirators. It was then represented as a political manifestation against the autocracy that had violated the constitution and the promises of Alexander. After the act of dethronement of Tsar Nicholas, it became a national struggle for independence with revolutionary elements inherent in it. Militarily it amounted to a regular Polish-Russian war. Fighting spread into Lithuania, attesting to the reality of the old commonwealth, and volunteers came from Galicia and Prussian Poland. The Polish command committed many strategic and tactical mistakes; the political leadership was undermined by internal dissensions. The hope of receiving Western backing remained unfulfilled, although European liberals showed great sympathy for the Polish cause. The insurrectionary leaders failed to emancipate the peasantry, which was a serious mistake. Not that enlisting the participation of the masses could have changed the final military outcome, although Polish radicals then and later asserted that it would have done precisely that. It was rather than an independent Polish government wasted the unique opportunity of showing its determination to integrate the masses into the fabric of the nation, and demonstrating that the struggle for Poland's freedom was inextricably linked with social emancipation. While Warsaw journals praised the United States, there were no attempts to invoke the American model of government. The Polish press even voiced the opinion that while a republic may be excellent in America it could be harmful in European conditions.

The collapse of the insurrection in the autumn of 1831 was followed by severe Russian reprisals. The kingdom's constitution was suspended; its parliament and army abolished; Warsaw University closed. The semi-independent status of the Congress Kingdom was gone, and many Poles condemned the insurrection as foolhardy. From a historical perspective, the November insurrection was one of the national liberation struggles so characteristic of the nineteenth century, and it emphasized the determination of the Poles to translate aspirations for independence into political and military action.

A sizable emigration resulted from the failure of the insurrection; it was composed of the political and literary elite of the nation and became known as the Great Emigration. The moderate wing, grouped around Czartoryski, concentrated on seeking the support of Britain and France for the Polish cause against Russia. By contrast, the radicals (the Democratic Society) put their trust in the cause of a European revolution. The Canadian historian Peter Brock rightly called the Democratic Society the first democratically run, centralized, and disciplined political party of Eastern Europe. Its ideal was a kind of Jeffersonian agrarian democracy, and its concept of agrarian revolution appeared to Marx to be a crucial Polish contribution to European revolutionary thought. Polish political writings and philosophy of the post–1830 period became indeed highly important, rich, varied, and original. The emigration included the three giants of Polish Romantic poetry: Adam Mickiewicz, Juliusz Słowacki, and Zygmunt Krasiński, whose national message of freedom and sacrifice was to have a lasting impact on the Polish psyche. In music, the emigration was epitomized by Fryderyk Chopin. A

Messianic creed arose which in its more extreme and mystic form represented Poland as the Christ of nations who redeemed through the national Golgotha not only itself but all oppressed mankind.

The Americans learned about the outbreak of the insurrection in Poland by January 1831, and the popular reaction was most friendly to the Poles. Already in the preceding years the autocratic regime in the kingdom had been the object of occasional criticism in the press as was the collaboration of Polish nobles with Russia. Now pro-Polish articles appeared, groups of young men in New York, Boston, Philadelphia, and New Orleans volunteered to fight alongside the Poles (Edgar Allan Poe was one of them), and committees of aid to Poland were formed in which priests and Masons were prominent. Poems with titles like "Freedom! Freedom! Hear the Shout," "Rise, White Eagle, Rise" or "The Autocrat's Prayer," were written expressing sympathy to Poland which "wakes from slavery's chains." Americans criticized France and England for their inactivity with regard to Poland.

No one assumed that the United States government would embroil itself with European problems. Washington informed the prospective volunteers to Poland that American laws did not permit enlisting in foreign armies, but when Dr. Paul Fitzsimons Eve of Augusta, Georgia, then working as a surgeon in Paris, went to join the Polish insurgents he was received on his return in 1832 by President Jackson. Eve served the Poles with distinction, and his report on the Polish events is of considerable interest.

Paris became the leading center of American action for Poland, and on the initiative of the septuagenarian Lafayette, James Fenimore Cooper—who had become friendly with Mickiewicz—organized a Polish-American Committee. Samuel Morse, Ralph W. Emerson, and Dr. Samuel G. Howe were its most distinguished members. Cooper's appeal to form aid committees throughout the United States recalled that Poland had once been the fifth power in Christendom and although sometimes guilty of political and economic wrongs, its real crime was "too much liberty." Cooper's appeal produced a drive in America, several mass meetings, the sending of two flags purchased in Boston for the Polish army, and some $20,000 dispatched to Lafayette. The money was mainly used to assist the needy emigrés, and two Polish leaders thanked Cooper feelingly: "May America, the model for all free countries, preserve the remembrance of our efforts and of our wrongs; the recollection of her spontaneous and generous sympathy will ever be dear to the Poles."

The pro-Polish sentiments and acts seem to have arisen purely from a sympathy for a people struggling against autocracy, rather than in connection with American views on Russia and American-Russian relations. Poland's partitions, which the well-known clergyman Charles H. Wharton characterized as the "most flagrant violation of national justice and international law," were recalled. The prominent Yale alumnus and Presbyterian clergyman William Buell Sprague wrote in a preface to *Remembrances of a Polish Exile*: "What American has not felt his heart beat sympathetically to the sad and tragical story of the destinies of Poland?" Another theme was also sounded. Dr. Eve, departing for Poland, spoke of wishing to repay the debt to Pułaski's countrymen; Sprague also mentioned the "common gratitude under which they [the Poles] have laid us to their country." Sprague went on to say that "so long as we breathe the air of liberty, we will not cease to sympathize with her [Poland] in her calamities, and to pray that the rule of her oppressors may be broken." Howe, active in the Paris committee, argued for American involvement even to the disregard of "ordinary rules of diplomacy" because there were times and cases when "all considerations should yield to the claims of outraged humanity." Thus it seems clear that moral considerations, the memory of Polish contributions to American independence—some newspapers also mentioned that Polish insurrectionists seemed to emulate the American revolutionary fighters—and humanitarian feelings were decisive in shaping the attitudes of the pro-Polish circles in the United States.

Russian reprisals which followed the crushing of the insurrection evoked highly critical comments in the American press. The *Niles' Weekly Register* was particularly outspoken. The 1830–1831 events contributed to an increased interest in Polish matters. James Fletcher's *History of Poland* was published in the United States in 1831 in the Harper series. Jane Porter's novel *Thaddeus of Warsaw*, inspired to some extent by the life of Kościuszko, went through eighteen editions between 1817 and 1911. Robin Carver's *Stories of Poland*, a book for children, presented the Poles as a brave but unfortunate people that may yet be set free. It contrasted the unhappy fate of Polish youth with their fortunate counterparts in America.

Even though the relations between the United States and Russia had as yet no real impact on American attitudes toward Poland, they deserve to be briefly mentioned to understand long-range trends. There was a curious mixture of distrust and hopeful friendship. Contemporaries were struck by parallels and contrasts between the two peoples, and in 1835 Alexis de Tocqueville had some thoughts on this subject. Americans and Russians, he felt, "tend

towards the same end, although they started from different points."
Both were expanding nations but while the American "struggles
against the natural obstacles which oppose him; the adversaries of
the Russians are men." The former conquer "by ploughshare" and
the latter "by the sword." It may not be too far-fetched to assume
that Americans and Russians were early drawn to and repelled by
each other. The image of Russia as the Muscovite menace persisted
in Washington, and St. Petersburg would on occasion view the
United States as a revolutionary upstart. There were common interests, notably commercial, as well as some friction connected with
the Russian presence in California and Oregon.

The pro-Polish views of the American press at the time of the
November insurrection gave rise to a minor diplomatic incident
between the United States and Russia. It centered on some critical
articles in the Washington *Globe,* which the Russians regarded as
a mouthpiece of the administration. The overzealous Russian
chargé d'affaires drafted a protest attacking the State Department
and making insinuations about President Jackson. The United
States demanded the withdrawal of these accusations and instructed
its envoy in St. Petersburg to lodge a protest. This James Buchanan
did, although he privately advised Washington that the *Globe* had
better become more circumspect. The minister was greatly concerned at this point with the delays of the commercial treaty with
Russia—signed eventually in 1832—and attempted to minimize the
reports of Russian cruelties in Poland. Still, the Russian chargé was
recalled from Washington, which showed St. Petersburg's desire to
be accommodating. By 1834 the diplomatic incident was forgotten
and President Jackson in his inaugural address singled out the Russian treaty for some laudatory remarks.

Only between 3 and 4 percent of the postinsurrectionary Polish
emigration came to America, some of them deported from Austria.
Among them were former soldiers, some artists and representatives
of other professions, but no outstanding political leaders. The
vicissitudes of the Polish emigration in Jacksonian America have
been told in detail elsewhere, and they do not properly belong to this
story. What concerns us is their impact on American attitudes
toward Russia and Poland. The Polish exiles produced a few books,
pamphlets and articles of clearly political portent. Major Józef
Horodyński wrote *The History of the Late Polish Revolution* (1833);
August A. Jakubowski contributed the *Remembrances of a Polish
Exile.* Politically the most active was Major Kasper Tochman, who
addressed numerous meetings, including state legislatures, on the
Polish subject and in 1844 published his speeches under the telling

title *Social, Political and Literary Condition of Poland and Her Future Prospects, Conjointly with the Policy of Russia towards these United States.* Tochman was instrumental in organizing a short-lived Polish Slavonian Literary Association in the State of New York whose members included such prominent figures as Albert Gallatin and William H. Seward.

Some of the Polish exiles tried to argue their national case not only in terms of public morality but also by pointing out that Russia, while occupying Poland, held a key geographic position in Europe. Tochman stressed that "the ocean is no longer a barrier," a bold view for mid-nineteenth century America. One United States senator also invoked balance of power considerations. Presenting in 1834 a petition to the Congress for a grant of land to Polish emigrés, he stated that "the cause of Poland is closely associated with the cause of peace" and that one half of Europe cannot survive if the other half is enslaved. Three years later the *Democratic Review* commented that Western ideas acquired by Russian troops in Poland might help to undermine tsarist autocracy—a statement with a familiar post-World War II ring. St. Petersburg worried about Polish emigrés "plotting against Russia" in the United States; most likely it overestimated their impact on America, which was clearly limited.

General interest in Polish matters was sustained in the mid-1830s, among others by John L. Stevens's letters on his travels in Poland published in the *Monthly Magazine*. Polish themes appeared in American music, to mention only the principal aria "The Fair Land of Poland" in a then popular opera, *Bohemian Girl*. The political significance of all this was obviously minimal. It may well be that the anonymous antagonist of Tochman who wrote that to expect a resurrection of Poland was "about as rational as to hope for the resurrection of the Roman Empire" represented more accurately the views of an average American.

As the 1840s progressed, interest in Poland and its problems declined. Individual political exiles kept coming to the United States, for instance the hapless dictator of the short-lived Cracow Revolution of 1846, Jan Tyssowski, and Henryk Kałussowski. The former became a prominent government official; Kałussowski was, briefly, an unofficial representative of Poland during the 1863 insurrection and played a role in the American acquisition of Alaska. Tochman continued to be active in Polish and American politics. In 1852 the Democratic Society of Polish Exiles was set up in the United States. Three years earlier Adam Gurowski, destined to play a somewhat sinister role in Polish-American relations, had come to

America. But by then another East Central European country had fired the imagination of the American people. That was Hungary in 1848, and for a while Louis Kossuth became a hero of the New World.

The American Civil War and the Insurrection of 1863

The Great Emigration displayed much activity through the 1830s and 1840s. The Czartoryski camp waged a gigantic diplomatic duel against Russia, concentrating on Turkey and the Balkans. Co-operating with France and Britain, the prince strove "to have the rights of Poland engraved on the walls of the parliaments." He instructed the homeland to avoid rash acts and to await a favorable international situation. Czartoryski appreciated the need for a solution of the peasant question and proposed voluntary emancipation, but did not advertise this position for fear of antagonizing the more conservative groups of the nobility and the gentry. He advocated a sustained effort in cultural and economic spheres to strengthen national resistance—a program known as organic work. The rival Democratic Society and its sympathizers put their trust in a national-social revolution in the homeland and in close coopera-tion with European revolutionaries. A wave of conspiracies, largely inspired by emigrés, passed through Galicia, affected Cracow, and swept the lands under Prussia and Russia. The conspiracies pro-voked intensified police persecutions and produced martyrs. The two trends of organic work and political conspiracy began to coexist, taking various forms in the different parts of dismembered Poland.

Some economic progress was noticeable throughout the divided country. The first railroad appeared in Congress Poland in 1845. In Prussian Poznania, the Poles began to practice successfully the precepts of organic work. A Polish middle class had consolidated, competing against the German element and the Jews, most of whom sided with the Germans. A growing movement of cooperatives, self-aid institutions, and farming circles made Poznania resemble western European countries more than other parts of Poland. The lands under Austrian and Russian rule faced somewhat different problems, the most important of which was the solution of the agrarian question with its far-reaching political ramifications.

Tsar Nicholas well summed up the Russian position toward the Poles: "If you persist in nursing your dreams of a distinct national-ity, of an independent Poland," he said, "you can only draw the greatest of misfortunes upon yourselves." The tsarist policies toward the Congress Kingdom sought to maintain full controls; in the western provinces of Lithuania, Belorussia, and the Ukraine they aimed at speeding up full absorption into Russia. They implied the elimination of Polish cultural and political influences, and the destruction of the link with Catholicism, the Uniate Church. Polish or polonized landowners continued, however, to be the most important cultural and economic element in these lands, and in view of the socioeconomic structure of tsarist Russia the government could not easily tamper with their social status. To do so would have implied a virtual revolution in agrarian conditions.

The peasant question in all its aspects was perhaps the central and the most difficult issue faced by the Poles under Russia and Austria. The peasantry had already been emancipated in Prussian Poland and, along different lines, in the Cracow Republic—the only example of an emancipation carried out by Polish authorities. It was evident that some form of peasant reform had to come in tsarist Russia and the Habsburg monarchy if these countries were to evolve economically toward a modern, capitalist society. But what form was it to take? A conversion of labor obligations to rent and the institution of perpetual tenancy, or liquidation of the corvée or *robot* accompanied by erection of peasant freehold farms? Who would compensate the landowners and how? Politically, these questions were of utmost importance, because their solution could determine whether the peasantry would be turned into loyal subjects of the emperor or the tsar or integrated into the fabric of the Polish nation. The radicals believed that only a social revolution in which the vested interests of the landowners were sacrificed to the needs of the peasantry could successfully advance the cause of Poland's independence. The people (*lud*) was the real backbone of the nation and it had to be gained at all cost.

Short of a national-social revolution the Poles could hardly win the battle for the peasants' souls against the partitioning powers. But, the real leadership still came from the upper classes; this was true for both the Czartoryski camp and the Democratic Society. The peasantry was backward, mostly illiterate; its level of national consciousness was low. It was easier to idolize the people in emigré meetings in Paris than to face realities in the Polish countryside. Not unnaturally the landowners were doubtful of the wisdom of the sacrifices that were demanded of them. They could and did point to the difficulties of a sweeping emancipation that might ruin their estates and the country's economy. Thus if the need of a reform was widely recognized, for patriotic, propagandistic, even economic reasons, the exact mode of carrying it out was not agreed upon.

There were other difficulties. In Galicia the local diet began seriously to consider the agrarian question in the early 1840s. The attitude of Vienna, anxious lest radical proposals of change in the Galician agrarian structure adversely affect other parts of the monarchy, restrained the scope of the diet's deliberations. Only by 1845 did it take up the issue of peasant emancipation, but it was already too late to avert a catastrophe.

The democratic camp, connected with the Democratic Society abroad, began to prepare a national and social revolution. Scheduled to begin in February 1846 simultaneously in various parts of the partitioned country, the revolt never got off the ground. Arrests destroyed the central organization and orders to call off the uprising led to confusion. Consequently only Cracow became for a short time a successful revolutionary center. A Polish National Government was proclaimed and issued a radical manifesto that decreed the emancipation of the peasantry without compensation to the landowners, promised land to the landless, and declared complete equality of the Jews. This was a bold move and Karl Marx characterized the Cracow Manifesto as marking the first social revolution on Polish soil.

Revolutionaries in nearby western Galicia who attempted to raise the masses against the government fell victim to clever manipulation of the peasantry by the local Austrian officials. The revolutionaries were predominantly drawn from the gentry, and in the strained manor-village relations in Galicia it was easy to provoke a peasant *jacquerie*. Peasant bands, regarding the revolutionaries as class enemies and rebels against the good emperor in Vienna, aided the Austrian troops against the insurgents. Soon a general massacre of landowners and their families began, accompanied by the burning and looting of manors. The peasant uprising of 1846 claimed over one thousand lives and came as a profound shock both to the democrats and their political opponents, who saw their worst fears justified.

Subsequent Polish revolutions in 1848 were inextricably linked with the Spring of Nations and directly influenced by the developments in the Habsburg monarchy, Prussia, and Germany. They were in a sense semilegal revolutions based on an assumed community of interests between liberal Berlin, Vienna, and the Poles as against counterrevolutionary Russia. Should Russia fight against the Germanic states, the Poles would be a useful ally. And from the Polish perspective, victory over the tsarist empire could mean the restoration of Poland. Fear of Russian intervention made Prussia condone a virtual Polish takeover of Poznania, including the formation of an armed militia. However, when that danger receded, German nationalism clashed with that of the Poles; the Poznanian revolution was doomed. While the assembly in Frankfurt wavered, the Prussian army crushed the Polish militia. Faced with a choice between nationalism and liberalism, the Germans opted, in the words of a Frankfurt deputy, for "healthy national egoism." Consequently the events of 1848 in Prussian Poland marked a transition from what was hitherto mainly a struggle between the Poles and the officialdom to a nationalist German-Polish strife.

In Galicia the Poles petitioned for autonomy which they regarded as a step toward eventual recreation of a united Poland. Again the Russian angle figured prominently in these calculations. At the same time the newly created Polish national councils appealed to the landowners to emancipate their peasants. The local Austrian governor forestalled and checkmated the Poles. First he announced the abolition of serfdom in Galicia ahead of the general emancipation in the Habsburg monarchy. Then he cleverly exploited anti-Polish feelings of the Ruthenians in the eastern part of the province by encouraging them to demand a separation of Galicia into two parts. The use of the peasant and Ruthenian issues as political weapons kept the Poles on the defensive until the Austrian counterrevolution was able militarily to restore its full control. The emancipation of the peasantry remained the sole although a lasting result of the 1848 revolution in Galicia. Only the peasants in Congress Poland and in the formerly Polish eastern provinces under Russia still remained unaffected, and naturally the peasant question there assumed an even greater sense of urgency.

The Spring of Nations in the Polish lands under Austria and Prussia had shown the depth and intensity of nationalist feelings, and it is appropriate to ask what the Poles meant when they spoke of a future independent and reunited Poland. To virtually all of its leaders Poland meant the old prepartition commonwealth, which had been a multinational state in the ethnic sense even though its politically conscious stratum was Polish or polonized. In 1848 Friedrich Engels too believed that a recreated Poland must have "at least" its borders of 1772. A sincere democrat and a great historian, Joachim Lelewel, regarded Lithuanians or Ukrainians as Poles in the sense of their political as distinct from ethnic nationality. The Poles accused Austria of trying to invent a Ruthenian question in Galicia; they would later attack Russia for purposefully setting the Lithuanians and Ukrainians against the Poles. While these accusations were not groundless, a national revival was beginning to take place among the non-Polish nationalities of the old commonwealth, and subsequent events would accelerate it. Similarly Polish national consciousness began to grow in Upper Silesia or parts of East Prussia that had not belonged to the commonwealth. Some Poles came slowly to recognize these developments as natural and unavoidable, and to speak of a future resurrected Poland not as a unitary state but a "federation of all these racially distinct lands." This was a somewhat novel idea that would dominate the thinking of the Polish left especially at the turn of the nineteenth and early twentieth century.

In 1854 the Crimean War, in which Britain and France fought Russia, appeared to create the favorable international constellation the Czartoryski camp had been hoping and working for so long. But once again, Polish expectations were unfulfilled. The Crimean War lasted both too long and not long enough: too long not to awaken Polish hopes and stir activities; too short to make it expedient for England and France to play the Polish card against Russia.

The United States could not view the Crimean War with indifference. Even if pro-Russian feelings in America had been temporarily weakened by the tsarist intervention in the Hungarian revolution in 1849, the prospect of a victorious Anglo-French alliance was not pleasing to the United States. It raised possibilities of a clash of interests in the Caribbean and in Central America. American economic stake in Russia, such as the construction of Russian vessels in American shipyards, some participation in Russian railroad building, and need of Russian exports, for instance hemp, could not be dismissed lightly. Pro-Russian attitudes were encouraged— of all people—by the brilliant Polish emigré, Adam Gurowski. Once a radical member of the Democratic Society, Gurowski went to the other extreme and began to preach Panslavist doctrines. The future of Slav nations, Poland included, lay, according to him, in a federation presided over by Russia. Regarded as a renegade by the Poles, Gurowski moved in influential circles in Washington which included Charles Sumner. After 1851 he was put in charge of the foreign section of the New York *Tribune,* and in this capacity allegedly caused the rejection of anti-Russian articles of Marx and Engels who understandably viewed him as an agent of Tsar Nicholas. In 1854 Gurowski published *America and Europe* in which he argued the case for cooperation between the United States and Russia.

It is difficult to estimate the extent of Gurowski's impact on American thinking about Russia, but his views seemed to coincide with American foreign policy. There was certainly no thought in Washington of any European entanglements. President Millard Fillmore had asserted in his annual message to Congress in 1851 that it was America's "imperative duty" not to interfere in internal policies of other governments. The United States sympathized with the oppressed who struggled for freedom but would tolerate no participatory acts, instigations of revolutions abroad, or preparations of military expeditions on American soil. The Crimean War, however, could start a chain reaction in Europe which the United States had to take into consideration.

In March 1854 the Polish democrats presented a memorandum to the U.S. minister in London, James Buchanan, containing information on the Polish situation "indispensable to any state preparing to influence actively the future destinies of Europe." The possibility of a Polish uprising for which American moral support would be very important was mentioned. Buchanan, while strongly condemning the partitions of Poland, was doubtful whether the Crimean War would produce speedy changes on the map of Europe. Still it could free Italy, Hungary, and Poland from foreign rule. By Poland he probably meant the Congress Kingdom. Should these countries establish regular de facto governments, the United States would doubtless recognize them; such a recognition would provide them "powerful moral aid" without "giving just cause of offence" to the powers that held them in subjection.

Buchanan's remarks to some of the Polish leading emigrés in London made Lelewel believe briefly that America had "the cause of the peoples in mind" and would "not be inactive." The leadership of the Democratic Society noted with appreciation "manifestations of American sympathy with the elements of the European future" but also recognized the official reserve imposed by the American position in international relations. The Poles thus did not seem to have expected too much of America. Plans of raising Polish volunteers in the United States to fight Russia in the Crimea misfired; some recruitment of volunteers via Canada provoked a minor American-British incident. Eventually, certain Poles from America did join the Polish division in Turkey.

The Crimean War shook the Russian empire and opened the era of the great reforms of Alexander II. As regards the Congress Kingdom, the tsar was only willing to offer limited concessions. Addressing a Polish delegation with admonition "no daydreaming, gentlemen," Alexander affirmed the correctness of his father's Polish policies. Still, he took some conciliatory measures in cultural and religious matters, and permitted the establishment of the Agricultural Society. This was a union of reformist landowners, led by a popular magnate, Count Andrzej Zamoyski, which quickly grew into a substitute parliament and a sounding board for ideas of change in the all-important agrarian sector. Zamoyski, fearful of being accused of collaboration with the Russian government, attempted to keep the Agricultural Society clear of politics. That was hardly possible when the government asked it in 1859 to prepare a project of land reform that was bound to have political repercussions. Around the Agricultural Society a political movement crystallized, later known as the Whites. It represented not only the landowning class but also the rising capitalist stratum in which several bankers of Jewish origin, notably Leopold Kronenberg, were active. Indeed, the kingdom's enlightened Jews were demonstrating strong patriotic feelings; an era of Polish-Jewish cooperation set in.

Zamoyski's political rival was Margrave Aleksander Wielopolski, whose standing stemmed from his strong personality and ideas rather than popular appeal. A stern and lonely aristocrat, contemptuous of public opinion, Wielopolski did not fear to maintain that the Congress Kingdom stood no chance of being restored to its 1815 position, not to mention any concessions in the Lithuanian and Ukrainian provinces. Wielopolski regarded as politically feasible a limited program of polonization of the educational system, some measures of local self-government, a tenantry status for the peasants, and full emancipation of the Jews whom he regarded as Poland's third estate.

While the Agricultural Society was timidly tackling the agrarian-peasant question, and eventually recommending an ambiguous program of limited emancipation, a semirevolutionary situation developed in Warsaw. An underground, referred to as the Reds and composed of students, younger army officers, artisans, and members of the lesser gentry, was growing and contributing to patriotic manifestations in the capital. In 1861, the year of the peasant emancipation decree in Russia, the demonstrators acting as a pressure group on the Agricultural Society clashed with Russian troops. A score were wounded and killed.

St. Petersburg and the Russian viceroy were all in favor of dealing firmly with the radicals; they wished, however, to begin a dialogue with the representatives of the upper classes. Since Zamoyski, ever sensitive to public opinion, could not become a political partner, the Russians turned to Wielopolski and named him a member of the administration. Wielopolski took stern measures of assuring order; he dissolved the Agricultural Society and admonished the Polish clergy not to meddle in politics. Psychologically, these were mistakes, for the Poles were not prepared to submit to another oppressive regime that disregarded their national feelings.

Wielopolski and the government were confronted with a "moral revolution." Heavily influenced by Romanticism, it took the form of fraternization between classes and religious denominations, Poles

76

and Lithuanians. New clashes occurred and crowds were massacred by the military on Warsaw's Castle Square. When demonstrators took refuge in churches, troops forced their way in. It seemed that the Russians could govern only by constant exercise of force. Wielopolski was therefore hastily summoned to St. Petersburg, where he won over the government to his program and returned in early 1862 as the de facto prime minister accompanied by a new viceroy, the tsar's own brother. The reforms he brought with him were impressive. The university of Warsaw was reopened under a new name and the school system was polonized; some self-government was introduced; and equality was granted to the Jews. Wielopolski's peasant reform, however, was conservative and totally inadequate, although de facto it put an end to compulsory labor obligations.

Defying public opinion, Wielopolski did not seek to gain support for his program. He uttered the long remembered and often quoted phrase: "one could do something *for* the Poles but nothing *with* the Poles." The Russian viceroy realized that Wielopolski moved in a political vacuum and approached the popular Zamoyski. But the count's insistence on a separate Polish army, a constitution, and concessions in the eastern lands struck the viceroy as the ravings of a maniac. Zamoyski was ordered to leave the country.

In the course of 1862 politics in the kingdom were further radicalized. The Whites gradually departed from adherence to legality and organized their own clandestine directory. The Reds developed their organization, set up a National Committee, and became a genuine political force preparing for a revolutionary showdown. They reached an agreement with Herzen and his *Kolokol* group in London and tried to form a common Polish-Russian revolutionary front. The thorny issue of Lithuania and the Ukraine was to be resolved by self-determination of these borderlands.

Meanwhile the margrave, to use the words of the prominent Polish historian Michał Bobrzyński, "instead of curbing" the Red movement "decided to break it." His means were particularly objectionable: a recourse to the draft for the Russian army so devised as to be, as Wielopolski himself put it, a proscription rather than a conscription. The National Committee was forced to take up the challenge and after much soul searching decreed an armed uprising on January 22, 1863. It appealed to the nations of Poland, Lithuania, and Ruś (Ukraine) to rise in arms, and simultaneously decreed full emancipation of the peasants, granting them property rights to the land they cultivated. The landless who joined the insurrection were promised plots out of the state domain. Another appeal was addressed to the Jews, called "Brother Poles of the Mosaic faith"; yet another warned the Russian people not to side with Poland's oppressors.

Thousands responded to the appeals of the National Committee (it later changed its name to National Government), although it was an anonymous body operating in a clandestine fashion. Its subsequent orders continued to be obeyed which meant that they corresponded to the real feelings of the nation. Altogether some 200,000 partisans, a large number given the kingdom's total population of over 4 million, fought at various times in the insurrection. The fighting spread into Lithuania and Belorussia, where not only the gentry but also the peasants rallied under the old Polish banner. The insurrection flared up briefly in the Ukraine, where the local population opposed it. Volunteers from Galicia and Prussian Poland, as well as foreigners, joined the fighting units.

In contrast to the 1830–1831 insurrection, the Poles had no army but only guerilla units armed with improvised weapons. They were no match for the Russian troops. Still, the bitter strife went on until the autumn of 1864 when the last leader, Romuald Traugutt, was executed in Warsaw. Sporadic skirmishes went on even beyond that date.

The insurrection had been started by the Reds; in the spring of 1863 the Whites joined in, bringing their financial resources and political experience. Their participation prolonged the uprising and made it a truly national affair. Were the Whites encouraged by the Franco-British-Austrian diplomatic representations to St. Petersburg, which seemed to internationalize the uprising, or did they use the great powers' move as a pretext to abandon their original reserve? Recent historiography inclines to the second view. The attitude of the peasantry toward the insurrection has been the object of some controversy. The National Government offered the peasants more than any of the partitioning regimes, and it attempted to enforce its decree. To offset the attraction of the insurrection, the Russian government amended its emancipation *ukaz* of 1861 in the Lithuanian and Ukrainian provinces to the advantage of the local peasantry. Evidence on peasant reactions is somewhat contradictory, but it is known that more peasants fought in the insurgent ranks than in any previous Polish uprising including that of Kościuszko in 1794.

Was the January insurrection a folly or a necessity? The question may be badly put for it presupposes the existence of rational choices. As in most revolutions, the Red and the Whites were not completely free agents. Circumstances pushed them in a certain direction until they reached a point of no return. On balance, the insurrection undoubtedly destroyed all the achievements of Wielopolski and opened a dark era of persecutions and russification. But one must bear in mind that had Wielopolski's policies prevailed, the Poles would have also had to pay a price. It is likely that the upper classes would have become more dependent on Russia and the peasant question not resolved along the radical lines the 1863 insurrection made unavoidable. The subsequent socioeconomic changes, which eventually operated to the country's advantage, would have taken a different form. Finally, Polish political thought would have stagnated; for all its failures the insurrection acted as a powerful shock that forced the Poles to reconsider their present dilemmas and the past.

The outbreak of the January insurrection came twenty-one days after Lincoln's Emancipation Proclamation, but the United States learned about it only by mid-February 1863. Polish questions had not occupied the Americans in the turbulent years preceding the Civil War, but there were occasional reports from travelers in addition to regular communications from legations abroad. In the mid-1850s Bayard Taylor, later to become American chargé d'affaires in St. Petersburg, noted that the Poles seemed to be gradually accepting Russian rule, although they were not likely to lose their feeling of a separate nationality. Another traveler, Captain George McClellan, the future commander of Union forces, had little good to say about the Poles. He found them unpleasant, unintelligent, and degenerate, and wondered how such people had ever achieved any historical prominence. In the State Department a pro-Russian stance was urged by the notorious Gurowski who in 1860 served in its press section. But Gurowski—called "Lincoln's Gadfly" or "Amadeus in spectacles"—was becoming ever more obnoxious and spared neither Lincoln, Seward, Chase, nor Sumner. So at that time his influence may have been on the wane.

The American minister to Russia, John Appleton, reported on unrest in Congress Poland in 1861, commenting rather favorably on Alexander's intentions and showing impatience with the stubborn Poles. Since the first revolutionary events in Poland coincided with the emergence of the Confederacy in February and the attack on Fort Sumter in April 1861, one can hardly blame the United States government for not devoting much attention to Polish affairs. Still, the Northern press printed some news about Poland, mainly in connection with the reforms of Alexander II. The Northern liberals' sympathies seemed divided between the tsar-liberator and the Poles.

The Polish emigrés in the United States tried to play the difficult role of interpreting events in the homeland and enlisting the sympathy of the Americans for their cause. By 1860 there were Poles in every state and territory of the United States, Dakota excepted, and their number has been estimated at 30,000. Some came after the upheaval of 1848, and the first Polish settlement called Panna Maria was established in Texas by immigrants from Silesia in 1854. Several Poles were involved with the abolitionist movement, and later served in the Union ranks. Among the most prominent was a post-1846 exile Włodzimierz (Vladimir) Krzyżanowski, known as Kriz in the army, where he served under Karl Schurz and rose to the rank of brigadier general. Tochman, who was perhaps best qualified to represent the Polish cause in America, had become a friend of Jefferson Davis, took the side of the South, and offered to raise a Polish contingent for the Confederate army. His position had seemingly nothing to do with the pro-Russian trends in the North, and his stand earned him severe censure by the Polish Democratic Society in France and Britain.

After the outbreak of the January insurrection, Poles in America attempted to stir public opinion through meetings and rallies in many cities including New York and San Francisco. Krzyżanowski and other Polish officers in the Union army were mainly responsible for the creation of a Polish Central Committee which appealed to the American people. Responses were mixed. Most of the supporters came from among those who fled Europe after 1848, as for example Karl Schurz. Polish Jews reacted sympathetically. The Irish, inspired by appeals of William Smith O'Brien and other Irish nationalists from Europe, gave staunch support to the Polish cause. Some of those who had been active on behalf of the Poles in 1831, however, were conspicuously absent. The total amount collected for Polish aid reached only $16,000. Given the Civil War in the United States, the international implications of the Polish insurrection, and the meager resources of Poles in America, probably little more could have been achieved.

The first news of the insurrection came from Russian sources. The official version was given without comments, except for the New York *Tribune* and the *Sun,* which voiced sympathy for the Poles together with criticism of a hopeless undertaking. The influential *North American and United States Gazette* of Philadelphia termed "making war without a reasonable prospect of success" a "crime" and a "blunder." It was not a light matter to disturb the peace of the world, the paper said, and while it wished the Poles "another chance of becoming a nation" it also wished them to make "a better use of their independence than they had when they were one." Russian policies toward the Poles, however, were also criticized. This was a distinctly chiller reaction than that toward the November insurrection of thirty-two years earlier. In 1863 and early 1864 there were changes in the attitude of the American press toward Polish developments; two remarks seemed to reflect most accurately the prevalent opinions. One, by the pro-Polish Horace Greeley in the New York *Tribune,* said that sympathy for Poland had "gone queerly out of fashion in America." The other came in a letter from John Harper of Philadelphia to his son in August 1863: "The Poles have our sympathies," he wrote, *"though* they rebel against Russia." (Italics added). The hopelessness of the Polish case was generally noted, and the chargé in St. Petersburg, Taylor, opined that history taught "that there is no resurrection for a nation once dead." Other American diplomats and politicians—Seward, Sumner, Judah Benjamin—showed more generosity and understanding toward the Poles, especially in private.

American views and policies were particularly influenced by two factors: the international implications of the insurrection and the supposed analogies between the Russian-Polish and the North-South struggles. In the spring of 1863 the Polish issue became the concern of Britain and France and there appeared the possibility of an international conflict in Europe. The United States' diplomacy could not fail to appreciate the fact that the insurrection had warded off the dangers of Anglo-French interference in the Civil War by turning the attention of Napoleon III away from America. For the Confederacy the insurrection came at an unfortunate moment, diminishing the chances of British and French recognition.

Several Northern journals, for instance the New York *Tribune, Weekly Tribune,* the Pittsburgh *Post* and the Catholic papers, viewed Poland favorably at least in part because of the involuntary service it had performed for the Union. Polish events appeared variously relevant for contemporary America and were commented upon in this context. The Boston *Daily Courier,* whose editor sympathized with the Confederate cause, used heavy irony in writing about American reactions toward the insurrection: had the Polish rebellion broken out three years earlier, there would have been much pro-Polish enthusiasm, declamations about Kościuszko and Sobieski, and denunciation of the tsar. Now a rebel was a rebel and deserved hanging. Other papers made veiled comparisons between the draft in Poland and the conscription introduced in the North. The Southern press attempted to compare the tyranny of the tsar to Lincoln. So did the famous cartoon in the British *Punch,* which pictured Lincoln and Alexander shaking hands against the background of gallows and destruction inflicted on their respective rebels.

The *New York Times,* on August 19, 1863, drew additional parallels between the Polish and Southern rebellions. The Poles demanded that the tsar "submit to a dismemberment of his empire," and Americans fighting for unity could not question his right to oppose it. Only a minority of Poles as only a minority of Southerners favored rebellion, but the abstaining Polish peasants seemed wiser than the "poor white trash." The Southern press also used the Polish case for polemical purposes. When a Confederate paper printed a comparative list of misdeeds of "Alexander II and Abraham I" this did not necessarily imply sympathy for Poland, referred to by another journal as "the political dream land of poets and patriots." At one point the Southern press argued that international neglect of the Confederacy was much more scandalous than neglecting Poland, which was "but a galvanized corpse that never had a government worthy of the name"; by contrast, the South was a "family of giants."

The Union was determined not to be involved in anti-Russian diplomacy of the European powers. On April 23, 1863, Paris addressed a note to the State Department suggesting that the United States associate itself with a mild pro-Polish memorandum to be jointly submitted to St. Petersburg. The document appealed to the tsar to devise means of placing Poland in conditions of lasting peace. Secretary Seward's reply indicated a polite approval of the French initiative but contained highly flattering words about the tsar. Seward made clear that the United States could not be associated with a joint démarche and cited historic reasons for a policy of noninvolvement with other countries. The American minister to St. Petersburg, the odd, Bowie-knife-wielding Kentuckian Cassius M. Clay, communicated Seward's reply to Chancellor Gorchakov and agreed to the Russian's request to have it published. Reporting back to Washington, Clay dwelt on the moral support Russia would gain "in defense of the integrity of her Empire." The envoy's bias showed again when he delightedly commented on Russian rejections of Franco-Austrian-British notes, or when he wrote that he was all on the side of Russia, "liberal Russia—against reactionary, Catholic and despotic Poland."

The Polish insurrectionary diplomats headed by Władysław Czartoryski, Prince Adam's son, regarded Seward's note as a "symptom of the Union's weakness" and "an act of petty spite against the stand which the Western Powers take in favor of the Confederacy." The Poles in general paid little attention to the Civil War, which they felt had no direct impact on the insurrection. Only in 1864 the National Government appointed Henryk Kałussowski as its political representative in the United States; Washington never granted him recognition.

Pro-Russian sentiments in America received new stimuli in the summer and late autumn of 1863. Russia gave its consent to the long sought-after telegraphic connection between San Francisco and St. Petersburg via Alaska. In September a Russian fleet came to New York, and shortly thereafter another squadron weighed anchor at San Francisco. The Russian fleet was dispatched to American waters not to bolster the United States against England and France, as the public naively imagined, but to escape a possible blockade in the Baltic and to be used if need be to threaten British maritime communications. The New York press enthusiastically welcomed the Russian navy; at one time forty editorials in nine dailies were devoted to it and of thse only one displayed a consistently anti-Russian and pro-Polish stand. The *Herald* drew comparisons between the American and the Russian march toward power, territorial extension, and population growth. Some papers even advocated an alliance between the United States and Russia. The official city reception for the Russian navy happened to coincide with St. Petersburg's rejection of the last Western representation concerning Poland. Prominent New York families—the Roosevelts, Fishes, Jeromes and others—sponsored a ball for the Russian officers. President Lincoln himself boarded the warship *Alexander Nevsky* and officially toasted the tsar. True, there were also discordant notes. Charles Sumner, for one, echoed West European criticism of American russophilism. Several newspapers suddenly dropped lavish praise of Russia and spoke once again about the iniquity of Polish partitions. There were remarks questioning the aptness of analogies between Poland and the South. It appears that in some instances a personal pique of newspaper editors offended by the Russians explained the sudden shift. Be that as it may, San Francisco's welcome of the Russian fleet fell short of the early euphoria of New Yorkers.

During the stay of the Russian fleet in New York an ugly incident occurred. A Polish sailor, one Aleksander Milewski, jumped his ship, escaped, was hunted down, discovered in an artillery regiment he joined in Virginia, and returned to the Russians. Milewski was court-martialed and hanged, but the whole episode failed to produce a stir comparable to that which followed a similar case of the Lithuanian Soviet sailor, Kudirka, in the early 1970s.

By the end of 1863 pro-Russian feelings had cooled, which may have prompted Lincoln to ask for some lectures on the emancipation of Russian serfs. Their effect was a weakening of sympathies for the Polish insurrection. In early 1864 came new attacks on Poland, with strong anti-Catholic overtones. One article boldly asserted that the extinction of Poland was "truly a gain to the cause of civilization." Polish exiles responded heatedly. Commenting on the new peasant emancipation decree in Congress Poland, Kałussowski stressed that the tsar gave only what had already been given by the Poles themselves in 1863. Other progressive aspects of the insurrection, for instance the emancipation of the Jews, were also brought out.

The period of the January insurrection left a deep mark on subsequent American-Polish relations. In handed down a legacy of comparing the defense of American unity with Russian determination to maintain the integrity of the empire. The newly advanced view that in the Russo-Polish strife the elements of progress and liberalism were not necessarily on the Polish side was also of importance. Alexander's reforms had of course a great deal to do with this opinion, promoted by people like Clay. The feeling also persisted that the mighty Russian empire had affinities with America and shared with it certain comon interests against Britain and France.

Postinsurrectionary Decades at Home and Mass Emigration to America

The decades that followed the collapse of the January insurrection ushered in a new phase that marked the beginnings of modern Polish society. The period also witnessed a new phenomenon in American-Polish relations: mass emigration from partitioned Poland to the United States. In mid-1860 the situation in Poland looked desperate. Congress Poland was reduced to a mere province of the Russian empire and called the Vistula Land (*Privislinsky krai*). Prussian Poland became the object of ever-increasing germanization that threatened the survival of its national character. Galicia, together with Cracow (annexed by Austria after 1846), achieved local autonomy but the price paid for it seemed a perpetuation of conservative loyalty to the Habsburgs and economic backwardness. In Lithuania, the historic ties with Poland and the old tradition of the commonwealth were opposed by rising Lithuanian nationalism. Ukrainian nationalist revival posed a threat in Eastern Galicia, which for some five hundred years had been an integral part of the Polish state. The Russian Ukraine, despite the visibility of its Polish element, was already outside the political and ideological orbit of Poland.

The Polish question virtually disappeared from the agenda of European cabinets, and the means by which the Poles had hitherto attempted to further their cause appeared discredited. Conspiracies and armed uprisings were condemned as suicidal, and a new philosophy of positivism arose—the term was borrowed from Auguste Comte—seeking the cultural and material advancement of the nation. Coinciding with the rapid spurt of industrial growth in Congress Poland, it produced some results but not without degenerating into an *enrichissez-vous* outlook. In the political sphere, the corollary of positivism was loyalty to the governments of the partitioning powers, a Triple Loyalty that stood in danger of becoming conservative servilism and an endorsement of the existing threefold division of Poland.

The provisions of the 1864 tsarist decree emancipating the peasantry in Congress Poland need not be spelled out in detail here. Nor is it necessary to dwell on the various measures undertaken to russify the country and to hold it in a state of permanent subjection. We might look, however, at the Russian objectives and the actual effects they produced. Working on the assumption that the Catholic church and the landowning gentry—though not necessarily the magnates—were the chief obstacles to Russian domination, the government hoped to break them by reliance on the peasantry, by abolishing the Uniate church in 1875, and by harassment of the Catholic hierarchy. The position of the gentry became undermined by confiscation of land of the insurrectionists or by heavy financial burdens imposed on the estates. The long-range results were somewhat unexpected and hardly welcomed from the Russian viewpoint. By emancipating the peasantry and withdrawing it from dependency on the manor, the Russian administration could no longer pose as the peasants' defender and protector against the landowner. Coming into direct contact with an alien administration, irritated by the Russian-language schools, antagonized by measures which flouted the Poles' attachment to the Catholic church—for instance, the provocative construction of a huge Orthodox church in the heart of Warsaw—the peasantry could hardly identify itself with the tsarist regime. The déclassé members of the gentry, driven to towns, reinforced the intelligentsia and stamped it with their own outlook. Unlike the Russian intelligentsia which became largely alienated by the tsarist regime within its own state, the Polish intelligentsia, precisely because it was deprived of its own state, assumed the responsibility for national leadership. From its ranks came those who would provide guidance to radical movements that spread to the peasants and industrial workers, producing a new form of struggle for social and national freedom.

The most important developments in Congress Poland in the three decades after 1863 centered around the Industrial Revolution and Warsaw positivism, and the reaction which the two engendered. Only some features of the industrialization of the kingdom need to be mentioned here. The capital was not provided by the state, and much of it came from foreign investors who thought they would penetrate the vast Russian markets via Poland. In fact, some 70 percent of Polish exports in the years 1880–1890 went to Russia or through Russia to the Far East; finished products took the lead over raw materials. This was particularly true of textiles, which occupied the first place among Polish industries. Coal mining and the iron industry came next in importance. The output of coal went up in the years 1870–1890 from some 300,000 to 3 million tons. The production of iron almost quadrupled during the same period. A third branch that enjoyed phenomenal growth was sugar refining. All this did not make Congress Poland an industrialized country by Western standards, but transformed it into the most advanced part of the Russian empire. Importation of up-to-date machinery permitted an almost simultaneous growth in various branches of the economy, although it interfered with the development of native machine-producing industries. Technological progress contrasted with socioeconomic retardation. The partitions' borders and the policies of the three powers worked against economic unity of the Polish lands. Congress Poland had to import coke from the distant Donets Basin rather than from neighboring Silesia, and oil from Baku, not from Galicia. Railroads connected each part of Poland to the empire to which it belonged rather than to other Polish lands.

Industrialization brought with it the growth of a proletariat and a bourgeoisie, both of which included many Germans and Jews, some of whom became polonized. Class conflicts naturally were a fact of life as were illegal strikes; trade unions were forbidden in the tsarist empire.

Positivism was a reaction against Romanticism and all it stood for. The positivists rejected the insurrectionary tradition and praised the "heroism of a reasonable life." They demanded that outside winds "ventilate Poland's stuffy hut," and called on their countrymen to concentrate on work in all walks of life lest Poland remain hopelessly behind the rest of Europe. Positivist literature extolled the heroism of physicians fighting against illness, of teachers struggling against obscurantism, of engineers mastering the forces of nature. Although the trend produced a number of important novelists—Bolesław Prus, for one—positivist literature had a limited appeal. The writings of the most influential literary figure of the period, Henryk Sienkiewicz—whose *Quo Vadis* later won him the

Nobel Prize—heralded a reaction against positivism. Sienkiewicz's *Trilogy,* the great historical novel, sought to give hope and inspiration to the Polish reader. The past became also the main subject of the great canvases of the realist painter Jan Matejko, whose impact on the Poles was comparable to that of Sienkiewicz.

In Galicia the shock of the collapse of the January insurrection contributed to the rise of a conservative movement centered on Cracow. Within this group arose a new historical school which subjected the Polish past to searching criticism. The Cracow historians, of whom Michał Bobrzyński was the most brilliant, put stress on historical errors and warned against their repetition. Just as liberum veto had become the sinister symbol of old Polish anarchy, so liberum conspiro (freedom to conspire)—a term one of the conservatives invented—led Poland to repeated catastrophes in the course of the nineteenth century. The Galician conservatives sought to educate a new generation of Poles in the principles of work, social order, and political realism. The Habsburg monarchy provided the opportunities—Galicia enjoyed an autonomous regime from the 1860s—for the Poles to serve their political apprenticeship, and the conservatives felt that by cooperation with Austria they were not betraying the ultimate and far-off goal of Polish independence. At a later date they began to confuse patriotism with their control over Galician politics. In the last decades of the nineteenth century Galicia became the freest of all Polish lands, and its universities and schools the only ones where Polish was the language of instruction. Economic progress, however, was slower than under Russia and Prussia. The rising challengers to the conservative rule, the Populists and especially the Socialists, somewhat demagogically but not without reason likened Galicia to an estate leased to the Polish nobility. The situation in Eastern Galicia was further complicated by the Ruthenian (Ukrainian) problem which one of the contemporaries defined as a social issue with a national content.

Like Congress Poland and Galicia, Prussian Poland exhibited features of its own. Here the central figure of Bismarck dominated the three distinct periods between the 1860s and 1890s. During the first one up to 1871, Prussia achieved the unification of Germany, and despite strong Polish protests Pomerania and Poznania were incorporated into the North German Confederation and then into the empire. The second phase up to 1885 was characterized by the famous *Kulturkampf,* launched by Bismarck largely to strengthen the cohesion of the Reich against regionalist tendencies and the Catholic church. For the Poles the Kulturkampf was a menace to the Catholic and Polish character of the provinces, Catholicism being a pillar suporting Polish nationalism. The net effect of the Kulturkampf was a closing of Polish ranks under the double watchword of defense of Catholicism and "Polishness." Polish national consciousness was being strengthened also in the long-germanized Upper Silesia and other areas in which people formerly thought of themselves as Polish-speaking Prussians.

A third phase, starting in 1885, marked the beginnings of new policies based on the government's realization that a distinction between the inimical Polish gentry and clergy and the potentially loyal masses was growing obsolete. It was necessary to resort to large-scale measures of germanization and colonization of the Polish provinces. In 1885 the government brutally expelled some thirty thousand Poles and Jews, long settled in the area, who were not Prussian citizens. A year later Bismarck announced the creation of the colonization commission, which was endowed with large funds and designed to buy land in Poznania and West Prussia. The land thus acquired would then be parceled out among German settlers.

In opposing German policies the Poles perfected their system of agricultural circles, associations of industrialists and artisans, credit and savings associations, land and agrarian-industrial banks, as well as cultural and educational self-aid institutions. The Poznanians became disciplined and hard-working. But the prospects of their strife were not rosy, for although Prussia took pride in being a *Rechtsstaat* (law-observing state), it could and did use ruthless administrative pressures. What is more, on the German side voices were raised (for example the philosopher Edward Hartmann's) favoring complete germanization and elimination (*ausrotten*) of inimical alien minorities. Strongly believing in their superior culture, the Germans viewed such extreme policies as the fulfillment of their civilizing mission.

The last decades of the nineteenth century witnessed a new phenomenon that deeply affected American-Polish relations. This was the beginning of a mass emigration from the Polish lands to the New World. The story of the immigrants in America cannot be told in detail in this book; it is a subject that has been tackled by many writers although a definitive and authoritative study is still wanting. Here only a general picture will be sketched to enable the reader to place the emigration, later called the American Polonia, in the broad context of American-Polish relations.

The size of the emigration is still subject to doubt. Exact figures are hard to establish because Poles coming from the three empires were generally classified as natives of Russia, Austria, or Germany. Not only Poles but also Jews and Ruthenians were part of the emigration wave. According to recent calculations, there were about 50,000 Poles in America in 1870; by 1889 their figure increased to roughly 800,000. During the 1870–1914 period some 1.3 million Poles arrived from Russian Poland, around 1.2 million from Prussia's Polish provinces, and roughly 1.1 million from Galicia. Emigration from the Congress Kingdom declined after 1880; from Prussian Poland and Galicia it increased.

Most of the immigrants who had left their homeland in search of better living conditions were peasants. The newcomers had generally few skills and, except for those from Prussian Poland where there was virtually no illiteracy, they were uneducated and none had any knowledge of English. Most of them were Roman Catholics who saw in the church and the priests their natural leaders and protectors. A recently published collection of letters, confiscated by the tsarist censorship, gives a good insight into the mentality of these people, but the pioneering sociological study of the peasant in Poland and America by Florian Znaniecki and William Thomas still remains a most valuable treatment of the subject.

Polish immigrants, like most of their counterparts from southeastern and eastern European countries, had to make their way up from the lowest position on the social ladder. They frequently experienced discrimination and contempt. "It goes against the grain in an English-speaking man to fetch and carry for a Slovak or a Pole," one contemporary observer remarked. Yet they persevered, and their capacity for hard work was noted and won them the grudging respect of their neighbors. A Polish New England farmer became the hero of Edna Ferber's popular novel, *American Beauty*. The question of national self-identity of the immigrants needs to be further studied, but many of them became more clearly aware of their Polishness in a narrow ethnic sense than they had been at home. No doubt the alien environment drove them closer together, but the role of Polish parishes and sociopolitical organizers must also be noted. Already in 1866 a Polish Commune (*Gmina*) connected with the post-1863 political emigration in Europe was set up in Chicago. Polish newspapers and periodicals catering to the immigrants appeared; some of them have survived to the present. The need for mutual aid societies gave an impulse to the rise of organizations that later showed cultural and national political aspirations.

It was out of an association of Polish parishes that the first mass organization, the Polish Roman Catholic Union, emerged in 1873.

The union put emphasis on religious and national education and fostered Polish schools. Not all of the parishes, however, came into its fold. Partly as a reaction against the German and Irish church hierarchy—the first Polish bishop was named only in 1908—several Polish parishes showed separatist tendencies. Eventually, between 1900 and 1904 some twenty-four parishes united to form a separate Polish National Catholic Church; Reverend Francis Hodur was elected its first bishop and head.

A second mass organization, more numerous than the Polish Roman Catholic Union, came into existence in 1880. Called the Polish National Alliance, it partly owed its existence to post-1863 emigrants, among them one of the past members of the National Government, who publicly called for the creation of a Polish organization in America. Viewed askance by the Roman Catholic Union, the alliance put the stress on a national mission of representing the Polish cause abroad. The bulk of its membership came from first-generation immigrants, mostly workers of peasant background. The Polish National Alliance combined successfully its national mission with the operations of a life insurance company. Its membership grew from some 7,500 in 1895 to over 100,000 on the eve of the First World War. Subsequently many other Polish organizations, notably women's and sports clubs, emerged on American soil.

The immigrants, although beginning their new life in extremely hard conditions, frequently depicted America in their letters to their families and friends as a land of opportunity. Some returned home with their savings and became a living illustration of success overseas. Others assisted their families financially; in Galicia this aid mounted up to millions of dollars. The image of America as the land of plenty appealed to the imagination of the Poles, particularly the young and the more ambitious.

If the immigrants contributed to greater popularization of America in Poland, their impact on the United States was somewhat more ambiguous. As a labor force in the rapidly expanding post-Civil War America, the Poles were undoubtedly needed and they played their part in the growth of the country. At the same time their low standard of living, their devout Catholicism and clericalism, as well as their peasant customs evoked contempt and concern on the part of the Anglo-Saxon and northern Protestant stock. In a much publicized passage of Woodrow Wilson's *History of the American People,* published in 1902, the future president spoke in disparaging terms about the new mass of immigrants, Poles included. He regarded them as the dregs of European society washed on American shores and questioned the skill, energy, initiative, and intelligence of the immigrants of "the meaner sort." Ten years later, Josiah Strong's *Our Country* pictured the new, lowly, Catholic immigrants as endangering Anglo-Saxon and Protestant values embodied in the United States. A special presidential commission appointed in 1911 to study immigration patterns concluded that the new immigrants were largely undesirable elements. It opined that the Poles were highly strung, revolutionary malcontents, with a high record of criminality. Thus the American image of Poland as a country of unruly nobles historically incapable of successful conduct in public affairs was reinforced by the bigoted view of Polish masses as primitive, hard drinking, and uncouth.

A continuing trickle of Polish intelligentsia either visiting or settling in the United States did not seem to have affected the American image of Poland. The impact of these people, some of whom were acclaimed and admired, on the United States would require further research. The same is true for their role as interpreters of America to the Polish public.

In the 1870s the noted Polish actress, Helena Modrzejewska, better known to the Americans under her simplified name of Modjeska, arrived with her husband and a few friends. Their idyllic notion of California, where they planned to establish a small colony, was too unrealistic and the would-be farmers abandoned their venture. Modjeska resumed her stage career and won great acclaim in America as a Shakespearean actress. Her friend and companion, the novelist Henryk Sienkiewicz, returned to Poland. His letters from America, later translated into English, provide a sophisticated Pole's view of the United States and are highly interesting.

Sienkiewicz observed that "the man who departs for America is still a rarity among us." Although one could compile a fairly long list of Polish intellectuals or artists who left their imprint on the United States in the late nineteenth century, this was an essentially correct view. Among great writers only Cyprian Norwid had stayed in New York in the early 1850s, and he expressed his disillusionment with the American dream. Sienkiewicz's letters show the author's admiration for American democracy, the vigor and the greatness of the country. They also reveal his dislike of some American manners, materialism, and the absence of gracious living. Reactions of other contemporary Polish travelers to America, including clergymen, priests, aristocrats, and scientists, were somewhat similar. Probably many of them would have agreed with Sienkiewicz's judgment that "our people's national character is exactly opposite to that of the Americans."

The image of America as reflected in a few contemporary Polish novels, short stories, and political writings has not been fully studied, but superficial observation shows that America was not then a popular theme in Polish literature, anymore than in the twentieth century. Furthermore, although several people were impressed by American democracy and its free institutions, only a few wrote extensively about it. Most prominent among them was Stefan Buszczyński, a member of the Cracow Academy of Learning and a liberal who believed in a federalist solution of European problems. In his *America and Europe: A Historical and Financial Study,* a somewhat pessimistic view of Europe is contrasted with the United States. The latter he clearly deemed a model worthy of imitation by Europeans.

Among individual Poles who left their mark on the United States were educators, musicians, scientists, engineers and representatives of many other professions. Reverend Franciszek Dzierożynski served as vice-president of Georgetown University and was instrumental in the founding of St. John's College in Maryland and Holy Cross College in Worcester, Massachusetts. Artur Grabowski was the president of Defiance College in Ohio. Albert Michelson, born in Prussian Poland, a famous professor of physics at the University of Chicago, was the first American Nobel Prize winner in 1908. Modjeska's son, Ralph Modjeski, acquired some fame as an engineer in California. Among musicians, Jan and Edward de Reszke and also Adam Didur won acclaim as opera singers. Other names familiar to music lovers were Edward Sobolewski, Julian Fontana, and Marcelina Sembrich-Kochańska. The fact that they were Poles was duly noted. When in 1906 Artur Rubinstein came for his first series of concerts, he was referred to as a "young Polish pianist." Were any of them active in propagating Poland's cause? Modjeska did speak on behalf of Polish women at the Chicago World's Fair in 1893; one knows less about the others. A place apart is, of course, occupied by Ignacy Paderewski, whose debut in 1891 captured American audiences and made him the most beloved and admired Polish virtuoso. But the story of Paderewski's successful combination of a great pianist's career with an ambassadorship of the Polish cause belongs to the next chapter of this book.

Contemporary American writers and educators were devoting little attention to Poland and its history. In the 1870s the story of Russian reprisals against patriotic Poles was told in two American *Sixth Readers,* published in Pittsburgh and Cambridge. Both carried the poem entilted "The Polish Boy" by Ann S. Stephens, a New England novelist, which depicted in somewhat melodramatic terms the death of a boy threatened with exile in Siberia. In 1881 there appeared an anthology called *Poets and Poetry of Poland,* edited by Paul Sobolewski. More than two decades later, Sienkiewicz's historical novels influenced Louis E. von Norman's *Poland the Knight among Nations,* published in New York in 1908. It is more than doubtful that these publications or references to Poles had a wide appeal to the American public.

Polish history barely figured in college curricula of European history. Indeed, European history itself began to be taught fairly late in the century; Yale established its first professorship only in 1865. American historians were frequently trained at German universities where the new seminar techniques had originated. Their glimpses of the Polish past were largely through German eyes and publications. Three major European history textbooks published in this country between 1899 and 1907 and written respectively by George B. Adams, Ferdinand Schevill, and James H. Robinson and Charles A. Beard contained brief discussions of Polish partitions. While condemning them on moral grounds, Adams called the dismemeberment of Poland a "well-merited punishment of the selfish corruption of the ruling class." Schevill wrote that Poland had "herself to thank . . . for the ruin that overtook her." Robinson and Beard also talked at length about Polish "feudal anarchy," but at least provided some historical background by mentioning Poland's past. The ground for serious American scholarship on Poland was broken when in 1893–1894,, Archibald C. Coolidge began to teach a pioneering course on northern and eastern European history at Harvard. A year later Coolidge visited Poland, and his student Robert H. Lord chose as the topic of his dissertation the story of the second partition. The result was an outstanding monograph, published in 1915, a classic in the field and a real contribution to Polish historiography.

In the realm of politics Polish issues were of no concern to the United States in the 1880s or 1890s. Diplomatic dispatches from Russia duly reported on the abolition of the Uniate church and other problems affecting Russo-Polish relations. An American consular office was established in Warsaw in 1871; C. De Hoffman served as vice-consul. Yet Poland, and by that Washington presumably meant Congress Poland, appeared essentially a Russian domestic affair. After the American acquisition of Alaska from Russia, the latter was referred to as "the old and faithful friend of the United States." Nothing seemed to disturb American-Russian relations, least of all the Polish question.

Toward the First World War

Between the 1890s and 1914 the United States and partitioned Poland moved along totally different paths. Few contemporaries could have predicted the coming of a world war that would involve the United States and bring about Poland's reemergence as an independent state. There was indeed little to indicate that United States policy would converge with Polish national objectives and that the Polish emigration in America would become a politically important link between the two nations.

The 1890s saw the beginnings of new processes taking place in the United States and in the Polish lands. In 1885 President Cleveland still repeated in his inaugural address that old slogan of "Peace, commerce, and honest friendship with all nations; entangling alliances with none," but the United States was shortly to leave its self-imposed continental confinement. The victory over Spain in 1898 was the most dramatic turning point in America's rise to the position of a world power and heralded its entry upon the path of imperial expansion. American foreign trade rose, and exports of manufactured goods increased proportionately faster than those of agricultural products. Clearly the United States stood in need of expanding foreign markets. In 1880 the American navy was the twelfth in the world, by 1900 it became third. "The power that rules the Pacific," said Senator Beveridge in 1900, "is the power that rules the world," and that power "will forever be the American Republic." In the words of the historians Morrison and Commager, President Theodore Roosevelt established for his country "a right she did not at that time want—to be consulted in world politics." Another American historian, Robert Ferrell, said that the United States rose to a position of power but not to the understanding of what its power could mean in terms of responsibility for the peace of Europe. This may have been at least partly the fault of Taft's administration, which did not fully comprehend nor make clear to the American people that the security which the country had enjoyed throughout the nineteenth century was largely due to Britain as the balancer of the European equilibrium. A successful German challenge to Britain would upset this balance and pose a serious threat to America. The relative positions of Austria-Hungary and Russia seem to have been even less clearly perceived in Washington. Russia was not regarded as a threat to the European balance, which was true in one sense, but much less so if one thinks of Russian-Austrian rivalry. The idea that Eastern Europe, of which so little was known, would provide the spark for the great conflagration of

1914–1918 was probably a most extravagant notion to most Americans.

In Poland the rise of mass political movements, Socialist and National Democratic, was the single most important development at the turn of the nineteenth and early twentieth centuries. Economically, the increasing integration of Polish lands in the three partitioning empires raised doubts whether an independent and reunified Poland could ever become a reality. Processes of industrialization continued in Congress Poland, but their future could be called into question by the program of industrialization of Russia itself. Attempts at a Russo-Polish conciliation made by Polish conservatives and some liberal intellectuals showed no results. In Galicia there was an increased radicalization of politics—along both social and national lines—that corresponded to the general pattern throughout the Dual Monarchy. In Prussian Poland, the program of German colonization and linguistic and political germanization received a new expression through the foundation in 1894 of a German Eastern Association popularly known as the HKT (after the initials of its founders). The term Hakatism acquired wide currency as an expression of extreme German nationalism and a fighting anti-Polish creed. The Prussian Poles kept up their resistance, but difficulties and conflicts multiplied.

Polish responses to these new challenges came from the right and the left: nationalism and socialism. The National Democratic movement had its origins in the Polish League, a revived version of the old Democratic Society, centered in Switzerland. By 1893 the league transformed itself into the National League with headquarters in Poland; the center in Switzerland supervised a fund, the National Treasury. Its purpose was to assist political actions in Poland that rejected Triple Loyalty and promoted national resistance, even insurrection at an opportune moment. The National League gradually evolved in the direction of "integral nationalism" and adopted flexible tactics. The man who more than anyone else stamped it with his ideas and his personality was Roman Dmowski, who deserves to be called the father of modern Polish nationalism.

Dmowski came from a poor Warsaw family of small gentry origin, but he never identified himself with any social class. A natural scientist by training, influenced by contemporary biological and sociological theories, he excelled in clear formulation and ruthless application of ideas. He regarded nationalism as the mainspring of human and social action and rejected its Romantic, liberal, moralistic, and humanitarian version. The nation to Dmowski was a living organism, and life among nations was characterized by struggle for survival. He thus came close to social Darwinism and a basic distinction between individual and national ethics. Dmowski virtually dismissed some of the most cherished traditions of the old commonwealth—Polish toleration and the Jagiellonian eastward expansion—which he regarded as signs of political weakness. Poland fell not because it grew old but because the noble nation reflecting the outlook of the szlachta had lost its virility. Thus he turned to the masses, which were young and dynamic. To mold them in the precepts of modern nationalism became Dmowski's objective. He hoped to assimilate non-Polish nationalities, but not to appease them. The Jews, individual cases excepted, he considered as unassimilable. Anti-Semitism became a basic ingredient of the National Democratic theory, and following the influx of Russian Jews into Poland after 1880, it gained wide currency on both emotional and economic grounds. Dmowski desired and believed in Polish independence as a future goal, but for tactical reasons did not include it in the National Democratic Program of 1903. A pragmatic politician, he took into account the fact of the threefold division of Poland, but simultaneously developed his movement throughout the partitioned country under the slogan "all-Polish" (*wszechpolski*).

If the National Democratic movement was a reaction against conservative Triple Loyalty, socialism was also a reaction and a challenge to the existing order. The first socialist organization on Polish soil was the Great Proletariat, which elaborated its program in 1882. Led by Ludwik Waryński, it postulated a violent overthrow of the tsarist regime. But although a victorious social revolution would end national oppression, an independent Poland was not the primary goal. The early advocates of socialism viewed it as a greater and loftier idea than patriotism.

By 1890 many Polish Socialists began to see an insoluble connection between the revolution and the recovery of Polish independence. They invoked the authority of Marx and Engels for their stand and visualized future Poland as a federation of the nations of the old commonwealth. At a conference held in Paris in 1892 a Polish Socialist party (PPS) was called into existence. It was to operate in Russian Poland but to maintain close relations with the Polish Social Democratic party, which had arisen in Galicia roughly at the same time under the leadership of Ignacy Daszyński. The most charismatic leader of PPS, who came from Lithuania and belonged to a gentry family with vivid memories of 1863, was Józef Piłsudski. PPS was quickly challenged by the 'internationalists," who set up a rival organization later called Social Democracy of the Kingdom of Poland and Lithuania (SDKPiL). Its theorist was Rosa Luxemburg; one of its leaders was Feliks Dzierżyński, better known later as Dzerzhinsky, the dreaded head of the Bolshevik secret police.

It has been rightly said that the socialist fatherland was as real to Rosa Luxemburg as Poland was to Piłsudski. Luxemburg developed the thesis of an "organic integration" of the Congress Kingdom into Russia and viewed the emergence of an independent Poland as contrary to the laws of historical materialism and the logic of capitalist development. For the Polish proletariat independent Poland would mean regression, not progress. Luxemburg and her associates felt that Marx's views on Polish independence had become obsolete since the rise of socialism in Russia, which had replaced Poland as the driving force of the future revolution.

Piłsudski and some, though by no means all, leaders of PPS were only moderately drawn to the concept of class struggle or to Marxist economic theories. Piłsudski saw the historic role of socialism in Poland as a defender of the progressive West against reactionary tsardom. He regarded the industrial proletariat much in the same way in which the earlier Polish radicals had viewed the peasantry, namely as a new force that would carry on the old struggle for social justice and national liberation.

The Russo-Japanese war of 1904–1905 sharpened the basic differences between Polish political trends. The National Democrats saw the war as creating possibilities for concessions from Russia, and they proceeded cautiously. PPS felt that by exposing the weaknesses of the tsarist regime, the war was a golden opportunity for revolutionary-national actions. Bent on exploring the chances of cooperation with Japan, Piłsudski went to Tokyo. There he met Dmowski, who had come to argue the case against any Japanese-supported diversion in Congress Poland. The two approaches were irreconcilable, but Japan was not particularly interested in getting seriously involved in the Polish question in any case. Dmowski's and Piłsudski's Japanese experiences, however, were important, for they strengthened the former's belief in the force of nationalism and the latter's conviction of the importance of military actions.

The road of the Polish leaders to Japan led through the United States and both briefly stopped in this country; Piłsudski, accompanied by Tytus Filipowicz, in June, Dmowski in April and on his way back to Europe in August 1904. This visit of the two greatest figures of Polish twentieth-century history passed virtually unnoticed. Piłsudski addressed a small meeting of the Union of Polish Socialists in New York, an organization formed in 1890, in which Aleksander Dębski, a ranking PPS member, played a leading role.

Piłsudski also talked to Poles in Chicago. He was mainly concerned with two issues affecting American Poles: a representation of PPS in the United States and the question of a loan to bolster PPS activities. The first was satisfactorily resolved; the second apparently was not. As for Dmowski, he held talks with prominent American Poles, mainly in Chicago, about the activities of the Polish League and its relations with American Polonia.

At this point the Poles in America had already developed organizational forms that enabled them to become politically more active and to cooperate with the new movements in the emigration and in Poland. The Polish National Alliance came to stand for the recovery of Polish independence and aspired to the role of representative in America of a "free, independent people's Poland." The alliance supported the Polish League in Switzerland as a substitute Polish government. In 1894 a North American section of the National Treasury was set up. The subsequent evolution of the league and the National Democratic movement raised some doubts about continued financial support. Should not the collected funds be kept in America rather than automatically handed over to Switzerland? After 1895 the National League had its own representatives in the United States who strove to gain a leading position within the Polish National Alliance and neutralize the pro-PPS trend of Dębski and his supporters. Two ranking National Democrats came to visit the United States in 1895 and 1900, and Dmowski's American talks were doubtless meant to strengthen the league's standing in American Polish circles.

The expression Poles in America may most accurately reflect the status of the Polonia at the beginning of this century. This is how it appeared from the Polish perspective, but even the American Polish organization used the term Poles, American citizens, prior to 1914. At that time Polish immigrants were seen as a fourth segment of the partitioned nation—after all, people in Poland were also citizens of other countries—rather than as permanent settlers to whom even an independent Poland would be the "old country." To Americans of older stock the Poles seemed to belong at best to hyphenates, as Wilson called them—people with divided loyalties or uncertain identity.

Dmowski and Piłsudski felt that Poles in America were called upon to play an auxiliary political role, partly providing financial assistance, partly engaging in the propagation of the Polish cause. The emphasis seems to have been on the former. Using them as political leverage to affect the United States' policies toward Poland was not seriously considered. Polish voters hardly counted as yet.

Presumably many of the immigrants did not hold American passports; some because they failed to qualify on literacy or language grounds, others because they saw no clear advantage in becoming United States citizens. There was also no likelihood of interesting the American government in Polish matters, and it is characteristic that neither Dmowski nor Piłsudski tried to go to Washington or attempted talks with American politicians.

At the end of 1904 and into 1905 dramatic events took place in Congress Poland. A school strike erupted; PPS-led demonstrators battled with Russian police; then a general workers' strike produced a revolutionary situation. The 1905 revolution in Russia and Congress Poland was in full swing. Dmowski tried to convince the Russian government that only a Polish autonomous regime could reestablish law and order, but if he sought to be another Wielopolski, the Russians were not interested. Socialists and National Democrats clashed ideologically and politically; there were even some armed encounters and bloodshed.

In October 1905 Russia officially became a constitutional monarchy and in April 1906 elections were held to the Duma. The Polish Socialists boycotted them, which permitted the National Democrats to capture all the seats from Congress Poland. The Poles also won roughly one fourth of all the seats in the western provinces. In the first and second Dumas, the Poles tried to put forward a program of autonomy, or at least achieve significant concessions in Congress Poland. They hoped to exploit the existing divisions in the Duma to their advantage, but the government would not tolerate this state of affairs. The Duma was dissolved, and non-Russian and lower class representation cut down to a bare minimum. The Polish deputies led by Dmowski were put on the defensive, and their original demands had to be scaled down. The question was raised whether further Polish participation in the Duma made any political sense, and the National Democrats found themselves at crossroads.

The Socialists were also in a predicament. A conflict between the "old," led by Piłsudski, and the "young" split the PPS in 1906. The Piłsudski-led faction, reappraising the costly failure of the revolution, began to center its activities on organizing military cadres for a future insurrection. The other group, called the PPS-Left, moved closer to the Social Democrats (SDKPiL), and out of their union in 1918 the Polish Communist party eventually emerged.

During the six years that preceded the outbreak of the First World War the two political trends, headed by Dmowski and Piłsudski, crystallized. In 1908 Dmowski published his *Germany, Russia and the Polish Question*. In essence the book was an offer of cooperation with Russia and an attempt to resolve the impasse in the Duma by raising the Polish issue to a higher, international level. Dmowski argued that the greatest threat to the Polish nation came from Germany and since Germany was also challenging Russia and the West there was a community of interests between the Poles and the Entente. Thus, the Polish question would no longer be a stumbling bloc to French-Russian cooperation. Dmowski showed interest in Neoslavism, seeking to reassure Russia and meet her more than half way. Russia was not eager to start a meaningful dialogue. Neoslavism had no future, and Dmowski's conciliatory policy in the Duma produced no results. Worse still, Russia decided to detach the district of Chełm (called Kholm by the Russians) from the kingdom and annex it directly. The dispirited National League became torn by secessions and internal controversies. Financial suport from the National Treasury in Switzerland ceased after 1908.

Withdrawing from the Duma, Dmowski sought to repair the image of the National Democratic party and singled out the Jewish issue for attack. He accused the Jews of standing in the way of Russo-Polish cooperation. In 1912 when he was defeated in an election that was strongly affected by the Jewish vote, he launched the slogan of economic boycott. Anti-Semitism and a determined anti-Ukrainian stand in Galicia rallied Polish Nationalists. In Prussian Poland the strongly anti-German policies of Dmowski had already made the National Democratic movement a political power in that region. There was more competition in Galicia, where a populist-peasant movement assumed a new impotance with the emergence of the Piast party led by Wincenty Witos. Still, although opposed to the National Democrats, the Populists did not treat them as implacable enemies; for a time Witos himself was a member of the league.

As the World War approached, the National Democratic movement, all difficulties notwithstanding, was a real force in Polish politics. The Dmowski camp was tying Poland's cause to the Franco-Russian alliance and was ready to work for a reunification of Polish lands around the Congress Kingdom under the slogan of autonomy. Dmowski naturally hoped that the size of a reunited Poland as well as French assistance would turn this autonomy into de facto independence under Russia's aegis.

The Piłsudski camp had also undergone changes; without abandoning socialism, it outgrew the party. Piłsudski's main concern was the creation of a Polish semimilitary force in Galicia, and in 1908 his associates, the future generals Kazimierz Sosnkowski and Marian Kukiel, organized the Union of Armed Struggle which was placed under Piłsudski's command. Military work freed Piłsudski's masterful personality from former constraints. He became the blindly obeyed and worshipped "commander," as his followers addressed him. His qualities of leadership became even more pronounced. Although Piłsudski still held an important position in the PPS, he mentally distanced himself from the party. With the Balkan wars raising the specter of a European conflict, the pro-Piłsudski forces consolidated themselves. In 1912 there emerged in Galicia the Commission of Confederated Independence Parties, grouping the leftist and progressive organizations and providing a political platform for Piłsudski's military program.

The Piłsudski movement stood for Polish independence, to be gained by means that his opponents viewed as less than clear and consistent. The prerequisite was Russia's complete collapse, but the goal transcended the so-called Austro-Polish solution that envisaged a future Poland composed of the Congress Kingdom and Galicia and tied to the Habsburg monarchy. Speaking in Paris in January 1914, Piłsudski speculated on the course of the forthcoming war: in the first phase Russia would succumb to the Central Powers, in the second victors would be defeated by the superior forces of the West. Only a defeat of all three partitioning powers could bring full independence; hence Piłsudski felt that the Poles would combat Russia in the first phase and turn against the Central Powers in the second. This was no blueprint or master plan, and the pragmatist Piłsudski was prepared to adjust tactics to the changing scene. He insisted, however, on the premise that the war would so exhaust the three powers that a Polish policy of *faits accomplis* would be of crucial importance. Even a small Polish armed force would be decisive when the time came for the Poles to shape their own destiny.

Piłsudski's military-insurrectionist plans echoed the wave of Romanticism or Neoromanticism which under the name of Young Poland was then greatly affecting Polish literature and the mental outlook of the Poles. The dramas of such literary giants as Stanisław Wyspiański and the novels of Stefan Żeromski had a great impact on the Polish intelligentsia, Piłsudski and Dmowski included. It was the intelligentsia that led the way in Polish politics, and its leaders looked forward to the reemergence of an independent Poland, the dream of their fathers and grandfathers.

The opposing political currents in Poland naturally affected the American Poles, and the conflict between the Dmowski and Piłsudski camps found a reflection in the United States. In the Russo-Japanese war and the 1905 revolution, Poles in America took generally an anti-Russian stand. The National Alliance cautiously appraised the National Democratic policies and there was implied criticism in the caution. The leaders of the alliance stressed that their organization was not a political party and did not wish to identify itself with any political party in Poland. Doubtless the great distance did not permit an easy evaluation of the complex developments in the Polish lands, and local American problems claimed the attention of the alliance. There seems to be no doubt, however, that the 1905 revolution increased the influence of leftist groups within the National Alliance; Polish Socialists in America showed great activity. In 1911 the senior Socialist from Galicia, Daszyński, visited the United States. A year later Dębski returned from Poland to enlist the support, ideological and financial, of the National Alliance for the Commission of Confederated Independence Parties in Galicia. The result of these endeavors was the creation of the Committee of National Defense (KON), which obtained the backing of virtually all American Polish organizations and signified the endorsement of the pro-Piłsudski line.

American Polonia was not, however, a passive force that merely responded to impulses coming from Poland. Seeking to improve the Polish standing in the United States and to display its own initiative, the National Alliance gave the impetus to a Polish Congress that was to deliberate about Poland's independence. Held in 1910, it publicized, through the unveiling of the monuments of Kościuszko and Pułaski in Washington, Polish contributions to the independence of the United States. An information and press bureau, established in 1908, was another sign of the role American Poles were assuming in Polish political activities. In 1912, the National Alliance founded a Polish college in Cambridge Springs, Pennsylvania, named Alliance College.

The pro-Piłsudski Committee of National Defense did not long enjoy the undivided support of American Poles; the pro-Dmowski groups won the upper hand by establishing the Polish National Council in 1913. It gained the adherence of the leadership of the National Alliance and of the Roman Catholic Union, which in the past had opposed Dmowski's league. By 1914 the bulk of American Polonia, the Committee of National Defense excepted, swung to the pro-Entente program as advocated by the National Democrats.

All these complicated moves and countermoves had no visible impact on American opinions and the foreign policy of Washington. If the image of Russia suffered in America, it was largely because of the military defeat in 1905 and the reprisals against the revolutionaries. The wave of Jewish pogroms provoked strong anti-Russian agitation on the part of American Jewry. The Jews reiterated the themes of tsarist autocracy, social oppression, pogroms, and knout-yielding Cossacks more effectively than the Poles who denounced Russian reprisals. True, the issue of religious liberties in Poland brought forth pro-Polish comments by some American papers, notably the Catholic journals. Occasional American travelers to Polish lands contributed articles that attempted to portray the prevailing situation. The *Outlook* and *North American Review,* for instance, published reports that were friendly but included a good deal of criticism, notably of socialist schemes and of a "slavonization peril" provoked by policies of germanization.

Washington's relations with Russia were not very close. Theodore Roosevelt's policy during and after the Russo-Japanese war sought to achieve a balance in the Far East between Russia, Japan, and China, and the president's successful mediation brought about the peace of Portsmouth, the first major international peace treaty signed on American soil. The Russo-American commercial treaty of 1832 was abrogated in 1911, but the same year the United States fleet paid a courtesy visit to Kronstadt. If Russia was having a bad press in America, the Polish question had nothing to do with it. The government was well informed of the developments in Russian Poland through factual if slightly pro-Russian diplomatic reports from St. Petersburg. Lip service continued to be paid to Polish contributions to American independence and to the unhappy fate of Poland. In 1908 William H. Taft said in a speech in Milwaukee that the "dismemberment of Poland deserves the most severe condemnation" as a "historical fact lamented by nearly every heart." But as a writer in the *Nation* aptly put it in 1914, the partition "was long the favorite example for American orators of a great international crime" and "the interest of our people in Poland remained largely rhetorical and literary." The next few years were to bring a dramatic change in that respect.

3
Wilson and the Rebirth of Poland

Polish Efforts and Neutral America

THE First World War reopened the Polish question. While to the man in the street Poland's independence seemed little more than a beautiful dream, political leaders showed immediate activity. Dmowski and his followers saw the greatest threat in a German victory and worried lest a compromise German-Russian peace be realized at Polish expense. Hence, they greatly welcomed the eloquent Russian manifesto issued on August 14, 1914, by Grand Duke Nikolai Nikolaevich, Russia's commander-in-chief. "May the boundaries vanish which had cut asunder the Polish people! . . . May it once again be united under the scepter of the Russian Emperor." The manifesto carried promises of unification, autonomy, and religious and linguistic liberties.

The document was largely propagandistic, and since the tsar had not signed it Russia's hands were not tied. Autonomy was to apply not to Congress Poland but to provinces conquered from the enemy. Furthermore, as Foreign Minister Sergei Sazonov told Allied diplomats, Russia sought the annexation of Eastern Galicia and the lower course of the Niemen River. Hence by unified Poland the Russians meant Congress Poland enlarged by the western part of Galicia, Poznania, and a part of Silesia. Still, Russia's initiative indicated that once the war had begun, the Polish question could not be ignored.

On the other side, Piłsudski, operating within the Austrian framework, immediately resorted to military action. On August 6, the first detachment of his Riflemen marched into Congress Poland, and Piłsudski addressed them as the cadre of Poland's future army. Austria had been led to believe that this action would provoke an anti-Russian uprising in the kingdom; Piłsudski probably did not seriously count on it. "Agitating by means of war," as he put it, he strove to establish a base in the kingdom and show that the Poles were an element to be seriously considered in political and military calculations. Trying to achieve maximum independence he issued a fictitious proclamation of a secret Polish government in Warsaw, naming him supreme commander and calling on the Poles to rise.

Piłsudski's bluff was exposed, but the Polish political establishment in Galicia could not abandon the Riflemen to Russian vengeance or to dissolution by the Austrians. A Supreme National Committee (NKN) representing all political parties in Galicia was set up as a political umbrella for Piłsudski's activity. Furthermore, Vienna imposed certain limits. Two Polish legions were formally organized under Austrian high command; only one unit, later called the First Brigade, was commanded by Piłsudski. The legions were to be part of a larger scheme promoted by the Galician politicians— a future Poland linked with the Habsburg monarchy transformed into a trialist state. Berlin and Budapest, however, were not keen on the idea and successfully applied brakes. The already-prepared manifesto of Emperor Franz Joseph was never issued. The Polish question became a bone of contention between Germany and Austria.

In the first months of the war the NKN and the rival Dmowski organization became consolidated, but were unable to exercise much influence. Russia insisted that the Polish question was a domestic issue, and having occupied Eastern Galicia started to russify the province. Seeking to diminish his dependence on Austria and maintain some freedom of action from the NKN, Piłsudski ordered his followers in Russian-held Poland to organize a secret Polish Military Organization (POW); he also established contact with the West.

After the inconclusive military operations in 1914 that brought most of Eastern Galicia under Russian control and a part of Congress Poland under the Central Powers, an Austrian-German offensive broke through the Russian front in May 1915. In August Warsaw fell, and by the end of September the Russians evacuated the entire kingdom and Lithuania. The kingdom was divided into a larger German occupation zone which included Warsaw, and a smaller Austrian part. The German zone was subjected to ruthless economic exploitation; the Poles felt they were being treated as a colony.

After losing the kingdom the Russian government belatedly attempted to make concessions, but, as a minister said, "our aim is not to satisfy the Poles but to keep them from separating." In November 1915, Dmowski decided to go to the West, and Russia permitted him to do so in the hope that he might neutralize Polish trends there that were clearly inimical to the tsarist empire. Poles in Switzerland, Paris, and London were active setting up organizations that ranged from humanitarian relief institutions to political agencies. August Zaleski, representing the pro-Piłsudski trend, acted in London, and the Allies tolerated him since they were not yet bent on the destruction of Austria-Hungary, which they regarded then as a possible counterweight to Germany.

Berlin and Vienna continued to debate the Polish issue. Chancellor Bethmann Hollweg admitted that from Germany's point of view there existed no satisfactory solution. One plan might be to return the Congress Kingdom to Russia; another, to link it with Galicia—in either case Germany claimed a strategic band of territory (*Grenzstreifen*)—or, thirdly, to associate it closely with one of the Central Powers safeguarding the interests of the other. As the idea of a vast Central European bloc (*Mitteleuropa*) under German leadership began to emerge in 1916, the Congress Kingdom assumed a particularly important role in this scheme. As the German historian, Fritz Fischer, phrased it, "Poland was not only a war aim, but also the key to Germany's hegemony in Europe." A return to the prewar state of affairs was no longer possible.

Polish leaders attempted to exploit the new situation. In March 1916 Dmowski presented a memorandum to the Russian ambassador that was clearly addressed to the Western Powers. For the first time Dmowski used the word "independence" and urged the Allies to declare in favor of a unified and independent Polish kingdom linked with Russia. St. Petersburg was alarmed and Sazonov, who favored autonomy for Poland, fell from power. Paris and London observed the utmost caution but they too realized that they could not simply ignore the changing realities.

In the occupied kingdom, Piłsudski played a subtle game trying to enhance the value of Poland for the Central Powers. He opposed massive recruitment to the legions, continued building up his clandestine military organization, and clashed with the NKN and the Austrian command, which wanted manpower without being willing to pay a political price for it. By the spring of 1916 the German military governor in Warsaw, General Hans von Beseler, began to advocate a close association of the kingdom with Germany. Although military reasons predominated—the kingdom had a reservoir of over one million men of military age—political motives were not wanting. Since Poland was a key to Mitteleuropa, Germany wanted to have it. Beseler offered concessions to the Poles: Warsaw University was reopened and elections to municipal councils authorized. Poles willing to coperate (so-called Activists) were encouraged; even the abstaining Passivists, mainly National Democrats and their allies, were aware of opportunities that could be exploited.

On November 5, 1916, the Two Emperors' Manifesto announced that Germany and Austria-Hungary were establishing a Kingdom of Poland composed of former Russian lands but not yet definitely delimited. It was a statement of intentions rather than a founding charter, and it represented a temporary Austrian-German compromise rather than a final settlement of differences. For all its shortcomings, however, the document had far-reaching domestic and international repercussions. Many Poles were deeply moved by the manifesto, which spoke of a Polish state, Polish army, and self-government. They sensed that a great step had been taken that might well prove irreversible. The French Chamber of Deputies said that the manifesto "stamped the Polish question with an international character." Russia protested against this breach of international law, for the kingdom was still legally Russian, but felt obliged to renew its pledges to unify Poland. The Western Allies acknowledged the Russian stand and in so doing emphasized the international nature of the Polish issue.

Piłsudski's stand may well have contributed to the decision of the Central Powers. In the summer of 1916 he had insisted that Poles could fight only for Poland. Rejecting an Austrian offer to assume command of all the legions, he resigned in September 1916. Many of his officers and soldiers followed suit, and the legions, verging on mutiny, were transferred from the Austrian to the German zone. Would they fare better with the Germans, who had lauded the military exploits of the legionnaires? Four days after the manifesto, Beseler, acting against his better judgment, appealed for Polish volunteers, confirming the suspicions of those Poles who had said that the Central Powers only wanted cannon fodder. The left raised the slogan of no Polish army without a Polish government, and the occupying powers had to promise the creation of a Polish political organ. Called the Provisional State Council and set up in mid-January 1917 after some consultation with Polish representatives, it was composed mainly of rightist and center Activists. Piłsudski joined it as an independent—he had severed his ties with PPS around 1916—and became the chairman of the military commission. Other departments, which had merely advisory and preparatory functions, were finance, political affairs, interior, economy, labor, justice, and education and religion.

The month of November 1916 witnessed another event that was to prove highly significant for Poland. This was the reelection of Woodrow Wilson to the presidency of the United States.

The war in Europe had come as an unpleasant surprise to the United States. Not only the average American, but President Wilson too felt that the United States ought to stand clear of European struggles. But aloofness did not mean total abstention, and Washington early began to sound out the belligerents about a negotiated peace. In turn, neutrality did not exclude a certain partiality toward the Allies, particularly Britain and France, and opposition to the militarist autocracies of the Central Powers.

Volumes have been devoted to Woodrow Wilson and his policies, yet given the part he played in the reemergence of Poland, it is impossible not to say a few words about him as a man and a president. A moralist in politics, at least in the sense in which he perceived historical developments, Wilson was neither a narrow doctrinaire nor an impractical idealist. Autocratic in dealing with his collaborators, he was irascible and allowed his policies to be swayed by annoyance, but he respected facts and, called to deal with extraordinarily difficult international problems, slowly learned how to handle them. Originally a rather conservative isolationist, he became an internationalist. From a belief in peace without victory he moved to a position of championship of "war to end all wars." A man of vision, he sought to make the world "safe for democracy." Deeply drawn into international affairs, he continued to seek inspiration and guidance from American history. Other nations "do not seem like ourselves," he once said, and he was never particularly at ease with foreigners. The disparaging remarks Wilson once made about Polish immigrants were recalled during the presidential campaign of 1912, and Polish associations, among others, described Wilson as "narrow and unjust" in his opinions. Wilson was embarrassed, offered unconvincing excuses, and even promised to delete the offending passage from the next edition of his book. He professed admiration for Poles as well as interest in their history. Whether the whole episode, as some historians claim, made Wilson more cautious in his utterances and contributed to his conscious effort to enlist the support of hyphenated Americans in the 1916 elections, needs to be more carefully explored.

A man who proved very important for American-Polish wartime

relations was Colonel Edward M. House, a gifted dilettante in politics and, unlike Wilson, adroit in dealing with foreigners. House genuinely adored the president and flattered him. But the colonel himself was susceptible to flattery, and this trait was to be very useful to the Poles. Even if House exaggerated his influence over Wilson, for a time he was indispensable to the president as his confidant and agent in foreign policy matters. Wilson and Secretary of State Robert Lansing never got on well with one another.

The outbreak of the First World War activated the Polish emigration in the United States, and deepened the split between the pro-Piłsudski National Defense Committee (KON) and the more powerful pro-Entente camp. The two groups competed over fund raising for relief to Poland and clashed over the matter of sending volunteers to Europe. Within the important organization of Polish Falcons (*Sokół*) some members agitated for the legions while others favored forming Polish military units on the Allied side. The pro-Entente groups set up in October 1914 an organ later called the Polish Central Relief Committee, which competed with a charitable organization in which the Metropolitan Opera singer, Marcelina Sembrich-Kochańska, played a major role. The second body, active and successful, was eclipsed in 1915 by the Polish Victims Relief Fund sponsored by Paderewski and the pro-Entente Poles who sought to extend complete control over fund-raising in this country.

These conflicts may have been unavoidable but they did little to dispel the image of Poles as quarrelsome and disorganized. Local disputes added to the basic division in Polish politics. Personal ambitions of some Polish American leaders, to mention only John Smulski, a banker and a prominent figure in the National Alliance, also entered into the picture. Feelings ran high and accusations of russophilism or germanophilism were freely traded to discredit opponents. It was not an edifying spectacle, and Paderewski deplored it then and later. Another prominent pro-Entente Pole wrote that Poles ought to work "on both sides of the barricades, paying attention, however, not to injure each other." After the war Piłsudski also called on his supporters to work for the reconciliation of the two camps which, "having unnecessarily fought each other with such ruthlessness and passion, all too often, helas, gave the impression as if the Poles had taken the sides of the two inimical belligerent partitioners."

In 1915 Polish political activity in the United States received a powerful boost with the arrival in April of Ignacy Paderewski, who enjoyed a great reputation among Poles not only as an artist but as a most generous patron of Polish causes, cultural and political, and a great patriot. Prior to his arrival to America he had assumed the vice-presidency of a nonpartisan Committee of Aid to War Victims in Poland founded in Switzerland by Sienkiewicz. This committee must not be confused with another one also operating in Switzerland but with clearly political-propagandistic objectives. The latter grouped at first adherents of both Piłsudski and Dmowski and received subsidies from Polish organizations in America. It later evolved into a pro-National Democratic body and became known as the Lausanne Agency. Paderewski sympathized with the agency but was not a member of any political party. He had a high regard for Dmowski and considered him the most outstanding Polish politician in the West, but did not share all his views, notably regarding the Jewish question. Nevertheless, Paderewski was strongly attacked by American Jews as an anti-Semite, a groundless accusation.

Paderewski's initiative to give a series of concerts in America with proceeds going to war victims in Poland came at a politically propitious moment. Allied propaganda had done its best to shock the Americans with descriptions of German war depredations in Belgium; the public was receptive to news about German exploitation of Congress Poland. Subsequent efforts of Herbert Hoover and the Rockefeller Foundation to provide relief to the Poles had no effect, but all the activity drew attention to Polish political problems.

In early 1916 Paderewski assumed the honorary chairmanship of a Polish National Department, an executive agency directing the Central Relief Committee. The department acted as a spokesman of all the major Polish organizations in the United States, which claimed jointly some two hundred thousand members. It might be added here that the Poles were then the largest immigrant group from Eastern Europe. The activities of the department overshadowed those of the KON which continued to agitate for the restitution of the Polish kingdom through memoranda addressed to the administration. But it was not well subsidized nor did it enjoy massive support. Paderewski's National Department was more attuned to American pro-Allied currents, and it was Paderewski who helped in persuading Wilson to proclaim January 1, 1916, as the day for donations "for the aid of the stricken Polish people."

Paderewski's effectiveness was greatly strengthened through his personal contacts with high-placed Americans. He was introduced to Colonel House by Robert Woolley, director of the Mint, and visited him in November and December of 1915. House, who had imagined Paderewski to be a rather offensive egotist, was impressed by his personality and flattered by the famous artist's attentions. Paderewski spoke of Poland's plight and of his committee, which had the support of prominent Americans including former President Taft, but little money. House conveyed all this to President Wilson and to Mayor Baker of Cleveland, and it may well have been the mayor's advocacy that convinced the president to proclaim the day of aid to Polish people.

In December 1915 House sailed as Wilson's special emissary to Europe. During his talks in Paris he intimated to the Allies that the United States would remain neutral but, should the Entente be losing the war, American assistance might be forthcoming. In London he raised the Polish question but met with Balfour's argument that if Poland were to emerge as a buffer state between Germany and Russia it would deprive France of direct Russian assistance in any future conflict. It is likely that House mentioned Poland because of Paderewski's personal pleas. The colonel, who was already inclining toward the Allies, may have felt that Paderewski was strengthening the pro-Allied attitude of the Polish community in America and thus rendering important services. What is more, the case of Poland fitted well with the developing Wilsonian championship of the small and oppressed nations of Europe. Finally, the year 1916 was an election year and the Polish American vote, if solidly united behind Wilson's candidacy, could not be lightly dismissed.

In May 1916 Wilson emphasized in a major speech the rights of all nations to self-government and equal treatment. The president also spoke about his hopes for a future association of nations and used the phrase: "What affects mankind is inevitably our affair." A profession of faith rather than a program, Wilson's speech was well received by the oppressed nationalities. The administration was also making friendly gestures to hyphenated Americans, mainly those of pro-Allied leanings. In July Washington appealed to all belligerents to consider what could be done to facilitate relief to stricken Poland.

In his study on Wilson and the Poles, Louis Gerson has suggested the possibility of a deal between Paderewski and the administration. Paderewski would be recognized as a spokesman of American Poles in exchange for a promise to deliver their votes to Wilson. This does not seem plausible. There is no evidence of a real division among American Poles with regard to Wilson's candidacy, and the pro-Piłsudski organization, which House recognized as dynamic beyond its numerical strength, would not accept Paderewski's leadership in any case. In 1916 the KON was engaged in clandestine training of volunteers for Piłsudski's legions and kept sending its own political memoranda to Wilson.

Paderewski's personality undoubtedly played a great role in influencing American sentiments on the Polish question. He was a great orator, a forceful speaker, a personal charmer. Paderewski was unusually persuasive. Josephus Daniels wrote later that, "with an audience of one," Paderewski "was as much moved as if he were speaking to a multitude." Wilson compared Paderewski's oratory to Patrick Henry's. Mrs. Wilson recalled the pianist's face, "so fine, so tragic, so earnest," and his eyes reflecting "all the suffering and degradation of his countrymen." There were also some negative reactions: Lansing was occasionally annoyed by Paderewski's passionate espousal of ideas with "little regard to logic or practical considerations," and even House commented at times on Paderewski's childish naivete. Still, while foreign policy trends in America were essentially favorable to Poland, a symbol of Polish national strivings was needed and Paderewski, famous and admired, became it. Thus he advanced Poland's cause in a way that no one else in America could have done at the time.

The exact date of the first encounter between Wilson and Paderewski is uncertain and may have taken place in the spring of 1916. On the day of presidential elections in November 1916 Paderewski, heading a Polish delegation, visited Wilson at Shadow Lane and thanked him for his attitude toward Poland. Whether the president responded by making any political promises is rather doubtful. The Polish question, however, found its way into Wilson's famous Peace without Victory speech of January 1917, and legends have accumulated about Paderewski's contributions to this statement. While it is true that House did consult Paderewski, who produced a thirty-six page long memorandum, it is doubtful that House studied it closely. Furthermore, Wilson's speech was already prepared when House was summoned to the White House, so he could hardly have persuaded Wilson to use any of Paderewski's ideas.

Paderewski's memorandum outlined a proposal for the reconstitution of his country in the form of a United States of Poland, a federation composed of the Kingdom of Poland, the Kingdom of Lithuania, the Kingdom of Polesia, and the Kingdom of Galicia. A multinational state roughly corresponding to prepartition Poland, it would, as Paderewski put it, "mean the disintegration of the Russian Empire." Such an idea could hardly appeal to Wilson. More appealing to the Americans was Paderewski's reference to Jews as "all Poles from the very day of Polish independence" and his stressing their complete equality with all other nationalities. At best, Paderewski's memorandum could have served as another reminder to House and Wilson of the Polish question, and House was undoubtedly sincere when he assured Paderewski that he was promoting Poland's fortune at every opportunity and that the Poles would be highly pleased with Wilson's speech.

The presidential address put emphasis on the principle of government by consent of the governed as a sound basis of peace without victory. Before the speech, in response to Wilson's inquiry about belligerents' war aims, the Central Powers had indicated that they promoted a free Poland (the Two Emperors' Manifesto had already been issued), and the Allies invoked the tsar's Christmas Day 1916 order which spoke of "the creation of a free Poland from all three of her, until now, separated provinces." The Polish case could thus be effectively used as an illustration of international consensus on national self-determination. As Wilson put it, statesmen everywhere were agreed that "there should be a united, independent and autonomous Poland."

The speech did not propose drastic changes of the map of Europe or liberation of oppressed nationalities. The American ambassador reassured Berlin that when the president used the term Poland he referred mainly to the Congress Kingdom. Nor did the phrase about nations' rights of access to the sea—which elated the Poles—imply designs on Prussian Poland or Danzig. It was meant to acknowledge Russian right to access to the Mediterranean through the Straits. Nevertheless, the statement was of great importance for Poland. Paderewski and his supporters, as well as the pro-Piłsudski National Defence Committee, voiced their gratitude to the president. Poles in Russia were enthusiastic. The Provisional State Council in Warsaw rightly pointed out that for the first time a head of state "officially declared that according to his conviction an independent Polish State is the only fair solution of the Polish question and the indispensible condition for a just and durable peace." Indeed, such a declaration by an uncommitted world power then assuming the role of a mediator in the war was a godsend to the Polish nation.

The Decisive Years: 1917 and 1918

The two revolutions in Russia and the entry of the United States into the war opened a new, more intensely ideological, phase of the world conflict. The Poles greeted the fall of tsardom with jubilation, and principally thanks to their efforts the Petrograd Soviet of Workers' and Soldiers' Deputies declared on March 28, 1917, Poland's right to national self-determination and full independence. The manifesto of the Provisional Government, following two days later, was more guarded. It acknowledged that the creation of a Polish state composed of lands with Polish majorities constituted an element of European peace, but made border delimitations subject to consent of the Russian constituent assembly and spoke of a "free" military alliance between Poland and Russia. Lenin termed this provision as tantamount to "a complete military subjugation of Poland," and Poles were repelled by the idea. The Russian state, however, was crumbling, and out of the disintegrating tsarist army Polish military units began to be organized. A Polish army in Russia—largely a domain of the pro-Dmowski Right—came into existence, and its potential political and military role would later occupy Polish and Allied statesmen.

With the collapse of Russia, the Central Powers appeared as the chief obstacle to Poland's rebirth. The Austrian-Polish solution was moribund, and even Galician conservatives supported a resolution demanding a united and independent Poland with access to the sea. German imperialism in East Central Europe boded ill for a Polish state under their aegis. A conflict between Piłsudski and Beseler about the character of the Polish army erupted in the early summer of 1917, and Piłsudski and his chief of staff, Sosnkowski, were imprisoned in Magdeburg. Piłsudski appeared now as a double martyr, first at Russian and now at German hands. It became clear that the kingdom's days were numbered, although it continued to serve as a "school of fresh political life," as a Polish historian put it, and had accomplished a good deal in educational and administrative matters. New Austrian-German concessions, like the creation of a Regency Council, a cabinet, and an elected State Council, all achieved between October 1917 and June 1918, could not change this course of events.

The entry of the United States into the war against Germany in April 1917 raised the hopes of those Poles who favored the Allies. Plans could be entertained about a Polish army in America and a more effective form of political representation. Already in February 1917 Paderewski had tried to interest House in a Polish military contribution; four months later he wrote to him about the Polish army being organized in Russia. House was cautious, for the whole Russian situation baffled Washington. In the months to come the issue of Russia and the fear of a separate Russian peace with the Central Powers was the subject of discussions in which the British played a major role.

While Paderewski and his department were in close touch with House and the administration, the rival KON gained a spokesman in the recently arrived Jerzy Sosnowski. A somewhat mysterious figure, he originally came to the United States with a Russian purchasing team and had established contacts with the comptroller of currency, who introduced him to Lansing. Sosnowski corresponded with and met Lansing on several occasions in 1917 and 1918, urging American recognition of the Regency Council in Warsaw, the formation of a Polish army in America, and the establishment of a Polish government in the United States that would officially proclaim Poland's independence. Sosnowski's and Paderewski's paths occasionally crossed; the former attacked the latter's policies. Yet whatever impact Sosnowski's activities may have had on American thinking about Poland, Paderewski's position as recognized spokesman for the Polish nation remained unaffected.

In the spring of 1917 House tried to convince the British that a Polish state separating Russia from the rest of Europe would be most useful, for an aggressive Russia could be a greater menace than Germany. House passed Paderewski's memorandum on to Balfour and received in exchange a lengthy memorandum of Dmowski, which advocated the creation of a large centralized Polish state comprising the Congress Kingdom, Lithuania, parts of Belorussian and Ukrainian lands, Austrian Poland plus Teschen Silesia, and Prussian Poland with southern parts of East Prussia. There was no basic disagreement between the two about the size of the future Poland, but Dmowski's centralist views clashed with Paderewski's federalist concepts.

During the summer and autumn of 1917 a series of complex moves and countermoves took place with reference to the Polish question. The United States, Britain, France, and Russia as well as Polish politicians active in these countries attempted to shape developments in accord with their views and interests. There were three principal issues: the creation of a Polish army in the West and its connection with the Polish army corps in Russia; the organization of a supreme Polish representation in the Allied camp; and a formal Allied recognition of and commitment to an independent and allied Poland. Only a broad outline of this complicated story can be presented here.

In June 1917, France authorized the creation of a Polish army on its soil, thus indicating that Paris wished to exercise control over Polish developments. It is likely that Russia also preferred them to be under the safe French tutelage. At the same time, however, the idea of a Polish army organized in America had taken root in Washington. In late June, Lansing suggested to Wilson that in order to "utilize the intense longing of the Poles" for independence, a Polish military establishment, financed by the United

States, be set up, and "of course, it will have to be done in this country." Lansing also advocated the organization of a Polish provisional government in the United States, which he regarded as a logical place in order "to avoid all suspicions as to the genuine purpose of this step." Besides, since America would give a loan to this Polish government, it was only natural that Washington would wish to keep an eye on expenditures.

This plan may have been inspired by the projects Sosnowski had presented to Lansing. Paderewski did not seem to have proposed it, but he did share the view that there be a broadly based Polish representation in the Allied camp, and that Polish organizations in America apply some pressure, mainly financial, to promote unity between warring Polish political trends. Dmowski thought otherwise. In May his representative, Jan Horodyski, who also had close ties to British Intelligence, came to America to gain Paderewski's membership in the National Polish Committee, an outgrowth of the Lausanne Agency, to be set up under Dmowski's chairmanship in August. Horodyski also tried to convince Lansing that, although a much-needed Polish army in the West would be drawn mainly from American Poles, the political center should be in Europe.

Bombarded by memoranda from the pro-Piłsudski KON arguing against the recognition of a Dmowski-led organization, Lansing probed into the difficulties of establishing a united Polish front in the United States. The KON persuaded William R. Wilder, Wilson's former classmate, to write to the president suggesting that a special American envoy be sent to Switzerland to consult with representatives of *all* Polish parties. The KON later claimed that Wilson was friendly to the idea and Cyrus McCormick was selected as a candidate for this mission. While Washington deliberated, Dmowski succeeded in persuading Paderewski to become a member of the National Polish Committee and its representative in the United States.

Paderewski agreed reluctantly. He objected to the one-sided composition of the group, and unsuccessfully urged that it be enlarged by Socialist, Populist, and even Jewish representatives. He had doubts about Dmowski's chairmanship, and gave in only after arguments about his "exceptional position" in the United States and assurances that the committee, appreciating his nonpartisan stand, wanted "only a part" of him. Even after having consented, Paderewski continued to press for broadening the membership of the committee.

The National Polish Committee was formally set up in Lausanne on August 15, 1917, but shortly thereafter moved to Paris. France quickly recognized it as the official spokesman of Poland. The United States delayed its recognition for several months; again the story is complicated. Worried by the delays and suspecting some intrigue, Paderewski urged House to expedite matters. He heaped praise on the colonel, a man "sent by God to deliver Poland," and the first statesman since Napoleon to understand Poland's importance. He appealed to Wilson, calling him the "foster-father of a chiefless land" and "Poland's inspired protector." Meanwhile Lansing gathered information about the composition of the National Polish Committee and received appraisals from the American ambassadors in London and Paris, who described Dmowski and some of his collaborators as belonging "to the best class" of Polish statesmen.

The ensuing delays were caused by Russia. The Russian government asked that American recognition be coordinated with Petrograd, and Lansing admitted that a failure to consult Russia in a matter "that concerns her so intimately" could only lead to difficulties. Was Russia mainly concerned to keep the Polish question under some control in the spirit of the March 1917 manifesto, or did Polish democrats in Russia try to affect the ultimate composition of the committee? Both seem probable. Dmowski assured the American ambassador in Paris that he had no desire to ignore Russia, but opposed the inclusion of a Polish Socialist with revolutionary tendencies on his committee.

In November 7, 1917, the Bolshevik Revolution swept the Kerensky government from power. Three days later Lansing issued instructions to recognize the committee; the official American statement given to Paderewski and released to the press bore the date of December 1.

By then the organization of a Polish army, largely recruited in the United States, was well under way. Already in September the Paderewski-led National Department had organized a military commission, and the Secretary of War gave it the official blessing in early October. Thousands of men volunteered and began their training at Niagara-on-the-Lake in Canada and at Fort Niagara, New York. Eventually over 24,000 were sent overseas and constituted the bulk of the Polish army deployed in France and placed under the command of General Józef Haller. Dmowski's National Polish Committee gradually obtained political and military control over the Polish forces.

The great issue the committee faced toward the end of 1917 was a binding Allied declaration on independent Poland. From late November to early December an Inter-Allied Conference deliberated in France. Colonel House was the U.S. representative and sought to persuade the Allies to formulate a broad statement of war aims and to refrain from making specific territorial settlements. On the Polish question, House, keeping in touch with Dmowski and Horodyski, sought a formula acceptable to the committee and the Allies. Dmowski wanted either a formal convention, or a statement that an independent and united Poland was one of the Allied war aims. The British and French were reluctant, and House proposed a compromise wording that a free Poland was a condition of sure and lasting peace. The Western Allies, however, were only willing to speak of the desirability of an independent Poland, to which Paderewski bitterly objected.

Polish relations with the Allies cooled considerably. Wilson, suspicious of Allied secret diplomacy and of their unresponsiveness to his idea of an international society to enforce peace, was also annoyed. Unable to persuade the conference to issue a satisfactory statement on war aims and failing to secure a pronouncement on Poland, House returned to America convinced that President Wilson would have to assume the burden of making such a declaration.

Wilson's famous Fourteen Points of January 8, 1918, resulted not only from Allied failure to issue a stirring message to the world but also from developments in Russia. The Bolshevik Peace Decree, calling for a termination of war through an openly negotiated peace without indemnities and annexations, appealed to the war-weary masses of Europe. The Declaration of the Rights of the Peoples of Russia recognized the principle of national self-determination including secession and formation of independent states. These Leninst principles were of course to be interpreted in a revolutionary spirit. The Bolsheviks did not seek a liquidation of the old empire but its transformation along communist lines. Peace meant revolution. But this was not obvious to contemporaries and Bolshevik slogans proved an admirable weapon in negotiations with the Central Powers that began in Brest-Litovsk on December 22, 1917.

Debating the Polish question at Brest-Litovsk, the Bolsheviks denied that they claimed the old imperial borders and demanded that the Central Powers permit the Poles, not represented at the conference, to determine their own fate. Given the German record in East Central Europe, German counterarguments that the Bolsheviks themselves were not respecting self-determination in the Ukraine did not carry conviction. The Bolsheviks scored propagandistically and their statements echoed beyond the conference room. Both Wilson and Lansing were impressed by Bolshevik advocacy of national self-determination; Lansing, however, felt that such a universally applicable principle could lead to international anarchy. Wilson, who interpreted the principle more in the sense of consent of the governed, was inclined to agree with him. But Bolshevik propaganda was making the need of a general Western statement on war and peace all the more imperative.

Wilson began to draft his Fourteen Points unaware that at the moment, on January 5, 1918, Prime Minister Lloyd George had come out with a declaration that said: "An independent Poland, comprising all those genuinely Polish elements who desire to form part of it, is an urgent necessity for the stability of Western Europe." This meant that a future Poland would be not only narrowly ethnic but constituted through an unspecified form of public expression of desire, not an easy thing to bring about in mixed areas disorganized by war. Nor was Poland said to be Britain's war or peace aim. Lloyd George's formula was weaker than an earlier Italian pronouncement, in which "independent and united Poland" figured as constituting "one of the elements of a just and lasting peace and the respect of law," and a fairly emphatic French declaration favoring a "united, independent, indivisible [Poland], with all guarantees of free political, economic and military development, and with all the consequences which could result therefrom."

These declarations were available in Washington when Wilson and House discussed a statement on Poland to appear in the presidential message. As background material House gave Wilson a memorandum prepared by a new group of American experts, which has assembled in September and was called the Inquiry. While supporting in principle an independent, democratic, and unified Poland, the document dwelt on difficulties confronting a Polish state. If Poland were to be fully unified, this would involve separating East Prussia from Germany, which did not appear "within the bounds of practical politics." On the other hand, a Polish state denied access to the sea and deprived of Prussian Poles would be exceedingly weak and exposed. Hence the authors of the memorandum wondered if Poland might not be better off as a federal state within a democratic Russia, or an autonomous state within a reorganized Habsburg monarchy. Although House talked to Paderewski toward the end of December 1917, he did not involve him in the actual preparation of the statement on Poland. As House recalled, he and the president took a crucial paragraph out of the document that had been submited by the National Polish Committee to the Inter-Allied Conference in France and rephrased it, keeping it as close to the original "as we felt was wise and expedient." Thus Point Thirteen was born.

This often-quoted point needs to be reexamined here. "An independent Polish state," it said, "should be erected which should include the territories inhabited by indisputably Polish populations, which should be assured a free and secure access to the sea, and whose political and economic independence and territorial integrity should be guaranteed by international covenant." The statement made Wilson a hero in Polish eyes and encouraged the Wilsonian cult. Yet some Polish politicians also saw the limitations of the pronouncement. The word "should" instead of "must" was noted by Paderewski who came to House "to kneel at your feet," while House explained that the United States could not treat the restoration of Poland as an ultimatum. More disquieting was the term "erect" rather than "resurrect," for it implied that Wilson and House looked upon Poland as a new state, deriving its existence from ethnic criteria rather than from old historic rights. The expression "indisputably Polish," later used jokingly by the American delegates at the Peace Conference when addressing their Polish colleagues, came close to Lloyd George's "genuine" and was inspired by the phrasing of the manifesto of the Russian Provisional Government of March 1917.

Insistence on ethnic Poland had undoubtedly much to do with preoccupation with Russia. The empire had disintegrated and its troops had been driven out by the Central Powers from the Congress Kingdom, the Baltic countries, parts of Ukraine, and Belorussia. These non-Russian nations were striving after their own statehood. Washington refused to recognize these developments and the Fourteen Points explicitly mentioned "the evacuation of all Russian territory." Wilson considered that Russia's misfortunes "impose upon us at this time the obligation of unswerving fidelity to the principle of Russian territorial integrity." Lansing believed that the United States, which had once denied the South the right of self-determination, could not insist on applying this notion to Russia. Since Washington did not yet invoke self-determination with regard to the nationalities of the Habsburg monarchy, there was no discrepancy between the attitudes toward Austria-Hungary and Russia. Such a discrepancy arose later in 1918, and Colonel House wondered if one could pretend that Russian territory was synonymous with that of the old tsarist empire.

If Point Thirteen carried the implication that in a Russo-Polish conflict about the borderlands Poland would not have American support, the phrase "free and secure access to the sea" did not necessarily mean a transfer of Pomerania and Danzig from Germany to Poland. In this context, the absence of the adjective "united" that had figured in Wilson's pronouncement on Poland in the Peace without Victory speech of 1917 was also disquieting.

The Treaty of Brest-Litovsk between the Central Powers and Bolshevik Russia in March 1918 administered the *coup de grace* to the Austrian-Polish conception. The transfer of the district of Chełm to the Ukraine and a secret Austrian promise to divide Galicia into Polish and Ukrainian parts provoked a violent Polish reaction against Vienna. France, stunned by the Russians' signing a separate peace treaty, showed increased interest in Poland. The outcome was the first joint Allied statement of June 3, 1918, which said that the "creation of a united and independent Polish state with free access to the sea" constituted "one of the conditions for a just and lasting peace and for the rule of law in Europe." But if Polish chances in western Europe looked bright, there was not much visible progress in America, and Paderewski told Dmowski, who came to the United States in August, that things looked bad.

Indeed, several of Paderewski's initiatives produced little or no result. The resolution in favor of an independent Poland introduced on Paderewski's prompting by the Democratic congressman from Illinois, Thomas Galagher, and the senator from Nebraska, Gilbert M. Hitchcock, foundered on Wilson's opposition. The president felt that Poland should not be singled out for such a congressional declaration. Paderewski's attempts to interest the United States in the Polish troops in Russia, which could help in the formation of a second front and bolster anti-Bolshevik forces, met with an unfavorable reception by House. The colonel's view was that the whole Russian situation "had gotten beyond our depth at that moment." The White House was also lukewarm toward proposals to finance the National Polish Committee's relief program in Russia, although American money was approved for Polish activities in the West. Finally, House greatly exaggerated when he wrote later that the Fourteen Points had united all Poles for common action. Divisions continued to exist, and Paderewski was still making efforts to gain wider support for his policies.

In the course of his visit to the United States (August-November 1918), Dmowski sought to establish better contact with Wilson's administration, associate Paderewski closer with the work of the committee, and oversee organizational matters concerning recruitment and relations with Polish American groups. Dmowski displayed great activity. He made public speeches, participated in Polish American gatherings, inspired press articles, conferred with Jewish leaders, and held talks with Wilson, Lansing, and House. Attending, together with Paderewski, the great Polish congress in

Detroit in late August, which brought together about 1,000 delegates and was the high watermark of Polonia's activities, Dmowski consolidated the influence of his committee in the United States. The KON, however, had not disarmed, and its members boycotted the Detroit gathering. John Dewey, acting on its behalf, wrote to Paderewski and Wilson protesting against the nationalist-reactionary outlook of Dmowski, which he contrasted with the democratic pro-Piłsudski trend.

Paderewski took Dmowski to the White House on September 13 and the two outlined the Polish territorial program, which Dmowski later put in writing. Wilson, as he later recalled, qualified Polish territorial demands as "immense claims in all the directions," and said that Poland ought to comprise uniquely Polish-inhabited territories. Reminiscing about his encounter with Dmowski and Paderewski, the president showed some dry humor at their expense.

Dmowski's territorial program has already been described, but one aspect of it has to be mentioned. Wishing to avoid an outcry about the severance of East Prussia through the creation of a Polish "Corridor," Dmowski proposed that the German core of East Prussia be made either an independent state associated through a customs union with Poland or linked with Poland by federal ties. During his stay in America Dmowski concentrated on German-Polish issues and claimed later that he scored a great success in this area. According to his story, he discovered the existence of the Inquiry group and that it was asked not to concern itself with Prussian Poland and managed, with Polish American support, to include that issue. Although such a change did occur, Dmowski's claims cannot be fully substantiated, and it is still uncertain whether Polish pressures were responsible for it.

The establishment of the Inquiry stemmed from the need to collect data for the peace conference to come, and Poland as an object of study had been mentioned by House to Paderewski already in April 1917. The first memoranda concerning Poland came from Albert H. Putney of the State Department. Submitted in May, June, and July, they emphasized the impossibility of drawing borders coinciding with ethnic divisions. Putney was critical of Polish nationalism in relation to the Ukrainians and the Jews, and doubted the possibility of recreating the Polish-Lithuanian Commonwealth. He suggested that Eastern Galicia be linked with the Ukraine and united with Russia. As for the western borders, he opined that Poland ought to reach the sea and regarded a Polish takeover of Danzig as beneficial for that city. The Poles, in his view, were also entitled to all of Prussian Poland, including Upper Silesia.

Putney's memoranda were incorporated with the material prepared by the Inquiry—a small research group unrelated to the State Department and comprising several scholars and writers. House was the official supervisor; his brother-in-law, Sidney E. Mezes, later succeeded de facto by Isiah Bowman, the future president of Johns Hopkins University, served as director. Coolidge headed the East European Division which later devolved on his former student Robert Lord, who was also in charge of the Polish section. Two Polish scholars, Henryk Arctowski and St. J. Zwierzchowski who used the anglicized name Zowski, worked under Lord's guidance, and a historian of the Inquiry has blamed them for passing information to Dmowski and seeing "nothing improper in serving two masters." This seems an unduly harsh criticism, for there were numerous exceptions to the secrecy rule of the Inquiry. House wrote Wilson that Jewish representatives were determined "to break in with a jimmy if they are not let in"; Masaryk and some French diplomats gained confidential insights, and so did Britain's Intelligence delegate.

At the time of the formulation of the Fourteen Points, the first two reports of the Inquiry bearing on Poland were available and a preliminary report, chiefly prepared by Arctowski and covering all three partitions, followed. It was a statistical analysis with a wealth of material. Since Coolidge insisted that Lord was "the one man in the United States who really knows anything about Polish history" and would be wasted if used only to compile statistics, in March 1918 Lord prepared a long "Comparative Study of the Various Solutions of the Polish Question." The document considered the possibility of Poland being fully independent or linked in a federation with Austria. It examined several variants of territorial settlement, namely (1) Congress Kingdom enlarged by the provinces of Białystok, Suwałki, and Chełm, plus western Galicia, three-fourths of Teschen Silesia, and Prussian Poznania; (2) the same minus Poznania, in case Germany were not fully defeated, but plus Eastern Galicia; (3) excluding both Poznania and Eastern Galicia; (4) Congress Kingdom enlarged merely by Białystok and Bielsko in Teschen Silesia.

Lord made clear that he had excluded from consideration Upper Silesia, West Prussia, and the southern parts of East Prussia not because he rejected the validity of Polish claims but because, in view of the military situation—German victories in the east and no signs of collapse on the western front—their fate was unlikely to be changed. It may well be that these reasons accounted for the fact that the Inquiry did not proceed to gather more data on Prussian

Poland, although in May 1918 the area still figured among objects of study. Similarly, Lord's report on Poland prepared in the summer of 1918 was still based on the assumption that complete victory over Germany was unattainable, hence Polish access to the sea might be achieved through an internationalized Vistula. Lord did not hide that this solution would be wrought with great difficulties.

Differences of opinion among members of the Inqury are reflected in the forty-two reports about Poland. Yet another was a memorandum from Lansing to Wilson, during Dmowski's visit, in which the secretary of state advocated an independent Poland comprising Russian, German, and Austrian parts and the port of Danzig. Lansing's views became less definite in October. Finally, in November 1918 after Germany collapse, the Inquiry recommended in a special report the inclusion into Poland of Poznania, Pomerania, parts of East Prussia, and Upper Silesia—roughly the Dmowski program.

As the war was drawing to its end, Polish matters stood well in the United States. At a meeting of Oppressed Nationalities of Central Europe, held in Carnegie Hall in mid-September, a resolution was passed favoring "reconstitution of a united and independent democratic Poland"—to which at Paderewski's request was added, "with access to the sea by Danzig, the natural and historic harbor of the Poles." A Mid-European Democratic Union emerged from the meeting, but although Paderewski welcomed it as a harbinger of a future federation of East Central European states, friction between Poles and Ukrainians led to a Polish withdrawal from this interesting but ephemeral venture.

On the eve of the armistice on the western front, Dmowski went to see William Phillips at the State Department to warn that if the Germans evacuated all the territory they occupied in the east and no Allied troops were dispatched to replace them, Poland would be open to a Bolshevik invasion. Dmowski sincerely believed that the subsequent provision of the armistice which authorized the Germans to remain in the east as a protection against Bolshevism was due to his suggestion, but in fact this provision stemmed from German insistence. Another belief of Dmowski, that American troops might be deployed in Poland and Central Europe, also proved erroneous.

On armistice day Dmowski was invited to listen to Wilson's speech in the senate and was not greatly impressed. His chief worry, which Paderewski shared, was that the war had ended without a complete defeat of Germany. Before taking leave of the president, Dmowski insisted on Polish rights to German-controlled lands. He recalled that many Poles in America came from these regions and would not understand it if they were not allotted to Poland. Wilson allegedly promised not to disappoint them, but how effective was Dmowski's veiled reference to the Polish vote in America is debatable.

With the guns falling silent on the western front, Polish lands were in a state of turmoil. In Warsaw, the regents attempted to efface the stigma of being German appointees and, invoking "peace proposals proclaimed by the President of the United States," declared Poland's independence. They dissolved the State Council and promised regular elections, announced the formation of a representative government, and took control of the Polish troops that had been under Beseler's command. Galicia separated itself from the disintegrating Habsburg monarchy and set up a Liquidation Commission. The latter's jurisdiction extended only to the western part of the province; in Eastern Galicia the Ukrainians declared on November 1 the formation of a West Ukrainian Republic and tried to seize Lwów. An armed Polish-Ukrainian strife began. In Teschen Silesia, the local Czech and Polish committee agreed on November 5 to a temporary and provisional demarcation line roughly in accord with ethnic criteria. In Prussian Poland, a Polish Supreme People's Council and a provincial diet were formed in Poznania, but the Poles refrained from creating any faits accomplis in revolution-torn Germany. Declaring themselves for an independent and united Poland with access to the sea, they awaited the formal decisions of the forthcoming peace conference.

In the vast eastern borderlands—Lithuania, Belorussia, Ukraine—the situation was dangerous and fluid. German troops held some areas but were spontaneously evacuating others. National native governments were battling the advancing Bolsheviks who had repudiated the treaty of Brest-Litovsk. Nascent counterrevolutionary Russian armies complicated an already complex picture. In supplementary treaties signed by the Bolsheviks with the Central Powers in August 1918, the former had denounced a number of old agreements, among them the partitions of Poland, and the Poles could claim with some logic that Russia had thus renounced its part of the former territories of the old commonwealth. The Bolsheviks, of course, insisted that their advance into these lands did not stem from historic rights but constituted a natural extention of the revolution. Was this revolutionary tide also to submerge Poland, which stood on the way to Germany?

Political developments in the former Congress Kingdom and western Galicia showed the birth pains of renascent statehood. The

Polish left, giving precedence to a democratic coalition over national union or revolution advocated by the extremists, proclaimed on November 7, 1918, in Lublin, a provisional government of the Polish People's Republic. With the Socialist Daszyński as premier and the legionary colonel, Edward Rydz-Śmigły, in charge of the army, the government represented chiefly the leftist supporters of the imprisoned Piłsudski. Its manifesto declared the abolition of the regency and introduced a republican form of government. It announced elections to a constituent parliament and promised radical social reforms. Viewed as revolutionary by the propertied classes and regarded by the Bolsheviks as taking the wind out of the sails of a proletarian revolution, the Lublin government was short-lived. On November 10, 1918, Piłsudski returned from Magdeburg to Warsaw and was greeted as savior by a wide spectrum of public opinion. The next day the regents transferred to him the command of the army and three days later all their powers. The regency then dissolved itself and Piłsudski persuaded the Lublin government to follow suit. Assuming virtually dictatorial powers and the title of Chief of State, once used by Kościuszko, Piłsudski appointed a new cabinet, roughly similar in composition to the Lublin government. He announced then a speedy holding of elections to a constituent sejm. Most important, Piłsudski succeeded in arranging for the evacuation of German troops from the Congress Kingdom. He was thus master in the Kingdom, western Galicia, and parts of Teschen, all areas then under full Polish control. But he lacked recognition by the Allies, who were committed to Dmowski and his committee.

On November 16, Piłsudski notified the Allied powers of the formation of a Polish state and asked that their diplomatic representatives as well as the Haller army in France be dispatched to Poland. In a message addressed to Wilson, calling the president Poland's "first champion," Piłsudski asked that Polish troops serving under the American flag—an indication that he was not well informed—be also sent to the country. In an unofficial communication to Lansing, Warsaw conveyed the idea that the United States should not confine its relations to the National Polish Committee abroad, representing "only one political party of Poland."

The Allies were in a quandary. France deeply mistrusted Piłsudski as a Socialist who had cooperated with the Central Powers, and wished to recognize Dmowski's committee as the Polish government. The British opposed the French view. The American took a wait-and-see attitude and sent a fact-finding mission to Central Europe presided over by Coolidge. Representatives of Hoover's American

Relief Administration went to Poland a little later. Before examining the allegedly decisive role of the Hoover mission in the eventual creation of a coalition government in Warsaw, one needs to look more closely at American views on Poland and at the course of developments in that country.

Americans quickly realized that to send the Haller Army to Poland ahead of Dmowski's committee would mean cutting it off from his authority. If the committee went to Poland alone it could exercise little control. A simultaneous dispatch of the committee and the army would look like an attempt to suppress the government in Warsaw. The American Commission to Negotiate Peace probably expressed the general consensus by stressing the need to bring about a political truce in Poland. Piłsudski and Dmowski also felt that a compromise solution was necessary and some hard bargaining began. The compromise was facilitated by a British suggestion that Paderewski go to Poland and attempt a political reconciliation. Although a member of Dmowski's committee, he was not a partisan figure; he enjoyed great prestige in Poland as well as American and British trust. Traveling on a British cruiser, Paderewski landed in Danzig and proceeded to Poznań in late December 1918, where public manifestations in his honor turned into a spontaneous uprising against the Germans. The uprising delivered much of Poznania into Polish hands.

Although the first talk between Paderewski and Piłsudski in January 1919 was inconclusive, it is probable that Piłsudski, who toyed with the idea of a coalition cabinet headed by Paderewski, rejected its proposed composition rather than Paderewski's leadership. Sometime earlier the chief of state had confided to his collaborators that he seriously counted on Paderewski, with whom he agreed on most counts and who would be a moderate influence on Dmowski. Paderewski had a "common language" with the Allies even if he appeared too humble toward them. Piłsudski felt that as long as he had the army under his control, "I will have everything in hand."

After an unsuccessful and mysterious attempt at a coup by some rightists on January 5, it was fairly clear that a predominantly left government in Poland would be too weak and one one of the right unfeasible. Piłsudski and Paderewski began serious negotiations that lasted for several days. In telegrams to Colonel House, Paderewski painted the Polish situation in dark colors. The country was in danger of a Bolshevik invasion and the existing government was too weak to cope with it. He appealed at first for 50,000 American troops and French and British contingents, and then only for war material and aid. From Smulski came telegrams expressing strong support of American Poles for Paderewski's attempt to form a coalition government, and informing him that the Congress had approved food for liberated nations, especially for Poland. Smulski authorized Paderewski, if he so wished to transfer some funds to Piłsudski, but there was nothing in the telegrams to indicate any suggestion of blackmail to force Piłsudski's hand. The arrival in Warsaw of the representative of the Hoover mission, Vernon Kellogg, was construed as a direct American intervention in the Piłsudski-Paderewski negotiations. Hoover's recollections, not devoid of errors, mentioned that Kellogg had been authorized to inform Piłsudski that unless Paderewski became premier, "American cooperation and aid were futile." Wilson later referred to a letter allegedly given to Paderewski which promised American aid to Poland only as long as Paderewski "was in charge." In December, however, the president,on his way to Europe, told his collaborators that the Poles may have any form of government "they damned please." No doubt, the United States favored and supported Paderewski at this juncture, but evidence for decisive pressures is wanting. After he was offered the task to form a cabinet, Paderewski cabled House with a plea for aid: "what could I do with the moral support of the country alone,without the material assistance of the Allies and the United States?" It seems also that Piłsudski received Kellogg after having made his offer to Paderewski.

Hoover was not the only one to ascribe to his mission the role of a kingmaker. House's assistant, Stephen Bonsal, told an absurd story about how he made the Poles in Paris accept Dmowski and Paderewski as the Polish delegates at the peace conference, and a ·Canadian journal credited the formation of the coalition cabinet to a prominent Canadian scholar. "W. J. Rose brought order in Poland," was the title of the news item about the Paderewski cabinet.

In a confidential letter to his representative in Paris, Piłsudski convincingly outlined the reasons for the compromise that had been worked out. Poland needed arms, financial assistance, and food from the Allies and the easiest way of obtaining them was through Dmowski's committee. A domestic political truce was essential to avoid sharp conflicts when the parliament would convene. It was also necessary to overcome the negative attitude of Poznania, a National Democratic stronghold, and to assure Poland a strong bargaining position at the forthcoming peace conference. Paderewski's international reputation and prestige at home predestined him for the premiership. Since his appointment legitimized Piłsudski's position as well as that of the outgoing cabinet, Warsaw made important gains. A wedge was driven between Paderewski and Dmowski, and the former moved closer to the chief of state.

According to the compromise, Piłsudski remained head of state and Paderewski became the president of the council of ministers—hence subsequent references to Paderewski as president—and minister of foreign affairs. He would be Poland's first delegate at the peace conference and Dmowski the second. The National Polish Committee in Paris, enlarged by Piłsudski's appointees, would represent Poland abroad. The new cabinet was largely nonpartisan and several former ministers remained in it. Three Poznanian bankers joined the ministry, which was indicative of the role the province would play in Polish economics. The United States officially recognized the Polish government on January 30, 1919; the other Allies followed suit.

What was then the real role of the United States in the revival of the Polish state? In a speech to the sejm, Paderewski exclaimed that without "the powerful support of President Wilson whose heart has been won to our cause by our best friend, Colonel House," Poland "would undoubtedly still remain an internal question of Germany and Russia." This was a typical piece of Paderewski's flamboyant oratory, though most likely it was sincere. The Polish road to independence had been long and arduous. The war between the partitioning powers was bound to internationalize the Polish question in spite of the wishes of Berlin, St. Petersburg, or even Vienna. The swift current of international events carried the Polish question from the Nikolai Nikolaevich Manifesto through the Two Emperors' Manifesto and the declarations of the Russian Revolution to the Western Allies' statements, favoring a free Poland. In this respect the two pronouncements of Wilson—the Peace without Victory speech and the Fourteen Points—carried special weight and placed the Polish question on a yet higher level of diplomacy.

Strenuous Polish efforts, diplomatic, military, and propagandistic, did not allow the statemen to forget about Poland. There is no doubt that Poles in America, already a political factor of some consequence in the United States, signally promoted the Polish cause. The National Department and the Relief Committee alone had contributed between the autumn of 1915 and the spring of 1918 over 4.5 million dollars. Polish chances increased when Paderewski took the leadership and gained access to House, and indirectly to Wilson. It is too simplistic to speak of Polish votes or "deals" between the Wilsonian administration and Paderewski. He struck a responsive political chord and played it with a sincerity and appeal that were hard to resist. Yet were it not for a combination of many factors, Wilson's support to Poland may have been less effective than it ultimately proved to be. Neither Wilson, Piłsudski, Dmowski, Paderewski, nor the Russian Revolution alone was responsible for Poland's rebirth—all had their share in it. The American share during the war was indubitably large and important.

The Paris Peace Conference

The Polish settlement in Paris was one of the most difficult questions the peacemakers had to face. How could Polish territorial aspirations be satisfied without making Poland the perennial object of German and Russian revisionism and hate? True, Germany had been defeated, but its power was not broken. Russia was in turmoil, but its vast potential and the fighting Bolshevik creed made it a perennial challenger to a European settlement that went against Lenin's aims and the Russian *raison d'état*. Then, as Wilson had put it, it was necessary to agree on what constituted Poland and such agreement was wanting. The Poles considered that the war had destroyed the verdict of partitions and that Poland ought to comprise as much of its historic territory as feasible, whether in the form of a centralized state or a bloc of federated or associated units. Both Piłsudski and Dmowski felt that between the two neighboring giants there was no room for a small and weak Polish state; only a drastic redrafting of the map of Eastern Europe could guarantee a stable peace. The Allies differed in their views among themselves and with the Poles. The British sought to restrict the Polish state to its inner ethnic core so as to minimize the antagonism of its mighty neighbors. France, true to its old policy of having allies east of Germany, advocated a strong Polish state, a possible replacement for the lost Russian ally. Hoping, however, for a reemergence of a non-Bolshevik Russia, Paris opposed any schemes that would prevent future Russian cooperation with the Poles.

Wilson believed that any unavoidable injustices of a territorial settlement and resulting frictions could best be resolved through the League of Nations. The League would be a guardian of peace and order in a way in which the balance of power or strategic safeguards had never been. Wilson shared his colleagues' view that it was up to the great powers to make decisions binding on the smaller states. The Americans, as Masaryk astutely observed during the war, were "wont to look upon the liberation of small peoples and the creation of small States as a bothersome process of political and linguistic Balkanization." At the peace conference the representatives of the smaller states were looked upon as "suitors and suppliants." House considered that even in the future League, the smaller countries would have, not unlike the territories in the United States Congress, a representation without voting powers. That an independent East Central Europe already existed prior to the conference and in spite of conflicts was consolidating itself, was all too frequently underemphasized.

The principal peacemakers combined a great-power mentality with little knowledge of East European problems and conditions. The British diplomat Sir Esme Howard said that ignorance of Poland was such that "it was practically necessary to go through a course of instruction on the subject," which most of the delegates had neither the time nor the inclination to do. British and Dominion statesmen did not allow this lack to deter them from making sweeping judgments. Jan Smuts opined that "Poland was an historic failure, and always would be a failure, and in this Treaty we were trying to reverse the verdict of history." The great economist Keynes wrote that Poland was an economic impossibility with no industry except Jew-baiting. Balfour, no great friend of Poland, questioned why some of his colleagues assumed optimistically that Germany was repentant, yet claimed there was no hope of Poland "behaving as a reasonably civilised State." The Poles "have no special monopoly of vice," wrote Headlam-Morley to Lewis Namier.

It is not surprising that Lloyd George, who shared these negative views, would be annoyed with any Polish success, which he ascribed to the French and Americans. Wilson, according to Lloyd George, came to Europe "an enthusiastic pro-Pole" and the Poles unscrupulously exploited him. The reason was allegedly the "powerful Polish vote" in America that gave the Poles "a hold" on the American delegation. As for American experts, they were "fanatical pro-Poles" whose judgment in Polish matters was "vitiated by an invincible partisanship." Lloyd George gave no explanation why the Polish vote carried so much more weight than the Italian or the Irish, but then the title of his book should really have been "Half-Truths about the Peace Conference.

Reality was different from Lloyd George's version. The American delegation, acting in accord with general Wilsonian principles, heavily relied on the carefully prepared and reliable documentation of the Inquiry, and British and French experts acknowledged their preparedness. Charles Seymour recalled a meeting at which the suggestions of an American expert were accepted without documentary evidence, for hitherto "the facts presented by the Americans have been irrefutable; it would be a waste of time to consider them." A memorandum on American war aims and peace terms interpreted the Thirteenth Point to mean that Polish boundaries would be based "on a fair balance of national and economic considerations, giving due weight to the necessity for adequate access to the sea." This is roughly how Wilson himself saw it, and he insisted that nationalist desires of a particular nation could not always be fully satisfied.

There were diferences among the American experts, and some were better informed than others. Major General F. J. Kernan, who reported to Wilson about Polish imperialism, "could not understand what it was all about," in the words of one of his American colleagues. Recollections, memoirs, and letters of American experts in Paris reveal both friendly and condescending feelings toward the Poles with occasional sarcasm exercised at their expense.

The Paris Peace Conference opened on January 18, 1919, and its governing and decision-making organ, the Supreme Council, comprised the Americans, British, French, Japanese, and Italians. Only the first three—Wilson, Lloyd George, and Clemenceau—were the really decisive peacemakers. The Supreme Council concentrated first on Germany and the Covenant of the League, but constantly turned to other issues. It was the Supreme Council that made the final decision on Poland, but Polish questions were also handled by several other subordinate bodies, notably the Noulens Inter-Allied Mission—General Kernan and Lord served on it—which went to Poland, and the Commission on Polish Affairs established in February 1919 in Paris. The latter dealt at first with the Noulens reports. Later is prepared recommendations on the territorial settlement.

Until March 1919 Dmowski was the principal Polish delegate, firmly in control of the large Polish representation. From April on Paderewski played the main part, and when Dmowski fell ill in November, Paderewski acted largely alone until his resignation as premier a month later. The Poles could address the Supreme Council and the later-established Council of Foreign Ministers when invited to do so, and to communicate orally and in writing with the Commission on Polish Affairs. They were also allotted a number of seats on various commissions of the conference.

Territorial questions apart, the conference had to deal with other issues affecting Poland. For instance, it concerned itself with the dispatch of the Haller army and its use in Poland; it arranged a German-Polish armistice in Poznania, and also promoted a cease-fire between the Poles and Ukrainians in Eastern Galicia. It put an end to the Czechoslovak-Polish armed clash in Teschen. The question of the Haller army raised complex problems. The French wanted to send it quickly through Danzig, raising British fears of unilateral Polish faits accomplis in the area. The British, Churchill excepted, also worried that the Haller army might be used as an interventionist force against the Bolsheviks. The Americans, who favored a dispatch of the army if only to strengthen Paderewski's hand, were concerned lest the Haller troops, which included American citizens, be used against the Ukrainians or the Bolsheviks. The Secretary of State alerted Wilson to this danger, and Lansing obtained assurances from Dmowski that the Poles would stop recruiting in the United States.

Dmowski presented the Polish case to the Supreme Council on January 29, 1919, and roughly a month later submitted a note on the western borders of Poland. The Poles have often been criticized for using any arguments that would advance their case with little regard for logic, but although they may have seemed inconsistent, there was an inner logic governing their presentation. Regarding the three partitions as invalid, Dmowski took at his point of reference the last legal Polish boundaries, namely those of 1772. However, he did not claim the restoration of these boundaries and made it clear that national developments in the course of the nineteenth century required their revision. In the east, revisions would be to Poland's disadvantage; in the west, particularly in Silesia, they would benefit the Poles. From Germany Dmowski claimed Poznania, Pomerania with Danzig, Upper Silesia, and portions of East Prussia. These territories had an overall Polish majority and a sizable German minority.

Dmowski's proposal did not differ sharply from the American outline of tentative report and recommendations drawn up prior to his presentation. The document was the work of the Division of Territorial Economic and Political Intelligence, a result of the merger of the Inquiry and the American Commission to Negotiate Peace. For simplicity's sake we will continue to call it the Inquiry. Nor was the unanimous report of March 12 of the Commission on Polish Affairs, utilizing the Prussian population census of 1910, contrary to Dmowski's program. The report, however, cut the latter's claim by some 30 thousand square miles and reduced the German minority from 2.9 to 2.1 million people. It also inserted provisions for a plebiscite in the Allenstein (Olsztyn) district in East Prussia.

The commission's report met with opposition by Lloyd George. He specifically opposed the transfer of Marienwerder (Kwidzyń) and in general was against a large German minority in Poland. Wilson, supported by the French, backed the report. In mixed areas sizable national minorities were unavoidable, said the president, and he also expressed his concern with Poland's vulnerability in the face of German territorial ambitions. Poland was a new and a weak state not only because of historic failures but also because of likely internal divisions. While agreeing that nothing should be done to revive German antagonism toward Poland, he felt that the proposed settlement appeared equitable. But Lloyd George was adamant, largely for reasons that went beyond the merits of the case, and under his pressure the report was returned to the commission for reexamination.

The American experts, encouraged by Wilson's instructions to preserve as much of the report as possible, maintained their position. Other experts, seemingly sharing the view that the Polish interests here were vital and German interests secondary, supported the Americans. The commission returned its report unchanged.

In the weeks that followed, Lloyd George's insistence on a plebiscite in Marienwerder and on nonincorporation of Danzig into Poland prevailed over the objections of Clemenceau and mild reservations of Wilson. The reason must be sought in vaster problems concerning the German peace treaty as a whole, and the issue of French security, which transcended the question of the German-Polish border. These general matters cannot be discussed here, except to remark that Wilson eventually found himself closer to the British point of view and in opposition to the French. Yet he was profoundly uncomfortable about the concessions to Germany that were to be made at Poland's expense. At first he favored the inclusion of Danzig in Poland, but for some reason he came to feel that if Danzig went to the Poles then Fiume would have to become Italian, which he opposed. After mid-April the president said that all economic and strategic reasons favored uniting Danzig with Poland, yet these had to be ignored in order to give effect to the "general principles on which the peace was being based." This meant in effect an attempt to conciliate Germany.

Wilson worried that a decision against Poland would weaken Paderewski's position, but once it was decided that Danzig would become a free city the president paid no heed to Paderewski's eloquent pleas and even tears. Wilson was moved, but he told his French and British colleagues that being an artist, Paderewski had an unusually great sensitivity. He tried to console the Pole by a soothing letter but did not change the American position. An appeal by Polish Americans also failed to impress Wilson.

The peace terms were then presented to the German delegation and provoked its passionate reply. In the German notes, to cite H. W. V. Temperley, the British historian of the Paris Peace Conference, "every possible concession to Poland was refused, every possible territorial claim denied, every possible attempt made to depreciate Polish civilisation and capacity." Not only German nationalists but a liberal intellectual like Walther Rathenau held, in a talk with House's assistant, that in the case of Czechoslovakia and Poland "nothing will last except the shame of them; nothing that will advance humanity; nothing that will resound to the credit of civilization."

Fearful lest Germany refuse to sign the peace treaty, Lloyd George proposed to change the decision of granting Upper Silesia to Poland, and to hold a plebiscite instead. Heated exchanges with Wilson followed in which Lloyd George adroitly used the principle of national self-determination to advocate his case, professing to believe that a plebiscite would be won by the Polish side. The president was outmaneuvered. In vain did he argue that the Thirteenth Point had covered Upper Silesia and that all ethnographic data showed a Polish majority. The Americans knew that the German clergy and industrialists exercised a powerful hold on Upper Silesia and that a plebiscite at that time would not reveal the true nationality picture of the area. Wilson made the telling point that while the Allies were unwilling to make concessions themselves, "it was proposed to place the sacrifice on the Poles." He insisted that Paderewski and Dmowski be granted another hearing, and the Poles were duly heard but not listened to. In June 1919 it was decided to have the plebiscite, and the American experts were appalled. They spoke of Wilson's acceptance of it as a "black day." Why did Wilson compromise his convictions? It is likely that the concession, which House also considered sinister, was intended to save the treaty, and with it the Covenant of the League of Nations. Wilson was sacrificing Polish interests to achieve a lasting peace settlement.

The Upper Silesian plebiscite was eventually held in March 1921 and resulted in a German majority of 56 percent. In spite of the confident predictions of Lloyd George, bloodshed was not avoided, as two Polish uprisings before the plebiscite and one after it ravaged the province. The final decision, made under the auspices of the League of Nations in October 1921, divided Upper Silesia between Germany and Poland and established an elaborate system of regulations in the area. By that time the United States was no longer involved, and Paderewski's earlier appeals that American troops occupy Upper Silesia during the plebiscite could have as little effect as later Polish attempts to mobilize American support for their cause.

The Poles had to swallow other bitter pills. In spite of Wilson's representation that Poland be freed of the financial burden of war, the Polish state had to assume a part of the Russian debt and so-called costs of liberation from Austria. Although Poland suffered great material damages during the war, it was not deemed eligible for reparations. Together with other "new" states, Poland also had to assume through formal treaties unilateral obligations toward national minorities. No great power, victorious or defeated, undertook similar engagements. Since the question of minority protection was closely tied to the Jewish issue, it will be discussed in the last section of this chapter.

Worn out, Wilson left Paris after the signing of the Treaty of Versailles, to which the Covenant of the League was attached, and began his campaign in America for its ratification. In these circumstances it was natural that he should have declined Paderewski's pressing invitation to visit Poland. Herbert Hoover, whose name was linked with American economic aid, went in his place and was given a hero's welcome, which he described somewhat sarcastically in his memoirs. The Poles felt that although Wilson had not been able to assist them more effectively, he had been on their side during the arduous peace negotiations. His name was given to public squares and streets in Polish cities; his legend took a firm root in the country.

The Paris Peace Conference had dealt with but did not resolve all Polish borders. The final delimitation of the Czechoslovak-Polish frontier, particularly in Teschen, and of the eastern borders—reserved to the peacemakers' decision by Article 88 of the Treaty of Versailles—was effected much later. These matters, however, exercised the great powers in Paris and must now be briefly surveyed.

The Polish-Czech dispute in Teschen (Těšín in Czech and Cieszyn in Polish) was essentially trivial. The disputed area was small, some 850 square miles, but had rich coal deposits, mines, and iron-works. A railway that traversed it was the only railroad connection between Bohemia and Slovakia. The Poles were in the majority in three districts and the Czechs in one. There was also a sizable German minority. Piłsudski's attempt in late December 1918 to begin a dialogue with Prague and bring about a friendly settlement proved unsuccessful; the Czechoslovak government, confident of French support, did not wait long to undo the provisional arrangement of November 5 that had divided the area roughly in accord with ethnic criteria. On January 23, 1919, after a vain attempt to force the Poles out by invoking an alleged mandate of the Allied powers, the Czechoslovak troops attacked. The fighting produced a bad impression at the Peace Conference, not only because two allied states were involved but also because the Czechs had resorted to underhanded methods. Representatives of the Coolidge mission followed events closely and in their reports put the blame squarely on the Czechs. The Noulens mission reached similar conclusions. The peacemakers in Paris then stepped in and imposed a cease-fire and a new demarcation line that involved some Czech withdrawal.

Various bodies at the Peace Conference dealt with the territorial settlement in Teschen. The Poles claimed three-fourths of the area in virtue of ethnic principles. The Czechs claimed all of it stressing mainly economic and historic reasons. At first, the territorial commission in Paris favored the Czechs; later, an Inter-Allied commission dispatched to Teschen urged a division similar to the one proposed by Poland. The American delegation took an attitude friendly to the Poles, but seemed reluctant to become deeply involved. Acting on the American initiative, the peacemakers called on Czechs and Poles to settle the matter through direct negotiations. Lansing's motive in proposing this action was largely to remove the impression that France had a monopoly for arbitration among East Central European states. Direct talks failed, and the commissions on Poland and Czechoslovakia jointly recommended on August 22, 1919, a division favoring the Polish standpoint. Czechoslovak Foreign Minister Eduard Beneš, backed fully by France, then asked for a plebiscite, and his request was reluctantly granted. With the conditions on the spot deteriorating, the Poles, rather unwisely, declared that a plebiscite would be unfeasible. An arbitration by the king of the Belgians was proposed and dropped; finally, the Teschen question came up before the Allied Conference at Spa in July 1920. At this moment the Poles were asking for Allied assistance against Soviet Russia, so their representative agreed to abide by the decision of the Allies on Teschen. The decision, prepared beforehand by Beneš in cooperation with Allied experts, was formally rendered by the Conference of Ambassadors and resulted in a division of the Teschen area. Czechoslovakia obtained all that was vital to its interests; Poland lost some 130,000 Poles.

The Americans had no part in the final settlement. They were not present at Spa and cooperated with the Conference of Ambassadors through an observer only. Paderewski tried unsuccessfully to mobilize House's assistance, asking dramatically whether the United States "would tolerate such a defiance of her principles." Judging by the exchange of notes between Washington and United States ambassadors in Paris and London, American diplomats had serious doubts about the settlement, but refrained from voicing them publicly. Polish bitterness was intense and universal, and when Paderewski signed the agreement on Poland's behalf—although no longer as premier and foreign minister—he said that the Polish government could "never convince the nation that justice had been done." Undoubtedly the whole handling of the dispute by Prague, beginning with the thinly disguised armed coup and ending with a diplomatic victory achieved when Poland was weakest, left a scar that proved hard to heal. Although the Teschen issue was not the real cause of Czechoslovak-Polish estrangement in the subsequent period, it was its most visible and inflammable part.

In contrast to its attitude on the Teschen affair, the United States played an important role in Poland's eastern settlement. Here one must distinguish between the issue of Eastern Galicia, and the connected but much vaster problem of the eastern borderlands that separated ethnic Poland from Russia proper.

Since Galicia had been part of the Habsburg monarchy, a decision on it had legally nothing to do with Russia. The eastern part of the province, however, had been a war objective of prerevolutionary Russia; the majority of the population consisted of Ukrainians, who in November 1918 proclaimed a West Ukrainian Republic and soon afterward announced its union, more nominal than real, with the Ukrainian People's Republic (Russian Ukraine). Thus when Austria ceded Galicia through the Treaty of Saint Germain of September 1919, it ceded to the Allies and not to Poland. The reason was the uncertainty on the part of the peacemakers about how to dispose of its eastern part. Should it go to Poland, whose integral part it had been from the fourteenth century to the partitions? Was it to be linked with the Ukraine and then with Russia, the non-Bolshevik Russia pursued like a will-o'-the-wisp at the Peace Conference? Or was it to become part of a separate and independent Ukraine if such a Ukrainian state was to be seriously contemplated?

The Allied statesmen in Paris professed concern for and paid lip service to the Ukrainian cause. In reality they were preoccupied with the repercussions of a Ukrainian solution on Russia, and saw the Ukrainian issue in the context of the general Russian dilemma. The Poles, for genuine and tactical reasons, emphasized the connection between Eastern Galicia and defense against Bolshevism. The argument carried some conviction on military-strategic grounds; it was propagandistic when the Poles described the nationalist Ukrainian troops as Bolshevik bands.

Dmowski had included the Eastern Galician question in his general presentation of Polish territorial claims. He admitted the presence of a large Ukrainian population but argued against separate Ukrainian statehood on the grounds that 60 percent of the population was illiterate and politically immature. He derived Polish claims from history and from the dominant cultural and economic position of the Poles. Besides, in this ethnically mixed area the Poles were in a majority in many towns, including Lwów, and in some rural districts. Dmowski honestly doubted the reality of a Ukrainian nation, and believed that to encourage and nurture it was contrary to Polish interests. An independent Ukraine would dig a chasm between Poland and Russia, and the Ukrainians would, as some of them had done in the past, look for support to Germany. The only solution was to split the Ukraine between Russia and Poland, Eastern Galicia naturally belonging to the latter.

Dmowski's program, often called "centralist" or "annexationist," contrasted with the "federalist" trends of his Polish opponents. The federalists, who included people from Piłsudski's entourage, although Piłsudski himself was not a doctrinaire federalist, had a spokesman in Paderewski. They believed in the creation of a bloc, within the old prepartition borders, comprising Poles, Ukrainians, Belorussians, and possibly even the Baltic peoples. The Ukraine was not viewed as a member of the projected federation but as closely associated with it. The federalists were willing to make concessions in Eastern Galicia, but not to the extent of abandoning Lwów and the oilfields. They argued that the Polish group that would necessarily remain in the Ukraine would be balanced by a Ukrainian group in Poland. The Poles were unwilling to accept the fact that to East Galician Ukrainians the province had acquired the status of a Ukrainian Piedmont that could not be the object of barter. Hence, Poles could more easily talk to Ukrainians from Kiev to whom Russia and not Poland was the principal foe.

The Inquiry had taken an ambiguous stand on Eastern Galicia. It recommended borders that would leave the region outside of Poland but qualified its recommendation by mentioning the possibility of adding Eastern Galicia to Poland. Nor did the American peace delegation have strong feelings about the future settlement as long as it did not cripple Russia. What mattered at first was that Polish-Ukrainian fighting be stopped before the Bolsheviks endangered the area militarily. Wilson and his advisers were also conscious that the Eastern Galician issue was feeding Polish nationalist passions that could undermine the stability of the Paderewski government.

In early January Coolidge recommended an armistice that would free Ukrainian and Polish troops to fight the Red Army. For the time being Eastern Galicia could be treated as an autonomous province administered by the Ukrainians, except for Lwów, placed under a joint Ukrainian-Polish control. A little later the Noulens mission attempted to impose an armistice, but since it proved only briefly successful, Lord went to report to the Supreme Council. He urged that an immediate truce be imposed assuring the Poles control of Lwów, whose Polish character "had been strikingly demonstrated." The Council agreed on the need of a cease-fire and set up a special commission to work it out. The commission failed to get Dmowski's agreement to an armistice that would leave the oilfields to the Ukrainians. Dmowski argued that such an arrangement would expose Poland to Bolshevik military advance. Although Dmowski may have exaggerated this danger, it is true that Lenin did consider at that time a Soviet advance into Galicia and Bukovina to establish a link with Soviet Hungary.

Dmowski's opposition together with the news that, contrary to a promise made by Paderewski to Lloyd George and Lansing, Haller's troops were participating in hostilities against the Ukrainians, incensed the peacemakers. Paderewski tried to explain that this had happened prior to his return from Paris and that he had already ordered that the offensive be halted. Assuring Wilson of his desire that "everything here would take place in accord with your wishes," Paderewski added that the Poles could not remain passive. Should the government attempt to restrain them, a revolution in Poland would force its resignation, which, Paderewski wrote, "would not greatly improve matters." There is no doubt that Paderewski sincerely tried to follow Wilson's wishes. Speaking to the sejm, he lauded the United States to the skies, enumerating American military supplies, Hoover's aid mission, and prospects of an American loan. He stressed that Wilson, while recognizing the need for Poland's defense against the Bolsheviks, strongly desired a cessation of Polish warlike operations.

The Peace Conference, and especially Wilson, were placed in an awkward position. The Poles were seemingly defying Allied orders and Paderewski avowed that he might have to resign. The American envoy to Warsaw, Hugh Gibson, confirmed the premier's difficulties and suggested that the Supreme Council either release Paderewski from his commitments, or scrupulously hold him to the promises, in which case, however, Paderewski's cabinet might fall and a less desirable one emerge in its place.

Extremely annoyed, Wilson opted in May 1919 for a hard line. If Poland continued the military operations, he said, it might be asked to withdraw from the Peace Conference; perhaps one should even stop further transports of Haller's troops. The president proposed an ultimatum addressed to Piłsudski, for nothing should be done to create even a suspicion that Paderewski was not being supported. It was on this occasion that Wilson recalled that Paderewski had a letter from Hoover informing him that aid to Poland would be avaliable only as long as Paderewski was in power. The sequel was a stiff note to Piłsudski, which brought the reply that the offensive had been stopped. Emphasizing the distinction between the two Polish statesmen was not very helpful and it failed to enhance Paderewski's position in Poland. In spite of his standing with the Allies, he had failed to save Danzig and had been forced to accept the minority treaty. The Teschen issue was unresolved. Now the Allies were interfering with Polish operations in Eastern Galicia and Paderewski's prestige was at stake.

Invited to Paris in early June, Paderewski corrected Lloyd George, who accused the Poles of advancing into the Ukraine. Eastern Galicia was not the Ukraine, which had its own government. Paderewski did not add that he had concluded a short-lived agreement with a representative of the Ukrainian People's Republic, which carried Ukrainian renunciation of Eastern Galicia. The agreement was a political card to be played later. Asked point-blank whether Poland claimed Eastern Galicia, Paderewski replied in the affirmative but added that the province would receive autonomy. The effect of the hearing was Wilson's remark that "one ought to delimit also the border between Poland and the Ukraine." The president agreed with Lloyd George that a plebiscite in Eastern Galicia should be held, and the whole matter was referred to the Council of Foreign Ministers and the Commission on Polish Affairs.

The commission offered four different solutions: total independence, inclusion in Poland with or without autonomy, autonomous regime under a mandatory power, and a transition regime with a plebiscite to determine the final settlement. If Eastern Galicia were to be part of Poland, it would be so delineated as to comprise Lwów and the oilfields; an administrative line (A) would divide it from Poland proper. If the province were to be independent, its boundary (B) would be so traced as to leave Lwów and the oilfields to Poland.

The Allied foreign ministers differed in their views on Eastern Galicia. The French and Italians inclined toward its inclusion in Poland with provisions protecting the Ukrainians. The British favored a temporary Polish military occupation, administration under the League of Nations, and a plebiscite to determine the final status. Lansing took a middle position. Taking note of American reports praising Polish behavior and denouncing the brutalities of the Ukrainians, Lansing advocated a mandate to be entrusted to Poland and an eventual plebiscite. Because of the latent Bolshevik danger, the ministers agreed that Polish military occupation had to be recognized. On June 25, Lansing proposed a resolution that was adopted with minor modifications. It authorized the Poles to occupy Eastern Galicia, with Haller's troops if necessary, up to the river Zbrucz (the old frontier between Austrian Galicia and Russia), and to establish a civil authority that would "preserve as far as possible the autonomy of the territory and the political, religious and personal liberties of the inhabitants." The final settlement was "predicated upon the ultimate self-determination of the inhabitants of Eastern Galicia as to their political allegiance" and the time "for the exercise of such choice" was to be later determined by the Allied and Associated Powers.

Although the decision legitimized Polish control of Eastern Galicia, the Poles were indignant about the very idea of a mandate and a plebiscite in a province they regarded as an integral part of their state. Paderewski was blamed and in July he attempted to modify the verdict. The Americans clearly tried to avoid hurting his position. Lansing wrote Paderewski lauding his services to Poland that gained him admiration and the "respect of the world." He hoped the premier would be able to continue with his "splendid" work until Poland attained peace and happiness. More concretely, Lansing suggested to his colleagues a Polish mandate for thirty years instead of a shorter period that had been envisaged. This was still unacceptable to the Poles, and Paderewski appealed to the conference not to impose a solution that Poland "was at a loss to understand."

The matter dragged on through September to December 1919. The American representatives in Paris, Frank Polk and then Henry White, tried to meet Paderewski's wishes. They stressed that the Poles controlled and pacified the province and that it was impossible to determine an "ideal settlement." What mattered was the maintenance of a functioning stable administration. The Americans pressed for a mandate of indefinite duration, but they were unable to prevent the final decision of a twenty-five-year mandate. White then insisted that "his attitude were recorded in the minutes so that in twenty-five years Poland should not consider America responsible." Lansing on his side tried to bolster Paderewski's government by advocating increased material aid to Poland.

The twenty-five-year mandate, basically a British victory, was never implemented. After the United States had withdrawn from further work at the conference following the rejection of the Treaty of Versailles by the Senate, France persuaded Lloyd George to suspend the decision on December 22, 1919. The move came too late to save the Paderewski cabinet. Attacked from many sides, Paderewski felt bitter and hurt, and resigned on December 9, 1919. Just as Paderewski's installment in office had not been due to Hoover, so his resignation was not caused by a partial withdrawal of the Hoover mission. His break with Polish politics was not total and in 1920 he would represent his country at international conferences and at the League of Nations. The resignation almost coincided with Wilson's eclipse in American politics, although there was no connection between the two. Perhaps both statesmen suffered the penalty for not having been able to perform miracles at the Peace Conference. While totally different as men and as statesmen, neither of them was a thick-skinned, professionally flexible politician. In Poland, foreign policy was now exclusively in the hands of Piłsudski, who increasingly felt, in dealing with Russia and the intricate Eastern problems, that guns and bayonets mattered more than conventional diplomacy.

The Soviet-Polish War

The Peace Conference could have settled Polish eastern borders only if it had been able and determined to tackle effectively the entire Russian question. This it failed to do, and inconclusive deliberations in Paris contrasted with policies of faits accomplis in the vast eastern borderlands.

With the collapse of Germany the Bolsheviks began to advance along their western front. A successful revolution in Russia alone seemed impossible, and it was necessary to link forces with the biggest proletariat of Europe, that of Germany. In the path of a western advance lay the nascent Baltic states, Belorussia, the Ukraine, and Poland. The Bolshevik denunciation of the Treaty of Brest-Litovsk meant also nonrecognition of regimes in the borderlands that Russia had been forced to abandon. As the Red Army advanced, communist regimes were installed through a process of farcical revolutionary self-determination. As Lenin put it, "independent" Soviet states in the borderlands were necessary to deprive the chauvinists "of the possibility of treating the offensive of our troops as an occupation."

Even if one were to assume that the Soviet "operation Vistula" did not imply a Bolshevik occupation of Poland and opening the way to Germany, Warsaw had plenty of reasons for apprehension. Soviet offers to establish diplomatic relations with Poland were thinly disguised attempts to undermine the emerging state from within and to isolate it from the Allies. The organization of Polish

Red Army units and the propaganda pursued by Polish Communists occupying the leading positions in Soviet Lithuania were hardly re- assuring. Nor could the Poles watch with indifference a Bolshevik conquest of borderlands which had been part of prepartition Poland and where a sizable section of the propertied class was Polish. By February 1919 the Polish troops gained the right of passage through the crumbling German lines in the east and clashed with the ad- vancing units of the Red Army. A Soviet-Polish front came into existence in the Belorussian-Lithuanian area.

It was under these circumstances that Dmowski presented the Polish territorial claims to the Supreme Council. As mentioned, Dmowski admitted that the prepartition eastern frontiers of Po- land "should be curtailed." He claimed the more western, largely Catholic lands imprinted with cultural, historic, and economic Polish influences; the eastern he conceded to Russia. The frontier he proposed roughly coincided with the line of the second Polish partition.

Polish federalists, whose voice until Paderewski's arrival had not been heard in Paris, wished to force Russia back to the pre-1772 bor- ders and organize in the liberated lands a vast, vaguely defined federal structure. Piłsudski shared the view that Poland had a unique chance of driving Russia back to its ethnic borders and he favored federalism, but did not regard it as a panacea. He pointed out that the Poles were entering the borderlands by force, "which is contrary to the principles of federation." He wanted to create faits accomplis and argue with a "revolver in my pocket." But in view of "American palavers" at the Peace Conference about brother- hood of nations, he would "gladly lean toward the federalists."

It was ironical in a sense that Wilson was far from advocating national self-determination in Russia or urging federalist solutions there. Had the president fully believed that Russia was even more a prison of nations than Austria-Hungary, and had he been will- ing to give full support to non-Russian nationalities, he may have simultaneously achieved the disintegration of Russia and the col- lapse of Bolshevism. House insisted to Wilson in early 1919 that the West was bound to "give moral, material, and if necessary military support" to the border states against the Bolsheviks. The colonel had earlier noted his disagreement with Wilson and Lan- sing about the necessity to preserve Russia intact. Lansing also realized that Wilson's policy toward Russia was inconsistent with the principle of national self-determination but since he approved of the policy he only gained an argument against the principle.

The maintenance of Russian territorial integrity had been elevated almost to a dogma of American foreign policy. Historical analogies between the Union and indivisible Russia played a certain part in this attitude, but there was more. As Lansing put it, the United States would never support policies of splitting Russia up into separate units not only because to do so without Russian consent would be morally wrong but it would also remove the last obstacles to Japanese territorial ambitions and would revive German imperialism. The two powers, Lansing wrote, were far more dangerous than a "united, democratic Russia, well able to defend itself, but not disposed to attack." Thus, the United States did not seriously think of combating Bolshevism through a policy of assisting non-Russian nationalities. Direct intervention was also disliked, the Siberian interlude being a matter of necessity rather than choice, and wholehearted support to Russian counterrevolutionary armies did not appeal to the Americans.

Wilson felt he could sympathize with the "latent force behind Bolshevism." The idea that there was an analogy between the revolutionary republican America of 1776 facing a hostile world of monarchies and Bolshevik Russia defying capitalist Europe was not far from Wilson's mind. As George Kennan aptly remarked, Americans who are so often "inveterately conservative at home" seem to be "the partisans of radical change everywhere else." Wilson's overtures to the Bolsheviks need not concern us here, but it should be evident that as far as Poland was concerned, only those Polish claims that did not injure the territorial integrity of Russia had any chance of being sympathetically viewed by Wilson and Lansing.

Continuing Polish-Soviet clashes, punctuated by unofficial exchanges, lay outside any effective control of the Peace Conference. In April 1919 Piłsudski captured Wilno and addressed an appeal to the inhabitants of the former Grand Duchy of Lithuania, calling on them to determine their own fate. Hopes for the creation of a local government combining Polish, Lithuanian, and Belorussian elements did not materialize, but to keep the federalist option open Piłsudski did not annex this area to Poland. The Dmowski camp reacted angrily to his initiative; Paderewski endorsed Piłsudski's stand. The Peace Conference disliked the Polish move as indicative of eastern expansion, but temporarily treated it as dictated by military exigencies.

At the end of 1919 Piłsudski revealed his thoughts to Paderewski. The settlement of Poland's *western* borders, he wrote, depended on the good will of the Allies, and until it was completed one had to procrastinate in other matters. Once Paris made its decisions, Poland would become a force in the east with which everyone would have to reckon. Piłsudski stressed that the Poles had to dispel the notion that Russia proper bordered on the Bug River (the old line between the Congress Kingdom and Russia), and instead advocate the idea of "union of all nations and people who live between us and Russia proper with Poland and not with Russia, naturally on the basis of federation."

In early summer the Peace Conference decided to extend its support to the Russian counterrevolutionary leader Admiral Kolchak, provided he promised to honor Russian debts, summon a constituent assembly, recognize the independence of Finland and Poland—their borders to be settled by direct agreement and failing that by the League of Nations—and grant autonomy to Baltic, Caucasian, and Transcaspian provinces. This was the closest the conference came to recognizing the claims of non-Russian peoples (Ukraine and Belorussia excepted), and it was satisfied with Kolchak's somewhat evasive reply.

The specter of counterrevolutionary Russia worried Warsaw. Paderewski made an offer to the peacemakers: the Polish army could advance on Moscow if the Allies so desired and provided support and equipment, but the Poles wished to know where the conference stood for they had received advantageous offers from the Bolsheviks, had reached a line roughly coinciding with their territorial aspirations, and "could not fight indefinitely." Paderewski failed to force the hand of the Allies, and Clemenceau, speaking on their behalf, said that "he would not make peace nor would he make war." Warsaw understood that its role was to assist the Whites, whose victory it neither desired nor expected, and forego its own initiative. Piłsudski was not prepared to do that, and he began to listen to secret Soviet overtures. The hard-pressed Bolsheviks were trying to neutralize the Baltic states, which the Allies still refused to recognize, and they made overtures to Poland.

Secret talks between Piłsudski's and Lenin's representatives began in the summer of 1919 and continued again in late autumn. Piłsudski's objectives were clear; to push Russia back to her ethnic borders and create a new order in the vast Ukrainian-Belorussian-Lithuanian borderlands. This was a revival of the historic Russo-Polish strife, and Lenin astutely observed that "Poland cannot abandon this old perennial struggle even now."

Piłsudski sought to achieve his objectives by imposing peace terms if the Bolsheviks were sufficiently weak to accept them, or by war if they refused. He let Lenin know that Polish troops would not advance or assist the White General, Anton Denikin, because this did not lie in Poland's interest. He demanded, however, that the Bolsheviks abstain from attacking the national Ukrainian leader Semon Petliura, abandon Daugavpils (Dvinsk) to the Latvians, and stop all communist activity in Poland. The Bolsheviks were willing to negotiate but not to accept a dictate and were adamant about the Ukraine. Piłsudski assumed that they wanted to enmesh him in negotiations, gain time, and having triumphed over the counterrevolutionary armies, confront Poland from a position of strength. He became even more convinced that a favorable peace could only be achieved after a military victory over the Red Army. This was a view that the Polish sejm and a large part of public opinion did not share. Nor was it appreciated or approved by the Western Powers.

The West did not wish to equip the Polish army for offensive purposes, and the American delegate, Polk, voiced doubts whether the strength of the Polish army was justified. The United States would not provide arms or munitions to Poland. The part of American credits and supplies then going to Poland that could be classified as military equipment was small indeed, and only by ignoring or juggling figures could Soviet historiography have presented its misleading picture of massive military assistance. We shall return to this point in the next chapter, when discussing American loans and credits.

By September 1919, the Peace Conference had not yet made any definite statement on Poland's eastern frontiers. It was trying to provide some stability in Eastern Galicia, but the situation further north also required attention. The Commission on Polish Affairs reported that it was impossible to foresee when a regular Russian government, whose cooperation was "necessary to the definitive determination of the Eastern frontiers of Poland," would come into being. It suggested therefore a provisional recognition of the prewar boundary between the Congress Kingdom and Russia, with Chełm assigned to Poland. The border would be definitive as regards territories west of it, which Russia did not contest, and provisional "to the extent that, in the future, other territory situated to the East of that line may be incorporated with Poland." This was an ambiguous proposal. The Poles were already in physical control of large territories situated east of the line, and the conference did not intend to demand Polish evacuation for obvious military reasons. While the arrangement sought to dispose of territories *west* of the line, it created the impression that this was a Russo-Polish boundary as seen by the peacemakers. In fact, both the American and the French members of the Polish commission "believed that the final frontier should be farther to the east."

Polk was aware of these difficulties, and he proposed that the Polish government be given the choice of accepting the border without prejudice to a final settlement, or to consider the question open until Poland and Russia resolved it themselves. The American delegate believed that the Poles should be informed about the stand of the conference through a unilateral declaration which need not be binding on them. There was thus some uneasiness surrounding the declaration, dated December 2, 1919, and communicated to Poland on December 8. The document repeated that "the rights that Poland may be able to establish over the territories situated to the East of the said line are expressly preserved." The Polish government was distressed, and vainly argued against the publication of a document that General Denikin for one took as an Allied endorsement of a frontier between Poland and Russia. In truth, the December 8 declaration evaded the issue of a territorial settlement just as a Franco-British agreement to strengthen Poland not "for an attack on Russia, but rather for future contingencies" evaded the pressing matter of war and peace in the east.

The Bolsheviks masterfully exploited the confused situation. On January 28, 1920, the Council of People's Commissars addressed Warsaw, reiterating proposals for peace negotiations on the basis of Poland's independence and sovereignty. The Red Army would not cross the existing front line, the note said, intimating that this line would become the future state frontier. Were the Bolsheviks sincere? An editorial in a weekly close in its views to Piłsudski said that "peace must be the embodiment of our program in eastern affairs, and one can risk it only at that price." To diminish the risk Poland needed either full endorsement of the Allies or victory in the field. Piłsudski prepared for the latter, but he dispatched Foreign Minister Stanisław Patek to sound out London and Paris. The United States was already largely out of the diplomatic picture.

Piłsudski prepared the ground for an alliance with the Ukrainian leader, Petliura. The agreement was embodied in a full-fledged alliance signed in April 1920 that involved Ukrainian renunciation of Eastern Galicia. To Piłsudski this was a bold experiment seeking to overcome past Polish-Ukrainian bitterness. Petliura felt that Ukrainian independence could be achieved only with Polish aid, for which a price had to be paid. Thus the driving force behind the alliance was not the Polish landowners' vested interest—in fact, Warsaw was far more interested in the Ukrainian industrial potential—nor the idea that the Ukraine would become a Polish colony, but the need of a political and military barrier against Russia. On the

148

other hand, fear of an independent Ukrainian state was one of the main objections of the National Democrats to Piłsudski's policy.

Patek's negotiations in the West confirmed Piłsudski's opinion that one could not expect Allied commitment to Polish objectives. The French warned him against trusting the Bolsheviks and continued to advocate a "no peace, no war" approach. Lloyd George gave Patek, in the words of a British diplomat, "lots of advice" but "carefully avoided taking responsibility for it." Patek's principal question, as to what guarantees Poland could have that a treaty with the Bolsheviks (who were unrecognized by the Allies) would be internationally binding, was never answered.

The Poles, as Patek put it, were "particularly anxious to know whether American sentiment would be offended if they yielded to necessity and made the best terms possible." There was no clear response, but Poland's envoy in Washington, Prince Kazimierz Lubomirski, reported that the secretary of war was accusing Poland of imperialism and holding territories east of the December 8 line. A possibility of support existed only in the case of a defensive war. A sharp attack on Piłsudski, calling him an autocrat and a German agent who had ousted Paderewski for his American and Allied sympathies, appeared in the *Washington Post*. The American minister in Warsaw, Hugh Gibson, flooded the State Department with cables and reports. He warned that if no Allied aid was forthcoming the United States must face the likelihood of either a Soviet-Polish peace or the conquest of Poland by the Bolsheviks. In February 1920 Lansing finally summarized the American position. The United States could not "take responsibility for advising Poland on policy toward Russia," he wrote Gibson, but Warsaw must not refuse to negotiate on the assumption that American military or economic aid would be available. From Washington the Polish minister reported that the United States apparently left Poland a free hand. Gibson's view that the Western Powers "cut Poland adrift" was more accurate.

Polish peace terms, evaborated in March 1920 and showed to Allied ministers, demanded Russian "disannexation" of all lands west of the prepartition borders. The Poles explained that the fate of these lands would be settled in conformity with the wishes of the local population—Piłsudski had previously mentioned a plebiscite to the Allies—but the general impression remained that Poland had resolved to restore the historic borders of the old commonwealth in defiance of national self-determination. The Polish note was politically clumsy, and Gibson commented on "poor Polish propaganda which is almost unbelievably stupid although conducted by an undoubtedly intelligent people."

The Polish note was not officially communicated to the Soviet government, which, however, knew its content. Hence the Bolsheviks could fulminate against Polish brigandage and portrayed Warsaw as an "obedient lackey of the Entente." Direct exchanges between Warsaw and Moscow dealt with technicalities of a peace conference, although in contrast to the Poles the Bolsheviks seemed neither to have prepared their own terms nor appointed a peace delegation. At least no Soviet historian has revealed that they had. A controversy began about the meeting place and a cease-fire. The Poles insisted on a small frontline town of Borisov and a local armistice. They probably desired to prevent the conference from becoming another Brest-Litovsk show—Borisov was not readily accessible—and retain the ability to interfere with a concentration of the Red Army. These demands were not as outrageous as Moscow made them appear, for the Bolsheviks themselves had negotiated with Estonia without a general armistice. The 1953–1954 negotiations between the United Nations and the Chinese and North Koreans were also held in a frontline locality. But Soviet propaganda succeeded in presenting the Borisov affair as a major case of Polish bad faith and gained international sympathy for Russia.

American attitude naturally mattered to the Poles. Lubomirski reported that the State Department seemed to understand the Polish position. The new Secretary of State, Bainbridge Colby, wrote Gibson privately that the Poles did not appear to be genuinely interested in peace, though Gibson was not to repeat this to them. Beginning in mid-March, Gibson's dispatches were stamped with "sent to the President," but Wilson's views cannot be readily ascertained. It is likely that he continued to disapprove of a policy prejudicial to Russia's territorial integrity, although he was also becoming more anti-Bolshevik and thus sympathic to the Poles. Warsaw still hoped for some advice and moral support from America, "the only country which had no selfish interest to serve in her dealings with Poland," as Piłsudski told Gibson.

April 25, 1920, was the decisive day. The Polish army accompanied by two Ukrainian divisions began an all-out offensive and on May 7 it captured Kiev. This was no new war, although the expression "the war of 1920" has been commonly used, but the climax of a year-old conflict. Piłsudski and Petliura launched liberation appeals to the Ukrainians. There was some response when Eastern Galician brigades serving with the Red Army went over to the Poles and partisan fighting intensified in the Ukraine. But there was no mass rising of the war-weary population that had seen so many different occupants since 1917. The Ukrainians felt that they stood to lose Eastern Galicia and perhaps the land they had taken from the Polish landowners during the revolution in exchange for unspecified ties with Poland and the end of Bolshevism. The masses were not fired by this prospect, and the organization of Ukrainian units proceeded slowly. Equipment was scarce and discipline in the lower echelons of the Polish army left something to be desired. Still, the American legation reported that the Polish policy toward the Ukraine "has been carried out with great tact and cleverness" and that the inhabitants of Kiev were "all delighted to be ridden of the Bolsheviks." In Warsaw Piłsudski received a hero's welcome; he seemed sanguine about the outcome of the struggle.

Soviet propaganda first attempted to portray the Polish offensive as the "third intervention of the Entente"—a term that Stalin coined and which is still used by Soviet historians. Class slogans, however, mingled with nationalist appeals for "one and indivisible Red Russia." A number of tsarist officers joined the army in defense of the Russian fatherland. A statement of Bolshevik war aims prepared by Trotsky stressed the inviolability of Poland while predicting an ultimate victory of communism in that country. The emphasis was on defensive war, but there were hints about a European revolution. Only one document (of May 7) promised that after victory "the Soviet government will leave to the Polish nation the right to build your own life in accord with your own views." Most appeals spoke of Poland of Workers' and Peasants' or of a Soviet Poland.

The Polish offensive failed to destroy the opponent. Attacks and counterattacks followed until on June 5 the famous cavalry army of Semon Budenny broke through the Polish front. The Poles had to evacuate Kiev and then the Ukraine. In the north the main Soviet offensive led by Mikhail Tukhachevsky began on July 4 and started to push the retreating Polish armies toward Warsaw. On July 12, the Bolsheviks signed a peace treaty with the Lithuanians and handed over to them the captured Wilno. The campaigns were fought under primitive conditions. Troops were underfed and badly clothed; there was lack of effective communication. This was a war of movement with rapid advances and retreats demoralizing the poorly trained soldiers. Contrary to Soviet assertions the Poles did not enjoy a great technical superiority; their few planes were unable to stop the advancing cavalry masses.

Defeats on the front produced a political crisis in Poland and directed all the animosities against Piłsudski. A new cabinet under Władysław Grabski was formed and a State Defense Council set up to control Piłsudski. Overriding the latter's objections, the new premier went to seek Allied assistance at the Spa Conference. Upbraided by the French and the British for reckless Polish imperialism. Grabski promised that Poland would abide by Allied decisions in such unresolved matters as Wilno, Teschen, and Danzig, withdraw to the minimum boundary of December 8, 1919, and participate together with Russia, the Baltic states, and delegates of Eastern Galicia in a peace conference to be held in London. In exchange, the Allies promised to mediate between Warsaw and Moscow and provide assistance if the Bolsheviks rejected a proposed armistice and crossed the December 8 line. Since military assistance was excluded, it was not clear what form this aid would take.

The mediation effort was embodied in the famous Curzon Note sent on July 11, 1920, which created some confusion regarding Eastern Galicia. Here the line of actual hostilities, to which Grabski had consented, and Line A (the administrative border mentioned at the Peace Conference) were simultaneously indicated as the cease-fire line. The second would place all of Eastern Galicia outside of Poland. Whether it was a mistake or an underhanded move by the Foreign Office may never be known, but the December 8 line extended to Eastern Galicia entered history under the name of the Curzon Line. More would be heard about it in the years to come.

Polish gloom, deepened by the fact that the plebiscites in East Prussia went against the Poles, contrasted with Soviet jubilation. The Bolsheviks rejected the Curzon Line and demanded that the Poles approach them directly. At the same time Lenin resolved the debate about further advance by deciding to continue the offensive into purely ethnic Poland. The stakes were high, for as Lenin later put it, had Poland collapsed and become communist "the Versailles Treaty would have been shattered, and the entire international system built by the victors would have been destroyed."

Under these circumstances direct Soviet-Polish armistice exchanges were largely meaningless. Britain still believed in them; France did not; and the Inter-Allied Mission sent to Poland as the only manifestation of Western aid could not be too helpful. The representative of the French army on the mission, General Maurice Weygand, did render important military services to the Poles.

On July 28, 1920, the Red Army took the first sizable town west of the Curzon Line, Białystok, and two days later a Polish Provisional Revolutionary Committee was established there. Its leadership included Julian Marchlewski and Feliks Dzerzhinsky. Mysterious Soviet contacts with Germany hinted at the possibility of a territorial deal at Poland's expense between Moscow and Berlin. High German and British officials believed that as a result of Soviet victory Germany might recover the "Corridor" and retain Upper Silesia. A Soviet trade mission was in London, and talking to it, Lloyd George still thought he might preside over a Soviet-Polish peace settlement. In reality new Soviet secret political directives of July 21 enjoined that it was inadvisable "to say openly that we shall conclude peace only with a Soviet Poland."

Soviet armistice and peace terms presented to the Poles—and unofficially to London—provided for demobilization of the Polish army and dismantling of war industries, Soviet control of a strategic railroad to East Prussia, and the creation of a workers' militia armed by the Bolsheviks. Pending a peace settlement, the Poles were to withdraw in such a manner that the Red Army would control Warsaw. The final frontier would roughly correspond to the Curzon Line with minor modifications to Poland's advantage. It is obvious that these terms were designed to make a truncated Poland a Soviet satellite.

The country meanwhile was rallying around a broad coalition government led by the Populist leader Witos and the Socialist Daszyński. On August 1, 1920, Witos addressed a message to Wilson, perhaps to show that the Poles still counted on him. On August 15, Piłsudski launched a counter offensive that shattered the Red Army. The victory, which Lord D'Abernon called the Eighteenth Decisive Battle of the World, was quickly termed the Miracle of the Vistula by Piłsudski's adversaries and ascribed to Weygand. Although the Weygand legend is hard to destroy, all evidence points to the plan being prepared by the chief of staff and then reworked and adapted by Piłsudski. Since a commander-in-chief is invariably blamed for defeats, it seems only just to credit him also with victories.

The battle of Warsaw was followed by other victorious struggles that took the Polish army over the Curzon Line and further east. Simultaneously Polish-Soviet negotiations started again, after their deadlock at the abortive conference at Minsk, which had preceded the battle of Warsaw. It was obvious that Lenin's plans were no longer realizable and that Piłsudski lacked the support of the nation for another attempt to achieve his eastern program. The stage was set for the Peace Treaty of Riga.

What were American reactions and moves during the climax of the Soviet-Polish war in 1920? The press closely followed the events and in the crucial month of August news from Poland temporarily pushed items about the presidential candidates off the front page.

Reliable reporting mingled with fantastic stories, for instance about Piłsudski's collusion with the Bolsheviks. Jewish problems, on which more later, played a part in the unfriendly tone taken by many newspapers toward Poland; at one point House advised Paderewski to issue an explanatory statement to the American press. The specter of a Russo-German alliance based on the ruin of Poland appeared serious to House, who was quoted as saying that Germans would welcome the Russians as liberators. Pro-Polish sentiments took the form, among others, of volunteering for the Polish army. One of the units of the small Polish air force, renamed the Kościuszko Squadron and commanded by Cedrick Fauntleroy, was largely American in composition. In the interwar years a monument to the fallen American avaitors was built at the military cemetery in Lwów.

In spite of Gibson's urgent pleas in July for a declaration of principles, official Washington preserved silence. There were rumors of a special session of Congress, and Colby advised Wilson to make a statement that would have a beneficial effect upon Polish public opinion and help to steady a perilous situation. Somewhat wistfully Wilson replied that although he would willingly do anything to help Poland, he was hesistant because the time had passed when "personal intervention on my part or suggestion in regard to foreign politics would be of service." The administration "has adopted an attitude of cool reserve toward us," wrote Lubomirski. War supplies could be bought but there was not much chance to get indirect financial assistance and Washington was discouraging efforts to send war material. Appeals by Polish Americans for assistance to Warsaw failed to change the United States policy, but the Polish National Department succeeded in collecting over $600,000 for the Polish cause.

In early August, when the Red Army was racing toward Warsaw, Colby informed missions abroad that the time was not ripe to publicize American views. While the government was sympathetic to efforts to save Poland's integrity through an armistice, it could not participate "in plans to extend the armistice negotiations so as to bring about a general European conference involving the recognition of the Bolshevik government" and probably entailing a partition of Russia. Dwelling on the second point, Washington explained that this was the reason for its refusal to recognize the Baltic states. All such arrangements would collapse when a "restored Russia" would vindicate its territorial integrity and unity. American opposition to a conference, at that time advocated by Lloyd George, was additionally strengthened by suspicions that British-Soviet trade negotiations would harm the chances of future American economic penetration of Russia.

Then a *Washington Post* columnist raised the question of a possible revision of the Treaty of Versailles, and went on to attribute certain views on the Polish-Soviet war to the State Department. Allegedly, Washington believed that Polish aggression had rallied all Russians to the defense of the fatherland and thus saved the disintegrating Red Army. "The spirit of the Russian Army today," the paper wrote, "is the spirit of the American Army of 1776." The French, wishing to provoke Washington to take a public stand, commented on these newspaper articles, and thus probably contributed to the release of the Colby Note of August 10, 1920.

The note took the form of a letter to the Italian ambassador, which was circulated and released to the press. It said that the United States could not recognize the Bolshevik government, which was based on the negation of honor and good faith, and with which no treaties could be negotiated. The note repeated that America could not take part in a peace conference that would recognize the Bolsheviks and lead to a dismemberment of Russia from which "this country strongly recoils." Poland, Finland, and Armenia excepted, Russia's borders should be decided by the Russian people when it regained control of its own affairs. The American people also stood for "Poland's political independence and territorial integrity," the note stated, and the government had the intention of employing "all possible means" to preserve it.

All this was not very helpful. As an American diplomat in Warsaw put it, Colby "read a statement about what America thought about Bolshevism, bowed to the audience, and made an unapplauded exit." If Piłsudski could derive some comfort from American disapproval of an international conference, he could not fail to see that Washington seemed to be more concerned with Russia than with Poland. Good intentions toward Warsaw remained purely platonic. While the White Russians welcomed Colby's statement, Soviet Commissar Chicherin cleverly used it to give Washington a lesson in nationality problems. Chicherin recalled that non-Russian nations had all been forcibly annexed by the tsarist regime, and that American "discrimination" in favor of some nationalities could only stem from gross ignorance. By contrast, the Bolsheviks upheld the right of self-determination of the working people of every nationality.

The American chargé and his colleague stayed on in endangered Warsaw even after the diplomatic corps had left the city. If their action enhanced American prestige in Poland, a message from Washington, coming after the Polish victory, lowered it. After polite words of sympathy and praise for the gallant Polish troops, the State Department warned Poland on August 21 not to cross the Curzon Line. "The United States believes," the document read, "that the Polish Government might well take the opportunity afforded by the favorable turn of events to declare its intention to abstain from any aggression against Russian territorial integrity, to state that its policy is not directed against the restoration of a strong and united Russia, and that pending a direct agreement as to its Eastern frontier, Poland will remain within the boundary indicated by the Peace Conference." The United States could not promise to render Poland material assistance if Warsaw continued war operations.

The Poles were annoyed. Gibson explained that not only Piłsudski but all the military experts considered the Curzon Line "disastrous from a military point of view." American policy of abstention during the Soviet-Polish war hardly entitled Washington to proffer advice at this juncture. The Poles replied by pointing out that they did not acknowledge the Curzon Line as corresponding to ethnic criteria, and recalled that they had received no help when the Bolsheviks had crossed it in July. The Polish government's intention was to reach a peace settlement based on mutual territorial concessions, taking into account the will of the interested population, national claims, and economic necessities. Washington was not convinced and its worries centered on Wilno. Since the United States continued to deny recognition to Lithuania, the concern was less for Lithuanian rights than for Russian interests.

The Poles captured Wilno on October 9 by a stratagem. Piłsudski secretly ordered a division to "rebel" and seize the city and the surrounding territory, and the commanding general, Lucjan Żeligowski, then proclaimed a separate state called Central Lithuania. Piłsudski hoped that this "state," together with a slice of Belorussia to be gained at the peace conference, could serve as bait to induce Lithuania to federate with Poland. The reverse proved to be true, as for years to come Lithuania considered itself in a de facto state of war with Poland and the two had no diplomatic relations until 1938.

The Riga Peace Conference began on September 21, 1920, and resulted in preliminaries signed on October 12. The Soviet delegate, Adolf Ioffe, described the outcome as a peace of understanding that gave "a guarantee of stability." He characterized the territorial settlement by using the term "compromise boundary." The frontier corresponded by and large to Dmowski's proposed line, and in that sense Riga was a National Democratic peace rather than Piłsudski's.

Poland had to abandon its ally, Petliura, and the Ukrainians bitterly compared the settlement to the seventeenth-century Russo-Polish treaty of Andrusovo, which had divided the Ukraine between the two powers.

A second round of negotiations for a final treaty lasted from mid-November to March 18, 1921; the length of the proceedings was chiefly caused by wrangling about economic issues. The Bolsheviks considered that they had made significant territorial concessions and tried hard to avoid economic sacrifices. Eventually they agreed to pay the Poles their share of the gold reserve of the former imperial state bank—a concession that turned out to be a dead letter.

Did the Riga settlement really represent a compromise if one looks at the extreme demands of both sides, the long span of historic Polish-Russian relations, and the fundamental objectives of Soviet Russia and Piłsudski's Poland? With regard to the first aspect, there was a compromise and a reciprocal abatement of extreme demands. Historically speaking, the boundary decided at Riga lay almost halfway between the prepartition Polish frontiers and the most westerly borders of the Russian empire. Regarding the basic objectives of Piłsudski and Lenin, however, far from being a compromise the Treaty of Riga was a negation of both: the Polish leader's eastern program, and the Russian's plan of making communist Poland a bridge to the West. Dramatic Polish victories notwithstanding, Poland was not the long-term victor. Its basic problem of being a medium-size state situated between two giants was not resolved; a centralized Poland was burdened with large national minorities The Bolsheviks realized it. Solemnly recognizing the treaty and turning inward to build up their industrial power, they viewed the settlement as a temporary expedient. Their long-range goals remained virtually unchanged, and Soviet reentry into European politics in 1939 began with their tearing up the Treaty of Riga.

The signing of the treaty, the Upper Silesian plebiscite, and the adoption of a constitution, all in 1921, ended the turbulent period of consolidation of the country. By coincidence, the final treaty came two weeks after the inauguration of Warren G. Harding as president of the United States. The Wilsonian era was over.

The Jewish Issue

The story of American-Polish relations from 1914 to 1921 would be incomplete without the examination of the Jewish aspect to which only passing references were made. The subject is complex and controversial; a brief survey can scarcely do justice to it, yet it cannot be left out.

A tolerant attitude toward the Jews in the old commonwealth as well as the growth of modern anti-Semitism in Poland at the turn of the nineteenth and twentieth centuries have been already noted. Looking at the Jewish side, one must recall that the goal of emancipation combined with a denial of a separate Jewish nationality prevailed in Western Europe, but underwent fundamental changes in the eastern part of the Continent. With the emergence of Zionism and other trends, national and not only religious identity began to be stressed by the Jews, as well as demands for recognition of their separate national rights. The Bund, a mass Jewish workers' party in Russia and Poland, adopted the slogan of national-cultural autonomy. Galician Jews raised nationalist demands. After the fall of tsardom, a Jewish conference held in Petrograd in July-August 1917 requested guarantees of "civil and national rights of the Jews in independent Poland."

Since new Polish borders were not yet drawn and within those of 1772 there lived the largest Jewish group in the world, the nature of Polish territorial settlement was very important to the Jews as was the Jewish question for the reemerging Polish state.

The future of Jews in Eastern Europe was naturally of deep concern to American Jewry. In 1914 the mass of the Jewish population in the United States was of recent East European background but displayed little sentiment toward their original homelands. On the other hand, the elite was largely composed of assimilated German Jews who were frequently older immigrants with pro-German sympathies and anti-Zionist views. To this category belonged, for example, the prominent lawyer Louis Marshall, the great banker Jacob H. Schiff, Simon Wolf, and Julius Rosenwald. They dominated the American Jewish Committee, which opposed Zionism and promoted assimilation and civic and political equality. The Zionist Organization of America counted among its leaders such influential men as the Supreme Court Justice Louis D. Brandeis, Justice Julius W. Mack, and Rabbi Stephen Wise, all of whom had easy access to Wilson and House. The Zionists sought to displace the American Jewish Committee and make their own goals prevail, which included the recognition of separate Jewish nationality. Zionism became the dominant trend of American Jewry and operated largely through the American Jewish Congress set up in 1916. By the end of the war, however, both trends compromised on a formula that emphasized national rights "in lands in which national rights were or ought to be recognized." This obviously referred to Eastern Europe.

Paderewski appreciated the importance of the Jewish organizations in America and sought to find a common language with them. As mentioned, he urged Dmowski to include a representative of Polish Jews on the National Polish Committee, and in early 1918 participated at Rosenwald's initiation in a Polish-Jewish conference, where he appealed to the Jews to "support our cause." In the autumn he requested Dmowski's committee to send him the text of their statement issued in Paris, which said that in reborn Poland "Polish citizens without distinction as to origin, race or creed must all stand equal before the law." Paderewski transmitted the text to Marshall. The lawyer was skeptical about the practical application of the principle, and suggested a meeting with Dmowski that could lead to "a more acceptable formulation of principles so far as they affect the Jews of Poland."

Dmowski's subsequent conversations with Marshall and Brandeis were ostensibly cordial but fruitless. Marshall demanded that an end be put to the economic boycott of Jews and that Dmowski's policy toward them be changed. Dmowski retorted that only a large Polish state could accommodate the conflicting Jewish-Polish interests and insisted that Jews commit themselves to support his territorial program. Marshall would not consider this prior to Dmowski's commitment. Marshall summarized their conversation in a lengthly report he sent to Wilson, together with a memorandum spelling out the demands of the American Jewish Committee for the treatment of Jews in Poland. These were: citizenship rights to all with the possibility of retaining former state citizenship, repudiation of all discrimination, linguistic freedoms, religious and cultural Jewish autonomy, and a provision that the observance of the Sabbath would not interfere with Jewish business activities on other days (Sundays). These provisions were to be part of the Polish constitution and a condition of the organization of the new Poland. Dmowski learned about these points, possibly from a talk with Brandeis, and concluded that the Jewish demands were too far-reaching.

In December 1918, at the meeting of the American Jewish Congress, Marshall and Mack delivered low-key speeches on national rights, but for the sake of solidarity accepted a Bill of Rights to be applicable to Poland, Galicia, Lithuania, Russia, and other East European areas with a sizable Jewish population. The bill went beyond the demands submitted to Wilson and stipulated also for minority representation secured by the law of the land. Regarded as a guideline for the Jewish representatives at the forthcoming peace conference, the bill was to be treated as a lasting condition for the recognition of autonomy or independence of East European states.

Jewish political activity within reemerging Poland ranged from neutrality in Eastern Galicia and the Polish provinces to resolutions, like one passed at a conference in Warsaw in late December, demanding the recognition of Polish Jewry as a national minority with all the rights such a status entailed. Although this stand did not reflect the attitudes of all Polish Jews, it was bound to increase friction and inflame mutual antagonism. Conditions in the country were not conducive to rational dialogues or moderation. The Poles were drunk with their independence. As one Socialist wrote: "it is impossible to describe this vertigo, this passionate joy that affected the Polish population at this moment." Everything Polish excited enthusiasm, even "the sight of Polish policemen and gendarmes." This patriotic euphoria operating in the context of hardship, hunger, disease, and social and political turmoil was not easily controllable by the emerging administration. Patriotic passions took positive forms, or translated themselves into hatred of everyone and everything that seemed to stand in the way of Poland's rebirth and unity.

Toward the end of 1918 news began to reach the West about anti-Jewish riots and pogroms in Poland A Jewish correspondent of the Hearst press stationed in London was among the first to send gruesome telegrams, accompanied by pictures that on closer scrutiny turned out to be old photographs of the Kishnev pogrom in tsarist Russia. The Viennese *Neue Freie Presse* reported a pogrom in Lwów that allegedly claimed between 2,500 and 3,000 victims. The Poles were branded as savage anti-Semites, a charge that German propaganda quickly picked up by referring to Poland as the "pogrom zone." The American government was alarmed and asked its envoys abroad and the Coolidge mission to investigate. Their reports showed a wide discrepancy between reality and propaganda. The event in Lwów was reduced to its true, however reprehensible, proportion—sixty-four Jews had been killed until Polish military patrols restored order.

American reports drew attention to two aspects of the riots, one economic—attacks on Jewish shops, mostly in eastern Polish towns—and the other political—identification of Jews with Communists. The latter was a phenomenon not restricted to Poland. American investigators concluded that it was unfair to blame the Polish authorities and the nation as a whole for the outbursts of anti-Semitism. The United States minister in Bern wrote that the nascent

Polish government would, in fact, welcome an Allied fact-finding mission.

Neither Piłsudski nor any of the leading cabinet members was an anti-Semite. The short-lived Lublin government had included in its manifesto a statement on full equality of political and civic rights for all, "irrespective of origin, faith and nationality," and the electoral law adopted in November 1918 provided for universal, direct, secret, proportional, and equal suffrage. In the elections held in January 1919, candidates representing national minorities, mainly Jews, polled 12 percent of the votes. On the other hand the Polish right, led by Dmowski, gained 37 percent of the votes and became the single largest parliamentary group. But the left followed very closely with 34 percent.

In December 1918 Dmowski returned to the idea he had broached in his conversation with Marshall. He instructed his associate to contact Jewish leaders abroad and propose a deal: if the Jews sent a delegation to Paris ready to support the Polish territorial program, Dmowski would personally assume the leadership of a campaign to put an end to anti-Semitism in Poland. Was Dmowski sincere? Was he naive enough to imagine that his word would be taken at face value by the Jews? One could hardly expect him to abandon suddenly his long-standing anti-Jewish position. Perhaps he only envisaged stopping the economic boycott to which Marshall had so strongly objected. At any rate, Dmowski tried to appear moderate, and when he came to Paris House instructed his aide, Stephen Bonsal, to find out his views on the Jewish question. Bonsal found Dmowski reasonable, and House also believed that the Poles would be fair but that it would take time before animosities subsided. At the time anti-Semitism in Poland was real enough, even discounting the obvious exaggerations, and House tended to agree with Wilson that an "iron pledge" on just treatment of minorities had to be exacted.

In March 1919 the Jewish lobby at the Paris Peace Conference consolidated itself. While British and French Jews retained their own outlook and a separate status, a powerful Committee of Jewish Delegations at the Peace Conference emerged under American leadership. It represented organizations of the United States, Canada, and Eastern Europe, but the Americans were clearly the most influential. Trying to moderate the more extreme demands of the nationalists, they became the champions of Jewish autonomy in Poland and Eastern Europe. Mack and Marshall were the first two chairmen of the committee; from mid-May 1919 the East European leader, Nahum Sokolov, took over.

The committee judged that to ask for a special status for the Jews would single them out and increase the existing hostility against them. Hence they advocated the rights of all national minorities, stressing that the Jews were one of them. This policy was bound to lead to a confrontation between Jews and Poles at the Conference. Dmowski in particular felt that his program of a unitary Polish state, which he had to defend against Polish federalists, was now jeopardized by Jewish advocacy of autonomy for national minorities. Embittered by his struggles in Paris, Dmowski later came to see the Jews behind every Polish defeat at the Peace Conference.

At the same time that the Commission on Polish Affairs was preparing its territorial reports, Jewish representatives sought quietly to influence the peacemakers while widely publicizing the alleged pogroms in Poland. Simultaneously, the American Jewish Congress exercised pressure of its own and in March adopted a new memorandum which was forwarded to Wilson. It emphasized the right of the inhabitants of Galicia and Prussian Poland to retain their former citizenship if they so desired, and repeated demands for guarantees of national rights. Wilson, although long sympathetic to the Zionist cause, was noncommittal. Marshall, Mack, and Sokolov continued to operate secretly so as not to alarm the "new states." In talking with the American Peace Delegation, the Jewish leaders were confirmed in their belief that they should not make their claims on Poland public. House hesitated between his sympathy for Poland and his desire to satisfy legitimate Jewish grievances. Hoover favored political equality and religious liberty, but not any specific minority provisions. Lord opposed minority protection in general. At House's request, David H. Miller and another American expert began to cooperate with the Committee of Jewish Delegations on a modified version of a bill of rights and on April 19, 1919, came up with a draft proposal.

The proposal made the basic claim that a minority of at least one percent of the population was entitled to an autonomous organization that included participation in administrative organs. Miller had succeeded in eliminating such terms as representation on "national" institutions and "governmental functions," but went along with the principle of some proportional minority representation and the inclusion of an irrevocable bill of rights in the Polish constitution. Mack and Marshall complemented the draft by justifying autonomy on the grounds that polonization of the Jews should be prevented. They also stressed the principle of proportional control of funds and representation on all elected bodies.

Polish territorial acquisitions were to be made conditional on the acceptance of a minorities' bill of rights.

The Jewish leaders in Paris fully utilized the news about anti-Jewish outbreaks in Poland as proof that extensive guarantees were indispensable. The incidents in question occurred in the eastern lands into which Polish troops were then advancing. Marshall gave an interview to the *New York Times* in which he spoke about "murders, tortures, robberies" committed in Wilno. In fact, Piłsudski, who was there personally, had difficulty in restraining an impending pogrom in reaction to some Jews shooting at his soldiers. Later excesses did occur in Wilno, where sixty-five people lost their lives, and in Lida, where thirty were killed. In Pińsk, a trigger-happy local commander, allegedly mistaking a Jewish meeting for a Bolshevik gathering, ordered the execution of thirty-five Jews.

The circumstances surrounding these deplorable acts and Polish countermeasures received little attention in the American press. Gibson reported from Warsaw that the sejm had appointed a Polish-Jewish committee of investigation and that in Wilno Piłsudski included the Jews in the city administration. In the eastern borderlands, where the Jews often constituted the majority of the small town dwellers, the proletariat frequently sided with the Bolsheviks giving rise to the commonplace: Jew equals Bolshevik. It was less noticeable that the Jewish bourgeoisie often fell victim to the commissars. Life for civilians was at best uncertain in the type of warefare waged in the east, and the Jews as shopkeepers, tradesmen, or local moneylenders were particularly vulnerable.

May and June 1919 were spent on the crucial phase of working out minority provisions in Paris. After House had received a final report from Miller, Wilson told the Supreme Council that, his attention having been drawn to the position of Jews in Rumania and Poland, he favored the creation of a special commission to draft provisions for the protection of minorities. Since this meant interference with domestic affairs, the council ruled that although Poland and the other "new states" had been recognized, they could hardly be said to have been created before the signing of peace treaties. This odd formula was not likely to facilitate Polish acceptance of minority provisions with good grace.

The commission on which Miller was the American representative was instructed not to associate Poles or Jews with its work nor even to reveal its existence to them. Working rapidly, the commission produced a draft by May 3 in spite of serious differences between the American and British members. The British claimed that Miller was "very much in the hands of Marshall" and said that the Americans were more concerned with "the vote of the New York Jews than [with] the real advantages to be won for the Jews in Poland." Controversy centered on whether the Polish Jews were to have a state within a state with "the right to elect a proportion of the entire number of representatives in all state, departmental, municipal and other public elective bodies based upon the ratio of its numbers in the respective electorial areas to the entire population therein," or enjoy a status that would guarantee their rights as individuals. Since provisions applicable to Jews were to extend to all national minorities within the country, the first arrangement would have made Poland a conglomeration of autonomous minorities, hardly operative as a state.

The Committee of Jewish Delegations redoubled its efforts. It insisted that without real minority provisions Ukrainians, Lithuanians, Germans, and Jews faced the danger of "annihilation of their ancient civilization," and stressed that minorities must have the right to appeal to the League of Nations. The peacemakers argued that these and other demands were excessive. For example, Miller for one thought that to grant Jews the right to keep their shops and institutions open on Sunday would be "rejected as legislation by all modern States." Such provisions "would endanger the Treaty in the Senate." President Wilson was more sympathetic, but in his turn doubtful about a recognition of "national rights." Eventually a watered-down version that was still favorable to the Jews was adopted. Disregarding the secrecy rule, Miller acquainted Marshall with the text. The British member's sense of propriety was offended: "it will have a disastrous effect if the Poles learn that a copy has been given to the Jews before the Polish official representatives have seen it," he commented. Marshall naturally appreciated Miller's gesture and told Wilson that Miller has been "very helpful"; the president was allegedly pleased to hear it. Five days later the document was officially given to the Polish delegation and another copy was sent directly to Warsaw. The smaller states had already successfully rebeled against the Supreme Council's policy of showing them peace terms only twenty-four hours before they were to be given to Austria. Now, they openly attacked the minority provisions. The Poles seemed to have adopted a wait-and-see strategy which may explain why Warsaw had made no counterproposals and why Paderewski had failed to respond to soundings by the Committee of Jewish Delegations. Perhaps this strategy was a mistake. The Rumanian delegate led the charge of the smaller states and incurred the wrath of Clemenceau. Paderewski's speech was brief and sounded "tactful and sonorous." Poland, he said, was perfectly willing to grant its minorities the same rights minorities enjoyed in the West. If international protection of minorities under the League of Nations was to be introduced, let it apply to all members. Wilson replied in a conciliatory but firm speech. Avoiding any reference to the Jews, he asserted the right of great powers which had won the war and had to exercise ultimate authority. He was, however, tactful enough not to offend unduly the susceptibilities of the smaller Allies.

The final stages of discussion were again accompanied by wide publicity given to anti-Semitic outbreaks in Poland. The new riots were on a very small scale. In Kolbuszowa eight Jews, three peasants, and two soldiers quelling the riot died; violence at Częstochowa claimed five Jewish victims. American newspapers carried paid advertisements stating that Jews were being slaughtered and a wave of pogroms was sweeping Poland. Jewish people were said never to have been set upon by an enemy more merciless and brutal. A huge demonstration of some 15,000 Jews was held in Madison Square Garden; Marshall sent a long cable to Wilson protesting the pogroms. A resolution was introduced into the House of Representatives asking the president to take steps to prevent a "recurrence of massacres of men, women and children."

The American legation in Warsaw was growing weary, for two out of every three telegrams dealt with the pogrom issue. Gibson flippantly remarked: "If a Jew is injured it is called a pogrom. If a Christian is mobbed it is called a food riot." Gibson was suspicious of Zionist propaganda and indirectly raised doubts about the representatives in Paris being true spokesmen of all Polish Jews. In atempting an analysis of the structure of Polish Jewry, he mentioned the assimilated group on whose behalf Stanisław Posner came to Paris. He spoke of the Orthodox masses which cared little for being considered a nation. He mentioned the Litvaks, recent Jewish newcomers from Russia, who "give open provocation to public feelings" of the Poles. He drew the attention of the State Department to the opinion of some Jewish members of the sejm that Poland was being coerced "through the influence of foreign Jews." Gibson, unfriendly to the Jews, was not an uncritical admirer of the Poles either, and one can consider his dispatches as fairly objective. He reported Piłsudski's confidential remarks about the excesses of Haller's soldiers, who were cutting off beards of Orthodox Jews and maltreating them, and speculated about the causes of such behavior. While Piłsudski was genuinely indignant at the soldiers' conduct, and Haller threatened the anti-Semitic offenders with court martial, Gibson was doubtful whether matters could change overnight. Food shortages, anxiety over border settlements, fears of Germany, continued hostilities, large unemployment—all this was likely to feed anti-Semitism. The atmosphere was also poisoned by rumors about a special treaty of protection to minorities and stories of Jewish-German collusion.

It was imperative that a fact-finding mission be sent to Poland to calm the excitement and help toward long-range improvement of Polish-Jewish relations. Hoover allegedly suggested this course to Paderewski and urged it on Wilson. The president chose three men, including Henry Morgenthau, Jr., a German-born Jew and a former United States ambassador to Turkey, and General E. Jadwin, of whom Morgenthau said that he could evaluate facts with the precision of a mathematician. Paderewski officially requested Lansing to send the mission, and the Secretary of State instructed it not only to investigate excesses but also to analyze their causes and suggest remedies for the future. Amelioration of the status of the Jews, Lansing wrote, would benefit Poland and what benefited Poland ought to be of advantage to its Jews.

House and Gibson welcomed the choice of Morgenthau as promising to clear "much of the misrepresentation and falsehoods." Morgenthau hesitated, for he was strongly opposed by the Zionists, but gave in to Wilson's pressures. Morgenthau believed that the Jew "in most lands and down the ages" has been like "the fringe of the carpet, the loose end over which every foot has stumbled, every heel has left its injuring impression on the disconnected individual strands." He wished him to be "a part of the pattern of the carpet itself." In his reminiscences of Poland, Morgenthau showed later a tendency toward errors and oversimplifications, particularly when speaking about Piłsudski and Dmowski. But he clearly admired Paderewski, who was "not only not an anti-Semite" but "infinitely the greatest of the modern Poles."

Morgenthau's report of October 1919 stated that there is "no question that some of the Jewish leaders exaggerated these evils." He also blamed the "malevolent, self-seeking mischief-makers both in the Jewish and Polish press." His remark about an ambitious minority of Jews, who had intensified the trouble by believing that the "solution lay only in official recognition of the Jew as a separate nationality," reflected his anti-Zionist feelings. Analyzing the excesses—and the figures of the dead in this chapter are based on Morgenthau's report—he drew attention to the fact that only two outbreaks had occurred in former Congress Poland; four involved soldiers in a combat zone; and one resulted from the orders of a junior officer. In most though not in all cases, the guilty were tried and sentenced. The concluding remark of the report deserves to be cited in full:

> Just as the Jews would resent being condemned as a race for the action of a few of their undesirable co-religionists, so it would be correspondingly unfair to condemn the Polish nation as a whole for the violence committed by uncontrolled troops or local mobs. These excesses were apparently not premeditated, for if they had been part of a preconceived plan, the number of victims would have run into the thousands instead of amounting to about 280. It is believed that these excesses were the result of a widespread anti-Semitic prejudice, aggravated by the belief that the Jewish inhabitants were politically hostile to the Polish state.

The climax of the Polish-Soviet war in 1920 produced fresh accusations by some American papers of anti-Semitic outrages perpetrated by the Poles. The source was often Bolshevik propaganda, which naturally did not dwell on the anti-Semitic exploits of Budenny's cavalry corps. The Polish legation demanded information from Warsaw, but given the chaotic conditions and the shifting front, little was forthcoming. There doubtless was a strong belief in Poland that the Jews identified with the Bolsheviks. News about Białystok, where the commissars recognized only Russian and Yiddish as official languages, did nothing to dispel it. In the increasingly charged atmosphere Jews and Polish Socialists became suspect in many quarters. A batallion of the PPS militia sent to the front was disarmed by gendarmes as crypto-Communists; a special section of the internment camp at Jabłonna was suddenly reserved for Jews—a clear aberration if one thinks of Jewish officers including regimental commanders serving with distinction in the Polish army. The Jabłonna episode lasted for twenty-five days and occasioned a protest of Polish deputies, writers, and scholars who demanded the punishment of those responsible.

Rabbi Wise, acting as president of the Committee of the Status of Jews in Eastern Europe, complanied to Wilson about the "concentration camp" and other alleged atrocities. The *New York Journal* appealed dramatically: "Stop killing Jews." A vicious anti-Semitic campaign waged by the *Dearborn Independent,* invoking the Protocols of Zion and decrying the Treaty of Versailles as a Jewish instrument designed to humiliate Poland, was hardly the kind of help the Poles needed. The *New York American,* exploiting the Jewish issue for its own ends, wrote that it was the League of Nations that had enabled Poland to invade Russia and perpetrate pogroms: hence the League must be opposed. When matters calmed down a little in October, Lubomirski sought a dialogue with Jewish leaders and a conference took place in the Waldorf Astoria Hotel in New York.

Apparently, animosity still prevailed, as evidenced by a Jewish meeting in December at which some Polish posters were displayed allegedly proving that the Polish government had encouraged the murder of Jews. In January 1921 the State Department opposed General Haller's visit to the United States on the grounds that it would provoke new Jewish-Polish polemics.

Polish-Jewish relations are not, of course, an object of analysis here; we are primarily concerned with their impact on the United States and Poland. Dmowski's inability to reach an understanding with American Jews weakened the Polish cause in the United States and at the Paris Peace Conference. On the other hand, it is doubtful that American Jewish influence had played a large part in shaping Wilson's policy toward the Polish territorial settlement. It is unlikely that Jewish support would have helped Poland to get better borders in the west and the east; unfriendly as they might have been, the Jews in Paris were far from being omnipotent, as Dmowski obsessively asserted. In the matter of protection of national minorities the Jewish Committee of Delegations scored a partial victory, but if one looks at later events he cannot help wondering if it was not a Pyrrhic victory. All efforts centered on gaining protection from Poland and the other "new" countries. But when during World War II the mortal blow fell on East European Jewry, it was delievered not by the states which had been obliged to sign the minority treaties but by Germany on which no such demands had been made.

Jewish-Polish tensions in 1919–1920 adversely affected the American image of reborn Poland. While outrages committed against the Jews must be strongly condemned, onesided Jewish accounts of events had their share in picturing all Poles as anti-Semites, imperialists, and oppressors of national minorities. A recent and otherwise excellent study of American foreign policy in the interwar period by Selig Adler characteristically says that "Pro-Polish sentiment, so marked during wartime, was dissipated as the Warsaw government persecuted racial minorities and pushed its boundaries eastward in blatant violation of the principle of national self-determination." This is an unfair oversimplification, for Warsaw did not organize or approve anti-Jewish outbreaks and the conflict with the Bolsheviks over the borderlands was hardly a unilateral Polish violation of national self-determination. No neighboring state had a good record in handling its nationalities yet it was not subjected to such criticism. The Jewish question, of course, provides an insufficient explanation of the change of American feelings toward Poland and one must probe deeper into the subject.

Already in the course of the nineteenth century Americans who favored the Polish cause did so for moral and not political reasons. During the war and at the Peace Conference Wilson, House and indeed a part of American public opinion believed that a moral wrong to the Poles had to be undone; Paderewski with his emotional and idealistic oratory strengthened this belief. The re-creation of Poland appeared as a quasi-philantropic undertaking. One of the first Polish representatives in the United States, Franciszek Pułaski, perceived it clearly when he wrote: "Poland is treated rather as a romantic cause that lends itself to humanitarian action than as a political issue."

But the Polish nation, like any other, was not a conglomerate of suffering martyrs and selfless idealists. Nor was there any reason to suppose that Polish political leaders were made of different stuff from politicians throughout the world. The Polish nation, which had worked and fought for its national existence, was not a charity case. In resented and resisted attempts to be confined to economically and strategically impossible borders. It had ambitions, dynamism, and will to power. This seeming discrepancy between poor and persecuted Poles and a virile people attempting to establish the best possible place under the sun baffled many Americans. That this Poland, which Wilson and House were prone to hail as their creation, should show ambitions similar to other powers appeared somewhat reprehensible. Perhaps in the final analysis one should point toward the American inclination to oversell policies, allies, and causes. That tendency, when confronted with realities, hurt the image of reborn Poland just as it hurt Wilson and last but not least the Treaty of Versailles and the League of Nations.

4

From Peace to War

INTERWAR Poland, or the Second Republic as historians increasing call it, faced innumerable problems, international and domestic. Covering an area of roughly 150,000 square miles with 27.2 million inhabitants (35 million by 1939), the Polish state was the sixth largest in Europe, but still much smaller than the prepartition Polish-Lithuanian Commonwealth. The French historian, Louis Eisenmann, aptly characterized its international position when he wrote: "It was a tragedy for Poland to have been reborn too weak to be a power, and strong enough to aspire to more than the status of a small country."

The vulnerability of the Second Republic was obvious. Most of its long borders (2,600 miles) were contested, and it had only some 90 miles of seashore. The Free City of Danzig was Poland's only harbor and the complex relationship between the two caused friction. Berlin refused to accept the German-Polish settlement as final and spoke of the "burning frontiers." The Treaty of Versailles was of course the hated Dictate, and Poland was called a *Saison-staat,* an artificial creation that would not last long. Franco-British disagreements and the way Polish territorial problems had been handled provided grounds for German revisionism. As a British member of the Court of International Justice opined, "If Danzig had been given out and out to Poland before Germany had recovered from the first shock of her defeat and of her political upheaval, the situation would not have been so bad and in time would have been accepted." The prolonged agony of settling the status of Upper Silesia poisoned the relations between Berlin and Warsaw. Pomerania (Pomorze), dubbed the "Corridor," stood out as a symbol of German humiliation; German propaganda successfully pointed to the iniquity of isolation of East Prussia.

Soviet Russia too resented the borders of the Treaty of Riga, for a sizable Ukrainian and Belorussian population in Poland raised fears of an irredenta. But, although Moscow harped on Polish aggressiveness, it found the lack of a common border with Germany far more aggravating. Speaking about the revolutionary upheaval in Germany in 1923, Trotsky emphasized "the counterrevolutionary significance of the Riga treaty for the fate of Europe," for the situation would have been very different if "we had a common frontier with Germany."

Polish foreign policy strove to prevent German-Soviet pincers from closing on it. Since the possibility of Polish cooperation with Germany against Russia or vice versa was virtually unthinkable, the Second Republic searched for a working security system. But the League of Nations, particularly without the United States, could hardly fulfill this requirement. Poland's natural ally against Germany was France, and in 1921 Piłsudski concluded an alliance with Paris accompanied by a secret military convention. This alliance, however, was insufficient against the Russian threat and Warsaw strengthened its eastern defenses by an alliance with Rumania. The emergence of a larger bloc of East Central European states that could stand against the great neighbors foundered on lack of cooperation between the so-called new states, particularly Czechoslovakia and Poland. The vulnerability of the Second Republic restricted its freedom of maneuver in international relations, where it appeared a risk and a liability. This fact in turn affected Polish domestic problems, economic and political.

The hundred-twenty-odd years of partitions had vitiated Polish economic development, and the war years 1914–1920 had taken a terrible toll of the country's resources. Population losses amounted to nearly half a million people killed and several hundred thousand dead from epidemics and hunger. In 1920 the population was 2 million less than in 1910. According to the Polish delegation at the Peace Conference, material losses were of the magnitude of some 73 million French francs. In the countryside large areas lay fallow and the production of the main crops dropped in some cases to half of the prewar figures. The number of cattle, pigs, and sheep diminished by 40 to 50 percent. More than half of the railroad stations and bridges were destroyed and almost as great a number of locomotives. Some 18 percent of buildings lay in ruin. Much of the industry had been dismantled by the Germans and the Russians, and metallurgical and textile production came almost to a halt. Where 8.9 million tons of coal had been produced before the war, only 6.4 were mined in 1920. Oil output dropped from 1.1 million tons to 0.7; crude iron from 330 thousand to 119.

The war with Soviet Russia brought new hardships. Even though war orders temporarily assisted industrial production, eliminated unemployment, and brought up real wages, shortages of coal, transportation problems, and lack of qualified workers prevented a real recovery. Financially, war expenses absorbed nearly half of the Polish budget between 1918 and mid-1919 and 62 percent from mid-1919 to March 1920. Indebtedness to the Allies, especially to the United States, and Polish shares of German and Austro-Hungarian state loans constituted another burden. In 1920 the budgetary deficit amounted to 91 percent.

Comparable devastations and losses would have been a serious strain on a well-integrated and rich country, and Poland was neither. The reborn Polish state had to weld together three distinct parts and create out of them a new economic, legal, administrative, and political unit. It had to grapple with different legal codes, taxation systems, and currencies; it inherited a railroad network that did not connect the principal centers of Poland with each other. Prewar trade patterns changed abruptly; the once important trade with Russia, for instance, dwindled to insignificance. A common currency in the form of Polish marks could only be established in 1920.

In the interwar period Poland's industrial production amounted to 0.7 percent of world production; her population was 1.5 percent of the world population. Only coal was abundant and Poland occupied the fifth place among coal-producers in the world. In relation to world production the output of oil had dropped and Poland could export some of it only because of the low level of domestic consumption. Oil deposits were becoming gradually exhausted, although natural gas output rose. The country had essentially an agrarian economy and was the world's third largest producer of rye. Three-fourths of Poland's population lived in the countryside and only one-fourth in towns. If one looks at the principal occupations in 1921, 63.8 percent of the people worked in agriculture, 17.2 in mining and industry, and 6.2 percent in trade and business. As compared with other countries Poland was more advanced economically than the Balkan countries, less than Italy, and lagged far behind highly industrialized central or western European states. Having one of the highest birth rates in Europe, its rapid population increase produced a large, economically unproductive rural population—81 persons per 100 hectares of cultivated land as compared to 49 in Germany—a phenomenon known as hidden unemployment. Accompanying it was the factor of "price scissors"—a gap between low prices of agricultural products and high prices of industrial goods.

Land-hungry peasant masses demanded redistribution of the land held by private landowners, the state, and the church. Particularly offensive were the large although not numerous domains, and the fact that less than 30,000 families possessed a quarter of all estates. Seeing it from another angle, farms and estates over 50 hectares occupied 31.2 percent of all arable land but constituted a mere 1 percent of all farms. The first agrarian reform was voted in July 1919 and followed by a law a year later, but only in 1925 a large-scale program of reforms was instituted. Even if it had been more fully implemented, it was no panacea, for purely economic reasons. The agrarian problem was insoluble without an industrialization of the country.

Industrialization required capital as well as labor, and native capital was wanting. The war and inflation had wiped out many savings. Within the Polish economy, big capitalists were few and state participation was high. The state owned virtually all railroads, armament factories, post, telegraph and telephones. Salt, tobacco, liquor, and matches were state monopolies. The state's share in coal and oil production was roughly one-fifth of the total, a little more so in metallurgy. Foreign capital, which already played a significant part in prewar Polish lands, appeared as the only available source, and although invested at high rates of interest in existing plants and taking its profits and dividends outside the country, it could hardly be replaced with native resources. This was an unhealthy economic situation that boded ill for the future.

The society reflected a retarded stage of development. The bourgeoisie was small (1.1 to 2 percent, depending on the method of calculation) and so was the working class (20 to 27.5 percent). The lower middle class accounted for about 11 percent, landowners made up 0.3, and the peasants between 52 and 53.2 percent of the entire population. This social breakdown is somewhat different when we add the factor of national minorities. Because official statistics are not fully reliable, let us accept the figure that two prominent Polish economists, Z. Landau and J. Tomaszewski, had arrived at by correcting the official census. According to them, Poles constituted 64 percent, Ukranians 16 percent, Jews 10, Belorussians 6, and Germans 3 percent. The overwhelming majority of the

Ukrainians and Belorussians were peasants, which means that ethnic Polish peasants were proportionally a smaller group than shown in the overall figures cited above. Most of the Jewish population was completely unassimilated and lived in conditions of extreme poverty; a small minority was conspicuous in the rich upper bourgeoisie. Two-thirds of the Jews engaged in small trade and crafts, which made them the predominant group in the lower middle class category and reduced ethnic Polish representation in it to a bare minimum. While the general figure for the intelligentsia (including white-collar workers) was only about 5.1 percent, the Jews constituted a significant percentage of that small figure. In the free professions they made up almost half of the total. The distribution of the German population was more even and the Germans were also represented in the industrialist and the landowner class. The uneven distribution of national minorities throughout the various strata of society created social as well as political problems.

Geographic maldistribution was also significant. About 60 percent of the Germans lived in formerly German territories. Jews were mainly concentrated in urban centers of former Austrian and Russian Poland, and constituted in several of the smaller eastern towns the majority of the population. Ukrainians and Belorussians, of course, were a minority that lived in compact blocs in the east. All these imbalances help to explain the persistence of national friction and point to some socioeconomic causes of anti-Semitism.

Particularly important in Polish society was the intelligentsia. "From the point of view of ownership of intellect," wrote the Polish sociologist, Józef Chałasiński, it was "a strictly defined class," the entry to which was opened through a diploma. In background the intelligentsia stretched through all social classes but, as already noted, it had adopted many characteristics of the gentry with which it was often connected. It was the intelligentsia rather than the aristocracy and the landowning gentry, whatever the social prestige these two enjoyed, that dominated Polish society and politics. Largely endowed with prerequisites for leadership, it believed that it was ordained to rule the country as its true elite.

Polish political life was still affected by the heavy burden of partitions and struggles for national independence. As the Polish sociologist, Jan Szczepański, put it so well, "in the nineteenth century, the Poles had proved their ability to endure and their capability to resist," but institutions developed for this task and energies mobilized to preserve national identity were "ill-suited to the task of organizing a state administration and to solving not only the problems unsolved in the nineteenth century but also those newly arising in an independent state." For many of Piłsudski's former soldiers, independence and its preservation were goals rather than prerequisites for normal political life. While many Americans, as we saw, were shocked to find that the new Poland had some of the features of a country governed by harsh rules of power politics, there were also prominent Poles who were disillusioned. Many had fought and died for an idealized image of Poland as a land of freedom, fairness to all, and social justice. A confrontation with realities that included party strife, vested interests, and struggle for power was painful even to Piłsudski. Patriotism alone was no substitute for political programs that sought solutions to complex social, economic, and ideological problems. Polish individualism complicated the picture.

The Poles saw Poland as a national state albeit comprising large minorities, and their outlook was comparable to the view of most other "new nations" in East Central Europe. In reality, Poland might be called a halfway state with all the problems resulting therefrom. The minorities were too large to permit a well-functioning, purely national state, and yet it was not a union of distinct nations, like Yugoslavia.

At first it seemed obvious that Poland must be a democracy. Piłsudski quickly arranged for elections to the constituent assembly, sejm, which met in January 1919, and to this body he resigned his dictatorial powers. The sejm unanimously reelected Piłsudski as chief of state, with powers restricted by the provisional "little constitution" of February 1919. According to that document, the sejm was the "sovereign and legislative authority" of the republic, although in practice it left control over foreign policy and the army to Piłsudski. During the critical months of the Soviet-Polish war the sejm did not meet, and some of its prerogatives were exercised by the State Defense Council.

The constituent sejm was an arena of factional infighting and a far cry from an ideal institution working harmoniously for lofty goals. The wartime Piłsudski-Dmowski split continued and deepened. The right, the left, and a volatile center emerged, and the electoral law produced a multitude of political parties organized in ten parliamentary clubs. If the working of the sejm disillusioned Piłsudski, his strong personality frightened the deputies, particularly of the right and center. Together with a certain crudeness in Polish parliamentarianism and an evident lack of experience, there was also considerable idealism. One of its manifestations was the highly democratic franchise that included women's right to vote, and which the former Galician conservatives criticized as too liberal in the prevailing Polish conditions.

Let us now turn to American-Polish relations during these formative years, particularly in the economic sphere. After World War I, the prestige and power of the United States rose to unprecedented heights. America became a creditor nation and the world's banker, and it was anticipated that the United States would play a leading role in international politics. Instead, popular sentiment in America turned against the peace treaties and continued involvement in European affairs. Such issues as Fiume were said not to be worth one dollar or a single American life. For the millions loaned to Europe during the war the Americans had a right to be left in peace. Americocentric attitudes combined with xenophobia and such phenomena as the Red Scare and the growth of the Ku Klux Klan, as well as general suspicions of Europe. Disillusioned liberals criticized the Paris settlement and European squabbles. German-Americans, Italian-Americans, and Irish-Americans denounced the misuse of the principle of national self-determination.

The Senate voted against the Treaty of Versailles and the League of Nations in November 1919. Ill and for a while incapacitated, Wilson refused to compromise, and the final vote took place in March 1920. A separate treaty between the United States and Germany put an end to the state of war and assured America the benefits of Versailles, without committing it to maintain the territorial provisions. America embraced isolationism, a term that has been frequently misunderstood and misrepresented. Isolationism did not mean that the United States turned is back on the outside world and abstained from participation in international affairs. The need to collect European debts alone would have made it impossible. Rather, it meant deliberate avoidance of entangling alliances or involvement in the League of Nations. Isolationists put stress on unilateralism and rejected the thesis that foreign wars could be prevented by cooperative actions. They questioned the assumption that an international organization was essential to preserve peace and even more that it required American presence.

United States foreign policy was fairly vigorous in Asia and Latin America. In the case of Europe, Washington kept a free hand while cultivating economic and cultural contacts. Isolationism was only a frame of reference and a mood; American foreign policy was not based on a coherent system of thought on matters international. In everyday operations it was largely pragmatic. Global economic expansion was not considered inconsistent with political reserve but rather as complementing it. A feeling of superiority made Americans believe that by pursuing their national policies they were providing an example to Europe and the rest of the world.

Diplomatic relations between the United States and Poland were established early in 1919, and the first American minister was Hugh Gibson, a man with "a scintillating mind and razorlike wit," as a subordinate described him. In May, he was received by Piłsudski and stressed American friendship for Poland going back to Kościuszko and Pułaski. He also spoke of the 4 million Poles in America. These were phrases that frequently recurred at American-Polish functions. Gibson also conveyed American expectations of Poland, namely that it would consolidate itself "without regard to former political or social differences" and take its place in international life as a "great, peace-loving and happy nation." Piłsudski in reply paid tribute to Wilson and saw in Gibson's words "a precious pledge" of American support and assistance. The first Polish minister to Washington, Prince Kazimierz Lubomirski, who was chosen for his alleged business talents, handed his letters of credence in November 1919 and was received in the White House in mid-May 1920.

Gibson, whom the Polish foreign minister described as a "great friend" to the country, was sympathetic to Polish needs and showed it by his stand during the Soviet-Polish war. In 1921 he argued that the absence of final Allied recognition of Polish borders undermined Polish credit and the viability of the state. At the same time, Gibson viewed Poland as a small country that had to be accommodating to Washington's wishes, and his reports were not free from condescension or even outright mockery of the Poles. In business dealings he was hard and unyielding.

By 1921, American thinking about Poland showed, as noted. a certain decline of sympathies. The Polish military attaché wrote from Washington that the press was on the whole projecting an image of Poland as a weak and barbarian country specializing in the murder of Jews. In diplomatic and governmental circles another image prevailed. Poles were thought to be politically immature, charming but naughty children not appreciative of the great powers' advice. They lacked realism and conducted business in a chaotic and shoddy fashion. True, there were also pro-Polish enthusiasts. Charles J. M. Phillips, of the American Red Cross, described the country with sympathy and respect in his book *The New Poland,* published in 1923. There were other publications that pictured Poland and its past in a friendly fashion: Kenneth Robert in *Europe's Morning After,* James Roy in his *The Pole and Czech in Silesia,* and more critically, Arthur Goodhardt in *Poland and the Minority Races.* The Polish past was presented in attractive terms by Monica Gardner. Some translations of Polish literary works became available. Yet one can assume that by 1921 American feelings toward Poland were a mixture of indifference, occasional impatience, and condescension. In the intellectual leftist circles antipathy was more pronounced. "How Long Will Poland Last?" was the headline of an article published in the *Nation* in February 1921.

How did Warsaw perceive America's role in international relations and Washington's position on questions of vital interest to Poland? Diplomatic reports from the Polish legation in early 1921, deemed important enough to be forwarded to Piłsudski, stressed the United States' crucial position because of its economic might and good relations with Britain. Washington sought a normal trade balance, economic recovery, and stabilization of Europe. To these ends, Russia's natural resources and the industrial might of Germany were of considerable interest to the United States. What is more, Russia was from Washington's point of view a counterweight to Japan. While the Poles assumed that the United States would stand by the Versailles territorial settlement, they worried lest the continuing emphasis on the indivisibility of Russia reflect unfavorably on Polish eastern borders. The legation urged that attempts be made to persuade the United States to approve the Treaty of Riga before America withdrew even farther from European matters. The same was said about interesting the United States in Upper Silesia. In neither case, however, did Polish diplomacy register a success.

An elaborate analysis of American foreign policy with special emphasis on the Polish aspect came from the commercial attaché in Washington in 1923. For the United States, the attaché wrote, Poland was neither essential, as it was for France, nor an obstacle in foreign policy, as for Germany and Russia. Poland "represents no special interest" to America, and one "cannot even hope to gain America directly for our policy." At the same time, the United States as world power and center of finance was most important to the Poles, and they ought to devise ways of influencing Washington's policies. The Polish diplomat believed that the United States was bound to be drawn into international matters despite its professed lack of interest, and enumerated three areas that had to be watched: the Russian question, problems of oil, and international finance. With regard to Russia, it was up to Polish diplomacy to convince Washington that it made no sense to place hopes on a future united and democratic Russia. Rather than await the chance of doing business with Russia, America ought to expand economically in Eastern Europe. To the slogan of indivisible Russia one should oppose that of indivisible China. As for oil, the attaché recommended attempts to arouse American interest in Eastern Galicia. With regard to general financial and commercial matters, the Poles should argue that American interest required bolstering Poland to stand up to Germany. Surely Upper Silesia in Polish hands weakened Germany as an American competitor, and the Free City of Danzig could attract American carriers operating between Poland and the United States.

All these objectives, as the Poles realized, were difficult to achieve given the one-sidedness of American-Polish relationships. Even in the economic sphere the 1918-1920 contacts between the two countries were more humanitarian than businesslike. The circle of high finance, the Polish legation reported, was frigid toward Poland and viewed possibilities of investment as too small to be of interest to American business.

The existing economic activities fell roughly into two categories: first, aid, handled mainly through Hoover's American Relief Administration (ARA) to which small credit operations should be added, and second, the Polish loan floated in the United States. Connected with these were the first attempts to establish normal trade relations between the United States and Poland.

In early January 1919, Herbert Hoover, named director-general of Relief for Allied and Associated Powers, received direct reports from his representative in Warsaw about the terrible conditions prevailing in Poland. Given the difficulty of access—the Allied blockade of Germany was lifted only in April—American food shipments began coming through Switzerland. Later supplies went by ships to Danzig. The cargoes originating with the Food Administration and the War Department were to be paid for right away, but Hoover arranged for delayed payments. The U.S. army surpluses placed at Hoover's disposal by presidential orders were sent on credit. In February 1919 a Congressional appropriation for Polish relief regularized the operations, and two months later an agreement between the ARA and the Polish government provided for $8.5 million worth of foodstuffs. Theoretically, all goods were to be handed over to the Polish government, but in reality distribution remained in the hands of the American mission. Meals were provided through a canteen system, and some of the food for children was sent as a gift. By February 1920 a million children were being fed. In the summer the program was reorganized with the creation of the Polish-American Children Relief Committee. A new Congressional appropriation in late 1919 fell victim to a feud between the Capitol and the White House; the flour credit of March 1920 was the last one granted to Poland.

Alongside the ARA, other institutions engaged in relief for Poland, notably the Red Cross and the Quaker missions. A special program for Jews was operated and sponsored by the Joint Distribution Committee. To combat a typhus epidemic in eastern Poland, Hoover obtained the services of Colonel Harry L. Gilchrist of the Army Medical Corps with hundreds of assistants. Sanitation equipment and supplies were brought in and the mission performed very creditably under most difficult conditions.

In his dealings with Paderewski, Hoover insisted that greater order be brought into Polish economic life to facilitate better use of native and foreign resources. He advised setting up an economic council comprising delegates of the concerned ministries and foreign economic advisers. Several were indeed appointed in the summer of 1919. Colonel A. B. Barber of the Corps of Engineering became a technical adviser with assistants responsible for railroads, coal, oil and gas, and commercial matters. Dr. E. D. Durand, formerly of the U.S. Census, became food adviser. Irving Shuman, whom Paderewski had employed earlier, acted as counselor on commercial matters. Goodyear and Ferguson were supervising coal mining. The American technical mission, an outgrowth of the ARA, remained in Poland until 1922. On the termination of all American-assisted relief activities, Poland's premier expressed heartfelt thanks to the United States. The Poles, he said, "worship the name of Hoover." A deputy to the sejm declared that "there was never in the history of all the world an equal generosity of one nation to another." As a token of appreciation to the ARA, the Polish government later agreed to transport free of charge American relief supplies to Soviet Russia to help combat starvation in that country.

Some recent historiography, particularly Soviet, has insisted on the political motivation of the American relief activities. Hoover and his associates made the assumption that poverty and hunger bred social unrest and revolutionary upheavals. Although Hoover spoke of a stable Poland holding the "frontline of Europe against Bolshevik invasion," he criticized the Soviet-Polish war as ruinous to Poland and discouraging a flow of credits. Out of American aid to Poland only some 20 percent came under the heading of technical military equipment. Goods sent by the War Department were valued at $13.9 million and those by the Navy Department at $303,000. Roughly $18 million-worth of office equipment, mules, saddles, and sanitary supplies came from governmental sources and $337 thousand-worth from the Service Motor Truck Company. Only the second can be classified as military equipment. American reluctance to send armaments on credit had already been pointed out.

Polish search for private credits and money loans produced minimal results, roughly $8 million. Money loans did not exceed 1 percent of all Polish debts; all the rest were goods send on credit. Thus Poland purchased 160 locomotives from the Baldwin Locomotive Works headed by Samuel Vauclain, who later became the first president of the American-Polish Chamber of Commerce and Industry in the United States. Among other transactions was a contract with the Liberty Steel Products Company to buy merchandise in America and Asia. Some of these operations were economically unsound and reflected the unsettled character of American-Polish economic relations as well as confusion in Polish governmental and business circles. Gibson drily commented on "at least 100 commissions from America all aiming to save Poland," and added, "I somehow wish the cloven dollar mark was not so evident on many of them." Army surpluses were apparently often grossly overpriced.

In spite of its deficiencies, American assistance to Poland was of crucial importance. Out of all foreign credits which the Polish state received from abroad those from the United States constituted 65 percent. Polish total indebtedness to America (including interest) was calculated at the time of the debt-funding agreement in 1924 at $178,560,000. Although badly needed, these credits placed a heavy burden on the Polish economy, especially because Poland could not hope to repay them through its exports to America.

Polish interest in foreign loans was evident already during the war. Dmowski's committee had prepared projects of an international bank to be set up in Switzerland and issuing bonds backed by Polish American capital. At the first meeting of Paderewski's cabinet a resolution called for efforts to obtain an American loan. Paderewski was optimistic about contacts with American financial circles and prophesied "very extensive loans." The main part was to be played by American Poles, and Smulski was all in favor of floating a sizable loan on the American stock market.

In June 1919 the Polish government signed an agreement with Smulski, who himself was president of the North Western Savings Bank, called the Polish Bank, in Chicago. Smulski was to place a $100 million loan at 5 percent interest for a period of five years, with the property and income of the Polish Republic offered as security. Smulski, however, ran into difficulties in trying to finance the undertaking, and in October Paderewski received two highly recommended Americans (John C. O'Laughlin and Philip Patchin), who offered to act on behalf of the People's Industrial

Trading Corporation of the United States. Poland's finance minister then signed an agreement with them on October 27, 1919, granting far-reaching concessions to their corporation, and simultaneously canceled the agreement with Smulski. The operation was to consist of exchanging Polish 6-percent gold dollar bonds for American Victory and Liberty Bonds, and Polish Americans were viewed as the potential buyers.

The State Department and the Treasury opposed the transaction on the grounds that it would depress the market in American bonds and, indeed, Warsaw had acted foolishly in having failed to consult Washington. As for Polish Americans, Smulski and his adherents, supported by the National Democrats in Poland, started a campaign against the proposed loan, accusing Warsaw of selling out to an obscure American corporation headed by a Jew. Worried by the outcry, the Polish envoy, Lubomirski, counseled his government against the agreement, and the Polish government renegotiated the contract without obtaining much better terms. Signed in February 1920, it provided for a $100 million loan, the first issue of $50 million to be placed by the end of June. By going ahead with the scheme, Warsaw was running the risk of compromising this and future loans in the eyes of Polish Americans on whose attitude the success of the loan largely hinged. Warsaw made an all-out effort. Representatives of the Polish right and left were dispatched to propagandize the loan; the famous writer Władysław Reymont went on tour of Polish American centers; Joseph Conrad was induced to send a much-publicized telegram advocating support for the loan. The Polish American clergy was mobilized.

All these efforts notwithstanding, the loan was a failure. Subscriptions began in May and the operation was closed by October 1920, producing only $18.4 million minus commission and operating costs. The value of the bonds systematically declined. Polish Americans had been showing great generosity toward their native land: in 1919-1923 money sent to relatives in the old country was calculated at roughly $170 million, the purchase of stocks in Polish commercial firms at $49 million, and money left by tourists and returning emigrants at $75 million. But the conflicts and squabbles that accompanied the loan disgusted the Polonia and had diverse and far-reaching ramifications. The loan not only threw a shadow on relations between Poland and Polish Americans and disappointed Warsaw; is also adversely affected the United States' attitude toward the Polish state. The People's Industrial Trading Corporation accused the Polish legation in Washington of having slandered the company. It claimed damages for delays in commission payments, and a law suit followed. In Warsaw Gibson protested against Polish criticism alleging delaying tactics of the American administration; Polk sent a sharp note to the Polish legation. The conflict had repercussions on Polish food purchases in America.

American-Polish commercial relations were not developing satisfactorily either. In the first chaotic months following the reemergence of Poland, there were no means of transmitting money from America to Poland nor were there any arrangements for financial transactions or credit operations between American and Polish banks. The American Relief Administration, in collaboration with the Federal Reserve Board, served as a kind of an exchange bureau. During his visit to Poland, Morgenthau suggested to Paderewski the creation of a joint Polish-American-West European corporation with a capital of $150 million to assume responsibility for contracts in cotton and wool. The project may have been connected with an idea Hoover had earlier, to set up a commission of Polish businessmen with the help of local and foreign capital to act as the main Polish buying and selling agency. Apparently these projects had no sequel.

Commercial and financial matters occupied a prominent place in the correspondence between the State Department and the Warsaw legation. The question of remittance of funds and other technical aspects of payment transfers was not resolved until February 1921, when the Polish government empowered the Guaranty Trust Company of New York to act as Poland's agent in the United States. Such delays angered Hoover, who spoke of Polish financial incompetence. No trade agreement existed, and the Poles began only at the turn of 1921 to prepare a project of a commercial convention based on the Most-Favored-Nation clause. The trade turnover in 1920 was minimal from the American point of view. Exports to Poland constituted 0.8 percent of United States exports; imports amounted only to 0.01 percent.

The Years of Parliamentary Ascendancy

The constituent sejm adopted the first Polish constitution on March 17, 1921, roughly two weeks after Harding's inauguration. While America was going back to normalcy, Poland embarked on parliamentary democracy, and once again paid tribute in a moving telegram to the departing Woodrow Wilson. A year later the former president received Poland's highest order of the White Eagle, the only foreign decoration he accepted.

The constitution was largely patterned on that of France, the American model having been considered and rejected. Based on a division of powers, it made the lower chamber of the parliament, the sejm, the center of authority. The cabinet was dependent on parliamentary majority, and the president, elected by the two chambers, was largely a figurehead. The system was at least partly devised to prevent Piłsudski from exercising real power, and in response he disdainfully refused to be a candidate for the presidential office. Since the electoral law passed in July 1921 maintained proportional suffrage, the November 1922 elections again produced a proliferation of political parties ranging from right to left. The right was dominated by the National Democrats, fanatically opposed to Piłsudski, strongly nationalistic, anti-Semitic, and socially conservative. The center consisted mainly of the Populist party called Piast and lesser groups. Torn by conflicting trends, it could not easily act as a moderating force in Polish politics. The left was made up of the Polish Socialist party (PPS) and another Populist party called Wyzwolenie (Liberation). The split in the peasant movement prevented it from asserting itself as the numerically largest element in Poland. The national minorities combined in a powerful bloc that disposed of 20 percent of all seats. The Communist party of Poland (KPRP or KPP) had refused to register and remained a clandestine organization, but a few deputies represented its interests in the sejm. They never gained more than a few percent of the total vote.

No single group commanded a majority and there had to be multiparty governments. Given the obvious right-left incompatibility, only center-right or center-left coalitions could be formed, but even so the Populist center differed from the National Democrats and their conservative allies on social grounds; it distrusted the Socialists as demagogues and potential allies of Piłsudski. These deep-seated antagonisms reached their dramatic climax with the presidential elections of December 1922. After complex maneuvers, the candidate of Populist Wyzwolenie, Gabriel Narutowicz, was chosen president with the support of the national minorities. Savagely attacked by the right as a "Jewish-elected" president, Narutowicz was assassinated by a mentally unbalanced nationalist fanatic; Poland found itself on the brink of a civil war.

The murder of the first president of reborn Poland was a shock to the whole nation, and a nonparty cabinet led by General Władysław Sikorski took stern measures to maintain order. Stanisław Wojciechowski was elected the new president by the same majority as Narutowicz. Political tensions remained and combined with severe economic difficulties. Continuing inflation and deficits posed a serious threat and, given the internationally precarious situation, military expenditure still absorbed 30 to 40 percent of the budget. At first, inflation had some advantages. It helped to lower the cost of production and made Polish exports more competitive. Unemployment diminished and wages increased; in the countryside, the peasants were able to repay loans and mortgages more rapidly. With favorable world prices for agrarian products, both landowners and peasants began to fare better. Yet the inflation soon spiraled into hyperinflation and prices rose more quickly than the ratio between the Polish currency and the dollar.

In another area of latent trouble and conflict the figure of Piłsudski loomed large. The highest-ranking Polish officer—he had been named marshal in 1920—was regarded by many as the father of Polish independence; he occupied a lofty and unique place, and his views and policies could not be ignored. To assure that his beloved army would not be affected by partisan politics and preserved an autonomous position, Piłsudski had set up a system that placed the army outside the cabinet's control. As long as he personally remained minister of war the system functioned, but under the new constitution it was bound to come under attack. Matters came to a head in 1923, when a right-center coalition cabinet presided over by Witos came into power, and Piłsudski refused his collaboration. The marshal resigned all his functions and withdraw to his country home in Sulejówek near Warsaw.

The right-center coalition took over the government when the economic situation was getting out of hand. Inflation assumed staggering proportions. In 1922 one dollar equalled 17,803 Polish marks; by August 1923 it stood at 231,260, and reached the astronomical figure of 2,300,000 in December. Prices rose faster than the monetary inflation, and export ceased to be profitable. Credit became scarce. The social consequences of this situation were severe; the left was anyway already critical of the coalition's program in social matters and its attitude toward national minorites. The land reform was stalled; the emphasis put on the Polish character of the state sounded ominous to Ukrainians and Belorussians, especially as it was accompanied by utterances about a more nationalist policy in eastern parts of Poland. The Jews became alarmed by the prospect of *numerus clausus* (restrictive quota) at universities where the number of Jewish students exceeded their general percentages in the country.

Unrest in eastern Poland, fed by incursion of bands from Soviet Russia, became serious. Ukrainian militancy assumed wider proportions, which worried Gibson, since the State Department came upon evidence of anti-Polish Ukrainian activities in America and some mysterious links with American oil interests. This was highly embarrassing to Washington. Workers' strikes and riots erupted, particularly in Cracow in November 1923 where troops had to intervene. The cabinet lost its parliamentary majority and resigned in December 1923.

In the area of international relations, the Second Republic had concluded the two basic alliances with France and Rumania in 1921. The policy of the foreign ministers—Gabriel Narutowicz, Konstanty Skirmunt, and Count Aleksander Skrzyński—strove to demonstrate Poland's desire for peace and international cooperation. Skirmunt succeeded in relaxing tensions with Czechoslovakia and bringing Poland closer to the Little Entente. In connection with the Genoa Conference of 1922, which had met to deal with European economic reconstruction, Skirmunt and Paderewski vainly argued for some American cooperation as well as for a United States acceptance of Warsaw's view that in Eastern Europe Poland rather than Russia was of major political interest to America. An unexpected by-product of the Genoa Conference was the famous German-Soviet Treaty of Rapallo, which appeared as a serious threat to Poland. With clandestine military cooperation between Russia and Germany, the Second Republic could become most vulnerable. The only gain registered in 1923 was the official recognition of the Riga frontier by the Conference of Ambassadors on March 15, 1923. The United States confirmed it on April 5, apparently regarding it as a routine matter.

During the life of the Witos cabinet, the foreign ministry was briefly held by Dmowski. This was the only time he was a cabinet member, a fact that naturally raised many conjectures. Why did Dmowski avoid making a bid for power? The question cannot be fully treated here, but it seems that Dmowski strove above all for spiritual leadership of the nation, and particularly wished to mold the younger generation in accord with his philosophy rather than dissipating his energies in daily political strife. Already at this point Dmowski began to show some interest in the Italian Fascist model of government. As foreign minister he left no imprint on Polish diplomacy, which had to face a difficult international situation resulting from the French occupation of the Ruhr in 1923. It was up to the next cabinet to deal with all the multiple consequences of this crisis.

The new, nonparty cabinet headed by Władysław Grabski concentrated on economic reforms. The objective was to halt inflation and stabilize the currency by new property taxes, a raise in railroad tariffs, and cuts in state expenditure. For the first time receipts exceeded expenses. Grabski then moved on to create Bank Polski in April 1924 as a central national bank of issue. The newly introduced unit of currency, the *złoty,* was covered by gold and foreign and domestic securities and fixed to the dollar at a 5.18 to 1 ratio. In July 1925 the sejm passed the final land reform act providing for an annual parceling out of 200,000 hectares by private landowners, voluntarily under state supervision and compulsorily if the process did not move well. Until then some 750,000 hectares had been parceled out. With regard to national minorities, the government negotiated an agreement with the Jews whereby they declared their attachment to the principle of Poland's territorial integrity and received pledges for satisfaction of their grievances in educational, cultural, and economic matters.

Grabski's reforms, favorably reported by American ministers in Warsaw, ran into opposition from several quarters, notably the so-called Lewiatan (The Central Association of Polish Industry, Mining, Trade and Finance). The propertied classes felt that as a result of Grabski's fiscal policies they bore the heaviest burden in the state economy. In 1925 the country was severely hit by a tariff war with Germany. The production of coal fell off and the złoty was endangered. Throughout his tenure in office Grabski felt that his domestic reforms required a boost in the form of foreign loans and investments, but early overtures to the house of Morgan were unsuccessful, and talks with Hallgarten and Company inconclusive. Although some foreign credits were obtained, the Poles looked to the greatest financial power of the world, the United States.

Harding's administration had no vision of world affairs, and the president, as an American historian put it, "when he thought at all he thought in stereotypes." The able Secretary of State C. E. Hughes favored limited involvement in European affairs but had to steer a cautious course, especially because the Congress desired to regain the influence it had lost to Wilson. Consequently the United States was cool toward attempts to put teeth into the Covenant of the League of Nations in the form of the abortive Draft Treaty of Mutual Assistance of 1923, or the Geneva Protocol of 1924. Collecting the debts the Allies owed to America—in 1925 the United States held over \$22 billion in foreign obligations including war debts— preoccupied Washington and the country. But a vigorous and liberally conceived economic plan on a global scale was wanting. Even worse, new high tariffs reflected ignorance of the simple fact that European debtors could only pay if they were able to export to the United States. New immigration laws greatly restricting the flow of immigrants from poorer European countries, Poland included, added a burden to their economies. Simultaneously, American business insisted on an open door for American products and capital, in a somewhat naive belief that economic expansion took precedence over foreign policies. Only a small if articulate minority in the United States insisted that a world power could abdicate its international leadership and responsibility at the world's and its own peril.

There were differences of opinion in Washington about foreign loans and investments. Secretary of Commerce Hoover believed in governmental controls. The State Department considered advisability of loans from the point of view of the national interest, and the Treasury thought first of the connection to war debts. In 1922 a Debt Commission was created to supervise the funding of debts into long-range obligations, and until such arrangements were made —the Polish debt was funded on November 14, 1924—no government funds were available for loans. As for private loans, the Ruling of 1922 provided, much to Hoover's annoyance, only for general governmental supervision. This meant in practice a vetoing of loans to countries that were either unrecognized by the United States (Soviet Russia) or continued in default of payment of war debts.

Hoover's department actively promoted American commercial expansion and so did some of the United States diplomatic envoys, for example Gibson in Warsaw. Invoking Polish desires for a commercial agreement as leverage, the minister acted on behalf of American business firms dealing with Poland and between 1922 and 1924 lodged several protests against alleged discrimination of American businessmen. In some instances, as in the matter of the United States Lines, Washington eventually proved more accommodating than its representative. The balance of trade continued to be unfavorable for Poland. During the 1922–1924 period the value of American imports to Poland rose by 40 percent, that of Polish exports only by 16 percent. The United States ranked as the second largest importer after Germany, but Poland occupied only the seventeenth place among importers to America. The United States exported mainly corn, flour, edible fats, fertilizers, and later on, machinery. From Poland came foodstuffs, timber, and furs. The draft of an American-Polish commercial treaty was worked out in late 1924 and notes on a Most-Favored-Nation treatment exchanged in February 1925. A full-fledged treaty was to come six years later.

The first attempts by the Grabski government to obtain American loans took place within a complex context. The only recent American credits came from the Service Motor Truck, Baltic American Line, and the Radio Corporation of America and totaled about $720,000. Warsaw hoped to be able to capitalize on its domestic stabilization to obtain larger sums and to attract significant American capital. In early 1924 Grabski mentioned the figure of $400 to 500 million and asked Paderewski to sound out American circles. International problems, however, stood in Poland's way. One of them was the French victory over Germany in the Ruhr affair of 1923, which backfired mainly because of American and British financial pressures on Paris. Fearful lest French policies alienate and impoverish Germany and push it into Russian arms, the Dawes Plan was worked out to stabilize the German economy and provide a working system of reparation payments. Under the slogan "business, not politics," the American-inspired Dawes Plan in fact separated the issue of security from that of war reparations. Moreover, while providing for Allied-supervised German payments, it granted huge credits to the Weimar Republic. Between 1924 and 1930 American loans to Germany totaled $1,430,250,000, constituting two-thirds of the foreign credits that Germany received, and 18 percent of American export of capital.

The United States' vested interest in Germany could be ominous for the Poles. A gigantic buildup of Germany might promote its eastward expansion, or at least economic penetration. The beginnings of the German-Polish economic war in the summer of 1925 increased Polish fears. Economics went hand in hand with politics, and a German revisionist campaign encouraged the belief held in international financial circles that Polish possession of Upper Silesia and the "Corridor" stood in the way of a genuine stabilization of postwar Europe.

American-Polish economic exchanges in late 1924 took various forms. They concerned the trade agreement and the funding agreement mentioned before, a proposal by the American firm of Ulen and Company to advance $10 million in credits to a number of Polish cities, and an attempt to float a sizable loan in the United States. The agreement with Ulen signed in November 1924 provided for communal investments in four cities to which six others were added in July 1926. The terms of the loan were onerous—8 percent interest and 15 percent commission—the credit took the form of bonds issued by the Bank Polski and floated by Ulen in the United States. The execution of the constructions raised multiple problems, but the Poles had to go along, partly to encourage future foreign contracts, partly to alleviate the problem of unemployment through public works.

A Polish loan in the United States handled by the banking firm of Dillon, Read and Company was a much bigger and more ambitious undertaking. Clarence D. Dillon was, in the words of Stanton Griffis, "the greatest financier of our times," and his firm had ties to the house of Morgan. Attempts to interest Dillon in Poland, as one undertaken by Vauclain of the Baldwin Locomotive Works, went back to 1922, but conditions had been unfavorable. The Department of Commerce was informing potential investors that although the Poles offered the highest available interest, "due precaution" was necessary given Poland's inflation, industrial stagnation, and trade deficits. By 1924 the domestic scene changed, and Poland made a successful arrangement with American brokers to place the unsold $3.5 million of the 1920 loan. The main broker involved, Paul Klopstock, then succeeded in arousing Dillon's interest. In December 1924 the financier proposed a $25 million figure which the Poles rejected as too small, and after further talks the Polish government signed an agreement with Dillon in January 1925 for an 8 percent loan for investment purposes to be amortized in twenty years. Although the agreement spoke of $50 million, only $35 million were floated and Poland eventually netted $21 million. The conditions were not harsh, but extensive securities had to be provided by Poland, including pledges not only of existing railroad lines but of those to be constructed in the future.

The Poles went out of their way to cultivate Dillon and appointed him Poland's official banker. In turn, he declared that it was his ambition to be associated with a "great and famous nation" and to make it "recover its due place of a great power." Before floating the loan, Dillon, Read and Company publicly stated their belief that Poland was "a permanent part of the political structure of Europe," and that its territorial integrity was "not open to reasonable question." On the surface at least, the loan was a first sign of interest that American financial circles showed in Poland, but there were also shadows. Polish diplomats and economic historians regarded with some suspicion the alleged inability of Dillon to place the entire loan, as well as the delays that accompanied the operation. The quick decline of the bonds' value on the stock exchange also seemed to indicate a lack of determination to make the loan a success. Dillon's insistence on having a monopoly of all Polish loans to be floated in America raised doubts concerning his motives. Did Dillon, whose involvement with German investments was considerable, wish to limit credits to Poland so as to facilitate Germany's economic pressure on Warsaw?

The Polish agreement with Dillon preceded by a few weeks the proposal made by Germany's foreign minister Gustav Stresemann for a security pact in Western Europe. Seeking to stabilize the status quo on the German-French and German-Belgian borders under British and Italian guarantees, the proposal left open the question of Germany's eastern borders. Embodied eventually in the treaties of Locarno of October 1925, the western security scheme made Poland more vulnerable and weakened the French system of eastern alliances to which Warsaw attached basic importance. Poland was alarmed by the German proposal and Foreign Minister Skrzyński sought to counter their move by deciding in March 1925 to look for support in the United States. The Polish envoy in Washington, Władysław Wróblewski, opposed the trip, which turned out to be the only such visit by a Polish foreign minister in the entire interwar period.

Skrzyński believed that all existing international and domestic European problems were in the final analysis due to financial preoccupations. The United States held the key to world finance and, although it emphasized its aloofness from European politics, it was bound to determine them. While the Franco-British-German security talks were going on, Skrzyński wanted to explain the Polish position to Washington and gain American moral support. This involved counteracting anti-Polish propaganda, improving Poland's image, and strengthening the ties with Polish Americans. He also wished to encourage further American credits to his country.

The Poles had made several efforts to revive the wartime pro-Polish feelings in America. The sejm eulogized Wilson after his death; in June 1925, Colonel House received an honorary degree from Poznań University and later a monument was erected to honor him. Articles such as one by Herbert Feis in *Foreign Affairs* of July 1925, which predicted an increase of American investments in East Central Europe and linked the security of loans with "the success of the League of Nations in its task of maintaining international peace," sounded encouraging. But the recurrent criticism of the western Polish borders and remarks about the "Corridor" and Upper Silesia as unjustly taken from Germany caused anxiety.

The State Department suggested that Skrzyński's visit be centered on the July session at the Institute of Politics in Williamstown, Massachusetts, a prestigious institution often visited by prominent Europeans. This meant that the foreign minister would not come as an official guest of the government, and indeed the invitation to Skrzyński was signed by Harry A Garfield, the president of Williams College and of the institute. Skrzyński's visit thus became a public relations mission in which his personality would play a considerable part. The foreign minister, a nonparty man with a broad moderate liberal outlook, had many assets as a diplomat, and the American envoy reported from Warsaw that he was regarded as a very capable man with a forceful personality. With an apprenticeship in prewar Austrian foreign service, speaking fluent English, Skrzyński had engaging manners although his shyness occasionally produced *gaucheries* or took the form of haughty coolness.

Skrzyński sailed into New York on July 15, 1925, and remained in America until the first week of August. His contacts with the administration were limited. He had lunch with President Coolidge at White Court in Swampscott, Massachusetts, he may have seen Secretary Kellogg, and he did call on Undersecretary Joseph Grew. Skrzyński's comments on Coolidge understanding "us and our problems" sounded a little hollow, as did his report to Warsaw that the president was showing interest in European problems and that Polish policy could count on some American support. In fact, Coolidge strongly supported the security talks then going on in Europe as a welcome indication of the European states' resolve to tackle their own problems without involving America. Kellogg had already told the Polish envoy that the United States could not associate itself with any security pact and must be completely neutral toward boundary disputes.

The foreign minister displayed great activity. He made 19 speeches and gave 18 interviews. He was the guest of honor at a luncheon at the Century Club, given by the editor of *Forum* and presided over by the chairman of the Foreign Policy Association. He visited such great Polish American centers as Chicago and Detroit and met with a delegation of the American Jewish Congress, which expressed its gratification with the recent Polish-Jewish agreement. In this connection the *New York Times* commented that it was a good thing that the Poles had made amends to Jews for wrongs that "had created such bad feelings among Jewish financiers that Poland was finding it difficult to obtain credits." In his public speeches and interviews, Skrzyński stressed the indivisibility of European security and inviolability of Polish borders. Without the inclusion of Poland the European security talks could not bring lasting solutions. The minister rejected the accusations of Polsh militarism, defended the "Corridor," and emphasized recent achievements tending toward a stabilization of his country.

Skrzyński expressed Polish gratitude to America, denied that the United States immigration laws were harmful for the Polish economy, and refused to call the German-Polish conflict an "economic war." His references to Polish needs for American loans were tactful and he chose a low key approach. The matter of credits was of course very important, and prior to Skrzyński's visit the Bank Polski had reached an agreement with the Irving Bank and Trust Company for a $6 million loan secured by a gold deposit made by the Poles in Warsaw. The representative of Bank Polski, Feliks Młynarski, was then in the United States talking to Dillon and attempting to obtain credits from the Federal Reserve Bank. In the absence of its head, Governor Benjamin Strong, his deputy J. H. Case agreed to a $10 million loan for the purpose of sustaining the złoty. Whether this success was due entirely to Młynarski or whether Skrzyński could claim some credit is not quite clear. Skrzyński also talked about finances with the State Department, the Secretary of Treasury Andrew W. Mellon, and with prominent financiers at a luncheon given by Dillon at the India House. Although the Pole went out of his way to captivate Dillon, whom he decorated with the Grand Cross of Polonia Restituta, the prospects of obtaining a second part of the loan were dim. Skrzyński's remarks about the American "enviable privilege to be able to use some of this great [financial] influence for the development of universal prosperity and for the noble purpose of eliminating war" may or may not have impressed the financiers.

The climax of the visit came on July 30 and 31, when Skrzyński addressed the session in Williamstown on "American and Polish Democracy" and on "American Policy toward Europe." It was unfortunate, although probably accidental, that his speech was overshadowed by an address by William R. Castle of the State Department, which was regarded as an official statement of the policy of the Coolidge administration toward Europe. Castle characterized this policy as "helpfulness without impertinent interference; cooperation without entanglement; avoidance of promises which cannot be fulfilled and the scrupulous fulfillment of engagements." He made it clear that although the United States approved of the forthcoming security pact in Europe, it would not be party to it. "We cannot guarantee to protect by force the frontiers of different nations," he said, nor "become embroiled in political matters of purely European interest." Castle denied that Washington was rigid in the matter of foreign debts or was an exigent creditor. As for new loans, the administration was advising bankers about making loans consistent with American policy. It was, for example, a matter of policy that "we object to loans for building up armament."

After Castle's remarks, Skrzyński's task was doubly difficult: to make Poland's problems relevant for an administration that wanted to stay clear of European squabbles altogether. Skrzyński placed Polish issues in a wider context of postwar Europe, which he characterized as full of uncertainty, aggressiveness, and the menacing presence of two major ideologies: nationalism and communism. The victory of either of them he said, was likely to lead to war and the ruin of Europe—prophetic words. Skrzyński voiced his hope in democracy as the only alternative and spoke of an "Americanization of Europe in its fullest and noblest sense." He spoke of American moral influence and recalled that the Monroe Doctrine did not only stand for a hands-off policy but symbolized a refusal to deal with absolutism and reaction. Although the press oversimplified his address, the headline "Skrzynski says changes in Europe warrant United States giving up 'hands off' policy" roughly summarized his plea for American involvement.

Attempting a brief discussion of Polish historic evolution in terms of democracy and liberty, Skrzyński pointed to Germany and Russia and to nationalism and communism. "Wedged between the most powerful centers of these forces what course can Polish democracy adopt?" And he replied: "It can find salvation only in the inspiring ideal of that unique, essential, and powerful democracy the United States represents today." In subsequent remarks Skrzyński spoke again about Pax Americana and his hopes for a United States of Europe.

Whatever positive effect Skrzyński's speeches may have had, they promptly provoked rejoinders. The press quoted the Italian statesman, Francesco Nitti, who criticized the existence of the "Corridor", and reprinted the *Berliner Tageblatt's* attack on Skrzyński's position. The German ambassador in Washington, who spoke in Williamstown shortly thereafter, denied hostile German intentions against Poland but made it clear that the issue of Upper Silesia was "not settled." Ukrainian attacks on Skrzyński's description of Poland as a democracy were given ample space in the *Boston Transcript*.

The Polish press commented enthusiastically on Skrzyński's visit, perhaps partly for domestic reasons. A Polish historian calculated that Skrzyński's speeches appeared in 3,200 papers, but that indicates rather the existence of syndicated columns than a wide coverage. The *New York Times* once put a Skrzyński item on the fifth page; generally news concerning his visit were buried on pages 15 to 17. Skrzyński's speech was not reprinted in *Foreign Affairs,* unlike some others by prominent Europeans who spoke at Williamstown. The foreign minister's efforts and skill seem undeniable, and bitter criticism of his activities by F. Cunliffe Owen in a letter to Paderewski appears largely dictated by spite. Still Skrzyński could hardly have achieved any concrete results, for the views of the administration ran counter to Polish objectives, and the American mood was well expressed in a contemporary journalist's doggerel:

> The French are afraid of the Germans
> The Germans are mad at the Poles,
> And Latin America thinks Uncle Sam
> Is exploiting their bodies and souls
>
> We thought that democracy, peace and
> Good will,
> Had come to the dear human race
> But judging by all that we can recall
> The world is a . . . of a place.

While conscious of American disenchantment with Europe, the Poles were convinced that their lack of success in the United States stemmed from inimical German actions. Indeed, in a circular to missions abroad, Stresemann had written in June 1925 that it was essential to convince the world that German-Polish borders could not endure. This was not to be said openly but in private such opinions had to be expressed. The road to a revision of the German-Polish border led through an economic collapse of Poland. Berlin was seeking to end the economic war with Warsaw, but on terms that would greatly increase Poland's economic dependence on Germany. Simultaneously, it sought to discredit Poland in the West, undermine Polish attempts to obtain financial assistance without strings attached, and link the issue of loans to Poland with that of territorial revision. The German ambassador in Washington kept telling the State Department officials that Skrzyński's visit "spoke volumes for the poor economic condition of the country." His colleague in London exchanged views with the American ambassador on the alleged ruin of former German industry in lands transferred to Poland. Skrzyński complained bitterly to the German minister in Warsaw that hostile German propaganda accompanied his every step in the United States.

Developing German economic cooperation with Washington and London caused Stresemann to speculate about the possibility of an Anglo-American-German trust. Several Polish diplomats feared as much and believed that Britain sought to pull Poland away from France and subject it to German economic expansion. It seemed logical to some Polish diplomats and later to economic historians that the American buildup of the German industrial complex, in connection with the Dawes Plan, had to entail projections for a market for German goods. Surely the Anglo-Saxon powers were not interested in making Germany more competitive with themselves; hence German expansion would have to be directed eastward.

The Polish economic scene darkened in the second half of 1925 and a gradual collapse of the złoty necessitated governmental interventions. The $10 million American loan had been used to maintain monetary stability but more was needed. Dillon proved unwilling to activate the second part of his loan, and it was up to Strong of the Federal Reserve Bank to take the initiative. Large issues were at stake. Stresemann wrote that "whether Poland will receive further American loans will be decisive to her economic future," and he may have added political future, for internationally the Polish position looked bad.

In October 1925 the Locarno treaties were signed and, although France concluded new security accords with Poland and Czechoslovakia, the system of French eastern alliances was severely shaken. Stabilization in the West contrasted with insecurity in the East. As a member of the Franco-British-German triumvirate Stresemann became one of the leaders of Europe. Within Poland the pressures on the government led to Grabski's resignation, and Skrzyński became both premier and foreign minister in November. To avoid international isolation, Skrzyński had to go along, albeit reluctantly, with the new Locarno system; in internal matters deflationary policies were adopted that produced a strain in the relations with the Socialists, who objected to burdens falling on the working class.

The Polish search for a foreign loan was thus taking place under difficult conditions. The United States attitude was uncertain. Although basically pleased with Locarno, American diplomats felt that it did not resolve all questions and the open issue of the German-Polish frontier might lead to another war. To avoid it, European disarmament seemed the best course of action. Strong, cooperating closely with Montague Norman of the Bank of England and Hjalmar Schacht of the Reichsbank, listened to their arguments for an internationally supervised stabilization plan for Poland involving an internationally subscribed loan. The machinery of the League of Nations, through which Britain would have had a decisive say, was considered but the Poles politely declined such an arrangement.

After consultation with Dillon, Strong suggested that an American expert be sent to Poland to study the situation and formulate recommendations. Personally, Strong had a low opinion of Poles as businessmen, criticized the lack of coordination among Polish officials, and felt there were too many private bankers seeking Polish business. Professor E. W. Kemmerer of Princeton University was chosen. A former member of the Dawes Committee with wide experience in international finance and a consultant of Dillon and Read, he seemed to be an impartial and trustworthy expert whose views Washington could take seriously.

Kemmerer visited Poland during the Christmas season of 1925 and came back with recommendations. He suggested stabilizing the złoty at 9 to the dollar and urged outside credits of at least $15 million. He recommended austerity measures and "better publicity for Poland abroad," as well as different practices for the Bank Polski. The German press voiced criticism of Kemmerer's mission, and in early 1926 Schacht argued that a stabilization loan was useless unless the Poles balanced their budget and that could only be achieved by a reduction of their military expenditures and a commercial agreement with Germany. These conditions were impossible for Poland to meet. Stresemann informed his ambassador in London that his real objective was "to postpone the final and lasting stabilization of Poland until that country will be ripe for the settlement of the border question according to our wishes." Norman of the Bank of England seconded Schacht, appealing to financiers not to make any loans to Poland and promoting the idea of supervision by the League of Nations, which project raised the possibility of linking financial assistance with border revision.

Warsaw renewed its efforts in Washington. The Poles said they were not opposed to foreign advice, as evidenced by the Kemmerer mission, but could not follow the approach advocated by Schacht and Norman. Strong, who seemed to have moved away from the Norman-Schacht perspective and closer to the views of Emile Moreau, governor of the Banque de France, began to appreciate the Polish position. The French made their point, and the English government came to think that one ought not to link financial and territorial questions. The new American envoy in Poland, John B. Stetson, Jr., showed himself fully in accord with the Polish stand vis-à-vis Berlin and sharply criticized the anti-Polish activities of Germany.

Before the negotiations for a stabilization loan entered their final phase, a dramatic event took place in Poland that altered the course of its interwar history. In early May, Skrzyński's cabinet resigned and the new right-center coalition ministry headed by Witos was overthrown on May 12, by a coup staged by Piłsudski. He became the real master of the country. Although the event did not represent a turning point in American-Polish relations, its significance for Poland was such that it must be treated as a beginning of a new and distinct period.

Poland under Piłsudski

Piłsudski's coup d'état ended the era of parliamentary ascendancy. The new regime was at first a mixture of parliamentarianism and governmental domination and evolved later closer to an authoritarian model. The weaknesses of the past system were obvious. Until 1926 there had been no less than ten cabinets, either based on shaky coalitions or formed outside the party constellation. The right, the center, and the left all suggested constitutional changes to assure greater stability. The powers of the president needed strengthening, and the right and center also favored an increased role for the senate. There were demands for changes in the electoral law and the right sought to restrict numerically the representation of national minorities. A growing disillusionment with parliamentary democracy was noticeable, and Dmowski for one admitted that if Poland had a Mussolini he would not be against a dictatorship.

Piłsudski's position rendered the growing constitutional crisis particularly acute. Ever since his withdrawal, the marshal opposed projects to subordinate the army to political controls and in strong, even vulgar language ridiculed them as an assault on the army's "moral interests." He also believed the projects were designed to prevent his return to the army command. Piłsudski could count on fanatical devotion of the former legionary officers, now disgruntled, who in November 1925 staged a demonstration placing their swords at the marshal's disposal. A second center of opposition comprised the Socialists and the leftist Populists, who still thought of Piłsudski as a man of the left, and accused the right of harboring fascist designs. They denounced alleged government corruption, capitalist exploitation, and low public morality of the state apparatus. The dissatisfaction of national minorities, although not a crucial factor, was also real. An autonomous regime in Eastern Galicia, provided by a law in 1922, had not been implemented. Right-center governments encouraged colonization of the eastern borderlands by Polish settlers which provoked fresh outbursts of Ukrainian terror. The Belorussians were goaded into opposition by nationalist measures in education. The government's only successful venture in the area of relations with national minorities was the 1925 agreement with the Jews, but even so, Jewish sympathies lay clearly with Piłsudski and his camp.

A crisis was at hand. After Skrzyński's resignation, it was hastened by an ill-advised decision of the president to name a new cabinet headed by Witos, who launched reckless verbal attacks against Piłsudski. The marshal took up the challenge and on May 12, 1926, accompanied by troops loyal to him, marched into Warsaw. Most likely he envisaged an armed demonstration that would force President Wojciechowski, his old friend and colleague, to dismiss the cabinet and associate Piłsudski in a thorough reorganization of the state. Wojciechowski, however, refused to yield to pressure. It was a paradoxical situation. Piłsudski was amazed that he had to fight the president; the latter was shocked that the marshal had resorted to an illegal action; both Piłsudski and Witos were taken by surprise by the unexpected rigidity of Wojciechowski.

The brief but bloody combat that ensued bore the marks of improvisation and Piłsudski's cause was assisted by the railroad strike proclaimed by the Socialists. Even the Communists took the marshal's side, and their stand gave rise to a long controversy within the party about the "mistake of 1926." After two days of fighting, Wojciechowski dismissed the cabinet and resigned from the presidency. The transfer of power to the new regime was carried out by the speaker of the sejm, the Populist Maciej Rataj, who in accord with the constitution had assumed supreme authority in the country.

Piłsudski's Poland could have been based on two alternatives. One was the creation of a strong political party led by Piłsudski and assuring him a parliamentary majority. With constitutional changes strengthening the position of the president, Piłsudski seemed the natural candidate for that post. The second alternative was a dictatorship. In practice, neither was chosen, and the reason lay both in the complexity of Polish politics and Piłsudski's personality.

The supporters of Piłsudski were no political party in the normal sense of the word. Their slogan of a "moral regeneration" or "cleansing"—*sanacja*—reflected a *Weltanschauung* and a frame of mind rather than a clearcut program. Piłsudski believed firmly that as a result of partitions the Polish people were politically immature and the politicians, immersed in feuds, catered to vested interests. Piłsudski often voiced his almost obsessive suspicion of "foreign agencies." What he meant was that the Poles had learned to rely on foreign influences and had become subservient to foreign interests. Thus, the Socialists were affected by cosmopolitan pacifism, class consideration, and the International; the National Democrats served the French. The somewhat nebulous "Piłsudski ideology" stressed the value and the importance of statehood. The state had long stood for foreign oppression and to sabotage it had been a virtue. Now the people had to be reeducated in their approach toward statehood. Hence, the need for a "moral regeneration" accompanied by a relentless struggle against those who allegedly had either undermined or exploited the state for their own ends. Piłsudski himself was a puritan in financial matters, but his opponents had hardly been crooks. Sanacja's search for the corrupt politicians and embezzlers of state funds proved disappointing. There had been a few irregularities or transgressions but no real corruption.

To translate Piłsudski's ideas into practical politics was no easy task. By nature an autocrat, who had been attacked and reviled and had aged prematurely, Piłsudski became a bitter, suspicious, and solitary figure. He denied plans for establishing a dictatorship on the Mussolini model, and said that he "would try to see whether one could still govern Poland without a whip." But he showed his contempt for the parliament and told the deputies that the sejm and senate were among the most hated institutions in the country. He sought to accomplish his objectives by legal methods but would not shrink from using force. Piłsudski had a strong belief in his mission, and may have shared on occasion Margrave Wielopolski's belief that one could do something for the Poles but nothing with the Poles. His mental outlook, his belief in Poland's grandeur, and some of his policies are reminiscent of Charles de Gaulle, as the German historian, Hans Roos, has pointed out so well. It was Piłsudski's tragedy that he felt obliged to resort to force, which he strongly believed to be counterproductive in public life.

Piłsudski disenchanted the left by refusing to share with it the fruits of victory, and gradually drove it into bitter opposition. The National Democrats he weakened, especially by winning over the conservative landowners (the famous visit to Radziwiłłs' castle at Nieśwież) and some big industrialists. Indeed, Piłsudski believed that the old historic elite was more "state-conscious" than other groups and could be profitably enlisted for Poland's service.

In spite of original promises to hold general elections, it suited the cabinet, headed by Kazimierz Bartel, to deal with the same sejm, confused, chastened, and split. Piłsudski allowed it to elect him president of the republic and then refused the office saying that he had merely wished for a legalization of his coup d'état. His chosen candidate for presidency, Professor Ignacy Mościcki, was then elected and the presidential powers extended by a constitutional amendment of August 2, 1926. Bartel's ministry operated on the general assumption that good government meant cooperation among technocratic experts, theoretical advisers from the academic world, and informed and articulate interest groups. To govern was to implement policies, and the role of the parliament was to exercise general supervision and periodically voice approval or disapproval of these policies. This was not what the political representatives in the parliament believed their function to be.

The followers of Piłsudski organized a movement called the Nonpartisan Bloc of Cooperation with the Government (BBWR or BB). If grouped a wide spectrum of people holding different views but bound together by their confidence in Piłsudski and subscribing to his general state philosophy. The charismatic powers of the marshal, reinforced by a carefully cultivated image, helped the BBWR to capture the single largest number of seats, but not the majority, in the 1928 elections.

Piłsudski's own position was legally and constitutionally anomalous. He was formally in command of the armed forces and served as minister of war (and twice as premier), but in fact exercised the final authority. The president and the cabinet referred to him for ultimate decisions. Many of his old soldiers from the First Brigade, later known as the Colonels, surrounded him and became the post-1926 ruling elite.

After the coup a certain stability prevailed in the country, although Piłsudski's enemies showed no desire for reconciliation. Dmowski broadened his party through the creation in 1926 of the Camp of Great Poland (OWP), a movement that showed some influences of Italian fascism. Piłsudski sincerely sought to overcome the divisions resulting from the 1926 coup, particularly in the army; there were, however, some arrests and dismissals, although not comparable to purges that usually follow a revolutionary change of government. The marshal himself concentrated his attention on the army and to a lesser extent on foreign policies, leaving a good deal of freedom to the cabinet. Under Bartel that body tried to manage the parliament "without the whip," unless there were a direct challenge to the government. A complex series of maneuvers and countermaneuvers ensued. With regard to national minorities, attempts were made toward a liberalization of policies in the eastern parts of the country, and Bartel warned the school authorities that brutal polonization was self-defeating and reprehensible. The occasional and tacit practice of the anti-Jewish restrictive quota at schools of higher education was officially forbidden in 1927. But there was no sweeping program of winning over the national minorities.

The economic situation improved, including the balance of payments, but not so much because of the policies of the post-1926 regime. Already at the beginning of 1926 there were signs of economic recovery connected partly with the general return of European prosperity, partly resulting from the English coal strike, which opened new markets for Polish coal. Ill effects of the economic war with Germany were becoming offset by a reorientation of Polish trade. The new government initiated no strikingly original plans and Piłsudski himself had scant knowledge of and little interest in economic matters. Conscious of the need for foreign credits, the government sought to attract them through a four-stage program: first, to continue previous efforts to attract foreign capital; second, to balance the budget (which was achieved by the end of 1926) and stabilize the currency. Foreign economic experts were to appraise these achievements and express opinions that would reassure the foreign investors. The third objective was to secure a foreign loan so as to create a financial reserve and convince the world of the stability of the złoty. The last step was to launch a campaign to attract foreign, particularly American, capital on a massive scale.

The events of 1926 had no special repercussions on American-Polish relations. Secretary of State Frank Kellogg instructed American minister Stetson to treat the new Polish regime as legitimate, and the envoy assisted at the inauguration of President Mościcki and dealt with the Bartel cabinet. Stetson was in fact quite enthusiastic about Piłsudski who, he felt, had done more than any other Pole for the recreation of the Polish state. As he expressed it, Piłsudski was considered the father of Poland just as Washington was the father of the United States. If Stetson was at first more critical of Piłsudski's entourage, the envoy later revised some of his judgments.

In 1926–1929 and even after, American business circles were showing interest in Poland, although Stetson cautioned Washington that the Poles had much to learn about finances. Unless "they are willing to accept a close cooperation and rigid control," he wrote, "it will be difficult to find safe outlets for American capital in Poland." American financiers, however, were seeking profitable investments, particularly in view of some restrictions on capital movement to Germany, and throughout 1926 there was a good deal of activity. The second Ulen loan was completed; there was a series of visits of private businessmen and talks between the Poles and the Federal Reserve Bank, Harris, Forbes and Company. Negotiations with the director of the Bankers Trust began in connection with a planned tobacco loan. Dillon was less involved; as was rumored, Berlin threatened that if he continued with the second installment of the loan he could not expect to participate in credit operations for Germany.

The largest investment undertaken in 1925–1926 involved W. A.

Harriman. His interest was aroused by zinc production in Poland, which occupied the third place in the world, notably by the concern of Giesche in Katowice, then in danger of being compulsorily bought out by the Polish government for arrears in taxes. As Giesche in Poland was in reality part of Giesches Erben in German Silesia, the issue was politically sensitive. In 1926 Harriman signed an agreement with Poland to form an American company that would buy out the Polish Giesche's shares and invest no less than $10 million, half of the sum to be used for modernization of the mines. An increase in production was anticipated, particularly given the tax benefits that the Polish state granted to the zinc industry. Consequently a Silesian American Corporation (SACO) was set up in which the Anaconda Copper Mining (Rockefeller) and Harriman had majority shares, the rest being held by the German Giesches Erben. SACO obtained control over 20 percent of the world's zinc, and in a private agreement with Giesches Erben gave it monopoly for the sale of Polish zinc, lead and leaden products. The Poles worried that the operation seemed to work mainly to German advantage and complained that two Germans but only one Pole sat on the first board of SACO. By 1929 the SACO operations produced some $12 million, $4.5 of it going to the German concern.

Another venture of Harriman's, jointly with Anaconda and two German firms, was the Consolidated Silesian Steel Corporation, where most of the capital was German. The corporation assumed control over the largest Polish mining and smelting concern, Wspólnota Interesów, which produced half of Poland's iron and 20 percent of its coal. The Poles were unhappy again with what turned out to be a veiled promotion of German interests in Upper Silesia, for Giesche assessed the cooperation with Harriman as "obtaining American protection against the dominant Polish influences in areas which had fallen away from Germany." Harriman's other ventures will be mentioned later, but it is important to signal here his appointment to the largest Polish private bank, the Bank Handlowy in Warsaw, on whose board he remained until the mid-1930s.

Polish efforts to obtain a large loan continued. In July 1926 Kemmerer revisited Poland and prepared a detailed report on its economy and fitness for outside credits. He reemphasized the need of maintaining the rate of the złoty to the dollar and recommended increased production of raw materials and foodstuffs for export. Polish industry, he opined, stood no real chance of developing export capacities. Warsaw worried, for these views seemed to follow the concept of East-West trade in which the East European countries were treated as mere suppliers of agricultural products. There were additional fears lest foreign loans be made conditional on cuts in "unproductive" expenses such as the military.

To the Poles a large loan was important above all as an acknowledgment of Poland's economic soundness, and a green light to potential investors. Negotiations with Bankers Trust led to a preliminary option for a $125 million tobacco loan involving the lease of the tobacco state monopoly. Almost simultaneously, Foreign Minister August Zaleski entered into far-reaching talks with Blair and Company represented by Jean Monnet. The embarrassing situation of double negotiations was resolved by an agreement whereby Bankers Trust gave up its option and combined with Blair and Company and Chase Securities Corporation to undertake a stabilization rather than an investment loan. Blair, with Chase, agreed to be jointly designated as Poland's banker in the place of Dillon and Read who consented to withdraw.

Negotiations for the stabilization loan centered on two interrelated matters. The first was the size and the terms of the loan; the second concerned the recognition by the American, British, German, and French banks of issue of the correctness of the stabilization plan and of Poland's financial policies. In February 1927 a Polish delegation went to New York where it reached an agreement with its American partners and the Federal Reserve Bank to secure a $50 million loan, and to receive an American adviser and an international committee of experts attached to the Bank Polski. John Foster Dulles acted as the legal adviser of banks taking part in the negotiations. The Polish delegates, although less than happy with the arrangement, decided to accept it, thus in a sense placing their government before an accomplished fact. Piłsudski, increasingly critical of the entire stabilization scheme that involved foreign interference, manifested his displeasure by not receiving the delegates, but the government gave its sanction.

The second round involved the banks of issue, and here Strong of America, siding with Moreau of France, rejected the Norman-Schacht scheme of using the machinery of the League of Nations to oversee the loan. The French-American front also prevented the introduction of any political stipulations. Strong opposed, however, a joint Franco-American patronage of the operation, not wishing to tie himself too closely to France and its East European policies but agreed that the Banque de France work out the final details. These resulted in the curtailment of the powers of the American adviser and in the elimination of the international committee of experts. It was also the Banque de France that opened the reserve credit, serving as security, and invited other banks of issue to join the consortium. Consequently a $20 million credit was opened for the duration of a year, the Federal Reserve Bank contributing the largest sum of $5.25 million. The loan itself produced a total of $71,333 million ($62 million and £ 2 million). The American share amounted to $47 million, and the 7 percent bonds were sold mostly in the United States.

On the eve of the signing in October 1927 of the Bond Purchase Agreement, the Loan Agreement, and the Fiscal Agency Compensation Agreement, Piłsudski intervened. He shocked the American representatives by demanding that the American adviser stay clear of political issues, and insisting on a higher price of the bonds, for reasons of national prestige. His success had no effect on the subsequent steady decline of the value of the stabilization bonds— $89.7 in 1928 and $51 in 1932—which, when compared with the fluctuations of other foreign bonds on the New York exchange, may well have reflected a lack of confidence in Polish financial and political stability.

The sums Poland obtained were earmarked for an increase of the capital of Bank Polski, the creation of a treasury reserve, and for assistance of economic development of the country. The stabilization plan called for an increase in state revenue with simultaneous cuts in expenditures, a liquidation of loans from treasury surplus funds, and a strengthening of the autonomy of Bank Polski, which by now had the exclusive right to issue legal tender backed by gold. The American supervisor of the stabilization plan acting as adviser to Bank Polski was Charles Dewey, a former undersecretary of the Treasury. Allegedly in the good graces of Mellon and Hoover, he was not very influential in American financial circles. His chief enemies, however were in Berlin and London. Dewey handled his delicate job well and became popular in Poland. Some friction was of course unavoidable, but serious criticism of the adviser related only to his opposition to certain forms of loans he viewed as unproductive.

Refraining from undue interference with the Polish treasury and staying away from politics, Dewey made strenuous efforts to attract American capital to Poland. The State Department and the legation in Warsaw were critical of his "extravagant promises" of American financial input and suspected Dewey of seeking personal popularity. In a speech given in New York in 1930 and reprinted in the *Wall Street Journal*, Dewey expressed his belief that Poland was "destined to become the chief distributing center for Central Europe and the Near East" and urged American manufacturers and businessmen to meet Europeans' need for foreign capital. Dewey did his best to put Poland on the economic map, but the results were meager. High hopes for a mass influx of American loans and investments in Poland failed to materialize. While more capital was invested it was in the already existing enterprises, and although American interest in the Polish market grew, it was still quite limited.

According to the Federal Reserve Bank, American loans to Poland amounted, on January 1, 1928, to about $132 million, roughly one-sixth of the sum loaned to Germany. Only two larger loans followed thereafter: one advanced in 1928 by the First National Corporation of Boston and another by Stone and Webster and Blodget, Inc. The first was a $10 million loan to the city of Warsaw at 7 percent, the second of $11.2 million to the province of Upper Silesia. In each case only $8 million were issued. As for smaller operations, the Mack Truck Company loaned one million to a township near Łódź with the proviso that the community purchase Mack buses for a quarter of a million dollars. There were inconclusive negotiations with such diverse firms as Dillon, Bankers Trust, and International Telephone and Telegraph Corporation; credits were obtained only from the Irving Trust, and an agreement concluded with Standard Steel Car Corporation for financing the production of railroad cars.

A venture that produced a great deal of controversy and ended in failure was Harriman's ambitious plan of electrification of Poland. It was to cover an area that comprised 35 percent of Poland's population and 21 percent of its area. Proposed in 1929, the plan was tentatively approved by the ministry of public works, but then came under attack by consumers, local producers, and political and military quarters. The press asked whether Poland was to become Harriman's colony, and American diplomats in Warsaw reported Polish concern lest the whole scheme be German-inspired with Harriman acting as a figurehead. Strategic implications of foreign controls in such vital areas as electricity raised serious objections, and in 1930 the government formally rejected Harriman's bid.

To complete the picture a few words need still be said about American investments in Polish oil. Some capital was involved already prior to the First World War, and efforts to increase it were made in the early 1920s. Vacuum Oil Company, Standard Oil of New Jersey, and Standard Nobel were the principal investors, and the last two combined in 1927 to form Standard Nobel Company, which produced in 1933 about 5.6 percent and refined about 14.3 percent of Polish oil. Vacuum then joined forces with Standard to establish a new drilling company in which Harriman was also involved. About 10 percent of European investments of these American firms went into the distribution and marketing of Polish oil.

All in all, American capital in Poland was small by American standards but occupied, from the Polish point of view, an important place in the country's economy. Its concentration in such key branches as zinc, oil, iron smelting and coal mining, textiles and chemical industries further enhanced this importance. American shares in joint stock companies amounted to 22 percent in 1933 and were rated third after French and German. By 1934 German capital dropped to third place. All American investments constituted about 33.6 percent of all foreign capital and occupied first place in the Polish economy. A progressive reduction began in mid-1930, especially after the Polish government bought out Harriman's holdings in Upper Silesia. There was also a decline of shares in the petroleum industry. In retrospect, Washington opined that investments in Poland had not proved "a successful venture." By 1939 American capital dropped to little more than 18 percent and, according to State Department figures, did not exceed $50 million. A Treasury Department census published after the war came up with a figure of $26.8 million owned by American citizens and $33.6 million by corporations controlled in the United States. These assets included interest in controlled enterprises, bullion, currency and deposits, securities receipts and claims, personal property, real property, interest in estates and trusts, and insurance policies. When assets of aliens residing in America and those of corporations controlled abroad were added, the total came to $220.2 million.

Polish feelings about foreign investments were mixed. The Poles needed the capital and found the politically neutral American credits very desirable, but at the same time were displeased with the operations of foreign capitalists (especially the French and the Italians) and the real costs involved. It was not only that the rates of interest were high, but American capital did not raise the productive potential of Poland. The profits were seldom reinvested, no new enterprises were established, and dividends left the country. In 1929, for instance, 411 million złotys worth of dividends and profits were exported—a sizable sum, as the state budget amounted roughly to 2,888,000,000 złotys (one dollar then equaled 11.9 złotys). The funded debt was a serious burden on the economy, and repayments of capital and interest rose from $1 million in 1925 to $3 million in 1929. Prior to the Depression, the Poles made these payments largely out of the incoming foreign credits; later, when the influx of American capital virtually ceased, they were obliged to cover the balance of payments deficit through gold and foreign exchanges. To make matters worse, Poland suffered from a chronically unfavorable balance of trade with the United States. In 1928, for instance, Polish exports to America constituted 0.8 percent and imports from the United States 13.9 percent of the country's total trade. Finally, in political terms Warsaw was always concerned lest American capital serve as a camouflage for German economic expansion.

Let us now turn to the international context of these developments. The Locarno period, between 1926 and 1930, raised high hopes for European stabilization based on French-German reconciliation and the reinstatement of Germany in the counsels of Europe. The United States, and particularly its ambassadors in Berlin and London, encouraged these hopes and showed trust in the Weimar Republic. The British envoy in Berlin noticed the "close sympathy and instinctive understanding between Americans and Germans." Historical writings that questioned German guilt for the First World War and criticized the harshness of Versailles reinforced pro-German feelings. So did a steady flow of tourists to Germany, scholarly exchanges, the activities of American Germans, and financial investments. The State Department, however, began to worry lest payments to private investors jeopardize German reparations and adversely affect war debt payments by Britain and France.

Poland's fears that its interests might be sacrificed for the sake of cooperation between the West and Berlin were not groundless. German revisionism did not abate, and if Locarno had thrown a shadow on German-Russian relations, the 1926 Treaty of Berlin attested to mutual interests of the two giant neighbors of Poland. Polish-Russian relations were cool, and Moscow, sincerely or for propagandistic reasons, represented Piłsudski's return to power as a new threat to its security.

Under the foreign minister, August Zaleski, Poland steered a cautious course. The government sought to increase its security by advocating an eastern Locarno and exerted some pressure on France in that direction, but could not afford to appear as a liability and a burden to Paris. Zaleski tried to cultivate England and Italy, and Piłsudski unsuccessfully attempted to establish direct relations with Stresemann. Aristide Briand of France and Austen Chamberlain of England listened with equanimity to German arguments that real stability could only be achieved with a solution of German-Polish problems. Briand toyed with the idea of an exchange of the "Corridor" for a Polish outlet to the sea through Lithuania, a wild and impossible scheme that the Poles refused to envisage, reiterating that their territory was inviolable. The Second Republic obtained only a semipermanent seat on the Council of the League of Nations in contrast with Germany's position in Geneva. It had to resist French attempts to limit the working of the Franco-Polish alliance. Polish prestige and position suffered by Stresemann's bringing up of the German minority complaints before the League. Attempts to obtain security guarantees in connection with the evacuation of the Rhineland in 1930 proved futile.

American-Polish relations centered in 1928 on the famous Kellogg-Briand Pact for the outlawry of war. A year earlier the Poles had submitted to the League of Nations a project for a general non-aggression pact which, however, foundered on British-French-German opposition. In the spring of 1928 Kellogg submitted to the Locarno powers a plan for the renunciation of war that deftly disposed of Briand's previous initiative for a bilateral Franco-American alliance. The Poles viewed the American project with mixed feelings, for it could ensure neutrality of the United States in the event of a Franco-German war in which Poland would be most likely involved. Warsaw was particularly concerned with two issues: first, the fact that Washington had not included Poland in its original invitation to the powers; second, the possible restrictions the pact might impose on the Franco-Polish military alliance. Zaleski in Warsaw and the new envoy in Washington, Jan Ciechanowski, voiced concern that the United States had stressed the different international status of Germany and of Poland. Kellogg's explanations were not very convincing and the Poles were gratified when, seemingly through Briand's interference, Washington said that Poland would figure among the original signatories provided it accepted the proposed formula.

By late June 1928 Poland, together with other French allies in East Central Europe, was included in the Kellogg-Briand scheme. This less than spontaneous invitation saved Warsaw's face, and the Poles pointed out that after all Poland had been the originator of the plan. Furthermore, it was flattering to participate with other powers in the first major American initiative in the field of international security. As for Polish efforts to obtain assurances that the Kellogg-Briand Pact would not jeopardize the Franco-Polish alliance, it was more or less understood that outlawing war did not abolish the right of self-defense. Much of this was empty verbiage, and Piłsudski for one contemptuously regarded the pact as nothing but a scrap of paper.

American-Polish relations in 1928 seemed cordial. The stabilization plan was entering into operation, and on August 16, 1928, the

United States and Poland signed arbitration and conciliation treaties. To foster better public relations, a group of Polish journalists
visited the United States and an equestrian team from Poland was
invited to the White House. Paderewski came on one of his frequent visits to America, where he met with the president and three
former presidents, and as usual was widely acclaimed. Before the
election of Herbert Hoover, Paderewski was asked to influence the
Polish voters, and they were of great help in the Republican cause.
Hoover's victory evoked favorable comments in the Polish press.
The governmental journals commented that Hoover, as a great
economist, would not neglect Europe and voiced hopes for the decline of isolationism in America. Such articles, partly inspired by
the United States minister, Stetson, found counterparts in friendly
remarks about Poland in American newspapers. In March 1928 the
New York Times had a lengthy editorial commenting most favorably on Piłsudski and his government. The paper stressed Polish
achievements in economics and politics.

Indeed, Poland's economic picture looked quite good. There was
a growth in industrial output and investments corresponding to
general European trends. Unemployment was low and real wages
increased. Although in most areas of production the pre-1914 levels
had not been reached, in some they were surpassed. The Poles were
proud of the rapid transformation of the small fishing village of
Gdynia into a first-rate Baltic harbor, and in contrast to Danzig,
fully under Polish control. Another fast-growing new enterprise was
the chemical industry. A new railroad connection between the
Upper Silesian industrial area and the Baltic was completed. Agriculture prospered with high prices for agrarian products; the parceling out of estates proceeded at the rate foreseen by the land reform. Only toward the end of 1928 the first harbingers of the approaching Great Depression began to appear.

In politics the moderate period of Bartel was coming to its end.
Piłsudski insisted on far-reaching constitutional changes that were
bound to antagonize the parliament. The marshal and the sejm
were set on a collision course; the impeachment of the minister of
treasury, who had transferred public funds to assist in the electoral
campaign of the governmental BBWR, was a foretaste of a serious
crisis. Taking place in the summer of 1929, the affair predated by
a few months the Wall Street crash that opened a new era in America and Europe.

Before examining Polish domestic politics and the country's international situation, it is necessary to draw attention to the impact
the Depression had on Poland's economy. Few countries were hit

as badly by the crisis as Poland, where the Depression began in 1929, reached bottom in 1932, and continued longer than in the rest of Europe in the agrarian sector. During the years 1929 to 1933 Polish national income fell by 25 percent. Depression in industry meant a fall in production; in agriculture it meant a steady and catastrophic decline of prices for foodstuffs. The "price scissors" opened wide. Taking prices of 1928 as 100, in 1929 a farmer received 76 for his products and had to pay 101 for manufactured goods, whereas in 1933 he received 40 and paid 73. The result was hardship, even misery of the peasantry, a slowing down of land reform, a drop of yields per acre, and reduction of peasant consumption to a bare minimum. While industrial production declined throughout Europe on the average of 27 percent, in Poland it fell by 41 percent. Heavy industry was especially affected. Unemployment became a serious issue, and multiplying cartels seeking to preserve prices often contributed to a vicious circle. In foreign trade dumping practices became widespread, and the government, in order not to antagonize the foreign investor, delayed for too long the limitations on movement of capital. The gold standard was maintained, and the government fought the Depression by classic means of deflation—the memory of the hyperinflation of the 1920s was still alive—and attempted greater state intervention only after 1932. Budget deficits increased from 1930 onward and necessitated cuts in expenditures. Even the budget of the war ministry was reduced in absolute figures, although proportionately it increased from 30 to 35 percent between 1930 and 1935 because of the uncertain international situation.

The hardening of the Piłsudski regime was at least partly affected by the grim economic picture and the worsening international constellation. As some of his supporters put it, a hard-pressed Poland could not afford the luxury of a parliamentary democracy. A consolidated center-left actively opposed antidemocratic trends and faced the tough cabinet of the Colonels led by Walery Sławek. The latter's dictum that the constitution would be changed in one way or another and that it was "better to break the bones of one sejm deputy than to put up machine guns in the streets" reflected the feelings of Piłsudski's followers that unless the sejm were drastically curbed the country would plunge into civil war.

The center-left took up the challenge, and at a congress held in Cracow in June 1930 openly denounced Piłsudski as a dictator and criticized the president. What particularly infuriated Piłsudski, was their threat that the Polish people would repudiate foreign commitments made by an illegally constituted regime. In the night of September 9-10 a number of leading opposition deputies, including former Premier Witos, the Upper Silesian leader, Wojciech Korfanty, and a ranking Socialist, Herman Lieberman, were summarily arrested, manhandled, and thrown into the military fortress at Brześć. In the elections held shortly thereafter the BBWR gained 56 percent of the sejm's seats, but the Piłsudski camp lost many of its liberal intellectuals. The aristocratic supporters were also appalled; many of the staunchest supporters wavered.

The affair of Brześć was compounded, in the eyes of the international public, by a crackdown on the Ukrainians in Eastern Galicia. In reprisal for acts of terrorism, Polish troops were sent to the villages, causing much destruction of property and indulging in physical abuse. The new American ambassador in Warsaw, John Willys, reported that "Ukrainian intransigeance has met its match in Polish ruthlessness," but Western liberal public opinion was outraged by Polish "atrocities" of 1930.

The deplorable Brześć affair and the Ukrainian "pacifications" corresponded to the wave of brutality and radicalism that was rising throughout Europe. Compared to developments in Germany and Central Europe, Polish excesses were still relatively mild. The arrested politicians received short-term sentences and, except for those who went into exile, were released after a year or so. Ukrainian sources spoke of thirty-five people who had lost their lives in Eastern Galicia; the Poles contested these figures. It is indubitable, however, that democracy in Poland had suffered a severe blow.

Internationally the post-Locarno era was over by 1930, and after Stresemann's death German revisionism became more strident. In August a German cabinet member made a particularly aggressive revisionist speech that echoed throughout Poland. The Poles were on the lookout for German-Ukrainian contacts, but they followed above all the impact of revisionism on the great powers.

American sympathies for Weimar Germany underwent a subtle change. Previously, peaceful revisionism appeared as a way of settling problems left open by Locarno. Now, according to Polish diplomats, Americans reasoned that the Depression could not be overcome until Europe was pacified, and this "would not take place until the question of the 'corridor' would be resolved." Ambassador Willys reported in 1931 from Warsaw about Polish feelings that the United States "is so concerned over the security of its financial commitments in Germany that American influence is being aligned on the side of the Reich against Poland." There was plenty of evidence of American interest in some solution to the German-Polish question. The Secretary of State, Henry L. Stimson, and

President Hoover considered an international highway through the "Corridor"; Shepard Morgan, the vice-president of Chase National Bank, among others, suggested a return of the "Corridor" to Germany within the framework of an eastern Locarno. Stimson found the idea of peaceful revision "well worth while," and mentioned it to the French chargé d'affaires and to the British Prime Minister MacDonald. The United States, he said, only wished that border changes be carried out by peaceful means.

The question of the revision of German-Polish borders occupied a prominent place in the correspondence between the head of the Eastern European Division in the State Department, Robert F. Kelley, and the American chargé in Warsaw, John Wiley. Kelley lectured on the topic at Princeton, and although he recommended no specific solution, the thrust of his remarks was that a homogeneous Germany with more than 60 million inhabitants had obviously a better chance to determine the issue than a heterogeneous small Polish state.

In October 1931 the Poles were shocked by the remarks made by the powerful chairman of the Foreign Relations Committee, Senator William E. Borah. The occasion was the visit of Premier Pierre Laval of France, and Borah addressed French journalists at a big press conference arranged by the State Department. The senator stated bluntly that there would be no disarmament in Europe as long as certain problems existed, for instance, the Polish "Corridor," and he said: "I would change the Polish Corridor if it was possible to do so; and I would change the situation with reference to Upper Silesia." Borah explained that changes ought to be made by the interested parties themselves and, naturally, by peaceful means. In view of previous consultations between Borah and President Hoover it was hard to believe that the senator voiced only his private opinion, even if the form of his remarks was embarrassing to the administration. As Walter Lippmann, who at this time took over the editorship of the publication *US in World Affairs,* observed, Borah said publicly "what responsible statesmen were saying privately." The United States did not feel that the maintenance of the Versailles status quo was essential for European security; in fact the reverse might be true. Stimson felt strongly that a solution of the "Corridor" was essential for the success of the disarmament conference. Even the mood of American internationalists was hardly reassuring for the Poles. As Hamilton Fish Armstrong recalled, those present at a luncheon given by House in early 1931 for Paderewski "tried to pretend a deep interest in Polish affairs which were in a sad state."

The United States was attempting to exploit French desires for a rapprochement by hinting at greater flexibility in the matter of German-Polish borders. Wiley played with the idea of American financial aid if France and Poland proved cooperative, and this may have given rise to rumors in Warsaw about an American plan of advancing a $500 million loan to Poland for renouncing the "Corridor." The famous moratorium on reparations and war debts offered by President Hoover in 1931 was not accompanied by efforts to induce Germany to be less revisionist, as the Poles had expected. In talks with Polish diplomats Hoover said that although a strong Poland was the best rampart Germany had against Russia, a compromise solution of German-Polish antagonism would be most desirable. Hoover himself doubted Germany's aggressive designs against Poland.

Polish reaction against the Borah statement took the form of mass meetings and a press campaign protesting his remarks. Angry telegrams were sent to the State Department. Piłsudski instructed the Polish ambassador to tell Hoover that his country would fight to the last man to defend its borders. Washington was ill pleased, especially since the chargé d'affaires in Warsaw reported Piłsudski's remarks, that under certain conditions he might be obliged to march against Germany (a preventive war?), and commented that this was not an empty threat.

Paderewski made an impassioned speech (published as a pamphlet) in New York in June 1932, and the Polish envoy in Washington, Ciechanowski, contributed an article to *Foreign Affairs* entitled "The Polish Corridor: Revision or Peace?" The "Corridor" issue was hotly debated at the 1932 conference of the Institute of Politics in Williamstown. The State Department, desirous to obtain a clearer picture of the issues involved, instructed the embassy in Warsaw to prepare a memorandum on the German-Polish controversy. This lengthy document, dated March 19, 1932, took a strongly anti-German position. The "Corridor" issue was not a justified grievance but a propaganda argument against Versailles. While millions of Germans lived outside of the republic, Berlin seemed concerned only with those in Poland; the vicious anti-Polish campaign resulted not so much from the desire to liberate Germans but reflected a "tendency to enslave more Poles." German propaganda against the "Corridor" seemed to be a "convenient mask to create in the world an opinion which would connive at a German attack on Poland—an attack, the real object of which are territories larger than the 'Corridor.'" The memorandum denounced German foreign policy which, "outwardly professing good will to a neighboring country, at the same time is suspected of subsidizing revolutionary bands; poisoning of German youth with falsehood and hatred of its neighbor; professing peace but at the same time communing with Soviet Russia against the safety of another state; an olive branch for the West, and the seeds of destruction for the East." The memorandum concluded that until this attitude changed in Germany, an international agreement providing guarantees remained "the first need of Europe, as without it the only security for Poland consists in the strength of her arms and fidelity of her allies." This appraisal of the situation was accurate and tragically prophetic.

Bilateral American-Polish relations remained outwardly friendly. In 1930 the respective legations had been elevated to the rank of embassies. A year later the unveiling of Wilson's monument in Poznań served as an occasion to stress American-Polish ties. In 1932 Dewey revisited Poland, where he was lavishly entertained, and made speeches extolling Polish achievements that annoyed the opposition in Poland and the financial circles in the United States. The years 1931 and 1932 saw a visit of General Gustaw Orlicz-Dreszer to the United States, where he was appalled by the effectiveness of German propaganda, and a return visit of General Douglas MacArthur to Poland. In his reminiscences MacArthur gave a backhanded praise to Polish cavalry and sympathized with Piłsudski's dilemma of finding a way "to avoid certain disaster" for his country caught between Germany and Russia. The visit of the chief of the general staff was not an indication of direct American military interest in Eastern Europe; rather, it was part of MacArthur's campaign to strengthen the United States army by pointing at the unsettled state of affairs in Europe.

Hoover's activity on the international scene worried Warsaw. In 1930 the new Polish envoy had stressed in his accreditation speech American-Polish friendship, intensification of commercial exchanges, and reinforcement of sentiments of security in Europe, particularly in its eastern part; Hoover's reply expressed only a noncommittal "well-wishing interest." The president's unsuccessful proposal in 1932 for an across-the-board disarmament of one-third of existing strength clearly favored Germany. It evoked a Polish comment about the "American elephant in the European china shop." In the sphere of economics, however, the signing of the American-Polish Treaty of Friendship, Commerce and Consular Rights on June 15, 1931, providing for a Most-Favored-Nation clause was a welcome achievement. The usual amount of friction over American business in Poland, particularly in connection with Harriman's activities, was of no great import. Far more significant was the matter of Polish debts and their relation to the Hoover moratorium. The United States was Poland's largest foreign creditor, holding 54 percent of the state debt and 69 percent of the municipal foreign debts. Warsaw argued that the funded debt ought to be treated in the same way as war debts, but Washington refused to accept this point of view. From November 1932 Poland was declared in default, and defaulted on other loans in October 1936. But a year and a half later the Poles made a settlement on conversion of outstanding private loans at a reduced rate of interest and annual debt services. According to figures prepared by the State Department, total Polish indebtedness to the government of the United States amounted by 1939 to $259,346.55 and was in default.

The election of Franklin D. Roosevelt as president in November 1932 met with positive comments by the Polish press, although opinions differed whether it would mean a reorientation of American foreign policy. Roosevelt's administration brought no real change to the relations with Poland, but his outlook and stand on international affairs raised various questions. Was he a new Wilson who had learned from Wilsonian mistakes, or an opportunist and a hard-line realist? He had championed a United States expansion and in 1920 had to defend himself against charges of imperialism. In 1932 he won on a largely isolationist platform of no-entanglements and rigidity on European debts. While concentrating on domestic American policies—the New Deal—Roosevelt perceived, of course, the interdependence of domestic and foreign affairs and was not indifferent to European problems. In 1934 he approved the Reciprocal Trade Agreement Act that liberalized foreign commerce, but he had earlier contributed to the collapse of the London International Economic Conference by rejecting its stabilization plan.

Roosevelt's foreign policy was undoubtedly cautious. His representative at the Disarmament Conference in Geneva held out the promise of American consultation with the League if an international crisis occurred, and of noninterference with sanctions against an aggressor. But he made it perfectly clear that the United States would make no commitment whatsoever to use its armed forces for the settlement of any disputes. With regard to Nazi Germany—Hitler's chancellorship almost coincided with Roosevelt's inauguration—and Soviet Russia, American diplomacy was pragmatically rather than ideologically motivated. It was Nazi Germany, with its outspoken criticism of "Jew-ridden" and "Negroid" United States and with its defiance of the Open Door policy in international economics, that was responsible for a deterioration of relations between Washington and Berlin. Nazi domestic policies and warlike utterances added to the growing revulsion against the new regime, but in early 1934 American aviation firms were still selling large amounts of equipment to the Reich, thus assisting its air armament program.

Although Roosevelt and Secretary of State Cordell Hull assured the Poles that they would not discuss the "Corridor" behind their backs, they were not entirely honest. The president told a French minister that he saw no reason why "some mechanical arrangement" could not be devised to link East Prussia with Germany. When in September 1934 Roosevelt proclaimed a Pulaski Day, it was more a gesture of good will toward Americans of Polish descent than a sign of growing friendship for Poland. Once again the issue of the "Corridor" occupied the pages of *Foreign Affairs* in 1933, and Paderewski crossed swords in print with Clement Vollmer, who advocated a new corridor along the Niemen River.

United States recognition of Soviet Russia in 1933 appeared as a bold and dramatic political move, but its motivation was economic —hopes for Russia's trade—rather than political. The first United States ambassador, William Bullitt, a fervent advocate of American-Russian cooperation, found his stay in Moscow a bitter disillusionment. He established close relations with the Polish ambassador Juliusz Łukasiewicz, and subsequently became well acquainted with the premises of Polish diplomacy and sympathetic toward it.

International developments of the early 1930s made Piłsudski concentrate on foreign affairs, but a word needs to be said about the domestic scene. Within Poland, after the dramatic events of 1929-1930 a relative calm prevailed, but with strong undercurrents. The left-center opposition had been seriously weakened, but the two Populist parties, Piast and Wyzwolenie, finally combined in a single Populist party. After the Comintern adopted the Popular Front line, Polish Communists began to make overtures to the Socialists, who had serious misgivings of such an alliance. The Depression and the rise of a young generation with few career opportunities combined to give an impetus to radicalism of the right. The National Democratic party dropped the adjective "democratic," and its extreme splinter group, the illegal National Radical Camp (ONR) became virtually fascist. A youthful leader of one ONR group, Falanga, was Bolesław Piasecki.

The main difficulty of the Piłsudski regime continued to be the lack of a unifying political doctrine. Trying to divine the marshal's intentions from general directives, Piłsudski's followers often pursued unimaginative policies and resorted to administrative pressures. After the assassination of the minister of the interior in 1934, an isolation camp was set up in Bereza Kartuska which, although not comparable to Nazi concentration or Soviet labor camps, was a shocking testimony to the government's inability to adhere to norms of judicial procedure. Attempts to resolve Ukrainian-Polish difficulties brought a shaky arrangement with the Ukrainian moderates punctured by terrorism of the Ukrainian Military Organization (OUN) and Polish reprisals.

The principal target of the Piłsudski administration, a new constitution, was achieved in 1935. Rushed through the sejm in a manner that raised doubts about the legality of the procedure, it set up a presidential regime. The president became a supreme authority placed above other branches of government, namely the cabinet, the parliament, the armed forces, and the judiciary. He had the right to perform certain acts without the signature of ministers and was responsible for them only to "God and history." In case of war, when unable to discharge his duties, he could nominate his successor. The political system established by the 1935 constitution, for which the American example of a strong presidency was invoked, was a reaction against the 1921 constitution and a swing from one extreme to another. The new electoral law, eliminating the principle of proportional representation and introducing electoral assemblies that undercut political parties, completed a structure that was essentially authoritarian.

Polish foreign policy underwent a dramatic transformation in 1932–1934. Promoting his trusted undersecretary of state, Józef Beck, to foreign minister, Piłsudski seized the initiative and won significant even if temporary advantages for Poland. With regard to Russia, he exploited Moscow's desires for relaxation of tension on its western borders by concluding a Soviet-Polish nonaggression treaty in 1932. The Russians regarded it as a step leading them out of isolation; Piłsudski saw it as a measure of normalizing relations, but had no intention of assisting the USSR to reenter the councils of Europe. As regards Germany, Piłsudski showed his toughness in 1932 and 1933 on the matter of Danzig—the barometer of German-Polish relations—and by approaching France with the controversial and still somewhat enigmatic preventive war overtures. It was obvious that Paris was in no mood to consider any warlike action against Hitler's Germany and was emasculating rather than rejecting revisionist schemes such as Mussolini's Four Power Pact. Piłsudski concluded that reliance on France must not exclude attempts to increase Polish security by other means, and turned his eyes toward Berlin.

The Nazi movement was of course rabidly nationalistic, and their ideologue Alfred Rosenberg regarded the "disappearance of the

Polish state" as a "chief necessity." At the same time Hitler's grandiose ambitions and goals transcended the issue of the German-
Polish frontier that had obsessed the leaders of Weimar Germany.
Hitler acted by force and understood force, and he knew that for
the time being Germany was militarily weaker than Poland. The
preventive war idea was not regarded as a mere bluff in Berlin,
and Hitler, as dictator, could impose a policy of accommodation
with Warsaw without being accused of selling out German national
interests. A détente with Poland could be propagandistically exploited to show the Reich's reasonableness and at the same time
might undermine Franco-Polish cooperation. Hitler may have
thought that in the long run Piłsudski's Poland might align itself
with Germany against Soviet Russia.

For Warsaw a détente with Germany would allow room for diplomatic maneuver that an exclusive reliance on France had greatly
limited. Long regarded as a liability because of the unresolved
German-Polish problems, Warsaw could now expect to be treated
with greater consideration by Paris. Admittedly, a separately negotiated arrangement with Berlin would arouse suspicions, but that
would not worry Piłsudski.

A joint German-Polish communiqué of November 1933, followed
by the signing of a Declaration of Non-Aggression on January 26,
1934, took European and American diplomats by surprise. The
declaration, valid for ten years, recognized the binding nature of
previous international engagements of both signatories, which included the Franco-Polish alliance. Professing determination to
maintain peace and negotiate disputes, Germany and Poland agreed
"under no circumstances to use force to settle such disputes." The
declaration, Piłsudski told his associates, assured peace for at least
the next *four* years, and subsequent events did not prove him far
wrong. While France, Russia, and the Little Entente were profoundly disturbed and seethed with rumors of a secret Polish-
German deal or alliance, it is to the credit of American diplomats
that they never believed in the existence of any such secret clauses.
If the German-Polish declaration undermined to some extent the
French system of alliances and helped Nazi diplomacy, one must
not forget that Paris and London bore the principal blame for this
state of affairs. Had it not been for the attitude of the West, the
United States included, toward the "Corridor," and for the vacillating policies at the Disarmament Conference and at the time of the
Four Power Pact, Poland would not have been driven to resort to
a direct agreement with Berlin.

The declaration marked the beginning of a policy of equilibrium between Germany and Russia. The avowed enmity of Nazi Germany toward the Soviet Union seemed to preclude their collusion at Poland's expense. A neutral Poland, separating the two giants, diminished the chances of their clash, which would have to take place on Poland's soil. In spite of Beck's attempts to reassure Moscow that Poland would not lean toward Berlin, Russia remained suspicious. A subsequent Polish refusal to participate in a proposed Eastern Pact, sponsored by France and Russia, and Warsaw's dislike of French and Czechoslovak alliances with the Soviet Union, served only to confirm these suspicions. Was Poland wrong in trying not to jeopardize the newly won agreement with Berlin by refusing to participate in a diplomatic bloc to be led by Paris and Moscow? Was freedom of maneuver, illusory perhaps but still not perceived as such, worth exchanging for dependence on Soviet Russia? Warsaw did not think so. Until 1939 Paris kept trying to cope with the Nazi menace by purely diplomatic means, which the Poles thought ineffective. To Beck, the Franco-Polish alliance was principally a military accord guaranteeing that in case of war France and Poland would act in common. Until then divergences in foreign policies of the two allies were perfectly natural. To the French, who had tried to limit the automatic nature of the Franco-Polish military convention, the alliance with Poland was above all a diplomatic instrument assuring strict Polish adherence to the French line. The difference in interpretation was basic.

Beck symbolized and embodied the new Polish foreign policy, sharing with many Poles a sense of national vanity that had been badly hurt by France and the West. Gifted though he was, he was too dynamic and ambitious to realize that the delicate policy of equilibrium required a low profile and great restraint. The newly won diplomatic freedom went to his head and intoxicated many of his countrymen as well. The tone of Polish foreign policy changed and Warsaw was getting even for the years of diplomatic humiliations. The Treaty for the Protection of Minorities was repudiated in 1934. Although contemplated earlier, this was an unwise blow against the Versailles system. A tough line against Czechoslovakia only increased the circle of Warsaw's critics. Poland was a power, asserted the Polish press; an article by Casimir Smogorzewski in the July 1935 issue of *Foreign Affairs,* entitled "Poland, Free, Peaceful, Strong," contrasted strikingly with the defensive Polish articles in the early 1930s.

These features of Polish diplomacy became even more evident later, and it is questionable whether Piłsudski, with his uncanny grasp of opportunities, would have approved them. The question remains unanswered, for in May 1935 Piłsudski died of cancer, and Poland found itself a semidictatorial state without a dictator, professing a Piłsudski cult without Piłsudski.

Toward the Second World War

The Piłsudski men in power believed themselves ordained to govern the country, but as a minority without a genuine political party they could only base legitimacy on the marshal's inheritance. Could a political heritage and a legend be bequeathed? It seemed necessary to enlarge the basis of public support.

A complex inner struggle for power that involved Sławek, President Mościcki, and Piłsudski's successor in the army, General Rydz-Śmigły, eventually led to an accommodation between the president and the general (later named marshal). Sławek's cabinet gave way to one that inclined toward the liberal wing of the Piłsudski movement; that one was followed by what turned out to be the last ministry of interwar Poland. Headed by General Felicjan Sławoj-Składkowski, a man hardly suited for an important political post, the cabinet comprised the president's men and Rydz-Śmigły's adherents. Beck remained a power unto himself, recognized as the Piłsudski-chosen expert in foreign matters.

The parliament hardly counted. Political parties boycotted the 1935 elections at which only 46 percent of the voters participated. Besides representatives of national minorities, the parliament consisted only of various factions of the Piłsudski movement, with some nonpartisan figures. Realizing the slender basis of the regime, Rydz-Śmigły and his supporters launched a new organization in place of BBWR, which was dissolved by Sławek. The Camp of National Unity (OZN) came into being on February 21, 1937, and proclaimed a "national and Christian" program. A rightist journal sneered that the program was based on a recipe calling for 40 percent of nationalism, 30 percent of social radicalism, 20 percent of agrarianism, and 10 percent of anti-Semitism. Large segments of the Piłsudski movement took a dim view of the OZN and of its pseudofascist and anti-Semitic features that were largely designed to attract the national radical youth. In fact, a brief flirtation with the youth groups caused a stir and rumors of an impending massacre of the liberal and democratic wing. Thus, the OZN opened dangerous possibilities for a further evolution towards a rightist, pseudofascist regime. The Camp of National Unity increasingly became a haven for opportunists and career-seekers, whom old Piłsudski legionnaires contemptuously dubbed the Fourth Brigade. A certain outward consolidation was achieved, as attested by the rise of popular participation in the 1938 elections, but internal decomposition proceeded, and Sławek's suicide in 1939 became its dramatic and disquieting symbol.

The opposition grew vocal. The Socialists, deceived in their hopes for a democratization of the regime, led the working class. Communists were decimated when Moscow dissolved the Polish Communist party and liquidated most of its leaders in the 1937–1938 purges. The Populist party, in which Stanisław Mikołajczyk rose to prominence, found it impossible to come to terms with the regime. The peasants' strength was dramatically demonstrated in a strike organized in 1937 that prevented food deliveries to the cities and led to bloody incidents. In the circles of the liberal intelligentsia Democratic Clubs emerged which, shortly before the Second World War, consolidated into the Democratic party.

More to the center stood the newly formed Labor party, of Christian Democratic leanings. Its spiritual patronage came largely from prominent leaders living abroad, such as Paderewski, Korfanty, Sikorski, Witos—the term Front Morges, used to describe the group, came from the name of Paderewski's residence in Switzerland.

More powerful than the left and the center was the right, whose evolution conformed to the general European pattern. The aging Dmowski patronized the militant youth; the Nationalists (Former National Democrats) were conspicuous among the younger intelligentsia, lower middle class, and university or even high school students. The extremists came close to fascism. Given the dynamic character of the nationalist movement, the regime recognized it as an important force and on occasion sought to win it over. Although bitter memories of past antagonism and power competition precluded a reconciliation, trends operating in both comps militated against democracy and parliamentary forms of government.

The vitality and power of the opposition was vividly demonstrated in communal elections in 1938–1939. The governmental OZN gained 29 percent of the vote in towns with a population of over 25,000, compared to 26 percent for the Socialists and nearly 19 percent for the Nationalists. The political future of the system appeared uncertain.

Political developments in Poland affected the national minorities. The Germans, treated with circumspection after the Declaration of Non-Aggression, fared best. There was limited cooperation between the government and moderate Ukrainian parties, but open hostility between Polish and Ukrainian masses grew. The Jews were in the worst position. Official anti-Semitism, while opposed to violence and persecutions, condoned discrimination, particularly in the economic sphere. The government considered various emigration schemes. Here it found some common ground with the militant Zionists who favored exodus to Palestine. The Nationalists demanded exclusion of Jews from the free professions and the party-affiliated youth organizations engaged in anti-Jewish riots. At the universities they fought for a segregation of Jewish students (ghetto benches) and practiced violence. But although the Nationalists pressed for, and some of the OZN leaders considered anti-Jewish legislation of the type passed at that time in Hungary, none was enacted in Poland. Polish liberals and democrats, nonpartisans as well as those belonging to the left, center, and the Piłsudski camp, opposed with determination and civil courage anti-Jewish excesses and discrimination.

Political problems must of course be related to economic evolution. From 1936 on state intervention increased, largely as a result of the policies of Finance Minister Eugeniusz Kwiatkowski. The government sought to stimulate production through public works, taxes, customs, credits, railroad tariffs, and direct state orders. Some of the foreign-owned enterprises were bought out, and financial controls were established to prevent the flight of foreign capital. Quotas and licenses were introduced in foreign trade. In 1936 the budgetary deficit was liquidated although the balance of payments still remained unfavorable. The terms of American-Polish trade were increasingly unfavorable to Poland. In 1937 Polish imports from the United States (with cotton occupying the first place) stood at $28,188,000; exports to America (canned ham leading the list) came to $19,074,000. The following year the respective figures were $30,142,000 and $11,893,000.

In the agrarian sector some improvements were assisted by the rise of prices and increased domestic consumption, and stimulated by the radically inclined minister of agriculture Poniatowski. More land was parceled and small holdings were consolidated. Yet "price scissors" and rural unemployment could not be overcome except by general drastic reforms. Hard life in the countryside and continuing unemployment in towns led to the wave of economic-political strikes in 1936–1937.

An imaginative four-year investment plan, launched in 1936, was accelerated and completed by 1939. Its long-range objectives included the raising of technical levels of transportation and production, creating conditions for systematic industrialization, obliterating the regional differences within the country, and lowering the costs of production. The government assigned 15.7 percent of the national income in 1937 for accumulation—roughly the same amount as in the first post-World War II plan—and concentrated its efforts

223

on the so-called Central Industrial District (COP) that comprised 15.4 percent of the area and 18 percent of the population. The core of the district—a strategically convenient area—was the triangle between the Vistula, San, and Dunajec rivers, often referred to as COP proper. Works partly or fully completed included hydroelectric dams, airplane and truck factories, and chemical and armament plants. These were notable achievements, but Kwiatkowski rightly concluded that only a comprehensive fifteen-year plan could overcome Poland's structural backwardness. Such a plan was outlined in December 1938 but nullified by the outbreak of the Second World War.

The COP was meant to contribute to the strengthening of defensive capabilities of Poland. Influenced by the 1919–1920 model of war in which the cavalry had demonstrated its great usefulness, Piłsudski had not sufficiently modernized the army. Rapid German rearmament changed the military picture to Poland's disadvantage. French military doctrine, which influenced the Poles, assigned an auxiliary role to the air force and armor. Although Rydz–Śmigły began to modernize the army, its complete overhaul as well as the creation of a large air force were beyond Polish financial means. Some military credits were obtained from France, and domestic loans—Fund of National Defense and antiaircraft bonds—were oversubscribed. In the face of external danger the Poles showed great patriotism and solidarity, but the Polish army could no longer be a match for Hitler's Wehrmacht or the huge Red Army.

The aggressiveness of Berlin and Rome contrasted with the vacillating policies of London and Paris and their appeasement of the dictators. In March 1936 Hitler denounced Locarno and reoccupied the Rhineland. Beck notified Paris that Poland was ready to stand by France, but believing that the French would merely protest, he was careful not to burn bridges to Berlin. Hitler's boldness paid off and confirmed Beck's low opinion of Paris. Although a Polish-French rapprochement, demanded by Rydz-Śmigły and the opposition, followed, it did not alter Beck's policy. Warsaw assumed that the German thrust would be directed in the first instance against Austria and Czechoslovakia, and Poland did not intend to risk war in their defense.

In the mounting European crisis the voice of the United States was barely audible. In 1936 Roosevelt was reelected on a platform that almost ignored foreign policy. If the president was moving away from isolationism, the American people and the Congress were not. The Nye Commission, which had investigated in 1934 the role of armament manufacturers, popularized the view that bankers and profiteers had tricked the United States into the First World War. The Congress passed Neutrality Laws in 1935, 1936, and 1937 that played into the hands of aggressors by indiscriminately denying access to the American arsenal.

The reoccupation of the Rhineland brought no official response, although Ambassador Cudahy predicted from Warsaw that war would come within a few years. American public opinion did find the Nazis increasingly objectionable, while the liberals voiced their admiration of the Soviet Union and fellow travellers asserted that "Communism is twentieth-century Americanism." Roosevelt himself was worried as United States diplomats handed in gloomy reports about the continent: Germany constituted a real threat to peace while Soviet Russia posed the danger of communist domination. Yet nothing was done to prepare for future contingencies and the East European Division in the State Department was liquidated as too conservative in outlook.

In January 1937 the president requested from the U.S. ambassador an evaluation of Poland's capability for defense and an appraisal of the Polish economic situation. Cudahy's remarks on the latter score were pessimistic, and he wondered if Poland, which he called the poorest country in Europe, would survive economically the next decade. American economic aid, however, was not contemplated. A series of articles in the *New York Times* painted Polish politics in dark colors. The paper criticized the "strongly nationalist and authoritarian" Camp of National Unity and drew attention to its racist tendencies. The OZN also came in for criticism by American diplomats. The *Times* warned that current trends in Poland would alienate world public opinion from that country.

Polish foreign policy met with understanding of such diplomats as Bullitt and the new ambassador in Warsaw, Anthony Drexell Biddle. In cordial talks with Beck, Bullitt offered his services to help the Poles in Washington and suggested a meeting between Beck and Roosevelt. The president's famous Quarantine speech of October 1937, in which he advocated a "concerted effort" by "peace loving nations" to oppose violations of treaties and international anarchy, and spoke of a quarantine "against the spread of disease," elicited Beck's favorable comment. The speech, he said, was a "stop, look and listen" sign flashed from Washington. While the White House tried to educate the American people in international matters and strengthen European will to resist aggression, Bullitt came once again to Warsaw in late 1937. He suggested that Beck propose a European stabilization plan and support the idea of Franco-German rapprochement. A hint of a $50 million loan to strengthen Polish war industry was dropped but had no sequel. Other American projects of the time, including overtures to Neville Chamberlain of England, produced no practical results. United States diplomacy operated under heavy domestic constraints. The Ludlow Amendment to the Constitution, proposed in 1938, would have made a declaration of war by the United States dependent on public referendum, and the administration had to make an all-out effort to prevent it coming to a vote.

In 1938 events in Europe began to move with a frightening rapidity: the Anschluss of Austria in March, a Czechoslovak crisis in May, and finally the mutilation of Czechoslovakia through the Munich Conference in September. The able Assistant Secretary of State George Messersmith pointed out that German control of East Central Europe would relegate Britain and France to a secondary international position. The United States could not be indifferent to such prospects. Roosevelt was aware of the need to revise the Neutrality Laws but a sense of urgency seemed to be missing. It was important to avert war in Europe, but the United States continued to be passive. Roosevelt personally gave a stamp of approval to Chamberlain's appeasement at Munich by sending him the famous "good man" telegram.

Warsaw was not passive, but its policy gave the appearance of collusion with Hitler. The annexation of Austria almost coincided with a Polish ultimatum to Lithuania, forcing that country to restore diplomatic relations with Poland. The move was made to strengthen the Polish northern flank and to demonstrate the country's determination, but the ultimatum made a bad impression abroad. During the Czechoslovak crisis, Beck demanded that concessions to the German minority be matched by those to Poles in Teschen. Thus, the principal German pressure on Czechoslovakia was accompanied by a parallel pressure from Warsaw. Munich left the Polish issue open, and Poland resorted to a second ultimatum in 1938 in order to obtain Teschen. Whatever the merits of the Polish case and the economic importance of the district were (it produced five-sevenths of Poland's iron and seven-tenths of steel), the brutal move against stricken Czechoslovakia tarnished Poland's image. Washington disliked Beck's methods, and Roosevelt conveyed a personal message expressing hope that the Teschen question would be resolved by negotiations. When the Polish ambassador in Washington, Count Jerzy Potocki, sought to convince Cordell Hull that Poland had come out of the whole affair with increased prestige, the American disagreed.

The final disintegration of Czechoslovakia following the German entry into Prague in March 1939 produced a new situation. Western appeasement had proved ineffective in restraining Nazi Germany, and Beck's vague notion of a Third Europe stretching from the Baltic to the Adriatic and using Italy against Germany could not offset the loss of Czechoslovakia. Militarily and strategically Poland's position deteriorated, for not only had Germany gained the Czechoslovak arsenal but also surrounded Poland from the south. Already in October 1938 Germany's Foreign Minister Joachim von Ribbentrop raised the question of Danzig and the "Corridor." The Poles evaded the issue just as they had previously ignored renewed German proposals to join an anti-Soviet bloc. In January 1939, Berlin reiterated its demands. Britain then took a step without precedent in its diplomatic practice. In late March it offered a guarantee of military assistance to Poland if its independence were threatened. After Beck's visit to London in April this was transformed into a bilateral agreement and became in August 1939 a full-fledged British-Polish alliance. A British-French-Polish bloc opposing further German expansion was formed, and the position of Soviet Russia became particularly important, for its choice of joining either the West and Poland or Germany would determine subsequent events.

Only the essentials of the complicated and still controversial double Russian negotiations with the West and Germany will be sketched here. It seems fairly clear that Stalin played a lonely game. Unsure whether the international crisis would result in war or a new Munich, Moscow sought to gain advantages and assurances in either case. In talks with the French and British delegates the Russians insisted on a sphere of influence in the Baltic states and the right to send their troops into Poland to aid that country. The Poles, suspecting that once the Red Army entered their territory it would be likely to stay, opposed an a priori commitment. Indignantly claiming that Poland did not wish to be helped, Moscow made this issue a foundering rock of the negotiations. Soviet good faith appears suspect, for by then Stalin had virtually accepted German offers and needed a pretext for breaking off the talks with the West. The Soviet-German deal provided for a division of Eastern Europe into respective spheres of influence and assigned half of Poland to Russia in exchange for the Kremlin's neutrality. Naturally, Western-Soviet talks were permeated with mutual suspicions all along. Beck felt that a resolute Western-Polish front could deal adequately with Hitler, and Ambassador Biddle shared the Polish point of view. He felt that the West was wrong in wooing Russia and should instead lean fully on Poland. He thought that the West and the United States ought to assist Poland financially and voiced criticism of the American ambassador in Moscow, Joseph Davies, who adopted an uncritically pro-Soviet line. Other American diplomats looked on the European scene with forebodings. A Franco-British-Polish victory over Germany appeared to them unlikely, and they spoke of the "possibility of ultimate Bolshevism" prevailing in Europe.

The German-Soviet Non-Aggression Pact signed by Foreign Commissar V. Molotov and Joachim von Ribbentrop on August 23, 1939, came as a shock to the world and gave a green light to Hitler to unleash his armies against Poland. The temporary gainer was Stalin. As he once said: "Were the Soviet Union to participate in a warlike conflict, it ought to be in its final phase where the participation would in a decisive manner affect the political and military outcome of the war." This was possible only if Soviet Russia were left in peace to digest its territorial gains. The Poles proved to be the losers, but they felt they could not have acted in any different way. As Marshal Rydz-Smigły allegedly said: "With the Germans we may possibly lose our freedom but with the Russians we could lose our souls." Still, on the eve of the Second World War the Poles were sanguine. They believed in the effectiveness of Western military assistance, discussed in staff talks, and a concerted action that would defeat Germany. Beck had achieved the basic objective of Polish diplomacy, namely that in case of war his country would not be isolated.

Polish sang-froid in dealing with the crisis impressed foreign observers. Hitler's demands on Danzig and the extraterritorial corridor through the "Corridor" were rejected; both Beck and Hitler knew that the real issue was not Danzig but Poland's status as an independent state. The German ultimatum went beyond Berlin's original demands, and in the early morning of September 1, 1939, without a formal declaration of war and having fabricated "Polish aggressive acts," Germany attacked Poland.

The role of the United States before the outbreak of hostilities was minimal, not because the White House and the State Department were oblivious of the consequences of European war but because their hands were tied. American sympathies lay on the side of the anti-Nazi camp, and Bullitt was not the only one to believe that should war break out "likely we shall not take part in it at the beginning, but we shall finish it." It is debatable whether American diplomacy actually stiffened Polish and Franco-British resistance to Hitler. True, Washington ignored at one point British hints that the United States put pressure on Poland. The State Department commented that the British might be thinking of a new Munich and wished the Americans to do "their dirty work for them." It is also true that Warsaw believed that the United States supported it morally. But this could not determine Polish foreign policy. Roosevelt's letters to Hitler and Mussolini asking for assurances to respect the rights of other nations were primarily meant to educate the American people by identifying the aggressors and exposing their intentions. A die-hard isolationist like Senator Borah, who publicly stated that he saw no signs of an approaching war, could not be convinced, but others could and were. Roosevelt's notes to Hitler and Mościcki urging a peaceful solution of the conflict, which produced a favorable reply from the Polish president but none from Hitler, could also be seen as an object lesson for the American people.

Interwar American-Polish relations were drawing to a close. They had been largely one-sided and Poland per se of marginal importance to the United States. At the same time, Poland as part of the East Central European borderland between Germany and Russia could be neglected only so long as one of these two great powers did not show aspirations that affected world politics. As Raymond L. Buell wrote in his *Poland: The Key to Europe*—a report for the Foreign Policy Association published as a book in 1939—"If it were possible to localize a war between Poland and Germany, the Western world might be conceivably indifferent to Poland's fate." But a Germany that destroyed Poland and gained a common border with Russia would be in a position to destroy it in turn and make a bid for world dominance. Faced with such prospects the United States could not treat the Polish question as utterly divorced from American security. This important aspect of the Polish issue seems to have been noticed by only few if any of America's political leaders, and escaped almost completely the attention of the man in the street.

Ambassador Cudahy told Beck in 1933 that Poland was little known in the United States and advertised by people who did not understand the American mentality. The kind of information sent from Warsaw failed to arouse interest. The ambassador contrasted Polish propaganda and public relations efforts with those of Germany and France which were far more effective. He urged the creation of an American press bureau in Poland and suggested periodic press conferences with Beck. There was no sequel to these suggestions, but it is clear that to interest the American public in Poland was a difficult task. In this connection, let us look briefly at the cultural cooperation between the two countries, the role of the American Polonia, and the part played by diplomatic representatives in fostering good relations between the United States and Poland.

The monthly publication *Poland* carried information and news to the American, particularly the Polish American public. A reader could get some idea about Polish affairs from John Gunther's popular book, *Inside Europe,* where on the whole Poland did not come out as appealing. Several books by Americans (notably by Robert Machray) and Poles on Polish politics and history were available. To this group also belonged the volumes by Paul Super, the head of the highly successful and American-directed YMCA in Poland. A few contemporary novels were accessible in English translation; the *Trumpeter of Cracow,* mentioned earlier, held some attraction for American youth. Polish-American relations and history were surveyed in a series of pioneering studies by Miecislaus Haiman, the founder of the Polish Museum and Archives set up in Chicago in 1935. Arthur P. Coleman, who at one time taught Polish courses at Columbia, was, together with his wife, one of the first popularizers of Polish literature and history in this country. There were others, but attempts to establish a Polish chair at the University of Michigan or develop Polish studies at Dartmouth proved futile.

Scholarly exchanges operated on various levels, but in a small way. The Carnegie Endowment assisted Polish libraries and subsidized an occasional publication. The fellowship program of the Rockefeller Foundation brought 198 Polish scholars to the United States prior to 1941, and offered grants totalling $538,164. The foundation also spent nearly $1 million within Poland. The Kościuszko Foundation, established in December 1925 under the leadership of Henry N. MacCracken of Vassar, Samuel Vauclain of Baldwin Locomotives, and a dynamic Polish immigrant, Stephen Mizwa (its president for many years), concentrated its efforts on visits of professors and students and sought to cultivate cultural contacts between the United States and Poland. At the cost of $125,000, these exchanges benefited 101 Americans and 69 Poles. The foundation also sponsored publications and served as the outpost of American Polish cultural activities.

Numerous Polish scholars and artists were brought for longer or shorter periods to the United States, and several remained. The list is long, and only a few names can be mentioned by way of illustration. Stanisław Ulam, Marek Kac, Kazimierz Funk represented the sciences; Oskar Halecki, history; Oskar Lange, economics. During the war the great sociologist, Bronisław Malinowski, came together with several other outstanding scholars. Among artists, the names of the pianist Artur Rubinstein, the singer Adam Didur, the conductor Artur Rodziński, the violinists Paweł Kochański and Bronisław Huberman, stand out. Only studies in depth could reveal what kind of impact they made on America and whether they helped to promote the Polish image, and how effectively.

To what extent did the Polish American community serve as a bridge between the United States and Poland? Its financial contribution to the homeland has been mentioned earlier, although the full extent of this aid requires further research. Its influence on presidential elections is a mater of dispute. In the interwar period, the Polish American community underwent significant changes, although only those directly related to United States-Polish relations concern us here. The emergence of an independent Poland enhanced the self-respect of this group but also sharpened the question of their own national identity. Some 90,000 American Poles, perhaps a third of whom were American-born, returned to live in the Polish state. The vast majority remained. Naturalization processes accelerated, and the term Americans of Polish descent gained wider currency. At the second conference of Poles living outside the homeland, held in Warsaw in 1934, the World Association of Poles from Abroad (Światpol) came into existence. The delegation of American Polonia offered its collaboration, but stressed that Polish Americans regarded themselves as an integral part of the American nation. Indeed, a study of Polonia in Buffalo made in 1927 revealed that 57 percent of the people thought of themselves as Americans, 39 percent as American Poles or Polish Americans, and only 7 percent viewed themselves as Poles. The Polish leaders of Światpol were slow to grasp this evolution, and some friction developed between them and Polish Americans.

The Polish experiences of the volunteers in the Haller army were not uniformly positive, and the Polonia was bitter that Paderewski had not remained the head of government in Warsaw. The bad effects of the 1920 loan further strained the Polish American relations with Warsaw. If a new sentimental link with Poland had been forged, there were also grave disappointments and a growing realization that America was home. The small trickle of new immigrants—the quota established in 1924 was 5,982 annually—dissolved in the Polonia. What is more, the melting pot concept or the idea of cultural pluralism affected various segments of the Polonia differently. Some American Poles associated social advancement with a severance of all ties with the Polonia and a complete merger with the WASP society. Even to those who retained a cultural affinity

231

with Poland, politics in the Second Republic became remote and incomprehensible. The goals of the Polonia became ever more American-oriented, and successes of those of Polish stock in America—for instance, of Leopold Stokowski or the film actress, Pola Negri (Apolonia Chałupiec)—were often more relevant to the status of Polish Americans than achievements in the far-off "old country." Although an American historian wrote about "our increasingly influential Polish-American group" on the eve of the Second World War, it is unclear whether this should be taken to mean that the Polonia had become an effective Polish lobby and pressure group in the United States, a natural bridge between this country and Poland, or a more important ethnic group in America.

Contributions of American and Polish diplomatic representatives in the respective capitals have never been properly evaluated. Most United States envoys came from wealthy families, for the Warsaw post was expensive. It was also considered quite important. "The man you send to Warsaw," wrote Bullitt to Roosevelt in 1935, "must know French and, if possible, should know German, and if you want to get any information from Warsaw, should also be very much of a gentleman and acutely intelligent." Some of the ministers fulfilled these stiff requirements. Hugh Gibson, the only truly professional diplomat, left his imprint on American-Polish relations. Among his successors who spent several years in Poland, John Stetson, John Cudahy, and chargé Wiley made genuine efforts to present the Polish side fairly and to foster good relations. The last ambassador, Anthony Biddle, was one of the few foreign diplomats who was on excellent terms with Beck.

Among Polish ministers and ambassadors, Jan Ciechanowski, who stayed for nearly five years until 1930, established valuable contacts in Washington and was highly regarded even though he occasionally lectured the Americans. Filipowicz and Patek were largely political appointees to whom the embassy came as a crowning reward. Stimson disliked Filipowicz, and Hull found it difficult to understand Patek. The last ambassador, Count Jerzy Potocki, scintillated on the social firmament of Washington and got on well with Roosevelt. The quality of his dispatches left something to be desired.

Americans found much to criticize about interwar Poland. Skrzyński had already noted that the little they knew about his country was mainly detrimental to its image. This did not change over the years, and it may be useful to conclude this chapter with a rapid overview of the lights and shadows of the Second Republic.

In politics, the Poles proved unable to resolve successfully the constitutional-political dilemma and moved from a hegemony of the sejm to an authoritarian regime. Polish failures here are part of the general crisis that agitated Europe throughout the interwar period. Parliamentary democracy fell victim to totalitarianism in many countries, and it is to the credit of the Poles that they imitated neither the fascist nor the communist models.

The complex question of national minorities found no solution, but the same was true in other neighboring countries. Minorities were not wisely or consistently treated, but there was no discriminatory legislation or totalitarian oppression. Harsh Polish policies were so ineffective that, as a Ukrainian historian put it, "after nineteen years of suppression, [the Ukrainians] were better organized and had a greater national consciousness than had been the case in 1919." Anti-Semitism there was and it must be condemned, even if the anti-Semites and the Jews exaggerated its portent for different reasons. At the same time it is a fact that the intensely nationalist climate of the 1920s and 1930s precluded a working solution to the problem of a three-million strong unassimilated community.

There has been much criticism of the Polish economy, which, save in certain areas (coke, paper, cement, sulphuric acid), did not reach the prewar level of production. Yet one must remember that in addition to the difficult point of departure, the changed structure of production and a reorientation of trading patterns make comparisons misleading. True, the social structure did not change drastically, standards of living did not rise, and Poland remained a backward country, but whether its economic potential increased in absolute terms is hard to say.

There were also accomplishments. Polish social legislation belonged to the most advanced in Europe. The construction of Gdynia, the emergence of civil aviation, the building of new branches of industry—chemical, armament, electrical energy—were not negligible successes. Demographic trends militated against attempts to resolve the problem of rural overpopulation, but the land reform which led to a distribution of 2.7 million hectares (11 percent of agricultural land) should not be dismissed lightly.

A combination of socioeconomic, political, and minority problems affected Polish foreign policy and, in turn, Poland's international vulnerability compounded existing domestic difficulties. When one criticizes Piłsudski's and Beck's diplomacy, however, he has to ask what was a viable alternative in foreign policy. Part of a buffer zone between Germany and Russia, Poland had not been assisted or strengthened by the outside world. The policy of balance was often ridiculed, yet the fact that Poland did not open the gate to Hitler's eastern expansion accorded well with Europe's interest. Whether a Polish alliance with Russia against Germany would have benefited the international community is more than doubtful.

Polish achievements in the cultural and scholarly spheres received no mention thus far, although they belonged to the brightest pages of the Second Republic. The Polish intellectual group was second to none, and if it was elitist, mass culture and education were not yet familiar phenomena throughout most of interwar Europe. In literature, particularly poetry, the list of prominent authors is so long that only a few names can be mentioned. The Skamander group included such important authors as Julian Tuwin, Antoni Słonimski, Kazimierz Wierzyński, Jan Lechoń and Jarosław Iwaszkiewicz. Among prose writers there are many women, to mention only Maria Nałkowska, Maria Dąbrowska, and Zofia Kossak-Szczucka. Several avant-garde authors gained in stature after the Second World War; their works were translated into English and won the acclaim of American critics. The plays of Stanisław I. Witkiewicz belong to this category as do the books of Bruno Szulc, called the Polish Kafka, and the writings of Witold Gombrowicz and Czesław Miłosz. Janusz Korczak, a writer of children's books and an educator, became internationally known after his heroic death during the German occupation, and another victim of the Nazi terror, Tadeusz Boy-Żeleński, a critic, essayist, and translator, has remained a great name in Polish literature. This list of top writers could easily be expanded.

In the field of music, the composer Karol Szymanowski has stood out as the most notable figure of the interwar period. There were important painters and sculptors, like Xawery Dunikowski. In 1924 Reymont received the Nobel Prize for Literature; a golden prize in poetry was awarded at the Olympic Games to Wierzyński.

Compulsory education embraced all children between the age of seven and fourteen, and in the 1937–1938 academic year over 4.7 million pupils attended elementary schools, over 380,000 went to secondary and vocational schools, and more than 48,000 were enrolled at universities and institutions of higher learning (numbering thirty-two in all). In the 1930s there was one university student for every 700 inhabitants, a higher ratio than in contemporary Britain. Roughly a quarter of the student body received some financial aid. Although in education and social advancement the children of workers and peasants proportionately lagged behind those of the intelligentsia, individuals from the lowest stratum occupied important positions in the life of the country.

What is then the final balance sheet? Postwar Polish historiography had, during the Stalinist period, painted a uniformly black picture of the Second Republic. This is no longer the case, and historians admit that for all its shortcomings interwar Poland occupies a crucial place in the country's long history. The period of independence and statehood, regained after well over one hundred and twenty years of suppression, had incalculable political, economic, social, psychological, and moral repercussions. Had modern Poland not known the independence that one generation took for granted, its fate in the Second World War and even today would have been entirely different. This fact alone justifies the emphasis placed on the scanty twenty years between the two world wars, even if from the viewpoint of American-Polish relations they lacked the dramatic features of the preceding and succeeding periods.

5

Roosevelt and Poland in the Second World War

D The Polish War Effort

URING the Second World War Poles fought a relentless struggle against Nazi Germany at home and abroad, over years full of sacrifice, suffering, and almost unparalleled hardship. This period also witnessed the political strife waged to preserve the territorial integrity and sovereignty of the Polish state against the designs of the Soviet Union. Taking place in the context of the great powers' strategy and wartime diplomacy, Polish political efforts were particularly directed toward the United States, whose assistance was crucial. For the United States, however, the importance of Poland and indeed of all the smaller states of East Central Europe appeared secondary. As the war progressed the Poles began to realize that the fate of their nation no longer lay in their hands. Although a member of the finally victorious coalition, Poland saw its status and borders determined by the great powers, whose attitudes toward the Polish ally became a function of their mutual relations.

On September 1, 1939, the bulk of the German war machine was hurled against Poland. Had Hitler decided to attack in the West, a two-front war would have immediately begun, but his decision to strike first against Poland averted this danger. Britain and France did formally declare war on September 3, but they undertook no genuine military operations. Their strategy, only partly revealed to the Poles, assigned to their allies the role of an advance guard, condemned to annihilation but expected to dull the edge of the German war machine, thus gaining valuable time for them.

The 1939 campaign in Poland gave rise to legends. Two of them can immediately be disposed of: the destruction of the Polish air force on the ground and the heroic but useless cavalry charges against the German Panzers. Most of the greatly outnumbered air force was in fact destroyed in combat, inflicting heavy losses (some 285 planes) on the Luftwaffe. Sporadic cavalry charges were made, but against the infantry and mechanized units, not tanks. Given the length and the configuration of the Polish-German border (including Czech and Slovak sectors), the country was indefensible in a lonely war; a withdrawal from the exposed frontiers to meet the German onslaught along the Vistula and other main rivers was extremely difficult for political and strategic reasons. Although debates about Polish strategy in 1939 will probably go on, no adequate alternative plan has been suggested. Marshal Rydz-Śmigły hoped that Polish resistance would last long enough to permit an Allied offensive on the western front. Avoidance of strategic and tactical errors might have prolonged the struggle, but the sheer numerical preponderance of the Wehrmacht, its higher fire-power ratio, the use of 2,700 tanks versus some 313 light and medium Polish tanks and a couple of hundred armored cars, and the dominance of the German air force (nearly 2,000 planes versus some 400) could leave no doubt as to the final outcome of the struggle.

The tactics of a blitzkrieg, applied for the first time, hastened the inevitable collapse. Polish resistance was stubborn, and heroic episodes were not lacking. The tiny garrison at Westerplatte, near Danzig, fought for several days against overwhelming odds. Warsaw held out in a siege that lasted until 28 September. Fortifications on the Hel Peninsula did not surrender until 2 October; there were battles fought beyond that date. Polish losses amounted to roughly 66,000 killed and 133,000 wounded; indiscriminate bombing and machine gun strafing took a heavy toll of the civilian population. German losses in killed, wounded, and missing came to only 50,000, but the damage done to air force and armor was considerable. Measured in terms of artillery ammunition used per day of fighting, the German campaign in Poland was harder than the subsequent campaign in the west in 1940. The Poles had given a valuable respite to their British and French allies. They also gave the British intelligence a superb gift, the top-secret German cipher machine, the Enigma.

The last battles were still being fought when the Red Army had invaded Poland from the east. Urged by Berlin to intervene in virtue of the secret protocol of the Ribbentrop-Molotov Pact, Soviet Russia hesitated until September 17. Reminded that further delays would bring German troops into areas assigned to Soviet Russia, Moscow decided to move. The Polish ambassador was presented with a document announcing the Soviet entry in view of the total collapse of the Polish state. He protested this unilateral breach of all past Soviet-Polish treaties and refused to accept the communication. The official Soviet explanation of the Red Army invasion stressed protection to the Ukrainian and Belorussian population in Poland supposedly endangered by Germany. This caused some unpleasantness between Berlin and Moscow.

Given the hopelessness of the situation, the Polish command did not order armed resistance to the Red Army; some minor skirmishes, however, took place. Did the Soviet stab in the back prevent a possibly successful regrouping of the Polish troops? The question is virtually unanswerable, but there is no doubt that Soviet intervention hastened the end of the campaign. The president, accompanied by the government, the commander-in-chief and his staff, and thousands of Polish soldiers and civilians, crossed the Rumanian border on September 17. Others took refuge in Hungary. In spite of the expectations that allied Rumania would allow the passage of the Polish government and high command to France to continue the war from abroad, Bucharest interned the civilian and military authorities. The president had to use his constitutional right to appoint a successor free to perform his duties. Marshal Rydz-Śmigły also resigned his command.

The fall of Poland was a traumatic experience to the people. The army of which the Poles were genuinely proud had been shattered. After a mere twenty years of independence, the country was once more partitioned between Germany and Russia. Again the Poles had to fight abroad for the liberation of their homeland. No wonder that in despair and anger they bitterly denounced the prewar regime and the military leaders. No Pole, however, was ready to accept his country's defeat as final or willingly submit to the occupants, although few if any imagined what occupation by a totalitarian state held in store.

The final division of Poland was worked out in a German-Soviet treaty of friendship of September 28, 1939, and an additional chunk of Poland passed to Germany in exchange for assigning Lithuania to the Soviet sphere. The Ribbentrop-Molotov line placed under Soviet Russia almost half of Poland, inhabited by some 13 million people, 5 million of whom were ethnic Poles. The predominantly Polish Białystok area and Lwów came under Soviet control. The area comprised about 50 percent of Poland's forests, 63 percent of oil, and 90 percent of natural gas. On October 31, Molotov gloated about the fall of the Second Republic: "One swift blow at Poland, first by the German army and then by the Red Army, and nothing was left of this ugly offspring of the Versailles treaty." This often-quoted phrase was followed a little later by a speech which asserted that since there could be no question of remaking Poland, it was "absurd to continue the present war under the banner of restoration of the former Polish state." *Izvestiia* wrote that Russia and Germany meant to assure peace and order in these territories, and indeed a secret agreement provided for German-Soviet cooperation against Polish "agitation."

The Soviet government treated eastern Poland as subject to Soviet laws. A communist regime was introduced and officials brought from the Soviet Ukraine and Belorussia took over. The NKVD (Soviet security service) secretly classified several categories of people among various nationalities—Polish, Ukrainian, Belorussian and Jewish—as ipso facto enemies of the Soviet Union. Many would be later arrested and deported to the Soviet Union. The same fate befell former army officers and prisoners of war. Between February 1940 and the outbreak of the Russo-German war in 1941, around 1.5 million Polish citizens, possibly more, became inmates of camps scattered from Kazakhstan to Siberia.

Universities and schools were reopened and literary associations were allowed to function, but with a stress on Marxist-Leninist content of culture and education. True to their penchant for outward legality, Soviet authorities organized in late October 1939 elections in which 90 percent of the people participated. National Assemblies of Western Belorussia and Western Ukraine, thus elected, gathered respectively in Białystok and Lwów and petitioned by a show of hands for incorporation into Soviet Belorussia and the Ukraine. The city of Wilno with its surrounding area was handed over to Lithuania, which by 1940 became a Soviet Republic. While Russian Communists exercised real power, several Polish Communists were active in the process of incorporation of Poland's eastern provinces into the Soviet Union. Among them were Wanda Wasilewska, the daughter of a former Polish foreign minister and associate of Piłsudski, and Stefan Jędrychowski, both of whom were elected to the Supreme Soviet.

As nightmarish as conditions were for the Poles under the Soviet regime, life in the rest of Poland under Germany defied imagination. The fact that individual Nazi acts of terror, as for instance the destruction of the Czech village of Lidice, evoked greater feeling of revulsion than German atrocities in Poland can perhaps be explained on the grounds that at a certain point mass executions become statistics. Imagination cannot fully absorb the fact of the extermination of some six million Polish citizens during the occupation years. The Jewish massacres apart, the scale of German terror was reflected in the contemptuous remark of the governor of occupied Poland, Hans Frank: "If I wanted to put up posters for every seven Poles that had been shot, the Polish forests would not suffice to produce the paper for the announcements."

The impact of the occupation on the Polish psyche was profound, and it manifested itself in attitudes toward life and death, public morality, authority, individuals, and society. The German occupation brought to the fore noble, heroic and self-sacrificing traits along with corrupting and debasing features. Few if any people succeeded in having gone through this period unscathed, and one can hardly understand post-World War II Poland without reference to wartime experiences.

The German share of Poland was divided into territories annexed to Germany outright, and the General Gouvernement. The former comprised lands held by Germany at one time or another and newly added areas. Native Germans constituted less than 6 percent of the total population, but these territories were eventually to be fully germanized. During the wartime period only beginnings were made; all Jews and over 700,000 Poles were evicted to the General Gouvernement or taken as laborers to Germany. Baltic Germans were brought in as unwilling settlers. A thin German veneer covered the Polish character of these lands. Not only towns for which German names existed saw them revived, but new ones were invented. Gdynia became Gottenhaffen and Łodź Litzmannstadt.

The future of the General Gouvernement seemed at first uncertain. Hitler talked vaguely in late 1939 about a rump Polish satellite state, seemingly holding it out as bait to the antiwar circles in France and Britain. Shortly thereafter the true character of the General Gouvernement became clear. It was to serve as "a sink in which to empty the Jews," and its inhabitants, in the words of Governor Frank, were to be "slaves of the German Reich."

The intense terror served as a deterrent against Polish resistance and as the means of gradually destroying the people. In a sense, ruthlessness was inherent in the Nazi regime and manifested itself, among other things, in the extermination of patients in the lunatic asylums. The specific forms of Nazi terror and its objectives varied over the years. A Polish historian of occupied Warsaw distinguished between several different periods, characterized respectively by preventive arrests of the intelligentsia and secret mass executions; mass manhunts and deportations to concentration camps largely to get laborers; systematic massacres in prisons and in the woods and increased use of concentration camps; public executions and extension of terror to the labor class; executions of prisoners running up to 300 people weekly followed by a slackening of openly advertised terror. The high points seemed to coincide, in the spring of 1941, with preparations for the invasion of Russia and in late 1943 with the crucial developments on the eastern front. But these events need not have played the determining role.

Given Poland's destiny as a German colony, it was logical for the Nazis to concentrate their "devil's work"—a phrase ascribed to Hitler—on the Polish intelligentsia. A certain pattern already emerged from the first sporadic executions during the September 1939 campaign. A systematic annihilation of Polish culture took the form of confiscation or destruction of libraries, museums, and monuments of art; a prohibition of printing of books and newspapers; the outlawing of theatres except for cabarets designed for "primitive entertainment"; and toleration of only primary and technical education. All the faculty of the Jagiellonian University of Cracow was arrested in November 1939 and taken to a concentration camp, where several professors died. Many other members of the scholarly profession were to perish in the years to come, and many risked their lives teaching in secretly functioning university classes.

The economic exploitation of the General Gouvernement produced impoverishment of the population, rampant inflation, and a drastic fall in the GNP. Friction between Governor Frank and Berlin increased the confusion concerning the place of occupied Poland in the Reich's economy, and halfway solutions were adopted. Private property of Jews and absent or inimical Poles was confiscated; German trustees were assigned to landowning estates and industries; the peasantry had to deliver fixed quotas of foodstuffs. The market of the General Gouvernement became subject to regulations, and starvation rationing was introduced. In 1932 an unemployed worker of the lowest category consumed roughly 2000 calories; by 1943, in comparison, a Pole was entitled to 400 calories and a Jew to less than 200. Such measures combined with others created conditions of a surrealistic "make-believe" life, as a Polish scholar has called it. In these Kafkaesque conditions Polish farmers and landowners, whose mortgages rapidly dwindled, fared better than the city dwellers. The governor of Warsaw admitted that he had no idea of how the million and a half inhabitants of the capital earned their living. To the regimented market the Poles opposed a highly developed black market, which the Germans tolerated or even used themselves. The process of corruption of German official-dom reached tremendous dimensions.

Remnants of the Polish administration were preserved on the lowest level; this was also true for the self-administering Jewish units in the ghettos. A Polish welfare institution, the Central Social Council (RGO), was tolerated by the German authorities, as were similar organizations of the Jews and Ukrainians. After the German invasion of Russia, Eastern Galicia was included in the General Gouvernement in 1941 and the number of Ukrainians reached almost 30 percent of the population. The Ukrainians were able to engage in a political dialogue with the Germans.

For an average Pole living in a big city life would at best be uncertain. Even if he did not belong to the underground, he might suddenly be seized, sent to a concentration camp or taken as a hostage and publicly executed in retaliation for anti-German activities of which he knew nothing. If he sheltered a Jew he would be sentenced to death.

The Jews and the frequently forgotten Gypsies (hunted down and exterminated by the Germans) were beyond the pale. Early in the war Jews were herded into ghettos established in most larger cities and isolated from the rest of the population by stone walls. There they vegetated, hoping vainly that the genocide of several million was not feasible. At the turn of 1942 and early 1943 the Nazis proceeded, however, to "the final solution" and organized large-scale transports from the ghettos. Concentration camps, to mention only Oświęcim-Brzezinka (Auschwitz) and Majdanek, were filled with Jews and Poles. Later, Jews were also sent to special death camps, notably Treblinka, where they faced immediate extermination in gas chambers.

Did Poland become a Jewish graveyard partly because the Poles were inclined to anti-Semitism? Could a larger number of Jews have survived amidst a more amicably disposed population? These questions have to be carefully considered. It is necessary to reiterate that Poland was the only occupied country where aiding or sheltering a Jew was punishable by death, and where German terror was about the worst in Europe. If one can speak of indifference of the Polish masses to the fate of the separated and isolated Jewish community, it must be seen in the context of the ongoing struggle for survival. Sublime courage or villainy are always the attributes of a minority. Blackmailers and informers who denounced the Jews were threatened with severe penalties by the Polish underground. While anti-Semitism persisted and was fed by stories of pro-Soviet Jewish behavior in eastern Poland, some of the formerly notorious anti-

Semites helped Jews, and not only individuals but numerous churches and convents provided them with places of refuge.

Polish aid to Jews took organizational forms by 1942–1943, and a special council of assistance was set up in the underground administration. Its reports to the Polish government in exile alerted the Allies to the fate of the Jews and urged action, but it was only in 1944 that President Roosevelt issued an open warning to Germany concerning the extermination of Jews. Contacts between the Polish underground and the Jewish Fighting Organization (ŻOB) existed, and some assistance was extended during the heroic Jewish struggle in the Warsaw ghetto in the spring of 1943. On the basis of existing evidence one can conclude that without the help of the Poles a large number of the Jewish survivors (variously estimated as between 40,000 and 120,000) would also have perished in the Holocaust.

The Polish underground constituted a most important and complex chapter of the occupation period. Its origins went back to the final phases of the 1939 campaign and were linked with Rydz-Śmigły's orders to organize a clandestine military network. Given the all-embracing nature of German occupation, the underground had to extend its activities to almost all walks of life. A secret state emerged comprising military and civilian branches, with secret courts, education, press and publications, theaters, concerts, and exhibits. In 1940 a partisan force later called the Home Army (*Armia Krajowa*, or AK) came into existence. Its commander-in-chief was General Stefan Grot-Rowecki, acting under the orders of the supreme command abroad. In 1943 the AK numbered some 200,000 men or more; exact figures are hard to establish. Its activities branched in three directions: diversion and sabotage, information and propaganda, and intelligence work. Between 1941 and mid-1944 the sabotage branch damaged over 6,900 German locomotives and 20,000 railroad cars, derailed over 700 transports, damaged or destroyed over 4,000 army vehicles, and dynamited 38 bridges. Various acts of sabotage exceeded 5,700. In 1942, special AK units seeking to protect the population against raging German terror engaged in counterterror against Germans and their collaborators. When later in the year the occupants attempted to expel the Polish population from a large area around Zamość, the AK operating from heavily wooded area carried out offensive guerilla operations.

In addition to the AK there were other "woods units" associated with political parties, most of which followed the AK leadership. Only the National Armed Forces (*Narodowe Siły Zbrojne*, NSZ) on the extreme right, and Communist partisans of the People's Guard, later called the People's Army (*Armia Ludowa*, AL), refused to acknowledge the AK command. The underground soldiers, treated as bandits by the German authorities, fought under extremely hard conditions, facing torture and death if captured by the Gestapo. If the underground had some demoralizing effects on its youthful members, it also spurred them to heroism and selfless devotion. Their fighting spirit was very high. Intelligence work of the AK claimed such successes as capturing a German flying bomb, the V2, and sending the detailed description together with some vital parts to England. The information and propaganda branch played an important part in preserving the morale of the Polish people by issuing bulletins and publications undermining German propaganda efforts.

The relationship between the underground and the Polish government in exile went through several phases. The Home Political Representation, to use one of the changing names of the central organ in Poland was based on the major political parties and represented the overwhelming majority of Poles. Still, friction between politicians and the military—the former by and large representing the prewar opposition, the latter the professional soldiers educated in the Piłsudski tradition—was unavoidable. To enhance the power of the civilian authority, the government in exile appointed a delegate for the homeland who by 1944 had the title of deputy premier and headed a small cabinet.

The underground's ideological declarations stressed that the war for independence continued and that the homeland fought for a democratic state strong enough to give support to other countries situated between Germany and Russia. The government in exile was recognized as the supreme legal authority, but the underground denied it the exclusive right to take decisions prejudicial to Poland's territorial integrity or likely to endanger a genuinely democratic system.

Contact between homeland and abroad was maintained by clandestine radio communications and secret airstrips permitting supplies and parachute jumps into occupied Poland. These activities were supervised by the Allied Special Operations Executive (SOE) which had a Polish section. From 1941 to 1943 over 160 Polish officers and couriers were dropped by parachute. Supplies over the entire war period amounted to some 600 tons—in comparison, supplies to occupied France exceeded 5,700 tons and to Yugoslavia, 10,000. From 1944 three secret airfields operated permitting the landing of Allied aircraft.

The Polish government in exile was constituted in 1939 in France and moved to Britain after the French collapse. The new president,

Władysław Raczkiewicz, had been appointed by the interned president Mościcki, and in turn appointed a cabinet headed by General Sikorski who also assumed the command of Polish armed forces. Zaleski became foreign minister, and leading figures of prewar opposition filled the cabinet posts. A substitute parliament, the National Council, was headed by the aged Paderewski. The application of the 1935 constitution was modified so as to permit a more democratic operation of the regime, but the government strongly emphasized that it was the legal continuator of the former Warsaw government and consequently a successor to all prewar commitments and treaties entered into by Poland. It was recognized as a legitimate government by France, Britain, and virtually all the neutral states.

The Polish status of a full-fledged ally was, however, more theoretical than real. The military collapse, total occupation, and particularly the relationship with the USSR, with which Poland, but not its allies, was in a de facto state of war, placed the Polish government in a position of inequality toward France and Britain. The Poles made strenuous efforts to show that they could still signally contribute to the Allied war effort at home and abroad. Polish troops composed of refugees and prewar emigrants and organized in France reached the size of two divisions, a highland brigade and a motorized brigade. Polish airmen stationed in Britain made up Polish squadrons within the RAF; naval units sent out earlier joined the Royal Navy. A Polish brigade was organized in the Middle East. These troops fought in the Norwegian campaign, particularly at Narvik, and in France in 1940, although only a few units could be evacuated to England. There they were reorganized and expanded, and by the summer of 1940 the Polish army, navy, and air force comprised some 30,000 men. In the Battle of Britain Polish fighters were credited with destroying more enemy planes per pilot than any others in the Royal Air Force.

Increasingly regarded as the symbol of Polish determination to fight until victory, General Sikorski was a commander of high calibre and a capable politician. A determined and courageous man, he displayed great self-confidence although he lacked Piłsudski's intuition and charisma. Susceptible to flattery, he did not always choose his collaborators wisely. Although authoritarian by temperament, Sikorski was a sincere democrat opposed to the prewar Polish regime. Critical of Beck's foreign policy, he sought, with British support, to reach an understanding with the Czechoslovak government in exile headed by former President Beneš. In November 1940 a joint Czechoslovak-Polish statement appeared favoring a close postwar association of the two states, Sikorski's final goal being a West Slav federation constituting a nucleus of a regional East Central European bloc. Beneš insisted that any future larger unit in this area "will not and dare not be anti-Russian," whereas Sikorski opposed a subordination of that part of Europe to Russian interests. He viewed the future association of smaller East Central European states as strengthening them against both Germany and the Soviet Union.

Given the Soviet role in 1939 and their subsequent policies toward the Poles, one could hardly expect the Polish government to feel friendly toward Russia. Yet Sikorski was aware that Churchill, for all the initial indignation voiced over the Soviet stab in the back, was not absolutely committed to the restitution of Polish eastern frontiers. After the fall of France, London was inclined to recognize or at least not to question the status quo achieved by the Soviet Union. Informal exchanges between a Sikorski confidant and a representative of the Soviet Tass agency in London revealed that Moscow might favor a future restitution of a Polish state, provided it be confined to "ethnic" Poland and politically oriented toward Soviet Russia. Sikorski was not prepared to talk to the Russians in these terms, but he seemed to favor some secret agreement providing for the organization of Polish troops in Russia. In mid-1940 all this was highly unrealistic, but President Raczkiewicz and Foreign Minister Zaleski found Sikorski's attitudes, presumably influenced by the British, most disturbing.

In the spring of 1941 Sikorski went on a visit to the United States. He wished to tap the manpower reservoir of American Polonia for the Polish army and obtain Washington's blessings for such an undertaking. His political purpose was to acquaint Roosevelt with Polish war aims, particularly with the project of a Czechoslovak-Polish confederation and a future wider union in East Central Europe. Finally, he sought to establish closer cooperation with Polish Americans, as during the First World War, and enlist their support for the Polish cause. The first stage of American-Polish wartime relations began.

The outbreak of hostilities in 1939 revealed the strength of anti-war feelings in the United States. Roosevelt behaved with caution. In one of his fireside chats, however, he said: "Even a neutral cannot be asked to close his mind or his conscience," and in his tactics combined the isolationist "keep-out-of-war" slogan with the "prevent-the-war" outcry of the internationalists. War, Roosevelt argued, could be prevented by extending assistance to the Allies. After protracted debates, he was able to sign the new Neutrality Laws providing for a repeal of the arms embargo, but still stipulating that American supplies be paid for on delivery and transported in foreign ships.

Roosevelt followed the Polish campaign on a map hung in his White House office. His appeals to the belligerents against indiscriminate bombings had no effect on the Germans; the British used them as a pretext against launching their own air attacks. But the brutality of German warfare shocked the Americans, and the ambassador in Warsaw reported that he found it hard to ascribe the "wanton aerial bombardment" by the Luftwaffe to anything "short of deliberate intention to terrorize the civilian population and to reduce the number of child-producing Poles irrespective of category." Ambassador Biddle's detailed and long report on the campaign in Poland was submitted to the president. Americans could visualize what German air raids were like thanks to a reporter, Julian Bryan, caught in the besieged Warsaw, who provided a description of them with numerous photographs in his book, *Siege,* published in New York in 1940.

Guided largely by humanitarian motives, the United States offered refuge in America to President Mościcki who, however, settled in Switzerland. In the autumn of 1939 a Commission for Relief in Poland was organized under Herbert Hoover, and the American Red Cross undertook deliveries of supplies to the Polish population. Nearly half a million adults and 320,000 children (Polish, Ukrainian and Jewish) received aid administered through the Central Social Council. By the end of 1940, however, this aid could no longer get through to occupied Poland. The Jewish Joint succeeded in providing separate help to Jews in the amount of 4 million German marks in 1941 and 5 million the following year. Then it was stopped by the Germans. In subsequent years American Jewry seemed to show relatively little interest, other than verbal, in the fate of their coreligionists in occupied Poland.

The United States promptly recognized the Polish government in exile, declaring that "mere seizure" of territory "does not extinguish the legal existence of a Government." This statement, made by Secretary Hull on October 7, 1939, did not, however, contain a phrase from an earlier draft, that America did not and never would recognize the fruits of aggression. As Moffat of the State Department noted, the statement accomplished this purpose but did not "bind our hands for the future." Roosevelt protested neither against the Soviet invasion of Poland nor against the installation of Russian bases in the Baltic countries, and this abstention probably stemmed from a fear of bringing Moscow closer to Germany. Still, the Russian attack on Finland was severely censured, and in February 1940 Roosevelt called the Soviet dictatorship as absolute as any in existence. The poor showing of the Red Army against the Finns contributed to the bad press Russia had in the United States. In an opinion poll run by *Fortune* in early 1940, the question "which nation do you regard as the worst influence in Europe," elicited the answer: Germany (53.3 percent) and Russia (34.2).

In early 1940 Roosevelt dispatched his trusted Undersecretary of State Sumner Welles on a fact-finding mission to Europe. The findings provided the president with the argument that America was seeking a "moral basis for peace," which was unattainable if small nations had to live in fear of powerful neighbors and pay tribute for freedom from invasion. Sumner Welles met with Polish leaders and found that Sikorski, whose character and integrity (but not his intellect) he praised, was generally optimistic. On the other hand, Foreign Minister Zaleski, with whom Biddle, reappointed ambassador to the government in exile, was on friendly terms, was pessimistic and gave Welles a sober memorandum on the European situation.

Roosevelt's policy of educating American public opinion to the Nazi danger was accompanied, notably during the 1940 presidential campaign, by promises that "your boys are not going to be sent into any foreign wars." Exploiting the shock caused by the fall of France and the danger posed to the British navy, Roosevelt succeeded in getting congressional approval for massive armaments and arranged for the lease of 50 old destroyers to England in exchange for British bases—the precursor of Lend-Lease.

It was under these circumstances that Sikorski came to America in late March 1941. The ground for his visit had been prepared by the new Ambassador Ciechanowski, who had occupied the Washington post in the 1920s. The general was the first Polish premier and commander-in-chief ever to visit the United States. En route he stopped in Canada, where he reached an agreement about the formation and training of Polish troops. In Washington, the American side of the deal was completed when Roosevelt and Welles gave their blessings for discreet volunteer recruitment. The success of this operation naturally hinged on the support of Polish Americans, and Sikorski, thinking of the First World War experiences and impressed by the welcome he received in New York, Chicago, Buffalo, and Detroit, misjudged the feelings and attitudes of American Polonia. Then and later he was inclined to regard them as Poles under the moral jurisdiction of his government.

America's Polish community had been horrified by the fall of

Poland and manifested its feelings in the moving Pulaski Day Parade in October 1939. Mass meetings were held and addressed by Herbert Hoover and the Archbishop of New York, Francis Spellman, among others. But out of the millions of Polish Americans only some 450,000 still retained Polish passports. Even they increasingly thought of themselves as Americans of Polish descent and were willing to assist the cause of Poland but not by enlisting in the Polish army. Recruitment produced small results; about 1,000 volunteered and joined the training camp in Canada.

Roosevelt's interest in Sikorski propagandizing the Polonia circles was largely connected with his policy of gradually leading the Americans into the Allied camp. He had already told Ciechanowski that the ambassador could, by speaking to Polish American circles, help to educate the public in world problems.

The Polish premier obtained Washington's promise that Poland would be included in the Lend-Lease program. This type of help was most welcome, especially since Polish assets in the United States had been frozen after the outbreak of the war. But it was made clear to Sikorski that he would have to work out the practical arrangements with London. Sikorski presented a memorandum on the plight of Jews in ghettos and made a special effort to obtain American support and blessing for his postwar plans of political reorganization of Central Europe. He said that he came to America not only as a Pole but as a spokesman of the smaller European powers. He described the Czechoslovak-Polish rapprochement as a first step in the direction of a democratic, regional organization of East Central Europe. Roosevelt responded by calling the plan a "fine idea" and congratulated Sikorski on his cooperation with Beneš, but it is doubtful whether Washington attached any real importance to Sikorski's ideas.

There was interest in some quarters. An anonymous group calling itself American Military Experts contributed an article to the periodical *New Europe,* published in New York, which asserted that a federation of victims of German and Soviet ambitions would be most important. On military grounds, the article advocated that Poland's western boundary be pushed to the river Oder. Since the credit for the later Oder-Neisse (Odra-Nysa) border was given by Soviet and Marxist Polish historiography to the communist camp, it is worthwhile to recall that Poles abroad and the underground showed an early interest in it. In November 1940 the "West Slav Bulletin," appearing in Edinburgh in Polish, printed a map of the Czechoslovak-Polish union with a western frontier on the Oder-Neisse. Sikorski thought of the border as a security line important not only to Poland but to the entire East Central European region. At that point he did not officially present it in Washington but engaged in sounding out the American leaders.

Sikorski's first visit revealed certain elements of the pattern of wartime American-Polish relations. A general friendliness apart, one could notice Washington's cautious attitude toward Polish long-range political objectives as well as a tendency to treat Poland as being primarily a British concern. At this point Roosevelt found it useful to propagandize Poland's cause in order to mobilize American public opinion against Germany, and the Polonia served this purpose well. This was going to change later when Russia entered the Allied camp.

The Grand Alliance and Its Poor Relatives

The German invasion of Russia on June 22, 1941, opened a new phase of the Second World War. Britain's decision, backed by Washington, to welcome the Soviet Union as a comrade in arms and a principal ally, placed the Polish government in a quandary. Were the Poles to efface at one stroke the recent Soviet-Polish past and join in welcoming the much needed ally against Germany or should they insist, even at the price of disturbing Western-Soviet relations, on Russian amends and guarantees as a condition for collaboration? A great deal depended of course on the appraisal of the German-Soviet struggle and its impact on the final outcome of the war.

To Churchill the involvement of Russia was a godsend. The prime minister said that if Germany invaded hell, he would feel bound to make a favorable reference to the devil in the House of Commons. Churchill anticipated a long and exhausting war and was determined that Russia not be lost as an ally as happened in 1939. Without waiting for Soviet overtures and request for aid he extended his hand to Moscow.

American thinking was somewhat different. While Cordell Hull and old Russian hands such as Bullitt urged caution, Roosevelt and his advisers favored unconditional assistance in order to prevent a speedy Russian collapse. The secretary of war reckoned with a German victory within one to three months; even former Ambassador Joseph E. Davies, who was more optimistic, did not exclude a separate Soviet-German peace, although he believed there would be prolonged Russian resistance behind the Urals. Davies doubted that for many years to come the Soviet Union would be in a position to spread communism to the United States or even to Europe. Roosevelt shared this point of view. If the war in the east, he wrote to Leahy, proved to be more than a diversion, it would mean "the liberation of Europe from Nazi domination," and "at the same time I do not think we need worry about any possibility of Russian domination." Was this because Roosevelt deemed the USSR too weak to attempt it—both he and his entourage seemed to underestimate Soviet military potential—or because he thought it unlikely? The president probably devoted little thought to the possible effect of a Russian victory and, as some American historians believe, had a feeling toward Soviet Russia similar to that of Jefferson toward the French Revolution. For all its bad sides Bolshevism was surely an experiment for the improvement of the lot of man.

In July 1941 Roosevelt dispatched his confidant and alter ego, Harry Hopkins, on a perilous flight to Moscow. The president instructed him to impress on Stalin that the United States wished really to assist the Soviet Union. According to the American ambassador in Moscow, the Russians attached great importance to the mission; the ambassador felt it would have most beneficial effects on Soviet-American relations and on the Soviet war effort. This appraisal notwithstanding, it is hard not to believe that the solicitude of the capitalist Anglo-Saxon world struck the ever-suspicious Stalin as a cynical attempt to use Russians as cannon fodder. Hard pressed though he was, Stalin immediately exploited the fact that it was not he who had pleaded for Western help and, fully aware of the importance of the Red Army for the Allies, he would demand aid as his due and show annoyance that it was not large and speedy enough. He also wanted to start concrete political talks with the British to obtain confirmation of his territorial gains in East Central Europe. It was less apparent whether Stalin sought to treat all of that region as Russia's sphere of influence and planned a westward expansion of communism. But it is difficult to imagine that Soviet leaders did not have ambitious thoughts. The First World War had brought a victory of communism in Russia—the Second World War held the prospect of a communist revolution in Europe.

Preoccupied with dispelling Soviet suspicions of the West, Churchill and Roosevelt were offering aid to Russia first to prevent a Soviet military collapse, later to bring a German defeat in the east, finally not to endanger their postwar collaboration with a mighty power. The West was driven deeper and deeper into a kind of appeasement. As Charles Bohlen later put it, Roosevelt never entirely comprehended "the great gulf that separated a Bolshevik from a non-Bolshevik." The president's political tactics, which won him great successes in domestic affairs, proved ill-fitted to diplomacy, particularly in dealing with such a partner as Stalin. The discrepancies between Roosevelt's private and public statements, his constant worry about the American electorate, and his belief in having won over Stalin by charm and charisma, proved in the long run to be serious liabilities and put the president in a weak bargaining position against the Russian dictator.

Caught in the web of overt and undercover Anglo-American-Russian diplomacy, the Polish government faced great difficulties. Churchill's concern for Poland was genuine, and his exclamation to General Sikorski in the dark hours of the French collapse: "We shall conquer together or we shall die together," was not purely rhetorical. Churchill was also a realist, even if of an emotional type, and as the war progressed he realized that to maintain Britain on a footing of equality with the United States and Russia he would need allies on the Continent. Hence his inclination toward a European union, and a regional organization in East Central Europe based on Poland and Czechoslovakia. Churchill was willing to compromise with Russia, but could not disinterest himself in the fate of Poland. With most Englishmen, however, he believed that the Riga frontiers ought to be revised to Russia's advantage, especially if it meant Soviet acceptance of his plans.

Roosevelt, as an American historian pointed out, "had little genuine concern for Poland." His concept of the postwar world was based on great powers' domination and had little room for groupings of smaller states. The Poles could never be America's partners; they were not to ask the reason why, or to put it more crudely, not to rock the boat of great powers' cooperation. Roosevelt did generally subscribe to the Wilsonian principle of national self-determination and for domestic reasons found it necessary to emphasize the fact. The Poles were frequently misled by this and prone to contrast the seemingly ruthless Churchillian Realpolitik with American idealism. They did not fully appreciate the extent to which the president wished to stay clear of Russian-British controversies and avoid the Polish problem which, as Anthony Eden remarked, "terrified" the American administration for domestic political reasons.

Shortly after the German attack on Russia, Churchill assumed the "invidious responsibility," to use his own words, for making the Polish government reestablish diplomatic relations withRussia without insisting on any guarantees. The Sikorski-Maisky agreement signed on July 30, 1941, annulled the Ribbentrop-Molotov Pact, provided an "amnesty" for Poles in Russia, and prepared the ground for the formation of a Polish army on Soviet soil. The agreement led to a split in the Polish government, resulting in the resignation of General Sosnkowski and Zaleski. Of course Sikorski could hardly afford to defy British emphatic wishes, but he also believed that Russia would be bled white by the war and that the overwhelming might of the West could determine the future shape of Europe. Creating a Polish army in the east and freeing masses of Poles from Soviet camps appeared as immediate and tangible gains; if a détente in Soviet-Polish relations proved solid so much the better.

The Polish public was told that the agreement signified a return to the territorial status quo of 1939. This was misleading, because Russia claimed eastern Polish lands not in virtue of the pact with the Germans but because the inhabitants had voted for incorporation in the Soviet Union. A Soviet suggestion to create a Polish (as well as Czechoslovak and Yugoslav) national committee in Russia to supervise the organization of the armed forces carried dangerous implications. Moscow seemingly wished to have on hand a second Polish center that would be more amenable to its influence and a potential rival to the government in London. Meant as a trial balloon, the proposal was quickly withdrawn when even the conciliatory Beneš rejected it. In this connection one must remember that already before the German-Soviet break, the Russians had attempted to propagandize select groups of captured Polish officers, and among the questions the NKVD asked was: did they recognize that the Polish government in exile was a fiction and would they be willing to fight the Germans on the Soviet side? By November 1940 a few officers were moved to a comfortable house in the outskirts of Moscow which they called the "villa of bliss." Thus, Soviet attempts at gaining a pliable Polish instrument preceded all the later friction between Russia and the Polish government in London.

What was the American reaction to the reestablishment of Soviet-Polish relations and the role Britain played in it? Ambassador Ciechanowski, who presented a detailed report to Washington, gathered that the State Department was not uniformly happy about the means London had used to pressure the Poles into agreement. Sumner Welles was advised by Hamilton Fish Armstrong that an effort be made to gain Soviet acceptance of the prewar Polish-Russian borders. Armstrong felt that such a commitment might be "comparatively easy to obtain" at that moment, and it would represent a "moral sugar-coating" for the "pill which Americans must swallow if our government is to aid Russia." This counsel was not followed, and all that Ciechanowski could obtain from the State Department was a statement saying that American policy toward Poland had been made clear in 1939, namely, "not recognizing any change in her status of a free, sovereign, and independent nation."

The Soviet-Polish agreement, as understood by Washington, was "in line with the United States policy of non-recognition of territory taken by conquest," an encouraging if not a very precise formula.. But the real question remained open: whether Washington was willing to make use of its aid to Russia to support the Polish case. Paderewski had pleaded for this in his last message to Poles and Americans of Polish descent shortly before his death on June 29, 1941.

The Poles were given to understand that Roosevelt would use his influence with Russia at an appropriate moment, but that moment drew farther and farther away. Not fully comprehending the subtleties of Roosevelt's policy, the Polish government continued to regard Washington as more amenable to its representation than London. The inclusion of Poland in the Lend-Lease and a grant of $12.5 million for underground activities and the upkeep of Polish diplomatic missions confirmed the assumption of genuine American interest in Poland.

At that point Roosevelt's main concern was to convince a reluctant American public about the need for aid to Russia. The isolationists demanded that the two tyrannies be allowed to destroy each other. Some fifteen top Republicans regarded the German-Soviet war as a struggle unrelated to the issue of liberty and democracy versus totalitarianism. Taft was warning against the danger of a communist victory. Rather than urge the Soviet ambassador to make concessions to the Poles, Roosevelt suggested that Moscow publicize freedom of religion in the USSR, which might have an "educational effect" on the Americans. The president complained to the Russian about difficulties caused by prejudice and hostility against Russia held by large groups which exercised political power in Congress. He tried, jointly with the ambassador, to provide "sugar-coating" to American aid, but of a different kind from that suggested by Armstrong. The image of Russia had to be improved and the vision of the gallant eastern ally projected. This task devolved on the Office of War Information (OWI), which Durbrow of the State Department termed as "very definitely pro-Soviet." Its work done, Roosevelt could rejoice when an opinion poll indicated at the time that 73 percent of Americans hoped for a Soviet victory over Germany.

The Atlantic Charter, proclaimed on August 14, 1941, fell neatly into this pattern. The moralistic content of its principles fulfilled several functions. The Charter could be a reassurance to America's and worldwide worries about communist designs. It reflected Roosevelt's desire to put Churchill on record regarding the purity of

Allied war aims, and gain a safeguard against secret deals or spheres of influence without restraining Washington's freedom of action. The Soviet Union endorsed the Charter with subtly phrased but ominous reservations and emphasis on self-determination of nations.

In order to work out aid to and established cooperation with the USSR, the Harriman-Beaverbrook mission was dispatched to Russia toward the end of September 1941. A Polish attempt to join it was thwarted by Washington on the grounds that only an Anglo-American mission had been agreed upon. Hull, however, instructed Harriman to deal directly with Polish representatives in the Soviet Union, partly because Poland was a recipient of Lend-Lease, partly to strengthen the Polish hand. As an instrument of negotiations, the mission proved of little value. Stalin, alternating warmth and coolness, made it work on the principle of "give and give and give," as Harriman wrote, "with no thought of a *quid pro quo*."

American interest in Poland took the form of an inquiry into the fate of Polish priests, and a plea to Molotov to arm four Polish divisions. The second point stemmed from representations made to Harriman by the Polish commander, General Władysław Anders, and Ambassador Stanisław Kot. But the mission did not offer to provide Western equipment to the Poles, as not only Washington and Sikorski but also Molotov had suggested. Lord Beaverbrook did his best to sabotage any such plans. A month later the American embassy in Moscow transmitted Polish requests for American arms and equipment, in vain. By November 1941 both Churchill and Roosevelt inclined to the idea of moving Polish troops out of the Soviet Union to Iran, where they would be supplied with Western arms, trained, and then returned to Russia.

Toward the end of November, Sikorski went to Russia. The Anglo-American mission had not prepared the political ground for his talks, and American interest in Poland and Eastern Europe being undefined, could not have been explained to the Russians. Although Sikorski deluded himself that he was being treated as an equal ally, this was not the case. His requests that Poland be represented on the Supreme War Council and later on the level of the Joint Chiefs of Staff met with cool reception in London; Washington, as always, regarded these matters as Britain's business. Sikorski's main preoccupation, however, was the Polish army in the Soviet Union, for he believed that it would seriously strengthen the Polish position in the Allied camp. Mindful of the disaster that befell the Polish divisions in the French campaign of 1940, Sikorski wanted to preserve a large separate Polish operational group in Russia and prevent the squandering of his troops in small and scattered units.

Had Western equipment been available, this might have been possible to achieve.

General Sikorski went to Russia at a moment when the first signs of Polish-Soviet friction were already visible. The Soviets interpreted the so-called amnesty as applicable only to ethnic Poles and not to Jews, Ukrainians, and Belorussians who were Polish citizens. The Polish embassy protested. The Poles repeatedly inquired about the fate of several thousand officers, known to have been deported to Russia, who disappeared without a trace. Welfare missions seeking out Poles dispersed throughout Russia constantly ran into obstructions. Upon his arrival Sikorski received two ominous warnings. On December 1, the Russians officially declared that all inhabitants of eastern Polish provinces were Soviet citizens; the exception made for ethnic Poles was only a gesture of goodwill. A day later *Izvestiia* reported on a Polish meeting in Saratov, presided over by Wasilewska and Jędrychowski among others, which issued a manifesto to the Polish nation and foreshadowed the creation of the Union of Polish Patriots. The Soviets were letting Sikorski know that they had at their disposal the nucleus of a rival Polish center. Unknown to Sikorski was a third move, the parachuting of several Polish Communists to Warsaw, who began to reconstruct the party which they renamed the Polish Workers' party (PPR). Its objectives comprised not only the creation of a broad leftist front but also the organization of fighting units, supplied and assisted by the Soviets. The Russians also began to parachute their own partisans into Polish territories.

The Sikorski-Stalin talks began in a tense atmosphere. Stalin voiced his annoyance with the plan to remove Polish troops to Iran, which he regarded as a British intrigue. Eventually, it was agreed that the bulk of the army should remain in the Soviet Union to form five to seven divisions. Difficulties in locating missing people, particularly some 15,000 officers, and the problem of survival in primitive conditions occasioned further exchanges. Then Stalin raised the issue of the Polish-Soviet border. Constitutionally, the government in exile could not consent to cessions of state territory, but Sikorski probably made a mistake when he refused to listen to Stalin's ideas on the subject. Thus, the border question remained open, both sides insisting on the status quo respectively of 1939 and 1941. Stalin's remark about Polish territorial extensions in the west, in East Prussia, and along the Oder River was not taken up by Sikorski.

The visit ended in apparent harmony with the signing of the Sikorski-Stalin declaration on December 4, 1941, which spoke of a common struggle against Germany and future neighborly cooperation. Sikorski returned to London impressed with Stalin and quite hopeful about mutual relations. To his confidants he intimated the possibility of territorial concessions in Eastern Galicia and the recognition of Wilno as capital of Lithuania if that country agreed to a union with Poland. Sikorski also hinted that changes in the east with compensations in the west were not excluded.

Sikorski's visit was followed by that of Britain's Foreign Secretary Anthony Eden. By then the United States was already at war, and the State Department, knowing of Russian overtures to Britain, cautioned the latter against any special commitments and secret accords. Eden was thus highly embarrassed when Stalin proposed a Russian-British pact with secret territorial provisions. These included recognition of Soviet annexations and the special position of the USSR with regard to Rumania and Finland. The Polish-Russian border was to be settled jointly by Britain, the USSR, and Poland and correspond to the Curzon Line which, except in the Białystok area, was roughly similar to the Molotov-Ribbentrop border. Eden promised to refer the Soviet proposals to London and to consult with the United States. His advocacy of regional federations in Europe, dear to Sikorski and favored by the British, evoked Stalin's curt reply that "if some European countries wished to federate" he had no objections

Churchill was indignant about Soviet demands and felt that to abandon the Baltic countries "would dishonor our cause." Yet his indignation did not last long; at the same time Lord Beaverbrook insisted that the British press be allowed to champion the 1941 Soviet borders. With regard to Poland, Churchill began to develop the theory that the country would be able to preserve its sovereignty and political independence only at the price of territorial concessions.

Fearful of British pressures, Sikorski began a diplomatic counteroffensive by speeding up the Polish-Czechoslovak negotiations, encouraging a united front of the smaller Allies, and stimulating American opposition to a British-Soviet deal. A Polish-Czechoslovak declaration on a postwar confederation was issued on January 23, 1942. Ten days earlier Sikorski presided over a conference of the smaller Allies at which the British, American, and Russian delegates appeared as guests. With regard to America, Polish efforts seemed to coincide with Washington's determination to oppose Soviet demands. The State Department felt that any frontier agreements prior to a future peace conference could only sow mutual suspicions and discord in the Allied camp, have an unfortunate effect on smaller countries around the world, and undermine the moral force of the Atlantic Charter. Stalin, it was believed, wanted territorial commitments both to legitimize his past annexations and to make sure Russian claims would be recognized even if the war ended without Soviet physical control of these lands.

The American stand was not as close to Polish thinking as one might assume. Washington's was a largely negative formula that postponed but did not resolve the real issues. The United States had no program with regard to East Central Europe, and its seemingly anti-Russian stand was not tantamount to a pro-Polish policy. Ambassador Biddle worried lest Polish diplomacy arouse Soviet suspicions and he characterized Sikorski as too ambitious. The Pole's vision of his country as a center piece in a postwar Europe, Biddle thought, was clouding his judgment; other smaller Allies were beginning to be afraid to follow Sikorski's lead. Biddle was applying brakes and warning Washington that Sikorski might launch "a subtle anti-Russian play" among the Polish Americans.

Acting on the assumption that only an American veto could prevent a British-Soviet deal at the expense of East Central Europe, the Polish government dispatched acting Foreign Minister Count Edward Raczyński to the United States in February 1942. Raczyński went to seek an American "reinsurance" and possibly American credits and perhaps even a Polish-American agreement. He found Roosevelt and the State Department firmly adhering to the Atlantic Charter. Cordell Hull sincerely believed that it was preferable to take a firm attitude at that point rather than to retreat and be forced to be firm when "our position had been weakened by the abandonment of general principles." The Poles were gratified by Roosevelt's manifesto to the Polish nation, which stressed the invaluable Polish contribution to the war effort. They did not fully realize that, paradoxical as it may seem, Roosevelt's opposition to an Anglo-Russian deal was basically dictated by pro-Russian and domestic considerations.

In a contemporary memorandum Hopkins asserted that Russia was essential to the United States in war and in the postwar era and therefore, "we should be real friends." The relationship would not be one-sided because Russia would greatly need American products after the war. To improve relations Hopkins recommended that only personnel "loyal to this concept" be assigned to handling Russian problems. This referred to State Department professionals who feared that American moral and material aid to Russia would facilitate postwar Soviet domination of Europe. A future peace, Hopkins felt, would have to meet Soviet "legitimate aspirations," a notion shared by Roosevelt. The president and his aide had thus no substantive objections to Soviet demands and cared little about the areas claimed by the USSR, but 1942 was the congressional election year and it mattered a great deal that the image of Russia not be tarnished. It would not do to alarm the opponents of the Soviet Union, including the Polish American voters, by tolerating territorial agreements that could not remain secret for long. Nor would the Congress be likely to support aid to Soviet Russia unless, as Kennan put it, "an atmosphere of political intimacy with the Soviet government could be created and maintained."

Pro-Soviet propaganda was given the full-steam-ahead signal. The heavily propagandistic film "Mission to Moscow"—which the State Department officials had dubbed "Submission to Moscow"—was shown throughout the country. Charles Bohlen recalled that it was impossible to convince people that "admiration for the extraordinary valor of the Russian troops and the unquestionable heroism of the Russian people was blinding Americans to the dangers of the Bolshevik leaders." Prominent Americans, ranging from Reinhold Niebuhr, Henry A. Wallace, John Foster Dulles, Wendell Wilkie to scholars such as Ralph Perry of Harvard and George Vernadsky of Yale, were euphoric about the Red Army's resistance to the Nazis.

While Roosevelt and Hopkins kept reassuring Raczyński about their opposition to Soviet territorial demands, Assistant Secretary of State Adolphe A. Berle was more sincere when he told the Polish diplomat that Russia would emerge out of the war as a great power and would have to be granted special security rights. The unlimited sovereignty of the smaller states could not stand in the way.

Working on the assumption that Soviet demands for territorial expansion stemmed from a preoccupation with security—fears of a revived Germany and isolationism in America—State Department experts suggested a new worldwide system of collective security in the form of the United Nations. The idea appealed to Roosevelt, who later in the year told Molotov of his favorite idea: a four-policemen consortium maintaining peace and order in the postwar world. The policemen were the United States, Russia, Britain, and China; all other states, including France, would be disarmed. Minor issues such as the Polish question would be reduced to their true insignificant proportions.

The contrast between the main Allies and lesser associates was apparent in the launching of the United Nations in January 1942. Churchill stayed in the White House where Ambassador Litvinov joined him for lunch and the Chinese ambassador was consulted, while other Allies were addressed by Roosevelt and Churchill but not asked to express their views. After the United Nations document was signed by the great powers, others were invited to drop in at their convenience to affix their signatures. There was no pretense of equality. Similarly, only the big four were really involved in the creation of UNRRA (United Nations Relief and Rehabilitation Administration).

In these circumstances it was doubtful whether Sikorski's second visit to the United States in March 1942 could serve any useful purpose. Presumably the Polish government was still nervous about the possibility of a British-Soviet deal, and Sikorski believed that his personal intervention was needed. The American and Polish statesmen went essentially over the ground already covered by Raczyński. The president reassured Sikorski about American opposition to wartime deals and showed polite interest in the Polish underground and the plight of Polish Jews. Sikorski's defense of his confederation plans, then under attack by the Soviet Union, produced little response. No wonder, since Sumner Welles fully approved of Biddle's efforts to shelve Sikorski's projects. This was no time to offend Russia, Welles opined, although not all of its demands were acceptable. The Division of European Affairs of the State Department qualified Sikorski's efforts for a confederation free of Russian influences as "obviously doomed to failure."

It appears that Sikorski did not realize that his second visit to Washington was unsuccessful. Biddle reported that Sikorski returned to London "reinvigorated" and charmed by his contact with Roosevelt. In an interview to the British press, Sikorski asserted that the president and the people of the United States "fully realize the part that Poland can play after the war as a crystallizing center for a federal grouping in Europe." In his instructions to General Anders, Sikorski even stated that the Polish government would have "a decisive voice in all matters regarding the European continent," and that both London and Washington regarded Poland as the first among the subjugated nations. In private conversations with top Polish diplomats, Sikorski said that only a firm attitude of Roosevelt's could prevent an appeasement of Russia. He shared their views that Stalin's objectives regarding Poland were not merely territorial, but he still seemed optimistic about American interest in his country.

The attitude of the American Polonia was of some significance in that respect. The major organizations, including the Polish National Alliance and the Roman Catholic Union, set up in 1941 a Council of American Polonia which, however, did not engage directly in politics. In general it supported Roosevelt's and Sikorski's statements and contributed heavily to relief for Poland. The groups more critical of Sikorski's Russian policy centered around the editors of the two major American Polish newspapers: M. F. Węgrzynek of the New York *Nowy Świat,* and Frank Januszewski of the Detroit *Dziennik Polski.* Both were greatly influenced by a prominent prewar Piłsudski supporter, Ignacy Matuszewski, whom Sikorski had excluded from Polish emigré councils. Matuszewski undertook to mobilize public opinion in America in favor of Poland and signally contributed to the emergence of the National Committee of Americans of Polish Descent (known as KNAPP from a Polish abbreviation). With Węgrzynek presiding, the KNAPP constituted itself on June 20-21, 1942. Its formal establishment was preceded by a lengthy appeal addressed to Roosevelt in May, which expressed fears about Soviet designs on Poland and pleaded that the country not be diminished in size but rather augmented by territories in the west.

Worried by the activities of American Polonia, the Foreign Nationalities Branch of the Office of Strategic Services (OSS) looked with favor on the small pro-Soviet groups of Polish Americans. Probably manipulated by the Soviets, Leon Krzycki, a high official of the Amalgamated Clothing Workers of America, held in April 1942 an American Slav Congress which added its voice to the pro-Russian chorus of praise and admiration. An obscure and unsophisticated priest, Stanisław Orlemanski, and a prominent economist from Chicago, Professor Oskar Lange, a leftist who had come to America shortly before the war, later rose to prominence as representatives of the pro-Russian trend.

In late May 1942 the British-Soviet pact was signed without reference to territorial issues, but the Poles were mistaken in regarding this as their victory. Roosevelt went out of his way to humor his guest, Molotov, and besides mentioning the four-policemen idea, rashly promised the opening of a second front in Europe in 1942. The President did not want Molotov to depart empty-handed, but he failed to realize that an empty promise would not only increase Soviet suspicions but provide Stalin with valuable means of pressure. Such tactics, useful perhaps in an electoral campaign, were fatal in diplomacy. Roosevelt's message to Stalin stressing that the president believed in traditional Russian-American friendship stemming from "the character of the two peoples" could also be double-edged, for it might either be interpreted as a polite phrase or an assurance to Soviet Russia that American opposition to wartime territorial arrangements was in no way anti-Russian in nature.

Meanwhile Polish-Russian difficulties were mounting. General

Anders's decision to evacuate all Polish troops to the Middle East, a result of constant wrangles and conflicts, gave rise to mutual accusations. Incidents followed, such as the arrests of Polish employees in Russia, and culminated in the execution of two Polish Jewish Bund leaders, Henryk Erlich and Wiktor Alter, whom the Soviets declared guilty of collaboration with the Nazis. But this shocking episode had relatively little impact on American public opinion although Eleanor Roosevelt and Norman Thomas pleaded on their behalf.

The United States ambassador in Russia was instructed not to raise Polish matters with Stalin, and démarches on lower levels produced no results. He was finally told that the best policy for the United States would be not to meddle in Soviet-Polish affairs. The ambassador later wrote that Stalin held all the aces because he knew that "we had to play the game with him on his terms." The recommendation that Wendell Wilkie express, during his visit to Russia, some concern over the deteriorating Soviet-Polish relations was not heeded. Confronted with well orchestrated shouts for "second front," Wilkie played up to the Russians. As for Roosevelt, he professed his bewilderment over the state of Russian-Polish relations and promised Ciechanowski American assistance. There was no sequel, and once again Roosevelt could claim that he was not in a strong position to argue with the Russians. Moscow did not regard the Allied landing in North Africa as a fulfillment of the second front promise, and the West adopted a half-apologetic stance.

In December 1942 Sikorski came for the third and last time to Washington. In several memoranda the Polish premier outlined the confederation plans and Poland's territorial program that included an extension to the Oder River. Raising both political and military matters, he urged a strengthening of the moral and political unity of the Allies by an unconditional recognition of the sovereignty and territorial integrity of all members of the Grand Alliance. As for war strategy, he advocated an Allied offensive through the Balkans designed to cut off the German forces in Russia.

Sikorski's views struck no responsive chord. Although Roosevelt did mention in passing Turkey's usefulness for Allied operations, an offensive through the Balkans ran counter to American military thinking. Washington seemed more friendly toward the confederation idea, although the State Department opined that the United States could not discuss it before the great powers agreed on it among themselves. Sikorski's proposed draft of a letter by Roosevelt endorsing the concept of confederations in East Central Europe was watered down to such an extent that the endorsement became meaningless. While Sikorski later tried to assure the British that Washington shared his point of view, Sumner Welles made clear to London that Sikorski had done most of the talking. Roosevelt undertook no commitments, especially of a territorial nature. As for the Soviet-Polish border, the State Department considered a re-establishment of the Riga boundary impossible. While voicing official optimism, Sikorski began, for the first time, to fear that the United States was drifting toward a policy of appeasing Russia. Indeed, most signs pointed that way. In early 1943, Sumner Welles asked the Polish ambassador whether Poland was unwilling to sacrifice even an inch of its eastern territories. Returning from the Casablanca Conference, Roosevelt asked Ciechanowski not to press him to intervene in Soviet-Polish difficulties. The American ambassador in Russia was warning Washington that an expression of interest in Poland might have "far-reaching repercussions on American-Soviet relations" and even harm the Poles vis-à-vis Russia. He claimed that Sikorski's visit to Washington had done precisely that. In the ensuing months, the American contribution to the Polish problem was largely restricted to strong requests that the Poles not make public statements about their friction with Russia.

Displaying no initiative of his own, undermining Churchill's plans for a united Europe, and restraining the Poles, Roosevelt was coming around to the British viewpoint on Russian territorial demands. In March 1943 he indicated to Eden that he might agree to satisfy Russia in the Baltic area in order to use this as a lever to get concessions elsewhere. Roosevelt had no objections to Russian expansion to the Curzon Line, the importance of which Eden minimized. What mattered, Eden said, was that the right people were in control in Warsaw. This raised a fundamental issue that later would become central to the discussions of how to reconcile Russian desires for a "friendly" Polish government with the principle of a free democratic system. What could one do, Roosevelt asked, if the Poles had a "liberal government" at the time of the peace conference and threw it out "within a year?" Russian views on the matter were clear. Eden mentioned that Russia would not favor a Polish government of the type that existed before the war or in London. A friendly government was also a prerequisite for a Czechoslovak-Polish union, a point the Russians had made abundantly clear to Beneš.

Castigating unrealistic Polish hopes of becoming the main power in Eastern Europe—Roosevelt said that he liked Sikorski but did not think the Poles played their cards wisely—the president and

Eden agreed that postwar Poland would get East Prussia and minor extension in the west. But, as Roosevelt put it, it was up to the great powers to decide "what Poland should be," and he had no intention to go to a peace conference and "bargain with Poland or the other small states." Poland was to be set up "in a way that will maintain the peace of the world." This was a view the Russians approved of. Litvinov was telling Harry Hopkins that the United States and Britain should decide what to do with the Poles and "tell them" rather than ask them. Maisky in London was making similar points.

Was there a definite American policy or plan of how to work out a satisfactory Polish settlement? Harriman felt that it would mean trouble for the future "if we allow ourselves to be kicked around by the Russians." Roosevelt increasingly acted on the assumption that Russia would occupy a dominant position after the war, and therefore friendly relations with the Soviet Union were essential. Expectations of future economic cooperation with Russia as well as preoccupation with Japan reinforced this point of view. But this was still not a clear-cut policy, and the question arises whether an alternative policy could have been formulated.

The man who firmly believed so and whose experience in dealing with the Soviet Union went back to 1919 and the 1930s was the first American ambassador in Moscow, William C. Bullitt. In virtue of a private understanding with Roosevelt, Bullitt regarded himself as the principal White House expert on European problems. But in fact his star and influence were on the wane. Still, in 1943 Bullitt was submitting long memoranda for the president arguing for a different approach to international relations. Bullitt pointed out that there was no evidence of change in Stalin and that hopes to that effect were wishful thinking. His intentions ought to be approached with the "same admirable realism" with which Stalin treated all questions affecting the Soviet Union. Predicting with amazing accuracy the likely course of developments if Soviet ambitions were unchecked, Bullitt recommended agreements with the British concerning the future balance of power and integration of Europe, direct talks with Stalin, an immediate study of an invasion through the Balkans, and a reorganization of the State Department. By Europe Bullitt meant the continent west of the 1939 borders of Russia (minus Bessarabia, which he was willing to cede to the USSR). He urged the creation of a peace staff to prepare political objectives. Haste was essential because once Germany surrendered, American influence with the USSR would "reach zero."

With regard to Poland, Bullitt warned that the "eventual reduction of Poland to the status of a small Soviet republic" was part of a larger scheme. Unless checked, the Soviet sphere of influence like "an amoeba" would flow westward. America was at the peak of its influence and could apply pressure on Russia and Britain, but political pressure was insufficient to prevent a Soviet absorption of Eastern Europe. Hence, one had to mount a Balkan operation in order to get to the region before the Russians. In another memorandum Bullitt urged again that measures be taken to make it "difficult for Stalin to break his promise and overrun Central Europe."

Bullitt's views were contrary to everything Roosevelt considered to be the right approach toward Russia. He noted Bullitt's fears but felt that nothing could be lost by trying to work with the Soviet Union. Thus the president was committed to a vague and ill-defined policy that led with inexorable logic to Teheran and Yalta, and contained within it the germs of the Cold War.

The Road to Teheran

In the spring of 1943 the Poles suffered three heavy blows: the breach of diplomatic relations with the Soviet government, the arrest by the Gestapo of the commander of the Home Army, and the death of General Sikorski in a plane crash.

On April 13, the German radio announced the discovery of mass graves of Polish officers near the village of Katyn and accused the Russians of this murder. The Soviet reply, that the murder had been perpetrated by the Germans in 1941, was startling since Moscow had until then answered repeated Polish inquiries by professing complete ignorance of the officers' fate. The Polish government in London was shocked. In spite of Churchill's arguments that no action could bring the men to life, the Sikorski government issued a carefully phrased communiqué which, while denouncing German perfidious propaganda, asked for an inquiry by the International Red Cross. As Kennan later wrote, "it is hard, in retrospect, to see how the Poles could have done less."

Accusing Sikorski's government of collusion with Nazi Germany, Moscow severed diplomatic relations with it. Soviet-Polish relations had already been close to a breaking point. Four days before the incident, an American memorandum opined that underground Soviet activities in Poland and Russian treatment of the Poles suggested that the Soviets might desire a break in order to set up a Moscow-controlled "free Poland." Already in March Biddle had reported that Sikorski was prepared to "do all" in his power to avoid a rupture of relations, if only his government were met "with goodwill and some response on the other side." Biddle was not uncritically pro-Polish and in fact favored a quiet dismissal of several members of Sikorski's cabinet in order to placate the Russians. After the Katyn incident, Biddle commented that Moscow seemed to have awaited a pretext and warned that there were fundamental issues involved that went beyond the question of the Soviet-Polish border. The entire "Middle Zone" was at stake.

Soviet moves had indeed been disquieting for some time. In March 1943 the Union of Polish Patriots, headed by Wasilewska, came into existence and issued its political manifesto which carefully avoided any mention of a socialist or communist regime in Poland. Even earlier, in mid-February, Colonel Zygmunt Berling, who had remained after the departure of Polish troops from Russia, received Moscow's authorization to create and command a Polish division in the Soviet Union. The official announcement of the creation of the Kościuszko Division, politically subordinated to the Union of Patriots, came in May after the Soviet-Polish break. Hastily organized, the division was sent to the front in August and two months later suffered heavy casualties in the battle of Lenino. By that time Berling, promoted to general by Stalin, was entrusted with the organization of an entire Polish army corps. The British were alarmed since according to the official Soviet position of January 1943, there were no longer any Polish citizens remaining in Russia.

Roosevelt's reaction to Katyn and the breach of relations was one of annoyance. He scoffed when he was shown a special report pointing to Soviet guilt, an attitude he maintained even when the report was followed by documents and gruesome photographs. The president professed or appeared to profess belief in German guilt. Interceding with Stalin and defending Sikorski against the charge of collusion with the Nazis, Roosevelt called the Polish reaction "a stupid mistake" (corrected to "mistake" in the final version). Unlike the British government, however, Washington showed little sense of urgency. To Biddle's representations that one ought to press Sikorski for changes in his government and for curbing anti-Soviet Polish activity abroad, Welles replied that the United States did not wish to be involved either in a discussion of the Soviet-Polish border or in applying pressure on the government in London. In fact Roosevelt's attitude toward the Polish government became increasingly suspicious. The OWI and OSS memoranda, reinforced by opinions of Hopkins, Jonathan Daniels, and Davies, represented the government in London as a clique of reactionaries and inveterate russophobes who sought to arouse the Polonia against Roosevelt's Russian policy. The president's mood may be gauged by the fact that he was willing to acknowledge Wasilewska's congratulatory message from Moscow. But the State Department objected.

In a telegram to Stalin Roosevelt said that Churchill would make the Poles act with "more common sense," which meant that the matter of restoration of Polish-Soviet relations would be left to London. Largely for the record, the president asked whether he could be of any assistance and mentioned the adverse effect of the break on the millions of Poles in the United States. If this was also an attempt at veiled pressure, it was unlikely to succeed, especially since the United States, just like Britain, refused to take over the representation of Polish interests in the Soviet Union. This task was delegated to Australia. Sikorski's appeal to Roosevelt of May 4, 1943, which listed unfriendly Soviet activities prior to the break, complained about Wasilewska's Union of Patriots and their plans to communize Poland, and worried about the fate of Poles left in Russia without citizenship rights, produced little effect.

The American attitude toward the Russian-Polish problem appeared ever more alarming to the Poles. Welles made his annoyance about Sikorski's reaction to Katyn quite obvious. In a book published a year later Welles came out unequivocally in favor of Soviet claims to eastern Poland inhabited, according to him, by only 10 percent of ethnic Poles, a palpable untruth. Welles proposed the addition of East Prussia to postwar Poland, but simultaneously favored Polish territorial cessions to Germany in the region of Poznania and Pomerania.

In the summer of 1943, a questionnaire prepared by the National Opinion Research Center and sponsored by the OWI sought to ascertain the thinking of the Polonia on foreign matters and weigh the impact of anti-Soviet feelings. The phrasing of the questions alarmed the Polish embassy and the Polish American press. They felt that several were deliberately slanted in order to elicit answers that could then convincingly be used as an argument for a pro-Russian policy of Washington. The informants were asked, for instance whether they advocated American guarantees of Polish borders even at the risk of a war between the United States and the USSR. Other inquiries concerned the representativeness of the Polish government in London, and questions were raised about Matuszewski and his activities in America. The politically loaded questions were likely to deepen controversies among the Poles and weaken their position in America. Polish American organizations vehemently protested in many ways, including a telegram to Roosevelt; Polish American congressmen applied pressure. The Congress was perturbed, and the Washington columnist of the *New York Times* voiced sharp criticism of the questionnaire.

The result of the poll showed that 90 percent of the informants favored all possible measures to assist Poland, although only 45 percent were willing to push matters to the brink of war with Russia. One-third favored keeping the prewar boundaries; the majority said that they should be expanded. The poll may have given the Roosevelt administration some useful indications about the feelings of the Polonia as well as ideas on how best to handle Polish American public opinion. But Washington knew already that the National Committee of Americans of Polish Descent (KNAPP) was most outspoken in its warnings about Soviet designs on Poland. Drew Pearson sharply attacked the KNAPP and its spokesman Matuszewski. Sikorski had crossed swords with KNAPP by publicly castigating those who wished to disturb Polish-Soviet relations. After Katyn, KNAPP's criticism of Sikorski's Russian policy became widely shared in Polish American circles. In a dramatic telegram to Roosevelt they voiced concern that millions of fresh Polish graves should not be allowed to stand "before posterity as symbols of sacrifice made in vain."

Those feelings of Polish Americans could not be ignored in the year before the election, and Roosevelt had to tread cautiously. The directives given to the Office of War Information in June 1943 recommended emphasis on the ideals of the postwar world. "Make this picture so vivid and beautiful that the Poles will feel that we and the Russians are not only working for the same end, but for the only end which worthy men and women cherish." Broadcasts minimized Soviet-Polish friction and avoided taking sides in the dispute. The omnipotence of the United States was suggested.

All this was welcome news to Stalin. He had learned earlier through British channels that "among the supporters of President Roosevelt there are people who consider the prospects of the present Polish Government uncertain." They would like Sikorski to return after the war to Poland but doubted the chances of other members of his cabinet. Commenting on this useful piece of information, Stalin said that "the Americans were very near to the mark." There was little reason to be conciliatory or to mince words. *Izvestiia* carried a savage attack by Wasilewska on the Sikorski government. In his reply to Churchill's representations, Stalin accused the Poles of anti-Soviet propaganda and implied British connivance. There were "many pro-Hitler elements in the entourage of the Polish Government," he wrote, and Sikorski was "helpless and terrorized." Stalin described rumors about the formation of a Polish cabinet in Russia as nonsensical, but did not exclude the possibility of Britain, Russia, and America taking "measures to improve the composition of the present Polish government."

Roosevelt agreed with Churchill that a Soviet attempt to set up a rival Polish government was a danger that should be avoided at all cost, but the president preferred to discuss matters with Stalin without Churchill's assistance. His choice for this task of the uncritically pro-Soviet Joseph Davies showed that he wanted above all to humor Stalin. Davies reported that the Russians were suspicious, would insist on the Curzon Line, would oppose a "reactionary Poland," and would look with disfavor on the use of General Anders' Polish divisions in a second front in Yugoslavia. This last remark becomes clearer in the context of the military situation at the time. In the summer of 1943, the Allied invasion of Italy began, and rumors circulated about a possible descent in the Balkans. They aroused fears in Berlin and Rome and high expectations among the Balkan nations. A Balkan operation was advocated by Bullitt and others in order to forestal the Russians; in the opinion of the British historian, Elizabeth Wiskemann, a Balkan invasion might have ended the war in 1943. Stalin's concern about the use of the Anders troops becomes quite obvious. But he need not have worried, for the American command was fully opposed to any action in the Balkan peninsula. Operations in Italy, which Stalin refused to recognize as a second front, did not provide the Western Allies with any political instrument of pressure on the Soviet Union.

In mid-1943 the Poles suffered the loss of the Home Army commander Grot-Rowecki, arrested on June 30, and of General Sikorski, killed in a mysterious air crash at Gibraltar on July 3. We may never know whether it was an accident or an act of sabotage, but Sikorski's untimely death might have been convenient both to the British and to the Russians. Even Stalin preferred to accuse the Polish statesman of weakness rather than malice; Sikorski would have been a difficult person to ignore in a Western-Soviet deal at Poland's expense. His death encouraged the interpretation that he had been the most realistic of Polish politicians, conscious of the need to turn a new leaf in Soviet-Polish relations. A private Soviet epitaph came in the form of a curt remark made by the Russian ambassador, Bogomolov, to a Czechoslovak politician: Sikorski, the ambassador drily remarked, "had been anti-Russian."

Sikorski's successor to the premiership was Stanisław Mikołajczyk, the leader of the Populist party, a strong man but not of the standing or caliber of the deceased general. The new commander-in-chief, General Sosnkowski, was remembered for having opposed the original Sikorski-Maisky agreement. The one thing Sosnkowski and Mikołajczyk shared was a dislike for one another. A dangerous political-military dualism developed that affected relations with the homeland. There the post of commander of the Home Army went to General Tadeusz Bór-Komorowski, a brave officer but less sophisticated politically than Grot-Rowecki.

The main issue, which had been the object of numerous exchanges between Sikorski and Grot-Rowecki, was that of an uprising in Poland at the moment of German military collapse. Inextricably linked with it was the problem of how to use the Home Army to harass the Germans without suffering irreparable losses and exposing the population to savage Nazi reprisals. Some large-scale operations did take place in 1942, but the command believed that the bulk of underground forces had to be preserved for a final uprising. Polish Communists sharply criticized this policy and insisted on continuous and costly partisan actions meant above all to relieve the Soviet front.

At the turn of 1942 and early 1943 the new Communist leader in occupied Poland Władysław Gomułka, opened talks with the representatives of the Polish government and the Home Army. He offered to collaborate in an intensified campaign, provided the Communist partisans were represented on the general staff of the Home Army and on local levels while retaining their separate identity. Gomułka advocated that, even before the end of hostilities, a government be formed in Poland and based on a broad representation. Grot-Rowecki regarded these overtures as an attempt to penetrate the Home Army and to legitimize the Polish Workers' party (of some 8,000 members) in the eyes of public opinion. He demanded therefore formal recognition of the government in exile and its delegate in occupied Poland, a statement that Communists would act independently of foreign decision-making centers, the acceptance of the principle of Poland's territorial integrity, and a commitment to oppose any aggressor. Naturally the talks collapsed.

The reference to any aggressor was connected with the anticipated entry of the Red Army into Poland and the attitude to be adopted toward it. Was the Home Army to treat the Russians as liberators and allies? Sikorski's dialogue with Grot-Rowecki, before it was ended by the premier's death and the commander's arrest, produced some measure of agreement. Both men felt that once the German occupation began to crumble, the AK ought to seize control and, stressing its character of a partner and ally, act as a host to the entering Red Army. The AK commander insisted that such a policy be predicated on some previous Anglo-American guarantees to the

Polish underground, otherwise it might be forced to remain secret and in some form oppose the Soviet takeover of the country. Sikorski ruled out any active resistance and Grot-Rowecki accepted this position. Local anti-German uprisings preceding the Soviet advance were to be encouraged, particularly in the Lwów and Wilno regions to emphasize their Polish character. The AK commander also urged political concessions to the Ukrainians and Belorussians as well as the preparation of radical social reforms.

The dialogue continued between Sosnkowski and Bór-Komorowski. The former favored a general uprising—called Storm *(Burza)*—to be staged either if the Western Allies were close enough to help and permitted the premier and commander-in-chief to direct it, or if the German military control had completely collapsed. Cooperation with the Red Army could only be envisaged after a reestablishment of Polish-Soviet relations. In its absence a conspiratorial network would be maintained in Russian-occupied areas. The underground authorities modified these instructions in the sense that the Home Army units would come out into the open and identify themselves to the Red Army; those active in the lands claimed by Russia would try to remain there in conditions of semiconspiracy. Fighting against the Red Army was ruled out. All these decisions were made with a strong presumption that the West would retain a decisive voice in Polish matters. Even hopes for an eventual entry of Anglo-American troops persisted.

Partly in response to Polish urgings but also in order to create a better climate for a resumption of Soviet-Polish relations, American diplomacy tried to intercede on behalf of the Poles in Russia, while staying clear of territorial and political issues. Classified as Soviet citizens and denied the chance of leaving the country, these people evoked American sympathy. Stalin however, made it clear that he did not attach much significance to such matters nor did he feel that they caused Soviet-Polish estrangement. The severance of Soviet-Polish relations, he affirmed and reiterated, was due to "the generally hostile direction of the policies of the Polish Government in relation to the USSR." There was no good reason for Stalin to alter his policy toward the Poles. As far as the Western Allies were concerned, the dissolution of the Comintern and the re-creation of the Patriarchate of Moscow, interpreted as indications of Russian liberalization, were quite sufficient to improve Stalin's image in America and Britain.

Stalin's agreement to an Anglo-American-Soviet conference of foreign ministers in Moscow in late October 1943 was enthusiastically received in the West. The conference was to serve as a preparatory session for the forthcoming meeting of the Big Three, and the Poles hoped that it would provide an opportunity for Anglo-Saxon defense of the Polish position. The British attitude was not encouraging, for Eden favored the 1941 borders and changes in the composition of the Polish government. Still, London wanted to salvage the idea of confederations in East Central Europe to which the Poles attached great importance.

On the surface, the American attitude seemed more promising. Ciechanowski attempted to win over Cordell Hull to an arrangement whereby Soviet-Polish relations would be reestablished first, and the frontier issues would be left for a later settlement. The Polish ambassador warned of likely trouble if the Red Army entered Poland prior to the reestablishment of relations. He urged the presence of symbolic American and British detachments in Poland and argued his government's right to be represented on Allied councils. Hull agreed that Poles should act as hosts to the Red Army and stressed his belief that no territorial changes should occur before the end of the war. He also showed interest in the confederation plans and promised to defend generally the Polish side. Still, the Poles had cause for concern. They learned that plans for Home Army operations had been omitted from the general Allied strategic plans for Europe and were only to be considered in the event of an arrangement with the Soviet side. Nor was Washington likely to take the initiative, for it viewed Poland as a British strategic responsibility.

At the Moscow Conference the Polish question was handled in a somewhat perfunctory way that the Russians could only interpret as indicative of little real interest on the part of the United States and Britain. Eden's plan to discuss Polish matters hinged on American support, but Hull was lukewarm and unwilling to extend it. The foreign secretary's advocacy of regional confederations in East Central Europe brought forth Molotov's rejoinder that he doubted the value of confederations organized by exile governments which were not representing the will of the people. Harriman, appointed at that time American ambassador to Russia, pressed Hull to talk to Molotov about Poland, but the secretary of state did not wish "to deal with the piddling little things." Hull limited himself to platitudinous remarks about American concern for the rights of smaller nations and made no reference to the Soviet-Polish borders. This was likely to give the Soviets the impression that the United States would not object to their territorial claims. As for Harriman, he spoke about the need to compose Soviet-Polish differences and pointed to the existence of pro-Polish and pro-Russian groups in

America which wished for a reestablishment or Polish-Russian relations.

Eden's transmittal of Polish requests for arms for the Home Army elicited a Russian reply that supplies of arms were a good thing as long as the arms "fell into reliable hands." Accusing the Polish government of an unfriendly attitude toward Russia and treating Eden and Harriman to a "torrent of abuse against the Poles," the Russians mentioned the Kościuszko division fighting on their side. Eden countered by praising the Anders troops then fighting in Italy.

A report to the Joint Chiefs of Staff claimed that Eden and Hull made efforts to have the Soviets resume relations with the government in London, but as their suggestions were not well received, "the subject was dropped without much discussion." Harriman reported to Roosevelt that the Russians clearly insisted on the 1941 frontier and on a "friendly" Polish government. Although they made no reference to extending communism to Eastern Europe, Harriman suspected this would be attempted "if the kind of relationship they demand from their western border states can be obtained no other way." The Russians would act unilaterally in establishing relations with those countries in a way "satisfactory to themselves."

Starting from a position of relative weakness, the Russians scored on all fronts. Their lack of opposition to the possible inclusion of Turkey in the war or to a Balkan operation may have meant that they were willing to pay a price for a more speedy end of hostilities. But they were not asked to pay any price, and they saw that the West was not seeking to bind their hands in Eastern Europe. Soviet "concessions" took the form of agreements to cooperate on the top level with the Western powers, and Hull hailed the Four Nations Declaration as a great American victory. He visualized a bright future when "there no longer [would] be need for spheres of influence, for alliances, for balance of power." Harriman was closer to the mark when he diagnosed Stalin's objectives as a "pulverized Europe in which there would be no strong countries except for the Soviet Union."

The Moscow Conference meant a further deterioration of the Polish situation. Hull informed Ciechanowski that the Soviets seemed to regard territorial concessions as a prerequisite to a renewal of diplomatic relations. Stressing the strategically superior Russian position, he hinted that sacrifices had to be made. There would be no British-American representatives on the eastern front just as there were no Soviet delegates in the western theater. The Combined Chiefs of Staff informed the Poles that the arms and technical equipment deliveries to the Home Army previously promised by Roosevelt had to be canceled. The Poles protested against the Big Three decision of leaving the administration of liberated territories to the power that liberated them, for it implied that Poland, although an Allied nation, was put on the same footing as the former enemy territories. Partly to soften all these blows, after repeated urging by the State Department, Roosevelt invited the Polish Premier Mikołajczyk to visit Washington in January 1944.

The Soviet Union and Polish Communists increased their efforts to undermine the government in exile. At home Gomułka began to lay foundations for a future "anti-fascist national front" and tried to gain support from Populist and Socialist leaders, whom he assured that communism would not be introduced in Poland by force. The Polish Workers' party denounced the government in London as incapable of organizing a democratic regime in postwar Poland. In America, Father Orlemanski set up a Kościuszko League in November 1943 in Detroit, which passed resolutions directed against the government in London and attacked the KNAPP. Naturally all this was publicized by the Tass Agency. Soviet and Polish Communist partisans intensified their activities, and Bór-Komorowski ordered his units to combat bandits (who also operated under the guise of partisans) and subversive groups. The order was understood by some as a green light to fight the Communists in the underground and although the AK commander later explicitly forbade it, this was grist to the mill of Soviet propaganda. The stage was being set for representing the Soviet-Polish conflict as essentially a domestic strife between Polish progressive and reactionary forces.

On the eve of Roosevelt's departure for Teheran, the Polish government submitted a lengthy memorandum reiterating hope for the reestablishment of Soviet-Polish relations and subsequent Anglo-American guarantees of Poland's independence and territorial integrity. It appealed for Roosevelt's intervention with Stalin, and spoke of an uprising scheduled to break out at a moment agreed with the Allies either just before or during the entry of the Red Army. Hull also received an oral message from Mikołajczyk wishing to convey to the president suggestions for a solution of the existing difficulties. Mikołajczyk was ready to undertake the necessary journey at any time and in secrecy. This phrase and the reference to an uprising were both underlined—perhaps by Hull or Hopkins—as deserving attention.

Hull reported that the Polish ambassador was very agitated and had to be calmed by assurances that the secretary was "a friend of Poland." The situation was indeed becoming desperate, and Miko-łajczyk said that even a man condemned to death had a right to a last word. He warned of serious repercussions among Poles in Britain and America, in the armed forces and in the underground, if the Polish government were not consulted prior to Allied decisions affecting Poland. Hull recommended to Roosevelt to work for a resumption of Polish-Soviet relations, and if this proved temporarily unfeasible, exert "all our influence to persuade the Polish Government to give instructions to its underground army to launch at the opportune moment a full-fledged attack on the Germans" and "to assist the Red Army in its battle." This would help Britain and the United States to convince the Soviets of the Polish government's firm desire to contribute to the shortening of the war.

Preparing for the Teheran Conference, Roosevelt planned to appeal to Stalin "on grounds of higher morality" to respect self-determination in East Central Europe and be conciliatory toward Poland. It was to be an appeal, not a demand, and the president took no position paper with him. He wanted to play the Polish question by ear. "I think I can personally handle Stalin better than either your Foreign Office or my State Department," he wrote Churchill. "He likes me better." This was a risky assumption since, as the Russian-born British interpreter noticed Roosevelt had no understanding of Soviet psychology. The president told his collaborators that he was willing to accept the Curzon Line as the Soviet-Polish border but hoped to save Lwów for Poland and have plebiscites held in areas to be taken over by Russia.

The Teheran Conference (November 28 to December 1, 1943) represented a turning point in the course of Poland's history during the Second World War. It was there rather than at the much more publicized and debated Yalta that irreversible decisions were taken. Roosevelt showed his hand to Stalin and presided over a policy that led to subsequent American-Soviet confrontations on terms less favorable to the United States. The very choice of the site was an American concession—Teheran was inconveniently located for communication with Washington—and Roosevelt's acceptance, for security reasons, of hospitality in a villa in the Russian embassy compound that was presumably bugged. was a tactical error. Instead of attempting to impress Stalin by a united American-British front, Roosevelt chose to exaggerate his differences with Churchill and sought to appear as an arbiter between the British and the Russians. He seemingly enjoyed Stalin's needling of Churchill, for instance, when the Soviet dictator spoke about the need to shoot

50,000 German officers. Coming after Katyn this was a grim joke at best and it incensed Churchill. Roosevelt laughed.

The conference resolved two major issues: the operation Overlord (Allied invasion of France) and the Polish question. With regard to the former Stalin acted as a hard interrogator, constantly implying his doubts in British and American sincerity and resolve. In contrast to the Moscow Conference, he now firmly opposed the involvement of Turkey and a Balkan operation. Roosevelt was forced into a defensive position to which his own tactics also contributed. Far from dominating the conference and winning Stalin over, he found the Russian leader tough and on occasion capable of deliberate discourtesy. In discussing the postwar international organization, Roosevelt admitted that the United States could contribute only maritime and air forces; land armies to police the world would have to come from Britain and Russia. Stalin must have been delighted to learn that Washington anticipated pulling out of Europe, thus reducing its political influence on the Continent.

Churchill was the first to raise the Polish question with a somewhat reluctant Stalin. Receiving confirmation of Soviet support for an extension of Poland up to the Oder River, Churchill demonstrated with three matches how Poland would be physically moved in the westward direction. Then Roosevelt closeting himself with Stalin, gave him a most candid exposition of his stand on the Polish question. The president would like to see the eastern Polish borders revised in Russia's favor and the western shifted to the Oder, but he had to fight a presidential campaign in 1944 and could not afford to risk losing the large Polish American vote. Hence, he could not commit himself publicly. Stalin understood only too well. Roosevelt's omission of any reference to Lwów may have meant that he did not want to irritate Stalin or did not think it worth mentioning. The Russians had good reason to assume that Roosevelt had given his consent to the Curzon Line.

The president's interpreter, Charles Bohlen, was "dismayed" by Roosevelt's stand, which not only contradicted previous American insistence on no territorial deals during the war, but placed Roosevelt at a tactical disadvantage with Stalin. First Churchill and then Roosevelt were willing to recognize major Soviet territorial acquisitions in Poland without asking for anything in return, such as reestablishment of Soviet-Polish relations or pledges of respecting Poland's independence. No wonder that at subsequent formal discussions of the Polish question Stalin felt no need to make any concessions. The burden of making them was shifted onto the

Poles, and at no point did Roosevelt or Churchill insist that the Polish ally be consulted.

In discussions on the reestablishment of diplomatic relations and on Poland's borders, Roosevelt voiced the hope that the former would be achieved, at least partly to placate public opinion at home. Stalin said it was virtually impossible to have relations with a government that was "closely connected with the Germans" and whose agents were killing Russian partisans, Roosevelt and Churchill were willing to recognize the fact that Moscow could only be induced to reopen talks with the Polish government in London if it became friendly; that is, changed its composition and accepted Soviet territorial demands. An examination of these led to arguments whether the Molotov-Ribbentrop Line and the Curzon Line were identical. Roosevelt abstained, and one senses from the protocols that he wished to have the discussion ended and a quick agreement reached. As Eden noted in his diary Americans were "terrified of the subject which Harry [Hopkins] called 'political dynamite' for their elections." It was Churchill who insisted that the Polish problem was "urgent" and Poland an "instrument needed in the orchestra of Europe." Finally, the Soviet side agreed to a most peculiar "compromise" by accepting the Curzon Line rather than the slightly more advantageous Molotov-Ribbentrop Line, and exacting as payment the northern part of East Prussia with Königsberg and the Tilsit area. It may be recalled that the Poles assumed that all of East Prussia would go to them; thus far Washington and London had raised no objections. Polish western borders would reach the Oder River, but a more specific frontier line was not traced. The Big Three decision, to be imposed on the Polish government, was to be justified in terms of territorial compensation to Poland in the west for its losses in the east. As for Polish Americans, Stalin gave the friendly advice to Roosevelt that some propaganda work ought to be done among them.

It was not only Isaac Deutscher, writing about Stalin with the benefit of hindsight, who believed that Teheran "was a moment of Stalin's supreme triumph." Summarizing the results of the conference, Bohlen wrote that the Soviet Union would be the only important military force on the Continent, and there were clear indications "as to the kind of Poland that the Soviet Union wished to see emerge from the war." These views were strikingly similar to the observations Harriman had made.

Roosevelt's message after Teheran, that "the doctrine that the strong shall dominate the weak is the doctrine of our enemies—and we reject it," sounds particularly hypocritical. The American people were assured in a Christmas Eve speech of Roosevelt's belief that "we are going to get along very well" with Stalin. Did he really think that when Russia's "legitimate claims and requirements" were fully recognized it would prove "tractable and cooperative?" It seems almost incredible but Roosevelt and Hopkins did view Teheran as the peak of their achievements in wartime diplomacy. On his side, Stalin assumed, not without reason, that he had obtained full Western recognition of a free hand in East Central Europe. Although no agreement on the division of operational responsibilities was made, and Britain and the United States still flew missions to Eastern Europe without advance notice, the previous decision to leave the administration of liberated territories to the respective liberator and the tenor of the whole conference could make Stalin feel that his control of the region would not be disputed. The months to come showed that this was not entirely the case.

Warsaw, Yalta, Potsdam

It is likely that at this junction Stalin's plans regarding Poland were to control the country through a voluntary acquiescence by a reorganized Polish government. The Soviet desire for the appearance of legality is strong, and in late 1943 and early 1944 Polish Communists and their fellow travelers comprised no names of prominence, whereas a "friendly" government could provide some semblance of legitimacy. A historian of that period, Vojtech Mastny, has called this approach Stalin's search for a Polish Beneš. Indeed, in the December 1943 talks with the Czechoslovak president, Stalin repeatedly asked about Polish politicians in London, and Voroshilov pointedly remarked that "people must have leaders, if they do not they count for nothing." Although Benes had no warm words for anyone, he did mention Mikołajczyk, to whom Stalin proposed a somewhat ironical toast. Could Mikołajczyk become a Polish Beneš? The chances were slight, for such a person would have had to persuade his countrymen to forget the 1939–1941 period, repent over the denunciation of Katyn, give up voluntarily the eastern territories in exchange for ill-defined compensation in the west, and adjust Polish policies to Soviet exigencies. No free Pole was ready to do that.

Churchill believed that if the Poles accepted a friendly government and territorial concessions, they could still escape complete Soviet domination of their country. But if Stalin's final aim was a takeover of Poland, then such a government would be little more than a transition regime. The British stand seemed partly in accord with Soviet policies, yet it did arouse Stalin's suspicions of ulterior motives; besides, the Soviet dictator never trusted Churchill.

Moscow worried less about the United States. Stalin appreciated Roosevelt's position, made so abundantly clear to him at Teheran, and seemed little concerned by the president's high-sounding declarations about the territorial integrity of Poland and strict American adherence to the Atlantic Charter. If Stalin knew of the remark attributed to Bismarck, that people never lie as much as before an election, during a war, and after a hunt, he would have found it perfectly applicable. Hull's warning not to try to impose a puppet government on Poland because this would adversely affect the American people's support for postwar international organization was hardly the thing to impress Stalin with. Beneš assured the Russians that Washington had guaranteed the Poles nothing but refrained from being explicit about it, and Molotov's comment was: "That's domestic politics: the Polish vote."

American public opinion seemed pro-Soviet. Although according to current polls, the number of Americans who believed that Russia could be trusted to cooperate with the United States after the war dropped from 54 percent in November 1943 to 42 percent in January 1944, the figure was still impressive. The press continued to shower praise on the gallant Soviet ally. The *Life* magazine comments of 1943 that the Russians were "one hell of a people" who "look like Americans, dress like Americans and think like Americans" were still believed in 1944. Early that year, the *New Republic* compared Russian claims to Polish territories to American rights to Texas and California. Davies' *Mission to Russia* appeared in a condensed form in the *Reader's Digest*. In his book published in 1944 Sumner Welles wrote that a Soviet-created regional system in Eastern Europe would be "one of the cornerstones of a stable world organization," in fact comparable to the Monroe Doctrine.

After Teheran, the Central Committee of the Polish Workers' party wrote to the Polish Communists in Russia to urge the creation of a national representation. In the night of December 31, 1943–January 1, 1944, a National Council for the Homeland (KRN) was established, under the leadership of Bolesław Bierut, a onetime Comintern functionary. In March 1944 Stalin decided to recognize it as a representative of the Polish nation but not yet as a provisional government. His caution visibly contrasted with the eagerness of the Polish Communists, but for the first time the Soviet press wrote that "most ancient Polish lands" west of the prewar boundary would become part of a new Poland.

Operating under increasingly adverse conditions, the Polish government, the underground, and Polish Americans did not remain idle. When the Red Army crossed the prewar Polish-Soviet frontier, the government in London declared its readiness to collaborate militarily with the Russians. The Soviets replied that their army had entered West Ukrainian and Belorrussian territories, not Polish lands. Still, Home Army units in the east were mobilized, made contact with the Red Army, and jointly fought the Germans in the Volhynia, Wilno, and Lwów areas. The uprising—Storm—that was taking place in eastern territories revealed a uniform pattern of Soviet behavior: armed assistance was accepted, brief periods of collaboration ensued, then officers were arrested and soldiers incorporated into the Berling army. Was this a foretaste of Soviet attitudes toward Polish partisans in areas west of the Curzon Line?

In March 1944 the Polish "underground parliament" was enlarged and adopted the name of the Council of National Unity. Its program, entitled "What does the Polish nation fight for," insisted on prewar borders with the addition of East Prussia, and parts of Silesia and Pomerania; advocated good relations with the Soviet Union but not its interference in domestic affairs; promised to work for a democratic regime with a strong executive, and for a socio-economic reconstruction of the country including accelerated land reform and nationalization of key industries and forests. The Polish governmest could thus point to progressive strivings of its supporters in the homeland as well as to its unity and determination to fight. It was hoped that the Western Allies would take it into consideration.

The British had the unpleasant task of informing the Poles about the decisions taken at Teheran, although for a while they concealed the fact that parts of East Prussia had been assigned to Russia. They tried to convince Mikołajczyk that by taking over lands up to the Oder River Poland would be "rendering a service to Europe." The Polish premier, fully aware of the strong Polish opposition at home and abroad to far-reaching concessions to Russia, tried to sound out Washington. Would the United States underwrite Churchill's plan that entailed concessions, compensations, and political guarantees, It became clear that no American guarantees would be forthcoming and that, although Washington opposed wartime territorial deals, Roosevelt would not object to them if arrived at by an "amicable settlement." Unknown to the Poles, Roosevelt had rejected a State Department suggestion to make a pro-Polish gesture when the Red Army had crossed the Riga frontier. The Poles also ignored an agreement between Roosevelt and Churchill that it would be wise to delay Mikołajczyk's visit to Washington until Churchill had forced the Polish government to accept the British position. It was feared that Mikołajczyk's visit could stir up the American Polonia, whose reaction was "likely to be anti-Russian" and cause embarrassment to the administration. Washington's contribution to the Soviet-Polish question was thus meager and unhelpful. Hull's instructions to Harriman—to impress on the Soviets that America's faith in Russia hinged on their willingness to talk to a Polish government that was not "handpicked"—puzzled the ambassador. Surely the Soviets had made their position clear at Moscow and Teheran and the United States had not objected, so why raise objections now? A subsequent message from Washington indicated that Roosevelt did not wish to interfere with Russian interests, that American public opinion stood behind the Moscow-Teheran decisions, and that Soviet difficulties in dealing with the Polish government were appreciated in Washington. Roosevelt clearly did not wish to annoy Stalin.

Left alone with Churchill, Mikołajczyk half-heartedly agreed to the prime minister's telegram to Stalin on February 21, which said that the Polish government would accept the Curzon Line but could not do so publicly until this concession was part of a general frontier settlement in the west and the east. Churchill hoped for Soviet permission for the return of the Polish administration at least to the territories west of the Curzon Line, and for a working arrangement with the Red Army. Regarding the composition of the Polish government, while foreign dictate was unacceptable, once diplomatic relations were reestablished only people committed to cooperation with Soviet Russia would be represented in the cabinet. Roosevelt agreed to support Churchill's stand, but he did it by merely asking Stalin for "favorable and sympathetic consideration."

Churchill believed he had finally found the right formula. Stalin had previously assured the British ambassador that of course the Polish government would be allowed to come back and establish a broadly based administration provided a number of ministers he objected to would resign. By agreeing to Churchill's formula, Stalin would have achieved his territorial objectives although not their immediate announcement, secured the reconstruction of the Polish government, and allowed Mikołajczyk to save face. But such apparently were not Stalin's concerns. His reply to Churchill was exceedingly brutal and showed that Stalin wished to detach Mikołajczyk from the Polish government in exile but not to permit the latter's survival. The British ambassador was told that the "Russians and British shed their blood while the Poles sat on your back or hid behind the Prime Minister's." Stalin was "more convinced than ever" that the members of the emigré government were incapable of establishing normal relations with the USSR. He called Churchill's allusion to Polish concern about Wilno and Lwów "an affront" to Russia. Finally, he informed the prime minister that he had written Roosevelt that the time was "not yet ripe" for a solution of the problem of Soviet-Polish relations.

Stalin's outburst may have been intended as a warning to the British to keep out of Russo-Polish affairs. Churchill had tried to dispel Soviet suspicions and in so doing showed some firmness; Stalin interpreted it immediately as a threat and called the British bluff. Roosevelt's intervention at this point may have been of crucial importance, but the president was unwilling. He suggested to Churchill to leave the Polish issue aside for a while and "let nature take its course." Perhaps, Roosevelt wrote, the advancing Russians might "recognize some other organization as more representative of the people of Poland." All the president was willing to do was to convey his hope to Stalin through Harriman that the Soviets would "give the Poles a 'break'."

At this point an incident took place which provoked an outburst of indignation of Polish Americans. Father Orlemanski and Professor Lange went on Stalin's invitation to Moscow. The State Department was perturbed by what could appear as a step in the direction of abandoning the Polish government in London. Stalin had already mentioned both men as possible members of a Polish coalition government. On the other side, the Foreign Nationalities Branch of OSS favored the trip as an indication to the American public of Stalin's benevolent attitude toward Polish "democrats". While insisting on the purely private character of the Lange-Orlemanski visit, President Roosevelt obviously had been instrumental in authorizing it. Orlemanski returned full of praise for Stalin's religious toleration and respect for Polish independence. Lange was far too sophisticated to indulge in such naive statements. Active in the pro-Communist Polish American Committee of Liberation of Poland he behaved more like a politician. In Moscow, he had urged Stalin to leave Lwów to Poland, and he also became convinced of the possibility of a coalition government especially since Stalin entrusted him with personal greetings to Mikołajczyk. Lange interpreted this as a political overture to the Polish leader.

The long-delayed visit of Mikołajczyk to the United States was at last going to take place. In late January 1944 Roosevelt's advisers voiced doubts about the wisdom of such a visit "in the near future." They argued that it might be misinterpreted and be "more detrimental than helpful" to the Polish cause. In April, Churchill asked that Mikołajczyk be received; after Churchill's verbal duel with Stalin it seemed the only way to break the deadlock. Roosevelt however, kept postponing the date of Mikołajczyk's arrival. There were of course pressing matters connected with the operation Overlord that made it hard for Roosevelt to attend to Polish business, but the president also had mixed feelings about the visit. He understood that it might help Churchill and "make the Russians more careful if they see that Poland is not entirely without friends," as the president put it, but at the same time it must not antagonize Stalin. Thus Roosevelt let Stalin know that he had been delaying the visit, warned Mikołajczyk about agitating in the United States, and intended to tell him to get rid of anti-Soviet ministers. Roosevelt was in favor of the Curzon Line although he would prefer to see Lwów go to Poland. Finally, he hoped that the USSR for its part would emphasize Polish independence so as not to harm Roosevelt's electoral campaign in the United States.

The last point needs stressing. To gain the Polish American vote, a visit by Poland's premier was an asset so long as he did not adversely affect American opinion toward Russia. Polish Americans and their friends were showing signs of uneasiness, and already in November 1943 ten members of the House of Representatives had asked Hull to reassure them on the future of Poland. Hull disliked "interfering minorities," but the issue was real enough. In early spring of 1944 several prominent educators, writers and publicists, including George N. Shuster and Harry D. Gideonse, made a public statement emphasizing that the Soviet-Polish dispute raised "a question of ethics in international relations." If Russia valued American friendship, the statement ran, it must not use its power "to impose either an unjust frontier or a puppet government" on the Polish people. The anniversary of the May 3 Polish constitution was the occasion for many speeches in the Congress. Senators and congressmen with Polish American constituencies expressed their concern. All in all eighty-five congressmen and eleven senators spoke, lauding the Poles and criticizing the USSR; among them were twice as many Republicans as Democrats. This could give cause to worry in an election year.

The administration was particularly annoyed by the activities of the KNAPP, which largely inspired the establishment of the Polish American Congress as representative of the Polonia, in Buffalo in May 1944. Matuszewski, Węgrzynek, and Januszewski were most active as organizers; the presidency of the congress went to Charles

Rozmarek, recently also elected president of the Polish National Alliance. A White House assistant was full of admiration for the organizational abilities shown by the Poles, but there was cause for alarm on two counts. The leaders of the Polish American Congress showed sympathy to the Republicans; their activity, whether coordinated with the Polish government in exile or not, had anti-Russian overtones. A memorandum from a White House staffer to Roosevelt suggested that American money advanced to the Polish government was being improperly channeled to support these activities. With regard to Matuszewski, the memorandum advised that he be forced to comply with the provisions of the Foreign Agents Registration Act.

Mikołajczyk reached Washington on June 5, almost on the eve of D-Day in Europe. Although extremely busy, Roosevelt proved to be a most affable host. During the first encounter he sounded optimistic about Poland's future and remarked that Stalin had not struck him as an imperialist or even a communist. After all, it was Churchill who had brought up the Curzon Line in Teheran. The president naturally said nothing about his own secret talks with Stalin. During the first meeting Mikołajczyk was under Roosevelt's spell and amenable to his advice for concessions. The president stressed that he could only be a moderator and not a mediator in the Polish-Soviet controversy, and seemed to advocate a personal meeting between Stalin and Mikołajczyk and a good discussion of the issues, as in a labor dispute.

Roosevelt seized on military collaboration between the Home Army and the Russians as the "missing link" in Soviet-Polish relations. A ranking officer of the Home Army, recently transferred to London, General Stanisław Tatar (Tabor), who accompanied Mikołajczyk, strengthened the president's belief in the necessity to intensify the activity of the underground. It is not clear why Roosevelt thought that Stalin would be so much interested in the Home Army. Surely as important as it was, it could not be crucial from a Soviet military point of view. Was it ignorance on Roosevelt's part, or a search for a gimmick to be used in negotiating with the Russians? In subsequent talks Roosevelt alternated between advising Mikołajczyk to make concessions—there were five Russians to one Pole, he said—and cheering him up—perhaps Stalin would relent about Wilno and Lwów.

The State Department persuaded Mikołajczyk to talk to Professor Oskar Lange who told him that Stalin was not interested in Polish domestic politics but vitally concerned with Poland's foreign policy. It may well be that Lange's objective in talking to Mikołajczyk was to persuade him to deal directly with Moscow. If so, the premier was not overly impressed.

At the farewell meeting Roosevelt sounded again an optimistic note. Contrasting the Polish government with that of de Gaulle, he described it as "assuring the continuity of the Polish State." A few months later Roosevelt would say just the opposite.

The president promptly dispelled Stalin's possible fears about the outcome of the Mikołajczyk visit. He assured the Soviet dictator that he did not attempt to insert himself "into the merits" of the Polish-Russian "differences," nor was he trying to press his views in a matter which was "of special concern to you and your country." To Churchill, Roosevelt wrote a little later to say that Mikołajczyk's visit did not seem to have advanced matters and that it was difficult to express an opinion on the advisability of the Polish leader's trip to Moscow. The Russians must have been reassured. As for Mikołajczyk, he returned seemingly believing in America's will to assist Poland, in the importance of the Home Army as a political weapon, and in the usefulness of direct talks with Stalin. On each count he was to be proved wrong.

Upon his return Mikołajczyk authorized the delegate in Warsaw to launch the uprising Storm at a moment chosen by the authorities in the homeland. This action would demonstrate the extent of the support the government enjoyed in Poland and show Polish readiness to cooperate with Russia against Germany. The decision was taken in spite of the tragic fate of the earlier uprisings east of the Curzon Line and those still taking place near Lwów and Wilno. Warsaw was to be originally excluded from the Storm, but on July 21 Bór-Komorowski decided to include the capital which, with its great concentration of Home Army units, could show most dramatically the effort of the Polish nation.

Mikołajczyk's anticipated encounter with Stalin raised problems. In late June the premier held a series of talks with the Soviet ambassador to various governments in exile, Lebedev. Prepared by exchanges that had preceded Mikołajczyk's trip to Washington, these talks were indicative of Soviet desires to detach Mikołajczyk from a pro-Western policy and cast him in the role of a Polish Benes. The premier had been evasive earlier and had become even less flexible after his talks with Roosevelt. On June 23, Lebedev suddenly presented harsh terms: the removal of the Polish president and the commander-in-chief, the dismissal of a number of ministers to be replaced by men drawn from among Poles in Britain, Russia, and the United States, immediate acceptance of the

Curzon Line as the Polish eastern frontier, and a public condemnation of the previous cabinet for its stand on Katyn. The Russians were asking in effect that the government in exile not only commit suicide but also dig its own grave. Clearly, Stalin was no longer interested in any agreement with Mikołajczyk, and the terms were presented one day after the Soviet dictator had received a delegation of the National Committee for the Homeland (KRN) and given it a green light to proceed with the organization of a de facto government in Poland. When on July 22 Chełm, the first Polish town west of the Curzon Line, was captured, the Polish Committee of National Liberation (PKWN) was set up and subsequently moved to Lublin. It declared itself the "legal, provisional executive power" and denounced the government in London as usurpers. The committee, Stalin explained to Churchill, was a mere administrative organ that had to be established since Russia did not wish to introduce Soviet administration into Polish territories and was obliged to rely on Polish democratic forces. This was hardly a truthful statement since the USSR had signed a treaty with the committee on July 26 regarding Poland's territorial settlement, indicating that it considered it a quasi-government.

Mikołajczyk, who had assumed that he would go to Moscow as the head of the only legal Polish government, was in a difficult position. Stalin agreed to his visit but intimated that Mikołajczyk should discuss matters with the representatives of the new Lublin committee. Thus Stalin assumed the posture of a mediator between rival Polish claimants, interested in a merger of democratic forces in Poland with democratic elements in the emigration. Mikołajczyk's appeal to Roosevelt to dispatch American officers to the eastern front and to parachute intelligence agents into Poland was unrealistic in the extreme. All the support Roosevelt was prepared to give was a telegram to Stalin expressing hope that he would "work this whole matter out" with the Polish premier "to the best advantage of our common efforts."

Arriving in Moscow, Mikołajczyk tried to impress the Russians with the news of an imminent uprising in Warsaw that would assist the common war effort. The Russians responded that the Red Army was already ten kilometers from the Polish capital. The next day the uprising began. It epitomized in a dramatic way Polish heroism, German brutality, Soviet ruthlessness, and Western lack of resolve. The call was given on August 1, 1944, when Soviet artillery could be heard in Warsaw and the German military might seemed on the verge of collapse. Politically, the uprising was meant to demonstrate that the Home Army could wrest the capital from the Germans and act as host to the Soviet troops. At the time, however, other causes had combined so as to make it virtually unavoidable. Soviet radio repeatedly called on the Poles to rise; these appeals could be discounted as routine, but there was also a proclamation of the commander of a Polish People's Army unit, which was more dangerous. It mendaciously announced the flight of the Home Army commander and decreed a mobilization of Poles in the city. In the tense atmosphere filled with understandable desire to get even with the Germans, a spark could ignite a fire. The Home Army faced the danger of being branded cowards and collaborators if it did not give the signal to fight. Its leaders were ignorant of the fact that the West, informed of the coming uprising only three days earlier, averred itself incapable of providing necessary help. Moreover, the Allied high command felt that an uprising had to be militarily coordinated with Russia. The Polish commander-in-chief, General Sosnkowski, who alone could have forbidden the uprising, shirked his responsibility by not issuing orders of any kind. Finally, the Home Army command misread the signs and failed to realize that the temporarily disorganized Germans were mounting a counteroffensive which threw the Red Army back and filled the capital with armored troops.

The controversial Warsaw uprising resulted in the death of some 200,000 Poles and transformed the city into smouldering ruins. The badly armed, hungry and sleepless partisans, denied the protection of the Geneva Convention during the first month of the struggle, fought for sixty-two days with tenacity and gallantry. The uprising became not only history but also a legend, and the long rows of crosses in the Powązki cemetery in Warsaw, covered on each anniversary of the uprising with flowers and illuminated by candles, display the defiant motto "Gloria victis"—glory to the vanquished. If this be deemed Polish romanticism which extols useless sacrifice, a thought might be given to the long-range consequences of the uprising. On the negative side, it deprived Poland of a highly motivated and dynamic elite some of whom perished and others were deported to German camps; but it also demonstrated once again to would-be aggressors that if pressed too far the Poles would choose near-hopeless resistance over meek surrender.

Far from assisting Mikołajczyk in Moscow, the uprising proved to be a terrible political liability. The Polish premier had to plead for aid, and the Russians first denied that an uprising occurred, and then denounced it. Stalin spoke of a "group of criminals" who started it; Molotov castigated the "adventure" launched without prior knowledge of the Soviet high command and interfering with its operational plans. The American embassy reported on the "campaign of invective" in the press and commented that the Soviets, unable to rely on logic, resorted to "fury and clamor." While the Red Army seemed genuinely unable to attack in the first two weeks of the uprising, its subsequent reluctance to bring any relief or permit the West to do so could only be explained by the desire to see the London-directed Home Army massacred by the Germans. Throughout the war the British and the Americans worked on the assumption that enemies of their enemies were allies, and those who killed most Germans deserved military aid. It was otherwise with the Russians, and Harriman reported Molotov's words that only those who accepted the Soviet position could be rated as friends. "The jealous and intolerant eye of the Kremlin," Kennan wrote, "can distinguish, in the end, only vassals and enemies."

The Soviet refusal to allow British or American planes to use Russian airfields in their relief flights to Warsaw came as a shock. Harriman was "shattered" and commented on Soviet contempt for world public opinion. He increasingly advocated a firm stand against the Soviet Union. George Kennan went even further in regarding the Warsaw uprising as a challenge and a chance for a showdown with Russia. Bohlen disagreed that one could accomplish anything by resorting to threat. At best the Russians might allow air drops, but a showdown could have harmed greatly the chances of a postwar united world.

The Polish government vainly pleaded for Western military and political aid. Roosevelt would not change his policy toward Russia, and its callous behavior, while shocking by Western standards, also showed how determined and obstinate Stalin could be. The president invoked public opinion and its reaction "if the anti-Nazis are in effect abandoned," but was unwilling to go along with Churchill, who advocated tough messages to Stalin and dispatching planes that would attempt to land in Soviet airfields. A major raid of flying fortresses on September 18 was the most tangible American support to the uprising. Supplies dropped from a high altitude fell mostly into German hands, and by that time the uprising was already in agony. Even the Russians agreed to make air drops; an "extremely shrewd statement for the record," Harriman commented. A few days before the end Stalin was even willing to admit to the American ambassador that the Poles had had some cause to stage the uprising. This was not a change of heart but of tactics. The only military attempt to help the partisans, made by a detachment of Berling's Polish troops which crossed the Vistula, was stopped, presumably at Stalin's order. General Berling allegedly paid for this initiative with a broken career, but the whole episode is still unclear.

Mikołajczyk waited for three days for an audience with Stalin and was told that Moscow insisted on an immediate recognition of the eastern frontier. As for the reorganization of the government, he was referred to the representatives of the Committee of National Liberation. After tense talks, they offered Mikołajczyk the premiership of a provisional government in which three other "London Poles" would join fourteen members of the committee. Stalin categorically assured Mikołajczyk that he had no intention of making Poland communist and the premier preserved some hope. Some eight months later Stalin would tell the top Yugoslav Communists that in this war "whoever occupies a territory also imposes on it his own social system" and that it "cannot be otherwise."

Mikołajczyk returned to London hoping that some possibility of agreement with Russia existed if Britain and especially the United States gave the Poles strong support. Harriman considered that Mikołajczyk had scored a success in Moscow by being offered the premiership, and believed that he should strive to merge the different Polish groups. Kennan, observing Mikołajczyk's efforts, "reflected on the lightheartedness with which great powers offer advice to smaller ones in matters affecting the vital interests of the latter." He wished "we had the judgment and the good sense to bow our heads in silence before the tragedy of a people who have been our allies . . . and whom we cannot save from our friends." After deliberations, the Polish government in London reiterated its adherence to a formula that had already been communicated to the Western Allies. It envisaged a reconstituted Polish cabinet with communists on par with representatives of the four major parties; a provisional territorial settlement leaving some hope of eventually saving Lwów and Wilno for Poland; reestablished diplomatic relations with the Soviet Union and regularized collaboration with the Red Army. After the end of hostilities all foreign troops would leave Poland; elections would then be held and social reforms initiated; finally, Poland would sign alliances with Britain, France, Soviet Russia, and Czechoslovakia and cultivate friendly relations with the United States. This was a program that was totally unacceptable to the USSR.

Once again, Churchill took the initiative and flew to Moscow to attempt a deal with Stalin that would preserve a modicum of Western influence in Eastern Europe. Roosevelt withheld his blessing, although he cabled Stalin that in this "global war there is literally no question political and military in which the United

States is not interested." Stalin understood that Churchill's views did not express a concerted Anglo-American policy. The famous Churchill-Stalin percentage deal, made in October 1944, delineated their respective influences in the Balkans. The Americans disliked the scheme as smacking of spheres of influence but, as Bohlen put it, this did not mean that the United States did not recognize the "fact that the Soviet Union exercises a considerable degree of control and influence over all the countries of Eastern Europe."

Poland did not figure in the Churchill-Stalin understanding, and Churchill virtually forced Mikołajczyk to go once more to Moscow (October 12-18) to accept the Curzon Line. The British prime minister kept arguing that if this concession were made and the government reorganized, perhaps the Polish Committee of National Liberation could still be bypassed. Churchill did not accept Mikołajczyk's suggestion that the great powers announce a decision on eastern borders without Poland's participation. The United States' contribution at this point took the form of Harriman's invoking American public opinion. He told Molotov that Americans regarded the Polish problem as the "first real test" of postwar collaboration.

In Moscow, Molotov stunned Mikołajczyk by saying that at Teheran *all three* great Allies had accepted the Curzon Line. The Polish premier looked at Harriman for a denial, but the ambassador kept silent. Mikołajczyk, however, had to know and he had to assure himself of Washington's position on the territorial settlement. In late October he appealed to Roosevelt. Explaining the difficulties a government in exile faced in consenting to a cession of nearly half its state territory, he emphasized the question of Lwów and recalled Roosevelt's encouraging remarks made in Washington. He also referred to Molotov's "one-sided" version of the president's attitude in Teheran. He pleaded for a personal message to Stalin supporting the Poles on Lwów.

If Mikołajczyk thought he could induce Roosevelt to make a strong statement on the eve of the elections he was badly mistaken. The president was using such campaign slogans as no abandonment of the Atlantic Charter and Poland's territorial integrity, but he was careful not to assume real obligations. A special press release issued in November 1944 publicized American aid given to fighting Poles and listed the armaments provided under the Lend-Lease Act and the supplies sent to Polish prisoners of war in Germany.

To counteract the danger of Rozmarek carrying the Polish American vote into Dewey's camp, Roosevelt received the president of the Polish American Congress twice in October. During the first conversation the president made no binding promises regarding Polish affairs and Rozmarek withheld his endorsement of the Democratic candidate. During the second, Roosevelt assured the Polish American leader that the principles of the Atlantic Charter would be applied to Poland, and he succeeded not only in offsetting Cardinal Spellman's criticism of the pro-Russian line of the adminstration, but in gaining Rozmarek's endorsement. The incident shows that since the Polonia did not control crucial positions either in the church hierarchy, labor unions, or the Democratic party itself, Roosevelt needed only to appease the Polish Americans rather than to bargain with them. The argument, however, that the 1944 elections did Poland harm by diverting the president's attention from Polish problems to that of appeasing the Polonia is not very convincing.

Roosevelt replied to Mikołajczyk in late November, after the election. Having expressed American interest in a strong, free, and independent Poland, he endorsed border settlements based on Big Three agreements and promised economic aid for postwar reconstruction. Once again Roosevelt made clear that the United States could not guarantee Polish borders. Harriman for his part warned the Poles not to overestimate American possibilities of pressure on Russia.

Caught between the unyielding attitude of the majority of the Polish cabinet, relentless British pressure, and the United States' unwillingness or inability to support or guarantee a territorial settlement, Mikołajczyk resigned together with most of his Populist party supporters. After his resignation he defended himself against the charge of unwillingness to compromise. He had been willing to compromise, he said, but what was asked of him was a capitulation. A new Polish cabinet headed by a veteran Socialist who had recently escaped from Poland, Tomasz Arciszewski, was still officially recognized, although for all practical purposes ignored by Britain and the United States.

Roosevelt's mention of economic aid for postwar reconstruction of Poland was not a mere phrase. The matter had been examined by the State Department and summarized in a memorandum of October 31, 1944, which assumed that Poland would be deprived of its eastern provinces but receive East Prussia and Upper Silesia. The document attempted to define American interest in Poland as both general—part of the reconstruction of all devastated countries of Europe that was essential for future world stability, peace, and prosperity—and specific. In the second case it was assumed that Poland would "necessarily be under strong Russian influence," but it lay in America's interest that this influence be not so dominant "as to affect international political stability or restrict the exercise of the legitimate rights of third countries." The United States could hope to exert some influence in East Central Europe only if one power did not possess exclusive privileges and some equality was preserved regarding "opportunity in trade, investment and communication, including access to sources of information." To gain the goodwill of the Poles and to bring about economic conditions "related both as cause and effect with a liberal policy of this nature," America should help Poland "to rehabilitate her economy at the earliest possible moment." When conditions of reasonable prosperity were reestablished, there would be less chance for "extreme ideological doctrines, dangerous to both democracy and peace to take root in that country."

Analyzing economic transformations likely to take place, the memorandum drew attention to the fact that prewar Poland already had a developed form of "state socialism," meaning a large percentage of state ownership, but private enterprise had been encouraged. The former seemed likely to continue; the latter was less certain. The land reform announced by the Committee of National Liberation was expected to involve efforts to increase farm productivity through mechanization. This would require large outlays for equipment. Although Soviet attempts to gain an exclusive position in Poland could not be easily appraised, it appeared that Russia could not become Poland's supplier on a large scale. The United States could, and American interest in a rebuilt and prosperous Poland would favor an extension of credits. Poland could be regarded as "a reasonable credit risk for reconstruction loans."

Several ideas expressed in this document merit attention: the notion of prosperity contributing to political moderation, a distinction made between Soviet exclusive sphere of influence and an "open door" bloc, and some concern for American economic presence in Poland. These ideas reflected long-range goals, but it is debatable whether they had an appreciable impact on Roosevelt's handling of the Polish question at the Yalta Conference held between February 4 and 12, 1945.

What was the international situation on the eve of the conference? In Poland, the new commander of the Home Army, General Leopold Okulicki (Bór-Komorowski had become a German prisoner of war) attempted to reorganize the underground network and in late December 1944 acted as host to a symbolic British military mission. On January 19, 1945, he announced the dissolution of the Home Army. Earlier on New Year's Eve, the Lublin committee had transformed itself into a Provisional Government, backed by an army in which Soviet officers occupied the leading posts. Roosevelt's appeal to Stalin to withhold recognition of the Provisional Government until the Big Three meeting proved of no avail, and Moscow recognized it on January 5, 1945. In the west, Polish troops comprised Anders's Second Army Corps in Italy, which in May 1944 won the spectacular battle of Monte Cassino, an armored division in Holland, a paratroopers' brigade, and air force and naval units. The Western Allies had liberated France, Belgium, and parts of Holland and were locked in combat in northern Italy. The Russian offensive progressed rapidly engulfing the Balkans and parts of the Danubian basin.

The days of Nazi Germany were numbered, but heavy fighting lay ahead in the Pacific and war against Japan preoccupied American leadership. Except for the Far Eastern war, where Russian aid would be most welcome to America, the forthcoming conference was to deal primarily with postwar issues: the organization of the United Nations and the fate of Germany. To reach agreement on these matters as well as on a general declaration of principles regarding liberated Europe was the paramount goal of the United States.

International relations reflect and are shaped by a combination of diverse factors and trends, but the actual conduct of diplomacy is still affected by individuals. Their skills, ideas, and moods cannot be overlooked. Never an outstanding diplomat and seriously handicapped at Yalta by bad health, President Roosevelt continued to rely on his political instincts. Harry Hopkins was also ill at Yalta and not very active, but his views mattered and, as Bohlen recalled, he only "faintly understood the importance of the ideological factor in Soviet thinking." Hopkins still regarded Stalin as a sensible, reasonable and understanding person. The United States and Russia, Hopkins thought, were "mutually dependent upon each other for economic reasons." Harriman leaned more toward realpolitik, and both he and Bohlen felt that Roosevelt's posture of an aloof moderator was not well calculated to impress the Soviets. The British suggestion of drawing up a list of issues on which the West wanted Soviet agreement and a corresponding list of prices that could be paid was unacceptable to Roosevelt. As on earlier occasions, he worried lest the Russians believe that the Anglo-Saxon powers were ganging up on them.

Was it possible to work out at that time a well-defined American policy toward Russia and Soviet objectives? Bohlen and Kennan considered the problem and came up with different formulae. Kennan started with the assumption that Russia's military cooperation was essential and had, up to a point, to "find its reward at the expense of other peoples in eastern and central Europe." He recommended that America write them off, "unless it possessed the will 'to go whole hog' and oppose with all its physical and diplomatic resources Russian domination of the area." A division of spheres of influence would be preferable to an unclarified position with respect to American wishes and interests in that part of Europe. By refusing to name limits to Russian expansion and responsibilities, the United States was confusing the Russians and making them wonder whether they asked too little or were facing a trap. The agreement on the United Nations eagerly sought by Roosevelt might in fact tie American hands and imply a commitment to defend the Soviet sphere as part of the postwar order. It was thus better to make clear what the United States security required and preserve American right to use armed forces where and when necessary. Bohlen agreed with much of Kennan's analysis but not with the conclusions. He argued that only totalitarian states could carry out such policies and if one wished to defeat Germany it was impossible to keep Soviet armies out of East Central Europe and Germany. As for spheres of influence, they would surely produce a "loud and effective outcry from our own Poles and Czechs."

Failing to face issues squarely and to coordinate a plan of action with the British, Roosevelt's policy at Yalta became largely improvisation that led to the "shabbiest sort of equivocation," to use Kennan's expression. Yalta was a mixture of moralistic phraseology with realpolitik at its worst. As an American historian remarked, Roosevelt was only saved from a complete loss of credibility by the fact that he "won his war."

From the Russian and British points of view the Polish question represented one of the main issues of the conference. As Churchill wrote later, some 18,000 words had been said on the subject. To Roosevelt and Hopkins it was essentially a subordinate matter. What is "the American interest in places like . . . Poland, Greece and so on?" Hopkins jotted down. Characteristically, there is not a single chapter entitled Poland in Stettinius' memoir devoted to Yalta. Roosevelt found the Polish issue irritating. "Poland has been a source of trouble for over five hundred years," he exclaimed, according to Churchill's account. Stettinius noted that the current trend seemed to be more "toward a three-power alliance than anything else," and it was Eden rather than any of the major American participants who described Stalin's attitude toward smaller countries as "sinister."

The Polish question consisted of two interrelated issues: territorial and political-constitutional. The briefing papers prepared by the State Department for Roosevelt advised the acceptance of borders in the east along the Curzon Line, with modifications in Poland's favor in the area of Eastern Galician oilfields and Lwów. In the west, Poland was to receive parts of East Prussia, a slice of Pomerania, Danzig, and Upper Silesia. The United States could recognize only a widely representative Polish government. At Yalta, Churchill, feebly seconded by Roosevelt, tried to secure Stalin's agreement in the matter of Lwów. The prime minister appealed to Stalin's "magnanimity"; the president suggested, without insisting, that Stalin's gesture would be appreciated since it would make matters "easier at home." Roosevelt added that the majority of Polish Americans favored the Curzon Line, which was not true. There was really no compelling reason for the Russians to make concessions and they made none.

Polish western borders raised problems since the Teheran agreement on the extension to the Oder was quite vague, and the Oder is a long river. Harriman alerted the State Department that Russia's position had stiffened. In the past, the Russians had spoken of Stettin (Szczecin) and Breslau (Wrocław) as "perhaps" being assigned to Poland. By December 1944 they mentioned a western frontier along the Oder-Neisse (Odra-Nysa) rivers. At Yalta, Churchill was very uneasy about allowing such an extension, especially since Stalin clarified that he meant the Lusatian Neisse (there were two Neisse rivers) which lay more to the west. Roosevelt also considered the proposed boundary excessive but was less outspoken in his opposition. The final agreement spoke of reserving the final settlement of Polish-German frontiers, after consultations with a Polish government of national unity, to the peace conference. Thus Poland definitely lost the eastern provinces without obtaining an iron-clad commitment in the west.

With regard to the political-constitutional issue, Churchill tried to obtain Russian guarantees in exchange for the acceptance of the Soviet point of view on Polish-Russian borders. Roosevelt acted mainly as a moderator, thus weakening the British stand. There was agreement that a Polish government would have to be friendly to Russia, but differences remained as to the degree of friendliness, the composition of the cabinet, and the method of setting it up. The British insisted that they were honor-bound to see that Poland was a free and independent country and recalled that some 150,000 Poles were fighting in the west against Germany. Churchill quoted the line: "the eagle should permit the small birds to sing and care not wherefore they sang." At the same time he had no qualms about a settlement without any Polish participation.

Stalin, to quote Bohlen, appeared as a "master of evasive and delaying tactics with no great regard for facts." He exploited the percentage deal to undermine Churchill's arguments and posed as a genuine defender of the Poles whose views had to be respected. For Russia, he said, Poland was a matter of security, for the Germans had twice used Poland as a channel to invade Russia. Hence Poland had to be strong. This was a distortion of facts since both in 1914 and 1941 the Germans had invaded Russia through a Poland *partitioned* between them, but no one corrected him.

Roosevelt, true to form, invoked public opinion. The United States had neither an alliance with nor a vested interest in Poland, but the American public and the lofty aims of Allied pronouncements had to be considered. By now the Russians had enough of American public opinion being thrown into debates, and Vishinsky told Bohlen tersely that the American people ought to learn to obey their leaders.

The British did not hide their view that the Provisional Government recognized by the Soviets was unrepresentative. The American attitude was less clear-cut. Harriman had been in touch with Polish Communist leaders in Moscow and reported in June 1944 that he was satisfied that they were not Soviet agents. Roosevelt admitted that he knew none of the Polish ministers in London except for Mikołajczyk, for whom he had a high regard. Given the existence of two rival centers, Roosevelt felt that one ought to start with a clean slate, "something new and dramatic—like a breath of fresh air." Possibly carried away by his own rhetoric, Roosevelt dealt the coup de grace to the government in London by saying that there "hasn't really been any Polish government since 1939." The president disliked the "idea of continuity" and opined that ⁺t was up to the Big Three to help in setting up a government which would have the support of all the great powers.

This line of approach unwittingly strengthened the Soviet position. If Poland had no real government since 1939 and something new and dramatic was wanted, then the answer could well be the new Provisional Government which, Molotov said, "enjoyed tremendous prestige and popularity in Poland." All that was needed was strengthen it by the addition of democratic leaders from Poland and abroad. Thus the issue was narrowed to whether the Provisional Government ought to be enlarged—the Soviet view—or a new government mainly based on the provisional one be set up— the British position. Roosevelt, whose proposal of having rival

Poles come to Yalta was rejected as impractical, adopted the viewpoint that the difference between the two positions was "largely a matter of words." He proposed a compromise formula of a "reorganized government." But how was it to be chosen? Following Mikołajczyk's suggestion, Roosevelt proposed the creation of a presidential council which would exercise authority in Poland until elections were held. This made sense, but the president dropped the idea, which the Russians disliked, and accepted instead a committee composed of Molotov and the American and British ambassadors in Moscow "to consult in the first instance" with Polish leaders about the composition of the government. The phrasing was purposefully vague, which later permitted Molotov to emasculate the committee.

The final formula spoke of a reorganization of the "Provisional Government which is now functioning in Poland" on a broad democratic basis "with the inclusion of democratic leaders from Poland itself and from Poles abroad." After reorganization it would become a provisional government of national unity. Even if the Russians did not gain the immediate recognition of the Provisional Government on which they insisted—perhaps for bargaining purposes—they won a resounding victory. There remained the matter of elections which, as Stalin mentioned in an offhanded manner, could be held within a month. Roosevelt and Churchill considered it part of the package deal that the Polish government of national unity be pledged to holding "free and unfettered" elections. This was accepted, but instead of a definite date the words "as soon as possible" were inserted. Roosevelt insisted that the elections be as pure as Caesar's wife, to which Stalin jokingly responded that Caesar's wife "had her sins." Stalin, invoking Polish pride, objected to any foreign supervision, and Roosevelt agreed to withdraw a stipulation about Allied ambassadors acting as observers and evaluators. Finally, the Soviets gained another point with regard to the elections by specifying that only "non-Fascist and anti-Fascist" Poles be permitted to participate. Given Soviet terminology, this was a meaningful qualification which could not be offset by a largely declamatory and ineffective Declaration on Liberated Europe adopted by the conference.

There is no doubt that the Polish settlement, arrived at in the absence of the government in London which the Americans and the British still officially recognized as an ally, was hardly an example of international morality. This "dawn of the new day," as Hopkins called Yalta, was breaking under somewhat sinister circumstances. Were the American leaders aware they had concluded a bad deal, their only justification being that they could not have done any better? As Hopkins recalled later, Roosevelt considered the Polish question "virtually settled." Writing to Thomas W. Lamont, he described it as "the most hopeful agreement possible for a free and independent Polish state.' We cannot know if he really believed that. To a note scribbled by Leahy and passed on to the president at Yalta that this was such an "elastic" agreement that the Russians could stretch it all the way from Yalta to Washington without technically breaking it, Roosevelt replied, "I know, Bill, I know it. But this is the best I can do for Poland at this time."

To be fair in criticizing Yalta, the conference must be treated in conjunction with the preceding three and a half years of Roosevelt's Russian policy. Washington had never really defined its objectives in East Central Europe nor alerted the Russians that the United States might object to Soviet controls in the area. Much was said of American public opinion, which had to be appeased, but U.S. spokesmen made it clear again and again that they did not wish Poland to disturb the harmony among the Big Three, especially between Russia and America. The Polish transaction was virtually completed, in stages, long before Yalta; the Crimean Conference witnessed the closing of the dead. Thus, to say that Yalta was unavoidable under the conditions of February 1945 is to miss the point. Relatively little could have been done at that late hour, although it may not have been necessary to concede virtually every Russian demand; but the roots of Yalta lay in the past.

Leahy recalled later that he had left Yalta "with the impression that the Soviet Government had no intention of permitting a free government to operate in Poland and that he would have been surprised had the Soviet Government behaved any differently than it had." This apparently shocked Stettinius, but Leahy's impression was fully justified. The argument that the Soviet side broke the Yalta agreements is not very convincing unless one accepts the naive notion that the West did not know how the Soviets used such terms as free elections, democracy, and liberty. When Harriman cabled later that, although it was hard for the West to believe, Stalin considered that at Yalta "we understood and were ready to accept Soviet policies already known to us," the only thing puzzling about this message is that the West found it hard to believe. There is force in the Soviet interpretation that the West accepted the Polish settlement at Yalta with open eyes. If it did not, it was guilty of naivete or self-delusion. How were the Russians to achieve a friendly government in Poland with genuinely free elections and democratic freedoms? And elections could not be free when all the safeguards had been removed with Western consent. In June 1945 Litvinov asked Edgar Snow to explain why the United States had waited until then to oppose the USSR on Eastern Europe and the Balkans. "You should have done this three years ago," the Soviet diplomat said. "Now it's too late and your complaints only arouse suspicion here."

Perhaps one reason for subsequent recriminations can be found in the time-honored practice of overselling foreign policy to the American public. In his speech of March 1, 1945, Roosevelt presented Yalta in shining colors. The Office of War Information received instructions to praise the conference and cover the Polish settlement briefly. In his speech Roosevelt repeated Stalin's false statement about Poland having been a corridor for German aggression, and stressed the compensation the country was to receive in the west. In America the criticism of Yalta was at first limited to congressmen and senators who disapproved of the new Polish-Soviet border, and to Polish American organizations, which protested vociferously. Senator Arthur H. Vanderberg, who had a large Polish American constituency, privately referred to Yalta as "awful," but the House Foreign Affairs Committee refused even to report on a resolution condemning the agreement. Possibly in order to calm the violent Polish reaction in the West, Roosevelt sent a message to Premier Arciszewski assuring him that Polish problems had received "most careful and sympathetic consideration." Stettinius told the Polish ambassador that, given Stalin's stubbornness, the president could not have risked the rejection of Soviet territorial demands, especially since Churchill advocated them also. The Big Three had agreed on an entirely new Polish government, Stettinius declared, but when faced with Ciechanowski's objection that this was not what the official communiqué said, he admitted the possibility of different interpretations. The Poles were not taken in, and Roosevelt's credibility as their friend and protector was damaged beyond repair.

The Poles could not fail to realize that while their frontiers with Germany were to await the peace conference the transfer to Russia of parts of East Prussia and of the lands beyond the Curzon Line had been concluded. By taking an equivocal position on Poland's western borders, the West had presented Stalin and Bierut with a psychologically important gift, for it appeared that it was only the Soviet Union that was trying to get the Oder-Neisse border for Poland. Given the anti-German feelings of the Poles, this was grist for the mill of communist propaganda.

Translating Yalta into practical terms, the Soviet side showed little regard for American public opinion or the sensibilities of Roosevelt and Churchill. In March 1945 the Russians arrested sixteen leaders of the Polish underground on the basis of the notorious article 59 of the Soviet Criminal Code which, as Solzhenitsyn put it, can be invoked against anyone in any situation. The arrested men were accused of plotting against the Soviet Union, and two of them, the last commander of the Home Army and the governmental delegate, eventually died in prison. The new authorities in Poland carried out arrests and some executions; the remnants of the underground countered with sabotage and attempts to kill Communist activists. In Moscow, the inter-allied committee supposed to assist in the formation of a government of national unity kept running into Soviet obstructions. The American side protested. The atmosphere grew tense, with Molotov's threats to boycott the United Nations meeting in San Francisco and Stalin's accusations against the United States plotting with the German Wehrmacht.

Churchill urged a tougher approach and singled out the Polish case. He cabled Roosevelt: at Yalta "Poland had lost her frontier. Is she now to lose her freedom?" The prime minister wrote that the West must not be maneuvered into becoming a party to Soviet imposition of its version of democracy on East Central Europe. Rather, the Big Two ought to confess "our total failure" and stand by "our interpretation" of Yalta. Churchill advocated that Anglo-American forces race the Red Army and occupy as much territory as possible so as to enable the West to bargain from a position of strength. The "Soviet menace," according to Churchill, had "already replaced the Nazi foe."

Roosevelt did not want Britain to bring the differences with Russia into the open and tried to persuade Churchill that it was all a matter of tactics. It would be courting certain refusal, Roosevelt argued, to demand that the "Lublin Poles" alone be forced to cease their persecution of political opponents. He consented, however, to ask Stalin to adhere to the Yalta formula regarding the creation of a Polish government, and even suggested the advisability of sending an American-British control commission to Poland. Stalin replied that the enlargement of the Provisional Government was under way. Washington did not attach the same importance to Poland and East Central Europe as London. Roosevelt's caution also stemmed from the fact that the United States, concentrating on the war against Japan, wished to avoid any confrontation with Russia. In his last days, Roosevelt oscillated between hoping to minimize the Soviet problems because they usually straightened themselves out, and a feeling that one "can't do business with Stalin" and "must be firm."

In April 1945 Roosevelt died and Harry Truman came to the White House. The new president had no intimate knowledge of international relations, and in consulting ranking politicians and diplomats received somewhat conflicting advice. Stettinius, Harriman and Forrestal favored a firm line; Marshall stressed the need for cooperation because of Japan. Stimson failed to perceive the significance of the Polish crisis for the United States and counseled moderation. Truman himself felt that agreements with the USSR had been so far a one-way street and spoke in his first message to Churchill of the "pressing and dangerous problem of Poland." Not that Truman was more willing than Roosevelt to follow the prime minister's lead and order the capture of Berlin, Vienna, and Prague. But he displayed a tougher attitude. Molotov's request that the Polish Provisional Government be represented at the United Nations sessions at San Francisco was turned down, and no Poles were present at the ceremony. Truman got rough with Molotov and authorized sharply-worded statements. In what appeared a pro-Polish gesture, he received Rozmarek, at the head of the delegation of the Polish American Congress, in the White House.

Truman then sought to reopen a dialogue with Stalin, and in May he dispatched Harry Hopkins to Russia. This looked very much like a return to Roosevelt's diplomacy. In talking to Stalin, Hopkins stressed that American public opinion was alarmed because the Yalta agreement on Poland had not been carried out. The Polish question, Hopkins explained, was not important in itself, but Poland "had become a symbol in the sense that it bore a direct relation to the willingness of the United States to participate in international affairs on a world-wide basis and that our people must believe that they are joining their power with that of the Soviet Union and Great Britain in the promotion of international peace." The United States had no special interest in Poland or its government as long as it was accepted by the Polish people and was friendly toward Russia. But Americans were disturbed by seemingly unilateral Russian measures and the complete exclusion of the United States. Hopkins harped on the theme that Americans attached great importance to fundamental rights and freedoms, and some, with whom Hopkins did not wish to be identified, felt that Soviet Russia strove to dominate Poland. In that connection, Hopkins pleaded for Soviet leniency toward the arrested Polish underground leaders.

Although amiable toward Hopkins, Stalin made it clear that he was fed up with constant references to public opinion, which he regarded as tactical devices. He blamed Polish difficulties on British interference and London's wishes to revive the *cordon sanitaire*. Yalta's meaning was plain, and the talk about Russian intentions to sovietize Poland was "stupid." The regime in Poland would be a parliamentary democracy. Stalin did recognize the right of a world power such as the United States to "participate in the Polish question," and explained the unilateral measures by security needs of the Red Army. As for the composition of the Polish government, roughly four cabinet seats could be given to people proposed by the Americans or the British.

Hopkins returned in a mood of guarded optimism. What Stalin seemed to have been saying was that he was prepared to respect American rights and prestige in order to regain Washington's confidence. If the United States had really no interest in Poland and the question was simply how to manage the susceptibilities of public opinion, Stalin was willing to be conciliatory as long as it did not interfere with Soviet interests. This was the old story over again, and there is truth in Adam Ulam's remark that the Hopkins mission, as previously that of Davies, effectively destroyed the hope that Stalin might relax his grip on Poland.

The only concrete result was a trade-off. Washington consented that only pro-Russian Poles be considered for the government of national unity, and the Soviets agreed to accept certain individuals, notably Mikołajczyk. Consequently, Mikołajczyk and four of his colleagues were added to the cabinet, presided over by Edward Osóbka-Morawski, which the United States recognized on July 5, 1945, as the Polish Provisional Government of National Unity. The holding of elections was not made a condition of the recognition, although Harriman recalled the Soviet promise. Ambassador Ciechanowski, who had vainly pleaded that Washington grant only a de facto recognition to Warsaw, was informed that the United States no longer recognized the government in London. The entire Polish embassy personnel in the United States and all the consuls resigned in protest. Trying to counter the criticism that the great powers had imposed the Provisional Government of National Unity on an unwilling nation, Washington took the official line that the government had been "set up by the Poles themselves."

On July 17, 1945, Stalin, Truman, and Churchill met at Potsdam. The main questions confronting the conference were: the German issue connected with the problem of reparations, preliminary arrangements for peace treaties with Germany's allies, and the matter of carrying out the Yalta Declaration on Liberated Europe. With regard to Poland the West was on the defensive. The Polish take-over of lands up to the Oder-Neisse line prior to the conference had produced sharp criticism in Washington. Kennan argued that such transfer of German territory to a Polish administration amounted to an evasion of Allied agreements and freed the West to dispose of German territories under Allied occupation. On legal grounds the Americans had a strong case, but politically the wisdom of opposing Polish interests was questionable. It was known that the United States continued to favor a German-Polish frontier that fell short of the Oder-Neisse Line. This only enhanced the Soviet image as a champion of Poland.

In discussing the German-Polish border at Potsdam, the Americans were secretly advised by Mikołajczyk, a member of the Polish delegation, to establish a connection between their acceptance of the border and a general agreement on basic conditions that alone could make Poland an independent state. In a memorandum handed to Harriman, Mikołajczyk spelled them out: a withdrawal of the Red Army and the NKVD from Poland, curbing of the local security police, and a return from the west of the Polish army and civilians. Elections should be held after the Russian withdrawal but not later than between December 1945 and February 1946. Truman singled out Mikołajczyk for praise and recalled the esteem in which Roosevelt held him. But although arguing strongly that the Polish government give pledges regarding free elections, the American side did not try to use the border settlement as a political lever. America's main preoccupation was with Germany and German reparations; consequently the German-Polish borders were treated in connection with a German not a Polish settlement. In a sense Poland was written off. The American motivation was both economic—how could Germany recover and pay reparations if deprived of all these lands—and political. Kennan argued that to place Poland's borders on the Oder-Neisse was "to make it perforce a Russian protectorate." But surely Poland's dependence on Russia was a fact, and a smaller Poland was likely to be more and not less dependent. The Poles could only see a pendulum-like Western policy, backing Russia against Germany or vice versa, but always at the expense of the states between the two.

Truman did not question the Polish claims on grounds of merit. As it was, Poland would emerge diminished in size and had a right to be compensated. After some bargaining, the Oder-Neisse Line was accepted but not as a permanent frontier. The former German lands were placed under Polish administration pending a future peace conference. Since at the same time the Allies authorized a transfer of the entire German population which lived there, it is hard to imagine that the border settlement could be other than permanent. In Lewis Namier's words, "it would have been more honest and more human" to make the settlement final.

By keeping the border settlement separate from domestic Polish problems, the West had no more leverage, except for American economic aid. Still, the British and to a lesser extent the Americans pressed Bierut, who protested outside interference but gave assurances that his government would hold free and unfettered elections in early 1946. He reiterated Stalin's remark to Hopkins that Poland would develop on the principles of Western democracy. With the heat turned on Bierut, Soviet Russia seemed by implication absolved from any direct responsibility for the Polish elections. Not that Stalin was willing to make concessions. When demands were made about the admission of observers and the press as well as for other means of supervision, Stalin half-jokingly announced that he wished to propose a compromise, namely to eliminate all such demands.

The question of Russian military withdrawal from Poland was settled by a provision permitting the presence of such troops as were needed for the control of two railroad lines that assured communication with the Soviet occupation zone in Germany. This was hardly a Western success. In the course of the Potsdam Conference Truman casually told Stalin about the atomic bomb. If this was intended as a means of diplomatic pressure, it produced no visible result. The chapter of wartime American-Polish relations was closed.

The United States policy toward Poland can be examined from various angles. Some historians have presented it in the form of a dilemma between the desire to promote national self-determination in East Central Europe and the determination to ensure cooperation with the Soviet Union. The first was an ideal, the second a necessity, and there was never any serious question which must be subordinated to the other. Still, Roosevelt hoped that necessary Polish sacrifices could be made palatable to the Poles and the Polish American voters by the discretion and restraint exercised by Soviet Russia.

But the question can also be viewed differently. By sacrificing to Soviet demands for security not only Poland but most of East Central Europe, the United States was jeopardizing the whole concept of the European balance of power, for Great Britain would no longer be able to act as a counterweight to Russia. This was a heavy price to pay, but it appears that Washington did not see it in this light. Balance of power and spheres of influence were notions considered dangerous by Americans. What mattered was general economic intercourse and worldwide political collaboration. Only the achievement of the two could prevent America from sliding back into isolation. It was through global collaboration that Soviet security interests could be satisfied. Here, it seems, Washington completely misunderstood Russia. Not only a historian writing in the 1970s but Kennan from his observation post in Moscow could point out that the whole concept of future collective security and international collaboration "seemed naive and unreal" to the Russians. But if the West wanted their assurances in that respect, "why not?" And Kennan prophetically concluded: "Once satisfied of the establishment of her power in Eastern and Central Europe," Russia would without much difficulty go through "with these strange Western schemes for collaboration in the preservation of peace." Seen in this light, the problem is not whether the United States was or was not in a position to counter Soviet designs on Poland and the rest of East Central Europe, but that it was willing to acquiesce in them in order to achieve these broad and somewhat chimeric goals.

Did the American policy makers appreciate that they were making real concessions, for Poland was not a burdensome local issue but an important piece in the European jigsaw puzzle? It has been often said that preoccupation with military victory obscured American thinking about political problems. That is true, but there was more to it. Thinking in global terms and concerned with domestic politics, Roosevelt and his collaborators including those of the OWI and OSS, took a basically sympathetic view of Russia often bypassing or circumventing the professional foreign service. These circles had limited knowledge of and even less concern with Poland and East Central Europe, yet the president listened to them and often bypassed his own secretary of state when dealing with the Soviet Union. Consequently, such officials as J. C. Dunn, H. F. Matthews, C. W. Cannon, G. Kennan, E. Durbrow, or C. E. Bohlen were not in a position to devise and implement a long-range program or authoritatively define United States interests in East Central Europe.

American diplomacy was frequently worried by Soviet moves and designs on Poland, but it responded to them by delaying difficult decisions, evading the issues, trying to mediate, and invoking the voice of public opinion. In practice this meant an abdication of responsibilities. The United States was finding itself increasingly in opposition to the Soviet Union, but not so much because of a dispute about principles as because of drifting policies. Adam Ulam's point that the primary defect of American diplomacy "was the failure to make itself respected" is well taken, as is his observation that the Polish case "demonstrated to Stalin that America was unsure about her policies and ignorant of the vast material and moral assets of which she disposed vis-à-vis the Soviet Union."

While Poland was one of the numerous issues the United States confronted, to the Poles it was naturally a matter of national survival. Not without reason, the Poles felt that their case rested on good moral grounds and was supported by the canons of international law. They had been victims of unprovoked German aggression; they continued to fight as part of the anti-Nazi alliance; none of the powers questioned the legitimacy of their government. Whether the eastern Polish border was a good one or not, it is difficult to argue that unilateral Soviet action undertaken in collusion with Germany abrogated the validity of the Treaty of Riga.

Yet moral claims and reliance on international law are no substitute for real power, and that Poland lacked. Neither the fighting underground nor the army, nor the Polish American assets could make up for the existing weakness. This fact was imperfectly understood by the Polish government in London. Furthermore, what continental Europeans had long called Anglo-Saxon hypocrisy operated against the Poles. Because the Soviet Union was badly needed it had to be represented as a paragon of all virtues; because the Poles were increasingly seen as an impediment to Western-Soviet cooperation, they had to be made into irresponsible troublemakers. The West had to persuade itself that by wronging them it was really acting in their best interest. Words, however, could hardly obscure the widening gap between morality and expediency, and the Second World War chapter in American-Polish relations ended by being an unedifying story.

6

In the Shadow of Stalinism and the Cold War

The New Poland

EMERGING from the Second World War, Poland was in many ways a new country. Its area of 120,350 square miles (roughly the size of New Mexico) was some 20 percent smaller than in 1939. The population of the Second Republic numbered around 35 million on the eve of the war; in 1946 it came to barely 24 million. As a result of phenomenally high birth-rate in the 1940s and early 1950s, the population reached the figure of over 34 million by the mid-1970s. This placed Poland in terms of size and population in seventh place in Europe.

Geographically the country was shifted some 150 miles to the west, assuming a shape closely resembling the early medieval kingdom of the Piasts. The capital, Warsaw, now lay east of the center, and the western or "recovered" territories, previously German, accounted for 48 percent of Poland's area and eventually for more than half of the total population. While the ancient cultural centers in the east, Wilno and Lwów, now found themselves outside Poland's borders, such major western cities as Wrocław (Breslau), Szczecin (Stettin), and Gdańsk (Danzig) were comprised within them. The length of Polish frontiers diminished by some 1,200 miles, and the country was no longer contiguous on seven but only on three states: the Soviet Union, East Germany, and Czechoslovakia. The tiny pre-1939 coastline of some 90 miles expanded to over 320; in addition to the port of Gdynia, Poland gained the important harbors of Gdańsk and Szczecin.

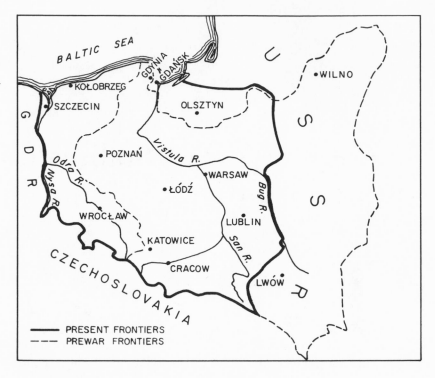

3. Poland before and after the Second World War

There was a radical change in the economic base of the country. By controlling the entire Silesian basin, Poland almost doubled its coal resources (estimated at 180 billion metric tons) and acquired new deposits of lead, zinc, copper, and lignite as well as some iron ores, cobalt, cadmium, and ceramic and porcelain clays. While in 1938 Poland produced nearly 4 billion kilowatt-hours of electricity, the area now within Polish borders had produced 7.4 billion. New Poland had 5 percent more arable land in proportion to the total territory than it had within the old borders. On the other hand, territorial cessions to Russia caused the loss of most of the country's oil and natural gas, significant potash salt deposits, and half of the forests.

Changes in population were equally drastic. The spontaneous flight of the Germans toward the end of the war was followed by mass expulsions, regularized by the Allied Control Commission agreement of November 1945 that provided for forcible transfers to the American, British, and Soviet occupation zones of Germany. The bulk of Jewry had been exterminated by the Nazis, and most of the Ukrainians and Belorussians were now outside the Polish state. After subsequent population transfers, notably a partial repatriation of Poles from the Soviet-annexed territories, a return of certain groups of emigrants and emigrés from the West, and a gradual exodus of the Jewish remnant from Poland, national minorities were estimated at between 1.5 and 2 percent of the total population.

Taking a coldly calculating view, postwar Poland had more compact and rational borders than in the past, and possessed a far greater economic potential. For the first time in modern history it was an ethnically homogeneous country. The "western territories" proved essential for the country's modernization; they relieved the demographic pressures in central Poland and absorbed the rapidly growing population. These were distinct advantages, although they could hardly be appreciated at a time when the war-devastated nation had its material bases severely damaged, its social structure dislocated, its morale shaken, and a government that would have been unthinkable without the presence of the mighty Red Army and NKVD.

War ravages were terrible. Some six million Polish citizens—almost 20 percent of the population—had perished during the war as compared to a quarter of a million Americans who had fallen in the struggle. Only a small fraction had died on the battlefield; nearly 90 percent had lost their lives in concentration and labor camps, were executed or died of privations. Proportionately, war losses of the intelligentsia were even higher (35 percent) and, if one adds the exiles and displaced persons, only a fraction (about 100,000) of the old intelligentsia lived in post-1945 Poland. Following deportations, flights, transfers and internal migration, about 33 percent of the Polish people resided elsewhere than in 1939.

Economically, the country was ruined, and war losses per capita of $625 were the largest of all war-ravaged countries. In industrial capacity and urban dwellings they amounted respectively to 60 and 45 percent. In the agrarian sector, about 40 percent of farm buildings and machinery was destroyed, 60 percent of cattle, 72 percent of sheep, and 45 percent of horses. Destruction in the city of Warsaw came close to 85 percent, and of the harbor installations of Gdynia to 50 percent. Several areas of the rich western territories were reduced to a wasteland. Wrocław suffered 80 percent damages; Gdańsk had been put to the torch by the Red Army. At first, controls over the former German economic establishment were in the hands of the Soviet army which treated it as war booty; even after the Potsdam Conference, large scale looting of the western territories continued.

According to Allied decisions the Polish part of German reparations was to come out of the Soviet share and was calculated at roughly 15 percent of its total. Then the Soviet side engaged in special arithmetic. The value of Polish territories lost to Russia was compared to those acquired from Germany and showed a surplus on the Polish side. After deducting the value of goods already taken out by the Russians from the western territories, Poland was still declared a debtor to the Soviet Union and obliged to deliver coal to Russia at $1.25 per metric ton while Sweden and Denmark were offering to pay $16. The coal "agreement" was to be valid only for the period of the occupation of Germany, then estimated to last for five years, but in fact continued much longer. The Poles succeeded, however, in avoiding a Russian proposal to set up joint Soviet-Polish companies in Silesia.

Cultural losses, incalculable in qualitative terms, were staggering. Libraries lost up to one third of their holdings, numerous works of art were destroyed, archives suffered badly. Some seven hundred university professors, one thousand high school and four thousand elementary school teachers perished. The five-year break in education and training of scholars, in publishing, in cultural and artistic activities produced gaps that were impossible to fill. While almost 8,000 scholarly publications had appeared in 1937, only 426 were printed in 1946. The corresponding drop in literary works was from 1,560 to 645. The general decline of cultural and academic levels went hand in hand with injuries done to the national psyche and mores. The war had not ended in the way for which most Poles had fought, waited, and prayed. Despair mingled with apathy, life had become devoid of meaning and was rated cheap. Some people developed a kind of schizophrenia.

Most Poles felt alienated in the new situation. A procommunist politician later recalled how the eyes of people he addressed in public meetings "burned with hatred toward us." The writer Z. Załuski described another type of a widely held attitude: "The Bolsheviks are in the country, the Communists are in power, Warsaw is burnt down, the legal government suppressed, nothing worse can happen to us, we have lost the war and have to think of ourselves." Idealism, devotion to duty, the public interest appeared to be empty words that should be forgotten. Instead, a cynical approach to life prevailed.

Dislocated, disoriented, insecure, experiencing leveling-down processes, Polish society was in the throes of a socioeconomic revolution, yet the real issue was not capitalism versus socialism. Kennan had recognized it already in 1944 when he observed that the real issue in Eastern Europe was "one of the independence of the national life or of domination by a big power which had never shown itself adept in making any permanent compromises with rival power groups." The need for a comprehensive agrarian reform was widely recognized and the question was only who would accomplish it and how. Already in 1944, before the hostilities ended, the state began to expropriate estates exceeding 50 hectares (roughly 120 acres), but their distribution to the peasantry led to heated debates between Communists and their Populist allies. Political rather than strictly economic considerations affected decisions on such questions as spontaneous distribution versus legal takeover, the size of the plots, and the amount to be allotted to state farms (PGR). The public was not sure whether the reform was meant as a first step toward collectivization—which the Communists denied—or an accelerated parceling out of the prewar type without compensation. Consequently there were peasants who greeted the reform with suspicion. All in all, around 6 million hectares were parceled out, creating new and enlarging some old farms. Except for the western territories, where holdings were sizable and seemingly designed with an eye to economic realities, small farms proliferated. There was no systematic consolidation of strips. For the time being lands belonging to the church were left alone. Although evictions of landowners often assumed brutal forms, there was no bloody agrarian revolution. Still, the way in which the reform was carried out added to the feeling of insecurity so characteristic in postwar Poland.

Nationalizaton of industry also began in 1944 and at first followed prewar legal procedures. It took its final form with a decree of January 1946 that provided for a seizure of mines, foundries, oil fields, power plants, gas, water works, and other large establishments. Private enterprises were allowed only if they employed a maximum of fifty workers per shift. The implementation of these provisions was often accompanied by arbitrariness and irregularities.

Did the new external and internal conditions leave any room for the rebirth of a genuine political life involving an interplay of competing forces? The Poles in the West believed that it did not, and a sizable emigration of several hundred thousand former soldiers and civilians rallied around President Raczkiewicz and the Arciszewski government in exile. Refusing to accept the fate of Poland as final, the emigrés loudly protested Yalta and the faits accompli at home. The emigration, much in the nineteenth-century Polish tradition, saw itself as the only free and authentic voice of Poland.

Believing in the unavoidable clash between the Soviet Union and the West, it concentrated on preserving the legality of the exile government. The watchword of a "state-in-exile" was born.

Some emigrés did return home for private and political reasons. They included prominent intellectuals, to mention only Słonimski, Tuwim, Władysław Broniewski and Ksawery Pruszyński. Pruszyński formulated his credo in a letter he left with a friend abroad. Asserting that he was not a Communist and loved freedom and democracy, Pruszyński wrote that he had no illusions about Russia. He had long trusted England and America and believed that they would not permit a Soviet seizure of Poland. But it did happen and the Poles had to adjust to Russia and "forget the West."

Within Poland, the main political parties, obliged to operate in secrecy during the German occupation, faced great problems trying to come back into the open. The National Democratic party was outlawed as a reactionary force; a splinter from the Polish Socialist party, which had entered into partnership with the Communists and participated in the Committee of National Liberation, proclaimed itself the reborn PPS; a populist faction, organized partly outside the underground Populist party, followed a similar course and adopted the name of the old organization. This placed formidable obstacles to the reemergence of the genuine PPS and Populist party, both of which had been the mainstay of the underground and the government in exile. Although the Home Army had been disbanded, not all its "woods detachments" had come into the open, and they were driven into an anticommunist underground. The Communists and their allies vociferously denounced the Home Army as a pack of traitors, German collaborators, and lackeys of reaction. A civilian underground came into being in September 1945 under the name WiN (Polish abbreviation for Freedom and Independence), but within a year its leadership was decimated by arrests. WiN did not preach armed resistance, but the Communists made no real distinction between it and the active partisans, especially the extreme rightist NSZ, or the Ukrainian Liberation Army (UPA). Soviet and Polish security forces ruthlessly hunted them down, and in the process many former partisan units degenerated into armed bands similar to the southern guerrillas active in the American Reconstruction period after the Civil War. Fratricidal struggle was going on in Poland, claiming thousands of victims.

Polish opponents to the regime ranged from an unconsolidated anticommunist political camp, through various underground resistance units, down to sizable but more passive groups that placed their faith in the Western resolve to ensure free elections and a democratic system. Then there were those who chose not to oppose the Communists or even went along with them hoping that the regime could be modified and steered in a more democratic and liberal direction. Communist appeals and promises were having a certain effect on the progressive intelligentsia, disillusioned with the West and fearful of the domestic extreme right, segments of the peasantry interested in the land reform, and some workers wishing for a speedy rebuilding of nationalized industries.

The Communists knew well that they were a small minority operating in a predominantly hostile society. In July 1944 the party had at least 5,000 and at most 20,000 members; by the end of 1945 its membership rose to almost 250,000. It was obvious that many of the new adherents were opportunists who would be purged in subsequent years, but at the moment the party could not be choosy. Nor was its leadership a monolith. The Moscovite faction headed by Bierut did not see eye to eye with the Natives, led by Gomułka. While the term "national Communists" can often be misleading, Zbigniew Brzezinski is close to the mark when he speaks of the phenomenon of "domesticism." People like Gomułka, who spent the war years in Poland, naturally viewed problems from a domestic perspective. Poland's national interest appeared to them indistinguishable from socialist revolution, but they felt that a Polish road to socialism could not be a blind imitation of the Russian model.

Polish Communist heritage carried with it liabilities which the Natives wished quickly to erase. These were: internationalism of the Rosa Luxemburg type, the prewar espousal by Polish Communists of German revisionism, and the stigma of Stalin's dissolution of the Polish Communist party in 1938 on the grounds of treason. Seeking to gain legitimacy in the eyes of the nation, the Polish Workers' party (PPR) justified its rule by invoking Poland's raison d'état and by claiming credit for the acquisition of the western territories. Few Polish Communists relished complete dependence on Moscow and they wished to govern Poland, insofar as possible, in their own right.

Another handicap for the Communists was the fact that so many Jews figured prominently in the ruling elite—a fact privately regretted by the Zionist leader Emil Sommerstein who himself collaborated with the new regime. Given the numerical weakness of the party and the traditionally high percentage of Jews in the leadership of the Polish Communist movement, it is not surprising that they became highly visible. The Polish right had always spoken of Judeo-Communism, and this preponderance confirmed it to the public, adding anti-Semitism as a factor in conflicts between the party and the population and within the party. The Moscovite faction was particularly vulnerable, with Polish Jews Jakub Berman and Hilary Minc occupying the key positions in the fields of security and economics. A somewhat grim joke circulating in Poland at the time said that the only difference between the Polish ministry of foreign affairs and Palestine was that the former had no Arabs in it.

Mikołajczyk's return to Poland in the late summer of 1945, as vice-premier in the Provisional Government of National Unity, introduced a new element into the Polish situation. "We had arranged and fostered his return to Poland," wrote later the American ambassador to Warsaw, Stanton Griffis, and indeed Mikołajczyk conceived his mission as a Western-backed attempt to shape Polish politics in the spirit of Yalta and Potsdam. Had Mikołajczyk aimed at becoming a junior partner of the Communists and sought to gain the trust of Moscow, he might have been allowed a certain leverage in the country. Insofar as he could assist in the legitimization of the Polish regime he was welcome. His limited objectives, such as amnesty to the partisans who came out into the open, repatriation of the Home Army fighters deported to Russia, and even the imposition of some limits on the police terror lay within the realm of the possible. Indeed, two amnesty acts passed by the government alleviated somewhat the position of the former partisans and permitted their reintegration into society. But Mikołajczyk's aims went further. Counting on American-British support, he strove to build a powerful party to challenge, through elections that were supposed to be free and unfettered, the Communists' rule.

Welcomed enthusiastically by many Poles, Mikołajczyk cast himself in the role of the opposition leader and succeeded in organizing a mass party called Polish Populist party (PSL), to distinguish it from the Populist party cooperating with the Communists. The PSL platform of January 1946 called for the end of police terror and the abolition of the ministries of security and propaganda. By early 1946 the Populists received wide support not only from the peasantry but also from important members of the intelligentsia and from the Catholic church. Regarded as the only genuinely anticommunist force in the country, PSL became a giant, but in the domestic and international context of 1945–1946, it proved to be a giant with feet of clay.

The Communists did everything to limit the effectiveness of the PSL and to circumscribe Mikołajczyk's power in the cabinet. In the crucial sphere of mass communication, PSL was allowed to publish only three newspapers which were subjected to rigidly enforced censorship. The previously agreed number of seats to be allotted to the Polish Populist party in the Council for the Homeland (temporary parliament) was cut. In the cabinet, the PSL held the ministries of agriculture, public administration, and education, but their scope was limited by others that were controlled by Communists. Thus the ministry of security checked that of public administration; Gomułka's ministry of recovered territories, which wielded great powers of patronage, interfered with agriculture and public administration; a special Council of Universities weakened PSL influence in education. To the Communists, Mikołajczyk became, to use Gomułka's words, "a symbol of all the antidemocratic elements, of all that is inimical to democracy and the Soviet Union." A campaign was launched to accuse him and his movement of counterrevolutionary designs and of collusion with the armed bands in the woods. Mikołajczyk was saddled with the moral responsibility for the fighting in the countryside, and represented as an instrument of Anglo-American imperialism. In the era of the nascent Cold War this was tantamount to saying that he was anti-Soviet by definition.

A detailed discussion of the origins of the Cold War obviously cannot be attempted here, but a brief review is needed because of its importance for American-Polish relations. History has shown that most wartime coalitions held together only by determination to defeat the common enemy do not survive beyond victory. The political-ideological gulf between the West and the Soviet Union, even if temporarily and purposefully obscured to promote wartime unity, was bound to cause a decomposition of the Grand Alliance. The Soviet Union was seeking to transform its influence in East Central Europe, including the German zone of occupation, into rigid controls, and displaying the ambitions of a super power. The victorious United States, enjoying great economic power and a monopoly on the atomic bomb, found it hard to condone such ambitions. Freed frm the German and Japanese threats, Washington saw the Russian might as the main international problem. Were there limits to a possible Russian expansion? Already in 1944 Harriman had worried that if one accepted the theory of Soviet right "to penetrate her immediate neighbors," penetration "of the next immediate neighbors becomes at a certain time equally logical." The domino theory was born. Acting Secretary of State Joseph Grew commented in May 1945 that Russian behavior in Eastern Europe could establish the "future world pattern." As Brzezinski put it, American interest in this area became "primarily a barometer reflecting the longer range Soviet interests and perspectives vis-à-vis the West."

Was American concern mainly of a political nature or did it also stem from preoccupations with markets and investments in East Central Europe? In view of the relatively small size of American capital involved and limited interests in the region, economic motivation could hardly have played a decisive role. Still, general assumptions of United States foreign policy were based on the belief in a free flow of goods and a worldwide economic community. A closed Soviet bloc in the eastern half of the Continent interfered with such goals.

In a speech of October 31, 1945, Byrnes praised regional arrangements such as the Monroe Doctrine and expressed sympathy for Soviet efforts "to draw into closer and more friendly association with her Central and Eastern European neighbors." He recognized Soviet claims to security but warned that there could be no lasting peace "in a world divided into spheres of exclusive influence." Wishing for an agreement with Russia for its political effect in the United States, Byrnes approvingly quoted from Marx, that if other powers held firm Russia was sure to draw back "in a very decent manner." Like many subsequent American pronouncements on the subject, Byrnes' statement exhibited both wishful and muddled thinking. How "exclusive" did Soviet influence have to be to arouse American opposition? What precisely constituted a "closer and more friendly association" which the United States approved? How firm had one to be to make Russia more accommodating, and if the Soviets disregarded vague warnings what was the United States to do about it?

Having largely convinced the American public that Soviet goals in East Central Europe were not unreasonable and did not represent a threat to American interests or security, Washington now had to tell the people that this was no longer true. Soviet behavior was not only morally reprehensible but threatened the free world. The Soviet side could and did retort that it was still open to cooperation provided that East Central Europe continued to be recognized as a Soviet sphere, a satisfactory solution was achieved regarding Germany's future, and American aid was extended for purposes of reconstruction. If America changed its outlook, that could only be regarded as a proof of hostility and provoke a tightening of the Soviet hold over East Central Europe. Already in August 1945 the *Bolshevik* warned that Marxists could not lapse into pacifism, because the imperialist forces that had triggered the Second World War were far from being spent. Nor could the Soviet Union lose interest in wars fought throughout the world to achieve liberation from the tyranny of capitalists and landowners.

The United States was on the defensive and was somewhat vulnerable to Communist accusations that it was the West and not the East that had departed from wartime cooperation. Nor did America have the means to pressure Soviet Russia into making concessions. Having condoned Soviet expansion, how was it going to roll it back? Ulam's point, that Stimson shared with the "revisionist" historians the fallacious view of American-Russian relations being "dominated by the problem of the atomic bomb," is well taken. There is no indication that the Soviet Union ever seriously worried about atomic attacks. As for "atomic diplomacy," Washington never could exploit the bomb monopoly nor did it try to share it in exchange for concrete Russian concessions.

At the first postwar conference of the Council of Foreign Ministers in 1945, the Russians were probing the limits of Western willingness to make new concessions. Molotov raised the question of Russian participation in the control of Japan and asked for a trusteeship of Tripolitania. He called Byrnes' insistence on free elections in East Central Europe an unwarranted meddling with sovereign states. Instead the West was pressured into recognizing the new regimes of former enemy states: Hungary, Bulgaria, and Rumania. It stiffened its attitude, however, on the all-important German issue. With the merger of the English and American zones of occupation (Bizonia), a supposed economic unity of Germany that included the Soviet zone came to an end. In a tough speech of February 9, 1946, Stalin asserted that peaceful international order was hardly possible in the face of the capitalist-imperialist conspiracy. A leading American liberal, Justice William Douglas, termed the speech a declaration of the Third World War. In March in his famous Fulton address Churchill spoke of an Iron Curtain that had split Europe into two halves.

Seen in this larger international context, what were the options open to American diplomacy with regard to Poland? It could accept Soviet controls as a fact of life, use face-saving devices, gloss over the matter of "free and unfettered" elections, and sacrifice Poland in the hope of improving American-Soviet relations. But since the trend in Poland and throughout East Central Europe seemed to indicate a general pattern of Soviet domination, such a policy made little sense. Thus Poland could not be forgotten and written off, and ways and means had to be devised to stem the tide sweeping it into a closed bloc and depriving it of essentials of political democracy. This was no easy task, for pressure had to be applied simultaneously on Moscow and Warsaw, and a distinction made between a friendly nation—the Poles—and their objectionable Communist regime. A State Department memorandum prepared at the time of the Potsdam Conference spelled out the problems and warned against "open interference" with Polish domestic politics. What remained was a policy of discreet backing of Mikołajczyk combined with verbal protests to the Polish government against any infringements of Yalta, and economic pressures. The use of these was difficult. Economic aid was likely to bolster the regime, but its denial would appear as inhumane punishment of Poles for the sins of the government imposed on them. Furthermore, to withhold economic aid would strengthen Poland's dependence on Russia. Finally, Poland could not be ostracized economically, for the United States sought an open international economic community, wished to dispose of its war surpluses, and needed coal from Polish Silesia for European reconstruction.

Thus, issues confronting American policy toward Poland were far from simple, and if we add to them the West-East confrontation over Germany, highly relevant to the Poles, a well thought-out and coordinated global plan would seem indispensable. But in 1945 the United States was ill-equipped to outline one. The Interdivisional Committee on Russia and Poland set up in the State Department in 1943 ceased to function after 1945. A professional intelligence service was of most recent vintage; the Policy Planning Staff would only be created two years later. There was a division of opinion in Washington on how to deal with Poland within the broad international context. The inexperienced Secretary Byrnes was hardly capable of sophisticated diplomacy and some of his moves were ill-calculated. Nor did he see eye to eye with Undersecretary Grew. Finally, the United States ambassador to Warsaw held views that were not always shared by the State Department.

The Period of Transition, 1945 to 1947

Arthur Bliss Lane had been appointed ambassador in the autumn of 1944, when the United States still recognized the Polish government in exile. Given the existing situation, he was not sent to London and, waiting to assume his duties, he had ample time to consider the Polish question and its importance for America. In a brief talk with Roosevelt in November 1944 he opined that the United States had to insist on Poland's independence, and met with Roosevelt's rejoinder: "Do you want me to go to war with Russia?" Lane was pessimistic about the outcome of Yalta and noticed with dismay Soviet indifference to Roosevelt's pleas not to create accomplished facts. He was critical of the apparent lack of concern for Poland on the part of the American policymakers. He later termed it incomprehensible, given the historical, geographical, and strategic position of that country and the presence of millions of Polish Americans in the United States. It was characteristic of the trends in Washington that Lane was allowed to see only one account of the Katyn massacre, on which the State Department tended to rely, furnished by Harriman's young daughter. Other intelligence reports on Katyn were kept under lock and key.

In the spring of 1945, Lane recommended that the American public be frankly told about the deterioration of American-Soviet relations over Poland. He agreed to accept the ambassadorial post in Warsaw, lest someone who might be willing to whitewash the Communist regime be sent there. At that point Washington still tried to pretend that the recently recognized government in Warsaw corresponded to the wishes of the Poles, and Truman assured Rozmarek that it had not been imposed on them by the Big Three.

Before his departure Lane received no real briefing, nor did Byrnes ask him to come to Potsdam to witness the handling of the Polish question at the conference. Lane, however, arranged to be there, met Bierut and Foreign Minister Wincenty Rzymowski, and got a closer look at the Communist leaders. Potsdam witnessed the beginnings of American-Polish talks concerning economic matters, and the American side stressed the important contribution Polish coal and food products, especially from the western territories, could make to postwar economic reconstruction of Europe. The Poles in turn showed great interest in Western aid for their economy. Exports from Poland, they said, would, until the end of 1946, pay for only half of Polish annual imports, estimated at $380 million dollars. Hence, credits of $190 million would be imperative and long-range credits of $500 million very important for reconstruction and development. The Americans favored economic aid, but while Byrnes and the State Department wished to use it to further European reconstruction, Lane hoped to wield it as an instrument of political pressure on Warsaw.

After his arrival in Poland, Lane used the first opportunity to discuss economic relations. Aid through the United Nations Relief and Rehabilitation Administration (UNRRA) raised minor difficulties connected with the distribution of goods. The UNRRA mission to Poland was headed by a Soviet official and distribution was entirely in Polish hands, but Lane agreed with Washington that this type of aid had to be given even if it were to benefit indirectly the USSR. Deliveries of food, cattle, clothing, machinery, locomotives, and other UNRRA items were of tremendous significance for Poland. Between mid-1945 and mid-1947, close to $500 million worth of goods was shipped, the American share amounting to 72 percent. The total value was calculated as equivalent to 22 percent of Polish national income in 1946. At one point some of the food deliveries were cut in size, which prompted an immediate Soviet and Polish outcry of food being used as a means of political coercion. Otherwise there was not much friction. In March 1946 Herbert Hoover, well remembered in Poland for his relief activities after the First World War, visited Warsaw in the company of the former American minister, Hugh Gibson. After General Dwight Eisenhower, who had paid a brief visit to Warsaw in September 1945, Hoover was the first prominent American to come to the new Poland.

Alongside with UNRRA other organizations were bringing aid to the country, particularly the American Relief for Poland directed by Henry Osinski, the War Relief Services—National Catholic Welfare Conference, Committee for American Relief in Europe (CARE), Quaker missions, and Joint Distribution Committee. The last one was assisting the Jews. The Red Cross contributed over $9 million up to the spring of 1947. This type of humanitarian aid met with the approval and gratitude of all Poles. Mikołajczyk urged Truman in November 1945 that it be given, and as Lane recalled, a high-ranking member of the Catholic hierarchy said that the United States must not "crucify the Polish people for the crimes of their government."

Assistance in the form of credits or exchange of technical experts raised problems that were partly economic and partly political. The availability of credits through the Export-Import Bank hinged largely on information about the Polish financial situation being made accessible to the United States. Lane suggested a scheme according to which Polish coal exports to Western Europe, especially Italy and France, would stimulate those countries' exports to the United States, making it possible for Poland to build up dollar reserves in New York. While Washington sought to gain Polish promises not to discriminate against American trade and investments, to respect the rights of American citizens, and behave in accord with the 1931 treaty—in short, not to grant any state a monopolistic position in the Polish economy—Lane pursued political objectives. Determined to use Warsaw's requests for loans and surpluses (cloth for the army) as a lever to "obtain fulfillment of Polish commitments under the Yalta and Potsdam decisions," the ambassador was going beyond his instructions; a certain dualism in American policy toward Poland became evident.

In the course of protracted negotiations held in Washington, the Americans expressed their concern over the emergence of a Soviet-dominated economic bloc in East Central Europe and sought assurances that the Poles would keep their economy open to contacts with the United States. Mikołajczyk emphasized this American concern when reporting to the Polish cabinet on the possibilities of United States credits. On his side, Lane worried over the political implications of a $500 million loan that Warsaw was interested in, and decided to consult some of the leading noncommunists in the country. They included Archbishop Stefan Sapieha (shortly to become cardinal), the ailing senior statesman of the Populists, Wincenty Witos, the foremost Socialist, Zygmunt Żuławski, still vainly trying to resuscitate an independent PPS, and General Juliusz Rómmel. All of them agreed that Poles would interpret an American loan as signifying acquiescence in the undemocratic and brutal policy of the regime vis-à-vis the opposition. Washington's refusal to make a big loan, they opined, would have important psychological effects, even though there was a danger that Poland would become economically more dependent on Russia. By December 1945, Washington seemed to have recognized the validity of Lane's arguments, but a small $25–50 million loan was still being considered.

Mikołajczyk concentrated on urging both Lane and the White House to try to make political conditions in Poland more bearable by demanding a speedy evacuation of the Red Army. The troops were authorized by the Potsdam agreement to guard communication lines with the Soviet zone in Germany.

The Polish government was seeking to reassure Washington. Oskar Lange, whose appointment as Poland's ambassador caused some uneasiness in view of his recent status as an American citizen, told the State Department that the Communists were now "a nationalist party working only for the better interests of Poland." But Lange did admit that some of the Polish leaders were taking their directives from Moscow. During Hoover's visit, Bierut emphatically asserted that there had never been a conflict of interest between Poland and the United States. Yet friction began to increase. Foreign Minister Rzymowski complained about the cool reception he had received on his September 1945 visit to the United States, having previously denounced Polish emigrés active in America as traitors to Poland. In June 1946 Warsaw officially termed the visit of General Bór-Komorowski to the United States as an unfriendly act on the part of Washington. Finally, the Polish government tried to discredit Lane by attaching to him the blame for the deteriorating American-Polish relations.

Indeed, Lane kept complaining to Bierut and other high-ranking Polish officials not only about improper treatment of the embassy and American citizens but also about the political climate in the country. Already in the autumn of 1945 he had warned Bierut that he could not recommend requests for economic aid unless there was real freedom of the press and the government stopped arbitrary police arrests. In December Lane and Bierut fought a verbal duel: the former stressing American obligations stemming from the Yalta agreement to assure some freedom of political life in Poland, the latter countering with charges of American interference in Polish domestic affairs. After the announcement of the January 1946 nationalization decree, the Polish government quickly construed Lane's insistence on safeguarding the rights of American citizens as an opposition to the decree itself. This was not true, but Lane had to take a stand on behalf of worried American investors like Anaconda, Vacuum Oil, and others.

Domestic political tension in Poland was on the increase as Communists and their allies prepared for a trial of strength through a popular referendum scheduled for the early summer of 1946. At the beginning of 1946, Mikołajczyk's PSL had some 600,000 members (his supporters claimed a higher figure), as compared with 235,000 for PPR, 165,000 for PPS, and 280,000 for the Populist party. Since the attempt to recreate an independent PPS failed, many of its former members joined the official party, weakening thereby its reliability for the Communists. They replied with pressures of various sorts. Mikołajczyk's supporters were exposed to constant harassment, arrests, even assassination; the British government publicly condemned murders of political opponents in Poland. Secretary Byrnes, driven by forceful representations on the part of Senator Vandenberg, whose constituency had a large Polish American component, endorsed the British position.

At the same time, the State Department began to incline toward a $40 million loan to Poland through the Export-Import Bank, and credit sales of $50 million worth of surplus war material. In return, the Poles were expected to make reassuring statements concerning former American property and give some promises regarding the elections. Lane was dismayed by Washington's stand even though he appreciated the fact that the army and navy wished to dispose of their surpluses before they became a total loss. The ambassador advised, in view of the Polish government's policy of simultaneously insulting the United States and asking for material aid, that America make it plain that "we do not intend to be backed farther against the wall." In April 1946, Senator Vandenberg stressed that American credits ought not to be granted before the implementation of the Yalta provisions. The Division of East European Affairs of the State Department tended to agree.

In May the loan agreement was stopped, but after minor Polish amends and explanations, Washington decided to go ahead with it. The State Department believed that if Warsaw gave proper publicity to American aid, the loan would show that the United States did not forget the Polish people. To Lane this seemed a most dangerous policy of appeasement. Already in March 1946 he had come to the conclusion that Mikołajczyk's political chances in Poland were nil. Hence, the United States should issue a public condemnation of police terror in Poland, abruptly terminate economic talks, and concentrate on educating the American public to the real aims of the Communists.

On June 30, 1946, the Polish government held a popular referendum. Its object was both to demonstrate the extent of support it enjoyed in the country and to test the strength of the opposition. The electorate was asked to answer three questions with "yes" or "no"; namely, did they support the abolition of the senate, did they support the land reform and nationalization of basic industries with some retention of private enterprises, and did they support the western boundary along the Odra-Nysa rivers? The nature of the questions made a negative response almost impossible, but, since the Communists called for a triple "yes," Mikołajczyk enjoined his supporters to vote "no" on the first question, although traditionally the Populists had never favored an upper chamber. Most likely, this was a double mistake, for it forewarned the Communists of Mikołajczyk's determination to seek a showdown, and would reveal the real strength of his camp. He might have been wiser to await the regular elections without showing his hand.

On the day of the referendum American teams of observers, meeting with only sporadic interference on the part of the authorities, reported no overt intimidation, and Mikołajczyk could only claim that the results of the vote were falsified afterward. Indeed, a delay of ten days intervened before the results were announced, and they showed that 68 percent of the voters answered the first question with a "yes." The PSL leaders vociferously protested tampering with the ballots, and the *New York Times* termed the referendum "a farce and a sham." Lane lectured the Polish government on what constituted a genuinely free suffrage, and Bierut exhibited signs of extreme annoyance. Warsaw came close to stating that the ambassador was a persona non grata, and Washington had to stress its full confidence in Lane.

While the vote was being counted and doctored, a tragic event took place in the town of Kielce that all but deflected the interest of Western public opinion from the referendum. There was an anti-Jewish riot, with some forty people killed and scores more wounded. Mikołajczyk called the outbreak a government-engineered provocation. Gomułka and the premier put the blame on the reactionary underground and pointed an accusing finger at Mikołajczyk and the Primate of Poland, Cardinal August Hlond. While this shocking outbreak undoubtedly played into the hands of the regime by providing ammunition against the opposition forces in the country, a Communist provocation seems doubtful. The riot appears to have been spontaneous and arose out of anti-Semitic feelings enhanced by the visible association of some Jews with the PPR and the security police. The majority of the Jewish population that attempted to remake its life in postwar Poland had returned from Russia, which rendered it doubly suspect in the eyes of anticommunist Poles. In the brutal and unsettled conditions of 1946 the Jews were particularly vulnerable. Attacks against them occurred at that time not only in Poland but also in Hungary.

News of the "Kielce pogrom" figured for three consecutive days on the front pages of the *New York Times* and tarnished Poland's image, but otherwise had no discernible impact on American-Polish intercourse. During the period that separated the referendum from the January 1947 elections, United States policy continued to exhibit a lack of coordination and inconsistency that worried Lane. This was most noticeable in the case of Secretary Byrnes' speech of September 6, and in the final agreements on American credits and loans to Poland of October and December 1946.

Advocating a vigorous policy, Lane listed American grievances: minor Polish obstructions of activities of United States citizens, press attacks, unfavorable rate of exchange, and housing difficulties of the embassy. He expressed dissatisfaction with Warsaw's indifference to American wishes, for instance regarding the proposed aviation agreement. The ambassador recommended to Washington a rejection of all Polish aid requests until the United States received satisfaction. He reiterated that Yalta and Potsdam accords had to be fully executed. The State Department was cautious and Acheson noncommittal; Byrnes held only a brief talk with Lane; conversations with Lange and Rzymowski were inconclusive.

On September 6, 1946, the Poles were stunned and Lane caught unawares by Byrnes' speech delivered in Stuttgart. After recalling that prior to Potsdam Russia alone had authorized the Poles to occupy the western territories, the secretary said that the Potsdam Conference accepted merely a Polish "administration" of these lands. The United States made no agreement "to support at the peace settlement the cession of this particular area." Calculated to embarrass the Russians on the eve of elections in Germany, the statement was part of a somewhat clumsy diplomatic offensive that sought to make Germany the pivot of American policy on the European continent. Its impact on American-Polish relations was bound to be unfortunate. In view of Allied wartime agreements about moving Poland westward, Truman's commendation of the Odra-Nysa frontier on August 9, 1945, and the authorized transfer of the German population, the Poles had every reason to believe that the territorial settlement was de facto final. A reopening of the issue at this point was, in Lane's words, "damaging to the cause of the opposition" in Poland, "as well as to the prestige of the United States." Communist propaganda made ample use of the speech, claiming that the United States was backing Germany against Poland. Mikołajczyk's supporters became the target of accusations that linked them with American-sponsored German revisionism. Crowds demonstrating in Warsaw in front of the American embassy proceeded to attack the headquarters of the PSL. Even though the manifestation was most likely engineered, it was a clever move. Mikołajczyk's own protests against the Stuttgart speech went unreported in the Polish press.

The Polish Populist party was facing a critical situation, although it still had some room for maneuver. The Socialists put out feelers to ascertain whether the PSL, if offered a sizable number of seats, would join an electoral bloc with the Communists, Socialists and Populists. These "defeatist" tendencies of the PPS, as a Communist historian has called them, revealed a greater fluidity in Polish politics than one would have expected. Mikołajczyk countered with proposals of an electoral bloc in the western and eastern provinces —where the Communists wielded greater power—and free elections elsewhere. He demanded, however, that within the bloc noncommunist parties (PSL, PPS, and SL) be guaranteed a total of 51 percent of parliamentary representation. Later Mikołajczyk would propose that the Populists (both factions) be granted 75 percent of the seats, roughly corresponding to the percentage of peasants in Poland. This was clearly unacceptable since the Communists were never willing to offer more than 50 percent to the two peasant parties or 25 percent to Mikołajczyk's party alone. The alarmed Communists intensified their efforts to bring the PPS into line, and brought the fast-rising Socialist star, Józef Cyrankiewicz, into the government. A consolidated electoral bloc emerged without the PSL, comprising PPR, PPS, SL, and two small parties—the Labor party (SP) and the Democratic party (SD). Not surprisingly, its program singled out foreign policy matters, and Byrnes' Stuttgart speech was a useful target. Lane also reported a whispered propaganda campaign asserting that a defeat of the bloc at the polls would signify a Russian takeover of Poland.

Intimidation, abuses, and ill-concealed terror provoked Mikołajczyk's protests and American warnings, which Bierut and the Soviet Union invariably countered by protests against unwarranted foreign interference in Polish affairs. But, terror apart, Mikołajczyk's party was weakening from the inside and showing signs of disorientation. The leader's tactics were subjected to internal criticism. To those Poles who imagined that Mikołajczyk had real guarantees of American and British support, the lack of a determined Western policy and Washington's interest in Germany came as a shock.

It was at this juncture that the United States decided to conclude economic agreements with Warsaw. In October 1946 a loan of $40 million was signed with the Export-Import Bank, followed by an agreement covering $50 million worth of surplus goods. In December the United States agreed to return the Polish gold (around $27.5 million), open the frozen accounts, and restore other Polish funds valued jointly at over $10 million. While the Polish minister of industry assured Acheson that Poland "did not wish to be absorbed either politically or economically into the Soviet system," did the State Department really imagine that economic aid granted on the eve of elections would help to guarantee their fairness? Perhaps Washington reasoned that by extending aid the United States would retain some voice in Polish matters and assist the government in Warsaw to preserve greater independence. It may well be that pure economic motivation also played a certain role. At any rate, neither Mikołajczyk's party nor the Polish nation interpreted the credits as a sign of American commitment to Polish freedom.

General elections, which according to Russian promises at Yalta were to be held within a few months, took place almost two years later, in January 1947. They resulted in an overwhelming victory of the Communist-led bloc. According to official figures, it gained 394 seats and Mikołajczyk's PSL only 28. Mikołajczyk immediately challenged the result and called the elections fraudulent. At the few polling stations where PSL observers had been present, the vote ran 65 to 85 percent in favor of Mikołajczyk's party.

The United States, acting together with Britain, condemned the elections as not fulfilling the provisions of Yalta and Potsdam. The Polish government, the State Department declared, "failed to carry out its solemn pledges." The United States would maintain its interest in the welfare of the Polish people but retain freedom of action in determining its attitude toward the government in Warsaw. President Truman repeated these points when receiving the newly accredited Polish ambassador, Józef Winiewicz, on February 4, 1947, thus departing from the customary ceremonies that accompany the presentation of letters of credence. Lane was instructed to absent himself from the opening of the sejm, and subsequently Truman accepted the ambassador's resignation on the grounds that Lane could do more good for relations between the American and Polish peoples as a private citizen. Stanton Griffis became his successor in Warsaw.

Washington agreed with Lane that a severance of diplomatic relations with the Polish government would be counterproductive. Cardinal Hlond made it clear that while he approved American protests, he opposed cutting off Poland from the West. Yet to distinguish between the government in Warsaw and the Polish people, however important that distinction was, raised problems both then and later.

In the absence of a breach of relations or denial of recognition to the new government, there was little concrete to be done. Senator Vandenberg proposed a conference of the signatories of Yalta; Sumner Welles advocated an open discussion in the General Assembly of the United Nations. Neither seemed to offer much promise and was not attempted. Observing a hardening of American attitudes toward Warsaw, the new Premier Cyrankiewicz had told Lane that if the United States cut off all assistance to Poland, it would become even more dependent on Russia. Ambassador Winiewicz used a somewhat similar argument when he said in Washington that a tough American policy would only aid those groups in Poland that wanted to rely completely on the Soviet Union. He was told that an improvement of American-Polish relations would depend on the evolution of the international situation and on the ability of the Polish government to win the support of its people and safeguard liberties to which the Americans were greatly attached. Neither seemed likely at that particular moment.

Mikołajczyk and the PSL were clearly finished as an independent force. The Populist movement was going through a deep internal crisis, and Mikołajczyk seemed to have become a liability and a symbol of mistaken faith in the West. Since the attempt of fighting communism had failed, a trend toward cooperation and adaptation surfaced. Mikołajczyk, regarded as the number one enemy of the regime, feared for his life, and in October 1947 fled the country. The American embassy had helped to engineer his flight, causing a diplomatic incident: the Polish government accused the embassy of complicity in the Mikołajczyk escape and Ambassador Griffis rejected the charges with feigned indignation. Still, it is likely that the Communists viewed Mikołajczyk's flight as good riddance. The way was prepared for a merger of the PSL with the Populist party, which began in May 1948 and eventually produced a pro-Communist United Populist party (ZSL) in late 1949.

At the meeting of the sejm in February 1947 the so-called little constitution was adopted and followed by an impressive-sounding declaration of civic rights and liberties. The sejm, however, went on record to say that any abuse of these rights and liberties for the purpose of overthrowing the regime would be "prevented by law." Bierut was elected president of the republic. A Council of State, composed of the president, the sejm's speaker, and six deputies, was set up to issue binding decrees when the sejm was not in session. Bierut and Gomułka—secretary of the party—vied for leadership of the Communist machinery, which by the end of 1947 controlled some 820,000 members. Together with such figures as Berman, Minc, and the feared head of the secret police, Stanisław Radkiewicz, they wielded the real power in the country. The army and the ministry of defense was, at least nominally, in the hands of General Michał Rola-Żymierski, a prewar general who had been dishonorably discharged, now named marshal of Poland.

Before proceeding to the new phase heralded by the little constitution and the elimination of Mikołajczyk, some features of the 1945–1947 transition period still need to be examined. It is obvious that the postwar situation in Poland differed drastically from that of Russia in 1917 and required a certain modification of the Marxist-Leninist formula of the revolutionary dictatorship of the proletariat. The concept of a People's Democracy, used by Tito in 1945, was adopted although its meaning was far from being clear. As applied to Poland, under the retained 1921 constitution modified by the July 22, 1944, Lublin Manifesto, it recognized the existence of different social classes that were not yet subject to the omnipotent dictatorship of the proletariat. Not only Gomułka but also Bierut admitted in 1946 the fact of important differences from the Soviet model. In early 1947, a leading Warsaw newspaper explained that the Communist parties had voluntarily abandoned the way of a violent social revolution and the dictatorship of the proletariat.

Polish social reforms were a long-postponed necessity rather than the introduction of socialism, much less communism.

At first the Catholic church was not persecuted, and given its excellent wartime record and the prestige of Cardinal Sapieha, this was a necessary policy. The church property confiscated by the Nazis was returned; destroyed churches were rebuilt; there was no open interference with religious education. The presidential oath taken by Bierut was couched in the old religious terms. True, in 1945 the prewar Concordat with the papacy was denounced and civil records were entrusted to the state. There also appeared the first signs of deviant trends seeking to undermine the unity of the church. The convergence of extreme nationalism with communism was promoted by the prewar Polish fascist, Bolesław Piasecki, who led an essentially political organization called Pax (after its publishing house). Another group, the "patriotic priests," made a rather unsuccessful appearance. These moves were denounced by the hierarchy, but already in 1947 Cardinal Hlond's criticism of Communist "paganism" evoked ominous responses from the parties of the bloc. They said that after the political bankruptcy of the emigration and Mikołajczyk's Populists, the church was taking over the role of the opponent to the regime.

In the socioeconomic field, the Communists insisted on the concept of public, private, and cooperative sectors of the economy. The peasants were constantly reassured that no collectivization of land was anticipated. Private enterprises accounted, in the 1944–1947 period, for about one-fifth of the national output, and craftsmen and tradesmen still operated under quite favorable circumstances. The prewar social structure had been largely shattered by the war, especially with regard to the upper and middle classes and the intelligentsia, but it was still capable of resurrection. This the Communists forcibly prevented. In 1945, the introduction of a new złoty with an unfavorable conversion rate wiped out many savings, thus weakening further the economic independence of an important stratum of the population.

In the foreign field, People's Democracy stood for a system guaranteeing close and friendly relations to the USSR but did not automatically signify a termination of old alliances with the West. In fact, the government attempted until 1947 to revive them, particularly one with France, provided they were adapted to the new situation. Although the autonomy of postwar Poland in the field of diplomacy was obviously restricted to the barest minimum, the pursuance of certain specifically Polish goals could still be observed, like the Odra-Nysa frontier and Teschen which led to a border controversy with Czechoslovakia.

For most Poles contacts with the West and the existence of a government in exile were still part of reality. People could listen to foreign broadcasts, and the habit of relying on the BBC survived the war. (The Voice of America, extolling the advantages of life in the United States, was less effective, as Lane for one did not fail to notice.) Polish political emigration continued to denounce the regime imposed on the subject nation, and the vision of a triumphant return of emigrés to a liberated Poland was not yet regarded as a fantastic dream. Even though the emigration had some links with certain clandestine groups in Poland, it warned against the dangers of domestic conspiracy and occasionally against exaggerated hopes placed in the American monopoly on the atomic bomb. The emigrés and Polish Americans were united in their defense of the Odra-Nysa frontier, criticized pro-German statements of Byrnes and later Marshall, and agitated for Western recognition of Poland's borders.

President Raczkiewicz's death in 1947 caused a process of internal splintering of the emigration. One group followed the new president in exile, August Zaleski, and attached great importance to the continuation of legitimacy of Polish authorities abroad. A second crystallized later around the Political Council established in 1949. It encompassed the major parties of the left and the right whose leaders invoked their prewar mandate of elected spokesmen of the nation. A third group, which came into existence after Mikołajczyk's escape, centered on the Populists (it was named the National Polish Democratic Committee in 1950) and claimed that it reflected more accurately than anyone else the strivings and political goals of postwar noncommunist Poles.

Until Mikołajczyk's arrival in the United States the American government was reluctant to have any dealings with Polish political emigration. Polish-American contacts and cooperation existed mainly on academic and scholarly levels and involved particularly those Polish scholars who had come to the United States shortly before or during the Second World War. Thanks to their initiative the Polish Institute of Arts and Sciences, the Polish American Historical Association, and later Polish Cultural Clubs came into being. The political activity of the Polish American Congress went on, of course, unabated. Its delegates had pleaded Poland's cause at the United Nations Conference in San Francisco and lobbied at the Paris Peace Conference in 1946. They repeatedly and publicly condemned Yalta and denounced the elections in Poland as fraudulent. They called for Western vigilance against the Soviet threat.

Without denying the importance of these activities and endeavors, it was the changing international scene that was making the question of Poland an acute issue in foreign policy. As on other occasions in the past it fell to Poland to be an object lesson to the Americans. In the 1945–1947 period Poland was seen as a test of Communist intentions and designs; after 1947 it was to serve as an example of Soviet tyranny and Russia's bad faith. To the developing great debate on American-Soviet relations, illuminated by such books as William Bullitt's *The Great Globe Itself* and James Burnham's *Struggle for the World,* Lane contributed his account of his mission in Poland, significantly entitled *I Saw Poland Betrayed.* Mikołajczyk's *The Rape of Poland* came out in the same year, 1948.

Stalinism, Containment, Liberation

Direct political, diplomatic, and economic intercourse between the United States and Poland dwindled after 1947 to near insignificance. At the same time, the Polish issue assumed a new dimension in American foreign policy and events in Poland increasingly became part of a general pattern variously referred to as the "cult of personality," "Zhdanovshchina," or simply Stalinism. Within the United States, a trend opposed to appeasement of Russia and communism gained prominence and affected the formulation if not the practice of American diplomacy. In discussing American-Polish relations during this period, there is a danger of losing the main thread in a maze of domestic and international complications. Yet without examining the larger context, these relations cannot be properly understood. Certain dates stand out as convenient landmarks and guiding posts, for instance 1948—the year of Truman's election and Gomułka's fall—or 1952, dating Eisenhower's election and the adoption of the constitution of the Polish People's Republic.

The "fifteen weeks" of 1947 witnessed the birth of the Truman Doctrine in March, the Marshall Plan in June, and the rise of the theory of containment, originating with Kennan's article in the July 1947 issue of Foreign Affairs. The Truman Doctrine came in answer to a concrete need of protecting Greece and Turkey against Russia, but it was couched in general terms. The presidential message spoke of "totalitarian regimes imposed on free peoples by direct or indirect aggression," which "undermine international peace and hence the security of the United States." Although the violation of Yalta with regard to Poland was mentioned, the doctrine was not thought applicable to East Central Europe, and the United States did not attempt to negotiate with the Soviet Union from a position of strength. At the Moscow Conference in March-April, the new Secretary of State George Marshall brushed aside as a Soviet trap the idea of a united, neutral, and disarmed Germany within its new frontiers, and formally reopened the Odra-Nysa issue. He suggested that while southern parts of former East Prussia and all of Upper Silesia remain with Poland—provided the coal resources were made available to sustain European economy—the remaining, mainly agricultural territories be divided taking into account the needs of the Germans, the Poles, and Europe as a whole.

Marshall's proposal, which evoked immediate Polish protests, was bound, as Lane warned the secretary, to produce "lasting resentment" in Poland and increase Warsaw's dependence on the Soviet Union. Marshall privately admitted that chances of border revision were slender, but he felt that the German-Polish border issue provided him with a "trading basis." The secretary genuinely worried lest Germany, deprived of the agricultural eastern lands, become over-industrialized and potentially explosive. His stand struck a responsive public chord in America. A questionnaire of May 1947, sponsored by the Council on Foreign Relations and addressed to community leaders in twenty-two American cities, showed a substantial support for an eventual transfer of part of the western territories to Germany. The question whether *all* the former German lands be relinquished by Poland was answered in the affirmative by 41 percent and negatively by 23 percent. Around 33 percent of those questioned were uncertain.

The Marshall Plan, designed to assist European recovery with massive American aid, did not exclude Russia and Eastern Europe although it seemed unlikely that Moscow would participate in a cooperative undertaking. Molotov, in fact, stressed that each country ought to prepare separately its own recovery plan and then ask the United States what kind of aid was available. This was contrary to Marshall's basic idea, and an Organization for European Economic Cooperation (OEEC) emerged that was limited to Western Europe.

At first the Polish government reacted favorably to the Marshall Plan. Warsaw believed that Poland should take advantage of any opportunity that would strengthen the country and the new regime. Moscow, however, made it clear that acceptance was unthinkable and Warsaw had no choice but to acquiesce. Subsequently, Ambassador Winiewicz denounced the plan as aiming at the "subordination of Europe to the United States and the rebuilding of the war potential of Germany," but in the autumn of 1947 Polish criticism was more guarded. The government was still striving to get a loan from the International Bank for Reconstruction and Development, which was favorably inclined if the loan would be used to increase Poland's coal production. Warsaw tried to convince Washington once again that American credits and agricultural surpluses were essential to prevent complete Polish dependence on Moscow. Ambassador Griffis caustically commented, speaking mainly of UNRRA aid, that Warsaw "has its left hand extended for help and its right hand is a fist constantly attacking the United States." This was true, but there was also a modicum of truth in Winiewicz's remark to Marshall, that when he had been serving with the Polish government in London, the West had applied constant pressure on the Poles to cede territory to Russia and reach an agreement with it. "Poland had done this, but the result was the deterioration of her relations with the West." Marshall replied evasively that Poland was "in no-man's land and we had great sympathy for her position."

At this stage American sympathy for Poland was largely platonic, and Kennan's new theory of containment conveyed the impression that East Central Europe had been written off as far as Washington was concerned. Containment was a policy of opposing with counterforce any expansion of the Soviet bloc, thus increasing the strain on Soviet policy, imposing upon the Kremlin a greater degree of moderation and circumspection, and finally promoting tendencies toward a breakup or gradual mellowing of Soviet power. Kennan later explained that some of his ideas were misunderstood, but he pleaded guilty to the inexplicable omission of Eastern Europe in his article. Whatever Kennan's intentions were, and this is not the place to analyze the concept and its application in detail, containment came to mean a freezing of the blocs and American abandon of East Central Europe. As such, it corresponded to contemporary American and West European moods; there were only few people like Churchill who would have supported an offensive American policy to force Russia out of the eastern part of the Continent.

The lines of division were becoming more sharply drawn. The Communist Bloc consolidated with the 1948 takeover of Czechoslovakia and the formation of the Cominform, although the excesses of Moscow hegemony produced the Yugoslav schism. The chances of regional East European cooperation heralded by the Tito-Dimitrov plans were killed by Moscow. A network of treaties spread over the entire bloc, and by 1949 Poland had alliances with the USSR (April 1945), Yugoslavia (1946)—subsequently denounced—Czechoslovakia (1947), Bulgaria and Hungary (1948), and

Romania (1949). The bloc appeared as a threat to peace, and Western responses were largely military. A Franco-British alliance was signed in 1947 and enlarged a year later by the inclusion of Benelux. The Treaty of Brussels set up a Western European Defense Union which no longer spoke of Germany as a potential aggressor. Finally, in 1949 the North Atlantic Treaty Organization came into existence.

To Americans war seemed a real possibility. An opinion poll of March 1948 indicated that 74 percent of respondents expected war within the next ten years. A smaller group (32 percent) anticipated war within a year, according to a poll taken in September. East Central Europe did not appear as a main cause of a warlike confrontation, and by itself became somewhat secondary in United States diplomacy. Americans looked toward China, won by the Communists in 1949, and spoke of a global threat. The Berlin question, dramatized by the Soviet blockade and American airlift, emphasized the importance of Germany as a pillar of Western military consolidation. The recognition of the West German Federal Republic was countered by Russia with the creation of a German Democratic Republic (GDR) in East Germany. Bonn and the militant West German circles usually referred to it as "middle Germany," the adjective "eastern" being reserved for the territories lost after the war to Poland. The Korean War of 1950 and the end of American atomic monopoly—Russia exploded her first nuclear device in late 1949, had an atomic bomb two years later, and the H-bomb in 1953—accelerated Washington's plans for German rearmament. Advocated only a few years after the end of the Second World War, the German rearmament issue played havoc with the developing movement of Western European unification. It naturally raised fears in the countries of East Central Europe.

The handling of the German question and increasing American involvement with Bonn deepened Polish preoccupation with German revisionism. Polish anxiety was real enough—war and the German occupation were fresh in people's minds—but Warsaw also fanned these fears for ideological reasons and represented the Soviet Union as the only shield against a renewed *Drang nach Osten*. There is little doubt that the June 1950 Zgorzelec Treaty between Poland and the GDR, which solemnly recognized the Odra-Nysa border, could not have been signed save under the aegis of Moscow. But would the Kremlin never be tempted to revert to a Rapallo policy? Were concessions at the expense of Poland's western territories an unthinkable price to be paid for neutralization of a united Germany? The Polish leaders could not lightly dismiss such sobering thoughts, which made them ever more determined to behave as an unwavering and needed ally of the Soviet Union.

In discussing the relations between the United States and Poland let us survey first the direct economic and political contacts. While in 1947 Ambassador Griffis still had fleeting notions of using the Poles as a go-between with Russia, soon afterward he felt as "Mr. Alice in Blunderland," helplessly watching the unbroken "curve of degeneration" in American-Polish relations. American exports to Poland were small ($0.7 million) and although in 1946–1950 Polish exports to the United States, mainly agricultural, were growing (reaching the figure of $17 million) and credits from the Export-Import Bank facilitated purchases of rolling stock and mining equipment, the days of expanding trade were numbered. Empowered by a 1940 act of Congress to exercise far-reaching controls over foreign trade, the president began after 1948 to place severe restrictions on commerce with the Eastern Bloc. A complex system of screening export licenses was introduced to deny these countries access to potentially strategic goods. The Export Control Act of 1949 and the Mutual Defense Assistance Act (the Battle Act) of 1951 imposed a virtual embargo on credits and trade. Congressional pressure forced the Truman administration to deny the Most-Favored-Nation clause to Poland, which it had enjoyed since 1931. The State Department was unhappy with this decision, which weakened the moral position of the United States without really contributing to American security. An acrimonious correspondence ensued between Warsaw, accusing the United States of a unilateral abrogation of a treaty, and Washington. By 1952 the breach was final; already two years earlier Poland had withdrawn from the World Bank and the World Health Organization on the grounds of being discriminated against. The country was economically isolated from the West.

The same was happening in almost every area of American-Polish relations, and protests and recriminations accompanied the curtailment of contacts. In 1949 representatives of the International Red Cross and the International Refugee Organization were asked to leave Poland. In January 1950 the Polish government terminated the services of the Catholic Welfare, which had cooperated with the Polish organization Caritas. In 1951 the United States Information Service in Poland and the Polish Research and Information Service in America were closed. The activity of a mixed commission working to determine the claims of individual Poles to American citizenship came to an end. Maritime communications between New York and Gdynia stopped after an incident which made Washington suspend the right of the Polish liner Batory to call on American ports. In the political field, Warsaw objected to the termination of Polish consular offices in the American zone of Germany and subsequently protested against the United States' recognition of West Germany and the promotion of its rearmament. There were more protests; against the so-called Guard Companies composed of Polish displaced persons under American command, against a congressional investigation of the Katyn massacre, and other matters.

The high point of the verbal duel was reached with the publication by the Polish ministry of foreign affairs in 1953 of a collection entitled *Documents on the Hostile Policy of the United States Government toward People's Poland.* In the introduction, which termed anti-Polish policies a part of the "pattern of American plans for world conquest," the editors presented a brief historical outline of mutual relations. The United States was said to have opposed Polish territorial claims vis-à-vis Germany at the Paris Peace Conference in 1919, and helped to revive German militarism and direct it eastward in the interwar years. It sought, by holding out prospects of economic aid, to establish an "American-controlled government" in Warsaw after the Second World War. Such a government was expected to restore capitalism and a landowners' regime, and act as an instrument of "economic and political subjugation of Poland." Unsuccessful in these efforts, the United States then tried to spread anarchy in the country by assisting fascist traitors and bandits and showed its true intentions by forming NATO, a "posthumous offspring of Nazism." The book was published in English, which meant that it was destined for foreign consumption, although many of its statements frequently appeared in the local press and publications.

The *Documents* were published at a time when liberation slogans were sweeping the United States under the Eisenhower administration, the Cold War was at its peak, and Stalinism reigned supreme in Poland. Hence to place it in a proper context requires a closer look at the course of developments in the United States and Poland between the years 1948 and 1953.

Containment policies quickly became the practice of American diplomacy and proved more enduring than their critics anticipated. Mental habits harking back to World War II also survived, and in 1950 the word Katyn was crossed out from a Voice of America broadcast. Although Acheson in a speech at Berkeley the same year voiced concern for the real independence of East Central Europe, he echoed the wartime belief that such independence could be compatible with Soviet security. Neither such pious wishes nor containment corresponded any longer to the changing views of a large part of the American public.

Polish American leaders and Polish emigrés were in the forefront of attacks on the appeasement of Russia and on the hated concept of containment. In 1947 a Justice for Poland group was organized and called on Truman to abrogate the Yalta agreements and demand the evacuation of Poland by Soviet troops. Twenty-one Polish American organizations united in their denunciation of Yalta. Worried lest the Polish voters abandon the Democratic ticket in the 1948 presidential elections, the Democrats inserted a last-minute and unprecedented reference to Poland in the national platform. It recalled that Poland had been "resurrected" by "our Democratic President Woodrow Wilson" and was "an outstanding example" of a country seeking independence and democracy that deserved American sympathy.

Opinions differ on the role that concern for Poland played in the voting pattern of Polish Americans in 1948. As regards their leaders, Rozmarek was virtually alone in supporting Dewey's candidacy. Although Truman appears to have made no promises of seeking Poland's liberation from Soviet controls when talking to the leading Polish editors who visited him at the White House, a map of prewar Poland displayed on the wall of the presidential office testified to the continuation of the traditional technique of playing on national sentiments. Truman did promise, however, to promote legislation facilitating the admission to the United States of Polish emigrés, and the Displaced Persons Act of 1948, modified two years later, opened America's doors to the victims of the Second World War.

The Polish American Congress formed a special body for the resettlement of Polish displaced persons, and a Polish Immigration Committee, headed by Monsignor Felix Burant, extended a helping hand. With a sizable influx of Polish immigrants, the United States became an important Polish center although the headquarters of the political emigration remained in London. The Polish American Congress intensified its activities. In the early 1950s an educational and cultural commission was created, and its report emphasized the need to defend the Polish good name and to improve information services. Polish Americans and emigrés signally contributed to the creation of the congressional committee for the investigation of the Katyn crime, which produced in 1952 a voluminous report included in the Congressional Record. The conspiracy of silence surrounding Katyn was broken. Polish cultural, scholarly, and information activities continued in New York, both in the Polish Institute and in the revived Piłsudski Institute for Research in Contemporary History of Poland.

Cooperation between the Polish American Congress and the leadership of the Polish political emigration met with some problems after President Raczkiewicz's death. The National Committee of Americans of Polish Descent (KNAPP), whose wartime activity had been surveyed earlier, gave its support to the new president in exile, Zaleski. It vehemently opposed Rozmarek's tendency to establish a working cooperation with Mikołajczyk, who came to the United States shortly after his escape from Poland. Rozmarek, however, acting on behalf of the Polish American Congress, concluded a two-year agreement with Mikołajczyk and his committee, and it may well be that Washington's sympathy for Mikołajczyk influenced that decision. Mikołajczyk was the Polish leader in whom the United States had confidence and with whom a common language could be found. Received in the State Department, he was able to establish contact with influential American circles and address meetings attended by such influential people as Leahy and Kennan.

As the Cold War expanded, other Polish leaders also received some attention. General Anders, the wartime commander in Italy and one of the chief figures in the Polish Political Council in London, visited the United States in 1950 and appealed to some Americans, like Congressman Orland K. Armstrong, who advocated the creation of an exile Polish army and mentioned it on the floor of the Congress. A combination of moral considerations and propagandistic and tactical objectives accounted for American support extended to political exiles from Poland and other countries of East Central Europe. It took the form of the National Committee for a Free Europe, created with the endorsement of Secretary Acheson in 1949. The committee was first placed under the aegis of John Foster Dulles, then Joseph C. Grew. It encouraged cooperation among East Central European political emigrés and sponsored various activities, for instance the impressive ceremony in Williamsburg in 1952 that resulted in a joint Declaration of the Emigré Representatives. To influence the nations behind the Iron Curtain, the Free Europe Committee set up Radio Free Europe, located in Munich, which went on the air in October 1951. The Polish section, called the Voice of Free Poland, was headed by a former Home Army officer, Jan Nowak.

Although containment continued to be practiced, a new semi-official American policy toward East Central Europe began also to operate. It reflected blighted American hopes of cooperation with Russia, and embodied goals related to the Cold War that were not always clearly formulated. General Lucius Clay spoke of helping those "trapped behind the [Iron] curtain to prepare for the day of liberation." The president of the Free Europe Committee, C. D. Jackson, envisaged the role of Radio Free Europe as that of creating "conditions of turmoil in the countries our broadcasts reached." Was liberation then the objective of American foreign policy, and if so, how was it to be achieved? Creating turmoil could mean simply diversion, and verge on activities that were only one step removed from acts of sabotage or espionage. It appears that some operations of this sort were pursued, especially by American intelligence in Germany, where Polish displaced persons could be used by a recruiting officer. Occasionally, odd incidents came to light and adversely reflected on Polish politicians in exile. Communist propaganda naturally elaborated on these aspects of the anticommunist campaign, and saw American spies and Polish traitors behind every move the regime disliked. American perfidy was said to have gone as far as alleged clandestine germ warfare in the form of a much publicized potato disease that broke out in Poland. Few Poles took these accusations seriously.

It was to the credit of the Polish section of Radio Free Europe that it did not hold out exaggerated hopes of liberation or incite people to rebellion. In a 1953 New Year message Zaleski, appealing to Poles at home to preserve the faith and the Polish way of life, said: "It would be a crime to make this task still more trying by exhorting the people to an armed rising." The president in exile stressed that any action aiming at "organized sabotage" or helping "foreign intelligence services" could "only multiply the futile sacrifices" of the nation.

As McCarthyism began to affect the American scene, the fear of a communist conspiracy became obsessive in certain quarters. After the wartime whitewashing of Russia and communism the mood swung to the other extreme. Senator Joseph McCarthy made it his business to combat communism at home; others advocated an extension of the struggle into enemy territory. In 1951 Senator Alexander Wiley proposed a "psychological and revolutionary penetration" of the "satellites" largely in order to embarrass the Soviet Bloc and force it to concentrate on internal issues. Congressman Charles J. Kersten proposed that recognition be withdrawn from the Soviet Union and the East Central European states in preparation for their future liberation. Advocating aid to underground movements, Senator Taft wrote in his *Foreign Policy for Americans* that "a comparatively small amount of money, if well spent, could succeed in substantially building up a love of freedom in Soviet-dominated territory." The advocacy of an East European emigré army commanded by Anders made some headway, and the Congress allocated $100 million for unspecified military assistance funds (Kersten Amendment). This last move evoked Moscow's protests and Warsaw's accusations that the Mutual Security Act of 1951 mentioned Poland as a sphere of subversive operations.

Truman and Acheson were visibly embarrassed by these reckless and irresponsible projects and moves that accompanied the great debate on American foreign policy, but had no new ideas themselves. In his last State of the Union Message, the president warned against forgetting "the suffering of the people behind the Iron Curtain" without making any proposals on how to alleviate it.

The elections of 1952 gave the Republicans a chance to denounce the Democratic foreign policy record, from Yalta to the "negative, futile and immoral" containment. Yalta had already become a dirty word comparable to Munich. The Republican party platform of 1948 had promised to repudiate it, and in 1951 the *New York Times* called Yalta "a triumph for Communist diplomacy." The new slogan greatly appealed to Americans of East European descent.

The Republicans set up an Ethnic Origins Division, with former Ambassador Lane heading its activities' group. It was largely thanks to Lane's efforts that a liberation statement was formally included in the Republican platform; the Democrats merely reemphasized the Wilsonian principle of national self-determination. The guidelines for Republican candidates said that Americans of Polish origin were "vitally concerned as to our foreign policy toward Poland," and recommended a working knowledge of Polish matters. Buffalo, one of the major Polish American centers, was chosen for Dulles' address outlining the policy of liberation. The future secretary of state publicly questioned Harriman's remark about the prematurity of the Warsaw uprising of 1944. There was nothing premature about it, Dulles declared. "What was wrong was that the Russians double-crossed the Poles." Eisenhower was more guarded in his speeches. Only Lane's pressure and the fear of losing Polish American votes made him speak, on two occasions, about the repudiation of Yalta provisions applicable to Poland. The vice-presidential candidate Richard Nixon, however, openly denounced Yalta on Pulaski Day.

The elections brought a resounding victory to Dwight Eisenhower. He managed to reduce the Polish American vote from the usual 70 percent cast for the Democratic ticket to roughly 50 percent, but it is still debatable whether the question of Poland was the decisive reason for this swing. Domestic affairs were of great concern to Polish Americans, and Eisenhower's appeal transcended ethnic divisions. The precise part the Polish question played in the 1952 elections still demands further study.

The twin aspects of Republican foreign policy, as formulated by Dulles, were: an emphasis on military power capable of instant retaliation, and a political-ideological offensive couched in terms of liberation. Eisenhower insisted all along that liberation was to be peaceful, but he also asserted the Americans would never accept the enslavement of any nation "in order to purchase fancied gain for ourselves." Liberation and a theory of a "roll back" officially replaced containment, although, as Churchill observed, Dulles' flood of words tended "to rob his utterances of real significance." The liberation concept left many questions unresolved. How could liberation be effected peacefully? If it meant self-liberation, would the United States intervene or stand by without giving any effective assistance? Were nations to be liberated from their oppressive regimes, or the regimes from the Soviet Union? The case of Yugoslavia had showed that this was not an academic question. Finally, and this seems clear today, liberation was to a large extent a psychological boost to America's morale, countering the feeling of frustration over wartime and immediate postwar concessions and losses.

The doctrine or liberation promised more than could be delivered, and in that sense it was bound to confuse or mislead the East Europeans. Many Americans took it seriously enough, and resolutions demanding a formal repudiation of Yalta appeared in the Congress. The Polish American Representative, Thaddeus Machrowicz, inserted in the Congressional Record an article describing General Anders and his former soldiers eagerly awaiting a new D-Day. The president, while sympathetic to a vague "peaceful liberation," was careful not to authorize any moves that could result in an open confrontation with the Soviet Union. In his State of the Union Message of 1953, Eisenhower repeated that the United States would not acquiesce in the enslavement of any nation, but at the same time he quietly killed proposals for the repudiation of Yalta. His choice of Charles Bohlen for the Moscow embassy provoked the anger of Polish Americans, who spoke of a new appeasement and called Bohlen the "gravedigger" of Poland. Yet only extremists and McCarthyites were likely to assail the administration for being soft on communism. A more valid criticism of the Eisenhower-Dulles team is that their foreign policy lacked a good combination of flexibility, firmness, and real sophistication in dealing with the complex European issues.

The new administration showed no greater appreciation of the German-Polish problem than had its predecessor. It is likely that many members of the American elite shared Leahy's view of the "western territories" as being merely a "Soviet-sponsored Polish land grab in eastern Germany." An article in *Foreign Affairs* advocated a repudiation of the Odra-Nysa frontier and a recognition of the prewar Polish-Soviet border, in order to sow discord among Russian, German, and Polish Communists. Dulles's close relationship with the West German Chancellor, Konrad Adenauer, appeared to affect American policies toward Europe and made Polish references to a Washington-Bonn axis not far off the mark.

To analyze in depth the connection between the Cold War and Stalinism in Poland is no easy task. It would be too simplistic to construct a model showing a cause-and-effect correlation between international tension and domestic repression. A transformation of the Polish regime did not *automatically* result from the Cold War, just as periods of international détente did not *automatically* trigger policies of internal liberalization. Developments in Poland and throughout the Eastern Bloc were to a considerable extent governed by their own inner logic and motivation.

Since 1947 Poland had been moving away rapidly from the transition model of the first postwar years. State and society were being molded in a uniform and rigid cast borrowed from Soviet Russia. The original notion of People's Democracy was revised, and different roads to socialism, influenced by local conditions, declared invalid. As the Czech newspaper *Rude Pravo* put it crudely in 1952: "Love of the Soviet Union does not tolerate the slightest reservation." The Stalinist period was characterized by an intensification of ideological struggle, a rapid and large-scale industrialization with emphasis on heavy industry, and an enforced collectivization of agriculture. Dictatorship of the proletariat was the central concept but, as Oskar Lange expressed it later, in practice it retreated before the dictatorship of a "centralist-administrative apparatus." Police terror rounded out the picture.

The Soviet Union was the initiator of processes designed to eradicate the diversity that existed in East Central Europe and was reflected in the policies of individual Communist leaders. The Cominform, inaugurated at a meeting in Poland in September 1947, was the means for promoting uniformity, and Andrei Zhdanov, the Soviet chief ideologue, provided the theoretical justification. The external American threat was extensively propagandized, and the need for an ideological offensive explained on the grounds of an American drive for world supremacy. Any deviation from the Stalinist line evoked accusations of American imperialist plots.

Gomułka's dissatisfaction with the new trend and his coolness toward the Cominform led to his being accused in the autumn of 1948 of "nationalist deviation" and deprived of secretaryship of the party. A year later he was thrown out of the party and subsequently imprisoned. Bierut, as secretary general, presided over the merger of the Communist party with the Polish Socialist party in December 1948. The merger, at first strongly resisted by the PPS, corresponded to similar consolidations in the neighboring countries and raised the membership of the new Polish United Workers' Party (PZPR) to over 1,300,000. Bierut became its chairman and Cyrankiewicz the secretary general. The remaining political parties were streamlined. As mentioned before, the two Populist parties were joined in a United Populist party (ZSL) and the Small Democratic party absorbed the Labor party. They were now hardly more than transmission belts of the Communists. Since PZPR was the only organization that had the word "party" in its Polish name—the others were called *stronnictwa*—the term party acquired a clear official connotation and will henceforth be capitalized.

The ideological platform of the Party indissolubly tied Poland's "independence and march toward socialism" to a "struggle for peace under the leadership of the Soviet Union." There was only one supreme leader, Stalin, after whom streets, squares, and even a city (Katowice-Stalinogród) were named. The "cult of personality" permeated the entire system, and in Gomułka's words was embodied in a "hierarchic ladder of cults." But the cult of local leaders was only "a borrowed light. It shone as the moon does."

Consolidating its supremacy, the Party tried to emasculate or crush all potential elements of opposition. The Catholic church in particular became a target of attacks.. In 1950, under the new Primate (and cardinal after 1952) Stefan Wyszyński, the church achieved a modus vivendi with the state, but the state did not intend to treat it as more than a temporary expedient. The government gave support to Pax and to the patriotic priests, who were excommunicated in 1949. The enforced separation of church and state decreed by the 1952 constitution facilitated encroachments on the right of ecclesiastical appointments, Catholic social welfare, and religious teaching. The land of the church became subject to agrarian reform and was confiscated; the welfare organization Caritas was taken away; in 1953 the main press organ of the Catholics, *Tygodnik Powszechny,* was handed over to Pax. By 1954 nine bishops and hundreds of priests languished in prison. Cardinal Wyszyński himself was deprived of liberty. The church became an *ecclesia militans* with martyrs to show.

Administrative pressures, a euphemism for police terror, were applied to other groups too. Several thousand people were imprisoned and some executed, and fear of a sudden arrest in the middle of the night became a nightmare of the Stalinist period. Yet unlike other countries of the bloc and Soviet Russia itself, Poland under Stalinism did not hold show trials of Party leaders accused of and confessing to most unlikely crimes. There were no mass executions, and purged intellectuals were not forced to earn their living by manual work. The Catholic University of Lublin was allowed to survive. Poland did not have a gigantic monument of Stalin, unless one thinks of its substitute, a huge Palace of Culture and Learning which Stalin donated to Warsaw and which has offended the Poles' good taste ever since. The pace of collectivization of agriculture was slow. The conclusion is that Stalinism in Poland was milder than elsewhere. Whether this was due to Bierut, to the Polish national character, or to other factors is hard to tell. Even so, the fact that conditions were worse in the neighboring states was hardly a consolation to the oppressed people.

The Stalinist model was all-pervasive. Socialist Realism became the official style in art and literature. Writers who had genuinely espoused the cause of socialist Poland were stifled in their creativity. Others were drawn into the system by processes described by Czesław Miłosz in his *Captive Mind*. Class content of writing and art was increasingly emphasized. Polish learning had to bow to imported dogmas, which restricted the free search for truth. Crude Marxism-Leninism became not only a compulsory subject of instruction but a yardstick to measure developments and accomplishments in different disciplines. Stalin was pictured as an authority in virtually every field. Isolated from its traditional contacts with the West, Polish cultural and academic life suffered and in some areas vegetated. Western radio programs were jammed; tourism came to a virtual halt; Western films, music, and publications became a scarce commodity.

The Party sought to capture and educate the youth in its own image through the Association of Polish Youth (ZMP), officially referred to as the "younger brother of the Soviet Konsomol." The Polish scouts were refashioned to resemble more closely the Soviet pioneers. The Party operated through various other channels, to mention only the trade unions, the veterans' association (ZBOWID), and the Society for Polish-Soviet Friendship. The Poles coined the term *dretwa mowa* (double-talk) to describe the artificial, lifeless, and slogan-filled discourse that reigned supreme at meetings and characterized official pronouncements. If a socialist vision of the future could appeal to young idealistic minds, a good deal of the propaganda was so crude as to be counterproductive. This was particularly true about the slogans extolling the Poles' love for Stalin and the Russians.

Although nationalism and anti-Semitism were condemned and international brotherhood of workers elevated to a dogma, it was obvious that some nations were more equal than others. The visible presence of Russians in Poland, particularly in the armed forces, was strengthened by the appointment of the Red Army Marshal Konstantin Rokossovsky to the ministry of defense, supreme command, and a seat on the Politburo. Rokossovsky, who was born a Pole (Rokossowski), was chiefly remembered as the commander of the Soviet armies that stood idly by burning Warsaw during the 1944 uprising. With little regard for the national sensitivity of the Poles, he was named marshal of Poland.

The country's formal administrative structure was institutionalized under the 1952 constitution, which made the state the Polish People's Republic. The constitution placed all sovereignty in the working people (proletarian dictatorship), to be exercised through democratic centralism. State organs included a legislative sejm, a council of ministers and the State Council—both elected by the sejm—the courts, the prosecutor general, and the supreme auditing commission (NIK). The concept of separation of powers and of checks and balances was expressly rejected. The council of ministers stood at the top of an administrative pyramid in which the people's councils represented local government. The State Council, somewhat similar to the presidium of the Supreme Soviet in Russia, came to act as a collective president since, after Bierut's death, there were no more presidents of the republic. The State Council as a law giver clearly overshadowed the sejm, and passed during this period some one hundred decrees as compard to eight parliamentary acts. The judiciary was theoretically independent, but state prosecutors on all levels acted as watchdogs exerting pressure and affecting the judicial process.

The leading role of the Party did not appear in the constitution although it was obvious that it was the governing force in the country. The Party hierarchy paralleled that of the administration, and the Central Committee (KC) with its politburo and secretariat was the real center of power. Similarly, the security police, unmentioned in the constitution, represented a law unto itself.

Economic developments in the Stalinist period deserve particular attention. The Three-Year Plan of Reconstruction (1947–1949) bore the imprint of thinking of Polish Socialists rather than Communists. It addressed itself to reconstruction of the ruined country, nationalization, redistribution of wealth, monopoly in foreign trade, and other structural, institutional, and administrative changes. The rebuilding of devastated Poland, especially of Warsaw, evoked a good deal of genuine enthusiasm. In 1947 Ambassador Griffis praised the Poles' industry and predicted rapid achievements. Indeed, if one bears in mind the colossal wartime destruction, the production figures in some key areas were impressive. Comparing the 1938 figures with 1949 (both for the territory of postwar Poland), the output of steel rose from 2.0 to 2.3 million tons; that of hard coal from 66.1 to 74.1, and electric power increased from 7.4 thousand million kilowatt hours to 8.3. The standard of living was also a little higher as compared with 1938. Among the chief problems was the lack of qualified personnel, but the quick pace of mass education, amounting to a veritable social revolution, raised hopes for the future.

The Six-Year Plan of 1950–1955, already under discussion since 1948, was much more ideologically motivated. Criticism of the preceding type of "bourgeois planning," which had maintained a balance between the three sectors of the economy (state, cooperative, and private), came with advocacy of a rapid industrialization program to be achieved at the expense of the consumer. The all-embracing Soviet model of planning was to be imitated insofar as possible. The plan put emphasis on development of production branches serving investment processes, and concentrated on heavy industry as the key to industrialization. As a result, the production of iron almost tripled between 1949 and 1955, the raw steel output almost doubled, and electric power increased more than twice. At the same time there was no comparable increase in coal output, and cement production showed only a slow growth.

The Six-Year Plan fell short of its ambitious goals and created imbalances and distortions in the country's economy. Dogmatic planning and dependence on the Soviet Union led to grave problems. Seeking self-sufficiency in accord with Soviet precepts—the intrabloc Council of Mutual Economic Assistance set up in 1949 played an insignificant role—Poland built uneconomic plants and produced the kind of machinery that perpetuated backwardness instead of being a modernizing factor. The example of the automobile factory in Żerań was later cited as an illustration of such policies. The Lenin steel works at Nowa Huta, a new town constructed near Cracow and regarded as a show piece of socialist building, had to operate entirely on Russian iron ore. Poland had received several loans from the Soviet Union and had to adjust its economy to Russian dictates. Polish coal, exported to the USSR at below market prices, was perhaps the most visible form of exploitation, but there were other ways in which the Polish economy was tied to Soviet policies. During the Korean War, for example, stress was put on military production and assistance to North Korea and foreign trade turned eastward. By 1953 nearly 72 percent of it was with the Eastern Bloc, out of which 33.5 percent was with Russia.

Industrialization of Poland was obviously necessary, but the ways in which it was carried out during the Stalinist period vitiated the results. A largely administrative approach to economic matters resulted in the creation of a huge and inefficient bureaucratic machine that stressed labor discipline and operated in terms of fulfillment or overfulfillment of quotas of production. Little regard was paid to production cost, efficiency, or quality of products. Overcentralization paralyzed the initiative of managers and deprived the workers of incentives. By juggling statistical figures, the economic dictator, Minc, predicted that by 1955 Poland would cover half of the distance which separated it, in terms of industrialization, from the United States.

Obsession with heavy industry and the ideologically motivated policy of discriminating against private businesses and crafts, crippled small producers and all those engaged in the vital service sector. The share of private enterprises dropped from 21 percent (in 1946) to 6 percent of the national output in 1955. Indiscriminate and arbitrary use of fines, licenses, and taxes stifled private initiative. Since most of the accumulated capital was reinvested, mainly in heavy industries, the consumer suffered severe privations. Housing was neglected, real wages remained low; a second monetary reform in 1950 was achieved at the expense of the people.

Agriculture fared badly. Bent on collectivization, the regime discriminated against the wealthier farmer and antagonized the peasants. Instead of rewarding them for higher productivity per acre than what the mismanaged state farms achieved, the government was forcibly pushing the peasants into collective farms. Because of their stubborn resistance, less than 10 percent of land was effectively collectivized, but a feeling of uncertainty worked against private farming. Noting the distortions and errors in planning and the gulf between grim reality and rosy statistics, a leading Party theorist, Władysław Bieńkowski, would later remark that the country was indulging in "lunar economics."

Contradictions, oppression, and mismanagement became the characteristic features of an era that was subsequently called in Poland the "period of errors and distortions." A wide gap separated the *pays légal* from the *pays réel*. In Gomułka's words, the Stalinist legacy was "more than alarming" to the Party, the working class, and the nation. The Party, increasingly bureaucratized and evolving into a new ruling class, was out of tune with the nation; the leadership was losing touch with its rank and file. The Communist intellectuals and the youth were increasingly disillusioned. The working class and the peasantry was more and more alienated. A system that relied heavily on police terror could not develop the organizational techniques needed in a modernizing society. In a predominantly Catholic country, antireligious policies backfired. When national Polish heritage was distorted, derided, and humiliated in the name of Soviet-style internationalism, a patriotic reaction was inevitable.

Toward the Polish October

The death of Stalin in 1953 marked the beginning of a new era, even if that was not immediately apparent. In the struggle for Stalin's succession, Khrushchev and Malenkov joined other Soviet leaders to eliminate physically the most dangerous contender, Laurentii Beria, the feared chief of the secret police. With Beria gone, the new party bosses gained an upper hand over the secret police and saddled it with all the responsibility for the reign of terror. Fearing a return of unlimited despotic power of one individual, they instituted a practice of collective authority. The implication of these developments for Poland and the other People's Democracies was to become clear shortly. The "accomplices of Beria" were to be curbed or purged; the political leadership had to become more adaptable to a changing atmosphere; the socioeconomic crisis, corresponding to a critical industrialization stage, was to be tackled with greater flexibility and imagination. These trends became known as the "thaw," a term used by the Soviet writer Ilya Ehrenburg but harking back to the Russian post-Crimean thaw of the late 1850s.

In foreign policy Moscow's goals remained largely unchanged. Khrushchev and the other leaders had no intention of presiding over a decomposition of the Soviet empire or permitting a rollback of the Eastern Bloc. But they adopted a less rigid diplomatic style. Attempts to mend the break with Yugoslavia succeeded in 1955; a year later the Cominform, regarded as a Stalinist symbol, was dissolved. The rehabilitation of Tito implied the acceptance of several roads toward socialism and proved important for the internal evolution in Poland.

What was Washington's response to the new trends in the USSR and what posture did it adopt toward the issue of East-West relations? Although the United States spoke of liberation, asked the somewhat rhetorical question whether Russia was prepared to grant its satellites a freedom of political choice, and asserted through Dulles that America could not accept "captivity as a permanent fact of history," Eastern Europe was not the real object of Soviet-American controversy. "The brink of war" strategy practiced by Dulles was not conceived with Eastern Europe in mind. Nor were the implications of "massive retaliation" for Eastern Europe clarified, although this region would be particularly vulnerable in case of its application.

The real stake of the West-East power game was Germany, and there the first moves and countermoves were made in the post-Stalin era. Moscow's new leadership tried to sound Washington on the possibility of an agreement; the United States was wary of any deal that could smack of a new version of Yalta or Potsdam. At the same time, the hollowness of the liberation slogans voiced in the United States became obvious in June 1953, when Soviet tanks suppressed an uprising in East Germany and the only American reaction took the form of a tribute paid on the Senate's floor to "a heroic resistance throughout Eastern Europe."

Unable to influence the situation in East Germany, Dulles pressed for a military integration of West Germany into NATO. Russia became alarmed and repeatedly tried to prevent German militarization by threatening to counter with an Eastern Bloc military pact. A great powers' conference held in Berlin in 1954 failed to resolve the German question, and in May 1955 three important events took place. Agreements providing for West German military presence were ratified by NATO members; the Soviet Union and the West agreed to a mutual withdrawal from Austria and its recognition as a neutral state; Russia announced the signing of the Warsaw Pact, presented as a military counterweight to NATO. All these moves were interrelated. By evacuating Austria, the Soviets wished to show to West Germany that a neutral stance carried special rewards. The Warsaw Pact seemed hardly necessary given Soviet control over the military establishments in Eastern Europe, but it assured continued Soviet military presence in Rumania and Hungary after the original reason of guarding the routes to Austria was gone. Secondly, the pact could be used for bargaining purposes and its dissolution offered in return for the dismantling of NATO.

Finally, in virtue of the pact, the Soviet Union would be able to justify its actions against a recalcitrant member of the Eastern Bloc.

All these moves lessened the chance of a negotiated settlement of Germany, but did not close the door to later exchanges—for example, the Geneva Summit in the summer of 1955. The meeting did not resolve German questions but it introduced an atmosphere of limited détente. Characteristically, the question of Eastern Europe occupied a low priority in the position papers drafted by Dulles. Nor did it come up for discussion, for the Soviets took the line that there was "no problem of the countries of Eastern Europe." In subsequent months, however, the German issue was linked to some extent with East European matters when the West gave support to Eden's plan for free elections and reunification of Germany, coupled with a security agreement through which the Big Four, with Germany, Czechoslovakia, and Poland would guarantee each other's security, renounce the use of force, and limit armaments in a 100–150 mile zone along German eastern borders. The Soviet side countered with a proposal for a general European collective security treaty, excluding all foreign troops from the Continent, and the dissolution of NATO. A deadlock ensued, but the Cold War atmosphere was affected by the Geneva spirit. Liberation was mentioned again in Eisenhower's messages and resolutions introduced in the Congress, but on the other hand, the United States abstained in the vote to admit Albania, Bulgaria Hungary, and Rumania to the United Nations. This abstention made their entry possible.

The year of Stalin's death and the two years that followed it brought no visible change or improvement to Poland or American-Polish relations. In January 1953 the Polish government charged that American aircraft had violated Poland's air space. In turn, the United States accused Warsaw of harassment of American diplomats. In September 1953, following the arrest of Cardinal Wyszyński, President Eisenhower expressed "the condemnation of the American people of this new act of terrorism against religion." At the beginning of 1954 the United States closed Polish consulates in New York, Chicago, and Detroit, and in the same year the defection of the crew of the Polish ship *Praca* was hailed as a sign of the Poles' unchanged hatred for communism. Other defections to the United States took place.

The appointment in 1955 of a supposedly hard-line Polish ambassador, Romuald Spasowski, did nothing to mitigate the tense atmosphere. American embassies in Warsaw and Moscow made official inquiries about the fate of the Polish underground leaders arrested ten years earlier and, as late as the spring of 1956, the State Department protested to the Polish embassy against unsolicited visits of its officials to Poles living in America and attempts to induce them to return to Poland.

Liberation policies implied the encouragement of Polish and other East European political exiles in the United States, and in September 1954 the Assembly of Captive European Nations (ACEN) was set up. The organization was to promote actions that could enable "the free world to help the enslaved people to help themselves." It would also supply Washington with reliable information about the situation in the Eastern Bloc. The ACEN stressed the illegitimate character of the communist regimes in Eastern Europe, called for free elections under the supervision of the United Nations, and warned against Soviet overtures to the West. The effectiveness of the ACEN as a pressure group in America is hard to evaluate; for the Poles it became an additional and important platform for political campaigns in the United States. Through the ACEN different Polish political centers were able to coordinate their efforts in the field of foreign policy without abandoning their individual channels of communication to the State Department. Jerzy Lerski, acting on behalf of the Political Council, and the unofficial representative of the Polish government in exile, former Ambassador Józef Lipski, were able to keep Washington informed about Polish goals and desires. Among problems raised in talks with the State Department figured the concern for the fate of Cardinal Wyszyński and of those Poles who had not yet been repatriated from Russia. Lipski urged that Washington make it clear that the United States would not be a party to any international arrangement that would "confirm or prolong" the "unwilling subordination" of Poland and the rest of East Central Europe to Russia.

The Polish representatives in Washington insisted that the interests of the East European countries vis-à-vis Germany be safeguarded in any future peace settlement. They unanimously defended the Odra-Nysa border and watched international developments with anxiety, for American commitments to Bonn as well as Soviet plans for a unified Germany carried with them the danger of a deal made at Poland's expense. American insistence on German rearmament had been responsible for the Warsaw Pact and a tightening of Soviet reins over the bloc. Dulles's pro-German stance sustained revisionist hopes in West Germany, thus forcing Warsaw to rely greatly on Soviet support. Washington's special relationship to Bonn cramped the effectiveness of liberation slogans and evoked unpleasant memories of United States assistance and support to the prewar Weimar Republic. For example, American unwillingness to antagonize the Germans resulted in censorship of references to the Odra-Nysa frontier in Polish broadcasts of Radio Free Europe.

The beginning thaw in Russia, and the ambiguous mixture of liberation slogans with the Geneva spirit and pro-German attitudes in Washington constituted the international context of Polish domestic developments. The thaw released various forces in the Polish society, initiating a highly complex process operating on different levels and revealing different objectives. In general, one could say that the advocacy of a Polish way to socialism, seen by the Party leadership as a way out of the crisis, converged with general Polish feelings for recognition and satisfaction of national aspirations. The two were not identical although for a while they appeared to be so.

The thaw released criticism, at first veiled, of the distortions of the Stalinist period. A previously orthodox Communist poet, Adam Ważyk, in a much publicized *Poem for Adults,* denounced the prevailing hypocrisy and the denial of reality within the system. Słonimski struck at dogmatism and errors in cultural policies. Other intellectuals joined in this ever-widening critique. The younger generation proved particularly responsive, and a series of discussions of contemporary problems began, touching even on those that had been taboo in the past. Voices were raised demanding a dialogue with the former members of the Home Army driven to the margin of society as enemies of People's Poland. The student paper *Po Prostu* (Straight forward) engaged in open polemics. Its editors were Communists who gradually moved to an openly revisionist position. The paper became well known almost overnight, and its circulation reached at one point 200,000 copies. Youth clubs and cabarets appeared and brought into the open a long-suppressed interest in Western cultural trends.

At this juncture, American and emigré Polish ideological offensive carried on by Radio Free Europe and the independent Paris-based monthly *Kultura* (edited by Jerzy Giedroyc) began to influence the Polish scene. Cut off from virtually all contacts with the Western world, the Poles eagerly sought information from abroad. Because of jamming of radio broadcasts, the Free Europe Committee launched balloon-carried leaflets, and although the Polish representatives in Washington voiced disapproval of this operation, likely to result in reprisals against the people at home, it went on for a while Anticommunist propaganda received an unexpected boost as a result of the flight from Poland of Lieutenant Colonel Józef Światło, a high-ranking officer of the secret security police. One could hardly pretend that Światło came to seek freedom in the West for ideological reasons. Most likely he was fearful of being purged as one of Beria's accomplices, but his revelations proved of great importance. Światło described the system of secret police files—even President Bierut had one—and of internal spying from which not even the top Communist leaders were safe. He described how evidence against Gomułka had been fabricated, and he exposed from inside the working of the terror system. Much of what had been previously surmised now received confirmation from a high source. Światło's story, broadcast in early 1954 through Radio Free Europe and also dispatched in balloons, had the effect of a bombshell. In December 1954 the ministry of public security was abolished and its head, Radkiewicz, transferred. In 1955 a notorious secret police official was sent to prison. Thus the anti-Beria thaw converged with the exposures that came from America and contributed greatly to the ongoing Polish ferment.

In February 1956 came the famous Twentieth Party Congress, where Khrushchev denounced the Stalinist cult of personality and lashed out at crimes and errors of the past regime. Just as the liquidation of Beria had opened the way to a shake-up of the secret police, so Khrushchev's speech undermined the communist monolith all over the Eastern Bloc. The repercussions of the Twentieth Congress on Poland were profound, and again Radio Free Europe performed an important service by supplying the text of the secret speech of Khrushchev to its listeners. In a short time the turmoil in Poland appeared to threaten the very survival of the communist system.

One of the reasons why the Polish Party proved able to weather the storm was connected with the person of Gomułka, in whom the Party had an alternative to leadership imposed from outside. Gomułka's advocacy of a Polish road to socialism seemed to offer guarantees against either dogmatic Stalinism or collapse. Gomułka was quietly released by the end of 1954. In April 1956, after the sudden death of Bierut in Moscow, the new Party secretary, Edward Ochab, freed the leading associates of Gomułka, made promises about rectification of past errors, and held out prospects of democratization of the Party and the country. Premier Cyrankiewicz echoed these sentiments by speaking approvingly of the need for healthy criticism. This was now in full swing; for instance, economic distortions were severely censured by Oskar Lange and the senior and respected Socialist economist Edward Lipiński. In early 1956 the prewar Polish Communist party (KPP) was officially rehabilitated, improving the image and the morale of old Communists and indicating a breach with Stalinist methods in interparty relations. Personnel changes in the top positions in Poland included, in addition to Radkiewicz's demotion, the resignation of the once all-powerful Berman. Some political prisoners were released. Change was in the air, but its direction was not yet clear. Open discussions and debates in which an intellectual club, the Crooked Circle (*Krzywe Koło*), began to play a major role, could either be construed as a safety valve releasing accumulated tension or a token of more radical structural and ideological changes to come.

On June 28, 1956, the workers in Poznań rose in a massive demonstration. They had been driven to despair by economic privations and goaded to action by the news of an alleged arrest of a workers' delegation. Reluctant troops had to be used to suppress them. The demonstration turned into a bloody uprising, and the news appeared on front pages of American newspapers. The outbreak took place during an international fair, which assured it maximum publicity, and the question arises whether this was a coincidence or whether there were groups in Poland that used a spontaneous outbreak or even provoked it to attain their own ends. This question would occur to people again in connection with the events in Poland in 1968, 1970, and 1976.

Certainly "imperialist provocateurs," whom Premier Cyrankiewicz singled out as instigators of the uprising, did not exist, and the Polish government quickly dropped this line of accusation. Washington was taken aback by the Poznań events, and the State Department, while expressing shock over the bloody suppression, rejected with unfeigned indignation charges of American complicity. There was uncertainty in Washington on how to react to a development that had some bearing on the doctrine of liberation. Dulles's statements were singularly cautious. At a press conference on July 11, the secretary of state rejected any idea of interference in Poland and invoked the "old historic American tradition of setting an example of the good fruits of freedom." Dulles indulged in beliefs and hopes. He believed that the second postwar decade would see the emergence of new forces that would contribute to a transformation of the international scene. He hoped that Moscow would adopt a genuinely new policy that would include greater independence for its satellites. A State Department statement said that all free peoples would closely watch whether the Polish nation would be allowed a government capable of remedying the existing grievances. In the meantime, as a measure of solidarity and compassion, the American Red Cross offered to provide free food for the Poles, but the Polish Red Cross retorted that there was no need for it. Disappointed by the meek stand of Dulles in the Poznań affair, Lane chided, in a letter to the *New York Times*, the Polish American leaders for being insufficiently critical of American foreign policy. Indeed, occasional bold words were no substitute for a vigorous policy. Two amendments to the Mutual Security Act were introduced in the Senate to propose the use of $25 million in order to keep "alive the will for freedom." This was an empty gesture that only provided material for Soviet propaganda and brought forth Moscow's accusations of the United States using its money to finance uprisings in Eastern Europe.

At the July 1956 plenum of the Central Committee of the Party, a split between a hard-line Natolin faction and a liberalizing Puławy group became fully evident. Still, the plenum resisted the pressures of Bulganin and Marshal Zhukov, then present in Poland, to condemn the Poznań uprising as counterrevolutionary and instigated from abroad. Instead, the plenum conceded that the outbreak was a tragic consequence of dogmatic and authoritarian policies. The meeting passed some important resolutions and approved personnel changes; Gomułka and his close associates were rehabilitated and restored to the Party.

In the unfolding of events the precise level and kind of interaction between the inner Party maneuvers and popular demands is hard to determine. Within the Party, the struggle went on between those who stood up for and had vested interests in the old model, and their opponents who professed the need for democratization. The people simply pressed for liberty from the Stalinist nightmare—like the workers in Poznań, they wanted "bread and freedom." Among the noncommunist forces in the country, the church ranged itself on the side of liberty; Piasecki's Pax chose the authoritarian side. A lessening of dependence on Moscow and a different relationship with Russia figured in the thinking of the liberalizing faction. On the other side, one of Piasecki's lieutenants declared: "We are for Russia because we believe she is going to win . . . We are against America because we think that she is going to be defeated in the forthcoming struggle." It was obviously out of the question to involve the United States in the Polish developments, and when the reformist Polish leaders looked abroad for support, it was toward China—then in the "hundred flowers" stage —and Tito's Yugoslavia. Still, a small step toward an improvement of American-Polish relations was made with the signing of a little-publicized agreement on the settlement of wartime Lend-Lease accounts. This prepared the ground for subsequent economic talks.

At the turn of September and into October 1956, those arrested after the Poznań uprising were tried in open court and received surprisingly mild sentences. The White House, which had earlier expressed its hope that Stalinist methods would be abandoned in the judiciary field, was gratified. In his statement of September 26 Eisenhower commented that the basic problem of Poland was not the type of social or economic system, but having the power to decide it through free and unfettered elections.

Gomułka was moving closer to the center of power, and one more pillar of the previous regime, the economic dictator Minc, was removed. The Eighth Plenum meeting on October 19, 1956, brought Gomułka and his collaborators into the Politburo. It was clear that the Puławy faction would succeed in electing him as the Party's first secretary and, to guard against a threatened coup by the Natolin Stalinists, the new commander of the Internal Security Corps (KBW) took precautionary measures; workers of the Żerań factory were put on alert and so were students whose sympathies lay with the forces of change. At the crucial moment it became clear that the Polish army would not follow the orders of Marshal Rokossovsky.

The climax to this extraordinarily tense situation came with the sudden appearance in Warsaw of Khrushchev, accompanied by top Soviet political and military figures. Their objective was to prevent Gomułka and his supporters from gaining power, and they set in motion the Soviet military force stationed in Poland. Ochab and Gomułka refused to talk under the menace of Russian tanks advancing on Warsaw. The whole country was in a state of commotion, and a spark could have ignited an explosion. Khrushchev realized that, if backed against the wall, the Poles would fight as they had fought in the Warsaw uprising twelve years earlier, and he gave orders to the Red Army units to return to their quarters. The Soviet leaders began to see reason in Polish arguments that a native way to socialism would endanger neither communism, nor the Warsaw Pact, nor Soviet-Polish relations. Changes and adaptations of the system were required by Polish realities; there was no danger of a counterrevolution. Moreover, Moscow's attention turned perforce to the revolt in Hungary that quickly went out of control, and Gomułka's victory had to be accepted albeit reluctantly. At home Gomułka, hailed as the man who had successfully opposed the Russians, became a national hero overnight. He climbed to heights of popularity that neither he nor anyone else in the country would have thought possible.

The dramatic weekend of October 19 to 21, when the Russians parlayed with the Poles and the fate of Poland hung in the balance, attracted wide international attention. In the United States, events in Warsaw again made front-page news. The sudden appearance of Soviet leaders in the Polish capital was reported under a big headline on the first page of the *New York Times*. The Sunday, October 21 edition carried extensive analysis with photographs and Gomułka's profile. Throughout the crisis the White House and the State Department maintained a cautious posture. Three days before the fateful weekend Dulles held a press conference in which he avoided any mention of Poland. On October 20 came Eisenhower's expression of sympathy for the Polish "traditional yearning for liberty and independence." The White House statement added that the president followed the Polish situation in close touch with the Secretary of State. The next day Dulles spoke on the radio and television, and "ruled out the use of United States armed forces to help Poland regain her freedom." Outside military interference, Dulles asserted, "could precipitate a world war as a result of which the Polish people could be wiped out." The secretary alluded to the Warsaw uprising of 1944, and went on to assure his listeners that "he did not expect the Russians to use 'mass military' means to halt the Poles' moves towards independence."

What prompted Dulles to volunteer such a statement when Poland's fate seemed so precarious? What he said contrasted greatly with his original stand on liberation policies. According to the scenario he had outlined on May 15, 1952, in case of a revolt in Eastern Europe American support would be forthcoming and any threat of Soviet intervention met with a warning of American reprisals. Confronted with a concrete situation, Dulles reversed his position. It is likely that he meant to warn the Poles not to expect too much of the United States, and may have believed that assurance of American nonintervention would strengthen the more conciliatory leaders in Soviet Russia. One cannot dismiss the additional hypothesis that the atmosphere of the developing presidential campaign, with Adlai Stevenson calling for an end to the draft and an abolition of the H-bomb, had something to do with Dulles' moderation. In any case, Washington did not keep Soviet Russia guessing; cards were put squarely on the table.

Fear of a general war arising out of the East European situation dominated the thinking in Washington. Dulles kept reassuring Moscow that the United States would not resort to force, had no ulterior motive in desiring the independence of the "satellite countries," and did not think of them as potential American allies. The president referred again to the Poles' yearning for freedom and national independence and praised them for moving to "secure a peaceful transition to a new government" that seemed to "strive genuinely to serve the Polish people." This was an indirect appeal to the Poles to support Gomułka, and Dulles thought privately that October events heralded the beginning of Polish independence. The American support was declaratory. As Eisenhower put it, the United States must "never compromise the fundamental principle" that nations were entitled to self-government and that freedom-loving people deserved help.

The Poles were lucky that their October Revolution did not get out of hand as did the revolutionary situation in Hungary. Washington did nothing to assist the Hungarians, and the critics who asserted that the first week of November was a calamity for United States policy, also embarrassed by the simultaneous Suez crisis, had a valid point. The Hungarian revolution and its collapse gave the death blow to the myth of liberation and served as an object lesson to the Poles. All that remained of the theory of liberation was a cautious American policy of limited, mainly economic assistance to East European countries that had entered a path of internal liberalization or weakened their dependence on Moscow. That policy had a precedent in the post-1948 aid to Yugoslavia, and events were to show how it would be formulated and applied with regard to Gomułka's Poland.

7

From Gomułka to Gierek:
Détente and Its Limits

The Aftermath of 1956: Gradualism

THE October unheaval inaugurated a new period and significantly affected American-Polish relations. Gomułka criticized the recent past severely and called the Poznań events a "painful lesson" that the working class taught the Party leadership and the government. He asserted that the only immutable element in socialism was the abolition of "exploitation and oppression of man by man" and stated that it was "a poor idea" that "only Communists can build socialism." Gomułka made it clear, however, that the Party would retain the leadership and head the process of democratization. Friendship with Soviet Russia was the essence of Polish foreign policy, but it would be based on equality and independence of the two partners. All this seemed realistic and honest, and for a while the will of the nation and Gomułka's program converged. Although Gomułka scornfully rejected the term "national communism" as an invention of Dulles and American sovietologists, many people believed that the Party had in fact become national. The traditional Polish birthday song *sto lat* (may he live to be a hundred), which greeted Gomułka's public appearances, became for a while an unofficial Polish anthem.

The multiple changes that took place in Poland have been extensively described and analyzed; only a summary of the crucial developments will be presented here. Departures in four areas were particularly striking and proved more or less enduring: cessation of the terror, abandonment of collectivization, establishing a modus vivendi with the Catholic church, and the end of the country's isolation from the West. An amnesty freed the majority of political prisoners, and activities of secret police were curbed. Collective farms fell apart spontaneously, and the peasantry was assured that collectivization would not be attempted by force. Compulsory deliveries of agricultural products were greatly reduced. The agreement of December 6, 1956, between Gomułka and the released Cardinal Wyszyński permitted limited religious teaching, alleviated financial burdens on the church, and led to the appointments of resident bishops in the western territories. These concessions signified a recognition of the important role of the Catholic church in Polish society. The ecclesiastical hierarchy in turn lent its support to the Party and the government, particularly to prevent any activities that could be construed as an open challenge to Russia, although the church knew well that communist ideology underwent no basic change as far as religion was concerned.

Let us now look briefly at the political, cultural-ideological, and economic processes engendered or accelerated by the Polish October. As Gomułka had promised, the sejm became a more meaningful factor in the state and people were allowed, within circumscribed boundaries, not only to vote but also to elect. Serving as a barometer of public opinion, "consent elections" to use the term of a Polish political scientist, came into being, and for the first time in January 1957 there was a larger slate of candidates (750) than places in the sejm (460). Gomułka appealed to the voters, however, not to use their right to cross out Party candidates. To do so, he said, would be tantamount to crossing Poland off the political map of Europe. The appeal was heeded, but it was indicative of public sentiment that a successful non-Party candidate polled an average of 94.3 percent of the vote as compared with 90.8 to 89.2 for a Democratic or a Populist candidate, and 88 percent for a Party member.

In the new sejm the Catholic group connected to the *Tygodnik Powszechny* was represented, having regained control of the newspaper, and assumed the name of Znak. Its leading member, Jerzy Zawieyski, entered the State Council. The Catholic group advocated a program favored by Cardinal Wyszyński and enjoyed great moral prestige in the country. Its willingness to cooperate with the Gomułka regime stemmed from a "positivist" attitude and was connected with the new church-state understanding. Pax, which followed a hard line in October, suffered a temporary eclipse and had no candidates in the elections. Some of its members joined Znak, but the power base of Pax, a virtually capitalist enterprise with its own press, publishing house, factories, shops and other tax-exempt institutions, survived. No wonder that people tended to explain this phenomenon by direct link to Moscow.

The exhilarating atmosphere of the Polish October was felt in all spheres of cultural and scholarly life. Relaxed censorship permitted genuine public discussion; a retreat from socialist realism in visual arts and literature opened the way to new talents and novel forms of artistic expression. Falsification of history was denounced together with distortions of the present by the media. Professors deprived of their chairs were reinstated. The Union of Polish Youth was dissolved and new student organizations came into existence. With the end of compulsory classes in Marxism-Leninism and the acceptance of hitherto rejected disciplines such as sociology, universities once again became open to freer exchange of ideas. The historical essays of Paweł Jasienica made history attractive to readers bored by dogmatic and schematic presentations of the past. Marxist philosophy, liberated from its rigid shackles, entered the path of revisionism. The name of Leszek Kołakowski became famous as its bold interpreter. Symbolic of the change in literature was the election of Słonimski to the chairmanship of the Polish Writers' Union. Among new literary talents, the "angry young man" Marek Hłasko saw a meteoric rise in popularity. His novels and short stories caught the spirit of the time and made him the idol of the younger generation.

Through the plays of Sławomir Mrożek the Polish theater came once again to the forefront of European drama, and in subsequent years the experimental theater of Grotowski represented the Polish avant-garde at its best. There was a surge of creativity in painting, mostly abstract, music, and sculpture. Polish film became for the first time noted at home and abroad for its content and techniques. As foreign observers reported, post-October Poland became an exciting country seething with ideas and vitality.

Economic errors and distortions of the Stalinist era needed particular attention, and work began on a new Polish economic model. A brain trust composed of leading economists prepared in 1957 theses that advocated far-reaching decentralization, price reforms, and a system of working incentives. Small private enterprises and handicrafts that proliferated spontaneously were to be encouraged. Workers' councils were introduced into factories. Yet, except for the councils which survived for a couple of years, sweeping economic reforms failed to be implemented. What is more, economic difficulties made Gomułka suspicious of the economic experts; thus only correctives were introduced into the new Five-Year Plan (1956–

1960). They provided for some reallocation of investments from industry to consumer goods, and included the changes in agriculture already mentioned. The economic situation of Poland was far from good, and it was imperative to alleviate at least the burdensome relations with the Soviet Union and to seek outside credits and capital.

The October events opened up the country to contacts with the Western world. The Poles insisted on ending the jamming of foreign broadcasts—Gomułka ordered that it be stopped—and on free access to information from abroad, including the circulation of the Paris-based monthly *Kultura,* which was denied. Although *Kultura* was not available, it had a great impact, especially the articles of its leading political commentator, Juliusz Mieroszewski; even Cyrankiewicz and Gomułka made reference to them. In turn, the political emigration was greatly affected by the Polish October. The previous model of the emigration as the state in exile had been based on the assumption that the existence of a Communist regime barred the possibility of changes in the homeland. Events of 1956 showed a need to revise this stand, and after heated debates a sizable part of the emigration espoused the idea that its role was that of an auxiliary in the domestic evolutionary process. Especially *Kultura* subscribed to the evolutionist theory, viewing the Polish October as the first phase of a development that would gradually enlarge the country's internal and external freedom. The evolution would obviously be influenced by two major outside factors: the United States that could assist it, and Soviet Russia, likely to stem it.

The immediate and crucial issue was that of Soviet-Polish relations. Official destalinization immediately restored the old name to Katowice and to the main boulevard of Warsaw. In their fervor Poles began to utter loudly the forbidden word Katyn. A rumor has persisted ever since that at that point Khrushchev was willing to admit Stalin and Beria's guilt for this wartime massacre and was only dissuaded by Gomułka, who feared the shock-effect of such an admission on the Polish masses. If true, it was an important psychological error, for a frank statement on Katyn could have cleared the air. Close relations with the Soviet Union were obviously essential to Gomułka not only because of ideological considerations but also for general reasons; the perennial problem of Poland's geographical position was on everyone's mind.

Gomułka went to Moscow in November 1956, and Polish fears about his safety reflected accurately the prevailing mood in the country. The mission was a success, and Khrushchev once again recognized that the first secretary was neither a Tito nor a Nagy. Most likely he felt a certain respect for the tough Pole who had stood up to him. Agreements concluded in Moscow regularized the status of the Red Army in Poland by allowing Warsaw to have a say regarding its moves within the country. An economic setttlement by virtue of which the USSR made sizable payments to Poland and advanced credits amounted to a compensatory arrangement for past economic exploitation. Finally, Russia agreed to repatriate Poles still retained in the Soviet Union. The agreements further bolstered Gomułka's stature in Poland, and people relished the spectacle of the departing Soviet generals and senior officers who had occupied key positions in the Polish army. Among them was Marshal Rokossovsky.

In foreign as well as in domestic matters a crude system of commands and overt domination made way for subtler means of manipulation. If Moscow regarded Poland's ideological influence in the bloc as dangerous, it appreciated Gomułka's ability not to overstep permissible boundaries. Temporarily the country gained a greater freedom of maneuver in international relations. Gomułka did not join the Eastern Bloc's condemnation of the Hungarian revolution, and two years later remained friendly to Yugoslavia when Belgrade's relations with Moscow worsened again. More important, however, was the reestablishment of better relations with the United States, which attested to a measure of autonomy. Warsaw sought American credits to improve its economy and to lessen dependence on the Soviet Union, and it attempted to seize the initiative in the West-East deadlock by proposing a nuclear-free zone in Central Europe, embodied in the Rapacki Plan. The course of these economic developments and the story of the Rapacki Plan will become more intelligible when we examine the United States' attitude toward Polish and East European trends.

Liberation slogans played a minor role in the American presidential election of 1956, even though the Democrats criticized the Republicans for their empty pledges and for failing to press before the United Nations for a Soviet military withdrawal from Eastern Europe. The Republicans pointed to a gradual evolution within the area which their policies had allegedly assisted. Some ambiguity remained as to whether the United States was chiefly interested in the liberation of peoples from communism or the emancipation of Communist states from Moscow's tutelage, and Washington argued that domestic evolution would both weaken dependence on Moscow and advance the cause of internal freedom. In practice American policy promoted pluralism in East Central Europe even if it entailed support to Communist governments; the term "national communism" gained currency. In his major speech of December 31, 1956, Dulles said: "In Poland, and in satellite countries generally, there is a rising tide of patriotism and insistence upon governments that will serve the people and respect national traditions." The question was how the United States would try to assist this trend.

Under the second Eisenhower administration, Washington emphasized American refusal to accept "permanent subjugation" of East Central Europe. Simultaneously the National Security Council, charged by the president with an examination of the problem, recommended policies oriented toward the prevention of such crises as the Hungarian revolution, which the United States proved to be powerless to help. This was one side, somewhat negative, of a policy to which the congressional Foreign Affairs Committee added a more positive component by recommending encouragement of the rising nationalism of "satellite countries." The exact form this encouragement was to take was harder to determine, but it was clear that two areas were open for American activities: the economic-cultural and the international-political. The first was less difficult to penerate, but it did require a reappraisal of economic policies toward East Central Europe and the initiation of cultural exchanges.

Broadly put, the issue was whether American interests would be served be expanded economic intercourse with countries like Poland, which had shown a degree of independence from Moscow. Would a relaxation of economic controls assist primarily the Communist rulers or the "captive nations"? Was economic aid to Gomułka's regime the best way of promoting "national communism"? A debate of these issues involved the Congress, a special task force representing business circles appointed by President Eisenhower, and the Committee for Economic Development. The press, academia, and various associations joined in the discussion.

As early as October 22, 1956, Eisenhower had indicated his willingness to grant some economic aid to Poland. A few weeks later an American delegation of housing experts toured Poland, and two months later the Department of Commerce announced that it might issue licenses to exporters of agricultural surplus commodities. In February 1957 a Polish delegation came to Washington for negotiations which, however, moved slowly. The administration worried about the reaction of the Polish American community and of the conservative forces in the Congress. Indeed, in March the minority leader in the Senate, William K. Knowland, publicly opposed any aid to Poland as long as it remained under Soviet domination. A similar stand was taken by, among others, the president of the Institute of Foreign Trade, J. Anthony Marcus. Worries about the adverse reaction of the Polonia and the political emigration proved to be less well founded. In a memorandum for the State Department of late March, emigré Ambassador Lipski wrote that "free Poles are in favor of granting appropriate economic help to Poland although that country has not yet attained full independence, and finds itself still in a compulsory situation owing to external conditions."

Cardinal Wyszyński's appeal to Polish American representatives to help Poland's economy found a favorable reception. The new Polish emigré Council of National Unity fully endorsed the position taken by Senator John F. Kennedy, who argued that if the United States could score only "by turning a deaf ear to Polish hunger and misery, then we will have won a dubious 'victory' at best." Yet doubts remained about what economic aid to Poland could accomplish. Secretary Dulles was asked if $75 million would suffice to tear Poland away from Russia, and he had to explain that it was not a question of buying Poland's friendship at such a price but of encouraging an evolutionary process in that country. Dulles characterized the resolve to aid Poland on the assumption that it was not completely dominated by the USSR as a "pretty close decision."

Lengthy negotiations in Washington produced two agreements between June and August 1957. The first provided credits of $30 million through the Export-Import Bank, mainly for Polish purchases of capital goods—mining machinery and transportation equipment—and for American sales of agricultural surpluses, largely cotton, fats, and oil evaluated at $18.9 million, to be paid for in Polish złotys. The second agreement was signed after the Congress had accepted a liberal interpretation of the 1954 Agricultural Trade Development and Assistance Act (PL 480), which permitted credit sales to friendly governments. As a result, the amount of farm surpluses, especially wheat and cotton, was increased by an additional $46.1 million. Thus, by the autumn of 1957, roughly a year after the dramatic events in Poland, the country received economic assistance totalling $95 million.

The size of the credits and the time taken up by negotiations are open to criticism. The Poles had originally requested $300 million and hoped for even more to loosen their ties to Russia. After the first round of talks in Washington, Gomułka commented that the credits America offered were modest given Poland's needs. But he added that economic intercourse between countries of different social systems could pave the way to general relaxation in international relations. Addressing the Senate in August 1957, Kennedy clashed with Senator Mansfield and asserted that the Poles were not a "satellite people" and that economic aid granted to Poland was "too little and too late." He went on to quote a Polish exile's remark: "I wish that Poland would become the world's business rather than the world's inspiration."

It is debatable, of course, what more generous aid given more swiftly could have accomplished, but psychologically the most favorable moment was allowed to pass, and American help lacked spontaneity and drama. The Polish emigrés had advocated American initiatives with greater appeal to the Poles' imagination; for instance, an offer to construct a huge hospital in Warsaw or a home for the war-crippled Home Army fighters, or rebuilding the royal castle.

Turning to the cultural field, in April 1957 the Ford Foundation announced the creation of a fund of half a million dollars to finance the exchanges of intellectuals, students and professors, and to assist Polish universities and libraries. Two months later the Rockefeller Foundation set aside $475,000 for similar purposes. A closer look at these figures, especially as compared with sums spent for other educational purposes, reveals how small they were. In 1957–1958, for instance, the research division of a typical midwestern state university received grants of roughly $3.5 million. As compared to some forty Poles, recipients of the Ford and Rockefeller grants to the United States, the number of Thai students brought in under international exchanges to Indiana University was double that figure. In the years to come the cultural activities picked up momentum. Between 1957 and 1959 about four hundred Poles came under the Ford and Rockefeller-financed programs. Between 1958 and 1964 the United States Information Media Guaranty Program allotted, through a yearly agreement with Poland, about $8 million in Polish złotys for books, films, newspapers, and copyright fees. Gradually several programs of cultural and scholarly exchanges developed either on a national basis—for instance, under the Inter-University Travel Committee and later continued by the International Research and Exchanges Board—or by way of direct agreements between individual American and Polish academic institutions.

Alongside with outright aid, cultural and economic—not forgetting assistance coming from private organizations as, for instance, the Catholic Relief—American Polish trade also revived. After 1957, certain goods destined for Poland began to be removed from the Consultative Group Coordinating Committee list, which meant that while they still required special licenses to be exported to the Eastern Bloc, they could be exported on open general licenses to Poland. Because of the new credits, American exports to Poland rose and in 1958 stood at $104 million. (The total exported to the Eastern Bloc was valued at $112.6 million.) Grain, fats, and cotton made up around 37 percent of these exports, and at first raw materials were also significant. To allow Poland to gain hard currencies Polish exports to the United States were permitted to grow and accounted for three-fourths of all American imports from the Eastern Bloc. In the first years following the October events, the structure of Polish trade was fairly constant. Ham and canned meat, which had not been affected by the withdrawal of the Most-Favored-Nation clause in 1951, still constituted about 72 percent of Polish exports. An increase in volume accompanied by very small changes in the nature of goods involved remained a characteristic feature of Polish-American trade for several years to come.

A certain reintegration of Poland in the international economic community, combined with new American-Polish agreements, facilitated the growth of economic intercourse. By 1957 Poland became an observer of GATT (General Agreement on Tariffs and Trade), and a year later rejoined FAO (Food and Agriculture Organization attached to the UN). In mid-July 1960 an American-Polish agreement was signed providing for compensation of United States citizens for nationalized property. The compensation figure was set at $40 million to be paid by Poland over twenty years. In 1960 the United States restored the Most-Favored-Nation clause to Warsaw, which placed it in a privileged position vis-à-vis the other East European trading competitors. The restoration of the clause was regarded by Washington more as a reward for the relative Polish independence and as an incentive to other East European countries, than dictated by pure economic motives. In the early 1960s the Polish share of total American imports never amounted to more than 0.3 percent.

United States policy toward Warsaw was one component of West-East relations as a whole. The events of 1956 had shaken the Eastern Bloc and damaged its monolithic features, yet Khrushchev still felt strong or reckless enough to combine advocacy of "peaceful coexistence" with attempts to undermine the West. Henry Kissinger, writing in 1957, suggested that the United States be "as ready to profit from opportunities in the Soviet orbit" as the USSR felt free to exploit Western weaknesses and troubles. This was sound advice, yet it is doubtful whether such a policy was fully and consistently pursued by Washington.

The maximum goals of both blocs were clearly unattainable, if we assume that the West sought German reunification and the elimination of Soviet dominance from East Central Europe, and Moscow an extension of its controls by separating West Germany from NATO and getting the American troops out of Europe. But some room for maneuver existed, and in that respect both Germany and Poland occupied important positions. George Kennan and Walter Lippmann advised a *iunctim* (connecting link) between German reunification and self-determination of satellite states. In the 1957 issue of the *Journal of International Affairs* (devoted in its entirety to East Central Europe), Zbigniew Brzezinski counseled a policy aiming at neutralization of the area accompanied by guarantees of the existing borders. The Poles were particularly interested in the guarantees, given the controversial question of the Odra-Nysa frontier. The Americans continued to be divided on its merits, and in May 1957 the Republican Congressman from Tennessee, Carrol B. Reece, argued in the House of Representatives with the Polish American Representative Machrowicz. Reece's defense of German revisionist claims caused heated debates that went beyond the floor of the Congress.

The question of a negotiated military withdrawal both from Germany and some East European countries and the creation of a neutral zone separating the two great blocs agitated several politicians and writers in the United States and Europe. The theory of disengagement found supporters in Kennan and the British laborite leader, Hugh Gaitskell, and opponents in Dean Acheson and C. L. Sulzberger, who regarded a withdrawal of American troops from Germany as tantamount to a Soviet takeover of all of Europe. Poland became actively involved in the debate when in October 1957 its Foreign Minister, Adam Rapacki, proposed in the forum of the United Nations a plan for a nuclear-free zone composed of both West and East Germanies, Poland, and Czechoslovakia. In February 1958 Rapacki presented to the new American ambassador in Warsaw, Jacob Beam, a somewhat amended plan which held out the prospect of an eventual reduction of conventional armies in the nuclear-free zone. Opinions differ as to the real authorship of the plan and whether it was primarily a Polish initiative. Ulam, for one, doubts that it was conceived in Warsaw; others claim that it was, and received only a grudging Soviet assent. From the Polish point of view the merits of the Rapacki Plan were obvious. It was likely to weaken Soviet military presence in Poland and East Germany, promote a relaxation of military tensions between the rival blocs, and prepare the ground for a recognition of the Odra-Nysa border. Lipski told the State Department that the plan was valuable only insofar as it could produce a recognition of the Odra-Nysa frontier alongside with a Soviet withdrawal from East Central Europe.

Washington did not treat the Rapacki Plan seriously. This may have been a mistake not only in the broad context of West-East relations but specifically in regard to Poland. Military objections to an evacuation of West Germany prevented even attempts to discuss the plan and gain a psychological advantage. It would surely have been useful, as Kennan and Lippmann intimated, to consider exchanging German reunification for self-determination of Germay's eastern neighbors. On the Odra-Nysa frontier, Henry Kissinger argued a year later in the *New York Times Magazine* (March 8, 1959) that a military guarantee of the frontier by NATO "would lessen the Soviet ability to control Poland through the fears of Germany."

In the absence of concrete negotiations over disengagement, the West and East sparred without advancing matters. Although Russia withdrew its troops from Rumania in 1958, and had a new quarrel with Tito, not to mention the widening split with China, the initiative belonged to Khrushchev. Characteristically, he met the difficulties with a diplomatic offensive and, while stressing the need for peaceful coexistence, applied pressure on West Berlin. The foreign ministers' conference in Geneva ended with a fiasco.

The United States showed little flexibility or imagination in tackling West-East issues, but went again on public record favoring emancipation of Eastern Europe. In July 1959 the Congress passed a Captive Nations Resolution and declared a Captive Nations week. The resolution asserted that enslavement of nations by communist imperialism made the idea of peaceful coexistence a mockery. The Eastern Bloc was said to pose a "dire threat to the security of the United States. It was vital to keep alive the desire for liberty and independence of the "conquered nations" among which the Ukraine, Belorussia, and the Baltic countries were enumerated. This was "vital to the national security of the United States." Khrushchev was incensed. "This resolution stinks," he shouted to Vice-President Nixon, who was visiting the Soviet Union in July 1959. Continuing his diplomatic offensive, Khrushchev came twice to the United States; in late 1959, and to attend the United Nations session in 1960. His trips abounded in colorful episodes but yielded no concrete results except for an agreement to hold a summit meeting in Paris which proved stillborn. As regards the American attitude toward the Eastern Bloc, a State Department spokesman reaffirmed that Washington had no desire to turn the East European nations against Moscow or to make them into American allies following the American way of life. It recognized that a return to the prewar situation was impossible, but the United States could not accept a status quo that prevented these nations from achieving freedom and establishing the kind of governmental, economic, and social institutions they themselves desired.

Seen against this international background, direct American-Polish relations continued to improve. On his way back from Moscow, Nixon stopped in Warsaw and was impressed by the enthusiastic reception of the Polish crowds. In his speech in Washington he asserted that there were "many areas in which cooperation between Poland and the United States can be developed, with real benefits to both countries." In 1960 Gomułka, traveling separately from Khrushchev and his retinue, came to attend the United Nations session in New York. Secretary of State Christian Herter received the Polish leader—the only Communist visitor to be so honored—and Averell Harriman conferred with him at length. That was when the Most-Favored-Nation clause was restored to Poland and the compensation agreement settled. New credits were advanced. During his stay Gomułka issued a message to Americans of Polish descent. Recalling the heritage of Pułaski and Kościuszko, Gomułka said that Polish Americans more than anyone else could contribute to American-Polish friendship, which lay in the interest of both countries. The common bond between them was the desire to maintain and strengthen peace. Gomułka mentioned the threat of German revisionism and said that the Odra-Nysa frontier was inviolable. He ended his message with a personal touch alluding to his family still living in the United States. Indeed, Gomułka's father had worked in the Pennsylvania coal mines, and he too spent some time in this country as a child. Whether these were happy memories and whether he still remained in touch with his relatives (sister?) in the United States is more than doubtful.

President Eisenhower did not receive the Polish leader. This was deliberate; already two years earlier, in June 1958, the president had noted with dismay—as reported by the press—that in spite of American concessions to Warsaw there was no evidence of increased independence of the Polish People's Republic. In 1959 a book was published in New York under a title that reflected this feeling. It was *Frozen Revolution: Poland a Study in Communist Decay,* by Frank Gibney. A deterioration in Polish domestic affairs was being reported at length in the American press.

It is clear now that Gomułka's basic objective in 1956 had been to bridge the gap between the Party and the nation and to achieve a higher degree of the Party's legitimization. At no time did he conceive of allowing the process of democratization and liberalization to transform basically the state and society. As the Communist ideologue, Julian Hochfeld, put it in 1957, "under no conditions can a revolutionary, workers' party think of ceding power to someone else." Such a cession of power would inevitably lead to a counterrevolution, civil war, dissolution of the whole social fabric, perhaps even result in a national catastrophe. The years following 1956 witnessed a retreat from the ideals of the Polish October as seen by the revisionist wing of the Party and the masses of the people. While the leading revisionist philosopher, Kołakowski, viewed an evolution toward real democracy a risk worth taking, his stand was not only unacceptable to the dogmatists, who regarded the October concessions as tactical and temporary, but to Gomułka himself.

Gomułka steered a middle course between the revisionist and the orthodox, trying to weaken both and increase his own control. His personal integrity was respected, but the austere life he preached and practiced appealed to few high officials of the apparatus. His increasing suspicion of the intellectuals estranged him from the innovative and bolder spirits. In 1957 the influential revisionist youth paper *Po Prostu* was closed, and for the first time since Gomułka came to power the police battled recalcitrant students. Censorship began to be tightened, and there was growing disenchantment with "socialist legalism." Although individual rights and liberties were infinitely more respected than in the past, people began to fear that what had been given could also be taken away. The state-church relationship was a good barometer of the political atmosphere, and while it registered no frontal attack on the church, it indicated much friction. There were renewed fiscal pressures and a controversy over the distribution of large gifts made to Cardinal Wyszyński by the Polish Catholic organizations in the United States. There were incidents of various kinds; in 1960 the matter of building a church in the socialist showpiece town, Nowa Huta, became a *cause célèbre*. In spite of shortages of qualified personnel in hospitals and kindergartens, religious orders which had hitherto attended to them were gradually forced out. Religion classes were removed from school buildings.

These antireligious measures were essentially political in nature. The church was a competitor of the Party for the allegiance of the masses, and a non-Marxist Weltanschauung could be tolerated only at the price of identification with the system. The Party reproached the episcopate for failing to endorse unreservedly the Polish People's Republic, and made it suffer the consequences of being a tolerated but never trusted rival institution.

In the economic life the gains of October were visible. Living conditions had improved and the production of both peasant holdings and state farms rose. Imports of American grains and food products alleviated shortages. Production and importation of such new and much sought-after articles as television sets, radios, motorcycles, and refrigerators appealed to the Polish consumer. Production statistics listed new achievements in chemical industries and shipyards, to mention but two branches of industry. The discovery of new deposits of sulphur and copper were most welcome. There was a slow but steady growth of national income, a balanced foreign trade, and relatively small foreign indebtedness. Yet there were many shortcomings. Crafts and services were artificially stifled and subjected to discriminatory taxation and chicanery. In spite of the often repeated assertion that the country needed more working incentives, more services, and smaller plants, private initiative was being driven into an economic underground, that fed on the black market and was only marginally useful to the producer and consumer. A mixture of economic dogmatism, lack of competence of many supervisors and directors, and Gomułka's own distrust of bold economic schemes arrested reforms of the Yugoslav type.

The Third Party Congress, held in 1959, consolidated Gomułka's leadership in the country, but as a foreign observer put it, there was a noticeable difference with the 1956 situation. The power that he had held then may have been precarious but was backed by national enthusiasm. By 1959 his power was more secure, but national enthusiasm was on the wane. A period began which was subsequently called the Little Stabilization, and the stress was on the adjective.

Although Eisenhower's unwillingness to receive Gomułka may have partly stemmed from such domestic American considerations as distrust of communism, it also reflected a certain disappointment with the course of events in Poland. Economic aid and cultural exchanges did not decisively influence the Polish regime to evolve in the direction of greater freedom and independence. Although the State Department realized the limits to Gomułka's ability of maneuver, Polish statements backing Russia and denouncing American imperialism and NATO were resented. In turn, such incidents as the defection in 1959 of the head of Polish military attachés, Colonel Paweł Monat, to the United States greatly embarrassed and annoyed Warsaw. The signing of a formal charter of the Council of Mutual Economic Cooperation (CEMA or COMECON) in 1960 was viewed with some concern in Washington as an indication of increasing Polish involvement in the economic integration of the Eastern Bloc. Projects of a tighter link with the Soviet economy through the Friendship Pipeline carrying oil from Russia into East Central Europe evoked unfavorable comments in the United States. There were new reservations about aid to Poland and a privileged treatment of its imports.

There is no doubt that over the years American economic assistance was sizable and beneficial to Poland. After the $95 million credits in 1957, $98 were granted in 1958 and $103, $130, and $44 million respectively in 1959, 1960, and 1961. By December 1961 Poland had received an equivalent of $460,900,000. While the amounts were large, it is only fair to add that fluctuations in the credits and a feeling of uncertainty that accompanied them diminished their value for long-range planning. Grain began to play an increasingly large part in American exports to Poland—74 percent of the total in 1960—while the share of raw materials declined. By far the largest part (85 percent by 1961) of the credits were to be repaid in Polish złotys—calculated at 24 to a dollar—and used within Poland. Only the unused balances were to be repaid in dollars. The remaining 15 percent of credits was repayable over a twenty-year period in dollars advanced through the Export-Import Bank.

Peaceful Engagement in the Early 1960s

The American presidential elections of 1960 showed that liberation slogans largely belonged to the past. Both candidates, John F. Kennedy and Richard M. Nixon, repeated the almost obligatory phrase about favoring freedom in East Central Europe, a desirable but distant goal. Both opposed revolutionary unheavals in the satellite nations. When addressing the Polish National Alliance, the undersecretary of state called the acceptance of the status quo a "temporary nightmare" but advocated as concrete policy economic aid to the Poles. It is likely that Kennedy's exuberant personality— "youth, brains, and elegance"—captured the imagination of many Poles and Polish Americans. His past advocacy of economic assistance, his suggestion to use the American accounts in Poland for the reconstruction of the royal castle in Warsaw, the presence at his side of a Polish brother-in-law, Prince Stanisław Radziwiłł, and his being a Catholic may have helped Kennedy with the Polish American electorate. To offset this appeal Nixon made a last-minute promise to visit Eastern Europe if elected, to remind the world of the plight of its nations. Yet in the end there is no proof that pronouncements on Poland rather than domestic American reasons brought Kennedy some 78 percent of the Polish American vote and helped in his victory.

Kennedy's term in office, cut short by an assassin's bullet in 1963, saw the beginnings of "Peaceful Engagement in Eastern Europe," a term borrowed from the title of Brzezinski's and W. E. Griffith's article in *Foreign Affairs* of July 1961. Based on the premise that change in the Eastern Bloc could only come about through internal evolutionary processes, peaceful engagement was designed to affect both the regimes and the peoples, stimulate diversity within the area, and increase the chances of a higher degree of external independence. In a sense, peaceful engagement was a conceptualization of the post-1956 trend in American policy toward Poland and an argument for its enlargement. The long-range objective was a neutral belt of East European states enjoying a status comparable to that of Finland, that is, staying clear of Western alliances, displaying no hostility toward the Soviet Union, and possessing a genuine freedom of choice in domestic affairs. But American means of promoting such a program were obviously limited.

The German question, as before, played an important part in the formulation of a policy toward Poland. Brzezinski urged an immediate opening of United States consulates in Wrocław and Szczecin, the two largest cities in the western territories, as a symbol of Washington's recognition of Polish territorial concerns. He advocated that Bonn be encouraged to adopt a more flexible stance with regard to the German-Polish controversy. Kennedy refrained from taking any concrete steps in that direction, although he began to depart from the axiom of the Eisenhower administration that unification of Germany was a condition for an eventual return to full independence of all of Europe. Under Kennedy and later Johnson the sequence was reversed, and it was believed ever more strongly that the division between Western and Eastern Europe must first be obliterated before a reunification of Germany became possible. This line of thought was to prove later favorable to a German-Polish settlement.

Kennedy made friendly gestures toward the Polish nation. In his State of the Union Message of January 1961 he spoke of economic aid and "our abiding friendship for, and interest in the people of Poland." He officially designated October 11 as Pulaski Day, and his administration periodically asserted American nonrecognition of the Soviet domination of East Central Europe. More significant than these assertions were attempts to persuade the Americans of the merits of peaceful engagement. In 1962 the Assistant

Secretary of State, William R. Tyler, explained at some length that the Eastern Bloc was no longer a monilith and that its nations, while obviously dominated by Russia ideologically and diplomatically, were more like "junior partners" than satellites pure and simple. Since full independence and freedom was only realizable gradually, Tyler said that one could take full advantage of liberalizing trends if the scope of American relations with the area was and remained broad. It was believed that this entailed some curbing of irritants in East-West relations, and the Captive Nations week was quietly dropped. Kennedy's successors at the White House continued to forget it.

The obvious area of contact and engagement was the economic sphere, but here the views of the administration and the Congress diverged. Previous economic policies toward Poland, including PL 480, a select decontrolling of exports, and the granting of the MFN clause required no new congressional approval. The same was obviously true for aid administered by nongovernmental agencies, such as the Red Cross or various foundations and committees that annually contributed some $18 million for Poland. But congressional opposition arose against a more generalized relaxation of controls under the Battle Act, and economic relations with Poland also came under closer scrutiny. A report by a study mission to Poland, presented on Capitol Hill by Congressman Clement Zablocki, led to new soul-searching. The thrust of the report was that although the Polish people appreciated American aid, the Warsaw government gave insufficient credit to the United States for its efforts. There were other causes for growing American dissatisfaction with Poland. Those who believed that Warsaw would show greater independence of Moscow in the realm of foreign policy were disappointed by the Polish government's stand on Cuba and Germany.

Warsaw denounced the "brutal attack" on Cuba in 1961, meaning the Bay of Pigs episode, and spoke of the "most aggressive imperialist forces" that were "again taking the upper hand in the formation of US policy." In his speeches Gomułka drew a distinction between the "militarist circles" and the "far-sighted" people in Washington. The American-Soviet confrontation over the missiles installed in Cuba in 1962 produced great tension in Poland and evoked fears of a worldwide confrontation between the two blocs. Official Polish propaganda spoke of American recklessness that threatened world peace. Under such conditions, another version of the Rapacki Plan presented to the United Nations Disarmament Commission in Geneva in 1962 stood no chance of being seriously considered. Washington viewed it as simply a Soviet stratagem. The new plan proposed a freezing of nuclear and missile weapons and a ban on new bases during the first phase, and a gradual elimination of nuclear arms and a reduction of conventional forces and armaments during the second. International control and inspection was suggested, as well as a possible enlargement of the nuclear-free zone.

The matter of American-Polish economic relations, as affected by the Cuban crisis, figured large in the 1962 congressional debates, which concentrated on the use of presidential discretionary powers in foreign trade. The Foreign Assistance Act allowed the administration to determine whether a country qualified as friendly and was eligible for credit purchases of agricultural surpluses. The Trade Agreement Extension Act permitted the granting of the Most-Favored-Nation clause, and President Kennedy asked for continued discretion under a new act. Both affected Poland; hence Ambassador John M. Cabot was called back from Warsaw to testify on the usefulness of economic aid. Polish American organizations also mobilized for supportive action. Nevertheless, the Congress amended a new Trade Expansion Act in a way which made it necessary to deny the MFN clause to Poland (and Yugoslavia, and modified another act (the Export Control Act), by making not only strategic goods but other commodities that could adversely affect security subject to export controls.

The battle between the White House and Capitol Hill continued, and by December 1963 the administration regained much of the lost ground. Additional alterations to the Foreign Assistance Act (in turn affecting the Trade Expansion Act) created legal loopholes which permitted the administration to continue applying the MFN clause. These complex legalistic wrangles created a feeling of uncertainty that hurt American-Polish economic relations. Still, the temporary denial of the MFN clause had little practical significance, and under Johnson in 1964 it was again officially considered as binding. While the suspension of credit operations through the Export-Import Bank somewhat restricted deliveries of agricultural surpluses, it proved possible to extend limited credits through the Commodity Credit Corporation. Even though a privately organized boycott cut into the sales of Polish imports, particularly ham, and discouraged American business dealings with Poland, Kennedy consistently advocated sales to Poland and kept authorizing export licenses to grain dealers. The whole situation was characterized by ambiguity.

Kennedy and Secretary of State Dean Rusk explained on several occasions the rationale for a liberal economic policy. In 1962 the president assured the American public that his policy did not imply a recognition of permanency of Soviet domination but sought to exploit opportunities presented by divergences within the Eastern Bloc. The example of Poland was invoked. In a major speech in 1963, Rusk spoke of the disappearance of the "darkest night of Stalinist terror" in that country. New trends toward "nationalism and individual freedom," he said, were "more likely to be furthered by a somewhat relaxed atmosphere than by an atmosphere of crisis or severe cold war.' The Assistant Secretary of State warned that if "we close our eyes to the changes which have taken place in Eastern Europe, we do so in disregard of the vital security interests of the United States." The criterion for polycentrism as applied to Poland and Yugoslavia was that these two countries were seeking to defend their independence while other East European states were not. The State Department spokesman insisted that it was not a matter of choice between communism and democracy but of ignoring or encouraging certain emancipatory processes. To deprive Poland of the Most-Favored-Nation clause, another spokesman said, meant for the United States to walk away from the competition. Surely Khrushchev would be glad to have the windows to the West "bricked over."

Kennedy's assassination produced a profound impression in Poland that almost resembled national mourning. Some 16,000 people signed the condolences books in the United States embassy, and the entries, later analyzed by a political scientist, revealed the Kennedy image in Poland. Condolences referred to the dead president as a "friend of Poland," a "great man," a "champion of peace." An often recurring phrase expressed "grief and sorrow;" many Poles were visibly moved and affected by Kennedy's tragic and premature death.

The year 1964 saw the reinforcement of certain existing trends and the emergence of new ones, connected with the passing of the Adenauer era in Germany, the worsening of Chinese-Russian relations, and the fall of Khrushchev. The dynamic spirit that had characterized Kennedy's diplomacy continued under Lyndon B. Johnson, and partly accounted for the increasing American involvement in Vietnam. A certain American-Soviet relaxation was symbolized by the "hot line" between the White House and the Kremlin, but otherwise produced no startling development. Khrushchev had tried direct overtures to Washington shortly before Kennedy's death and then sounded out Bonn shortly before his own removal from the political scene, but scored in neither area.

Warsaw had faithfully adhered to the Khrushchev line, and Gomułka achieved the position of his trusted junior ally. This personal relationship may explain why he did not join the chorus of criticism of the Soviet leader orchestrated after Khrushchev's fall. Polish loyalty to Moscow was undoubtedly strengthened by fears of a Russo-German rapprochement, and loyalty, other reasons apart, appeared to be the best policy. Preoccupation with Germany prompted Gomułka to propose in 1964 his own version of the Rapacki Plan, presumably in the hope of preventing West German participation in a multilateral Western nuclear force then under discussion. Within the Eastern Bloc, Warsaw supported economic cooperation through the CEMA; Polish military contribution to the Warsaw Pact was second only to that of Russia, and in 1961 Polish troops participated for the first time in joint military exercises held by the pact members. Gomułka's Poland continued to make material contributions to Cuba and other Third World countries although this imposed additional strains on the national economy. With regard to the United States, there were by now familiar differences between the official attitude and the friendship manifested by the Polish masses. An example of the former was Warsaw's insistence on the selection of candidates for cultural exchanges, which in 1963 resulted in the termination of the Ford program. The pro-American outlook of Poles was demonstrated once again when enthusiastic crowds acclaimed Senator Robert Kennedy during his 1964 visit.

On the domestic front, Little Stabilization was coming to its end and Gomułka's regime was facing serious economic problems. The new Five-Year Plan (1961–1965), which put greater emphasis on the development of raw materials, was running into difficulties. Its structural weaknesses, in combination with the hard winter of 1963–1964, called the winter of the century, and bad harvests produced a genuine economic crisis. In November 1964 the Central Committee plenum had to scale down investments. This was a serious blow to Gomułka's leadership and the Party's ability to resolve socioeconomic needs. The Polish leader appeared ever more rigid, autocratic, and intolerant; the gains of October 1956 were viewed as being in jeopardy. In 1962 the Crooked Circle Club, once an important forum for free discussions, was dissolved. Two years later thirty-four leading Polish intellectuals addressed a letter to Gomułka protesting the extension of censorship and repression of intellectual freedom. These developments, widely reported in the American press, increased doubts about the effectiveness of peaceful engagement or bridge-building to Eastern Europe as a factor assisting internal liberalization.

The Johnson administration—and the proportion of Polish Americans voting for Johnson in 1964 was almost the same as previously for Kennedy—defended bridge building, although the policy was beset by many ambiguities. Was Soviet Russia and East Central Europe to be treated as one entity or two, and was the latter to be encouraged in order to weaken the former? Did the state of affairs in East Central Europe justify the assumption that American aid and encouragement contributed to the survival of even limited freedoms?

In a major speech in February 1964 Secretary Rusk confronted those congressmen who felt that no real change for the better had taken place in Eastern Europe and electoral reforms were nowhere in sight. The critics could point out that in the case of Poland there had been only 616 candidates in the 1961 elections to the sejm in contrast to 750 in 1956, and that a general political regression had taken place. Rusk took the position that containing communism and negotiating agreements was not enough and that it was continually necessary to encourage the evolution toward "national independence, peaceful cooperation, and open societies." Poland, he recalled, had received a somewhat different treatment from the other states in the Eastern Bloc, and he claimed that the Poles had preserved "a good deal" of national gains won in 1956. The secretary cited as examples the noncollectivized agriculture, religious freedom, and broad relations and exchanges with the West. Invoking historic ties with Poland and the presence of Polish Americans in the United States, Rusk concluded: "We apologize to none for our efforts to help the brave people of Poland to preserve their national identity and their own aspirations."

Three months later President Johnson spoke of building bridges to Eastern Europe and emphasized trade, the flow of ideas, visitors, and humanitarian aid. Trying to define the purpose of his policies, he spoke of opening new relationships to countries seeking increased independence, of opening the minds of a new generation to values and visions of the Western civilization to which they belonged, of giving freer play to national pride, "the strongest barrier to the ambition of any country to dominate another," and of showing that the interest and progress of Eastern Europe could be identified with wide-ranging relations with the West.

Many members of the Congress continued to have doubts about American engagement in Eastern Europe, although often not for the right reasons. Nor were congressional moves always logical. Thus, although in February 1964 Poland concluded a new accord with the United States for credits of $60.9 million, the congress proceeded to impose new limits on trade. Purchase of agricultural surpluses for Polish złotys was to be discontinued, and Poland would henceforth be expected to pay in dollars. Such restrictions appeared punitive and tended to bring into question the continuity of peaceful engagement. Still, by 1964 some $500 million worth of agricultural goods had been delivered to the Polish People's Republic, and trade between the two countries had grown. In 1964 the United States occupied the fourth place—after Russia, Germany, and Czechoslovakia—among Poland's importers.

The Years of Crisis

The late 1960s were years of mounting crises both in the United States and in Poland. In America the impetus came from the prolonged military involvement in Vietnam, which polarized American public opinion and contributed to a radicalization of various groups and shades of the left. Intellectual and academic circles assaulted what they considered to be American imperialism and militarism; at the same time, racial confrontations swelled the wave of unrest and riots that swept many parts of the United States; university campuses became particularly agitated. A revisionist historical school questioned America's role in the Cold War and tended to exonerate the Soviet side. Pertinent criticism mingled with loosely formulated and emotion-loaded attacks on the very foundations of Western society.

In Poland the crisis had different origins and characteristics, but there were some similarities with the American events, such as the fact that intellectuals and students formed the backbone of the social and political criticism. Their movement too fed on both alienation and idealism. In Poland, where at that time only 1.5 percent of university students belonged to the Party, the youth was alienated in a different way from young Americans. Idealism took the form, for example, of an open letter to the Party written in 1965 by two young university assistants (J. Kuroń and K. Modzelewski), which postulated a fundamental reconstruction of the socialist society. The basic difference between the American and Polish crises lay of course in the nature of the political regimes the respective rebels were grappling with. The machinery of repression defied comparison; the tragicomedy of the Chicago trial was hardly comparable to political arrests and trials in Poland. No wonder some of the Polish rebels who later emigrated to the United States looked with a certain contempt on the middle-class "revolutionaries" who proclaimed non-negotiable demands together with ultimatums for their own immunity. To the Poles this appeared a travesty of their own struggles and sufferings.

As mentioned earlier, Gomułka's regime was increasingly losing contact with the masses and making the Party vulnerable to inner struggles. In the battle for power personal ambitions naturally played a great part but there were also differences of outlook between the contenders. The Puławy group which had assisted Gomułka in 1956 became estranged from the ever more authoritarian first secretary. Its "liberal" stance was in turn challenged by a new faction of hard-liners, the "Partisans," who differed from the old Natolin in composition, attitude, and tactics. The fact that several Puławians were Jewish and used to cry anti-Semitism whenever attacked by their opponents, which annoyed many people in the Party, was now exploited by the Partisans who accused the Puławians of being a clique. In the crude contest between the Partisans and the Puławians, the Puławy group was pushed out of the Central Committee. Gomułka, so far playing one faction against the other, faced the danger of Partisans' ascendancy.

The Partisans derived their name from their leaders' participation in the wartime underground. The faction was grouped around General Mieczysław Moczar, and combined an authoritarian outlook with a tendency to capitalize on Polish nationalism. Among other means, Moczar adroitly used the organization of war veterans (ZBOWID), which he headed, as a platform on which Communists and noncommunists could meet. Writers and historians with some affinity to the Moczar group sought to rehabilitate Polish national achievements, particularly of the interwar period, which official literature had long distorted and denigrated in the name of internationalism. Playing up to popular sentiments, the Partisans resorted at times to veiled anti-Russian remarks which fulfilled the double purpose of demonstrating their own patriotism and of discrediting their opponents, many of whom had belonged to the Moscovite group that had spent the war years in the Soviet Union. Moczar himself was a hard-boiled politician, chief of security as deputy undersecretary in the ministry of the interior and minister since 1964. He was not a person to dismiss lightly.

The brewing ferment in the Party and throughout the country was fed by economic difficulties. The 1966–1970 Five-Year Plan was somewhat more cautious than its predecessor and contained quite sound projections for a modernization of production processes through structural improvements and increased foreign trade. It operated, however, under adverse conditions. In addition to problems mentioned earlier, a sudden upsurge of the Polish birth rate had adverse effects on the standard of living. The Party spoke of controlling the population growth (it later abandoned this position), an idea which the Catholic church vehemently denounced on both religious and national grounds. The secular argument was that the Poles could not afford to become a small nation, and to reduce their numbers was a counsel of despair resulting from the regime's inability to run an efficient economy. On these as on other grounds friction with the church increased. There were periodic showdowns, as during the celebration of Poland's millenium in the mid-1960s, when the Catholics emphasized the country's thousand-year-old Christian tradition.

Signs of discontent came also from the peasantry. Suspicious of any moves that could jeopardize private farming, the peasants complained about legal obstructions in land transactions, criticized the shortages of consumer goods, and voiced other grievances. Clearly no stratum of society was satisfied or identified itself fully with Gomułka's regime in the late 1960s.

American involvement in Vietnam affected Polish-American relationships directly and indirectly. Warsaw's endorsement of the Viet-Cong imposed a strain on mutual relations and helped to antagonize the Congress and some segments of public opinion. On the other hand, domestic criticism of aspects of American foreign policy in turn gave rise to anti-Cold War sentiments in different American quarters and led to the questioning of the role of Radio Free Europe. Finally, Washington's preoccupation with Vietnam diminished the activity of its diplomacy with regard to Eastern Europe, leaving the initiative to Paris, London, and Bonn, although West European trade expansion with the Eastern Bloc worried American economic circles.

While officially echoing Russian denunciations of American imperialism in Asia, Warsaw feared above all an intensification and a broadening of the conflict. In late 1967 Rapacki angrily remarked that Dulles's "acrobatics on the brink of the abyss have now been replaced by crawling towards the brink of the abyss." Such remarks added to news about Polish ships carrying supplies to Hanoi and the Polish government's early recognition of the Viet-Cong as the government of South Vietnam, were bound to annoy Washington. Still, the Johnson administration did not wish to abandon its bridge-building policies and continued to defend them in the face of renewed congressional criticism.

In 1965 a special presidential committee on East-West trade reaffirmed that, in view of a weakening of ties between Soviet Russia and its satellites and the growth of nationalism in Eastern Europe, American peaceful engagement could in the long run promote changes in the bloc. The question, however, remained whether in

the tense atmosphere created by the war in Vietnam the Congress and
the business circles would go along with that view and authorize continued economic cooperation with Poland and other members of
the Eastern Bloc.

President Johnson was determined to accord preferential treatment to Poland, and his administration was discouraging spontaneous moves to boycott Polish imports. In 1966 the administration
introduced the East-West Trade Relations Act, but it was tabled
by the Congress. Since the Foreign Assistance Act of the previous
year had not removed the president's discretion to use the Export-
Import Bank credits to further trade, Johnson kept permitting
small-scale financial operations. The president also spoke of the
possibility of further expenditure of American holdings in Polish
złotys accumulated in Poland. A new agreement allowed Poland to
buy American books, films, periodicals, and newspapers for złotys.
In 1966, however, the Food for Peace Act removed presidential discretionary use of PL 480 (agricultural surpluses) and made Poland
virtually ineligible. In 1967 restrictive amendments to the Export-
Import Bank Act introduced an effective prohibition of using the
bank for further credit operations. The Congress threatened to
deprive Poland once again of the Most-Favored-Nation clause.

These vicissitudes in American-Polish economic relations were
harming one of the principal functions this relationship was supposed to perform, namely tying Poland closer to the Western economy. The Polish planners could never absolutely depend on continuity of United States policy. Ups and downs were reflected in
trade. After the Poles were denied the right to purchase agricultural
surpluses for złotys, American exports to Poland dwindled to $35.4
million. In 1966 and 1967 there was an upward trend, and Poland
imported from America respectively for $53 million and for $60.8
million. Polish exports during these two years stood at $82.9 and
around $90 million, and this favorable balance of trade was par-
ticularly important because of the need to repay American credits.
In 1967, for instance, $28.3 million were repaid of which $6 million
were in złotys. While the volume of trade between the two countries in 1966 was roughly equal to that of American commerce with
all other members of the Eastern Bloc combined, the United States
was lagging far behind the West European nations.

Cultural exchanges continued to be an important element of
bridge-building. After the breakdown of the Ford Foundation program, the American side conceded the Polish government's right
to select its own candidates. There were some exceptions, as in the
case of individual university exchanges, but the American Council

of Learned Societies remained the only national institution to which individual Poles could directly apply. In 1965 the Kościuszko Foundation in New York resumed its exchange program with Poland, which soon involved several hundreds of people. Cultural relations comprised artistic and musical activities, for instance, visits by the Cleveland Symphony Orchestra to Poland and of the famous folkloristic dance ensembles, Mazowsze and Śląsk, to the United States. Novel forms of interaction appeared, particularly of a humanitarian character. American or Polish American money made possible the building of a model children's hospital at Prokocim near Cracow and enlarged the CARE relief program and other similar ventures.

In the field of diplomacy Washington tried to maintain good contacts with Warsaw. In the winter of 1965 Averell Harriman, acting on the president's behalf, chose the Polish capital for secret meetings with the North Vietnamese delegations. Johnson's new hand-picked ambassador to Poland, John A. Gronouski (a Polish American), facilitated Harriman's talks in which Rapacki displayed a cordial and Gomułka a tough attitude. There were further secret exchanges related to the United States-Hanoi negotiations, as for instance in 1966 between Ambassador-at-large Henry C. Lodge and Polish diplomats. During this period American broadcasts to Poland and to the rest of Eastern Europe underwent some changes. The Voice of America reduced the number of its programs and eliminated hearings of the Committee on Captive Nations. Radio Free Europe received instructions to concentrate on reporting developments in the bloc and avoid any liberation slogans.

In 1967 the question of financing Radio Free Europe became the subject of a public debate in the course of which the administration was criticized for the use of clandestine subsidies from the CIA funds. Some senators, for instance William Fulbright, advocated closing Radio Free Europe altogether. Johnson and his advisers, of whom Brzezinski as a member of the Policy Planning Council was one, wanted its continuation and pointed out that influx of news from abroad was essential as long as free mass media did not exist in Poland and the bloc. At times, Western broadcasts played an unexpected role in domestic Polish politics. During the 1968 crisis, for instance, the jamming of Radio Free Europe was stopped once again; apparently the struggling Party factions found it useful to refer to the broadcasts, for which top-level information was secretly supplied from Polish sources. In the age of mass media, propaganda can indeed become a many-edged weapon.

While American attention was riveted on Vietnam, debates about the nature of United States policy toward Eastern Europe continued in the background. The issue whether nationalism in the area ought to be encouraged was discussed in the spring of 1967 in the pages of the *Department of State Bulletin*. One of the three discussants, Deputy Undersecretary of State Foy D. Kohler, felt that by developing its relations with Eastern Europe the United States had been encouraging nationalism. Harriman argued that, although nationalism had led to demands for greater independence from Moscow, trends toward cooperation among East European states could be a healthy development from the point of view of the entire Continent. Brzezinski seemed to agree that nationalism as exploited by the Party's conservative faction was harmful and counterproductive.

Brzezinski's critique of Polish nationalism went hand in hand with his advocacy of German-Polish reconciliation, an idea he had persistently developed in his works, including the 1965 book, *Alternative to Partition: For a Broader Conception of America's Role in Europe*. Indeed, there was a need for a more active or imaginative American policy toward Europe, for defeats in Vietnam had raised doubts about the United States' global involvement and produced attitudes with neoisolationist overtones.

The question of exactly defining the relationship between American policy toward Russia and toward Eastern Europe remained as perplexing as ever. The Pacific Northwest Assembly, which grouped educators, businessmen, government figures and others, attempted to resolve the dilemma in two recommendations included in its March 1968 report. One of them said that the "posture of the United States toward East European countries should also try to avoid agravating tensions between the Soviet Union and the United States, with the understanding, however, that U.S. relations with Eastern Europe do not require mediation via the Soviet Union." A second recommendation advocated pursuing "open relations with East European states independent of U.S. policy toward the Soviet Union, always remaining sensitive, however, to the vital interest of the Soviet Union within the East European orbit." These less than crystal-clear formulae attested to the complexity of the problem. A final report of the 31st American Assembly, under the honorary chairmanship of Eisenhower, which met at Columbia University in late April 1967, tried to stay clear of the dilemma. It asserted, however, the importance of Eastern Europe to the United States and went on record as favoring "evolution not revolution." The recommendation favored the acceptance by the United States, together with West Germany, of the Odra-Nysa boundary as a state frontier between Poland and the reunited Germany. The authors admitted, however, that Western Europe, being closer to the Eastern Bloc, was bound to play a leading role with regard to that matter.

The American discussants of Eastern Europe rightly emphasized the existence of two trends: a growing nationalism within the region and increased West European economic and diplomatic intercourse with the bloc, although there the Common Market tended to create difficulties. In 1967 Rapacki said that whether "you recognize it or not, the Common Market exists" and has to be included in Polish economic calculations. But, given the German role in the organization, Warsaw faced the thorny issue of how to handle the need for economic exchanges with Western Europe without making itself open to political pressures.

De Gaulle's France and West Germany (governed since 1966 by the Kiesinger-Brandt great coalition) were in the forefront of taking the initiatives vis-à-vis Eastern Europe. Contacts between Paris and Warsaw culminated in de Gaulle's state visit to Poland in 1967, and the French president's statements favoring the Odra-Nysa border were greatly appreciated by the Poles. But Gomułka made clear that any French attempts to woo Poland away from the Soviet Union were doomed to fail. The German diplomatic offensive aroused great suspicions. Although interested in the expanding trade, Warsaw regarded German overtures for the establishment of diplomatic relations with the Eastern European countries as a device for undermining the bloc's solidarity with regard to the German-Polish frontier. The Rumanian acceptance of diplomatic ties with Bonn in 1967 provoked immediate Polish responses; Warsaw signed new alliances with Czechoslovakia and East Germany, and Moscow applied pressure on Prague.

The danger of Poland's isolation through German policies appeared real not only to the Party but also to noncommunist Poles. A leading member of the Catholic Znak, Stanisław Stomma, stressed geopolitics as the determinant of Polish foreign policy. It was the key to Poland's alliance with Soviet Russia, he said, although he also asserted that Poland "has neither resigned itself to a policy of drift, nor will it ever forego its own initiative, nor will it lose its own coloring or abandon its own methods." This sounded overly optimistic, and in reality room for maneuvers was greatly limited. Gomułka's own worries about Germany became compounded by the growth of polycentric currents within the bloc—which he related or pretended to relate to the German threat.

Rumanian establishment of relations with Bonn was an unwelcome sign of Bucharest's increased independence in international relations. Kadar's continued economic reforms in Hungary evoked little enthusiasm in Moscow or Warsaw. Greatest apprehension, however, was caused by Czechoslovakia, where the extent of domestic liberalization appeared truly dangerous to Moscow, Warsaw, and East Germany. Should the evolution in Czechoslovak domestic affairs affect Prague's foreign policy, Gomułka as well as his East German colleague would feel doubly exposed. It was in this tense atmosphere that an event occurred which, although geographically remote, greatly affected the Polish scene and triggered developments that led to the March 1968 crisis.

The event was the Six-Day Arab-Israeli war of June 1967. Moscow's involvement on the Arab side had been evident for some time, and shortly before the outbreak of hostilities in the Middle East, Russia had pressed for a united front of the East European countries. The *Washington Post* reported an alleged Polish reluctance to be too deeply involved, which may well have reflected pro-Israeli sympathies in several Polish quarters. Israeli victories appeared to be Soviet defeats; on the second day of fighting Cardinal Wyszyński gave a sermon that was much publicized later, about Israel's right to independent statehood; jokes circulating in Warsaw made fun of Arab military failures.

Gomułka was greatly annoyed, and his irascible temper was whipped into a frenzy by reports about alleged celebrations of Israeli victories by Party officials of Jewish descent. The government officially condemned Israel and on June 12 severed diplomatic relations with Tel Aviv, as did all members of the bloc, Rumania excepted. Polish propaganda began to draw parallels between the Israeli attack on Egypt and the German aggression on Poland in 1939. Finally, Gomułka came out with accusations against some Polish Jews whom he called a fifth column. This was out of character, for Gomułka had never before shown anti-Semitic tendencies. There had been no political trials in Poland with anti-Semitic overtones; indeed, in the mid-1950s the Party had allegedly resisted Russian suggestions of making Minc and Berman the Jewish scapegoats for the sins of Stalinism. Memories of the Holocaust, traditional opposition of the Polish left to anti-Semitism, and the prominent role Jews had played in the history of Polish communism militated against any such moves. While Russia had for some time linked Zionism, American imperialism, and German revisionism, this line found only a faint echo in Warsaw. The reasons for the changed official position came largely from inner-Party factionalism. The Partisans aided by Pax launched an "anti-Zionist" campaign (anti-Semitism continued to be officially condemned) and Gomułka was swept by the current.

Wielding an anti-Zionist stick, the Party leadership confronted students and intellectuals clamoring for change and invoking the Czechoslovak example. The Polish Writers Union raised its voice in February and in March against discriminatory cultural policies and censorship; student demonstrators chanted the slogan "All Poland waits for its Dubcek." Reprisals followed, and March 1968 became another milestone in Polish postwar evolution. The banning of Mickiewicz's classical play, *The Forefathers' Eve* (Dziady), because of cheering that erupted whenever an anti-Russian line was spoken on the stage led to police intervention. Future historians may be able to determine to what extent *agents provocateurs* of the Partisans added fuel to the fire, but there are indications that they acted in order to make Gomułka crack down on groups within and outside the Party that stood in the way of Moczar's rise to power. Anti-Zionism proved a most useful weapon; Jewish names of liberal intellectuals and of highly placed Party opponents were singled out to convey the picture of a Jewish-Israeli-West German-American conspiracy.

Prominent Party members, parents of students involved in the demonstrations, were purged; reprisals spread to academic and other circles. A number of Jews were driven to emigration and, not surprisingly, they vented their bitterness abroad. Although some of the persecuted individuals had somewhat shaky liberal credentials in the past, others, genuine liberals and non-Jews, were also attacked by the use of slander and base insinuations. This happened to the Catholic writers Stefan Kisielewski and Paweł Jasienica. The poisonous atmosphere grew thicker as Czechoslovakia experienced its Prague Spring and proclaimed socialism with a human face. Gomułka became convinced that changes in Czechoslovakia constituted a danger to communism and to Poland, and he also came to believe in the existence of a link between domestic opposition in Poland and Zionism.

The participation of Polish troops in the invasion of Czechoslovakia may have been unavoidable, but Gomułka's attitude conveyed an impression of Warsaw's eagerness. Thus, at the same time that the anti-Zionist campaign revived Western notions of perennial Polish anti-Semitism, the participation in the invasion recalled the dark days of Munich. Engrossed in a struggle for power, Gomułka and the Party leaders did not hesitate to tarnish the national image and inflict severe moral and political wounds upon the Polish society.

The American press reported in great detail on the events of 1968. While some papers tried to present all facts of the complex situation, others concentrated on the Jewish aspect. It came to overshadow all others, and sometimes all prominent Polish intellectuals locked in struggle with the Gomułka regime were pictured as Jews. Just as some Poles at home were inclined to view the Jewish purges as an internal Party squabble, so some American papers tended frequently to see all the issues in terms of anti-Semitism.

The half-hearted American reaction to the Soviet-led invasion need not concern us here, except as an indication of Washington's inability to assist the East European quest for freedom. As for the New Left and American liberals, their concern with the rape of Czechoslovakia was minimal, which was hardly encouraging to Polish opponents of the regime.

Polish centers abroad made their position perfectly clear. Emigré scholars and those of Polish descent joined with American colleagues in public condemnation of oppressive and discriminatory acts directed against intellectuals, students, and Jews. Arthur Rubinstein, who had combined all his life Polish patriotism with a Jewish identity, appealed to Poland's Communist leaders to end the campaign. The Paris-based *Kultura* devoted particular attention to anti-Semitism, not because it failed to perceive the complexity of all other issues, but because it wished to go on record as condemning policies that were blackening Poland's historic image. *Kultura* also censured the use of Polish troops in Czechoslovakia as a betrayal of the old motto of Polish revolutionaries: "for your freedom and for ours."

Gomułka paid an exorbitant price for his triumph in 1968. His popularity in the country plummeted to its lowest point. Within the Party he was facing the competition of Moczar, who in July became a deputy member of the Politburo. Another contender for power was the head of the largest and most important Party organization in Silesia, Edward Gierek. The Partisans regarded Gomułka as damping Polish nationalism; the younger Party leaders resented his perpetuation of the rule of the old cadre. Gomułka was a spent force allowed to register only one last success in the field of foreign policy: the signing of the important treaty with West Germany.

Chancellor Brandt's *Ost Politik*, aiming at a normalization of West German relations with Soviet Russia and Poland, resulted in the conclusion of a German-Soviet treaty on August 12 and a German-Polish treaty of December 7, 1970. The first article of the latter affirmed that the Odra-Nysa border "shall constitute the western State frontier of the People's Republic of Poland" and asserted the "inviolability of their existing frontiers." The United States, acting jointly with Britain and France, had already notified its approval of the treaty when it was first initiated in mid-November. From the point of view of Poland this was a great achievement, but Gomułka was not destined to profit from the peaceful resolution of German-Polish relations. In late December 1970, shortly before Christmas, the government announced a substantial rise in prices of basic foods. The reaction took the form of a spontaneous movement of protest which quickly transformed itself into a workers' uprising in the Baltic ports of Szczecin, Gdańsk, and Gdynia. The dockers clashed with police, burnt down Party headquarters and fought against tanks. As in 1956 in Poznań, the working class showed its determination and power. The December events made headlines in the American and European press; Radio Free Europe enabled the Poles to learn of the extent of the revolt. Allegedly Gomułka wanted to call in the Soviet troops; if this were true, his policy had run a full circle. Deserted by the Party leadership, perhaps even maneuvered into this hopeless position in the first place, he was forced to resign and make the way for Edward Gierek who became the first secretary of the Party.

Gierek's Poland: The Limits of Détente

In 1971 the Polish People's Republic was a vastly different country from the "new" Poland that had emerged out of war ruins a quarter of a century earlier. There is no doubt that it had gone a long way in the direction of urbanization and industrialization. While in 1945 some 31.8 percent of the population lived in towns, by 1970 the figure had increased to over 50 percent. By 1974 the share of industry in national income reached 67 percent, that of agriculture only 15.5. This drastic transformation had been uneven; heavy industries grew disproportionately faster than those producing consumer goods. Services had lagged behind, and their quality remained low. The Gomułka regime had neglected housing as well as new hospitals, hotels, or restaurants. Health services, medical and dental care, and paid vacations constituted an important postwar gain, and the number of doctors per 1,000 inhabitants increased between 1938 and 1968 four times and that of dentists tripled; on the other hand, the shortage of hospital beds, for instance, was catastrophic. Even though Poland was and is the second largest producer of rye and potatoes in the world, the fourth of sugar, the sixth of milk, and the tenth of meat, food privations continued. The average consumption increased, but so did expectations, and manipulations of prices and wages bred tension; it was after all the sudden rise of basic food prices that was responsible for Gomułka's fall.

Essentially a society in transition characterized by tensions that usually accompany such far-reaching changes, the Polish society was and remains a young society. In 1973 some 64.5 percent were thirty-nine years old or younger, which is almost exactly the situation in America. This is important in order to understand processes that reflect both good and bad features of youth. The decades of Communist leveling-down processes have not made Polish society fully egalitarian or classless. Discrepancies between wages, differences between city-dwellers and peasants, the existence of privileged groups, even remnants of class snobbery have all militated against equality.

The workers have become numerically the most important and powerful stratum, although like other social groups they have not yet fully developed their own ethos and characteristics. A large percentage of the working class consists of villagers who have only recently moved into the industrial environment and lack the traditions of prewar proletariat. There is also the subgroup of peasant-workers. A frequently inefficient system of incentives has been partly responsible for absenteeism, neglect, waste, and low productivity. As a social group the workers are still evolving in the direction of fuller self-identity.

The peasants' living conditions had improved in the Gomułka era. For example, over 90 percent of the farms have acquired electricity, and an extended network of communications had alleviated the problem of isolation of villages. At the same time the peasants had been excluded from social and health insurance and, although reassured about collectivization, remained insecure about their rights to the land. As a group they appear even today as halfway between old-fashioned peasants and modern farmers.

Polish intelligentsia had significantly changed from its prewar predecessor, distinguished by a traditional humanist-shaped outlook and gentry-inherited patterns of value and behavior. Within the new intelligentsia a technological and managerial group constitutes the majority, although the creative component—roughly equivalent to Western intellectuals—has retained its importance as the carrier and defender of national tradition against both technological modernization and cultural "sovietization." Common concern about the preservation of a Polish way of life has brought the intellectuals closer, though not necessarily in religious terms, to the Catholic church.

Members of the younger generation, especially the half million or so university and college students, are a dynamic force; but having been repeatedly disillusioned and deceived, they have shown symptoms of being a "polluted generation," as a Polish journalist put it. Yet the young may have also learned to hide their latent idealism under a mask of cynicism and egoism. Their real outlook at the beginning of the 1970s could not be easily ascertained or surmised.

In postwar Poland there has been an impressive growth of mass culture, accompanied by serious restraints under which cultural activities had to operate. The state had done good work in the 1950s and 1960s by making the products of culture available to the bulk of the population. Even the smallest localities could boast public libraries and bookstores; the number of theaters, orchestras, recreational-cultural facilities had increased greatly. Polish theater and film, visual arts, literature, and music had made great strides in the post-October period. In music composer-directors Krzysztof Penderecki and Witold Lutosławski have gained world fame. The Warsaw Autumn Festival and the Chopin and Wieniawski international competitions have attracted wide attention. Several stage and film producers, to mention only Kazimierz Wajda and Roman Polański, became familiar names on both sides of the Atlantic. In literature, the science-fiction writings of Stanisław Lem appeared in English translation in America. But as vigorous and original as Polish contributions in the cultural sphere had been, the ideological restraints affected them again and again under Gomułka's regime. Whether Gierek's attitude to culture would basically differ from that of his predecessor was not yet clear in 1971.

In the field of education, particularly higher education, quantitative progress was most noticeable. The eighty-nine universities and colleges compared very favorably with the thirty-two under the Second Republic, although a postwar proliferation of higher schools was by no means a uniquely Polish or East European phenomenon. In Poland, the emphasis was on technical and professional colleges that have produced specialists needed in the ongoing modernization process. Thus, for instance, technical universities grew from three to eighteen; medical schools from one to ten. This shift from a traditionally humanistically-oriented higher education was bound to have definite repercussions on the cultural life of the country, and taken in conjunction with all other trends, socioeconomic and political, deeply affect Poland's outlook.

An observer of the Polish scene in the early 1970s could not fail to notice certain dichotomies or contradictions inherent in it. The socialist system had liberated social forces which could become its driving force, yet it had to prevent their assertion lest they threaten the ruling regime. Assuming continuing modernization and growth of technology, could a technocratic elite efficiently run a modern industrial society without a good deal of autonomy that could endanger the decision-making process of the Party? In view of the gap between the prevailing political culture and the official state ideology, no longer believed in even by its spokesmen, what constituted the justification of the regime and its claim to legitimacy? Finally, there seemed no satisfactory solution to the dilemma that Polish culture was basically Western yet had to operate within an Eastern, Soviet bloc.

Edward Gierek was fifty-seven years old when he became Poland's leader. He had the reputation of an efficient, tough, and able administrator, and having lived for many years in France and Belgium—he returned home only in 1948—was regarded as the least parochial and most Western of the Communist leaders. His advent did not produce the euphoria that had accompanied Gomułka's rise in 1956, but many Poles believed that Gierek would introduce a new, more pragmatic style and be more conscious of the challenges of the "technotronic age."

Gierek faced multiple problems. In the field of politics he had to assert himself as the undisputed leader of the Party and reaffirm the Party's primacy. This required the elimination of factionalism on the top, especially of Moczar, and a general streamlining of the Party's organization. The second was not easy, for as a Polish sociologist, Jan Szczepański, had written, there had been "too few safeguards against negative selection of Party members." Then there was the dualism of Party and administration, which resulted in a blurring of responsibilities and made a Polish writer ask in the spring of 1971: "Where is the locus of power, in the sejm or in the Central Committee?" If the dualism was to be overcome, should it be by a greater or lesser involvement of the Party in political-administrative matters? No simple answer was available. In spite of the Party's overwhelming might one could not entirely dismiss other forces in society, organized and unorganized. The Catholic church was obviously one of them, and Szczepański also observed that political organizations of the emigrés with their press, radio, and programs could "be regarded as a substitute for an opposition party."

Gierek did not promise immediate improvements and appealed for a concerted effort to pursue economic growth and achieve better living conditions. To create a receptive atmosphere in the country he sought to conciliate workers through personal encounters; his phrase "help me" indicated a departure from Gomułka's authoritarian manner. To win over the peasants, he extended to them in 1971 the benefits of health insurance, replaced compulsory deliveries by contracts, and introduced measures regulating property deeds, inheritance, and sale of land. Consequently, the peasantry regained a little of the confidence undermined in the last years of Gomułka's rule. There was some improvement in church-state relations, notably in the fiscal domain, and recognition of legal ownership of church lands in the western territories. All these moves indicated a pragmatic approach. With regard to the economic model, Gierek gradually introduced the so-called small reforms, which significantly enlarged the scope for the initiative and managerial autonomy of key industry enterprises and asserted the principle of efficiency and remuneration for achievements. The Polish government attempted to reassure the people that their needs would not be neglected. The slogan of building a "second Poland" held out the promise of a gigantic program of housing construction; the propagandization of one-family houses and private cars was meant to mobilize private capital that existed in the country but was not fully utilized.

Gierek's policies of rapid economic growth and modernization were to be promoted through an import of foreign technology and credits and vastly expanded trade, and indeed under the 1971–1975 Five-Year Plan the country moved rapidly ahead. One must remember, however, that the greatest accomplishments came at the beginning and that Warsaw had received important Soviet aid. A few figures might illustrate the progress achieved. National income increased by 60 percent, and industrial production by over 73. The level of investment stood at roughly 20 percent annually, and real wages increased annually by 8 percent. The growth in agriculture between 1971 and 1975 was roughly 22 percent. The production of hard coal rose from 145 to 172 million tons (which put Poland in fourth place in the world); that of steel from 11.8 to 15.1 (tenth place). Copper output grew from 92.7 to 249 million (seventh place). Poland came to occupy third place in the world in the production of sulphur and seventh in zinc. Building of trucks and locomotives constituted an important area of production, as did shipbuilding. In the construction of sea-going fishing vessels Poland came to rival Japan for first place in the World. During the Five-Year Plan impressive advances were made in the newer branches of production: the chemical and petrochemical industry, the car industry, and electric and electronic machinery. The last had already in 1970 accounted for some 45 percent of Polish output. The total cargo handled in Polish ports—Gdańsk, Gdynia, Szczecin, and

Kołobrzeg—rose from 36.6 million tons in 1970 to 56 million in 1975, and the construction of the Northern Port was a success.

The most staggering expansion took place in foreign trade, which in 1974 accounted for 22 percent of the country's gross national product. Polish exports grew by 153 percent, indicating the important role they played in the economic development. Even so, a greater increase seemed imperative, for the value of foreign trade per inhabitant in Poland compared unfavorably with that of the western industrial states—it was less than half of that of Italy and only one fifth of that of West Germany in 1950–1970. In the mid-1970s the value of trade turnover per inhabitant placed Poland in eighteenth place in exports and twenty-first in imports.

Capitalizing on the fact that Polish foreign indebtedness under Gomułka had been small and that international détente acted as a protective umbrella for dealings with the West, Gierek seized the opportunity for attracting American capital and technology and stimulating trade relations. A phase of close American-Polish economic involvement began. Politics were pushed into the background, although ultimately they continued to provide the rationale for American economic diplomacy toward Poland.

Highlighted by Nixon's one-day stay in Warsaw in May 1972 and Gierek's visit to the United States in October 1974, economic cooperation between the two countries increased dramatically. It manifested itself in such areas as credits, volume of trade and its changing patterns, institutionalized collaboration, and even joint ventures. Already toward the end of 1970 the assistant secretary for economic affairs noted a new situation in Eastern Europe arising out of Bonn's treaties with Moscow and Warsaw. He urged American businessmen to give serious thought to opportunities available for commerce and quoted the opinion of the exiled reformist Czech economic expert, Ota Šik, that trade with the West was working for internal liberalization of Communist countries. The National Planning Association and the Committee on Economic Development overcame their past misgivings about expanded relations with the Eastern Bloc and came out strongly in their favor. Nixon spoke in the same vein in his report to the Congress in 1971 and found a receptive audience. In 1971 an amendment to the Export-Import Bank Act authorized a resumption of loans, and the Nixon-Gierek talks in Warsaw proved a turning point in subsequent credit operations. An arrangement was made granting Poland extensions in repayment for the agricultural commodities furnished under PL 480. From 1973 new credits were made available, involving in 1973–1974 some forty projects totalling up to $300 million. During the same year the Commodity Credit Corporation underwrote exports of goods valued at $32 million.

The increase in turnover can be seen in the following figures (in millions of dollars):

	U.S. EXPORTS TO POLAND	U.S. IMPORTS FROM POLAND
1971	73.3	107.6
1972	113.6	139.2
1973	350.0	182.9
1974	395.6	265.9

Poland earned additional amounts of dollars through tourism and transfers by individuals (some $50 million in 1971), but began to have an unfavorable balance of trade with the United States after 1973. The Polish share in the total American imports remained 0.3 percent; the percentage of exports to Poland, however, doubled from 0.2 to 0.4 percent. From the Polish point of view the American share represented 2.4 percent of total Polish imports in 1974.

The basic transformation of Poland's economy was only partly and slowly reflected in foreign trade. In 1972, when the export of American technology just began, the trade between the two countries was still predominantly (85 percent) in agricultural and food articles. Chief Polish exports were ham, canned meats, and vodka; United States exports comprised wheat, soya beans, corn, fats, and hides. In 1973 machinery and industrial equipment made up only 12.1 percent of U.S. exports; but on the Polish side coal, steel, and zinc rose to 35.4 percent, and consumer goods (clothing, glassware, furniture) to 21.8 percent. Since 1973 some 30 percent of American exports consisted of machinery and industrial equipment, including turn-key plants, and were valued between 1973 and 1975 at $300 million. The Poles in turn began to sell sohpisticated electromechanical products, for which the United States became the second best customer in the West. For example, Americans placed an order in Polish shipyards for two liquified-gas tankers valued at $100 million.

Gierek's visit in 1974 marked a further expansion of economic relations. A headline in the *New York Times* on October 11 announced that "Poland Basks in Stability and Economic Prosperity," and the paper carried a full-page advertisement of Morgan Guarantee banking services in Eastern Europe together with a photograph of Gierek conferring with Morgan officials. Several accords were initialed: on joint funding of cooperative scientific and technological projects (up to $54 million), on cooperative research on methods of coal extraction, on double taxation, on collaboration in medicine and health care, and in environmental protection. A joint statement on agricultural trade spoke of three-year advance projections on crops and import needs. Both sides agreed to set up a joint economic council. As a State Department spokesman emphasized, these agreements would create more comprehensive cooperation between the United States and Poland than with any Communist country, the Soviet Union excepted.

Trade and cooperation were the key words. It was projected that American-Polish turnover would reach the figure of $1 billion by 1976 and $2 billion in 1980. Cooperation was institutionalized in a United States-Polish Trade Commission set up after Nixon's visit, and complemented by a U.S. Trade Development Center in Warsaw, the first of its kind in Eastern Europe. Operating under the auspices of the Department of Commerce, it was to assist Americans seeking business opportunities in Poland. A new Polish-American Economic Council resulting from Gierek-Ford agreements came into being in January 1975. Primarily a channel of communication, it was concerned more with policy formulation than actual promotion of trade. The American side was represented by the Chamber of Commerce, the Polish side by the Chamber of Foreign Trade. Other agreements that followed in 1975 included a protocol on commercial, industrial, and technical cooperation and an accord on the settlement of prewar Polish bonds on the American market. Nine types of bonds were affected (among others the 1920 loan, the 1927 stabilization loan, and the Silesian loan of 1928). The First National Bank of Chicago, the First National City Bank, Irving Trust Company, and Dillon, Read and Company assumed responsibility for the operation.

A detailed presentation of American-Polish business activities could easily become a catalog of names and agreements. A special bilingual issue of the Polish publication *Handel Zagraniczny* (Foreign Trade) of 1975 was entirely devoted to these transactions and contained a great deal of data. To provide a few illustrations of the American economic involvement in Poland, let us mention the principal types of activity and the main participants. Credit agreements were concluded between the Polish Bank Handlowy and several American banks. The First National Bank of Chicago was the first to set up a Warsaw branch. In 1972 only one American private firm had its office in Poland; by 1975 there were fifteen. Among companies active in Poland were: International Harvester, Clark Equipment Company, U.S. Steel Corporation, Singer, Westinghouse, Koehring, Allen Scott and Company, Swindler-Dressler, and Textron. In 1973 a joint venture Toolmex Corporation with headquarters in Washington came into existence. In general, American technology was made available to Poland in the form of licenses or agreements on joint production and sometimes sales. In several instances entire works, as for instance the copper rolling mills near Katowice, were constructed under American supervision. Joint ventures involved the training of Polish engineers in America and prolonged stays of American technical personnel in Poland. While most of the activities affected heavy industries, other areas were also explored. Among them we may single out the construction of a Holiday Inn in Cracow. Modernization involved expansion of old facilities and construction of new ones—the export of up-to-date technology being regarded as the main answer to Poland's economic progress.

Before exploring the connection between détente, economic involvement, and internal liberalization, a few words still need to be said about American-Polish cultural exchanges. As in the Gomułka period, they operated on various levels and took divergent forms; there were also some new departures. In 1973–1974 the Lincoln Lectureship program was launched in which Poles were included. In 1976 Fulbright-Hays fellowships became applicable to Poland. Because of frequent changes, the extent of inter-university exchanges is hard to estimate, but it is likely that they have grown in volume. The number of man-months allotted to Poland under the IREX (International Research and Exchanges Board) agreement has increased, although figures published by IREX indicate that numerically the American-Polish exchanges still trail behind those between the United States and Yugoslavia. Reports on exchanges issued by the Board of Foreign Scholarships, operating under the Fulbright-Hays Act of 1961, provide a good deal of data, but its analysis would transcend the limits of this study. Generally, one might conclude that cultural cooperation has proved very fruitful, although the Polish side has often been more interested in sending out scientists and graduates of professional schools than humanists; on the American side opportunities have not been fully exploited in the mid-1970s because of diminishing federal funding.

As compared to other Eastern Bloc nationals, Poles have traveled quite freely and extensively to the United States. This has been not only a cultural experience for them but has diminished the feeling of claustrophobia so characteristic of the Stalinist period. The resumption of regular communication by sea and the inauguration of direct New York-Warsaw flights by Pan-American and Lot symbolizes closer contacts. In the summer of 1976, eighteen Polish bishops led by Cardinal Karol Wojtyła (elected Pope John Paul II in 1978) came to the United States to attend an International Eucharistic Congress, and toured many Polish American centers. It was an event unparalleled in the past.

Interest in American studies at Polish universities and research centers was reflected among others in the publication of the first book in Polish on American diplomatic history. Although in 1972 there still appeared propagandistic works stressing the aggressive tendencies in United States foreign policy, genuine scholarly interest in the American field and especially in the Polonia has been growing.

To assess the seven years to date of Gierek's rule, we need a closer look at the difficulties that began to accumulate beginning roughly in 1973–1974. The gigantic effort made to produce more with the help of foreign credits and technology, and to export more in order to repay debts and accelerate the modernization process, was bound to produce a temporary disequilibrium between production and the consumers' needs and put a strain on the country's economy. The already mentioned 153 percent growth in Polish exports was to be followed by another 80 percent increase planned for the 1976–1980 period. Imports, however, grew at an even higher rate—196 percent—and Polish foreign indebtedness skyrocketed. According to some calculations it stood at well over $8 billion in 1976, a good part of it in debt to the United States. Some of the causes were beyond Poland's control: for instance, the oil crisis of 1973 and the subsequent sharp rise of prices of raw materials. The rampant inflation in the West, America included, began to spread into Poland, adversely affecting the terms of trade and domestic living standards. The question to what extent Polish trade with the Eastern Bloc, particularly Soviet Russia, has assisted and how far it has complicated economic developments in the country cannot be satisfactorily discussed here. One can point out, however, that while Russia has been a very important market for Polish exports and had on occasion extended credits to Warsaw, it has continued to exploit Poland economically in a number of ways. Nor must one forget that as an economic partner of Russia, Poland has been always at a severe disadvantage, being dependent on the USSR for virtually all natural gas, 77 percent of oil, and 80 percent of iron ore.

Another setback was the severe drought of 1974–1975, which proved catastrophic for a meat-exporting country. Inflationary trends combined with severe shortages of meat and other foods on the domestic market. For a population which had experienced some improvements at the beginning of Gierek's era this meant the crushing of inflated hopes and genuine difficulties.

Acting on the assumption that it would cost the country less in the long run to produce more steel in order to satisfy domestic consumption than to import it, Gierek decided on the construction of new huge steel works—Huta Katowice—which received top priority and contributed to a dislocation of resources, indeed threatening a breakdown of the Five-Year Plan. This development has also played a role in whipping up discontent. In addition, the need to operate within two diametrically different price structures—one governing foreign trade with the West, the other domestic relations—produced constant contradictions.

A combination of all these factors led to a crisis situation, and Gierek may have been guilty of two fundamental mistakes in his policies. The first, more basic and of longer standing, was the failure to match economic pragmatism with political liberalization. The Poles understood the need of constantly conciliating the Soviet Union and realized that there were limits to domestic freedoms, but they came to be outraged by the fact that Gierek was going much farther than seemed necessary. Secondly, in dealing with the economic crisis, Gierek has sought to overcome it by political means, resorting to "neo-Stalinism without terror," as an emigré writer called it—a contradiction in terms. In both cases, he was guilty of misjudging the Polish national character, for greater freedom was an important element in the sustained economic effort, and the Poles might have accepted economic hardships (more readily) if reassured that national values were not endangered.

Gierek was successful in gaining complete control over the Party in the sense of eliminating potential rivals, first Moczar and then other contenders. An administrative reform in 1975, which roughly doubled the number of *województwa* (provinces), was principally designed to diminish the power of provincial Party bosses. The Party gained in efficiency but in the process became more sovietized. When an ideological offensive was resumed, though different in tone from those in the past, it was still widely perceived as an attempt at greater orthodoxy and subservience to Soviet Russia. Other forms of streamlining appeared ominous and contrary to inbred Polish individualism. Youth organizations were unified and subordinated to Party controls. Gierek's remarks on the need for closer ties between private farmers and planned economy brought out the old fears of collectivization of agriculture. Pressures on the lay Catholic groups increased and, while the regime tried to exploit the Vatican's "eastern policy" to promote a church-state détente, it showed little willingness to be more conciliatory toward the Polish ecclesiastical hierarchy. In fact, a top Party official singled out the "reactionary wing of Polish episcopate" as the "main organized anti-socialist power in our country."

Indeed, it was in the sphere of culture and preservation of national tradition that the Gierek regime showed least imagination or understanding. Proposed educational reforms carried with them the danger of undermining the humanist tradition of Polish culture, and policies of censorship and interference with intellectual freedoms produced tensions. Historical works blamed for nationalist interpretations were censored, and the chairman of the State Council, Henryk Jabłoński, publicly admonished his fellow historians in 1973 about the primacy of "historical materialism." The Soviet ambassador in Warsaw, Stanislav Pilotovich, assuming proconsular poses reminiscent of Russian envoys during the period of Polish partitions, proved particularly active in meddling in Polish cultural affairs. Polish national pride was further offended when Gierek decorated Brezhnev with the prestigious Polish military cross Virtuti Militari. Castigating certain aspects of Gierek's cultural policies in 1974, Cardinal Wyszyński demanded the Poles' right "to live in accordance with the spirit, history, culture and language of our own Polish land."

A growing opposition of Polish intellectuals became particularly noticeable in 1974–1975. In connection with governmental interest in Poles abroad, including American Polonia, a letter by Słonimski accompanied by fifteen signatures expressed concern about the fate of the "forgotten" Poles living in the Soviet Union. In a letter printed in Paris Kisielewski denounced falsifications in history textbooks. The accumulated anger came to the surface when in late 1975 the Party revealed its intentions to introduce far-reaching changes in the Polish constitution. While largely of declaratory character and stemming possibly from a desire to gain further blessings from the Kremlin, the proposed amendments appeared ominous. Poland was to be named a Socialist Republic (marking closer affinity with the Soviet model), the directing role of the Party and Poland's fraternal bond with the USSR were to be embodied in the constitution, and civic rights made virtually conditional upon fulfillment of duties toward the fatherland.

The proposals evoked a storm of protests against what was regarded as official limitations on Polish sovereignty and citizens' rights. In December 1975 the senior economist Lipiński sponsored a letter of 59 intellectuals calling for greater freedoms; in January 1976 Cardinal Wyszyński spoke out; a flood of open letters followed. The Party was forced to water down the changes. Poland remained a People's Republic; the phrase about Russia spoke only of "friendship and cooperation"; the Party was called the "leading political force in Society"; and the article about civic rights was dropped. Only one deputy, Stomma, the leader of the Catholic Znak, abstained from the vote, which cost him the seat in the next sejm. A new *Znak*—the usurped name is contested by its former leaders—came to the fore as a parliamentary Catholic representation more amenable to Gierek's policies.

Forced to compromise, the Party took revenge on the protesters by resorting to chicaneries and discriminations, which provoked new protests. Cardinal Wyszyński warned against reprisals. In an open letter to Gierek, Lipiński stated that the "imposition of the Soviet system has devastated our social and moral life," and described the reassertion of Polish sovereignty as essential. Gomułka's former collaborator, Władysław Bieńkowski, struck out at the Russian envoy for doing incalculable harm to Polish-Soviet cooperation. The authors of these letters were veteran Socialists or Communists who had fought for a truly people's Poland all their lives. But manifestations of bitter criticsm came also from the younger generaton and students. A clandestine Program of the Polish Coalition for Independence (PPN) was circulated.

Because of this convergence of economic and political tensions, the Party should have behaved with utmost caution, yet in June 1976 it announced a drastic rise of prices for meat, butter, sugar, and other basic articles. As in December 1970, the reaction of the working class was instantaneous. Many great factories came to a standstill, and in Radom and Ursus the workers went into the streets and battled with the police. Party headquarters in Radom were burnt down. Gierek was wise enough not to repeat Gomułka's errors; within twenty-four hours the offending price increases were withdrawn and the police were forbidden to use firearms. Thus bloodshed was avoided but not police brutality, and workers in unknown numbers were dismissed, some imprisoned, still others convicted after hastily held trials. The workers' plight produced a phenomenon without precedent in postwar Poland—the emergence of a united front of workers, intellectuals, and the church. The Workers' Defense Committee (KOR) headed by Lipiński, was set up to collect funds for the jobless workers and their families, an initiative fully endorsed by Cardinal Wyszyński. In a series of new letters protesting the persecution of workers, the signatures of popular Polish artists and singers appeared beside those of other representatives of the creative intelligentsia.

As the year 1976 came to its end, the situation remained tense and the future uncertain and dangerous. Gierek's visit to Moscow resulted in promises of economic assistance together with demonstrative statements of mutual solidarity, but the ambitious Five-Year Plan for 1976–1980 outlined by Gierek at the Seventh Party Congress had to be revised and the foreseen increase of GNP by 28 percent, of industrial production by 33 percent, and of agriculture by 15 percent curtailed. At the time of the Congress the *New York Times* correspondent commented that the Polish leadership hoped that by 1980 "food queues will have disappeared, housing will be plentiful, washing machines available for all, traffic jams an everyday occurrence and Poland will be a major European industrial power." These hopes now seem unrealistic. A series of measures called New Economic Maneuver was adopted at the end of 1976, but it did not help to improve the economic situation. While some concessions to consumers were made, meat remained extremely scarce and other shortages continued to exasperate the Poles. Once again private initiative was encouraged, notably by extension of social and health services to the craftsmen, but uncertainty about long-range trends prevented a genuine development of services. Although prices were officially kept down, hidden rises and inflationary trends continued. The Central Committee in reviewing the economic situation in October 1977 sounded a somber note, and at the Party conference in January 1978 Gierek criticized inefficiency and bottlenecks in Polish economy. The foreign indebtedness evaluated in 1978 as between $12 and $14 billion is staggering, and modern technology has provided no immediate solution. The planners hope that cattle breeding on an extensive scale will improve the situation in the years to come, but until now a large part of arable land still lies fallow.

How can the crushing debts to the West be repaid at a time of rising cost for raw materials and continuing unfavorable terms of foreign trade? Even expanded coal exports (Poland is already the second largest exporter in the world) or new discoveries of natural gas deposits and sulphur would require time before Poland could cash in on them. Continued price increases appear unavoidable, as do days of austerity that Gierek will have to persuade the people to accept. Yet without massive and imaginative assistance on the part of the United States the country's outlook is likely to be bleaker.

To turn to American-Polish political relations within the context of détente, President Richard Nixon, who captured a sizable Polish American vote in the elections, adopted a low-key attitude toward Warsaw. After his visit to Poland in 1972 he announced that the United States did not wish to complicate the relations of East European states with their allies. It was up to them "to determine the pace and scope of their developing relations with the United States." Shortly thereafter a new American consulate was set up in Poland, although in Cracow rather than in the western territories perhaps because the United States has recognized the Odra-Nysa border *de facto* but not *de jure*. Newly appointed ambassadors assumed their respective posts: Witold Trąmpczyński, a prominent economist, in Washington; Richard Davies, an old hand in Polish affairs, in Warsaw. Gierek's visit to the United States in 1974 marked the first time a Communist party chief was received at the White House, Soviet dignitaries excepted. A long interview with Gierek in the *Washington Post* was also unprecedented; his remarks were well received and sounded persuasive to American journalists. The *New York Times* described Gierek in Washington as "Mr. Brezhnev's alter ego," which enhanced his importance in American eyes. The paper wrote that, speaking internationally, "Mr. Gierek's position is the envy of Eastern Europe," implying that the Polish way merited American approval and could serve as an example to other states of the bloc. As for Polish-American relations, they were characterized as "better than ever before."

President Gerald Ford, the press, and business circles went out of their way to show respect to Gierek and interest in People's Poland. A twenty-one gun salute, reserved for heads of state, was fired at the ceremonies on the White House lawn. The *New York Times* established another precedent by giving space to a Polish journalist, Mieczysław Rakowski, for an analysis of the Polish situation. Other media, however, devoted less attention to Gierek, and the CBS network largely ignored the Polish visitor.

On the whole Gierek handled his speeches and press conferences adroitly. At the General Assembly of the United Nations he mentioned the contribution of the smaller countries to détente and voiced his support for a permanent security system in Europe that would overcome the need for existing blocs. In his replies to journalists he even indicated the possibility of resuming diplomatic relations with Israel, the existence of which, he said, Poland had always supported. Friendly ties between the United States and Poland were mentioned both by Gierek and Ford, who also made customary references to Polish settlers in Jamestown, Kościuszko and Washington. Gierek traveled to New York, Jamestown, and Pittsburgh, visiting in the last city the university that has been involved in academic exchanges with Poland.

Gierek extended an invitation to the president to come to Poland, and the visit eventually took place in July 1975 when Ford was on his way to the Helsinki Conference. Ford visited Warsaw, Cracow, and the former Oświęcim (Auschwitz) Nazi concentration camp. Both sides exchanged cordial words, and Gierek lavishly praised Ford as a partner in the search for world détente and security. While the State Department officials commented on the president's stop in Poland—and his later visits to Rumania and Yugoslavia— as a sign of encouragement given to the three countries "least subservient to Moscow," it is doubtful if the Poles understood Ford's visit in those terms.

American journalists reported on "polite but undemonstrative" crowds that lined the streets of Warsaw. "Restrained Warmth Greets President in Poland" was the headline in the *Washington Post.* The spontaneous enthusiasm that had accompanied the visits of Nixon and Robert Kennedy was absent. Apparently Ford had not projected the image of a forceful or imaginative statesman that would appeal to the Poles. Besides, the Helsinki Conference he was about to attend was advantageous to Poland only insofar as it reaffirmed the inviolability of borders. But if this was welcome with regard to the German-Polish frontier, it was more significant as a recognition of Soviet territorial acquisitions. Solzhenitsyn, for one, denounced Helsinki as an American sellout of eastern Europe, a view shared by some Polish intellectuals. The somewhat illusory Basket Three declaration about free flow of ideas evoked skepticism.

The real thinking of the State Department on Poland, within the general East European context, was revealed dramatically through a press leak in early 1976. A news item appeared about a conference of United States ambassadors in Europe held in London in December 1975, where Secretary Kissinger's spokesman, Helmut Sonnenfeldt, presented a policy analysis subsequently dubbed the Sonnenfeldt Doctrine. As in the case of containment, it is less important what its author really meant than what the "doctrine" was understood to imply and how far it squared with American diplomacy.

The Sonnenfeldt Doctrine recognized the inflammable nature of the East European situation and its potential danger to international peace. It referred to Soviet inability of ruling the region by means other than force as "doubly tragic" and implied dissatisfaction with East European nationalism, which in the Yugoslav case was "obnoxious" toward Soviet Russia. Sonnenfeldt used a particularly unhappy expression—"organic relationship"—when describing the kind of ties between Soviet Russia and Eastern Europe the United States would like to encourage. Since he asserted that Eastern Europe was within the Soviet "scope and area of natural interest," his phrase sounded less like a preference for a more imaginative and liberal Russian treatment of the area and more like an advocacy of a more structured and streamlined system of controls. Given the existence of the Warsaw Pact, CEMA, and the network of bilateral alliances—in Poland's case, with the USSR (1965), Czechoslovakia, the German Democratic Republic, and Bulgaria (1967), Hungary (1968), and Rumania (1970)—the notion of more "organic unity" could be understood as a green light to Russia to proceed with further amalgamation of the region.

While Sonnenfeldt was concerned lest East European states rock the boat of East-West relations, he also defined American policy as one of responding to "clearly visible aspirations in Eastern Europe for a more autonomous existence within the context of a strong Soviet geopolitical influence." Poland was cited as an example: "This has worked in Poland. The Poles have been able to overcome their romantic political inclinations which led to their disasters in the past. They have been skillfully developing a policy that is satisfying their needs for a national identity without arousing Soviet reactions. It is a long process."

The Sonnenfeldt statement, coming in the year of presidential elections, embarrassed the administration and provoked a heated debate. Washington, and especially Kissinger, were accused of betraying the East European nations and counseling them to make the best of Soviet rule. President Ford's political rival, Ronald Reagan, denounced such a policy in strong and demagogic terms. Meeting with forty-two leaders of ethnic organizations of the Milwaukee area, Ford stated emphatically that "Our policy in no sense—and I emphasize, in no sense—accepts Soviet dominion of Eastern Europe." The president added that the United States strongly supported "aspirations for freedom, for national independence of peoples everywhere, including the peoples of Eastern Europe." These public pronouncements did not allay suspicions; several Polish circles abroad and in the homeland resented the accolade bestowed on the Gierek regime at a time when it prepared changes of the Polish constitution that were to bring Poland closer (organically?) to the USSR.

The Sonnenfeldt Doctrine was not strikingly novel when seen against the background of American diplomacy, and it fitted well into the context of détente. In the sense of relaxation of tensions between the West and the East, détente is not a new phenomenon either. Periodic easing of tensions had occurred earlier. In the 1970s, however, détente had acquired the meaning of a formalized, almost institutionalized relationship based on the idea that reduction of tension and removal of threats of confrontation amounted to a new theory of international relations. Indeed the 1970s saw a series of West-East agreements: in 1971 on Berlin, in 1973 on Vietnam, in 1974 on SALT, and finally in 1973 and 1975 at Helsinki. Several of these accords registered mutual gains or at least constituted a recognition of the fact that no other means for settling differences were currently available. At the same time it was imperfectly understood that détente also reflected some wishful thinking combined with a post-Vietnam and Watergate malaise. Vietnam had sapped American beliefs not only in the United States' ability to intervene effectively in foreign matters but even its right to do so. A Gallup opinion poll in May 1975 showed that only 37 percent of respondents would favor sending American troops to defend Britain against a communist-backed force; in the case of West Germany the figure was only 27 percent. If this were true for the two nations long considered pivotal to United States security, other states could not expect much of America. From the point of view of Eastern Europe this was highly instructive.

To bring about the abatement of tensions, certain American politicians, to mention only Senator Fulbright, tended to consider unilateral concessions worthwhile and again attacked Radio Free Europe as a relic of the Cold War. The argument prevailed that relaxation of tensions was not tantamount to discarding all propaganda weapons by the American side; the radio was saved, but its activities were drastically curtailed. In the words of Eugene Rostow, an "acute dissonance in the nation between what we thought and what we did in the name of foreign policy" contributed to a proliferation of foreign policy trends in the country. Rostow singled out eight: world government utopians, isolationists, balance-of-powerites, all-out anticommunists, adherents of realpolitik, pacifists, Communists and fellow-travelers, and missionaries of democracy (neo-Wilsonians). Small wonder that no coherent theory of American foreign policy could emerge and appeal to the country. The post-Vietnam era increasingly witnessed the growth of a belief that the objective of the United States' policy was not to transform domestic political systems but rather foreign policies of other countries. The intimate connection between the two was not always perceived. The linking of economic aid with specific provisions, as for example allowing emigration of Jews from Russia, constituted a case apart.

While détente, as mentioned earlier, provided an umbrella for Gierek's economic intercourse with the West, its effects for Poland were somewhat mixed. As the *Christian Science Monitor* observed in an astute article of July 1975 entitled "What Detente Means to Poland's Man in the Street," it has been "confusing" and it "comes in contrasts." Idealistic visions of détente as a panacea evoked highly critical comments in the emigré publications. As for Polish intellectuals, the views expressed by a Finnish political affairs analyst in the May-June 1975 *Freedom at Issue* might have well represented their opinions. The Finn wrote: "My confidence in American power is utterly destroyed. A country that does not know how to use the enormous power it has, has none . . . The disintegration of the morale of the American political establishment and the crisis of self-confidence which is rocking the whole American people does not augur well for the outcome of America's détente policies."

Détente, like other similar concepts, lends itself easily to different interpretations, and the official Polish definition of it followed by and large that of Moscow. To the USSR détente has seemed doubly beneficial, for it promoted stability on the intergovernmental level and brought in economic advantages, while permitting an ideological offensive. Domestically, far from promoting liberalization, it was seen as requiring increased ideological vigilance. Détente, Rakowski wrote in his book, *The Foreign Policy of the Polish People's Republic* (published in 1975 in English), "does not eliminate the historical contradiction between socialism and capitalism." While regarding détente as a welcome and lasting trend in international relations, the author warned against Western attempts to exploit it for their ends. Poland's place in the ongoing struggle against imperialist aggression was made clear, as well as its active support for national liberation movements and communism in the West and the Third World. These passages revealed the minimal degree of autonomy of Polish foreign policy. The days of the Rapacki Plan were gone and, while Warsaw was able to improve relations with West European states and advocated—in Premier Piotr Jaroszewicz's words—a "totality of integrational undertakings" within the Eastern Bloc, it had no means of influencing great power politics.

The 1976 presidential campaign in the United States and the victory of Jimmy Carter appeared to signal new departures in American diplomacy. Ford's slip in one of the public debates, when he alleged that Poland did not consider itself under Soviet domination, should not be construed to imply a basic difference of opinions between him and Carter, but the new administration brought a different style to East-West relations. It also put new emphasis on respect of human rights. The appointment of Polish-born Zbigniew Brzezinski as the presidential national security advisor, highly gratifying to the Polish ego, brought in greater East European expertise to the White House. In a speech given in Montreal in May 1975 Brzezinski stated his preference for détente. "The continuation of the cold war," he said, "heightened tensions between America and the Soviet Union, will narrow the margin of freedom and the opportunities for change in Poland." This sounded very reasonable as a general assumption, although Brzezinski doubtless realized that there was no direct and immediate correlation between détente and greater domestic freedoms. In his speech Brzezinski outlined four possible models for future Polish developments: (1) a return to the pre-1939 independence which he deemed unlikely except in the case of complete Soviet collapse; (2) relative independence that could result from evolutionary processes in Russia and a "Western policy which would encourage closer relations between Eastern and Western Europe without precipitating countervailing Soviet responses"; (3) maintenance of the present situation, and finally (4) absorption of Poland by the Soviet Union, presumably accompanied "by a major weakening of the West and particularly, by American disengagement from Europe." Brzezinski concluded by saying that the second alternative, a relatively independent Poland, was an attainable goal and implied that the United States could contribute to its realization.

Throughout 1977 and early 1978 Carter's adherence to the human rights program appeared to be mostly verbal. That, and the differences between the more determined Brzezinski and the cautious Secretary Cyrus Vance made people wonder about the real direction of American foreign policy. Carter's visit to Warsaw in late December 1977 resulted in promises of additional economic aid (grains) but the presidential press conference and Mrs. Carter's and Brzezinski's meeting with Cardinal Wyszyński produced no great impression on the Poles. The president handled the human rights issue with caution, on the whole lauding Gierek and the Polish regime.

It is true that at present there are no political prisoners in Poland but existing tensions and difficulties are in no way nearing a solution. Church-Party relations have great ups and downs, and it is too early to say how the election of the new pope will affect them. There was a KOR-Party confrontation in early 1977 that led to the arrest of a number of KOR leaders; they were, however, released in July. The KOR (transforming itself into a Committee for Social Self Defense), the newer Movement for the Defense of Human and Civil Rights (ROPCiO), the Students' Solidarity Committee, and the secret Polish Coalition for Independence (PPN) have shown much activity. A "flying university" came into existence to give lectures, among others on such taboo subjects as the history of the Polish People's Republic. Wide-ranging (from political journals and pamphlets to literary works) Samizdat-type literature has been spreading and unlike in the Soviet Union the editors' and authors' names have appeared on the publications. The dissenters have been subject to selective harassment and intimidation but not imprisoned. An unprecedented situation of half-freedom and half-repression is, however, unthinkable in the long run and it may now be possible because of the power of the church on the one hand and far-reaching disagreements on the top levels of the Party on the other.

Indeed, a group of prominent old Communists including Ochab has been unsuccessfully pressing for liberalization, and grappling with hard-liners. The fact that Party membership has been constantly expanding attests less to an ideological revival than to adding strength in numbers for the establishment. As compared with the past, the Party has few intellectuals left and contains vast numbers of critics of the current regime. Contemporary Poland is beset by paradoxes in the political, cultural, and economic spheres and in 1978 is at a crossroads. How Gierek handles the crisis will show whether he is merely an adroit politician or a statesman. It may not be too late to bring the leadership closer to the people and persuade Russia that Polish society requires a far greater margin of freedom to function smoothly. While Gierek's statesmanship and Polish political maturity are necessary to assure these limited goals, imaginative American diplomacy is an essential supporting element.

American economic involvement in Poland, understood as providing a stimulus to modernization, that in turn might promote liberalization, has not proved a panacea. Détente, naively assumed to lead automatically to greater domestic freedoms, did not have a simple effect—both regression and progress have been observed in the past few years. Yet, unless the United States is prepared to continue assisting the Polish economy and trying to influence the political climate in Warsaw, the alternative may be chaos and a dramatic reassertion of Soviet might. The aid has to be based on realistic assumptions, taking into account the inefficiency of Polish economy, and applied in a selective fashion. It should be publicized more extensively and connected, although in a subtle way, to American concern for human rights. The issue is then largely political and ideological and transcends economics.

It seems fitting to conclude with a few remarks devoted to the American Polonia, which in a sense constitutes the natural link between the United States and Poland. The term Polonia lacks precision and is often used to encompass a wide range of different groups. There is the old emigration that had come to this country for economic reasons and brought with it a parish-structure organization that fitted ill into the American system. In the twentieth century the Polish American community has become increasingly secularized but had not yet developed new forms of effective leadership. The old alternatives: americanization, which meant social and political advancement, or maintenance of ethnic identity at the price of parochialism and inferior status, lost some relevance in these days of "ethnic" revival in the United States. Consequently, the inferiority complex that had plagued the Polish Americans may be on the wane.

New waves of immigrants during the Second World War and in the last thirty years were of a different character from the old Polonia. Comprising a sizable group of intelligentsia, they were able to enter American life on a higher level and make their contributions more rapidly. Fully self-conscious, politically and nationally, the new emigrants were able to make a rational choice whether they were to become Americans of Polish descent, Polish Americans, or Poles living in the United States either as aliens or naturalized citizens, loyal to the new country but remaining essentially Polish in their outlook.

The diversity of the Polonia, used in the broadest sense, helps to explain the existing variety of its political attitudes toward Poland. The actual and potential contributions of the Polonia to American-Polish relations prompted the Warsaw government to cultivate it while asserting that it regarded the emigration as part of the American nation and had no wish to convert it to communism. Warsaw has been seeking, however, to sustain and encourage the Polish Americans' interest in and attachment to the "old country." This policy has been rewarded with some success. Although the bulk of the Polonia is instinctively anticommunist, it has found it difficult on occasion to grasp all the intricacies of the developments in Poland or respond to them with a determined and unanimous voice. The distinction between cooperating with Warsaw or being used by it has not always been clearly perceived.

The Polish American Congress representing the old Polonia and the articulate recent emigrés, some of whom had set up a North American Study Center for Polish Affairs in mid-1970s, have repeatedly taken a stand on Polish problems and attempted to influence American policies toward them. Differences of views within the Polonia have naturally surfaced. There are those who have favored limited intercourse with Poland, especially cultural and economic, others who go one step farther and speak of the Polish "diaspora" rather than of an emigration, and others still who take the extreme positions of either accepting or rejecting completely the realities of the Polish People's Republic. A 1978 meeting of representatives of Polonia organizations from all over the world has indicated, however, the existence of basic agreement on such issues as aid to Poland, support for the position of the Catholic church and of the dissenters, and condemnation of anti-Semitism as a political weapon.

Gierek's visit in the United States in 1974 was generally boycotted by Polish American organizations, and the Communist leader did not venture to address them. Placards carried at the Pulaski Day parade with "Poland—yes, Gierek—no" showed the feeling of animosity against the regime. The reaction of the Polonia to the Sonnenfeldt Doctrine was also instantaneous and highly emotional. One of the Polish American representatives in Congress, the Republican from Illinois, Edward J. Derwinski, said that the doctrine was "the straw that broke the camel's back." Writing to Gerald Ford, the president of the Polish American Congress, Aloysius A. Mazewski, stated that the doctrine "amounts to the United States underwriting the Soviet colonialism in Eastern Europe." With regard to internal Polish matters, Polish American as well as emigré groups voiced protests against the constitutional changes introduced by the Party in 1976. The Polish American Congress issued a statement saying that violence done to national and civic rights of the Polish nation may force the congress to reconsider its support for economic cooperation and cultural exchanges between the United States and Poland. The July 1976 upheaval and the governmental persecution of workers also occasioned strong Polish American support for them; collection of funds to assist their cause assumed sizable proportions.

It is quite evident that the Polonia or its most articulate and active members constitute an important although thus far not a decisive factor in American-Polish relations. Both Washington and Warsaw have on numerous occasions singled out this ethnic group as a special asset, but its potential is not yet fully utilized, given the relatively narrow base of power of Polish Americans and the low degree of political sophistication of the masses with regard to Polish needs and problems. The impact of intellectuals, often indirect, has been noticeable. Economically, the Polonia has been contributing to Poland's welfare not only through donations and voluntary contributions, but through aid to families and money spent while traveling to the country. The Polish American elite can serve as an interpreter of the United States to Poland and vice versa, provided it does not become a hybrid out of touch with both cultures operating within a miniculture of its own. This is a far more real danger than that of the "hyphenate" being torn by conflicting loyalties. The Polonia's attachment to the Western outlook and to freedom as well as to the Polish cultural heritage are not hard to reconcile. True, historical, temperamental, and multiple other differences between the American and Polish nations make the function of an interpreter difficult. But all difficulties and past failures notwithstanding, the actual and especially the potential role of the Polonia as a bridge between the two countries should not be underestimated.

Reflections

HﾓISTORY and geography have shaped American-Polish relations. The United States
is a superpower and virtually a continent; Poland is a middle-sized
state in East Central Europe. The two are divided by 4,600 miles
of the Atlantic Ocean and the land mass of Western Europe. A
liner leaving the New York harbor reaches Gdynia in roughly ten
days. Direct flights from New York to the Polish capital take only
hours, deceptively shortening the great distance which in every
sense of the word separates the two countries.

The remarks that follow are deliberately called reflections rather
than conclusions, for they do not pretend to offer a systematic
analysis or a summary. Some could be called speculations because
they cannot be easily verified or documented, yet they serve a purpose in touching on broad matters that transcend the frame of any
single chapter of this study. We begin with American and Polish
attitudes toward the past and then attempt to generalize about
Americans and Poles and their images of each other. We will then
recapitulate briefly the salient points of our story and ponder a
little about the future.

Americans, as the novelist Emily Hahn put it, "have never been
overly fond of history. We always think that what we are experiencing is new." Nor is such an attitude surprising. The successive
waves of immigrants to America were escaping European history
and its burdens. The call of the "new," whether in terms of a new

frontier or a new experience or a new deal, has been irresistible; at the same time large chunks of the past disappear each year from the American landscape.

The Poles, in spite of recent changes in attitudes, are among the most history-conscious peoples. Even if they wished to escape history, they could hardly do it; the past permeates the present and a Pole turns to the past centuries to seek inspiration, consolation, or justification for the actions of today. The careful and costly rebuilding of historical monuments, churches included, by the Communist government was a culturally necessary response to the long history of forcible attempts by Poland's enemies to deprive the nation of its old heritage.

"Typically American" and "typically Polish" outlooks, reactions, and habits are hard to define, but it would be foolish to deny their existence. Clichés and half-truths mix with observable data and form the images the Poles have of Americans and vice versa. Americans, racial differences notwithstanding, are what we call for want of a better word Westerners. English linguistic, cultural, legal, philosophical, even sporting traditions have put a mark on the American outlook and way of life. Other traits—a-historical, anti-elitist, egalitarian (in a special sense), and idealistic—have emerged as a result of specific environment and development. Even if it is questioned today, the concept of the "American dream" still has meaning and appeal. If proverbs and sayings are revealing of national character, and I think they are, such expressions as "nothing succeeds like success," "if you can't beat them, join them," "selling a program," are concepts largely alien to the Polish psyche.

The American notion of compromise, seen as a positive phenomenon since a compromise must be achieved, stands in contrast to the somewhat pejorative Polish usage of the term. Martin Duberman made a telling point when he spoke of the American "conventional view that adherence to principle is the equivalent to 'fanaticism' or, alternately, that a flexible conscience is somehow related to charitableness of heart." The mixture of pragmatism, materialism, and idealism may well derive from the Anglo-Saxon background influenced by the Protestant ethos. At least many European students of America, Poles included, have perceived it in those terms. A German observer wrote in the 1830s: "Happiness and prosperity are so *popular* in the United States, that no one dares to show himself an exception to the rule." Margaret Mead mentions the "extraordinary premium on achievement" set in this country; others have stressed the "compulsive competitiveness." A journalist, Tom

Wicker, put it more crudely when he remarked that "the pocketbook usually outweighs ideology among American voters."

Poles visiting the United States have been struck again and again by the limits that Americans set to their friendliness toward each other and to outsiders. No doubt many people in this country shun involvement and certainly over-involvement in the affairs of others. By contrast, the Poles like to be involved, even at a price to their privacy. The English word "friend" is not the same as the Polish equivalent *przyjaciel*, which implies a more intimate kind of relationship. Comparing emotional tones, in vague and somewhat simplistic generic terms to be sure, Anglo-Saxon reserve contrasts with Slav exuberance.

If violence is as American as apple pie, Americans seem to display in international relations a repugnance to initiate violent actions. Still, the word "aggressive" when applied to a salesman or a business executive has a positive connotation. Again no Polish equivalents can be easily found.

Both Americans and Poles proved on many occasions capable of being tough, yet one can perhaps contrast an "urban" type of toughness with an "agrarian" model. To clarify this distinction, Polish toughness might be closer to that of the American Southerner, particularly of the ante-bellum period, than to that of the persevering Yankee.

The essentially industrial society has imposed on American thinking the notion of supply and demand and of advertising. In the last fifty years American leaders had to "sell," indeed oversell their foreign policies to the electorate. World War I was to end all wars, the Paris Peace settlement was to make the world safe for democracy, cooperation between superpowers after the Second World War was to ensure peace. Even if the overselling was deliberate and necessitated by political considerations, there is truth in Adam Ulam's remark that American writings on international affairs show a constant search "for one master formula, a philosopher's stone, which when applied to American foreign policy would solve all the problems." There is an impatience in the search for the formula and a reluctance to think in long-range terms. As M. Y. Ostrogorski had remarked, the American does not give "a thought to remote consequences; he sees only present advantages."

The failure to fulfill promised goals, the collapse of grandiose dreams "sold" to the public provokes violent reactions. As two journalists, David Gelman and Stephen Lasher, commented on the attacks on the Kennedy myth: "nothing exceeds the American passion for making myths except its passion for unmaking them."

This vision of grandiose solutions combined with inherent belief in American righteousness has, however, suffered greatly in the last decade. American leaders, in William A. Williams' words, "are engaged in pulling back from the extreme involvements and commitments that have grown out of the traditional belief in the magic quality of a new frontier that will solve all existing problems, resolve all moral dilemmas, and guarantee happiness evermore." Whether the Carter presidency will reverse this trend is too early to tell.

The Poles are half-Westerners and half-Easterners in their outlook and habits. They belong to the cultural traditions of the West, are linked with it through Catholicism and the essentially Western political culture. But they are Westerners in the continental European, not Anglo-Saxon sense, and they have been exposed to and affected by the East. Poland's history, which for centuries had evolved in a different way from the other countries of Europe, produced a sense of uniqueness of Polish historical experience. The heritage of the past seems to contrast with both the West and the East. The drama of the partitions, which had ended Poland's role of a great power, opened wounds that have not been healed to this day, and Polish mentality in international affairs became that of a small country. Speaking of American-East European relations in 1968, William B. Slottman aptly remarked that "We will have to abandon our overriding sense of being the Great Power talking to our inferiors, and they will have to rise above the 'Small Nation Mind' that continues to mistake the national community for the entire cosmos."

The Small Nation Mind is not restricted to seeing everything through a nationally-tinted magnifying glass. Also proper to it are abrupt changes from naive faith in the promises of the mighty to bitter disillusionment when these promises have failed to materialize. Polish leaders on occasion and Polish public opinion frequently have been prone to seeing sinister machinations and conspiracies directed against their nation. Harsh experiences from the past justify suspiciousness, but a conspiratorial view of history is no substitute for cool analysis. Prominent Poles who have often been far more critical of their own nation than outsiders drew attention to this oscillation between hope and despair. In some respects this may have been the inevitable outcome of historical developments, but it made the Poles highly sensitive, with a tendency to think in extremes.

American clichés about the Poles abound, and like all clichés they contain a grain of truth. Reminiscing about Joseph Conrad, Al-

fred Knopf called him "typically Polish," by which he meant that
he was dramatic and emotional. H. F. Armstrong commented on
the "characteristic Polish exhibition of insouciance despite the
persistent hostility on every border." The Poles are generally regarded as romantic, nationalistic, gallant, troublesome, individual-
istic, and unreliable. They lack social discipline and display what
proves to be a short-lived élan. The Poles themselves refer to this
last phenomenon as a "straw fire" (*słomiany ogień*), and many a
Polish leader had said in exasperation that his countrymen can die
magnificently but cannot endure to live laboriously.

American views of Poles have been formed partly through contacts with the mass immigration, poor and backward, and partly
through fragmentary acquaintance with Polish history. The lower-
class immigrants were looked down upon, even despised, a phenomenon which has survived in the form of the crude "Polish jokes."
A superficial reading of Poland's past and occasional contacts with
representatives of the upper classes have perpetuated the image
of brave but impractical Polish aristocrats, oppressing the peasants,
terrorizing the Jews and responsible for their country's misfortunes.
The cliché of the slow-witted yokel and the one of the useless
nobleman found an unexpected synthesis in a cheap American
western, in which a kind-hearted but almost subhuman Pole bears
the proud name of Casimir Pulaski. This view may gradually
change, among others as a result of increased contacts and the growing number of translations of Polish literary works into English
in the last decades. As a result, some Polish authors have made an
impact on the American reading public. There is no doubt, however, that American literature in Polish translation—which has influenced several generations of Poles—is by comparison far more
influential and accounts for a major portion of the Polish intelligentsia's literary diet. From a selection of Benjamin Franklin's
Poor Richard's Almanac, which was published in Poland in 1793,
through Washington Irving and James Fenimore Cooper, virtually
all important American writers have appeared in Polish translation. If the knowledge of American history in Poland is on a relatively low level, the United States—as Jedlicki has rightly remarked
in his short but illuminating essay on "Images of America"—has
been on Polish minds for two hundred years. America invaded
Poland with its products, from the potato to sophisticated machinery
and gadgets. It has influenced mass culture, fashions, and manners. It has been the topic of conversation in millions of peasant
huts and figured to some extent in Polish writings. The Polish
youth, like their counterparts throughout Europe, have been play-

ing cowboys and Indians, for generations, and the romance of the Wild West has fired their imagination on a par with the Polish epic of the Wild Steppes.

Jedlicki was also right in stressing the compensatory nature of the attraction that the Poles feel toward America; America seemed traditionally to compensate them for their own wants—lack of freedom, poverty, a feeling of provincialism. American technology, skyscrapers, but above all the vision of the land of opportunity and riches as presented and distorted by Hollywood has exercised a strong appeal. An episode from the 1950s may serve as a good illustration. When *A Streetcar Named Desire* was shown on the Warsaw stage, it was thought necessary to improve the looks of the New Orleans slum lest the public regard the decor as politically motivated anti-American propaganda. True, the Polish image of America has had its shadows. Slavery had evoked passionate Polish criticism and the hanging of John Brown drove the poet Norwid to express perhaps the bitterest disillusionment with the American myth in Polish literature. Wiktor Weintraub convincingly spoke of the coexistence of a myth of America as a land of freedom with that of America as a land of Mammon. Admiration for American achievements also mingled at times with a feeling of Old World class superiority and snobbery vis-à-vis the rich but crude Americans. From the late nineteenth century to the present Polish travelers' accounts have exhibited that slight disdain typical of the genteel poor toward the nouveau riche.

The American-Polish relationship had been shaped from its inception by a one-sidedness that went deeper than would have been normal in contacts between a great and a smaller nation. In the nineteenth century there was no Poland to deal with but only a Polish question. During the First World War Poland was seen as a cause, and during the interwar period the little support that was given to it stemmed more from moralistic than from power-political reasons. The Poles could not easily live up to an image of a model, liberated nation, and they frequently became the object of criticism for their domestic and foreign policies. The Americans, priding themselves for having resolved nationality problems through the Melting Pot concept—the racial issue was conveniently forgotten—tended to combine aloofness with self-righteousness. During the Second World War Poland evoked sympathy as a victim of aggression but being a source of trouble with Soviet Russia, once again appeared as a bothersome suppliant. In Roosevelt's view, a small state was not to influence unduly the superpowers even with regard to its own destiny. The notion that Poland together with the rest of Eastern Europe was a weighty element in the all-European balance of power was absent from the thinking of the White House. The issue seemed not so much restoring Poland to a rehabilitated Europe but rather of making its adjustment to the Soviet sphere of influence as palatable as possible.

The Second World War determined to a large extent the nature of American-Polish relations in subsequent decades. Poland served as a barometer of the Cold War, and Washington's attitude toward it became once again expressed in moralistic terms—liberation— rather than political-economic. Lack of flexibility over the German-Polish border and denial to postwar Poland of the Most-Favored-Nation clause meant that the United States was writing off the state while ostensibly caring for the nation.

The special treatment accorded Poland since 1956, though subject to vacillations in the 1960s, showed a more imaginative stance but revealed new dangers and reinforced some of the old ways of thinking about Poland and Eastern Europe in general. Before turning to the present and the future, let us mention yet another aspect of Polish-American relations.

John Campbell has aptly said that Eastern Europe has been "something of a football of American domestic politics, kicked most vigorously at four-year intervals when presidential elections occur." This remark is applicable to Poland in a broader sense; the country had long served or been exploited as an object lesson for American domestic consumption. Polish partitions provided a convenient illustration of how a country could mismanage its domestic affairs, and they were invoked as a warning to avoid bad government. The Polish Insurrection of 1863 made the country a football of American politics, but it was not until the First World War that the Poles could for the first time derive some benefits from this domestic political game. Poland became an excellent illustration of the Wilsonian principle of self-determination and owed to it, at least partly, the place it occupied in the presidential policy.

In the opening years of the Second World War Roosevelt found the Polish case a most useful example to mobilize American public opinion against the Nazi danger. Poland was called the conscience of humanity and the inspiration of the world. Its usefulness declined, however, as we know, in the subsequent years of the great struggle. Then Mikołajczyk and those who supported him became an index of the correctness of the United States' Russian policy, and the Polish case proved a handy argument, though not the only one, in the Republican upsurge in 1948. Gomułka, who spared the heralds of the liberation doctrine the acute embarrassment caused by Hungary in 1956, in turn became an example of successful polycentrism. Gierek finally, in the Sonnenfeldt statement, was singled out to show the feasibility of Kissinger's policies of West-East détente.

Of course Poland has not been on the minds of American foreign policy makers consistently and for long periods of time. As Gabriel Almond remarked, the "orientation of most Americans toward foreign policy is one of mood, and mood is essentially an unstable phenomenon." Experts on Polish questions apart, Poland has always been of marginal interest to the average American. It is after all a remote and a weak country and per se of no direct importance to the security of the United States. But if one thinks of Poland in the context of East Central Europe, its significance increases dramatically and merits close attention.

The British geopolitician Halford Mackinder referred to Eastern Europe in the often quoted phrase: "Who rules East Europe commands the heartland, who rules the heartland commands the world." The American diplomat Adolph Berle, commenting in 1956 on the European balance of power "and with it the basis of world peace," saw it as dependent "upon a tier of states between the Soviet Union and the Western world." Problems of Eastern Europe were at the center of international politics in 1914–1918 and 1938–1945. In the case of Poland, it could even be argued that the partitions of that country had started a chain reaction that gravely upset the international balance of power and made possible the rise of Prussia and subsequent German hegemony in Europe.

It was not the "balkanization" of East Central Europe after World War I that made the area unstable but the great powers' designs on it. Poland was the gateway for German expansion eastward in the days of Hitler, and the German collapse allowed a reverse movement of Russian westward expansion. The present Soviet controls bring only an apparent stabilization into the region, and the division of the Continent which results therefrom helps to relegate Europe to a position of inferiority.

The importance of Eastern Europe was stressed anew in the already-mentioned Sonnenfeldt Doctrine. But the State Department official saw a solution to the area, regarded as a potential source of grave international conflicts, in an "organic" relationship between Eastern Europe and Russia. By recognizing an overriding interest of the Soviet Union, Sonnenfeldt revived in essence the earlier American notions of spheres of influence sui generis, as espoused among others by Byrnes. The "sphere of influence" theory, however, could only work if one assumed that Soviet foreign policy is static, not dynamic. Control over Eastern Europe can hardly be the ultimate goal of a superpower with global interests. From the Eastern European perspective it is paradoxical, of course, that the advice to accept the unpopular Soviet rule should come from Washington. The two extremes—liberation from the Soviet rule or counsels of its acceptance—surely cannot exhaust the range of options in diplomacy, where there are usually more choices than two.

Because of its size, population, resources, and strategic position Poland is a pivot of the East European region in more ways than one. The geographic location and historic experience make the Poles perfectly aware of the fact that when Russia and Germany fought it was on Poland's territory; when they cooperated it was at Poland's expense. The present pro-Russian orientation is the only option available to Warsaw, and even if one thinks about a far-off future Poland, he will still have to reckon with the existence of two neighbors that are far more powerful. But if the country's location in unenviable, the present situation is not uniformly bleak. Since the Second World War time has worked for Poland in regard to repopulation and integration of "western territories." German revisionism, so stringent after the First World War, ran a different course after the Second, resulting in the German-Polish treaties that solidified the status quo. Poland today is ethnically homogeneous and largely reconciled to the territorial losses in the east. That fact is important for future Polish relations with Ukrainians and Belorussians, which are no longer likely to be poisoned by territorial disputes and domestic irredentas. The industrialization of the country should eventually put Poland on sound economic foundations.

As we have seen, détente and economic cooperation as currently practiced produced mixed effects on Poland. Yet they might operate to its advantage on two conditions: one, that cooperation with the West, particularly America, decisively and consistently assist the country's economy; two, that in the process moral forces of the Polish nation are sustained in their struggle for the preservation and development of cultural values, belief-systems, in brief of a distinctive Polish way of life.

What should and could be an effective American policy toward Poland? Let us repeat that there are no magic recipes in diplomacy or solutions that dispose once and for all of existing problems. Foreign policy can at best be a constant search for best ways and means of dealing with existing situations, while remembering that immediate achievements must not jeopardize the possibilities of the future. Furthermore, a truly imaginative foreign policy must be based on the realization that reality comprises material and tangible elements together with imponderables. It is obvious that the United States Polish policy is a segment of a global policy in which certain constants have to be borne in mind. It may be banal to speak of the growing interdependence of our world, yet it is a fact. While great powers will continue to play a dominant part, the role of the smaller states is paradoxically both shrinking and increasing. As Tito told Nixon during the latter's visit to Yugoslavia in 1970: "mere negotiations and avoidance of confrontation between the big powers are in themselves no longer sufficient," and unless "the processes of diplomacy are widened to include smaller nations on a meaningful basis" there will be only "shorter or longer intervals of respite between periods of cold war." The oil crisis of 1973 dramatically demonstrated what smaller countries controlling basic raw materials can do even to the great powers. Past American and Western policies of either backing Russia against Germany or Germany against Russia, usually at the expense of the smaller states in between, and never seriously trying to promote an East Central European grouping or confederation, have been less than satisfactory.

The overriding role of the great powers cannot or should not be, of course, minimized. From the American point of view the huge and expansive Soviet-dominated bloc is threatening and will continue to pose the threat of overpowering the United States. That is what power politics is all about. The Achilles' heel of the bloc is Eastern Europe, in which Poland's position has already been stressed. On these grounds alone, to dismiss Poland as remote and powerless is shortsighted and naive. But that is not all. Traditionally, the United States had two powerful weapons in its arsenal: economic might and moral authority. The latter became much dissipated in the last decade; America could hardly export ideas that were questioned and attacked at home in an orgy of self-flagellation. Détente, which the Soviet Union found perfectly compatible with its own ideological offensive, cramped American style. Paradoxically, the Soviet Union, which is the last multinational empire, held the ideological initiative. Exhibiting a guilt complex, the West viewed the freedom of Africans as more important than that of Lithuanians or Ukrainians.

A successful American policy toward Poland presupposes a recovery of American self-confidence and a revived belief in the credentials of Western civilization. The Polish nation, laboring against great odds, had manifested its stamina and its attachment to native values in 1956, 1968, 1970, and 1976. The first public pronouncements of the Carter administration, heralded as a break with narrow pragmatism, appeared as welcome signs of an upsurge of American willpower and determination to recover a moral leadership in the world. If it is strengthened by processes that would fully mobilize the vast American potential, this development might usher in a new phase of American foreign policy that could benefit both the United States and the world. A sophisticated realism that would avoid the pitfalls of myth-making and not degenerate into cynicism is needed on the American side; the Poles, cured by now of exaggerated hopes placed in the West yet fully conscious of their unbreakable ties with Western civilization, must continue to be cautious yet defend their own heritage. To repeat once again, the United States cannot "liberate" Poland but can bail it out at moments of economic crises; it cannot change its domestic system but can sustain Polish efforts in the all-important cultural sphere. It must avoid holding out unrealistic expectations or, inversely, exhibiting a willingness to sacrifice the Poles for the sake of the superpowers' cooperation. Finally, Washington may occasionally ponder the Polish and East European story, have a clear notion of its minimal and maximal goals vis-à-vis Poland, and prepare for future contingencies rather than respond to them as they arise.

Appendix A. Diplomatic Representatives

U.S. Ministers and
Ambassadors to Poland

Hugh Gibson	1919-1924
Alfred Pearson	1924-1925
John B. Stetson	1925-1930
John N. Willys (first ambassador)	1930-1932
F. Lammot Belin	1932-1933
John Cudahy	1933-1937
Anthony D. Biddle	1937-1944
Arthur B. Lane	1944-1947
Stanton Griffis	1947-1948
Waldemar J. Gallman	1948-1950
Joseph Flack	1950-1955
Joseph E. Jacobs	1955-1957
Jacob D. Beam	1957-1961
John M. Cabot	1961-1965
John A. Gronouski	1965-1968
Walter E. Stoessel	1968-1972
Richard Davies	1972-1978
William Schaufele	1978-

Polish Ministers and
Ambassadors to the U.S.

Kazimierz Lubomirski	1919-1922
Władysław Wróblewski	1922-1925
Jan Ciechanowski	1925-1929
Tytus Filipowicz (first ambassador)	1930-1932
Stanisław Patek	1933-1935
Jerzy Potocki	1936-1941
Jan Ciechanowski	1941-1945
Oskar Lange	1945-1946
Józef Winiewicz	1946-1955
Romuald Spasowski	1955-1961
Edward Drożniak	1961-1966
Jerzy Michałowski	1967-1971
Witold Trąmpczyński	1972-1978
Romuald Spasowski	1978-

Appendix B. Selective Chronology

United States		Poland	
		966	Baptism of Mieszko and his countrymen
		1025	Bolesław the Valiant crowned king
		c. 1116-1119	Gall's Chronicle
		1138	Testament of Bolesław the Wrymouth
		c. 1208-1218	Kadłubek's Chronicle
		1226	Teutonic Knights arrive in Prussia
		1241	Battle of Legnica with Tartars
		1364	Cracow University founded
		1385	Union with Lithuania at Krewo
		1410	Battle of Grunwald with Teutonic Knights
		1425-1433	*Neminem captivabimus*
		1466	Peace of Toruń restores Pomerania
1492	Columbus discovers America	1492-1526	Jagiellonian system in Central Europe
		1525	Duke of Prussia renders homage
		1543	Copernicus's *De revolutionibus*
		1569	Union of Lublin
		1578	Wilno University founded
		1596	Religious Union of Brześć (Brest)
		1605	Battle of Kircholm
1607	Jamestown colony		
1608	Polish settlers in Jamestown		

United States		*Poland*	
		1610	Battle of Klushino
1620	Mayflower Compact	1620	Battle of Cecora
1630	Founding of Massachusetts		
1636	Harvard College founded		
		1648	Khmelnitsky rebellion in the Ukraine
		1648-1660	The "deluge"
		1652	*Liberum veto*
		1658	Agreement of Hadziacz with the Cossacks
		1667	Treaty of Andrusovo with Moscow
1676	Bacon's Rebellion		
		1683	Sobieski at Vienna
1701	Yale College founded		
1703-1713	Queen Anne's war		
		1740	Collegium Nobilium founded
1755-1763	French and Indian wars		
1763	The Treaty of Paris		
		1764	King Stanislas Augustus elected
		1768	Bar Confederation
		1772	First Partition
1775-1783	War of Independence		
1776	Declaration of Independence		
1776	Arrival of Kościuszko		
1779	Death of Pułaski		
1781	Articles of Confederation		
1787	Constitution		
		1788-1792	The Great Sejm
1789	President George Washington inaugurated		
		1791	May 3 Constitution
		1793	Second Partition
		1794	Kościuszko's Insurrection
		1795	Third Partition
1797	President John Adams inaugurated	1797	Dąbrowski's Legion in Italy
1797-1798	Kościuszko's second stay		
1803	Louisiana Purchase		
		1807	Duchy of Warsaw established

United States		Poland	
		1809	War with Austria
1812	War with Great Britain	1812	Napoleon invades Russia
		1815	Kingdom of Poland under Alexander
		1816	Warsaw University founded
1823	Monroe Doctrine		
		1830-1831	November Insurrection
1846-1848	War with Mexico	1846	Cracow Revolution and peasant *jacquerie*
		1848	Spring of Nations in Galicia and Poznania; emancipation of Galician peasantry
1850	The Compromise of 1850		
1861-1865	The Civil War		
		1863-1864	January Insurrection; emancipation of peasantry
1867	Purchase of Alaska	1867	Galician autonomy
1868	Fourteenth Amendment		
		1892-1893	Emergence of PPS, SD, and National League
1898	War with Spain		
		1905	Revolution in the Kingdom
1913	President Wilson inaugurated		
		1914	World War I begins; Polish Legions
1915	Arrival of Paderewski		
		1916	The Two Emperors' Manifesto
1917	Wilson's Peace without Victory speech (April) U.S. entry into war	1917	(March) Provisional Government and Petrograd Soviet declarations on Poland (August) National Polish Committee (November) Bolshevik Revolution
1918	(January) Fourteen Points (November) Armistice	1918	(March) Treaty of Brest Litovsk (November) Piłsudski returns to Warsaw; Polish Republic
		1919	Treaty of Versailles

United States		*Poland*	
		1919-1920	Polish-Soviet War
		1920	Battle of Warsaw
1921	(March) President Harding inaugurated Immigration Act	1921	Alliances with France and Rumania; Treaty of Riga; Polish Constitution
		1922	President Narutowicz's assassination; President Wojciechowski inaugurated
1923	President Coolidge inaugurated		
1924	Immigration Bill		
1925	Skrzyński's visit	1925	Locarno
		1926	Piłsudski's coup d'état; Mościcki named president
		1927	Stabilization loan
1928	Kellogg-Briand Pact		
1929	President Hoover inaugurated (October) Wall Street crash		
		1930	The Brześć Affair
1931	Borah interview	1931	Commercial Treaty with the United States
		1932	Nonaggression Treaty with USSR
1933	President Roosevelt inaugurated (November) Recognition of the Soviet Union		
		1934	Nonaggression declaration with Germany
		1935	Constitution (May) Piłsudski dies
		1939	Alliance with Great Britain (September) War with Germany and Soviet invasion; Raczkiewicz becomes president; Sikorski is premier and commander-in-chief

United States		*Poland*	
1941	Sikorski's first visit (August) Atlantic Charter (December) U.S. in World War II	1941	(June) German invasion of USSR (July) Sikorski-Maisky agreement (December) Sikorski-Stalin declaration
1942	United Nations declaration (March) Sikorski's second visit (December) Sikorski's third visit	1942	Polish Workers' party founded
1943	(October) Moscow Conference (November-December) Teheran Conference	1943	Katyn discovery; USSR breaks off relations (April) Warsaw ghetto rising (June) Bór-Komorowski is commander of AK (July) Sikorski killed; Mikołajczyk is premier; Sosnkowski commander-in-chief
1944	(June) Mikołajczyk's visit; D-day in Europe (November) Presidential election	1944	Battle of Monte Cassino (July) Polish Committee of National Liberation in Lublin (August-October) Warsaw Uprising (November) Arciszewski is premier
1945	Yalta Conference (April) Roosevelt dies; Truman becomes president (May) End of war in Europe (July) Potsdam Conference (August) End of war in the Pacific	1945	Provisional Government recognized by USSR (July) Provisional Government of National Unity recognized by U.S.
1946	Byrnes' speech in Stutgart	1946	Referendum
1947	Truman Doctrine; Marshall Plan	1947	Elections
		1948	United Polish Workers' Party founded
1949	National Committee for a Free Europe (April) NATO		

Selective Chronology

United States		Poland	
1950-1953	Korean War	1950	Zgorzelec Treaty with GDR
		1952	Constitution of Polish People's Republic
1953	President Eisenhower inaugurated	1953	Stalin's death
		1955	Warsaw Pact
		1956	Khrushchev denounces Stalinism (June) Poznań workers' rising (October) Gomułka is first secretary
		1957	Rapacki Plan
		1959	Vice-president Nixon in Warsaw
1960	Gomułka's visit	1960	Council of Mutual Economic Cooperation
1961	President Kennedy inaugurated		
1962	Cuban Crisis		
1963	Kennedy assassinated; Johnson becomes president		
1965-1973	Vietnam War		
		1968	The March Crisis
1969	President Nixon inaugurated		
		1970	Treaty with West Germany; workers' upheaval topples Gomułka; Gierek becomes first secretary
		1972	Nixon's visit
1974	Nixon resigns; Ford becomes president		
1974	Gierek's visit		
1975	Helsinki Agreement	1975	Ford's visit; administrative reform
		1976	Constitution amended (June) Workers' riots
1977	President Carter inaugurated	1977	Carter's visit

Suggested Reading

NUMEROUS books and articles touch on American-Polish relations, but relatively few address themselves directly to this topic. Those listed below are all in English and include neither collections of documents and diaries, nor studies specifically devoted to the internal problems of the American Polonia.

General

The three best bibliographies are: Norman Davies, ed., *Poland: Past and Present: A Select Bibliography of Works in English* (Newtonville, Mass., 1977); Joseph W. Zurawski, ed., *Polish American History and Culture: A Classified Bibliography* (Chicago, 1975), and the section on Poland in Paul L. Horecky, ed., *East Central Europe: A Guide to Basic Publications* (Chicago, 1969). To these one can add Marion M. Coleman, ed., *Polish Literature in English Translation: A Bibliography* (Cheshire, Conn., 1963). For international affairs, bibliographies published by the Council on Foreign Relations in New York are most helpful.

There are several one-volume outlines of Polish history by such prominent scholars as Oscar Halecki, Roman Dyboski, G. Slocombe, William J. Rose, Zygmunt Wojciechowski, and Olgierd Górka, but the two-volume *Cambridge History of Poland* edited by W. F. Reddaway (Cambridge, 1941-1950) may be most representative of prewar Polish historiography, just as Stefan Kieniewicz et al., *History of Poland* (Warsaw, 1968), may best reflect the current historical trends. A good survey is M. K. Dziewanowski, *Poland in the 20th Century* (New York, 1977). Books on Polish literature and culture by Manfred Kridl, Wacław Lednicki, and Czesław Miłosz are particularly recommended, especially Lednicki's *Life and Culture of Poland as Reflected in Polish Literature* (New York, 1944). For a discussion of Polish nationalism the reader should turn to Peter Brock's essay on Poland in Peter F. Sugar and Ivo J. Lederer, eds, *Nationalism in Eastern Europe* (Seattle, 1969). Adam Bromke, *Poland's Politics: Idealism versus Realism* (Cambridge, Mass., 1967), provides an interesting and controversial interpretation of the past and the present. Piotr S. Wandycz, "Poland in International Politics," *Canadian Slavonic Papers*, XIV, 3 (1972), is a short review of this problem. W. J. Wagner, ed., *Polish Law Throughout the Ages* (Stanford, 1970), surveys a millennium of legal thought. For a sympathetic American appraisal of Poland see Paul Super, *The Polish Tradition: An Interpretation of a Nation* (London, 1939).

The book that comes nearest to a general study of American-Polish relations, Samuel L. Sharp, *Poland: White Eagle on a Red Field* (Cambridge, Mass., 1953), is eminently readable but marred by facile "debunking" of the past and superficial treatment of multiple aspects of these relations. For a passionate rejoinder by O. Halecki, see "The United States and Poland," *Review of Politics*,

XVI (January, 1954). Four recent articles merit special attention: Jerzy Jedlicki, "Images of America," *Polish Perspectives,* XVIII (November, 1975); George J. Lerski, "Sources for the Diplomatic History of Polish-American Relations," *Polish American Studies,* XXVII (Spring-Autumn 1976); Keith Sutherland, "America views Poland: Perspectives from the Final Partition to the Rebirth of the Polish Nation," *Antemurale,* XX (1976); and Franciszek Lyra, "Grounds for Connections: The Pattern of Polish-American Literary Relations," *Polish-American Studies,* I (1976).

Some of the works centering on Polish emigration to the United States are: Miecislaus Haiman, *Polish Past in America, 1608-1865* (reprinted Chicago, 1974); Joseph A. Wytrwal, *Poles in American History and Tradition* (Detroit, 1969) and *America's Polish Heritage* (Detroit, 1961); E. Renkiewicz, *The Poles in America 1608-1972: A Chronology and Fact Book* (New York, 1973), Bogdan Grzeloński, *Poles in the United States of America 1776-1863* (Warsaw, 1976), and a popular book by Laura Pilarski, *They Came from Poland: The Stories of Famous Polish-Americans* (New York, 1969). More sophisticated and interpretative are the bicentennial issue of the *Polish Review,* XXI, 3 (1976) entitled "The Polish Americans" and edited by Eugene Kleban and Thaddeus V. Gromada, and the article by Irena Spustek, "Observations on Historical Studies concerning Polish Americans," *Polish-American Studies,* I (1976). There is much useful material in Frank Mocha, ed., *Poles in America: Bicentennial Essays* (Stevens Point, 1978). Joseph L. Lichten's "Polish Americans and American Jews: Some Issues Which Unite and Divide" in the *Polish Review,* XVIII, 4 (1973), is well worth reading. Thomas A. Bailey, *America Faces Russia: Russian-American Relations from Early Times to Our Day* (Ithaca, 1950), is recommended for a better understanding of the Russian angle in Polish-American relations.

Chapter 1. Partitions of Poland and the Rise of the United States

For prepartition Polish history a few studies may be singled out as particularly illuminating. On the controversial question of peasant enserfment Andrzej Kaminski, "Neo-Serfdom in Poland-Lithuania," *Slavic Review,* XXXIV (June 1975), is most stimulating. On religious issues see Janusz Tazbir, *A State without Stakes: Polish Religious Toleration in the Sixteenth and Seventeenth Centuries* (New York, 1973), and Wiktor Weintraub, "Tolerance and Intolerance in Old Poland," *Canadian Slavonic Papers,* XIII, 1 (1970). A revealing book is Bernard D. Weinryb, *The Jews of Poland: A Social and Economic History of the Jewish Community in Poland from 1100 to 1800* (Philadelphia, 1972). Robert R. Palmer relates Polish eighteenth-century developments to the great events of Europe and America in his monumental *The Age of the Democratic Revolution* (Princeton, 1959-1964). Very important is the classic by Robert H. Lord, *The Second Partition of Poland* (Cambridge, Mass., 1915). The literature on the partitions is large indeed, but we shall mention only one recent book and two polemical articles: Herbert H. Kaplan, *The First Partition of Poland* (New York, 1962); Jerzy Topolski, "Reflections on the First Partition of Poland," *Acta Poloniae Historica,* XXVII (1973), and Jerzy Łojek, "The International Crisis of 1791," *East Central Europe,* II, 1 (1975).

American-Polish contacts have attracted several writers, but important gaps remain. Janusz Tazbir, "Christopher Columbus in Early Polish Literature," *Acta Poloniae Historica,* XXV (1972), is a valuable contribution. For early Polish settlers see Miecislaus Haiman, *Poles in New York in the 17th and 18th*

Centuries (Chicago, 1938), and Sigmund H. Uminski, *The Polish Pioneers in Virginia* (New York, 1974). Irene M. Sokol, "The American Revolution and Poland: A Bibliographical Essay," *Polish Review*, XII, 3 (1967), is an indispensable introduction to the subject. Her short "The American Revolution as Seen in Eighteenth Century Poland," in Damian S. Wandycz, ed., *Studies in Polish Civilization* (New York, 1970), is useful. Among the important studies by the leading Polish specialist Zofia Libiszowska see "American Thought in Polish Political Writings of the Great Diet (1788-1792)," *Polish-American Studies,* I (1976), and "Polish Opinion of the American Revolution," *Polish American Studies,* XXXIV (Spring 1977). M. M. Drozdowski, *The American Revolution in the Polish Socio-Historical Literature* (Chicago, 1977), is a useful brief study. The older works by Miecislaus Haiman, *The Fall of Poland in Contemporary American Opinion* (Chicago, 1935), *Poland and the American Revolutionary War* (Chicago, 1932), and a two-volume biography of Kościuszko, *Kosciuszko in the American Revolution* (New York, 1943) and *Kosciuszko: Leader and Exile* (New York, 1946), still retain their usefulness although an up-to-date study would be most welcome. The same is true for Pułaski, whose biography is available only in a shortened English version by Władysław Konopczynski, *Casimir Pulaski* (Chicago, 1947). There is, however, a new popular book by S. Kopczewski, *Kościuszko and Pułaski* (Warsaw, 1976). A select bibliography on Pułaski prepared by J. A. Wytrwal appeared in *Polish American Studies,* XIX (1962). Izabela Rusinowa, "The Kościuszko Insurrection Through the Eyes of 'The (New York) Herald' 1794-1795," *Polish-American Studies,* I (1976), is interesting.

For Niemcewicz's American experiences see Metchie J. E. Budka, *Under Their Vine and Fig Tree* (Elizabeth, N.J., 1965). Janina W. Hoskins' articles "The Image of America in Accounts of Polish Travelers of the 18th and 19th Centuries" and "A Lesson Which All Our Countrymen Should Study: Jefferson Views Poland" appeared in *The Quarterly Journal of the Library of Congress,* respectively in the July 1965 and January 1976 issues. James H. Hutson, "The Partition Treaty and the Declaration of Independence," *Journal of American History,* LVII, 4 (March 1972), points at American fears of being partitioned like Poland. Bogdan Grzeloński, ed., *Jefferson-Kościuszko Correspondence* (Warsaw, 1978), is useful.

Chapter 2. The Polish Question in the Nineteenth Century

Nineteenth-century developments are surveyed in Piotr S. Wandycz, *The Lands of Partitioned Poland 1795-1918* (Seattle, 1974), but the Polish question in international relations still awaits a comprehensive treatment in English and in Polish although numerous monographs deal with its various aspects.

American-Polish relations in the era of the November 1830 insurrection are discussed by Jerzy J. Lerski, *A Polish Chapter in Jacksonian America: The United States and the Polish Exiles of 1831* (Madison, 1958); Maria J. E. Copson-Niećko and Zygmunt Wardziński, "Polish Political Emigration in the United States 1831-1864," *Polish Review,* XIX, 3-4 (1974)—a polemical article; Joseph W. Wieczerzak, "The Polish Insurrection of 1830-1831 in the American Press," *Polish Review,* VI, 1-2 (1961); Arthur P. Coleman, *A New England City and the November Uprising* (Chicago, 1939); Robert E. Spiller, "Fenimore Cooper and Lafayette: Friends of Polish Freedom, 1830-1832," *The American Literature,* VII (March 1935); and Ludwik Krzyzanowski, "Cooper and Mickiewicz: A Literary Friendship," in M. Kridl, ed., *Adam Mickiewicz* (New York, 1951). Very interesting is Wiktor Weintraub, "Three Myths of America in

Polish Romantic Literature," in Damian S. Wandycz, ed., *Studies in Polish Civilization* (New York, 1970).

The only book-length coverage of the United States and the Polish insurrection of 1863 is Joseph W. Wieczerzak, *A Polish Chapter in Civil War America* (New York, 1967). Wieczerzak also contributed an article on "American Opinion and the Warsaw Disturbances of 1861," *Polish Review*, VI, 3 (1962). Stanisław Bóbr-Tylingo's well-documented article, "The January Uprising and the American Civil War," *Antemurale*, XX (1976), concentrates on international diplomacy. George J. Lerski, "The United States and the January Insurrection," *Polish American Studies*, XXX (Spring 1973), is also important. Arthur P. Coleman and Marion M. Coleman explored the reaction of the American press in their monograph *The Polish Insurrection in the Light of New York Editorial Opinion* (Williamsport, Pa., 1934), while the Russian angle is given particular attention in Martin Kaufman, "1863: Poland, Russia and the United States," *Polish American Studies*, XXI (January-June 1964), and Harold E. Blinn, "Seward and the Polish Rebellion of 1863," *American Historical Review*, XLV (July 1940).

Abraham G. Duker contributed "Polish Political Emigres in the United States and the Jews, 1833-1865," *Publications of the American Jewish Historical Society*, XXXIX (December 1949), and George J. Lerski discussed "Jewish-Polish Amity in Lincoln's America," *Polish Review*, XVIII, 4 (1973). LeRoy H. Fischer provided a biography of the controversial *Lincoln's Gadfly: Adam Gurowski* (Norman, Okla., 1964), a subject analyzed in depth in Polish by Zygmunt Gross.

Joseph Svastek, "Polish Travelers in Nineteenth Century United States," *Polish American Studies*, II (January-June, 1945), is a useful introduction; Leon Orłowski, "Henryk Korwin-Kałussowski (1806-1894): Delegate of the National Government in Washington," *Bulletin of the Polish Institute of Arts and Sciences in America*, IV (1946), deals with the prominent Pole who made America his home. Charles Morley, ed., *Portrait of America: Letters of Henry Sienkiewicz* (New York, 1959), and Helena Modjeska, *Memories and Impressions* (New York, 1910), make most interesting reading. Victor R. Greene, "Pre-World War I Emigration to the United States: Motives and Statistics," *Polish Review*, VI, 3 (1961), is a good introduction to this complex subject; William I. Thomas and Florian Znaniecki, *The Polish Peasant in Europe and America* (New York, 1958), is a classic first published in 1918, and one may profitably read a commentary on it by Konstantin Symmons-Symonolewicz in the *Polish Review*, XIII, 2 (1968).

Chapter 3. Wilson and the Rebirth of Poland

The only monographic treatment of the subject by Louis L. Gerson, *Woodrow Wilson and the Rebirth of Poland* (New Haven, 1953), is unsatisfactory. It contains factual errors and insufficiently documented sweeping assertions. His "The Poles," in Joseph P. O'Grady, ed., *The Immigrants' Influence on Wilson's Peace Policies* (Lexington, Ky., 1967), is not much of an improvement. Titus Komarnicki, *Rebirth of the Polish Republic* (London, 1957), contains a wealth of information about American policies toward the Polish issue. For wartime relations the articles by Victor S. Mamatey, "Wilson and the Restoration of Poland," *The Florida State University Slavic Papers*, I (1967), and Eugene Kusielewicz, "Paderewski and Wilson's Speech to the Senate, January 27, 1917," *Polish American Studies*, XIII (1956), bring new materials and interpretations; parts of L. E. Gelfand, *The Inquiry, American Preparations for Peace 1917-1919*

(New Haven, 1962), are also relevant. *The Intimate Papers of Colonel House* (Boston, New York, 1926-1928), edited by Charles Seymour, are still very important; Clarence Dawson, "The Thirteenth Point: An Interview with Col. House," *Poland,* IX, 5 (May 1928), is disappointing. Informative are two articles by Stanley R. Pliszka (Pliska): "The 'Polish-American Army' 1917-1921," *Polish Review,* X, 3 (1965), and "The Polish American Community and the Rebirth of Poland," *Polish American Studies,* XXVI (January-June 1969).

A good biography of Ignacy Paderewski still hasn't been published. Rom Landau, *Ignace Paderewski, Musician and Statesman* (New York, 1934), is sorely inadequate, and two accounts by his prominent American friends—Edward M. House, "Paderewski: The Paradox of Europe," *Harper's Magazine* (December 1925), and Vernon Kellogg, "Paderewski, Pilsudski and Poland," *World's Work,* XXXVIII (1919)—are thin and not very reliable. Although there are several biographies of Piłsudski in English, notably by W. F. Reddaway, Grace Humphrey, Rom Landau, and Piłsudski's wife, Alexandra, none is well-documented and comprehensive. Zygmunt J. Gasiorowski, "Joseph Piłsudski in the Light of American Reports, 1919-1922," *Slavonic and East European Review,* XLIX, 116 (July 1971), is, however, most interesting. About Roman Dmowski there is virtually nothing available in English.

Eugene Kusielewicz, "Wilson and the Polish Cause at Paris," *Polish Review,* I, 4 (1956), may serve as a good introduction to the subject. Among the many reminiscences and studies by Americans present at the Peace Conference Edward M. House and Charles Seymour, eds., *What Really Happened at Paris* (New York, 1921), Charles H. Haskins and Robert H. Lord, *Some Problems of the Peace Conference* (Cambridge, Mass., 1920), Robert Lansing, *The Big Four and Others and the Peace Conference* (Boston, 1921), and his *The Peace Negotiations* (Boston, 1921), Stephen Bonsal, *Suitors and Suppliants: The Little Nations at Versailles* (New York, 1946), E. J. Dillon, *The Inside Story of the Peace Conference* (New York, 1920), and James T. Shotwell, *At the Paris Peace Conference* (New York, 1937), contain relevant passages and colorful anecdotes but also occasional misinformation.

For the Jewish aspects consult Morton Tenzer, "The Jews," in Joseph P. O'Grady, ed., *The Immigrants' Influence on Wilson's Peace Policies* (Lexington, Ky., 1967); the older but still most informative O. I. Janowsky, *The Jews and Minority Rights 1898-1919* (London, 1933); Agnes Headlam-Morley et al., eds., *Sir James Headlam Morley: A Memoir of the Paris Peace Conference 1919* (London, 1972), and Henry Morgenthau, *All in a Life-Time* (New York, 1922), which is revealing in spite of many small mistakes about Poles and Poland.

Newer monographs on the Soviet-Polish war of 1919-1920, notably Piotr S. Wandycz, *Soviet-Polish Relations 1917-1921* (Cambridge, Mass., 1969), Norman Davies, *White Eagle, Red Star: The Polish Soviet War 1919-20* (New York, 1972), M. K. Dziewanowski, *Joseph Piłsudski, A European Federalist 1918-1922* (Stanford, 1969), and Richard H. Ullman, *The Anglo-Soviet Accord*—third volume of his *Anglo-Soviet Relations*—(Princeton, 1972), do not concentrate on American attitudes toward the Russo-Polish conflict although they include them within the general framework of their studies. Hence the work of E. Malcolm Carroll, edited by Frederic B. M. Hollyday, *Soviet Communism and Western Opinion 1919-1921* (Chapel Hill, 1965), is still very useful, as is a section of the *Moffat Papers,* edited by Nancy H. Hooker (Cambridge, Mass., 1956). Robert F. Karolevitz and Ross S. Fenn contributed *Flight of Eagles: The Story of the American*

Kosciuszko Squadron in the Polish-Russian War 1919-1920 (Sioux Falls, S.D., 1974).

The old book by H. H. Fisher, *America and the New Poland* (New York, 1928), remains most valuable; Charles J. M. Phillips, *The New Poland* (London, 1923), written by a member of the American Red Cross, is less reliable and presents a somewhat idealized picture of the country. The accounts of American economic aid to Poland will be listed under the next heading.

Chapter 4. From Peace to War

American aid to Poland has been surveyed by William Grove, *War's Aftermath: Polish Relief in 1919* (New York, 1940), and it occupies an important place in Suda L. Bane and R. H. Lutz, *Organization of American Relief in Europe, 1918-1919* (Stanford, 1943), and in George J. Lerski, *Herbert Hoover and Poland: A Documentary History of Friendship* (Stanford, 1977). American-Polish economic relations in the interwar period have been briefly and expertly analyzed by Zbigniew Landau, "Poland and America: The Economic Connection 1918-1939," *Polish American Studies*, XXXII (Autumn 1975). Landau contributed several studies in depth of American loans and investments in Poland which have not been translated into English, but his "The Foreign Loans of the Polish State in the Years 1918-1939," *Studia Historiae Oeconomicae*, IX (1974), and "Poland's Economy against the Background of World Economy 1913-1938," *Acta Poloniae Historica*, XX (1969), are also relevant for our topic. An older article by Leopold Wellisz, "American Capital in Poland," *Polish Review* (March 7, 1946) is pertinent, as is his book *Foreign Capital in Poland* (London, 1938).

General works on Polish interwar economy comprise Ferdynand Zweig, *Poland between Two Wars: A Critical Study of Social and Economic Changes* (London, 1944), and the more recent one by Jack Taylor, *Economic Development of Poland 1919-1950* (Ithaca, N.Y., 1952).

The best study of the Second Republic, except for foreign policy matters, is Antony Polonsky, *Politics in Independent Poland 1921-1939* (Oxford, 1972). Also noteworthy is the section on Poland in Joseph Rothschild, *East Central Europe between Two World Wars* (Seattle, 1974). This author previously contributed a major book, *Piłsudski's Coup D'état* (New York, 1966). Hans Roos competently covers the half century after 1916 in his *A History of Modern Poland* (New York, 1966). Older studies by American authors which deserve attention are Raymond L. Buell, *Poland: The Key to Europe* (New York, 1939), books by Robert Machray, especially his *Poland of Piłsudski* (London, 1936), and Bernadotte Schmitt, ed., *Poland* (Berkeley, 1945), which contains an informative section on American-Polish problems. Paul Super, *Twenty-Five Years with the Poles* (Trenton, 1947) is a significant eyewitness account.

There are several studies on national minorities, among them those by S. Horak, S. Segal, C. Heller, R. M. Rabinowicz, but few if any contain a balanced treatment. For a factual survey see Marian M. Drozdowski, "The National Minorities in Poland in 1918-1939," *Acta Poloniae Historica*, XXII (1970). The social scene is penetratingly analyzed by Janusz Żarnowski, "East Central European Societies, 1918-1939: The Polish Example," in Polish Academy of Sciences, Committee of Historical Sciences, Institute of History, *Poland at the Fourteenth International Congress of Historical Sciences in San Francisco* (Wrocław, 1975). Also important are the articles by Peter Brock, "The Politics of the Polish Pea-

sant," *International Review of Social History,* I (1956), and Konstanty Jeleń-
ski, "The Genealogy of the Polish Intelligentsia," *Survey,* XXIX (1959).

Roman Debicki, *Foreign Policy of Poland 1919-1939* (New York, 1962), is
the only survey available in English, which may be supplemented with Thaddeus V. Gromada, ed., *Essays on Poland's Foreign Policy 1918-1939* (New York,
1970), and Alexander Korczyński and Stefan Świętochowski, eds., *Poland between
Germany and Russia 1926-1939* (New York, 1975). Many monographs deal with
various facets of Polish interwar diplomacy, notably the works of H. von Riek-
hoff, J. Korbel, P. S. Wandycz, Anna M. Cienciala, and Bohdan B. Budurowycz.
The essay by Henry L. Roberts, "The Diplomacy of Colonel Beck," in Gordon
A. Craig and Felix Gilbert, eds., *The Diplomats 1919-1939* (Princeton, 1953), remains valuable. Martin Weil, *A Pretty Good Club: The Founding Fathers of
the U.S. Foreign Service* (New York, 1978), contains a good amount of information on American diplomats' attitudes toward Poland in the twentieth century.

American-Polish diplomatic relations occupy an important place in Marian
Wojciechowski, "The United States and Central Europe between the Two
World Wars (1918-1939/41)," *Polish Western Affairs,* XVI, 1 (1975), not a very
successful presentation. The papers of Beck and of the Polish ambassadors in
Paris and Berlin have been published in English—the last two by W. Jędrzeje-
wicz—and recently those of the last United States ambassador to prewar Warsaw
appeared, edited by Philip V. Cannistraro, Edward D. Wynot, and Theodore
P. Kovaleff under the title *Poland and the Coming of the Second World War*
(Columbus, Ohio, 1976). A short article by Constantin Symonolewicz, "Polish
Travelers and Observers in the U.S.A. (1918-1939)," *Polish American Studies,*
II (January-June 1945), deals with a subject that merits further attention.

Chapter 5. Roosevelt and Poland in the Second World War

The numerous studies on the Second World War are frequently relevant in
one way or another for American-Polish relations. Only a few can be mentioned here; those that treat the period mainly as background to the Cold War
are listed in the following section.

Books directly concerned with our topic are: the most recent, Richard C.
Lukas, *The Strange Allies: The United States and Poland 1941-1945* (Knox-
ville, Tenn., 1979); Edward Rozek, *Allied Wartime Diplomacy: A Pattern in
Poland* (New York, 1958), already a little dated, and Jan Ciechanowski, *Defeat
in Victory* (New York, 1947), which is an account by the ambassador in Washington. Useful short studies include Peter H. Irons, " 'The Test Is Poland':
Polish Americans and the Origins of the Cold War," *Polish American Studies,*
XXX (Autumn 1973); Jack L. Hammersmith, "The U.S. Office of War Information (OWI) and the Polish Question 1943-1945," *Polish Review,* XIX, 1
(1974); Charles Sandler, "Pro-Soviet Polish Americans: Oskar Lange and Russia's Friends in the Polonia 1941-1945," *Polish Review,* XXII, 4 (1977); Har-
riette L. Chandler, "The Transition to Cold Warrior: The Evolution of W.
Averell Harriman's Assessment of the U.S.S.R.'s Polish Policy, October 1943-
Warsaw Uprising," *East European Quarterly,* X (Summer 1976); J. R. Thackrah,
"Aspects of American and British Policy Towards Poland from the Yalta to
the Potsdam Conference 1945," *Polish Review,* XXI, 4 (1976), and Damian S.
Wandycz, *Polish-Americans and the Curzon Line* (New York, 1954).

A great deal of information on the United States' Polish policy is scattered
through various memoirs and edited papers, notably of George Kennan, Charles
Bohlen, W. A. Harriman, H. Hopkins, William C. Bullitt, W. H. Standley,

J. R. Deane, Cordell Hull, Sumner Welles, E. R. Stettinius, and W. Leahy. Robert E. Sherwood's study of Hopkins and Roosevelt is also pertinent. On the Polish side memoir literature in English comprises books by Stefan Korboński, Zbigniew Stypułkowski, Edward Raczyński, General Władysław Anders, General Tadeusz Bór-Komorowski, Stanisław Kot, as well as a book by an emissary sent to President Roosevelt by the Polish underground, Jan Karski, *Story of a Secret State* (Boston, 1944).

Among works touching on various aspects of the wartime period one must mention J. K. Zawodny, *Death in the Forest* (Notre Dame, Ind., 1962), which is the best treatment of Katyn; and his *Nothing but Honor: Story of the Uprising of Warsaw, 1944* (Stanford, 1978); Jan Ciechanowski, *The Warsaw Rising of 1944* (London, 1974), a controversial and "revisionist" book on the origins of the uprising which is weak on the diplomatic side; Piotr S. Wandycz, *Czechoslovak-Polish Confederation and the Great Powers* (Bloomington, Ind., 1956); the somewhat popular Tadeusz Cyprian and Jerzy Sawicki, *Nazi Rule in Poland 1939-1945* (Warsaw, 1961); the brief but highly informative Józef Garliński, "The Polish Underground State 1939-1945," *Journal of Contemporary History*, X (April 1975), and his *Poland, SOE and the Allies* (London, 1969), and the most recent and comprehensive survey, Stefan Korboński, *The Polish Underground State* (New York, 1978). The two principal works on Polish aid to the Jews are Władysław Bartoszewski and Zofia Lewin, *The Samaritans* (New York, 1970), and Kazimierz Iranek-Osmecki, *He Who Saves One Life* (New York, 1971). See also the significant work by Philip Friedman, *Their Brothers' Keeper* (New York, 1957). Bartoszewski's *Warsaw Death Ring 1939-1944* (Warsaw, 1968) is important. The most recent and somewhat journalistic account of the uprising in the Warsaw ghetto is by Dan Kurzman, *The Bravest Battle* (New York, 1976). The topic is also discussed among others by Ber Mark and P. Friedman. Wiktor Sukiennicki, "The Establishment of the Soviet Regime in Eastern Poland in 1939," *Journal of Central European Affairs*, XXIII (July 1963), and Jan Czapski, *The Inhuman Land* (New York, 1952), are particularly important to understand Polish feelings toward the USSR. Sikorski's mysterious death is narrated in David Irving's *Accident* (London, 1967).

Vojtech Mastny, "The Beneš-Stalin-Molotov Conversations in December 1943: New Documents," *Jahrbücher für Geschichte Osteuropas*, XX, 3 (1972), throws new light on Stalin's thinking about the Polish question. Sections of Lynn E. Davis, *The Cold War Begins: Soviet-American Conflict over Eastern Europe* (Princeton, 1974); John L. Gaddis, *The United States and the Origins of the Cold War 1941-1947* (New York, 1972); Sir John Wheeler-Bennett and Anthony Nichols, *The Semblance of Peace* (New York, 1972), and several studies by Herbert Feis mentioned in this chapter are all important and relevant; Diane S. Clemens, *Yalta* (New York, 1970), is less good on the Polish issue.

Chapter 6. In the Shadow of Stalinism and the Cold War

The literature on the Cold War and the late 1940s in Poland is vast, and the titles listed below represent only a sample. Some of the books included in the preceding section are also relevant just as works cited here contain parts that deal with the later years.

Five studies are particularly useful: Bennet Kovrig, *The Myth of Liberation: East Central Europe in US Diplomacy and Politics since 1941* (Baltimore, 1973); Hugh B. Hammet, "America's Non-Policy in Eastern Europe and the Origins of the Cold War," *Survey*, XIX (Autumn 1973); Geir Lunstad, *The American Non-*

Policy Towards Eastern Europe 1943-1947 (Tromsö. 1978); Mervill A. White, "Some Considerations of United States Foreign Policy Toward Eastern Europe 1941-1964," *Polish Review*, X, 4 (1965), and Stephen D. Kertesz, ed., *The Fate of East Central Europe: Hopes and Failures of American Foreign Policy* (Notre Dame, Ind., 1956).

Among books dealing with broad issues that intimately affect Poland, one may recommend Herbert Feis, *From Trust to Terror: The Onset of the Cold War 1945-1950* (New York, 1970), Martin F. Herz, *Beginnings of the Cold War* (Bloomington, Ind., 1966), and Adam Ulam, *The Rivals: America and Russia Since World War II* (New York, 1971). Most of the "revisionist" works, to mention only those by G. Alperowitz and G. Kolko, are not particularly helpful for they are weakest on issues that particularly concern us. If, however, Thomas G. Peterson be counted as a semirevisionist, his *Soviet-American Confrontation: Postwar Reconstruction and the Origins of the Cold War* (Baltimore, 1973), is definitely valuable.

Directly relevant for postwar American-Polish relations are the memoirs of the two American ambassadors in Warsaw, Arthur Bliss Lane, *I Saw Poland Betrayed* (New York, 1948), and Stanton Griffis, *Lying in State* (Garden City, N.Y., 1952). They help us to recapture the atmosphere of the period, which the critical John N. Cable, "Arthur Bliss Lane: Cold Warrior in Warsaw, 1945-47," *Polish American Studies*, XXX (Autumn 1973), finds hard to understand. Among several contributions on Polish Americans, the interesting ones are: George H. Janczewski, "The Significance of the Polish Vote in the American National Election Campaign of 1948," *Polish Review*, XIII, 4 (1968); Athan Theoharis, "The Republican Party and Yalta: Partisan Exploitation of the Polish American Concern over the Conference, 1945-1960," *Polish American Studies*, XXVIII (Spring 1971); and in the same periodical Danuta Mostwin, "Post-World War II Polish Immigrants in the United States," XXVI (Autumn 1969), and Miecislaus Haiman, "Polish Scholarship in the United States 1939-1947" in IV (July-December 1947).

Zbigniew Brzezinski, *The Soviet Bloc* (Cambridge, Mass., 1960 and subsequent revised editions), is indispensable. Among many other studies, one may single out R. V. Burks, *The Dynamics of Communism in Eastern Europe* (Princeton, 1961), as particularly illuminating.

Reminiscences by leading participants include Stanisław Mikołajczyk, *The Rape of Poland* (New York, 1948); Stefan Korboński, *Warsaw in Chains* (New York, 1959), and *Warsaw in Exile* (New York, 1966), and Czesław Miłosz, *The Captive Mind* (New York, 1955), which became a classic. Oscar Halecki, ed., *Poland* (New York, 1957), contains a wealth of information; M. K. Dziewanowski, *The Communist Party of Poland* (Cambridge, Mass., rev. ed., 1976), is the only extensive historical treatment available in English. Z. Jordan, *Philosophy and Ideology: The Development of Philosophy and Marxism-Leninism in Poland since the Second World War* (Dordrecht, 1963), is a most learned study.

Economic problems are expertly discussed by Thad Paul Alton, *The Polish Postwar Economy* (New York, 1955), John Michael Montias, *Central Planning in Poland* (New Haven, 1962), and Andrzej Korboński, *Politics of Socialist Agriculture in Poland 1945-1960* (New York, 1965). The crucial German issue is analyzed among others by Z. Jordan, *Oder-Neisse Line* (London, 1952), W. M. Drzewieniecki, *The German-Polish Frontier* (Chicago, 1959), and Józef Kokot, *The Logic of the Oder-Neisse Frontier* (Poznan, 1957). Seen in a broader frame, the question occupies Elizabeth Wiskemann in her *Germany's Eastern Neigh-*

bours (London, 1956). Two pamphlets—V. J. Wagner, *The Gentleman from Tennessee is Wrong: The Truth about the Odra-Nysa Border* (n.d., n.p.), and Polish American Congress, *In Defense of Poland's Western Boundary: An Economic Study* (Chicago, n.d.)—are representative of Polish efforts in America on behalf of the territorial status quo. Lucjan Dobroszycki, "Restoring Jewish Life in Post-War Poland," *Soviet Jewish Affairs*, III, 2 (1973), explores the sad pages of Polish-Jewish relations in the late 1940s.

Chapter 7. From Gomułka to Gierek: Détente and Its Limits

The numerous studies on Eastern Europe in the 1950s and 1960s include those written or edited by Harold G. Skilling, Stephen Fischer-Galati, William E. Griffith, James F. Brown, Peter Bender, Kurt London, Peter A. Toma, Leopold Labedz, and Adam Bromke. An article by Charles Gati, "East Central Europe: Touchstone for Detente," *Journal of International Affairs*, XXVIII, 2 (1974), is informative and stimulating. Michael Kaser, *COMECON: Integration Problems of the Planned Economies* (London, 1965), is important. A very useful statistical compendium and guide is Paul Marer, *Soviet and East European Foreign Trade 1946-1969* (Bloomington, Ind., 1972). Thomas A. Wolf, *U.S. East-West Trade Policy* (Lexington, Mass., 1973), and Gunnar Adler-Karlsson, *Western Economic Warfare, 1947-1967* (Stockholm, 1968), are relevant.

Works on Poland ranging from outlines to monographs and specialized articles are very many. To the general category belong Richard Hiscocks, *Poland: Bridge for the Abyss? An Interpretation of Developments in Post-War Poland* (London, 1963); the journalistic account by William Woods, *Poland: Eagle in the East* (London, 1969); two useful surveys, Alexander J. Groth, *People's Poland: Government and Politics* (San Francisco, 1972), and James F. Morrison, *The Polish People's Republic* (Baltimore, 1968); the more detailed Tadeusz N. Cieplak, ed., *Poland since 1956* (New York, 1972); Tadeusz Drewnowski et al., *Poland 1944-1964* (Warsaw, 1964), which contains a good deal of data; Hansjakob Stehle, *The Independent Satellite* (New York, 1965), written by a well-informed German correspondent; and Konrad Syrop, *Poland between the Hammer and the Anvil* (London, 1968).

Very informative is Richard F. Staar, *Poland 1944-1962: The Sovietization of a Captive People* (Baton Rouge, 1962), even if one disagrees with some of his theses. More detached in his approach is Hansjakob Stehle, "Polish Communism," in William E. Griffith, ed., *Communism in Europe* (Cambridge, Mass., 1964). Tadeusz N. Cieplak, "Some Distinctive Characteristics of the Communist System in the Polish People's Republic," *Polish Review*, XIX, 1 (1974), is well worth reading, and so is the article by Jerzy Wiatr, written from the Polish Marxist perspective, "Political Parties, Interest Representation and Economic Development in Poland," *American Political Science Review*, LXIV (December 1970). J. G. Zielinski, *Economic Reforms in Polish Industry* (London, 1973), deserves attention. On religious-political problems, see Vincent C. Chrypinski, "Polish Catholicism and Social Change," in Bohdan R. Bociurkiv and John W. Strong, eds., *Religion and Atheism in the USSR and Eastern Europe* (Toronto, 1975). Adam Bromke, "The 'Znak' Group in Poland," *East Europe* (January-February 1962), remains a valid introduction to the topic. Lucjan Blit, *The Eastern Pretender* (London, 1965), is well informed on the Pax group, although he tends to demonize its leader, Piasecki. Stefan Cardinal Wyszyński, *The Deeds of Faith* (New York, 1966), contains excerpts from letters and sermons of this great figure of the Polish church. Jan Szczepański, *Polish Society*

(New York, 1970), written by a leading Polish sociologist, is indispensable reading, and David Lane and George Kolankiewicz, eds., *Social Groups in Polish Society* (New York, 1973), provides much useful data.

There are half a dozen books on the "Polish October." Those by Frank Gibney, S. L. Shneiderman, Konrad Syrop, and Flora Lewis are probably the best. Nicholas Bethell, *Gomułka: His Poland, His Communism* (New York, 1969), is very readable although it can hardly answer all the questions. A. Ross Johnson, "Poland: End of an Era," *Problems of Communism*, XIX (January-February 1970), and Adam Bromke, "Beyond the Gomułka Era," *Foreign Affairs*, XLIX (April 1971), are noteworthy. Andrzej Brzeski, "Poland as a Catalyst of Change in the Communist Economic System," *Polish Review*, XVI, 2 (1971), is stimulating. Adam Bromke and John W. Strong, eds., *Gierek's Poland* (New York, 1973), comprises an analysis of the Polish scene by scholars from the homeland and abroad. Adam Bromke, "A New Juncture in Poland," *Problems of Communism*, XXV (September-October 1976), is an important attempt to assess the five years of Gierek's regime. A panel discussion, "Poland in the Last Quarter of the Twentieth Century," *Slavic Review*, XXXIV (December 1975), presents educated guesses about the future. See also Adam Bromke, "The Opposition in Poland," *Problems of Communism*, (September-October 1978).

Joseph R. Fiszman, *Revolution and Tradition in People's Poland: Education and Socialization* (Princeton, 1972), is a thoughtful analysis. Z. Anthony Kruszewski, *The Oder-Neisse Boundary and Poland's Modernization: The Socioeconomic and Political Impact* (New York, 1972), makes an important contribution to a significant topic. John J. Lenaghan, *The Limits of Freedom: Poland in World Affairs 1964-1972* (Carleton University Occasional Papers, Ottawa, 1972), is very useful. The Rapacki Plan together with its subsequent versions is analyzed by Polish authors: Andrzej Albrecht, *The Rapacki Plan—New Aspects* (Warsaw, 1963), and Karol Małcużyński, *The Gomułka Plan for a Nuclear Armaments Freeze in Central Europe* (Warsaw, 1964). The emigré writer Mieczysław Manelli contributes some interesting remarks on the topic in his *War of the Vanquished* (New York, 1972). Mieczysław F. Rakowski, *The Foreign Policy of the Polish People's Republic; Sketches from Thirty Years of History* (Warsaw, 1975), provides Warsaw's point of view.

There is no monograph as yet on the United States and Poland in the post-1956 period, but a number of articles or books are concerned with certain aspects of it. Zbigniew Brzezinski, "United States Policy in Eastern Europe: A Study of Contradiction," *Journal of International Affairs*, II, 1 (1957), is penetrating, as are all the writings of this prolific scholar. Piotr S. Wandycz, "American Policy Toward East Central Europe: The Polish Case 1956-1958," *Proceedings of the Indiana Academy of the Social Sciences* (1958), argues in favor of aid; Milorad M. Drachkovitch, *United States Aid to Yugoslavia and Poland: Analysis of a Controversy* (Washington, D.C., 1963), takes a different point of view. The question of economic assistance is presented by Clement J. Zablocki, "American Aid to Poland" and by Rev. A. J. Wycislo, "American Catholic Aid to Poland," both in *Polish American Studies*, XIX (July-December 1962). John C. Campbell, *American Policy Toward Communist Eastern Europe: The Choices Ahead* (Minneapolis, 1965), devotes a good deal of attention to the Polish issue. Jacob D. Beam, *An American Ambassador's Unique Perspective on East-West Issues* (New York, 1978), came out after the completion of this book.

Jan Wszelaki, ed., *John F. Kennedy and Poland* (New York, 1964), illustrates through a selection of documents Kennedy's opinions as senator and president.

J. K. Zawodny, "The Polish Response to the Kennedy Assassination," *Polish Review*, X, 1 (1965), analyzes entries made in the condolences books in the Warsaw embassy. Walter M. Drzewieniecki, "The American Poles and the Odra-Nysa Frontier," *Polish Western Affairs*, IX (1968), is useful. The pamphlet *President Nixon's Twenty-Four Hours in Warsaw* (Warsaw, 1972), is a lavishly illustrated text. Louis Gerson, *The Hyphenate in Recent American Politics and Diplomacy* (Lawrence, Kan., 1964), brings a great deal of data, but the conclusions are open to question. Stanley P. Wagner, "The Polish American Vote in 1960," *Polish American Studies*, XXI (January-June 1964), deals with a topic that requires more systematic and comprehensive studies.

Scholarly periodicals exclusively devoted to Polish American problems are *Polish American Studies,* published in this country, and *Polish-American Studies,* printed in Warsaw, the first volume of which appeared in 1976. The *Polish Review* contains frequent articles related to this subject.

Index

Index

The American Foreign Policy Library

The United States and the Andean Republics: Peru, Bolivia, and Ecuador
Fredrick B. Pike

The United States and the Arab World THIRD EDITION
William R. Polk

The Balkans in Our Time REVISED EDITION Robert Lee Wolff

The United States and Burma John F. Cady

The United States and Canada Gerald M. Craig

The United States and the Caribbean REVISED EDITION
Dexter Perkins

The United States and China FOURTH EDITION
John King Fairbank

The United States and India, Pakistan, Bangladesh
W. Norman Brown

The United States and Ireland Donald Harman Akenson

The United States and Israel Nadav Safran

The United States and Italy THIRD EDITION, ENLARGED
H. Stuart Hughes

The United States and Japan THIRD EDITION
Edwin O. Reischauer

The United States and Malaysia James W. Gould

The United States and North Africa: Morocco, Algeria, and Tunisia
Charles F. Gallagher

The United States and Poland Piotr S. Wandycz

Scandinavia REVISED EDITION, ENLARGED Franklin D. Scott

The United States and the Southern Cone: Argentina, Chile, and Uruguay
Arthur P. Whitaker